P9-DLO-966

BARRON'S

Encyclopedia of Dog Breeds

Third Edition

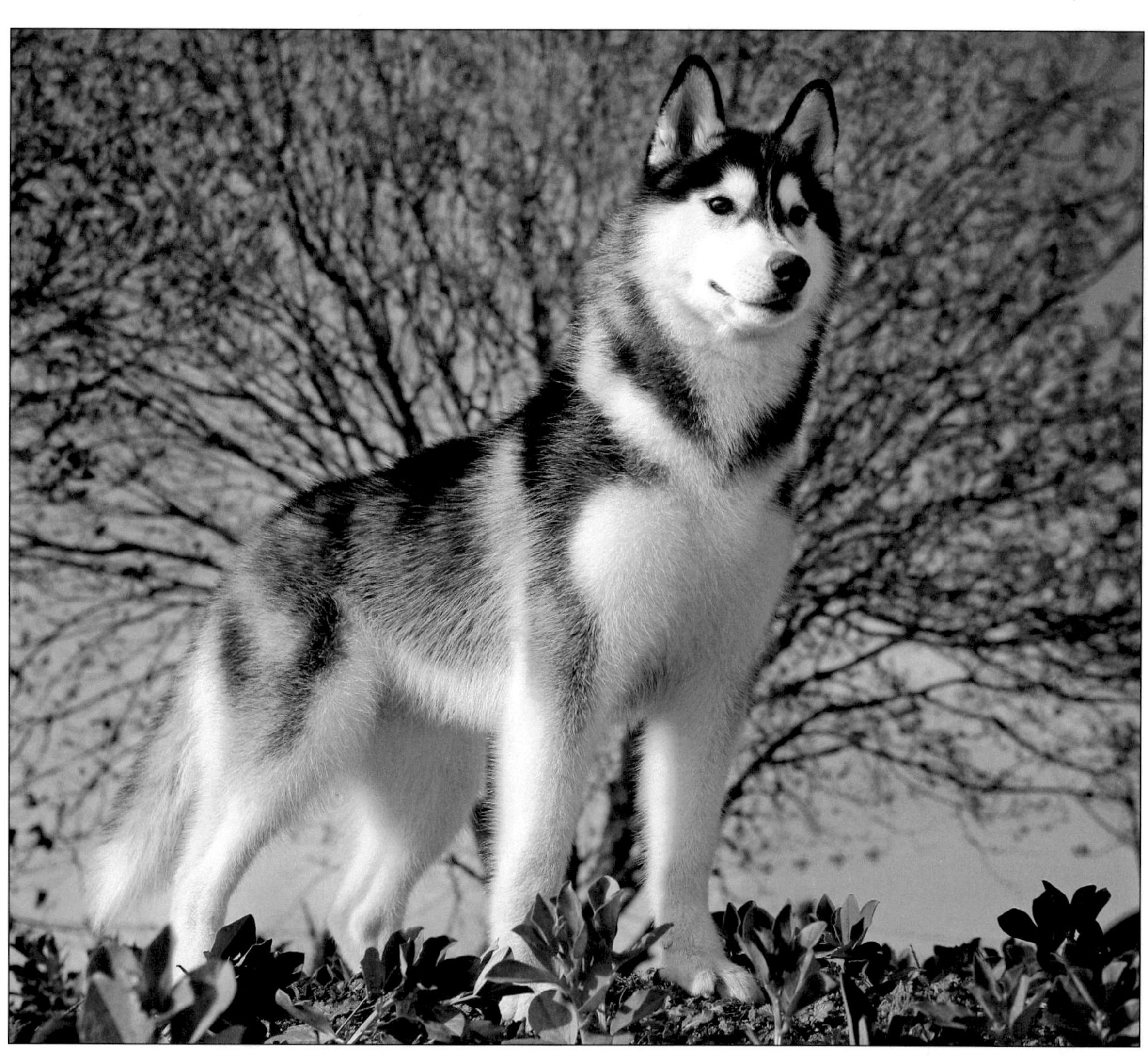

D. CAROLINE COILE, Ph.D.

ILLUSTRATIONS BY MICHELE EARLE-BRIDGES

COVER CREDITS

Front Cover

Main photo: Shutterstock, Ekaterina Brusnika; **Small photos**: Top: Fotolia, Claireliz; Middle left: Shutterstock, Pavel Shlykov; Middle right: Holly Simpson; Bottom left: Shutterstock, YAN WEN; Bottom right: Shutterstock, YAN WEN.

Back cover

Main photo: Patti Neale; **Small photos**: Top left and top right: Patti Neale; Bottom left: Shutterstock, YAN WEN; Bottom right: iStockphoto, Nwbob.

PHOTO CREDITS

123rf: Vitaly Titov: 145; **Kent Akselsen**: page 151; **Barbara Augello**: page 37; **Bergamasco Sheepdog Club of America**: pages 346, 347; **Kent Dannen**: pages 117, 199; **Dreamstime**: Willee Cole: 37; Cynoclub: 341; Veronika Druk: 366, 367; F8grapher: 254; Tom Flory: 335; Wenzhi Lu: 16, 23, 63, 210, 211, 292, 293, 371; Clement Morin: 295; Onetouchspark: 13, 155; Pavelmidi 1968: 303; PMKing: 333; Rodomír Režný: 31; Sunheyy: 153; Vivienstock: 384; Ankevan Wyk: 221; **Lynn Drumm:** page 363; **Cheryl Ertelt**: page 150; **Fotolia**: artSILENCE: 131; Sheila Atter: 232; Anna Auerbach: 25; Gianfranco Bella: 83; Callalloo Candcy: 175, 229, 362; Dogs: 15, 71, 75, 94, 125, 127, 167, 181, 191, 197, 204, 205, 217, 235, 239, 241, 257, 271, 299, 309, 321, 327, 337, 339, 342, 343, 344, 345; DragoNika: 53; Callalloo Fred: 286, 287; Hemlep: 20, 21; Jodi Mcgee: 310; Reddogs: 29; Paul Shlykov: 268; Thumber: 115; Callalloo Twisty: 212, 225, 231; Vincent: 207, 240; Waldemar: 353; Zottelhund: 168; **Christina Freitag**: pages 17, 82, 90, 119, 157, 161, 192, 193, 222, 224, 248, 336, 354; **Lee Grogan:** page 262; **iStockphoto**: AnimalInfo: 311; Dario Egidi: 5, 57, 62; Gary Forsyth: 185; Hyslop: 159; Nwbob: 291; Pawprincestudios: 227; S5iztok: 377; Paul Shlykov: 361; David Williamson: 33; **Joyce Mackay**: page 360; **Patti Neale**: pages 2, 3, 4, 6, 8, 9, 10, 11, 12, 14, 22, 24, 26, 28, 30, 32, 34, 36, 38, 40, 42, 43, 44, 45, 46, 48, 50, 52, 54, 56, 58, 59, 64, 65, 66, 68, 70, 74, 76, 77, 78, 80, 81, 84, 85, 86, 88, 89, 91, 92, 96, 97, 98, 99, 100, 101, 102, 104, 105, 106, 108, 109, 112, 113, 114, 116, 122, 126, 128, 130, 132, 133, 134, 136, 137, 138, 140, 141, 144, 146, 147, 148, 152, 154, 156, 158, 162, 163, 164, 165, 166, 169, 170, 178, 179, 180, 184, 186, 188, 189, 190, 194, 196, 198, 203, 206, 208, 213, 214, 215, 216, 220, 226, 228, 230, 233, 234, 236, 238, 246, 249, 250, 252, 255, 256, 259, 260, 261, 263, 264, 266, 267, 270, 272, 273, 274, 278, 282, 284, 285, 290, 294, 298, 300, 302, 304, 306, 312, 314, 315, 316, 317, 318, 320, 322, 324, 326, 328, 329, 334, 338, 340, 348, 352, 355, 356, 357, 358, 359, 364, 368, 370, 372, 374, 375, 380; **Rachel Rehberg-Gongre**: page 376; **Shutterstock**: Elisabeth Abramora: 384; Degtyaryov Andrey: 79; Rebecca Ashworth: 47, 49, 183; Capture Light: 200, 201, 223, 283, 382; Willee Cole: 296; Cynoclub: 171, 253; Jeff Dalton: 41; Daz Brown Photography: 381; Dezi: 1, 39, 61, 110, 139, 174; DragoNika: 93, 95, 269; F8grapher: 247, 313; Frank II: 149; Kirk Geisler: 19; Angela Giampiccolo: 349; Gillmar: 176; Glenkar: 27; Gp88: 279; Nicole Hrusthyk: v; Jkelly: 383; Tatiana Katsai: 111, 289, 297; Laila Kazakevica: 118, 319; Dick Kenny: 135; Rita Kochmarjova: 69, 172, 173, 187, 209, 305; Lenkadan: 7, 35, 55, 103, 323; L.F: 124; Ruben Lopez: 369; Dorottya Mathe: 258; Okeanas: 18; Otsphoto: 123, 129, 195, 265, 365; RHIMAGE: 87; Rodimov: 307; Pavel Shlykov: 67; Kazlouski Siarhei: 251; Anna Tyurina: 245; Svetlana Valoueva: 280, 281; Vojtaz: 373; Sally Wallis: 107; YAN WEN: i, 121, 142, 143, 177, 202, 218, 219, 242, 243, 275, 276, 277, 301, 331, 350, 351, 378, 379, 385, 386; WOLFAVNI: 332; Vera Zinkova: 160, 325; Zuzule: 51; **Holly Simpson**: pages 72, 73; **Patty Sosa**: page 308.

All inquiries should be addressed to:
Barron's Educational Series, Inc.
250 Wireless Boulevard
Hauppauge, NY 11788
www.barronseduc.com

ISBN: 978-0-7641-6729-4

Library of Congress Catalog Card No. 2015935573

Printed in China
9 8 7 6 5 4 3 2 1

CONTENTS

The Right Dog

You can choose your friends, but you can't choose your family—except, of course, for the family dog. In fact, humans have been choosing the dog's family for it for thousands of years, since the first time an arranged breeding between dogs with favored characteristics was carried out in an effort to produce more dogs of the same. In so doing, they gradually created from wolf ancestors the most diverse species in the world: *Canis familiaris*, the domestic dog.

FROM THE DOG FAMILY TO THE FAMILY DOG

The circumstances of the dog's initial domestication are forever lost in time. Early in the course of domestication, selection for traits that enabled this formerly wild species to share its life with humans was molding the dog that is such an integral part of human life today. Traits such as lack of fear, low reactivity, and dependence helped the first domestic dogs to live among members of another species.

As humans came to realize that "like begat like," they purposefully bred their best hunting dogs together, and their best guarding dogs together, creating the first canine specialists. Even in prehistoric times, considerable diversity in dogs existed, with distinct types or families—"breeds"—of domestic dogs arising at least by 3000 to 4000 years ago. Ancient Egypt was home to at least two distinct types of dogs, Greyhound and Mastiff, each specialized for a different job. By Roman times, most of the main types of modern breeds were in existence, with dogs specifically bred as guard, sheep, hunting, and lap dogs. The variety of dog breeds expanded greatly in Europe in the Middle Ages, with many breeds taking on importance as specialized hunters for either the aristocracy or poachers. Europe was not the only home of new dog breeds. Wherever humans lived, they shaped their dogs to do their bidding. Just as the needs of people change throughout history, breeds of dogs are not static. Many breeds have been born only to disappear into history, lost either because their work was no longer needed or another breed was developed that could do it better.

In the mid 1800s, a new pastime caught the attention of the European upper class: the exhibition of dogs. Before this time, it had been common to arrange contests between dogs based on coursing, fighting, or hauling ability, but the idea that any dog's worth could be estimated by its physical appearance was relatively new. As competition among breeds grew, the search for "new and exotic" breeds began. Travelers and dog buyers would spot prospective breed candidates, acquire a few, and exhibit them.

Dog shows spread quickly to America, where the American Kennel Club (AKC) was formed to register and promote purebred dogs. The requirements for breed recognition have changed somewhat through the years, but in general a breed must be backed by a national club that can demonstrate a sustained interest in the breed. New breeds are initially admitted into the Miscellaneous Class, and then later, pending demonstration of continued interest in the breed, admitted into one of the AKC's seven regular groups. The AKC breeds represent only a fraction of the world's breeds, but they are the most popular dogs in America.

ARE THEY GOOD WITH CHILDREN?

Every breed of dog can be good with children if raised with them the right way, and every breed can be bad with children if not adequately socialized with them. Sometimes a breed's job affects its interaction with children. Some herding breeds herd anything, including children, often by nipping. Some guarding breeds are protective of the children in their family, even against a roughhousing friend.

A large dog can accidentally topple a small child, and they have large teeth and powerful jaws that do more damage if they bite. Small dogs can be hurt by children.

Excitable dogs may become overly excited by the activity of children. Boisterous dogs can jump on children in play or simply annoy parents by adding to the household activity level. Inactive dogs are more likely to ignore children and perhaps even leave the room. Though they may help keep excitement levels down in the home, they may not be satisfying for children needing a playmate.

Independent dogs can be frustrating for children and may themselves be endangered by living with a child. Children may have difficulty taking an independent dog for a walk because it may wander away in search of adventure or game. Active, independent dogs may tend to run through gates and doors that children may inadvertently leave open. Playful, obedient, gentle, middle-sized dogs tend to make the best dogs for children.

HOW TO USE THE BREED PROFILES

The profiles are designed not only to inform you about a breed but also to provide information that will help you choose your best of breeds. Each profile is divided into several sections.

Popularity Breeds are ranked according to the AKC registration statistics at the time of writing, and are described as Most popular (AKC rank 1–10); Very popular (11–25); Popular (26–45); Somewhat popular (46–75); Somewhat uncomon (76–100); Uncommon (101–130); Rare (131–150); and Very rare (151 and above). Current rankings can be found at *www.akc.org*. These rankings underestimate the popularity of breeds that are primarily registered with non-AKC registries. Coonhounds, American Staffordshire Terriers, American Eskimo Dogs, and Rat Terriers, for example, are more heavily registered with the United Kennel Club (UKC); retired racing Greyhounds with the National Greyhound Association; and Foxhounds and many hunting breeds with various field organizations. More popular dogs are easier to locate, while very rare breeds may be in danger of extinction.

Family Many breeds belong to groupings of breeds associated by relationship or function.

Area of Origin The generally agreed-upon country or region in which a breed originated.

Date of Origin The approximate date at which a breed began to be recognized as distinct from other breeds.

Original Function Early uses for a breed.

Today's Functions Today's breed-specific uses and competitions. All breeds can participate in conformation shows, obedience trials, agility trials, tracking tests, and as therapy dogs. However, this is only mentioned if a breed is extraordinary in one of these functions.

Height and weight are the suggested values given in the AKC standards. Height is measured as the distance from the ground to the top of the withers. Those with an asterisk (*) indicate that no requirement was listed in the standard; these measurements are average reported values. Note that in any case, average values within a breed may differ from suggested values. Some breeders boast of weights or sizes that differ markedly from the AKC standard weights; such breeders should generally be avoided.

History

A breed's history describes the forces that molded its distinct features. Knowing the other breeds that have contributed to a new breed can help explain the traits that new breed displays; knowing what features a breed's creators were interested in accentuating can also help explain why a breed looks and acts as it does. A dog that has been bred to hunt at long range will have a lot of energy and tend to run at a great distance from its owner. A breed developed to dig out vermin will dig every chance it gets. Understanding a breed's history will help you decide whether a breed's innate characteristics will blend with your lifestyle.

Temperament

The same forces that shaped a breed's physical attributes have shaped its behavior and temperament. In fact, more often than not, the behavior of the dog was the initial trait that caused it to eventually become a breed.

Upkeep

The exercise requirements suggested here are average; dogs would usually do better with more but are usually given less. Note also that the requirements stated here are for adult dogs; never push a puppy to exercise beyond the time it is the least bit tired. Especially in giant breeds, such a practice can cause irreparable harm. Old dogs require considerably less exercise.

Apartment living is fine for very small dogs, and larger dogs with lower energy levels, or for owners who are committed to a regular exercise schedule. Some people want a dog that can live exclusively outdoors. No dog should be expected to live outside without human or canine companionship. Dogs are social animals; to a dog, solitary living is frustrating and so adverse that it can be considered severe punishment.

Coat care is another important consideration. Owners tend to underestimate the need for coat care, and overestimate their willingness to keep up a regular coat care regime. The dogs pictured in this book display the result of the maximum level of coat care. The coat care suggested here is average for the maintenance of an attractive coat typical of the breed; maintenance of a show-quality coat will require more commitment. Many wire coats require hand-plucking to maintain the correct harsh texture and deep coloration; clipping the coat will cause the coat to become soft and faded. Professional groomers seldom have the time or experience to hand-pluck a dog. Many breeds may require professional grooming; consider that this can be expensive. Pet owners can usually buy the proper grooming equipment and learn to groom their own dogs adequately.

All dogs need occasional bathing; long coats generally need bathing more often than short coats. Bathing removes oil and debris that can create matting. All dogs need occasional ear cleaning; only those in which ears are prone to problems are specifically mentioned as needing frequent cleaning. All dogs need tooth care, though many toy breeds suffer from tooth loss and periodontal disease and will need more attention to dental care. All dogs need regular nail clipping.

Many people are interested in finding a dog that doesn't shed. All dogs lose their hair; in some dogs, typically those with very curly coats, the hair is trapped by the other hairs instead of falling to the floor. In general, thick, double coats tend to shed in great amounts periodically; short, single coats shed less noticeably. No breed is truly hypoallergenic, as it is the dander of the dog, not the hair, that causes human allergies. A clean dog generally creates fewer problems for an allergic person.

Some dogs are just plain messy. Dogs with pendulous lips tend to drip water after drinking: many also tend to drool. Dogs with hairy feet tend to track debris into the house.

Although not specifically mentioned, food costs are higher for larger and more active dogs and for dogs that are outdoors in cold weather. Boarding and veterinary costs are also usually higher for larger dogs. Owners of giant dogs must take their dog's size into consideration when buying a car, or even a home. Tiny dogs need special precautions to avoid being injured, especially by other strange dogs. Obedience training is essential for all breeds of dogs; it tends to be more critical in larger or more aggressive dogs.

Health

Some health problems are seen more often in certain breeds due to various reasons. In some breeds, selection for particular traits may also inadvertently cause some health problems. Thus, flat-faced (brachycephalic) breeds have difficulty cooling themselves in hot weather and, sometimes, breathing. In other cases, a small number of dogs were used to found a breed, and if one of those dogs happened to carry a gene for a health problem, that undesirable gene could have become widespread throughout the breed because of the restricted gene pool. Finally, in breeds that have been extremely popular, careless breeding by owners not aware of health problems can cause genetic disorders to become more widespread. Parent clubs that have conducted breed health surveys have more information and thus their breeds may appear to have more health problems compared to those that have not conducted research. Thus, the health guide should be only a guide; a reported disorder does not doom a dog to having that problem nor does the absence of a disorder guarantee that the breed is free of it. The disorders are ranked as being of major concern (prevalent and serious), minor concern (either rare and serious or prevalent but not serious), and occasionally seen (reported, but not enough that it should dissuade anyone from choosing that breed). Note that the placement in one category versus another is at times a close or arbitrary decision. For disorders in which breed statistics are available, prevalent means that the disorder is reported in 10 percent or more of the individuals within a breed. Please refer to the Appendix at the back of this book for definitions of medical conditions.

Recommended tests refer to tests that the parents, or in some cases puppies, have. Tests reported in parentheses are suggested but not essential. Tests suggested by parent clubs for Canine Health Information Center (*www.caninehealth-info.org*) clearance are included. The Orthopedic Foundation for Animals (*www.offa.org*) maintains a registry for dogs evaluated as normal for several hereditary problems.

Form and Function

The physical features typical of a breed more often than not have their roots in functional requirements. This section describes the overall look, general proportions, substance, gait, coat, and expression of the breed, whenever possible explaining how that feature relates to the breed's function. Note that when overall proportions are available, unless otherwise specified, they refer to the proportion of the distance of height at the withers to the distance from the point of the breastbone to the point of the rump.

Illustrated Standard

The AKC standard for each breed is long and exacting. The illustrated standards point out some of the details that distinguish each breed. This is not a complete list of traits, and the reader is urged to consult the entire breed standard before evaluating a dog. Accepted colors are listed here, as well as breed specific disqualifications (DQ). These disqualifications (unless based on temperament or health) will in no way affect a dog's ability to function as a pet, but they do indicate that a dog is not show or (usually) breeding quality. The failure of one or both testicles to descend normally into the scrotum is a DQ in any breed. A dog with a DQ can still compete in all but conformation sports.

Note that many breeds traditionally may have docked tails and/or cropped ears. Tail docking is usually performed at a few days of age, so puppy buyers have little input if they do not wish this procedure performed on their prospective dog. If not performed at that time, it should never be performed. Ear cropping is usually performed at several months of age. Many pet owners elect not to have their puppy's ears cropped.

The following terms may be used:

COAT TERMS

Corded Coat intertwined in long, narrow mats.
Feather Long hair on the ears, backs of legs, and beneath the tail.
Ruff Profuse growth of hair on the neck.
Stand-off coat Coat that sticks out from the body rather than lying flat (example: Norwegian Elkhound).
Stripping Removal of the undercoat and dead outercoat without losing the harsh texture; plucking.

COLOR TERMS

Brindle Irregular vertical bands of dark hair overlaid on lighter hair.
Merle Dark patches overlaid on a lighter background of the same pigment type; also called dapple.

Parti-color Spotted.
Piebald Black patches on a white background.
Sable Black-tipped hairs.
Ticking Small flecks of coloring on a white background.
Wheaten Pale yellow color.

HEAD TERMS

Apple head Extremely domed skull.
Brachycephalic Broad head with short-muzzle.
Flews Upper lips, especially those that are pendulous.
Haw Exposed nictitating membrane (third eyelid), especially if unpigmented.
Occiput Highest point at the back of the skull, above where the neck joins the head.
Stop Transition area from backskull to muzzle, often demarcated by an abrupt depression.

TEETH TERMS

Level bite When upper and lower incisors meet evenly.
Overshot bite When upper incisors overlap lower incisors, leaving a gap between the teeth.
Scissors bite When upper incisors just overlap lower incisors, such that the rear surface of the upper incisors touches the outer surface of lower incisors.
Undershot bite When lower incisors extend beyond upper incisors

EAR TERMS

Button ears Semi-prick ears in which the top portion folds forward.
Bat ears Large, erect ears.
Drop ears Long, hanging ears.
Rose ears Small ears folded back in repose.
Prick ears Ears that stand upright.

BODY TERMS

Brisket Chest or sternum area.
Cobby Compact.
Loin Region between the ribcage and croup.
Topline Line formed by the withers, back, loin, and croup.
Tuck-up Area under the loin in a small-waisted dog.

FOOT TERMS

Cat foot Short, round foot.
Dew claws Toes on the insides of the front, and sometimes, rear legs.
Hare foot Long, narrow foot.

TAIL TERMS

Bob tail Very short, almost stump-like tail.
Gay tail Tail carried above the level of the back.
Saber tail Slightly curved, low-carried tail.
Screw tail Short, twisted tail.

MOVEMENT TERMS

Drive Strong thrust from the hindquarters.
Hackney High-stepping front movement.
Reach Length of forward stride.

At a Glance

Entries in this section range from *low* (represented by one box) to *high* (represented by five boxes). Most breeds vary over several rankings, and as such each ranking should be considered approximate for that breed. Individual dogs, like people, can show marked deviations from the average.

The information supplied in this section pertains to adult dogs.

Energy level. Note that there is no such thing as a low-energy puppy (or even adolescent), and buyers who need a low-energy dog from the outset are advised to consider a mature dog.

Exercise requirements. Exercise requirements are a combination of a dog's energy requirements and size or athleticism. Even a dog with very low requirements needs daily exercise.

Playfulness. Playfulness is related to energy level but focuses on whether that energy is aimed at interacting with people. Most people want a playful dog; however, the constant thud of a tennis ball dropped in your lap may be too demanding for busy people.

Affection level. NSome dogs, although devoted to their owners, are less demonstrative. A dog that ranks lower in this category does not mean that it does not need or thrive on attention and affection; it simply means that it may be less extroverted in its exhibition of it.

Friendliness toward dogs. Almost any dog can be aggressive toward strange dogs; those in which it is noted are a little more so than others. Similarly, in almost any breed, dogs may fight within a household, particularly dogs of the same sex. Dogs with higher ratings in this section tend to be less likely to fight than others, but they are not immune from it.

Friendliness toward other pets. All dogs can chase cats, and all dogs can learn to live peacefully with cats if they are raised with them. Some breeds, however, were bred to chase and kill small mammals, and these breeds are more likely to chase cats or other animals outside.

Friendliness toward strangers. Some breeds have never met a stranger. Some tend to be naturally aloof, shy, or suspicious.

Ease of training. Training ease does not necessarily reflect intelligence. Some dogs combine intelligence with a high energy level and a willingness to please that, taken together, result in a dog that learns quickly. Such dogs may be hard to live with if not trained, however, because they enjoy mental stimulation and need it in order to avoid boredom.

Watchdog ability. A dog that is alert enough to detect a stranger and will bark in response is given a high rating here, regardless of its size or protectiveness. Note that very high rankings may reflect a breed that tends to bark a lot.

Protection ability. The ability of a dog to be protective is a combination of its desire to act in a protective fashion, including its boldness, and its physical ability to enforce that desire.

Grooming requirements. This ranking is determined by coat type as well as size of the dog. A tiny dog with a lot of hair gets a lower ranking than a large dog with a lot of hair.

Cold tolerance. Small dogs and short-haired dogs are less heat tolerant than large, bulky dogs or dogs with thick, double coats.

Heat tolerance. Dogs, in general, are not heat tolerant. The shorter the nose, the bulkier the body, and the thicker the coat, the less heat tolerant a dog will be.

Important note: These ratings are based upon the assumption that a dog has been acquired from a reputable, qualified breeder. Qualified breeders will be willing to discuss temperament and health problems of their breed and will have proven their breeding stock in some sort of competitive area as well as screening it for breed typical health problems. They will have pictures of many of your potential puppy's ancestors. They will raise your puppy with plenty of human contact and proper health care. They will stand behind their dog and be available to you for advice for the rest of that puppy's life.

These breeds hunt in concert with a hunter armed with a gun, or in pre-gun times, a net. They work with the hunter to extend the hunter's abilities by either locating, moving, or fetching birds. Pointing and setting breeds locate game—they freeze in mid stride and "point" to game. Spaniels range back and forth close to the hunter, flushing game so that the hunter can shoot it. Retrievers bring back downed game—they mark where game falls and return with it over land or through water. Many breeds combine talents and are termed versatile hunters.

THE SPORTING GROUP

Brittany

AT A GLANCE

Energy level:	■ ■ ■ ■	Watchdog ability:	■ ■ ■ ■
Exercise requirements:	■ ■ ■ ■ ■	Protection ability:	■
Playfulness:	■ ■ ■ ■	Grooming requirements:	■
Affection level:	■ ■ ■ ■ ■	Cold tolerance:	■ ■ ■
Friendliness toward dogs:	■ ■ ■	Heat tolerance:	■ ■ ■
Friendliness toward other pets:	■ ■ ■		
Friendliness toward strangers:	■ ■ ■ ■ ■	WEIGHT: 30–40 lb	
Ease of training:	■ ■ ■ ■	HEIGHT: 17.5–20.5″	

POPULARITY: Popular
FAMILY: Gundog, Setter, Pointer, Versatile Hunting Dog
AREA OF ORIGIN: France
DATE OF ORIGIN: 1800s
ORIGINAL FUNCTION: Pointing, retrieving
TODAY'S FUNCTION: Pointing, retrieving, pointing field trials
OTHER NAME: Epagneul Breton, Brittany Spaniel

HISTORY

In the mid 1800s, French sportsmen crossed their small land spaniels with English Setters in attempts to produce a dog better suited for their needs. Some of the offspring were tailless, and their descendents continued to be tailless or stub-tailed. More importantly, they were excellent woodcock hunters with strong noses. These dogs soon became popular not only with the French gentry but also with poachers because they would both point and retrieve and were extremely obedient—essential qualities for the clandestine activities of the poachers. The first Brittany (or "Epagneul Breton") was registered in France in 1907. The Brittany came to America (Mexico) around 1925. The breed took a while to be accepted, mostly because hunters expected a pointing dog to have a long tail. When

ILLUSTRATED STANDARD

1. Nose some shade of brown or pink
2. Medium length, rounded skull
3. Short, triangular ears, set high
4. Short, straight back
5. Tailless to about 4 inches long, natural or docked

Color: orange and white, liver and white, or tricolored

DQ: under 17.5" or over 20.5" tall; black nose; black in coat

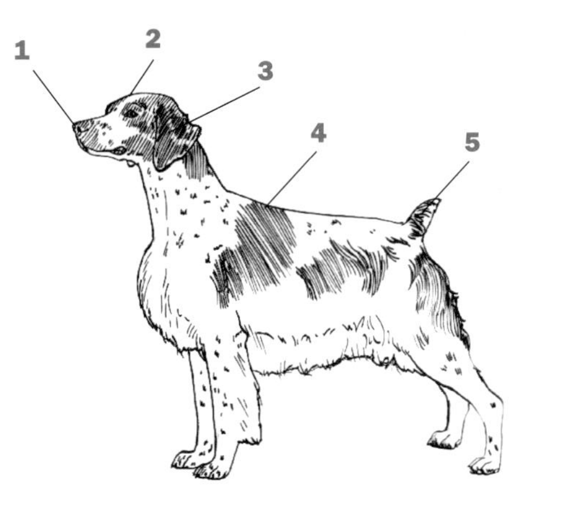

the dogs were given a chance, however, they proved their mettle and have since become the most popular of all pointing breeds at field trials. In fact, registrations eventually soared to place the Brittany among the top 20 in popularity, no doubt because of its bird-hunting abilities, close-ranging hunting style, small size, and tractable nature. Although registered as the Brittany Spaniel with the AKC from 1934, the word spaniel was dropped in 1982 in recognition of the dog's hunting style, which is more like that of a setter than a spaniel.

TEMPERAMENT

The Brittany is quick and curious, always on the lookout for birds or fun. It loves to run, scout, hunt, and play. It has an independent nature, befitting any pointing breed, yet it is sensitive and very responsive to human direction. The Brittany makes a good house pet as long as it receives daily mental and physical exercise. If not given sufficient exercise, it can become destructive.

UPKEEP

The Brittany is generally a hardy dog that requires little maintenance. Its major requirement is for abundant exercise, at least an hour of exertion—not just walking—every day. Its coat is not particularly thick or long, but it does require brushing once or twice weekly.

HEALTH

- Major concerns: CHD
- Minor concerns: epilepsy, hypothyroidism
- Occasionally seen: lens luxation, PRA
- Suggested tests: hip, thyroid, (eye)
- Life span: 12–13 years

FORM AND FUNCTION

The leggiest of the Sporting breeds, the Brittany is square-proportioned, the height at the shoulder equaling the length of the body. It stands slightly higher at the withers than at the rump. It is medium-sized with light bone. The combination of long legs and light bones endows the Brittany with remarkable agility and speed. In fact, the breed is very quick and is noted for its ground-covering side movement at the trot. The Brittany may be born tailless or have the tail docked to about 4 inches. The breed's coat is far less profuse than that of spaniels and is either flat or wavy. An overly profuse coat is detrimental when hunting in briars and is considered a severe fault. The Brittany's expression is alert and eager, but soft. The eyes are protected from briars by a fairly heavy eyebrow. The Brittany is an extremely athletic, eager dog that should be ready and able to run in the field for extended periods.

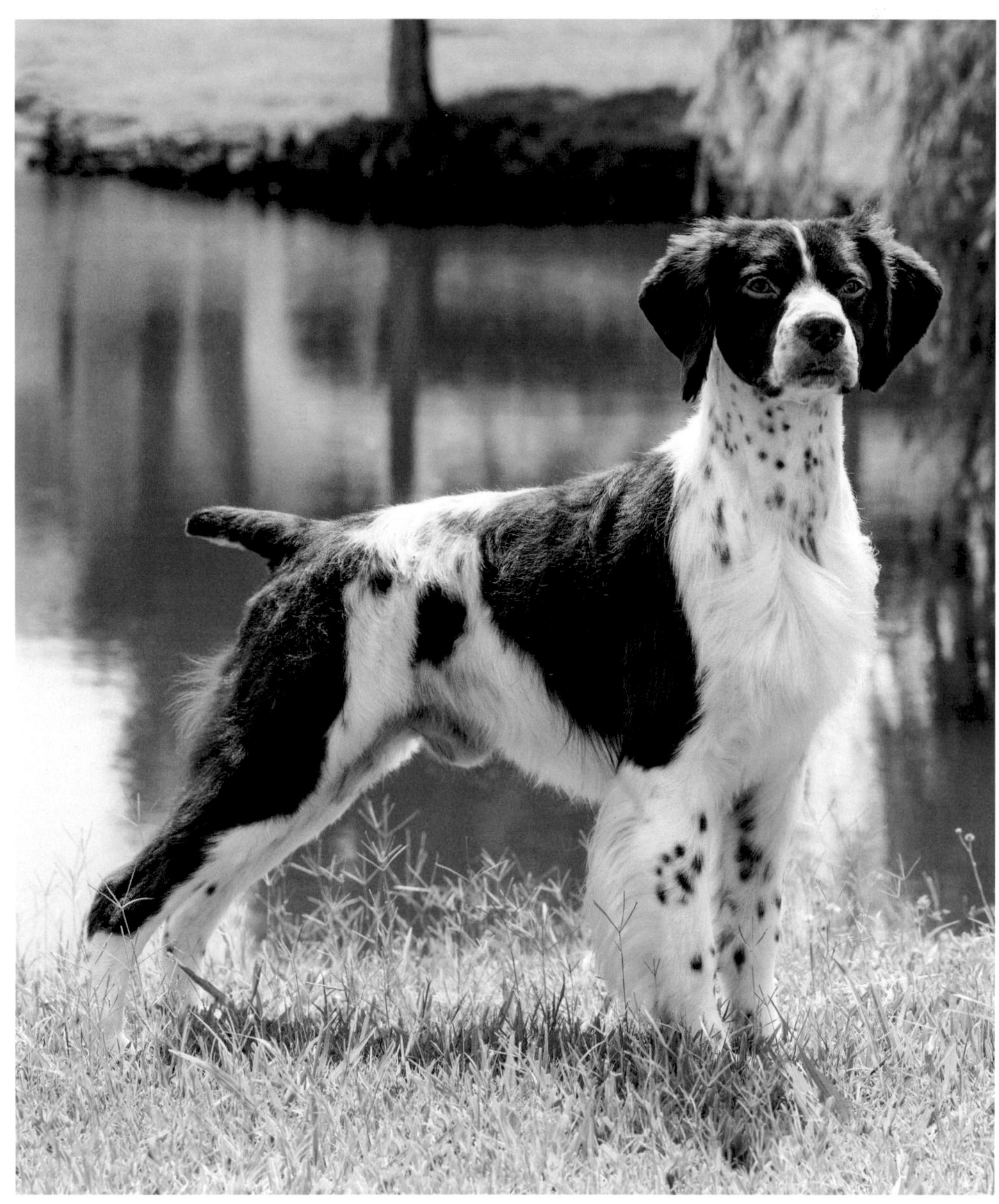

Pointer

AT A GLANCE

Energy level:	■■■■■	Watchdog ability:	■■■■	POPULARITY: Uncommon
Exercise requirements:	■■■■■	Protection ability:	■■■	FAMILY: Gundog, Pointer
Playfulness:	■■■■■	Grooming requirements:	■	AREA OF ORIGIN: England
Affection level:	■■■■■	Cold tolerance:	■■■	DATE OF ORIGIN: 1600s
Friendliness toward dogs:	■■■■■	Heat tolerance:	■■■	ORIGINAL FUNCTION: Pointing
Friendliness toward other pets:	■■■■■			TODAY'S FUNCTION: Pointing, pointing field trials, companion
Friendliness toward strangers:	■■■	WEIGHT: male: 55–75 lb; female: 45–65 lb		
Ease of training:	■■■	HEIGHT: male: 25–28″; female: 23–26″		OTHER NAME: English Pointer

HISTORY

The earliest Pointers were used in the seventeenth century not to point birds, but to point hare, which coursing Greyhounds were then unleashed to pursue. When wing-shooting became popular in the eighteenth century, the Pointer found its place as an adept bird locator. The ideal dog would find game, indicate its location, and remain still until the hunter could get ready to shoot—a task that was somewhat slow with the old flintlock guns. The early Pointer probably included in its genetic makeup some of the most talented breeds in existence: Greyhounds, Foxhounds, and Bloodhounds, as well as an old type of setting spaniel. Different countries developed different Pointer breeds. After the war of Spanish Succession (1713), British army officers returned home with heavy-

ILLUSTRATED STANDARD

1. Square, deep muzzle; nose slightly higher at tip than at stop
2. Long head with pronounced stop
3. Rounded eyes
4. Thin, soft, hanging ears, somewhat pointed at tip
5. Tail tapering, straight, carried near the line of the back
6. Muscular body
7. Oval feet

Color: liver, lemon, black, orange, either solid or mixed with white
DQ: none

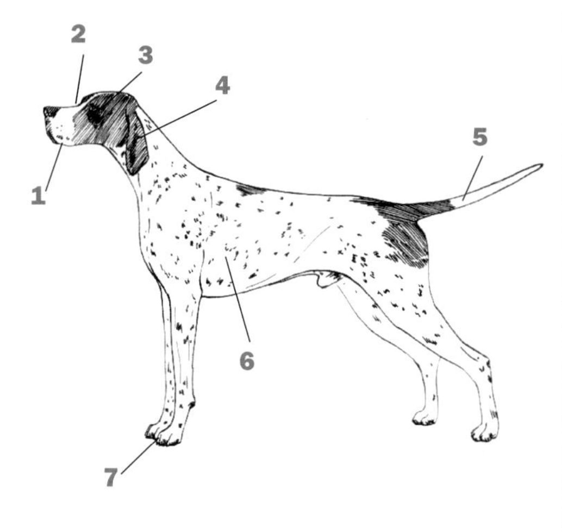

boned Spanish Pointers. These were later crossed with Italian Pointers to produce the modern Pointer. Pointers became popular for recreational hunting on large estates. Ideally, two Pointers were used so that the hunter could locate the bird precisely by cross-referencing the dogs' points. When dog shows came in vogue in the late nineteenth century, Pointers were among the most prominent of the breeds shown; in fact, the Westminster Kennel Club was organized primarily for Pointers. Pointers remain very popular as competitive field trial dogs and recreational hunters; however, they are not as popular as pets as many other sporting breeds.

TEMPERAMENT

The Pointer is a true wide-ranging hunter, which means that it not only is an excellent bird dog but also has the stamina to run for hours. Consequently, it needs lots of exercise or it can become frustrated and destructive. Because it is ever on the lookout for birds, it is easily distracted from everyday matters—but it is nearly impossible to distract once on point. It is gentle and sweet but may be too energetic and boisterous at times for very small children. Like many sporting breeds, it can be found in field or show types; the field type is generally smaller and perhaps more active.

UPKEEP

The Pointer needs exercise, and lots of it. It needs at least an hour of exertion every day. It is best when it has a regular opportunity to hunt, but it also enjoys running and searching the wilds on long jaunts afield. At home it needs space to exercise outdoors and should not be expected to sit inside all day. It requires only an occasional brushing to remove dead hair. Field lines may be more active.

HEALTH

- Major concerns: none
- Minor concerns: CHD, hypothyroidism, entropion
- Occasionally seen: cataract, deafness
- Suggested tests: hip, eye, thyroid
- Life span: 12–15 years
- Note: prone to tail-tip injuries

FORM AND FUNCTION

The Pointer combines athletic grace and power with a lean, muscular body, noble head, alert expression, and noble carriage. The gait is smooth and powerful, with head held high and nostrils wide, enabling it to cover a lot of ground while searching for airborne scent. The tail lashes from side to side when the dog gaits. The Pointer's close coat is short and dense, giving a clean streamlined appearance. Field type pointers tend to hold their tails upright when on point.

German Shorthaired Pointer

AT A GLANCE

Energy level:	■■■■■
Exercise requirements:	■■■■■
Playfulness:	■■■■
Affection level:	■■■■
Friendliness toward dogs:	■■■
Friendliness toward other pets:	■■
Friendliness toward strangers:	■■■
Ease of training:	■■■

Watchdog ability:	■■■■■
Protection ability:	■■■
Grooming requirements:	■
Cold tolerance:	■■■
Heat tolerance:	■■■

WEIGHT: male: 55–70 lb; female 45–60 lb
HEIGHT: male 23–25″; female 21–23″

POPULARITY: Very popular
FAMILY: Gundog, Pointer, Versatile Hunting Dog
AREA OF ORIGIN: Germany
DATE OF ORIGIN: 1600s
ORIGINAL FUNCTION: General hunting
TODAY'S FUNCTION: Pointing, pointing field trials
OTHER NAME: German Pointer (Shorthaired), Deutscher Kurzhaariger Vorstehund, Kurzhaar

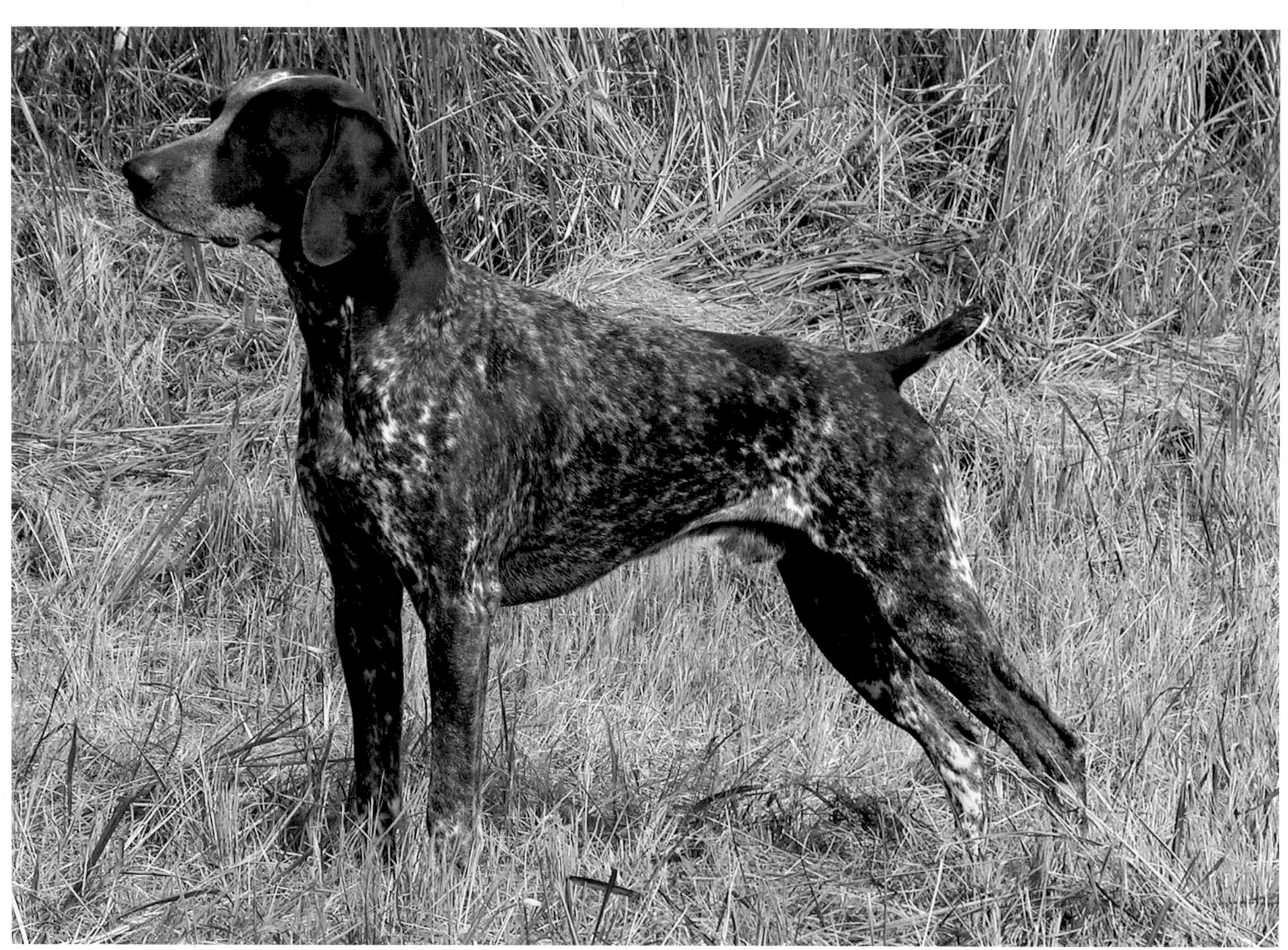

HISTORY

The German Shorthaired Pointer is one of the most versatile of hunting breeds, combining pointing, retrieving, trailing, and even game-killing abilities. This versatility arose through the purposeful blending of various breeds beginning as early as the seventeenth century. Crosses of the Spanish Pointer (a heavy type of pointer) with the Hannover Hound (a strain of scenthounds) resulted in a heavy houndlike dog that could both trail and point and was interested in both birds and mammals. When trailing, these dogs would bay; if needed, they would dispatch wounded game and even fox. Although all the early breeders agreed upon the goal of an all-purpose hunting dog, not all agreed upon how to achieve it. Crosses with the English Pointer were controversial but bestowed upon the breed a more

ILLUSTRATED STANDARD

1 Large, brown nose
2 Stop not as defined as in the Pointer
3 Almond-shaped eyes
4 Broad, high set, rounded ears
5 Short, strong back
6 Tail docked to 40 percent of length, carried down when relaxed or horizontally when moving
7 Defined tuck-up
8 Rounded feet

Color: liver or combinations of liver and white
DQ: china or wall eyes; flesh-colored nose; extreme overshot or undershot; any area of black, red, orange, lemon, or tan; solid white

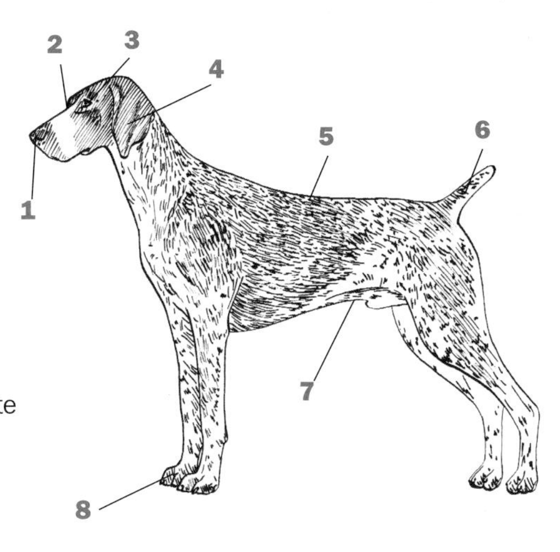

stylish look and nose-up hunting mode. It also imparted a dislike of water and an aversion to attacking quarry. Further breeding eliminated these unwanted pointer characteristics. In the early 1800s two Deutsch Kurzhaars (as the breed was originally known), Nero and Treff, distinguished themselves against other pointing breeds at the German Derby and, through the success of their descendents, are often credited as the modern Shorthaired's foundation. The breed was recognized in the late 1800s in Germany with the first Shorthaired coming to America in the 1920s. The German Shorthaired Pointer gained AKC recognition in 1930. The breed soon gained a reputation as the ideal dog for the hunter who wanted only one dog that could do it all. Besides being a gifted and versatile hunter, it is a handsome dog and obedient companion. These attributes helped the German Shorthaired Pointer become popular today.

TEMPERAMENT

The German Shorthaired Pointer's idea of heaven is a day hunting in the field and an evening curled up by its owner's side. This is an active dog that can become frustrated and "creative" if not given ample daily exercise, both mental and physical. It is a devoted family pet, although at times it is overly boisterous for small children. Because part of its heritage includes hunting mammals, some can be aggressive to small pets unless raised with them. It is a sensitive breed, responsive to gentle training. Some can whine or bark a lot.

UPKEEP

Bred to be an active hunting companion, this breed has a good deal of energy and requires a good deal of exercise. It thrives on mental and physical stimulation and can get both by hunting, hiking, or playing with its owner for a long period—at least an hour—every day. They like water and will swim if given the chance. Its grooming needs are minimal, consisting only of occasional brushing to remove dead hair.

HEALTH

- Major concerns: lymphedema
- Minor concerns: CHD, entropion, gastric torsion, vWD, pannus, OCD, hypothyroidism
- Occasionally seen: ectropion, PRA, cardiomyopathy
- Suggested tests: hip, eye, cardiac, (thyroid), (vWD)
- Life span: 12–14 years

FORM AND FUNCTION

The Shorthaired is an all-purpose close-working gundog that combines agility, power, and endurance. It is square or slightly longer than tall; although it has a short back, it should stand over plenty of ground. It should have a clean-cut head, graceful outline, strong quarters, and an athletic physique. The gait is smooth, light, and ground covering. The coat is short and tough.

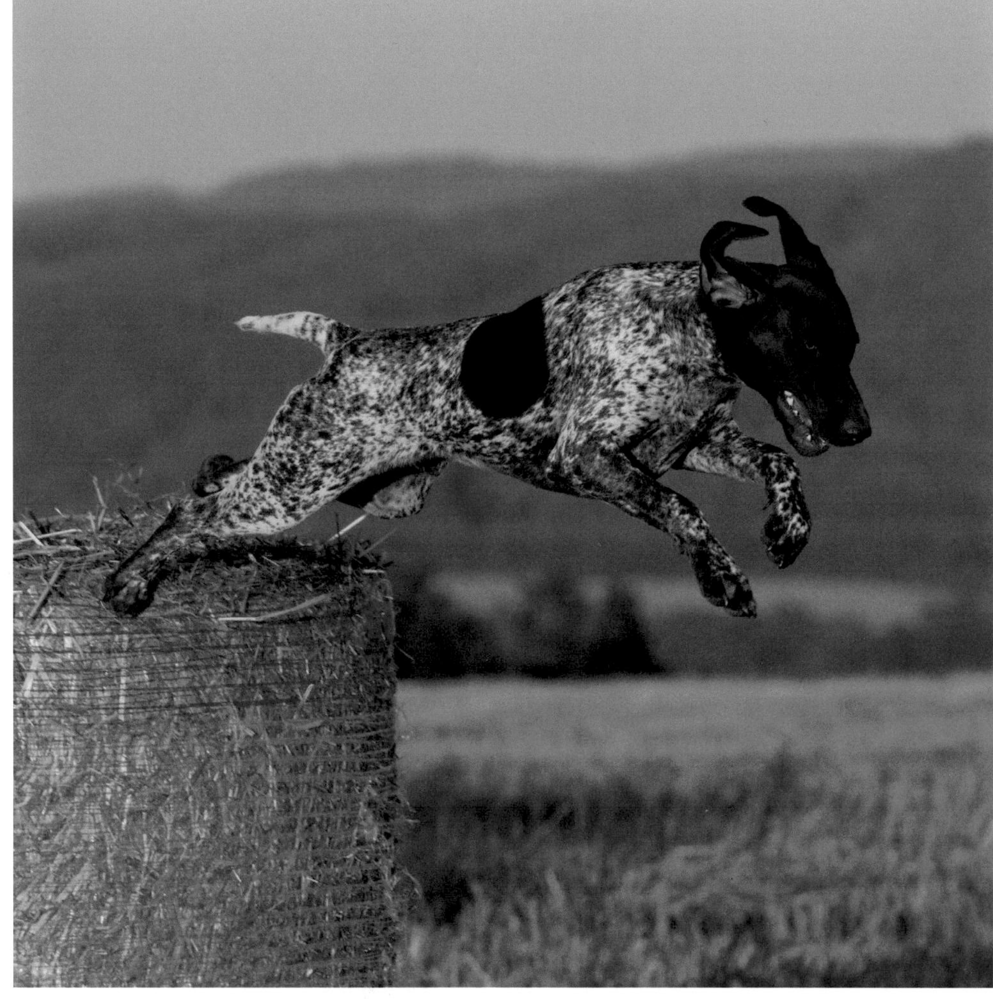

German Wirehaired Pointer

AT A GLANCE

Energy level:	■■■■■
Exercise requirements:	■■■■■
Playfulness:	■■■■
Affection level:	■■■
Friendliness toward dogs:	■■
Friendliness toward other pets:	■■■
Friendliness toward strangers:	■■
Ease of training:	■■■

Watchdog ability:	■■■■■
Protection ability:	■■■■
Grooming requirements:	■■■
Cold tolerance:	■■■
Heat tolerance:	■■■

WEIGHT: 45–75 lb
HEIGHT: male: 24–26″; female: smaller but not under 22″

POPULARITY: Somewhat popular
FAMILY: Gundog, Pointer, Versatile Hunting Dog
AREA OF ORIGIN: Germany
DATE OF ORIGIN: 1800s
ORIGINAL FUNCTION: General hunting, watchdog
TODAY'S FUNCTION: Pointing, pointing field trials, companion
OTHER NAME: Deutscher Drahthaariger Vorstehund, German Pointer (Wirehaired), Drahthaar

HISTORY

When game-bird shooting became accessible to persons of average means, demand for both specialist and versatile hunting breeds soared. The quest for versatile breeds reached its height in Germany, and the German Wirehaired Pointer represents one of its most successful results. Hunters wanted a dog that would locate and point upland game, track wounded game, confront tough vermin, retrieve waterfowl from land or water, and also function as companion and watchdog. It was developed to be a close worker over any kind of terrain. A rough wiry coat was needed to hunt through dense brambles. Its most important ancestor was the Pudelpointer (itself a combination of the old German Pudel and the Pointer), which was crossed with the early German Shorthaired Pointer,

ILLUSTRATED STANDARD

1 Beard and whiskers of medium length
2 Medium stop
3 Oval eyes, with medium length eyebrows
4 Short, straight, strong back
5 Tail docked to about two fifths of the original length; carried at or above horizontal
6 Defined tuck-up
7 Round, webbed feet

Color: liver and white, with ears and head solid liver, sometimes with a white blaze
DQ: none

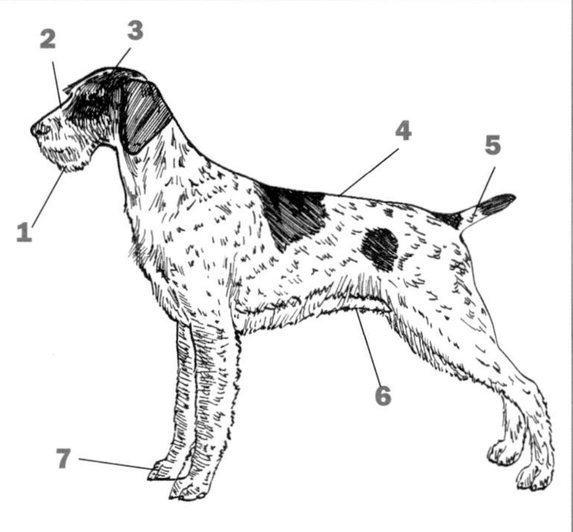

Griffon, Stichelhaar, and Polish Water Dog. The breed, known as the Drahthaar in Germany, has since become the most popular hunting breed in Germany. Nonetheless, it was not recognized there officially until the 1920s, the same time the first Wirehaired came to America. The German Wirehaired Pointer was recognized in America in 1959 but has never gained the popularity that they enjoy in their native land.

TEMPERAMENT

The German Wirehaired Pointer is both a rugged bird dog and amiable companion. It has the energy to hunt for hours, so it must be given a daily outlet lest it becomes destructive. It is a responsive breed, although it tends to be stubborn. It retains a guarding instinct, so it tends to be aloof, even protective, toward strangers as well as strange dogs. It is generally good, if sometimes overly boisterous, with children. It is ideal for the outdoor-oriented person wanting a tireless, weather-proof, intelligent partner.

UPKEEP

Exercise is a daily requirement for this energetic hunter. At least an hour a day of exertion is recommended, and the ideal situation would combine exercise with hunting or a chance to run and explore afield. Like most harsh coats, some minimal hand-stripping may occasionally be needed to maintain a sleek outline; otherwise, brushing about once a week will suffice. GWPs are low shedders.

HEALTH

- Major concerns: CHD
- Minor concerns: hypothyroidism
- Occasionally seen: seizures, entropion, elbow dysplasia, heart disease, gastric torsion, vWD
- Suggested tests: hip, elbow, cardiac, thyroid, eye, (vWD)
- Life span: 12–14 years

FORM AND FUNCTION

A sturdily built hunter, the German Wirehaired Pointer should be able to hunt all day through all types of cover. It is slightly longer than it is tall, enabling the gait to be free and smooth. The weather-resistant, straight wiry coat is an essential breed characteristic. The outer coat is about 1 to 2 inches long, long enough to protect against brambles but not so long that the outline of the dog is obscured. The eyebrows, beard, and whiskers are of medium length. The undercoat is thick in winter for warmth but thin in summer. The coat repels water, enabling the German Wirehaired Pointer to work almost as well in water as on land.

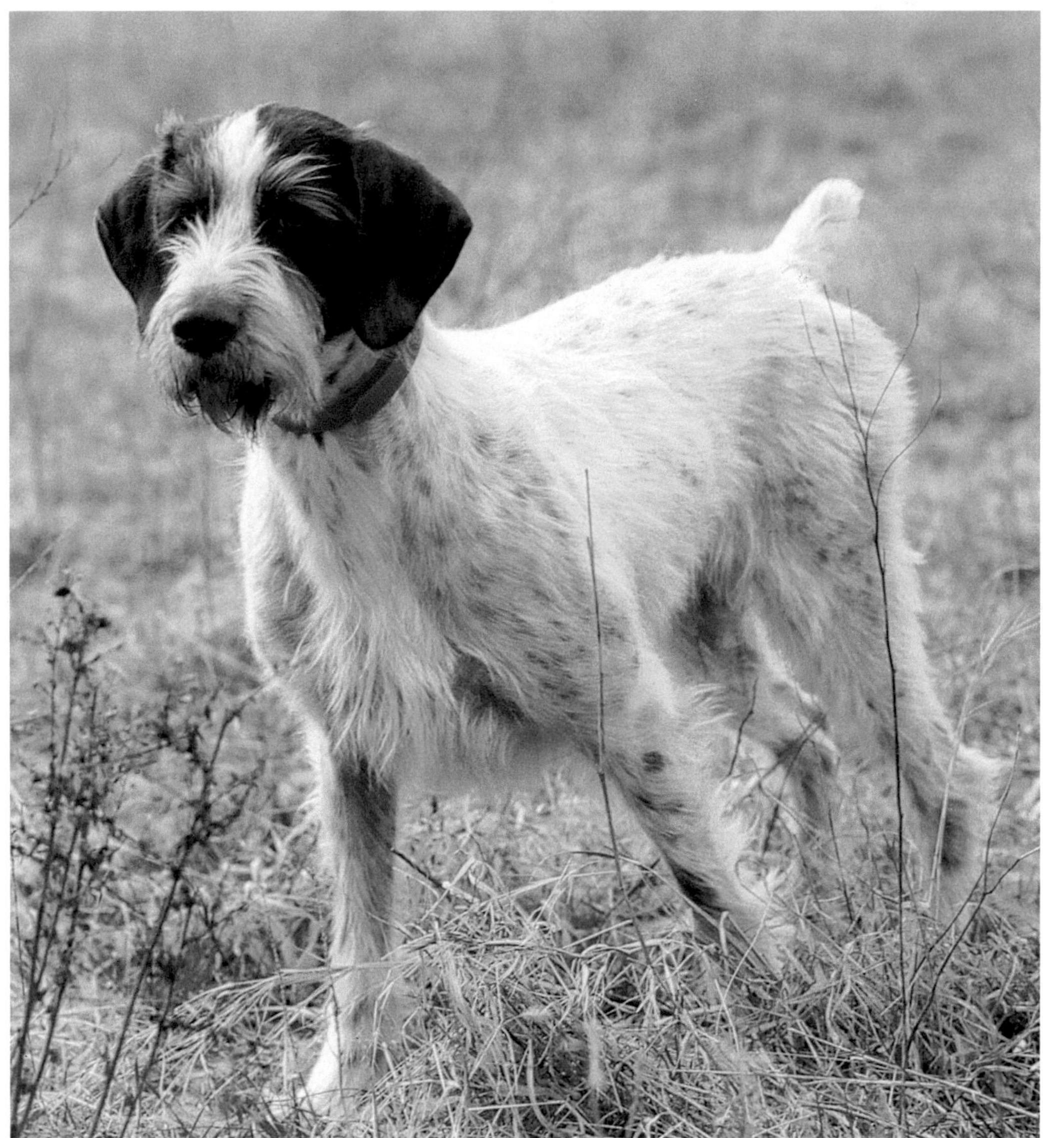

Chesapeake Bay Retriever

AT A GLANCE

Energy level:	■■■
Exercise requirements:	■■■
Playfulness:	■■■
Affection level:	■■■■
Friendliness toward dogs:	■■■
Friendliness toward other pets:	■■■
Friendliness toward strangers:	■■
Ease of training:	■■■

Watchdog ability:	■■■■
Protection ability:	■■■
Grooming requirements:	■■
Cold tolerance:	■■■■
Heat tolerance:	■■■

WEIGHT: male: 65–80 lb; female: 55–70 lb
HEIGHT: male: 23–26″; female: 21–24″

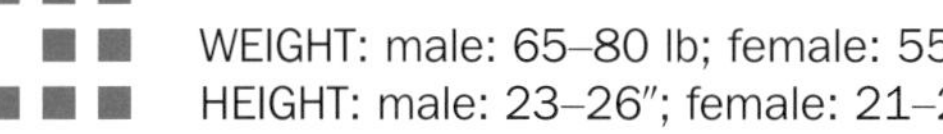

POPULARITY: Popular
FAMILY: Gundog, Retriever
AREA OF ORIGIN: United States
DATE OF ORIGIN: 1800s
ORIGINAL FUNCTION: Water retriever
TODAY'S FUNCTION: Water retriever, retriever field trials, companion
OTHER NAME: None

HISTORY

The history of the Chesapeake Bay Retriever is one of the most fascinating—and fortunate—in dogdom. In 1807, an American ship rescued the crew and cargo from a shipwrecked English brig off the coast of Maryland. Among the rescued were two presumably Newfoundland pups that were given to the rescuers. These pups (one black and one red) later proved to be skilled water retrievers, and as their reputations grew, many local retrievers of uncertain background came to be bred to them. It is also thought that Irish Water Spaniel, Newfoundland, Bloodhound, and other local hound crosses added to the development of the breed. Gradually a distinct local breed emerged, a dog that would repeatedly swim through the rough icy waters of the Chesapeake Bay and

ILLUSTRATED STANDARD

1 Broad, round skull with medium stop
2 Eyes amber
3 Hindquarters as high or slightly higher than shoulder
4 Especially powerful hindquarters for swimming
5 Tail straight or slightly curved
6 Webbed hare feet

Color: any color of brown, sedge, or deadgrass

DQ: lacking in breed characteristics; teeth overshot or undershot; dewclaws on hind legs; coat curly or with a tendency to curl all over the body; feathering on the tail or legs over 1-3/4" long; black colored; white on any part of the body except breast, belly, toes, or back of feet

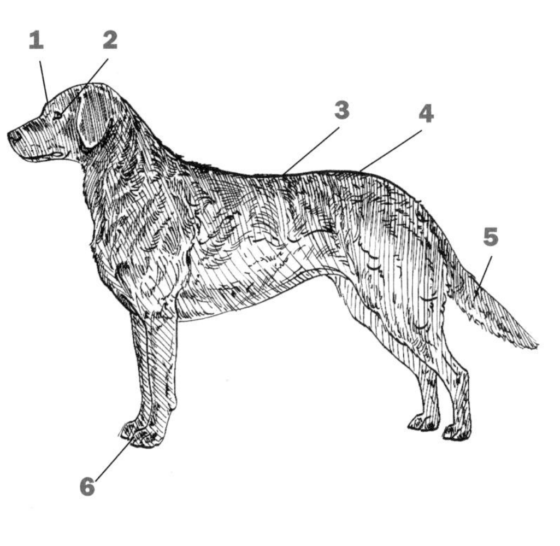

unerringly retrieve duck after duck. Even today, the Chessie is renowned for its remarkable ability to mark and remember where a bird has fallen. Its reputation spread well beyond the Chesapeake Bay area. By 1885, the breed was thoroughly established and recognized by the AKC. Despite being one of the oldest AKC recognized breeds, as well as one of the few breeds that can boast of being made in the United States, the Chessie's popularity has remained modest.

TEMPERAMENT

The Chesapeake Bay Retriever is hardy enough to not only withstand, but also relish, repeated plunges into icy water. It loves to swim and retrieve. Despite an active life when outdoors, inside it tends to be calm. The Chessie tends to be independent, although it is eager to learn. It is reserved with strangers and can be protective; it also can be aggressive toward strange dogs if challenged. This is the hardiest, most strong-willed, and protective of the retriever breeds.

UPKEEP

The Chessie is a large active dog that needs a daily chance to exercise. The oily, wavy coat needs weekly brushing but is generally easily maintained. It seldom needs washing; in fact, it's hard to get a Chessie wet! Bathing destroys the coat's oils and thus, its water resistance.

HEALTH

- Major concerns: CHD, gastric torsion
- Minor concerns: PRA, hypothyroidism
- Occasionally seen: entropion, OCD, elbow dysplasia, cerebellar abiotrophy
- Suggested tests: hip, eye, elbow, (thyroid), (cardiac)
- Life span: 10–13 years

FORM AND FUNCTION

The Chesapeake Bay Retriever was developed to hunt waterfowl under adverse conditions, facing strong tides in rough water, high winds, and sometimes even having to break through ice. It is an extraordinary swimmer, with a strong, yet tender, bite enabling it to carry birds. It has powerful limbs and webbed feet. The Chessie is slightly longer than tall, with its hindquarters as high, or higher, than its forequarters. Its coat is rendered virtually waterproof by virtue of its oily, harsh outer coat and dense wooly undercoat. The color matches its working surroundings: any shade of brown, sedge, or dead grass.

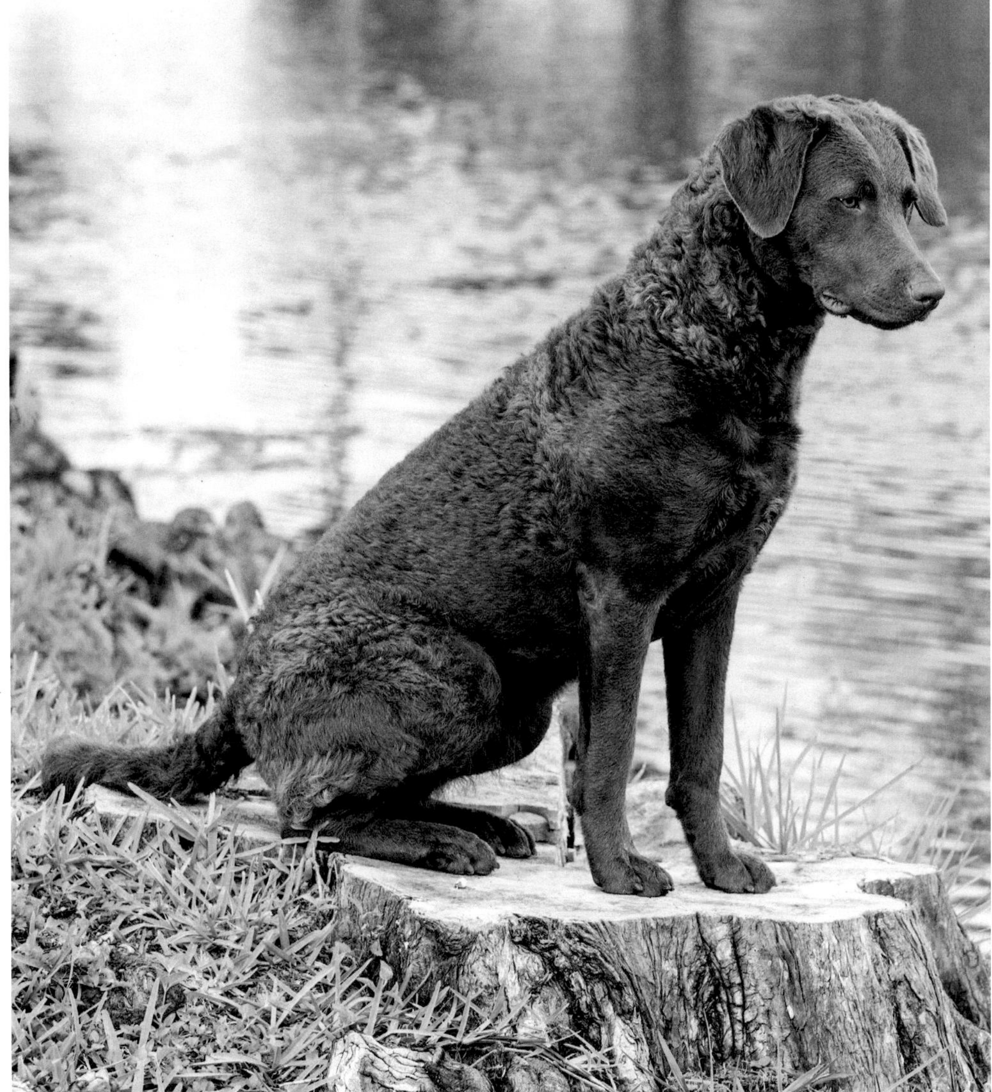

Curly-Coated Retriever

AT A GLANCE

Energy level:	■■■
Exercise requirements:	■■■
Playfulness:	■■■
Affection level:	■■■
Friendliness toward dogs:	■■■
Friendliness toward other pets:	■■■■
Friendliness toward strangers:	■■
Ease of training:	■■■

Watchdog ability:	■■■■
Protection ability:	■■
Grooming requirements:	■
Cold tolerance:	■■■■
Heat tolerance:	■■■

WEIGHT: 60–70 lb*
HEIGHT: male 25–27″; female 23–25″

POPULARITY: Very rare
FAMILY: Gundog, Retriever
AREA OF ORIGIN: England
DATE OF ORIGIN: 1700s
ORIGINAL FUNCTION: Water retrieving
TODAY'S FUNCTION: Water retrieving, retrieving field trials, companion
OTHER NAME: None

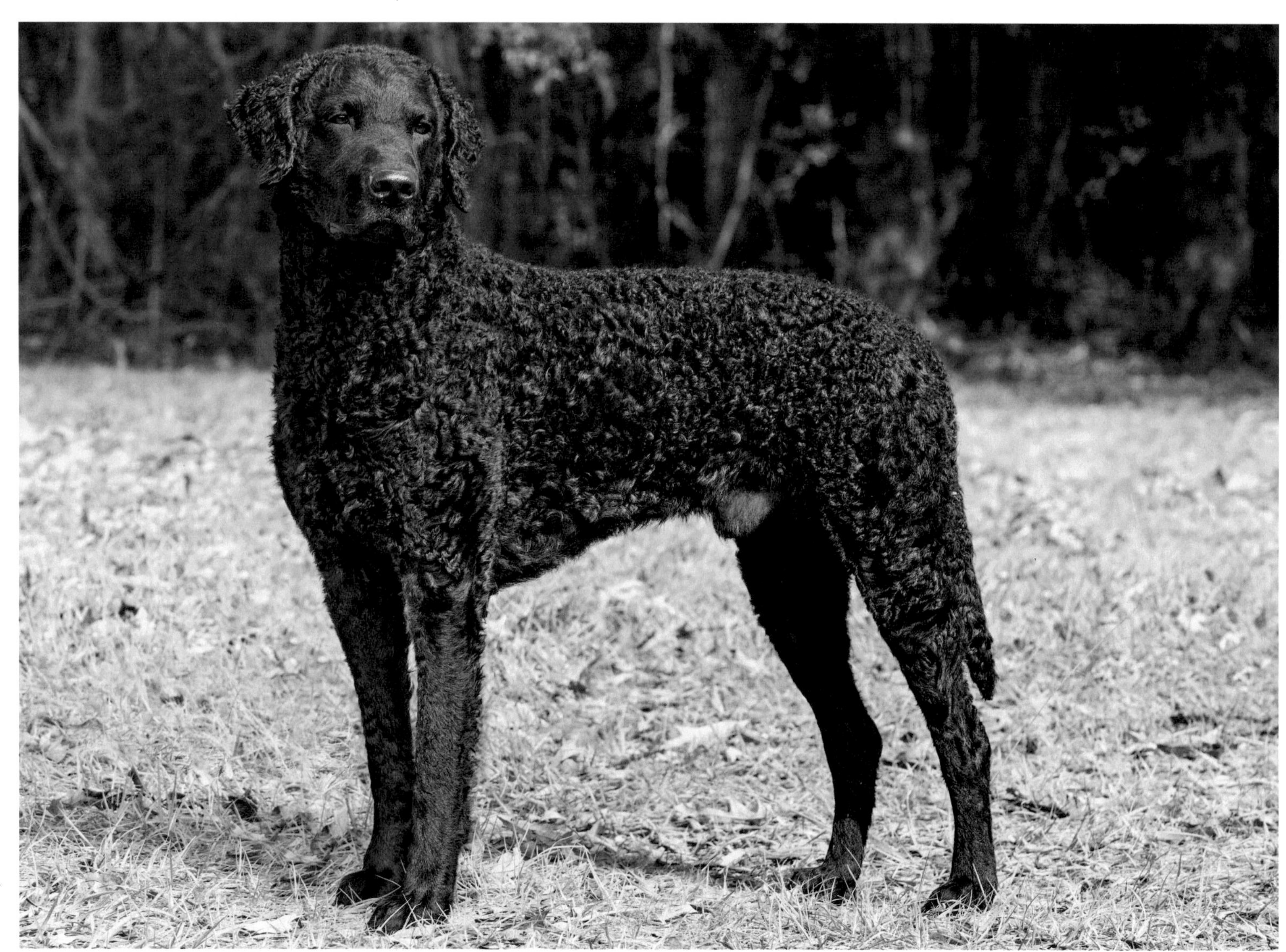

HISTORY

One of the oldest and most distinctive of the retriever breeds, the Curly-Coated Retriever may have been used in England for retrieving as long ago as the late eighteenth century. Although its exact origin remains conjectural, it probably stems from crosses of the descendents of the Old English Water Dog with the Irish Water Spaniel, and a small type of Newfoundland. These breeds together combined some of the finest water dogs in existence into one animal. Later crosses to the Poodle, a fine water retriever in its own right, served to further enhance the tight curls. By the mid 1800s, the Curly-Coated Retriever was the most popular retriever in England, prized not only for its unsurpassed retrieving abilities but also as a staunch and trustworthy companion.

ILLUSTRATED STANDARD

1 Tight lips
2 Head longer than wide; wedge-shaped with shallow stop
3 Rather large, almond-shaped eyes
4 Tail fairly straight, covered with curls
5 Round feet

Color: black or liver
DQ: none

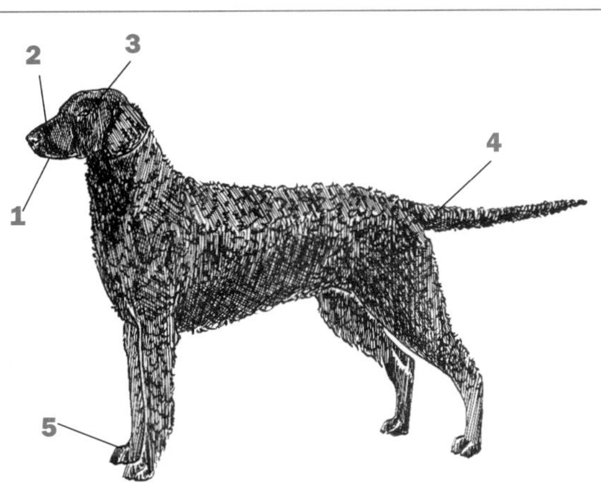

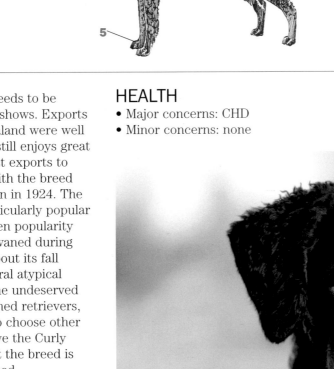

It was among the first breeds to be exhibited at English dog shows. Exports to Australia and New Zealand were well received, and the breed still enjoys great popularity there. The first exports to America were in 1907, with the breed receiving AKC recognition in 1924. The breed never became particularly popular in America, however. Even popularity of the Curly in England waned during the 1900s. One theory about its fall in popularity is that several atypical Curlies gave the breed the undeserved reputation as hard-mouthed retrievers, causing newer hunters to choose other retrievers. Those who give the Curly a chance have found that the breed is actually quite soft-mouthed.

TEMPERAMENT

The Curly-Coated Retriever is an eager and tireless land and, especially, water retriever outdoors, but a calm companion indoors. It is sensitive and gentle, very good with children, and responsive to commands. It is reserved with strangers. One of the most courageous of the retrievers, it is nonetheless quite sensitive. It makes an ideal partner for an active, outdoor-oriented person who also wants a loyal family companion.

UPKEEP

The Curly is an easy dog to maintain, requiring no unusual care. It needs daily exercise, preferably involving swimming and retrieving. Because brushing diminishes the tight curls, it should be combed only occasionally, preferably before getting wet. Some very minimal scissoring may be desirable to tidy up scraggly hairs. It does need regular brushing during its shedding seasons.

HEALTH

- Major concerns: CHD
- Minor concerns: none
- Occasionally seen: distichiasis, cataract, elbow dysplasia
- Suggested tests: hip, cardiac, eye, (elbow)
- Life span: 8–12 years

FORM AND FUNCTION

The Curly is the most graceful and elegant of the retrievers, appearing longer legged and more agile than the others. It has an alert upright carriage, enabling it to mark downed animals easily, be they fur or feather. It is an active land retriever and a hardy water retriever, able to withstand the rigors of repeated retrieves into heavy thickets or cold waters. Its distinctive coat provides protection from cold and briars and is made up of a dense mass of tight curls.

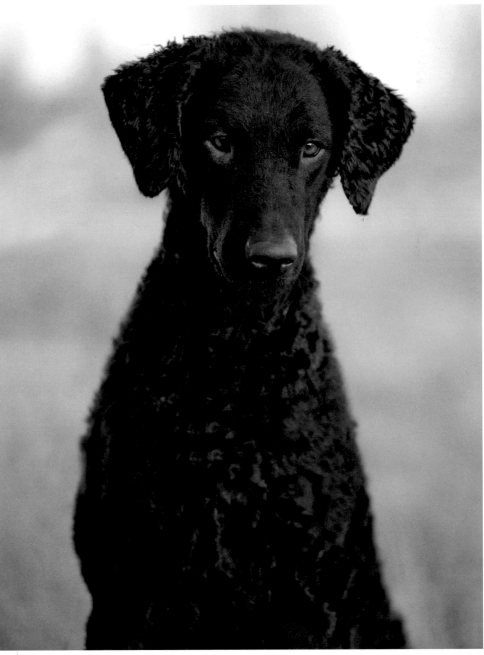

Flat-Coated Retriever

AT A GLANCE

Energy level:	■■■
Exercise requirements:	■■■
Playfulness:	■■■■
Affection level:	■■■■■
Friendliness toward dogs:	■■■
Friendliness toward other pets:	■■■■
Friendliness toward strangers:	■■■■
Ease of training:	■■■■■

Watchdog ability:	■■■■
Protection ability:	■■
Grooming requirements:	■■
Cold tolerance:	■■■
Heat tolerance:	■■■

WEIGHT: 60–70 lb*
HEIGHT: male: 23–24.5″; female: 22–23.5″

POPULARITY: Somewhat uncommon
FAMILY: Gundog, Retriever
AREA OF ORIGIN: England
DATE OF ORIGIN: 1800s
ORIGINAL FUNCTION: Water retrieving
TODAY'S FUNCTION: Water retrieving, retriever field trials
OTHER NAME: None

HISTORY

One of the earliest uses of retrieving dogs was to help fishermen retrieve fish and objects from the water. In the nineteenth century, such retrieving dogs were especially popular with the cod fisheries around Newfoundland. Of these dogs, the most popular breeds were the Labrador (not to be confused with the present Labrador Retriever) and several sizes of Newfoundlands. With the development of more advanced firearms, hunters were increasingly able to shoot "on the wing," but they needed a dog to mark the fallen bird and bring it back. The fishery dogs were unrivaled swimmers and natural retrievers, and crosses between them and British breeds such as setters or pointers honed the dog's bird sense. The result was the Wavy-Coated Retriever, and it became quite popular

ILLUSTRATED STANDARD

1 Long, deep muzzle
2 Long head with slight stop
3 Almond-shaped eyes
4 Small, hanging, thickly feathered ears
5 Fairly straight tail, carried near horizontal

Color: solid black or liver
DQ: any color other than black or liver

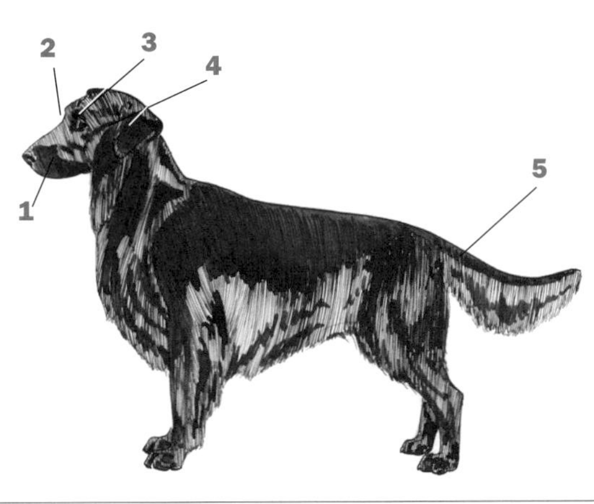

in America and England. In fact, it was among the earliest breeds to be shown at English dog shows. Near the end of the 1800s, crosses with a straighter-haired breed were made because the wavy coat was thought to be less water repellant. Crosses to setters and collies of the time may also have been made. The resulting Flat-Coated Retrievers became tremendously popular. The breed was not recognized by the AKC until 1915, by which time it had already begun to drop in popularity. By the end of the Second World War, the number of Flat-Coats had dwindled to the point that the breed was threatened with extinction. Concerted efforts to bring the breed back slowly succeeded, and the Flat-Coat now enjoys modest popularity as a companion and show dog, but has not regained its field presence.

TEMPERAMENT

The Flat-Coated Retriever is a sweet, exuberant, lively dog that loves to play and retrieve. It is on the go outdoors, but quiet indoors. This breed is among the most devoted and companionable of dogs, a true family dog. It needs regular exercise to be on its best behavior, however. It is a sensitive breed and very responsive to training. Its hallmark is its wagging tail.

UPKEEP

This active dog needs daily exercise and fun, and especially enjoys the chance to hunt or swim. This is a family-oriented dog that does best when allowed to live inside and play outside. Its coat needs only weekly brushing and little, if any, minor trimming occasionally.

HEALTH

- Major concerns: malignant histiocytosis
- Minor concerns: CHD, glaucoma, patellar luxation, hemangiosarcoma, osteosarcoma, lymphosarcoma, gastric torsion, fibrosarcoma
- Occasionally seen: seizures, diabetes
- Suggested tests: eye, hip, knee
- Life span: 8 years

FORM AND FUNCTION

"Power without lumber and raciness without weediness" is the traditional description of the Flat-Coated Retriever. It is strong but elegant, never cobby, among the most streamlined of the retrievers. It is slightly longer than tall, of moderate substance. The head is distinctive, long and of "one piece," all parts flowing smoothly into each other. The gait is ground covering, smooth, and efficient. The coat is thick and flat, of only moderate length, providing protection without adding weight. These attributes have resulted in a versatile and athletic hunter capable of retrieving over land and water.

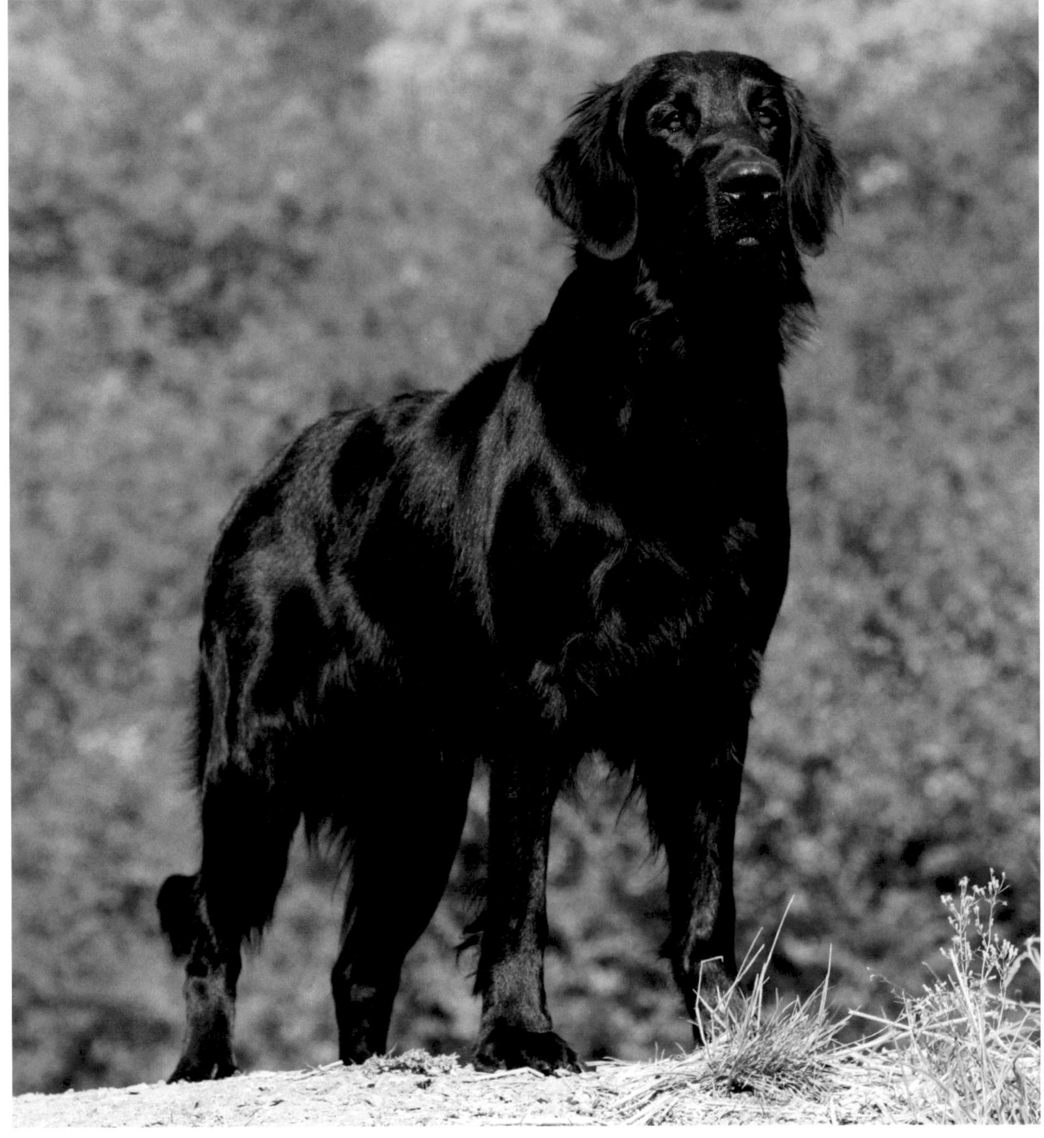

Golden Retriever

AT A GLANCE

Energy level:	■■■
Exercise requirements:	■■■
Playfulness:	■■■■■
Affection level:	■■■■■
Friendliness toward dogs:	■■■■■
Friendliness toward other pets:	■■■■■
Friendliness toward strangers:	■■■■■
Ease of training:	■■■■■

Watchdog ability:	■■■
Protection ability:	■■
Grooming requirements:	■■■
Cold tolerance:	■■■
Heat tolerance:	■■■

WEIGHT: male: 65–75 lb; female: 55–65 lb
HEIGHT: male: 23–24″; female: 21.5–22.5″

POPULARITY: Most Popular
FAMILY: Gundog, Retriever
AREA OF ORIGIN: England
DATE OF ORIGIN: 1800s
ORIGINAL FUNCTION: Retrieving
TODAY'S FUNCTION: Retrieving, assistance, obedience competition, retriever field trials
OTHER NAME: Yellow Retriever

HISTORY

One of the best documented and most fortuitous efforts to produce a breed resulted in the Golden Retriever. The man responsible for the breed was Lord Tweedmouth, who lived just north of the Scottish border along the Tweed River. With an increasing interest in retrieving dogs in the mid 1800s, a dog that could push through heavy vegetation, brave cold water, swim strongly, and retrieve gently was in demand. Lord Tweedmouth bred Nous, a yellow Wavy-Coated Retriever (a descendent of the small Newfoundland and the earlier Labrador breeds used by fisherman) to Belle, a Tweed Water Spaniel (a popular liver-colored retriever with tightly curled coat). They produced four puppies, which showed promise of being outstanding upland bird dogs. Subsequent judicious crosses were made

ILLUSTRATED STANDARD

1 Stop well defined
2 Broad skull, slightly rounded
3 Rather short ears
4 Thick tail, carried near horizontal
5 Little tuck-up
6 Round feet

Color: various shades of gold
DQ: deviation from height of more than 1"; undershot or overshot bite

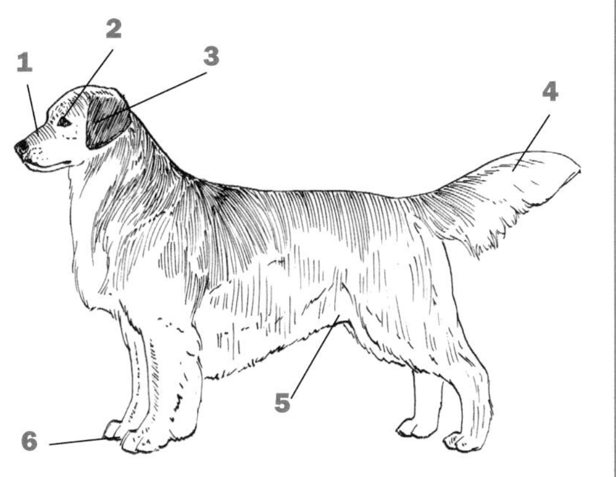

with other black retrievers, Tweed Spaniels, setters, and even a Bloodhound. The breed was first considered to be a yellow variety of Flat-Coated Retrievers, but was recognized as a separate breed, the Yellow or Golden Retriever, in 1912. A few of these dogs had come to America by way of Lord Tweedmouth's sons by 1900, but the AKC did not register them as a separate breed until 1927. The breed was valued for the hunting abilities so ably produced by the careful blending of foundation stock. It only later became popular as a pet, show dog, and obedience competitor. After it made the transition, however, its rise to the height of popularity was meteoric, and it remains one of the most popular of all breeds in America.

TEMPERAMENT

Everybody's friend, the Golden Retriever is known for its devoted and obedient nature as a family companion. It is an apt sporting retriever as well and yearns for a day in the field. Ignoring its active nature and powerful physique can lead to behavior problems, and it needs daily physical and mental exercise. Poorly bred Goldens may be overly exuberant and boisterous, but the correct Golden is eager to please and enjoys learning. Well-trained and exercised Goldens are calm and mannerly at home, and enthusiastic when invited to play. The Golden's achievements in competitive obedience are remarkable. It especially enjoys games that involve retrieving and loves to carry items in its mouth.

UPKEEP

The Golden Retriever needs daily exercise and human interaction. Challenging obedience lessons, active games, or retrieving sessions are all good ways to exercise the Golden's mind and body. The coat does not tend to mat but needs twice weekly brushing.

HEALTH

- Major concerns: CHD, skin problems (allergies, hot spots, ear infections), hemangiosarcoma, lymphoma
- Minor concerns: SAS, elbow dysplasia, eye disorders (entropion, CPRA), seizures, hypothyroidism, mast cell tumors
- Occasionally seen: osteosarcoma
- Suggested tests: hip, elbow, eye, cardiac, (thyroid)
- Life span: 10–13 years

FORM AND FUNCTION

The Golden Retriever is an athletic, strong dog, capable of carrying heavy game over land and water. For this, it needs a broad, powerful head with strong neck and well-developed fore- and hindquarters. It is just slightly longer than tall. The gait is smooth, powerful, and ground covering. The water-repellant coat is dense, with the outer coat straight or wavy.

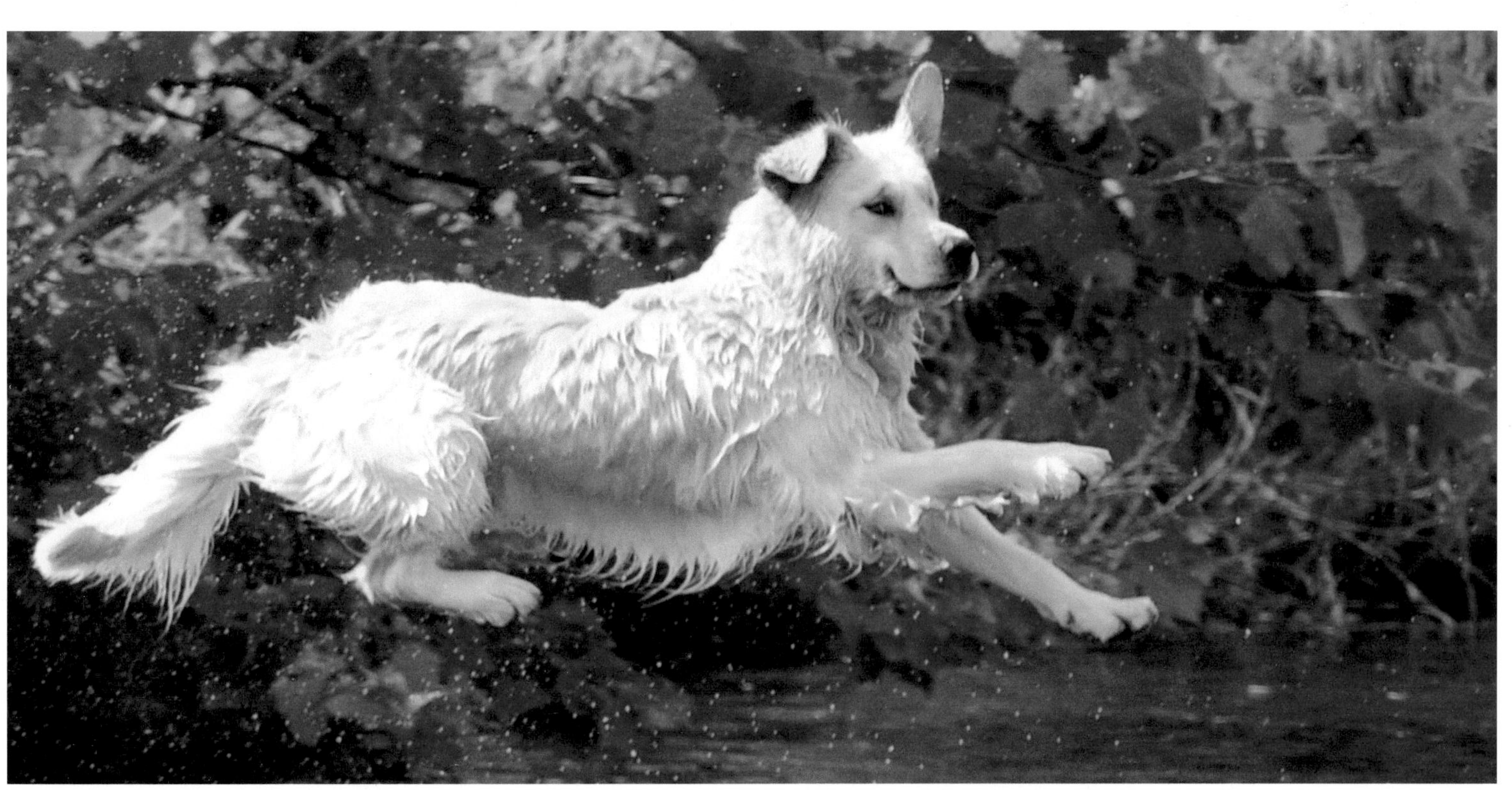

Labrador Retriever

AT A GLANCE

Energy level:	■■■■
Exercise requirements:	■■■
Playfulness:	■■■■■
Affection level:	■■■■■
Friendliness toward dogs:	■■■■
Friendliness toward other pets:	■■■■■
Friendliness toward strangers:	■■■■■
Ease of training:	■■■■■

Watchdog ability:	■■■■
Protection ability:	■■
Grooming requirements:	■■
Cold tolerance:	■■■■
Heat tolerance:	■■■

WEIGHT: male: 65–80 lb; female: 55–70 lb
HEIGHT: male 22.5–24.5″; female 21.5–23.5″

POPULARITY: Most Popular
FAMILY: Gundog, Retriever
AREA OF ORIGIN: Canada
DATE OF ORIGIN: 1800s
ORIGINAL FUNCTION: Water retrieving
TODAY'S FUNCTION: Water retrieving, assistance, obedience competition, retriever field trials
OTHER NAME: None

HISTORY

The original Labradors were all-purpose water dogs originating in Newfoundland, not Labrador. Not only did the breed not originate in Labrador, but it also was not originally called the Labrador Retriever. The Newfoundland of the early 1800s came in different sizes, one of which was the "Lesser" or "St. John's" Newfoundland—the earliest incarnation of the Labrador. These dogs—medium-sized black dogs with close hair—not only retrieved game but also retrieved fish, pulled small fishing boats through icy water, and helped the fisherman in any task involving swimming. Eventually the breed died out in Newfoundland in large part because of a heavy dog tax. However, a core of Labradors had been taken to England in the early 1800s, and it is from these dogs, along with crosses to other

ILLUSTRATED STANDARD

1 Kind, intelligent eyes
1 Broad backskull with moderate stop
3 Tail very thick toward base, with a rounded "otter-like" appearance, carried in line with topline
4 Little or no tuck-up; short-coupled

Color: solid black, yellow, or chocolate
DQ: deviation from prescribed height; thoroughly pink or pigmentless nose or eye rims; alteration of length or carriage of tail; any color other than solid black, yellow, or chocolate (a small white spot on the chest is permissible)

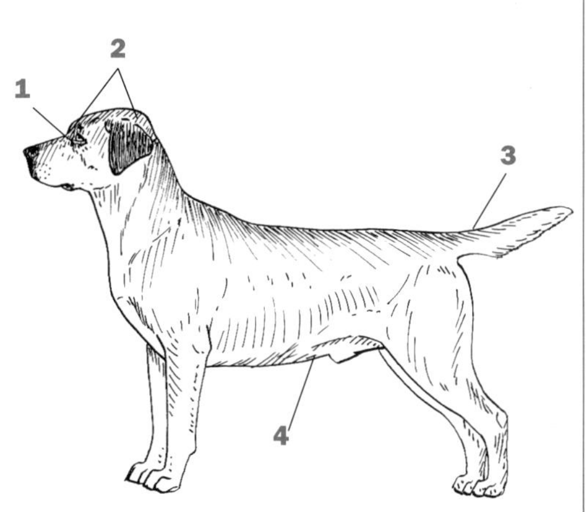

retrievers, that the breed continued. It was also in England that the breed earned its reputation as an extraordinary retriever of upland game. Initially breeders favored black Labs, and culled yellow or chocolate colors. By the early 1900s, the other colors had become acceptable, although still not as widely favored as the blacks. The breed was recognized by the English Kennel Club in 1903 and by the AKC in 1917. The popularity of this breed has grown steadily until it became the most popular breed in America in 1991 and remains so today.

TEMPERAMENT

Few breeds so richly deserve their popularity as does the Labrador Retriever. When trained, it is obedient and amiable, and tolerates well the antics of children, other dogs, and other pets. It will be a calm housedog, playful yard dog, and intense field dog, all on the same day. It is eager to please, enjoys learning, and excels in obedience. It is a powerful breed that loves to swim and retrieve. It needs daily physical and mental challenges to keep it occupied, however; a bored Lab can get into trouble. The Labrador's hunting instinct drives it to roam; breeders say "his home is under his hat."

UPKEEP

Labradors are active and sociable dogs. They need daily exercise, preferably in the form of retrieving and swimming. Owners with swimming pools either must fence them out or be prepared to share the pool with dog. The Lab coat sheds water easily. It needs weekly brushing to remove dead hair.

HEALTH

- Major concerns: CHD, elbow dysplasia, OCD, obesity, patellar luxation
- Minor concerns: cataract, CPRA, hot spots, retinal dysplasia, hypothyroidism
- Occasionally seen: diabetes, entropion, distichiasis, tricuspid valve dysplasia, centronuclear myopathy, exercise-induced collapse
- Suggested tests: hip, elbow, eye, exercise-induced collapse (DNA), (centronuclear myopathy), (knee)
- Life span: 10–12 years

FORM AND FUNCTION

The Labrador is a moderate dog, not extreme in any way. It is square or slightly longer than tall, of fairly large bone and substance. Its broad head and strong jaws should enable it to carry the largest game birds, such as Canada geese. Its heavy body set and strong legs enable it to swim and run powerfully. Its coat, which is short, straight, and dense with a soft undercoat, is weatherproof and helps to protect it from icy waters. The Lab is a working retriever and should possess style without over refinement and substance without clumsiness.

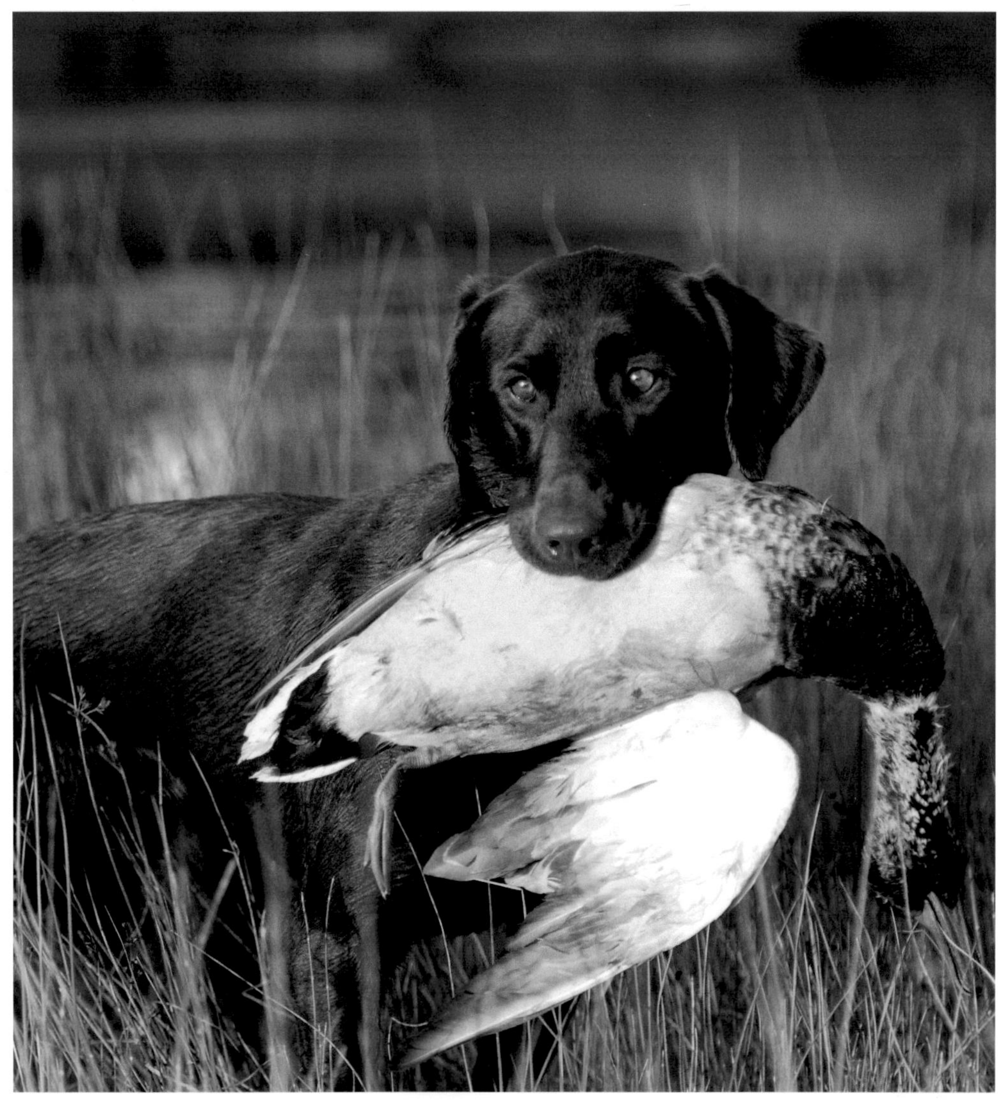

Nova Scotia Duck Tolling Retriever

AT A GLANCE

Energy level:	■■■■■	Watchdog ability:	■■	POPULARITY: Somewhat uncommon
Exercise requirements:	■■■■■	Protection ability:	■■	FAMILY: Gundog, Retriever
Playfulness:	■■■■■	Grooming requirements:	■■	AREA OF ORIGIN: Nova Scotia
Affection level:	■■■■■	Cold tolerance:	■■■■	DATE OF ORIGIN: 1800s
Friendliness toward dogs:	■■■■■	Heat tolerance:	■■■	ORIGINAL FUNCTION: Duck tolling and retrieving
Friendliness toward other pets:	■■■■■			
Friendliness toward strangers:	■■■	WEIGHT: male: 45–52 lb; female: 35–42 lb*		TODAY'S FUNCTION: Duck tolling and retrieving
Ease of training:	■■■■	HEIGHT: male: 18–21″; female: 17–20″		OTHER NAME: Little River Duck Dog

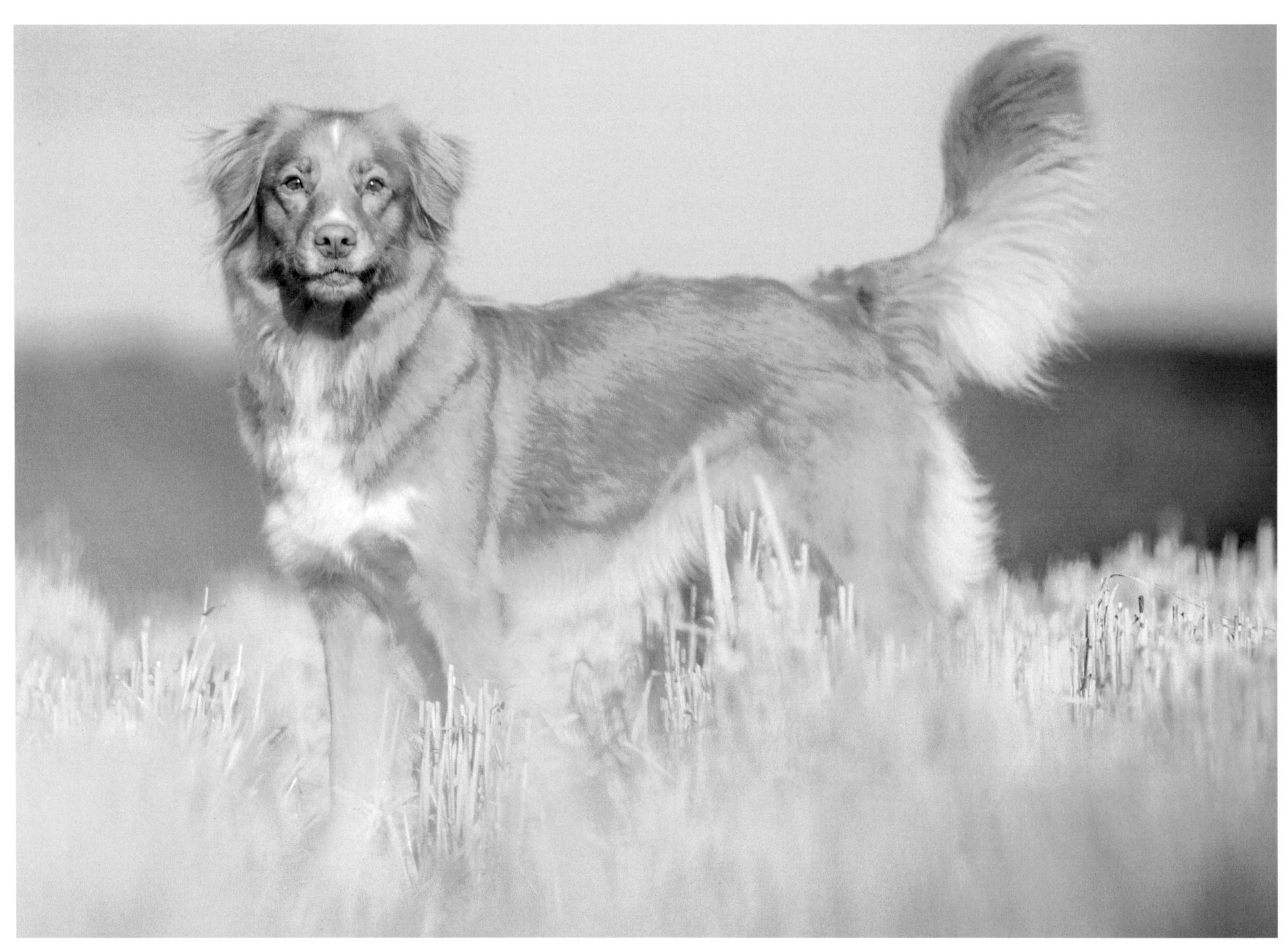

HISTORY

Europeans used dogs to toll (Middle English meaning: to lure or decoy) ducks into nets since the seventeenth century. Tolling is done by the dogs frolicking along the shore, chasing sticks, and occasionally disappearing from sight, an activity that draws curious ducks to the area. The tolling dog must continue in its animated fashion, tail wagging, retrieve after retrieve, ignoring the ducks. With the advent of guns, the ducks were then shot and the dogs sent to retrieve them. Such decoy dogs may have come with European settlers to the New World, where they were used to toll from the Chesapeake Bay to the Maritimes. The Nova Scotia Duck Tolling Retriever was developed in Yarmouth County, at the southern tip of Nova Scotia, in the early nineteenth century. It may have been

ILLUSTRATED STANDARD

1. Slightly wedge-shaped head
2. Almond-shaped eyes
3. High set ears, triangular with rounded tips
4. Level backline
5. Tail follows the slope of the croup, reaching to at least the hock, and covered with luxuriant feathering
6. Oval, medium-sized, webbed feet

Color: any shade of red, usually with white markings on the tail tip, feet, chest, or blaze

DQ: butterfly nose; undershot bite; wry mouth; overshot by more than 1/8"; rear dew claws; brown coat, black areas in coat, or buff (bleached, faded, or silvery); white on shoulders, around ears, back of neck, or across flanks

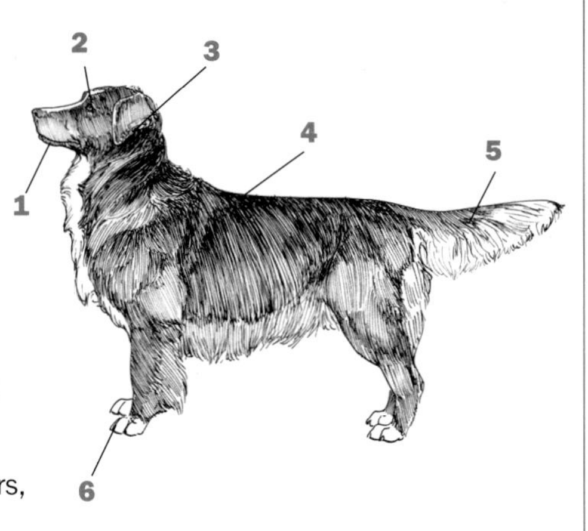

derived from the red European decoy dog and perhaps later crossed with spaniel-, setter-, or retriever-type dogs, as well as farm collies; an alternative theory is that they are derived in part from tolling American Indian dogs. Originally known as the Little River Duck Dog or the Yarmouth Toller, the breed later became known as the Nova Scotia Duck Tolling Retriever. It was recognized by the Canadian Kennel Club in 1915, with 15 Tollers registered that year. The first Tollers came to the United States in the 1960s, and it wasn't until 1984 that the Nova Scotia Duck Tolling Retriever Club (USA) was formed. The club offered a breed championship that required basic retrieving and tolling ability in order to qualify, and still offers a series of working certificates to ensure that the breed's instincts remain intact. In 2001 Tollers were admitted into the AKC Miscellaneous class, and were admitted as a regular member of the Sporting Group in 2003. Since then they have proven they are more than just tollers or retrievers, but excel at obedience, agility, tracking, and of course, companionship.

TEMPERAMENT

As befitting a dog bred to play and retrieve tirelessly, the Toller is very energetic and playful. You cannot throw a ball just once for a Toller! Everything they do is done with gusto, whether it's hunting, obedience, agility, or just walking around the block. They are alert but not hyperactive, and can adjust to many circumstances. They are affectionate and gentle, but young Tollers can be overly boisterous at times. They are good with children, other dogs, and pets. Tollers may be initially wary of strangers, but warm up quickly. They learn fast and are generally willing to please, but bore easily and then can be a bit stubborn. When excited, they can be very vocall and are known for the shrill "Toller scream."

UPKEEP

Tollers need lots of exercise, especially involving playing and retrieving. They love water! Tollers also profit from mental challenges, such as obedience and agility. They are devoted family companions that treasure their interaction with humans. Grooming consists of a thorough weekly brushing.

HEALTH

- Major concerns: none
- Minor concerns: CHD, PRA
- Occasionally seen: none
- Suggested tests: hip, eye, DNA for PRA
- Life span: 11–13 years

FORM AND FUNCTION

Because Tollers run as much as they swim when hunting, they are smaller and more agile than most other retrievers. Their powerful yet compact build enables them to rush around tirelessly, leaping and retrieving with tail always wagging. The jaws are strong enough to carry a duck. Because they were bred to work in icy waters, they have a water-repelling double coat of medium length. A longer coat is not appropriate for a working dog, although the tail feathering should be long, adding to the emphasis of the wagging tail. A white blaze, chest, tail tip, or feet is characteristic, and may serve to make the dog's gamboling more noticeable to distant ducks.

English Setter

AT A GLANCE

Energy level:	■■■■
Exercise requirements:	■■■■
Playfulness:	■■■
Affection level:	■■■■
Friendliness toward dogs:	■■■
Friendliness toward other pets:	■■■■
Friendliness toward strangers:	■■■■■
Ease of training:	■■■
Watchdog ability:	■■■■
Protection ability:	■■
Grooming requirements:	■■■
Cold tolerance:	■■■
Heat tolerance:	■■■

WEIGHT: male: 60–65 lb; female: 50–55 lb* (field types about 10 lb less)
HEIGHT: male: about 25″; female: about 24″

POPULARITY: Somewhat uncommon
FAMILY: Setter, Pointer
AREA OF ORIGIN: England
DATE OF ORIGIN: 1300s
ORIGINAL FUNCTION: Bird setting and retrieving
TODAY'S FUNCTION: Pointing, pointing field trials
OTHER NAME: None

HISTORY

Even before the advent of the shotgun, when birds were often caught with a net, dogs were trained to crouch when they pointed game. These "setters" were the forerunners of today's setters. The English Setter is the oldest known of this group, perhaps dating back to the fourteenth century. It was developed to locate game on the moors and then to freeze until the game was dispatched. The English Setter's ancestors probably included the Spanish Pointer, Springer Spaniel, and large Water Spaniel. The cultivation of the English Setter through concerted pure breeding was undertaken by Edward Laverack beginning around 1825 and continuing for over 35 years. These dogs formed the basis of all English Setters today. Incidentally, the term *belton* was coined by Laverack

ILLUSTRATED STANDARD

1 Muzzle long and square, with fairly pendant flews
2 Head long and lean with a well-defined stop
3 Eyes large and nearly round
4 Occiput moderately defined
5 Low-set ears
6 Topline level or sloping slightly to rear
7 Tail carried straight, and level with topline, tapering to a fine point

Color: orange, liver, lemon, or black ("blue") flecks over a white ground color; also a combination of black and tan flecks on white ("tricolor"); liver and lemon colors are rarely seen today; puppies born white, except for those with solid patches
DQ: none

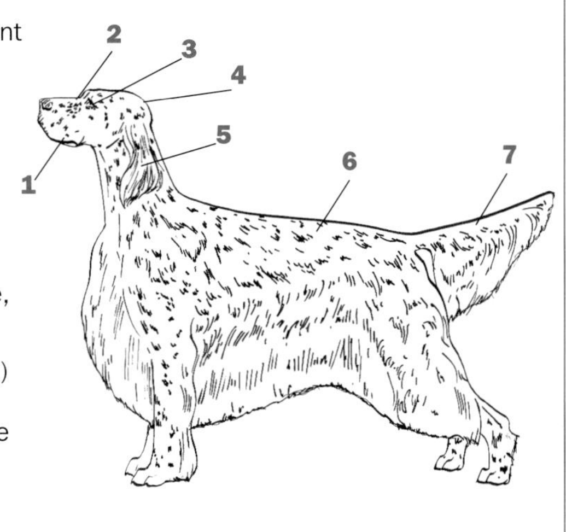

to describe the roan or ticked flecks of color and comes from the town of Belton, where Laverack hunted. The other most influential breeder, Purcell Llewellin, obtained his foundation stock from Laverack but based his breeding on field ability alone. Llewellin crossed his Laveracks with unrelated English Setters to produce such outstanding field dogs that many were imported to America. The Laverack and Llewellin setters diverged, with the Laverack providing the foundation for the show setters and the Llewellin forming the foundation for the field setters. Both types have enjoyed steady popularity in America.

TEMPERAMENT

Bred to cover a lot of area when hunting, the English Setter is a lively dog that loves to hunt and run. This is especially true of dogs from field lines. If not given sufficient exercise, they can be overly lively inside, but with daily exertion, they are calm and tractable housedogs. Those from conformation lines are particularly laid back and gentle and excel with children and less active adults. This is an amiable, easygoing breed that gets along well with children, strangers, and other dogs.

UPKEEP

The English Setter needs a lot of exercise every day, requiring at least an hour of hard exertion. The long coat needs regular brushing every two or three days. The white coat may be difficult to keep gleaming in some areas. Some clipping and trimming every month or two is advisable for optimal good looks.

HEALTH

- Major concerns: deafness, CHD, elbow dysplasia, hypothyroidism
- Minor concerns: PRA, OCD
- Occasionally seen: epilepsy
- Suggested tests: hearing, hip, elbow, (eye), thyroid
- Life span: 10–12 years

FORM AND FUNCTION

The English Setter is an elegant and athletic hunting dog with the ability to run tirelessly at a good pace. Its trot is ground covering and effortless, with the head held proudly and a lively tail. The coat is flat, with feathering on the ears, underside, backs of legs, underside of thighs, and tail. Its markings are distinctive, consisting of flecks of color, sometimes with patches, on a white background. The combination of good looks and hunting ability make the English Setter a perfect gentleman's hunting companion. The Laveracks tend to be larger, carry more feathering, often have deeper muzzle, and usually hold their tails nearly level when on point. The Llewellins tend to be smaller, faster, with less coat and often larger patches of color. They tend to hold their tails straight up when on point.

Gordon Setter

AT A GLANCE

Energy level:	■■■■	Watchdog ability:	■■■■	POPULARITY: Somewhat uncommon
Exercise requirements:	■■■■	Protection ability:	■■■	FAMILY: Gundog, Setter, Pointer
Playfulness:	■■■	Grooming requirements:	■■■	AREA OF ORIGIN: Great Britain (Scotland)
Affection level:	■■■■	Cold tolerance:	■■■	DATE OF ORIGIN: 1600s
Friendliness toward dogs:	■■	Heat tolerance:	■■■	ORIGINAL FUNCTION: Bird setting & retrieving
Friendliness toward other pets:	■■■■			TODAY'S FUNCTION: Pointing, pointing field trials
Friendliness toward strangers:	■■	WEIGHT: male: 55–80 lb; female: 45–70 lb		
Ease of training:	■■■	HEIGHT: male 24–27″; female 23–26″		OTHER NAME: None

HISTORY

Black and Tan Setters existed in Scotland at least by the 1600s, but it was not until the late 1700s that the breed became established as the Gordon Castle Setter. The Fourth Duke of Gordon (1743–1827) kept many of these dogs at his Gordon Castle, although most of these were reportedly black, tan, and white. Efforts to breed the finest setters at Gordon Castle continued through the efforts of the Duke of Richmond after the Fourth Duke's death. Black and Tan Setters, as they were initially named, were shown at the first dog show ever held, in 1859. The name was changed to Gordon Setter in 1924. Gordon Setters are the heaviest and slowest working of the setter breeds, and this distinction was accentuated when Gordons first entered the show ring. In 1875, the trend toward an overly

ILLUSTRATED STANDARD

1 Well-defined stop
2 Low-set ears
3 Short from shoulder to hips
4 Tail carried near horizontal, tapering
5 Cat feet
6 Pronounced forechest

Color: black and tan
DQ: predominantly tan, red, or buff dogs lacking the typical black and tan markings

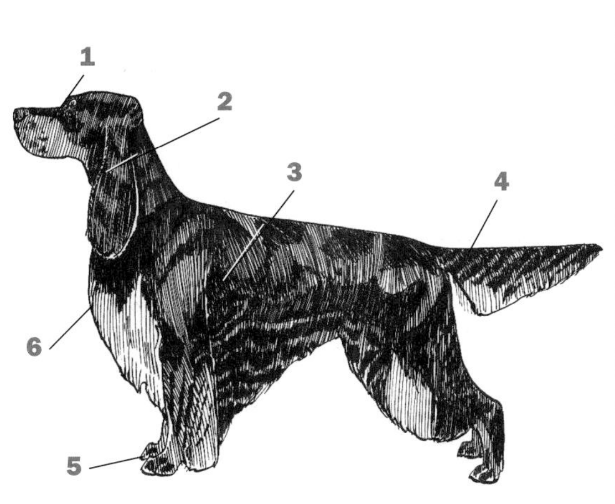

ponderous show Gordon was halted largely through the efforts of one man, Robert Chapman. Unlike many sporting breeds, little division between show- and field-type Gordons exists. Daniel Webster and George Blunt brought the first two Gordons to America in 1842. The dogs, named Rake and Rachael, were obtained from the Duke's stock and founded the breed in America. The Gordon Setter was among the first breeds recognized by the AKC, receiving the nod in 1892. The breed is a favorite among hunters demanding a one-man shooting dog, though it generally lacks the flash and speed of the other setter breeds. Although it has a steady following, it has never been as popular as the other setters as a pet.

TEMPERAMENT

The Gordon Setter is a capable, close-working bird dog. It can run and hunt all day, and this kind of energy needs a regular outlet or the dog is apt to become frustrated. Gordons make lively, enthusiastic companions, and need the company of lively people. Somewhat more protective than the other setters, it is reserved toward strangers and sometimes aggressive toward strange dogs. It generally gets along well with other family pets. The Gordon has earned its reputation as a devoted family dog.

UPKEEP

The Gordon needs much strenuous exercise every day in order to stay in shape. Its coat needs regular brushing and combing every two to three days. In addition, some clipping and trimming is needed for optimal good looks.

HEALTH

- Major concerns: CHD, gastric torsion
- Minor concerns: PRA, elbow dysplasia, cerebellar abiotrophy, hypothyroidism
- Occasionally seen: none
- Suggested tests: hip, elbow, eye, DNA for PRA
- Life span: 10–12 years

FORM AND FUNCTION

The heaviest of the setters, the Gordon is sturdily built with plenty of substance and bone. The suggestion should be one of strength and stamina rather than speed. It is square-proportioned, upstanding and stylish. The gait is bold, smooth, and effortless, with head carried proudly and tail constantly flagging. The Gordon Setter carries a thicker coat than the other setters. The hair is straight or slightly wavy, always soft and shiny. Longer feathering is on the ears, underside, backs of legs, and tail. The whole impression should be of a rugged dog capable of withstanding a long, active day in the field under a variety of conditions.

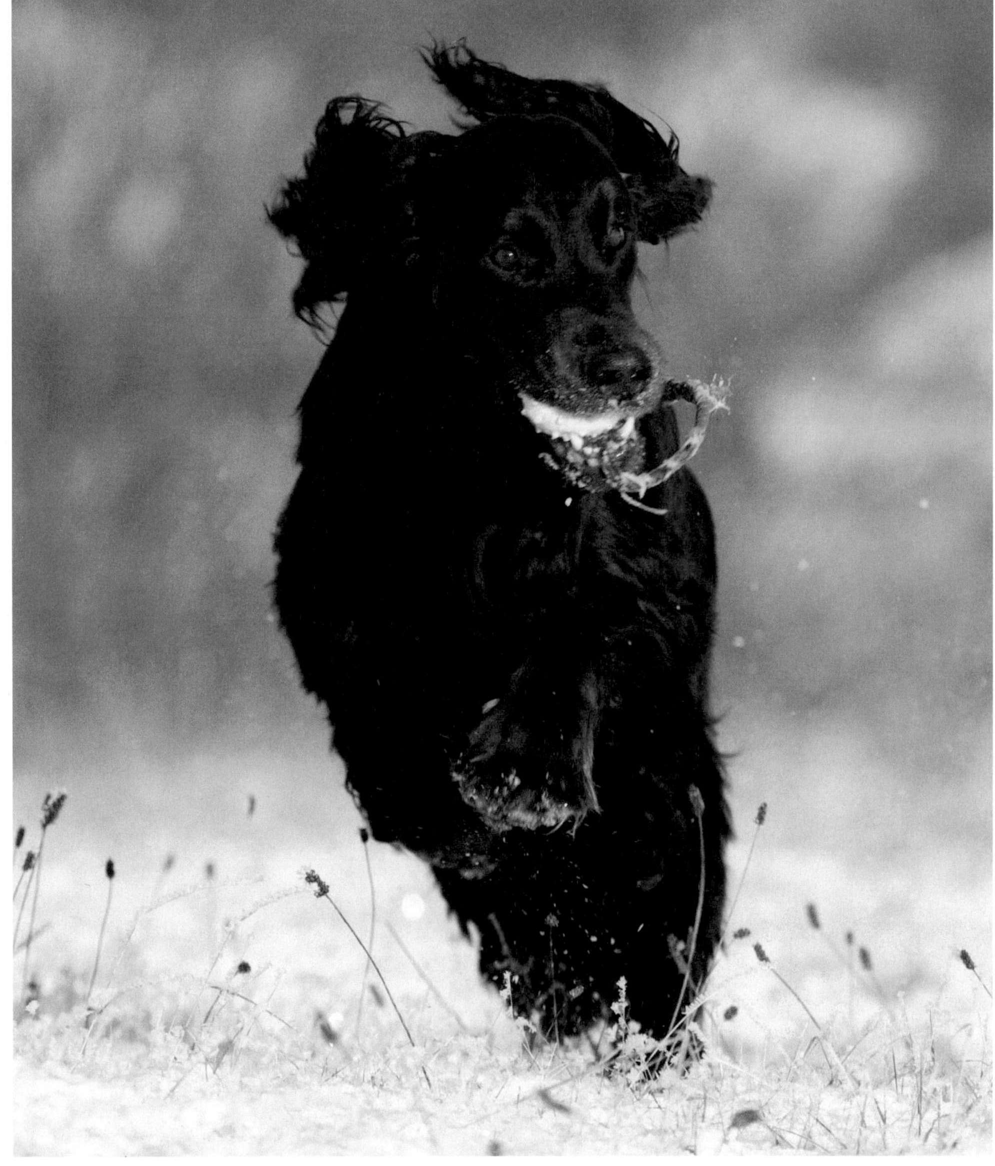

Irish Red and White Setter

AT A GLANCE

Energy level:	■■■■
Exercise requirements:	■■■■■
Playfulness:	■■■■
Affection level:	■■■■■
Friendliness toward dogs:	■■■■
Friendliness toward other pets:	■■■■
Friendliness toward strangers:	■■■■
Ease of training:	■■■■

Watchdog ability:	■■■■■
Protection ability:	■
Grooming requirements:	■■■■
Cold tolerance:	■■■
Heat tolerance:	■■■

WEIGHT: 50–75 lb
HEIGHT: male: 24.5–26″; female: 22.5–24″

POPULARITY: Rare
FAMILY: Setter
AREA OF ORIGIN: Ireland
DATE OF ORIGIN: 1700s
ORIGINAL FUNCTION: Bird setting and retrieving
TODAY'S FUNCTION: Pointing, pointing field trials
OTHER NAME: None

HISTORY

The Irish Red and White Setter predates its close relative, the Irish Setter. Its history can be traced to spaniel ancestors, many (if not most) of which were probably white with red markings. The dogs we now know as setters were larger and faster than spaniels, better for covering greater area. Setter litters contained red and white as well as solid red puppies, and they were all considered the same breed. During the early to mid 1800s, emphasis changed from breeding purely for hunting ability to including color preference, a practice spurred on by the onset of dog exhibitions. The solid red color became the fashion, and the red and white faded into the background by the early 1900s. The breed was almost extinct after World War I, but the Reverend Noble Huston

ILLUSTRATED STANDARD

1 Square muzzle
2 Distinct but not exaggerated stop
3 Round eyes
4 Skull domed and broad without noticeable occiput
5 Ears set level with eyes
6 Level topline
7 Moderately long tail, carried at or below backline
8 Feathering between toes

Color: white with solid red patches; flecking only on face and feet up to elbow and hock
DQ: none

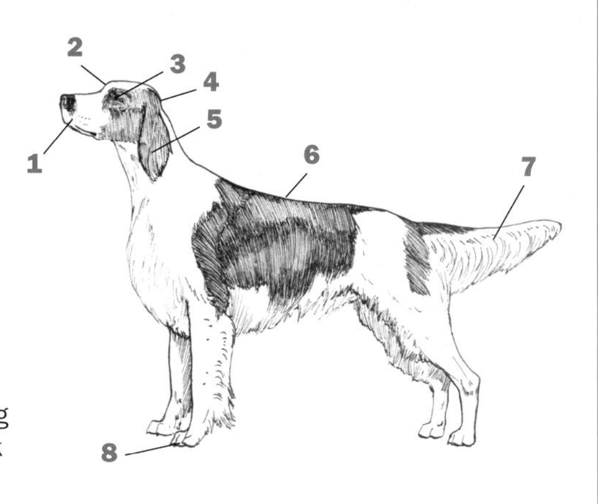

set out to revive them. He was followed by Mrs. Maureen Cuddy, whose female Judith Cunningham of Knockella is behind probably all Red and Whites today. In 1944, the Irish Red and White Setter Society was formed in London. Other breeders kept the breed going—but barely. Some came to the United States in the 1960s, and a concerted effort began in the 1980s to establish the breed in America. The Canadian Kennel Club recognized the Irish Red and White Setter in 1999; the AKC in 2009.

TEMPERAMENT

The Red and White is cheerful, lively, and friendly. It has a playful and outgoing disposition and gets along well with strangers, other dogs, and other pets. It is a natural bird dog with a strong hunting instinct that needs minimal training for the field compared to other breeds. Typically calmer than the Irish Setter, it learns easily though can still be distractable or stubborn. It is calm and quiet indoors if given sufficient exercise. It generally barks only when given a good reason.

UPKEEP

These active dogs are happiest when they're in the field, but they enjoy anything they can do with their families. They need about an hour of exercise each day. Training sessions for obedience and ability are also helpful. They welcome mental challenges and do well at obedience, agility, and other training activities. They are calm and easygoing inside, even if they miss a day of exercise. This sociable breed should not be relegated to a kennel. The coat should be brushed every two to three days. The Red and White should not be clipped, only tidied up.

HEALTH

- Major concerns: none
- Minor concerns: CHD, Canine Leukocyte Adhesion Deficiency (CLAD)
- Occasionally seen: vWD, cataract
- Suggested tests: hip, CLAD, eye
- Life span: 11–13 years

FORM AND FUNCTION

The Irish Red and White Setter is a working setter. It is strong and powerful, athletic rather than racy but without being lumbering. It is heavier in bone than the Irish Setter and square in proportion. The gait is long striding, very lively, graceful, and efficient—showing good reach and drive. Long, straight, silky feathering is present but not so much that could prove a hindrance in the field. The Irish Red and White Setter naturally crouches when it finds a bird, holding its tail horizontally rather than high.

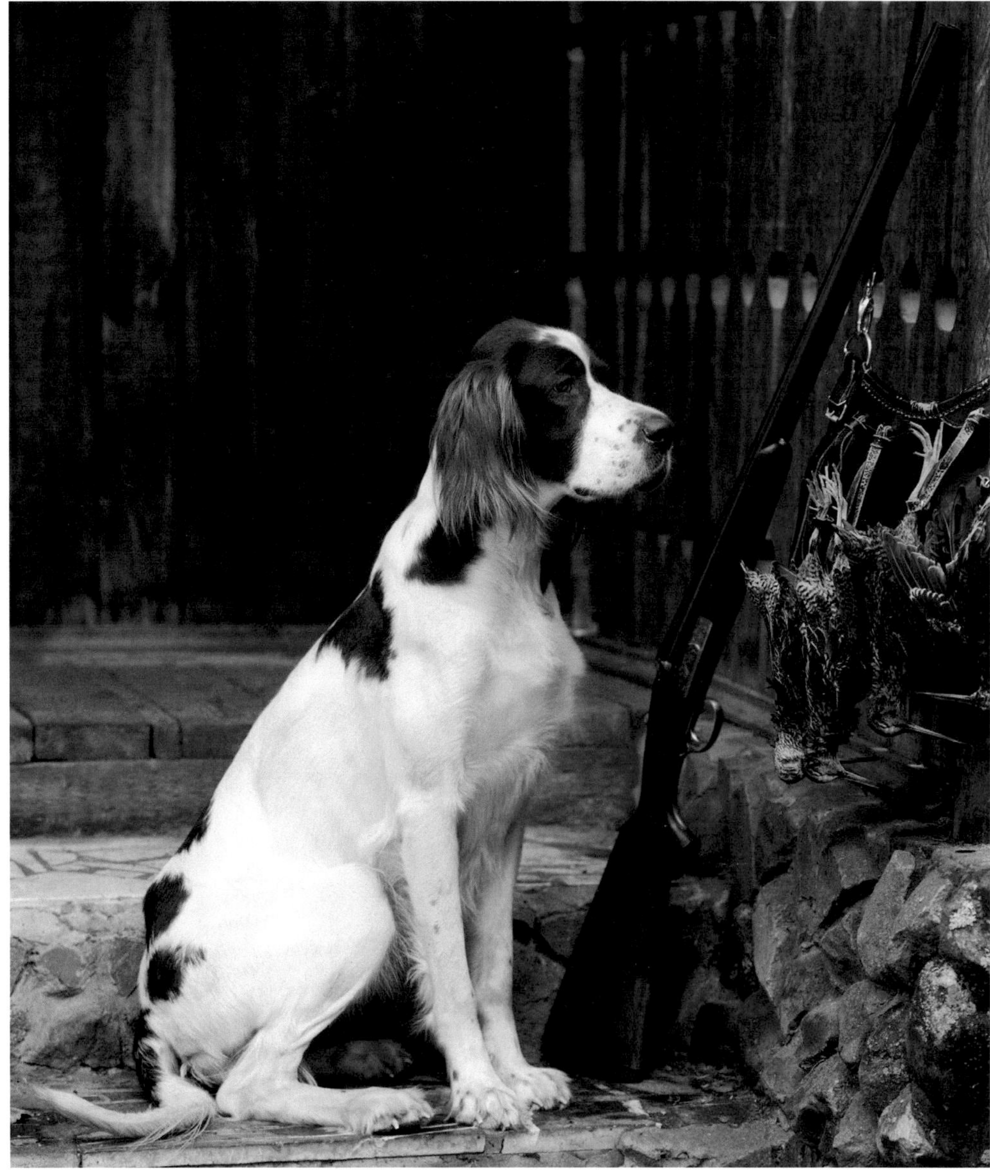

Irish Setter

AT A GLANCE

Energy level:	■■■■■
Exercise requirements:	■■■■■
Playfulness:	■■■■■
Affection level:	■■■■■
Friendliness toward dogs:	■■■■
Friendliness toward other pets:	■■■■
Friendliness toward strangers:	■■■■■
Ease of training:	■■■

Watchdog ability:	■■■■
Protection ability:	■
Grooming requirements:	■■■
Cold tolerance:	■■■
Heat tolerance:	■■■

WEIGHT: male: about 70 lb; female: about 60 lb
HEIGHT: male: about 27″; female: about 25″

POPULARITY: Somewhat popular
FAMILY: Gundog, Setter, Pointer
AREA OF ORIGIN: Ireland
DATE OF ORIGIN: 1700s
ORIGINAL FUNCTION: Bird setting and retrieving
TODAY'S FUNCTION: Pointing, pointing field trials
OTHER NAME: Red Setter

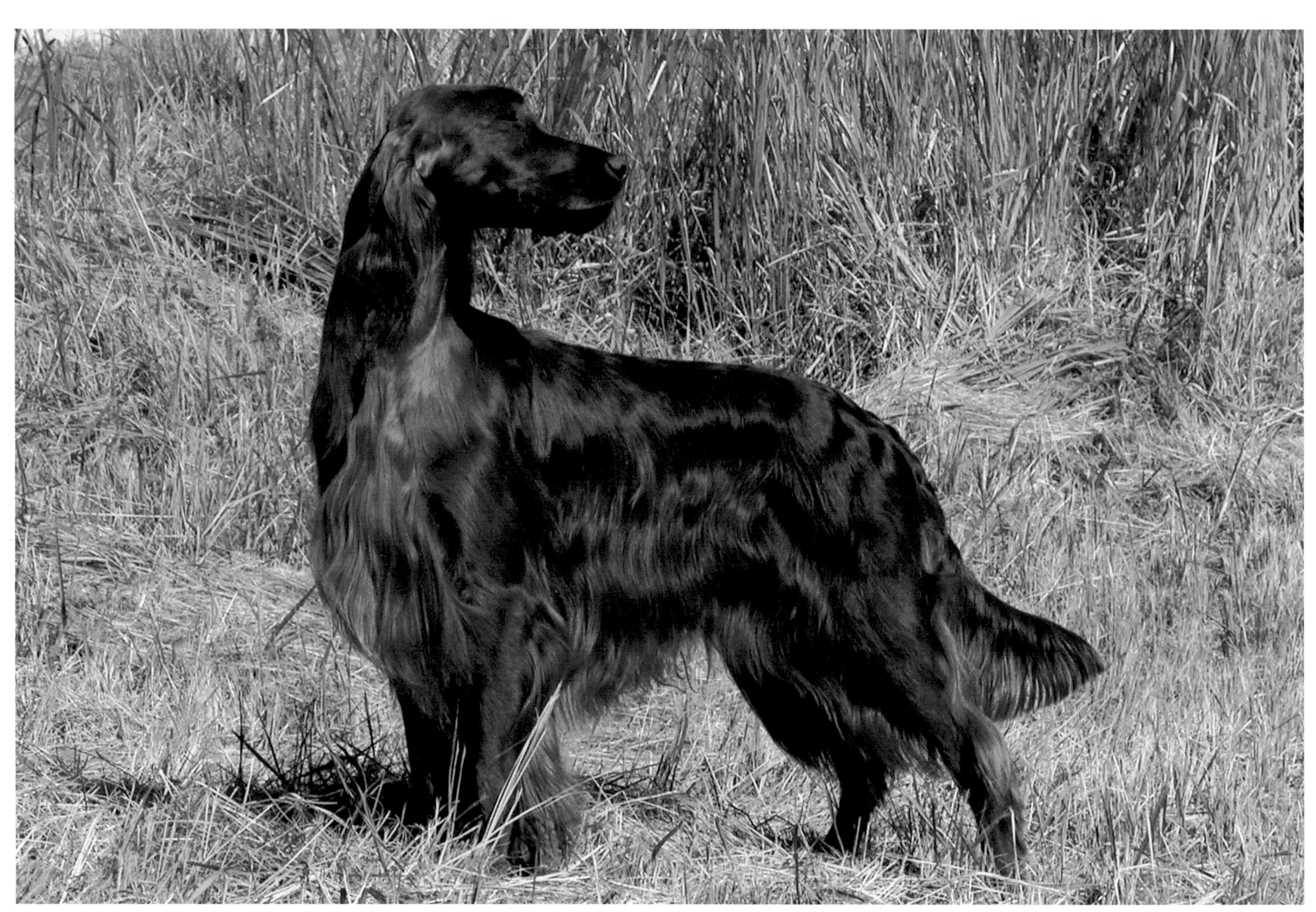

HISTORY

The precise origins of the Irish Setter are obscure, but the most reasonable theories consider it to have resulted from a blend of spaniels, pointers, and other setters—mostly the English but, to a lesser extent, the Gordon. Irish hunters needed a fast-working, keen-nosed dog, large enough to be seen from a distance. They found their dog in the red and white setters produced from these crosses. The first kennels of solid red setters appeared around 1800. In only a few years, these dogs had gained a reputation for their rich mahogany color. By the mid 1800s, Irish Red Setters (as they were originally known) had come to America, proving themselves as effective on American game birds as Irish ones. Back in Ireland, around 1862, a dog that was to forever change the breed, Champion Palmerston, was born. With an unusually long head and slender build, he was considered too refined for the field, so his owner ordered him drowned. Another fancier interceded, and the dog became a sensation as a show dog, going on to sire an incredible number of offspring. Virtually

ILLUSTRATED STANDARD

1 Muzzle moderately deep
2 Medium-size, almond-shaped eyes
3 Long, lean head with distinct stop and well-defined occiput
4 Low-set ears
5 Topline slopes to rear
6 Tail carried straight or slightly curving upward, nearly level with the back
7 Small feet

Color: mahogany or rich chestnut red
DQ: none

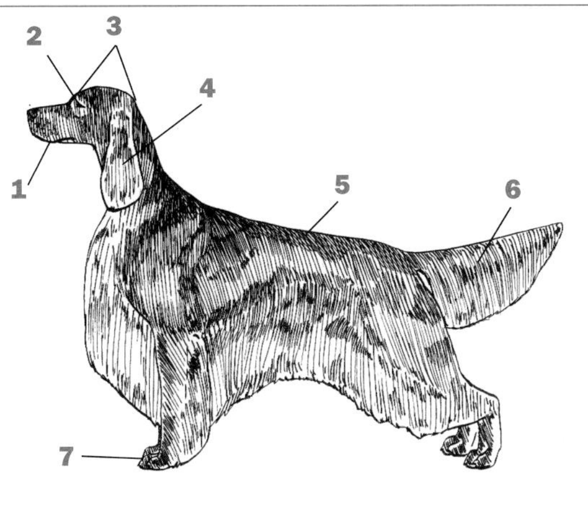

every modern Irish Setter can be traced to Palmerston. Interest changed from field trials to dog shows, and emphasis changed from hunting ability to glamour. Despite this, the Irish Setter remained a capable hunter, and dedicated breeders took steps to retain the breed's dual abilities. The breed increased principally in popularity as a show dog, however, and later as a pet. It eventually rose to a place among the most popular breeds in America in the 1970s, but has since plummeted in the rankings.

TEMPERAMENT

The Irish Setter was bred to be a tireless and enthusiastic hunter, and it approaches everything in life with a rollicking, good natured attitude, full of gusto and fervor. Given a daily outlet for its energy, it makes a pleasant companion. Without ample exercise, it can be overly active inside or become frustrated. It is an amiable breed, eager to please and be part of its family's activities. It is good with children, but can be too rambunctious for small children. It is less popular as a hunter than the other setters.

UPKEEP

The Irish needs exercise, and lots of it. It is not fair to take a dog selected for boundless energy and expect it to sit inside. A minimum of one hour of hard strenuous games and exertion a day is recommended. Because of its energy, it is not suited as an apartment dog. The coat needs regular brushing and combing every two to three days, plus some clipping and trimming to look its best.

HEALTH

- Major concerns: PRA, CHD, gastric torsion
- Minor concerns: megaesophagus, panosteitis, HOD, osteosarcoma, hypothyroidism
- Occasionally seen: OCD, epilepsy, hemophilia A, canine leukocyte adhesion deficiency (CLAD)
- Suggested tests: DNA for PRA, hip, thyroid
- Life span: 12–14 years
- Note: With the advent of DNA testing for PRA, this problem should no longer be a concern if both parents have been tested.

FORM AND FUNCTION

Among the most breathtaking of dogs, the Irish Setter's beauty is in part the result of necessity. Its elegant, yet substantial build enables it to hunt with speed and stamina. Its build is slightly longer than tall, giving ample room for movement without interference between fore and hind legs. The trot is ground covering and efficient. The coat is flat, straight, and of moderate length, with longer feathering on ears, backs of legs, belly, chest, and tail, providing protection from briars without becoming entangled in them. The rich mahogany color is just beautiful.

American Water Spaniel

AT A GLANCE

Energy level:	■■■■
Exercise requirements:	■■■
Playfulness:	■■■■
Affection level:	■■■
Friendliness toward dogs:	■■
Friendliness toward other pets:	■■■
Friendliness toward strangers:	■■
Ease of training:	■■■

Watchdog ability:	■■■■
Protection ability:	■■■
Grooming requirements:	■■■
Cold tolerance:	■■■
Heat tolerance:	■■■

WEIGHT: male: 30–45 lb; female: 25–40 lb
HEIGHT: 15–18″

POPULARITY: Very rare
FAMILY: Gundog, Spaniel
AREA OF ORIGIN: United States
DATE OF ORIGIN: 1800s
ORIGINAL FUNCTION: Bird flushing and retrieving
TODAY'S FUNCTION: Bird flushing and retrieving, spaniel field trials
OTHER NAME: None

HISTORY

Exactly when and where, or from what the American Water Spaniel was developed was never recorded. Its appearance strongly suggests a smaller version of the Irish Water Spaniel, and it is likely that it is derived from that breed or its earlier versions, the Northern, Southern, and Tweed Water Spaniels. The Curly-Coated Retriever and its forebear, the English Water Spaniel, may also have played a role. Some theories even credit the American Indians who lived in the Great Lakes regions as the creators of the breed. Whatever its origin, the American Water Spaniel first became established as a recognizable breed in the midwestern parts of the United States, where it was unsurpassed as a hunting companion. This small dog, then called the American Brown Spaniel, with the waterproof coat

ILLUSTRATED STANDARD

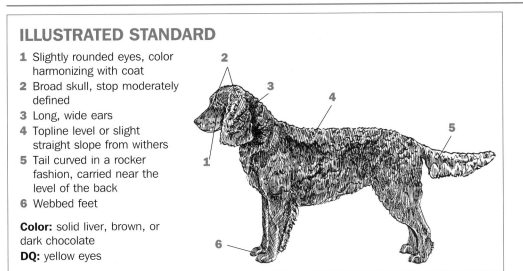

1 Slightly rounded eyes, color harmonizing with coat
2 Broad skull, stop moderately defined
3 Long, wide ears
4 Topline level or slight straight slope from withers
5 Tail curved in a rocker fashion, carried near the level of the back
6 Webbed feet

Color: solid liver, brown, or dark chocolate
DQ: yellow eyes

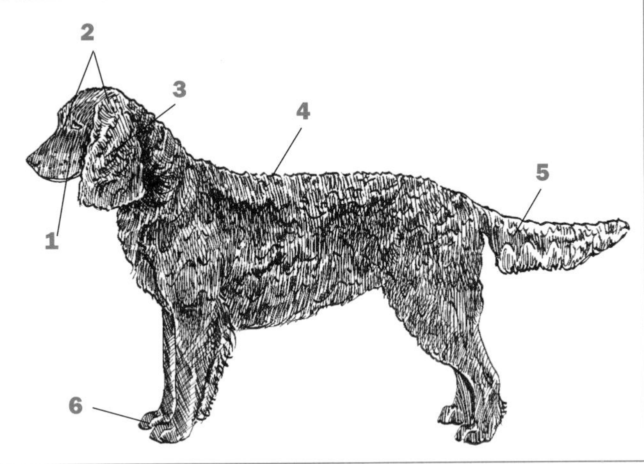

and keen nose could hunt through rough thickets, spring game, and retrieve all manner of game from land and water, often marking several fallen birds before retrieving them all unfailingly. The United Kennel Club recognized the breed as the American Water Spaniel in 1920, but until it was recognized by the AKC in 1940, no one ever considered breeding these dogs for anything but hunting ability. Even after recognition, the breed's forte remained in the field, and it is a rarity in the show ring or even the home. Today the American Water Spaniel is among the least known of AKC recognized breeds, despite being one of only two sporting breeds developed in America. In fact, the American Water Spaniel is the State Dog of Wisconsin.

TEMPERAMENT

As its name implies, the American Water Spaniel is a natural lover of water. Not only is it a skilled retriever and versatile hunter, but it is also a tractable fun-loving family dog—as long as it gets regular physical and mental exercise. It is sensitive and willing to please. Some can be timid. Generally good with other dogs in the household, some are aggressive toward strange dogs. Barking can be a definite problem; some also whine or drool.

UPKEEP

Like all hunting dogs, the American Water Spaniel needs daily exercise, although these requirements can be met with a long walk. The coat is oily and needs weekly brushing. Hair may be clipped from the feet and topknot. Ears should be checked regularly.

HEALTH

- Major concerns: mitral valve disease
- Minor concerns: PDA, pulmonic stenosis, CHD
- Occasionally seen: patellar luxation, PRA
- Suggested tests: cardiac, hip, eye
- Life span: 10–12 years

FORM AND FUNCTION

The American Water Spaniel packs a lot of ability into a comparatively small dog. Its muzzle is long and strong enough to carry a large goose, and it has strong quarters to propel it through water and over land. It is slightly longer than tall, solidly built and muscular. The coat can range from uniform waves (marcel) to close curls, with a dense undercoat. This combination provides protection against weather, water, or briars. The ears are well covered with hair, which should not grow into the ear canal. The gait is balanced, with reach and drive.

Boykin Spaniel

AT A GLANCE

Energy level:	■■■■
Exercise requirements:	■■■
Playfulness:	■■■■
Affection level:	■■■■
Friendliness toward dogs:	■■■■
Friendliness toward other pets:	■■■■
Friendliness toward strangers:	■■■■■
Ease of training:	■■■■

Watchdog ability:	■■■
Protection ability:	■
Grooming requirements:	■■■
Cold tolerance:	■■■
Heat tolerance:	■■■

WEIGHT: male: 30–40 lb; female: 25–35 lb*
HEIGHT: male: 15.5–18″; female: 14–16.5″

POPULARITY: Uncommon
FAMILY: Spaniel
AREA OF ORIGIN: United States
DATE OF ORIGIN: 1900s
ORIGINAL FUNCTION: Flushing and retrieving
TODAY'S FUNCTION: Flushing and retrieving
OTHER NAME: None

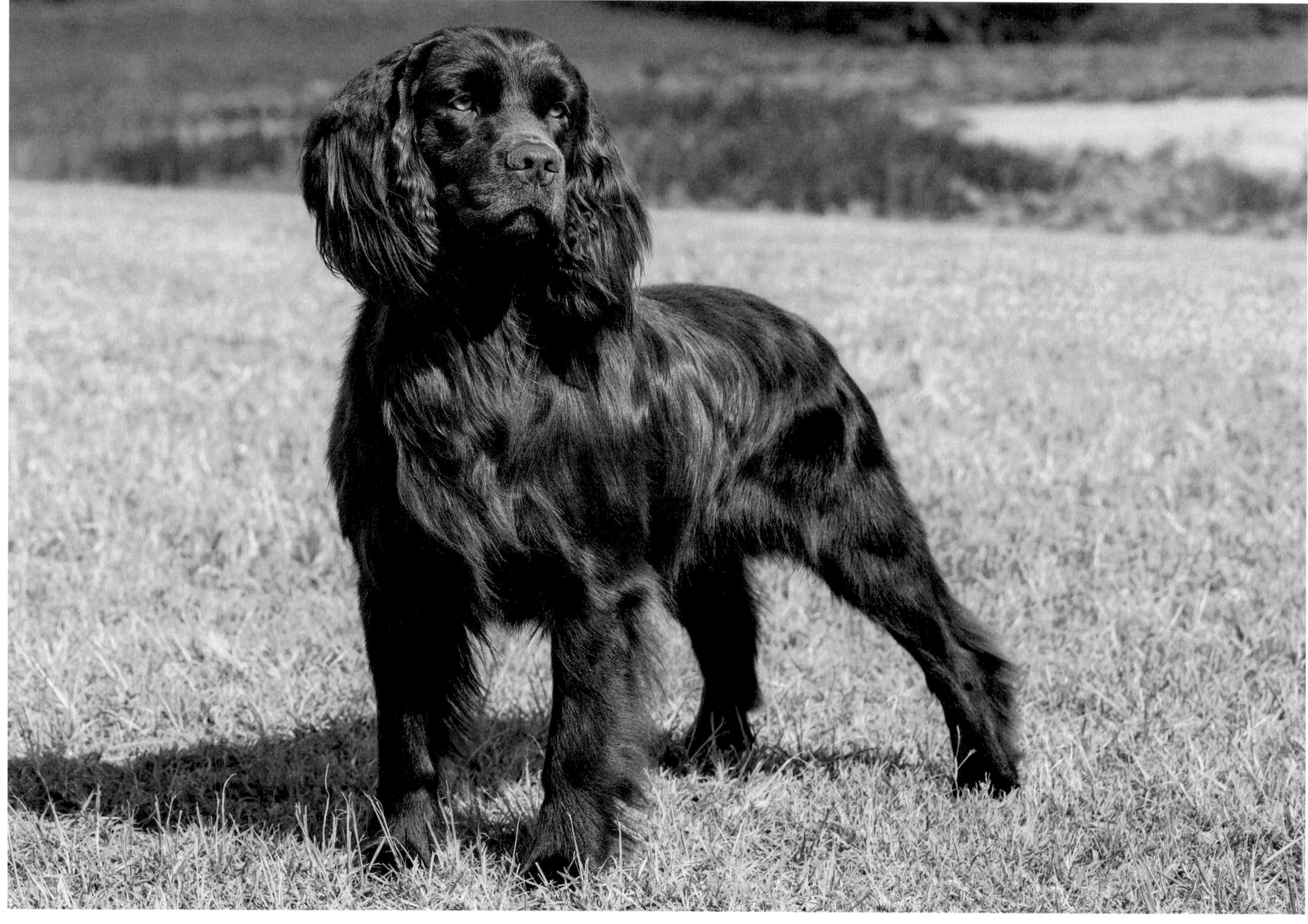

HISTORY

In the early 1900s, hunters on South Carolina's Wateree River used section boats, which were large boats that broke into smaller boats. They needed a small retrieving dog that could fit into these tiny sectionboats that could only fit one man and one small dog. L.W. "Whit" Boykin and his relatives tried several crosses to produce such a dog, finally hitting upon success with a small brown stray spaniel found by a friend in Spartanburg, South Carolina around 1905. The dog, named Dumpy, developed into an adept turkey dog and waterfowl retriever. Dumpy was bred to another stray brown spaniel, and eventually crosses were made with the Chesapeake Bay Retriever, Springer Spaniel, Cocker Spaniel, and American Water Spaniel. These dogs became known for their versatility, retaining the flushing abilities of a spaniel and adding water retrieving and even deer driving and tracking. The breed does not point, but flushes. They have excellent stamina and can hunt dove, pheasant, and other upland game even in hot

ILLUSTRATED STANDARD

1 Medium-sized, oval eyes, set well apart
2 Close-hanging, flat ears with thin leather, set slightly above or even with the eye
3 Moderate stop
4 Inconspicuous occiput
5 Dark liver nose
6 Straight level back
7 Tail carried horizontally or slightly higher; docked to 3 to 5″
8 Round, compact feet with webbed toes

Color: solid liver, brown, or dark chocolate
DQ: none

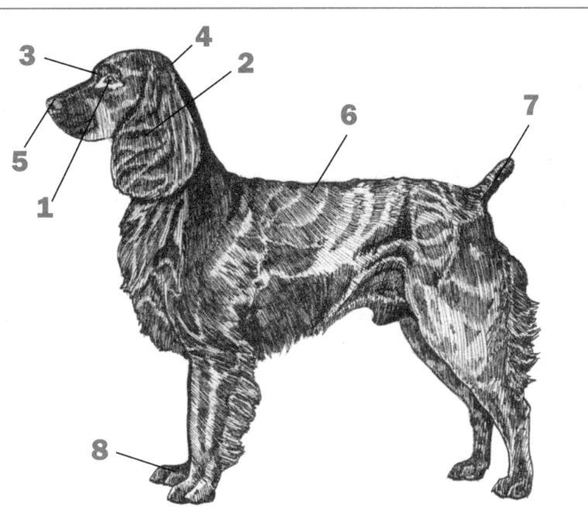

weather. Their forte, however, remains waterfowl, where they have been called "the dog who doesn't rock the boat." The breed's nexus was around Camden, South Carolina, where many hunters and wealthy families wintered. These families often left in the spring with little brown spaniels, distributing the Boykin around the country but especially along the eastern seaboard. The Boykin Spaniel Society was formed in 1977 and now has worldwide membership. In 1985, the Boykin Spaniel became the state dog of South Carolina, and in that same year it was recognized by the UKC. It joined the AKC Sporting Group in 2010. The Boykin Spaniel is more popular than its AKC registration numbers would indicate, as it is traditionally a dog used for hunting and companionship in the southeastern United States.

TEMPERAMENT

The Boykin is a friend to all, happy and eager to join any adventure—especially if it involves hunting, swimming, or traipsing through the woods. They are eager to please and relatively easy to train, fine for novice owners. They get along well with other dogs and pets. They don't bark excessively and are well-behaved house dogs as long as they get enough exercise.

UPKEEP

Boykins need a fairly high level of activity. A long walk or jogging venture, along with games of fetch, will usually satisfy their exercise needs each day. They also enjoy swimming. The coat is somewhat oily so requires weekly brushing and occasional bathing. Ears should be checked regularly.

HEALTH

- Major concerns: CHD, patellar luxation
- Minor concerns: cataract
- Occasionally seen: pulmonic stenosis, exercise induced collapse
- Suggested tests: hip, knee, eye
- Life span: 11–13 years

FORM AND FUNCTION

The Boykin Spaniel is a medium-sized dog built to flush and retrieve over all types of ground conditions with agility and reasonable speed. It has strong, but not overly heavy, bone and is slightly longer than tall. The jaws are long and strong enough to allow the dog to carry game easily. The coat has a medium length outer coat that can range from flat to slightly wavy, which protects it from the elements and repels water; and a short, dense undercoat for insulation. Movement is effortless with good reach and strong drive.

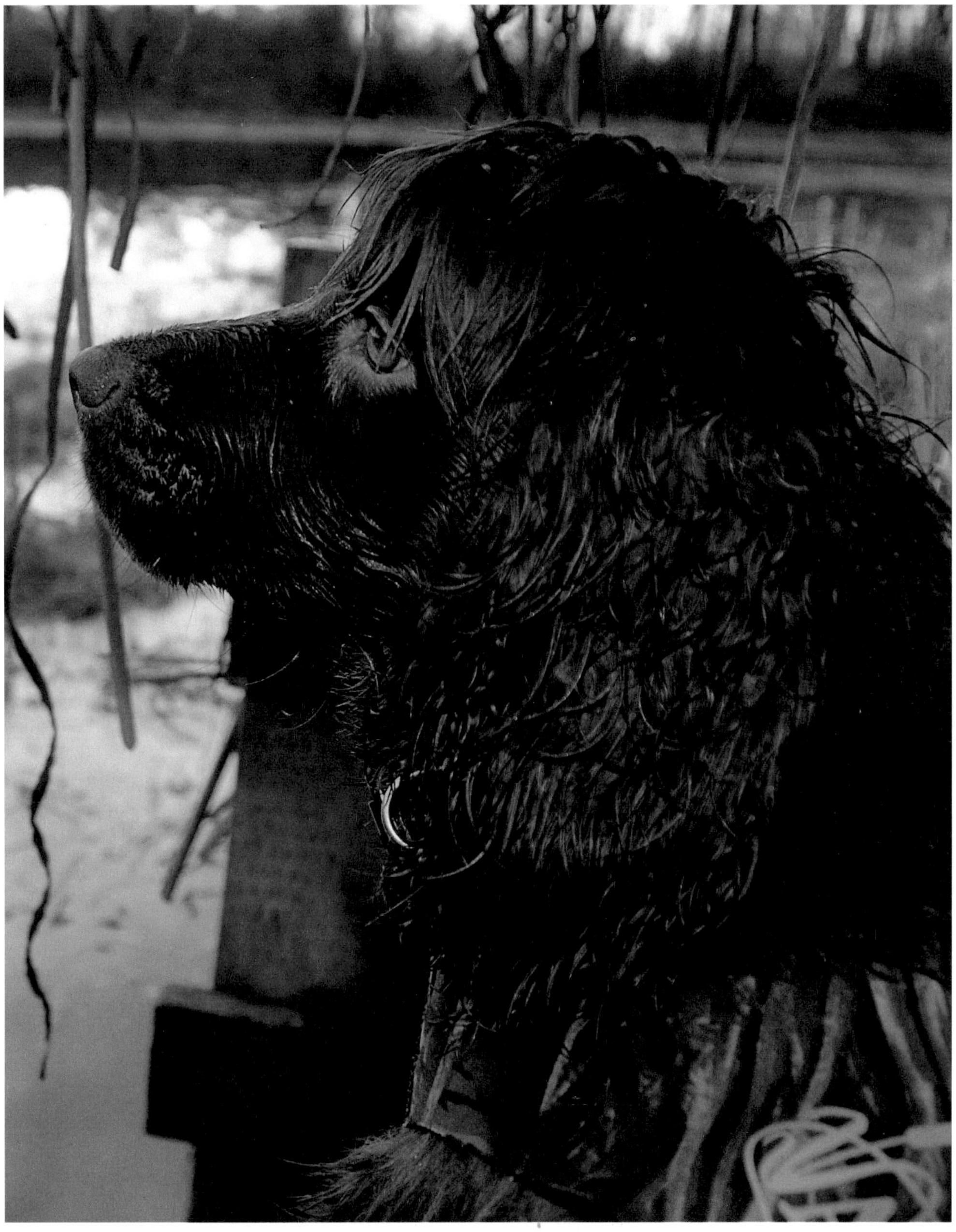

Clumber Spaniel

AT A GLANCE

Energy level:	■■
Exercise requirements:	■■
Playfulness:	■■■
Affection level:	■■■■
Friendliness toward dogs:	■■■
Friendliness toward other pets:	■■■■
Friendliness toward strangers:	■■■
Ease of training:	■■■

Watchdog ability:	■■
Protection ability:	■
Grooming requirements:	■■■
Cold tolerance:	■■■
Heat tolerance:	■■

WEIGHT: male: 70–85 lb; female: 55–70 lb
HEIGHT: male: 19–20″; female: 17–19″

POPULARITY: Rare
FAMILY: Gundog, Spaniel
AREA OF ORIGIN: England
DATE OF ORIGIN: 1700s
ORIGINAL FUNCTION: Bird flushing and retrieving
TODAY'S FUNCTION: Bird flushing and retrieving, spaniel field trials
OTHER NAME: None

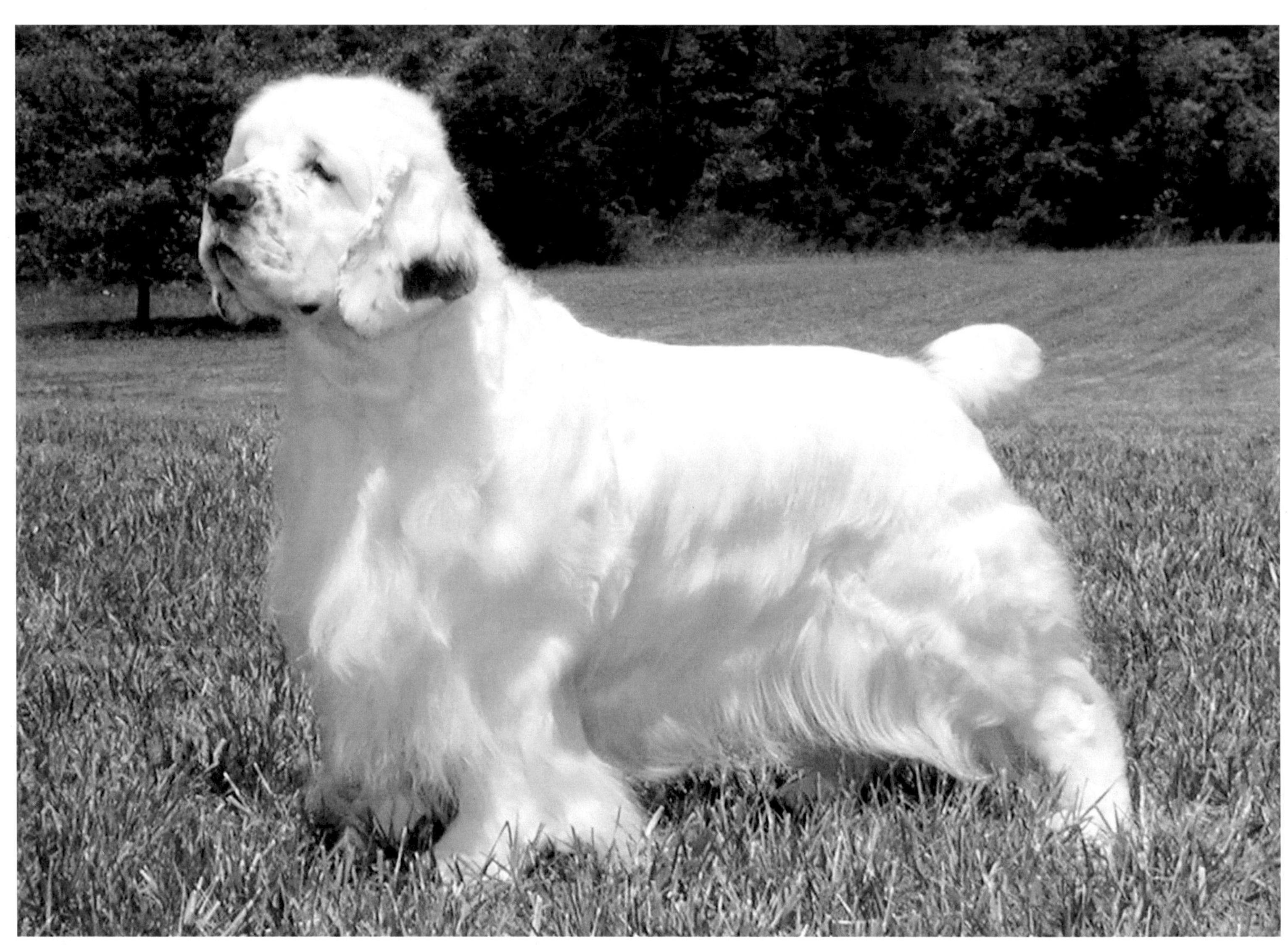

HISTORY

The stockiest of the spaniels, the Clumber is also one of the oldest, dating to the late 1700s. Although the exact derivation of the breed is unknown, it is likely that the old heavy-headed Alpine Spaniel and the low-bodied Basset Hound played prominent roles in its development. The breed did not get its name until around the time of the French Revolution, when it is believed that the Duc de Noailles of France moved his spaniel kennels to the Duke of Newcastle's English estate, Clumber Park. Clumber Spaniels appealed to the English nobility, who appreciated this slow-moving but especially keen-nosed hunter that was also an adept retriever. The breed was not readily available to commoners because the nobility dis-couraged its popularity except among

ILLUSTRATED STANDARD

1. Well-developed flews
2. Nose colored any shade of brown
3. Eyes large, deep-set, diamond shaped; some haw may show
4. Pronounced stop and occiput
5. Massive head
6. Low-set ears
7. Tail docked and carried near horizontal
8. Large feet

Color: white dog with lemon or orange markings (the fewer the markings on body, the better)
DQ: none

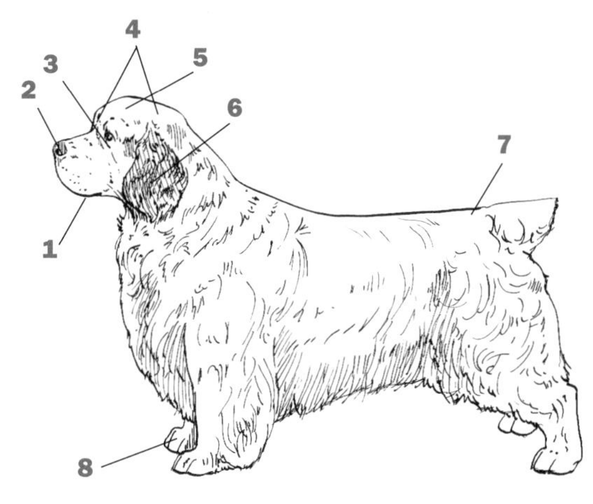

higher society. As befitting their high status, Clumbers were among the earliest breeds to be shown. They came to America in the late 1800s. Their popularity has remained strongest in the field, although Clumbers have attained high show honors. They remain generally unknown to the public despite their many attributes.

TEMPERAMENT

Among the most low-keyed and easygoing of sporting breeds, the Clumber Spaniel is nonetheless a hunter at heart, ever ready for a day in the field. At home it tends to be quiet and may even need to be goaded into exercise. It is one of the few sporting breeds suitable for city life, although it will relish walks and outings. The Clumber makes a good pet, especially devoted to one person.

UPKEEP

The Clumber enjoys a daily outing, but its exercise requirements can be met with a long walk on leash or a leisurely hike in the field. The coat needs brushing two to three times weekly, although in dirty areas it may need more frequent bathing in order to keep its coat a gleaming white. Clumbers tend to drool and, at times, snore.

HEALTH

- Major concerns: CHD, intervertebral disk disease
- Minor concerns: ectropion, entropion, otitis externa, PDP1, elbow dysplasia
- Occasionally seen: seizures
- Suggested tests: hip, eye, elbow, PDP1
- Life span: 10–12 years

FORM AND FUNCTION

The Clumber Spaniel is a long, low dog, rectangular in shape and with massive bone. This build, in combination with a deep chest, heavy brow, and powerful hindquarters, enables the dog to move through thick underbrush when hunting. The coat is straight, flat, soft, and dense, imparting resistance to weather. The white color helps the hunter locate the dog. The Clumber tends to hunt close. It moves easily, tending to roll slightly because of its wide body and short legs. The expression is soft.

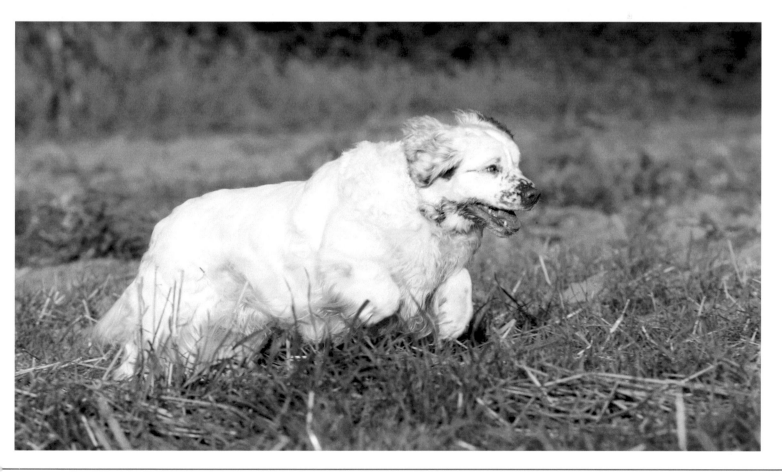

Cocker Spaniel

AT A GLANCE

Energy level:	■■■
Exercise requirements:	■■■
Playfulness:	■■■■
Affection level:	■■■■■
Friendliness toward dogs:	■■■■■
Friendliness toward other pets:	■■■■■
Friendliness toward strangers:	■■■■
Ease of training:	■■■■

Watchdog ability:	■■■■
Protection ability:	■
Grooming requirements:	■■■■
Cold tolerance:	■■■
Heat tolerance:	■■■

WEIGHT: 24–28 lb*
HEIGHT: male: 14.5–15.5″; female: 13.5–14.5″

POPULARITY: Popular
FAMILY: Gundog, Spaniel
AREA OF ORIGIN: United States
DATE OF ORIGIN: 1800s
ORIGINAL FUNCTION: Bird flushing and retrieving
TODAY'S FUNCTION: Spaniel field trials
OTHER NAME: American Cocker Spaniel

HISTORY

The American version of the Cocker Spaniel is derived from the English Cocker Spaniel. In the late 1800s, many English Cockers were brought to America, but American hunters preferred a slightly smaller dog to hunt quail and other small game birds. The American Cocker is smaller, with a rounder head, shorter muzzle, and more profuse coat than its English ancestor. Just how this smaller Cocker was developed is not entirely clear; some credit the dog Obo 2nd, born around 1880, as the first true American Cocker. But other evidence points to crosses of the English Cocker with even smaller toy spaniels (that nonetheless arose from the same ancestral stock). Initially the English and American Cocker Spaniels were considered varieties of the same breed, but they were officially

ILLUSTRATED STANDARD

1 Expression alert, soft, and appealing
2 Rounded skull with pronounced stop
3 Long, low-set, lobular ears
4 Topline slopes slightly to rear
5 Tail docked and carried in line or slightly higher than the topline
6 Round feet

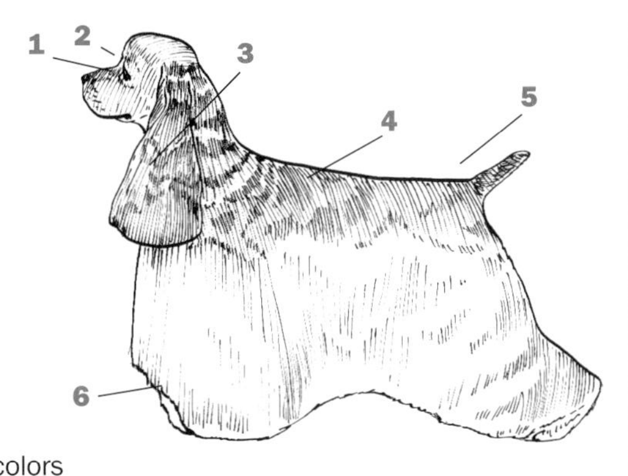

Color: Black variety: solid black or black and tan; ASCOB variety: any solid color other than black, including cream, red, brown, and brown with tan points; Particolor variety: any of the allowed solid colors broken up on a white background; also roans

DQ: males over 15.5"; females over 14.5"; colors other than those specified; white markings (other than on the chest and throat) in the black or ASCOB; primary color of more than 90 percent in the particolor in tan-pointed dogs, absence of tan markings in any normally tan-marked places or tan markings in excess of 10 percent

separated by the AKC in 1935. Although Cockers were already popular, after the separation the American Cocker surged in popularity and has remained one of the most popular breeds of all time in America. In fact, it was the most popular breed for many years. So popular was it that it was eventually divided into three color varieties: black, particolor, and ASCOB, which stands for Any Solid Color Other than Black. Only recently has its popularity spread to England, where it was recognized by the English Kennel Club in 1968, and it has gained admirers steadily since.

TEMPERAMENT

This breed is known as the "merry" Cocker, and the name is most fitting. It is playful, cheerful, amiable, sweet, sensitive, willing to please, and responsive to its family's wishes. It is not known for retaining its hunting instincts, but it is inquisitive and will appreciate a country outing. It is equally at home in the city and will happily walk on leash for its exercise needs. Some bark a lot; some are overly submissive.

UPKEEP

Although it enjoys a romp, the Cocker can receive adequate exercise with a long daily walk on leash. The coat of the Cocker requires a greater commitment than that of most breeds, although pets can be clipped short. In order to maintain a nice coat, it will need to be brushed and combed two to three times a week, in addition to professional clipping and scissoring every month. Special attention must be paid to ear and eye cleanliness in this breed. The profusely coated feet tend to carry debris. Cockers have a tendency to become overweight.

HEALTH

- Major concerns: cataract, glaucoma, PRA
- Minor concerns: CHD, ectropion, patellar luxation, entropion, allergies, seborrhea, otitis externa, liver disease, CHF, phosphofructokinase deficiency, urinary stones, cherry eye, cardiomyopathy, hypothyroidism
- Occasionally seen: gastric torsion, elbow dysplasia, epilepsy
- Suggested tests: eye, (knee), hip, (thyroid), DNA for phosphofructokinase deficiency
- Life span: 12–15 years

FORM AND FUNCTION

The smallest member of the Sporting Group, the Cocker should be compact and sturdy. Its gait is ground covering, strong, and effortless. The coat is silky, flat or slightly wavy, not overly long. Excessive coat can hinder the dog in the field. The head and expression are hallmarks of the breed; the expression is soft and appealing. Though seldom used for its original purpose, the Cocker should still be able to spend a day in the field and should be balanced and athletic. It is true, however, that most Cockers now have too much coat for field work.

English Cocker Spaniel

AT A GLANCE

Energy level:	■ ■ ■
Exercise requirements:	■ ■ ■
Playfulness:	■ ■ ■ ■
Affection level:	■ ■ ■ ■ ■
Friendliness toward dogs:	■ ■ ■ ■ ■
Friendliness toward other pets:	■ ■ ■ ■ ■
Friendliness toward strangers:	■ ■ ■ ■
Ease of training:	■ ■ ■ ■

Watchdog ability:	■ ■ ■ ■
Protection ability:	■ ■
Grooming requirements:	■ ■ ■
Cold tolerance:	■ ■ ■
Heat tolerance:	■ ■ ■

WEIGHT: male: 28–34 lb; female: 26–32 lb
HEIGHT: male: 16–17″; female: 15–16″

POPULARITY: Somewhat Popular
FAMILY: Gundog, Spaniel
AREA OF ORIGIN: England
DATE OF ORIGIN: 1800s
ORIGINAL FUNCTION: Bird flushing and retrieving
TODAY'S FUNCTION: Flushing and retrieving, spaniel field trials
OTHER NAME: Cocker Spaniel

HISTORY

The spaniel family is one of the largest groups of dogs, and one of the most specialized. The English Cocker Spaniel is one of the land spaniels. The land spaniels consisted of larger spaniels that were better for springing game, and smaller spaniels that were better for hunting woodcock. These different sizes appeared in the same litters and were essentially two variations of the same breed. Only in 1892 were the two sizes considered separate breeds, with the smaller size (under 25 lb) designated as the Cocker Spaniel. In fact, because both breeds shared the same gene pool, they still share many of the same hunting talents. In 1901, the weight limit was abolished. Cocker Spaniels became extremely popular in England, but American breeders strove to change the breed in ways that

ILLUSTRATED STANDARD

1 Slightly oval eyes
2 Slightly flattened skull, with moderate stop
3 Softly contoured head, with soft expression
4 Low-set ears
5 Topline slopes slightly to rear
6 Docked tail, carried horizontally
7 Cat feet

Color: solid black, liver, or red; black and tan, liver and tan, and any of these colors on a white background either particolored, ticked, or roan
DQ: none

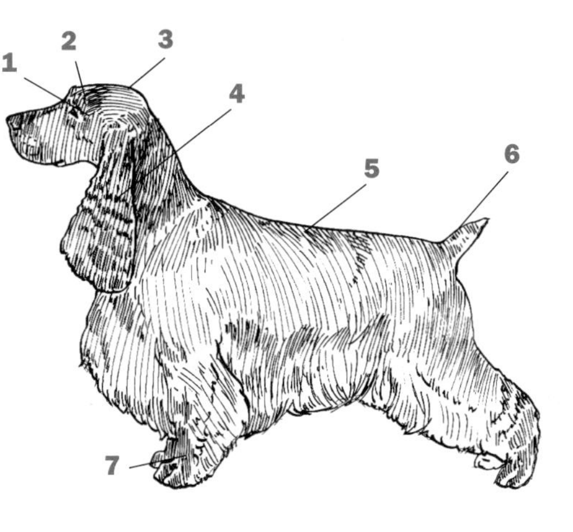

traditional English Cocker Spaniel enthusiasts objected to. English and American Cocker Spaniels were shown together until 1936, when English Cocker Spaniel Club of America was formed and the English Cocker received status as a separate variety. The English Cocker Spaniel Club discouraged the interbreeding of the American and English Cockers, and in 1946 the English Cocker was designated a separate breed. After the breeds were separated, the American Cocker eclipsed the English in popularity—but only in America. Throughout the rest of the world, the English Cocker is by far the more popular of the two breeds and is known simply as the Cocker Spaniel. It is one of the most successful show dogs and popular pets of all breeds in Great Britain.

TEMPERAMENT

The English Cocker Spaniel retains more of its hunting nature than does the American version, and it also needs a little more exercise. It is cheerful, inquisitive, demonstrative, devoted, biddable, loyal, and sensitive. This is a sociable dog that likes to stay close to its human family.

UPKEEP

Daily exercise is a necessity, either in the form of a long walk on leash, a good run in the field, or a lively game in the yard. The medium-length coat needs brushing two to three times per week, plus clipping around the head and ears and scissoring around the feet and tail every two months. The ears should be cleaned weekly.

HEALTH

- Major concerns: PRA, patellar luxation
- Minor concerns: cataract, CHD, kidney disease (familial nephropathy), hypothyroidism
- Occasionally seen: cardiomyopathy
- Suggested tests: hearing (for particolors), eye, hip, knee, (thyroid), DNA for PRA
- Life span: 12–14 years
- Note: deafness is a major concern in particolors; CHD is more common in solid colors; PRA is of PRCD type

FORM AND FUNCTION

The English Cocker must be able to find, flush, and retrieve upland game birds for a full day of hunting. It must be small enough to penetrate dense cover, but of sufficient size to retrieve larger game. The broad muzzle helps when retrieving. The dog is slightly taller than long, compactly built, and short coupled. This breed loves to hunt and shows it by the wagging of its tail when on the job. The English Cocker has a driving, powerful gait that covers ground effortlessly. The coat is of medium length, silky in texture, and either flat or slightly wavy. The feathering should not be so profuse that it becomes a hindrance in the field, but it should be long enough to protect the underside of the dog. The expression is soft and melting, yet dignified.

English Springer Spaniel

AT A GLANCE

Energy level:	■■■
Exercise requirements:	■■■■
Playfulness:	■■■■
Affection level:	■■■■■
Friendliness toward dogs:	■■■
Friendliness toward other pets:	■■■■■
Friendliness toward strangers:	■■■■
Ease of training:	■■■■■

Watchdog ability:	■■■■
Protection ability:	■■
Grooming requirements:	■■■■
Cold tolerance:	■■■
Heat tolerance:	■■■

WEIGHT: male: about 50 lb; female: about 40 lb
HEIGHT: male: 19–21″; female: 18–20″

POPULARITY: Popular
FAMILY: Gundog, Spaniel
AREA OF ORIGIN: England
DATE OF ORIGIN: 1800s
ORIGINAL FUNCTION: Bird flushing and retrieving
TODAY'S FUNCTION: Bird flushing and retrieving, spaniel field trials
OTHER NAME: None

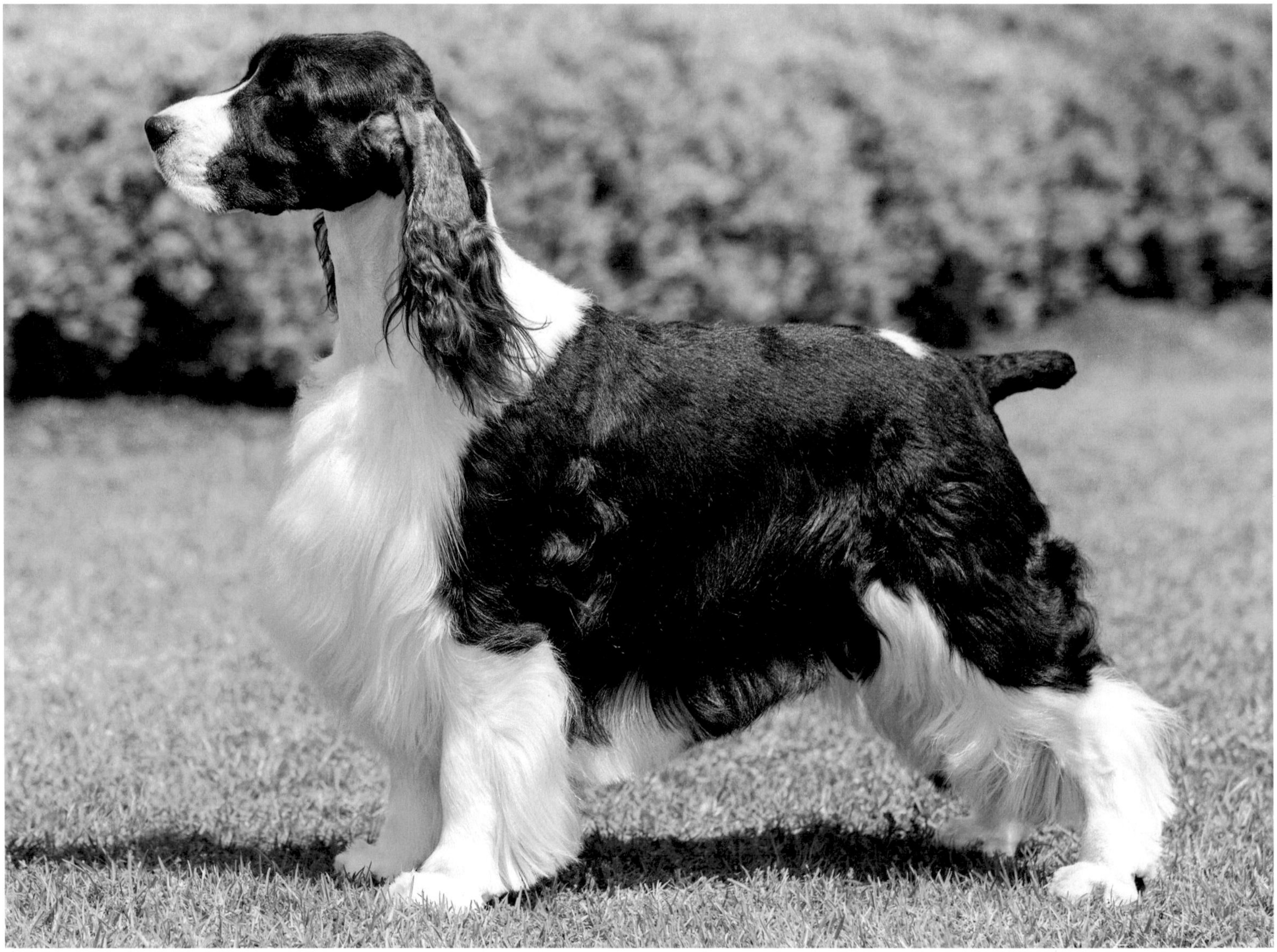

HISTORY

As the spaniels became increasingly specialized, the larger land spaniels that ranged farther afield became extremely useful at flushing or "springing" game. Before the advent of shotguns, the game was flushed into nets or then chased by falcons or Greyhounds. The first reference to springers referred to land spaniels in the late 1500s. Around 1800, distinct strains of carefully bred springers began to develop; one of the best known were those bred by the Duke of Norfolk. His dogs so heavily influenced the breed that for a while the breed was called Norfolk Spaniels. The name was changed to Springer Spaniel in 1900. The matter is complicated by the fact that the larger Springer and smaller Cocker Spaniels were simply size variations of the same breed. Only in 1902 did the

ILLUSTRATED STANDARD

1 Full lips
2 Oval eyes of medium size
3 Moderate stop
4 Long ears
5 Topline slopes slightly to rear
6 Docked tail carried horizontally or slightly elevated

Color: black or liver with white, black or liver roan, or tricolored (black or liver and white with tan markings); also white with black or liver markings
DQ: none

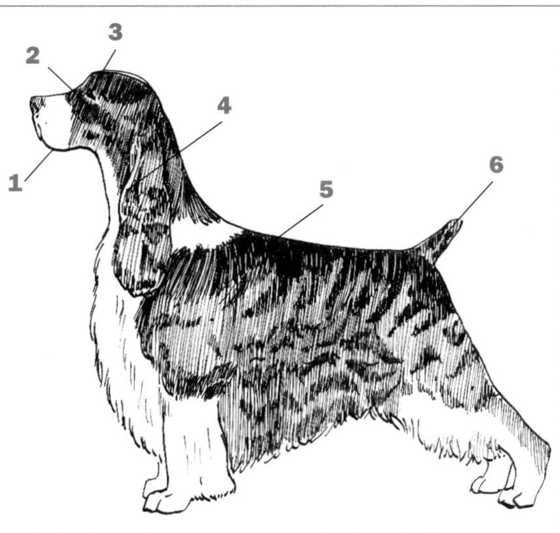

English Kennel Club recognize the Springer as a distinct breed. In America, the American Spaniel Club was formed in 1880 and began the task of separating the Springer and Cocker sizes. After separation, the Springer continued to thrive. It has remained popular with hunters demanding a versatile gundog that ranges fast and far and that can also flush and retrieve. It is also a popular show dog and pet.

TEMPERAMENT

The English Springer Spaniel is cheerful, playful, and energetic, ready for a day in the field and an evening by the hearth. It does everything with gusto and can be overly enthusiastic unless given plenty of exercise. The typical Springer is the ideal family companion.

UPKEEP

As an energetic and inquisitive dog, the Springer needs daily mental and physical exertion. Hunting is the first choice to satisfy both needs, but an outing in the field, long walk on leash, and good obedience lesson can go far to making the Springer a calm and well-behaved house dog. Its coat needs brushing or combing one or two times weekly plus clipping and scissoring every two to three months. Springers from field, rather than show, lines tend to have less coat.

HEALTH

- Major concerns: otitis externa, CHD, elbow dysplasia
- Minor concerns: phosphofructokinase deficiency, PRA, retinal dysplasia
- Occasionally seen: entropion, rage syndrome, seizures, gastric torsion, patellar luxation, fucosidosis
- Suggested tests: hip, elbow, eye, knee, (DNA for phosphofructokinase deficiency), DNA for PRA
- Life span: 10–14 years

FORM AND FUNCTION

The English Springer Spaniel is compactly built, upstanding with proud carriage, slightly longer than tall but with fairly long legs and a deep body. Its build should suggest a combination of strength, agility, and endurance, a dog capable of hunting tirelessly under the most difficult of conditions. The outer coat is medium length, either flat or wavy, and the undercoat is soft and dense. This combination protects the dog from weather, water, and thorns. The gait is long and ground covering. The expression—alert, kindly, and trusting—is an essential feature of Springer type. Field-bred Springers tend to be lighter boned, have less coat, and have more variable patterning than do show-bred Springers.

Field Spaniel

AT A GLANCE

Energy level:	■■■■	Watchdog ability:	■■■■
Exercise requirements:	■■■■	Protection ability:	■■
Playfulness:	■■■■	Grooming requirements:	■■■
Affection level:	■■■■■	Cold tolerance:	■■■
Friendliness toward dogs:	■■■	Heat tolerance:	■■■
Friendliness toward other pets:	■■■■■		
Friendliness toward strangers:	■■■	WEIGHT: 35–50 lb*	
Ease of training:	■■■■	HEIGHT: male: 18″; female: 17″ (±1 inch)	

POPULARITY: Rare
FAMILY: Gundog, Spaniel
AREA OF ORIGIN: England
DATE OF ORIGIN: 1800s
ORIGINAL FUNCTION: Bird flushing and retrieving
TODAY'S FUNCTION: Bird flushing and retrieving, spaniel field trials
OTHER NAME: None

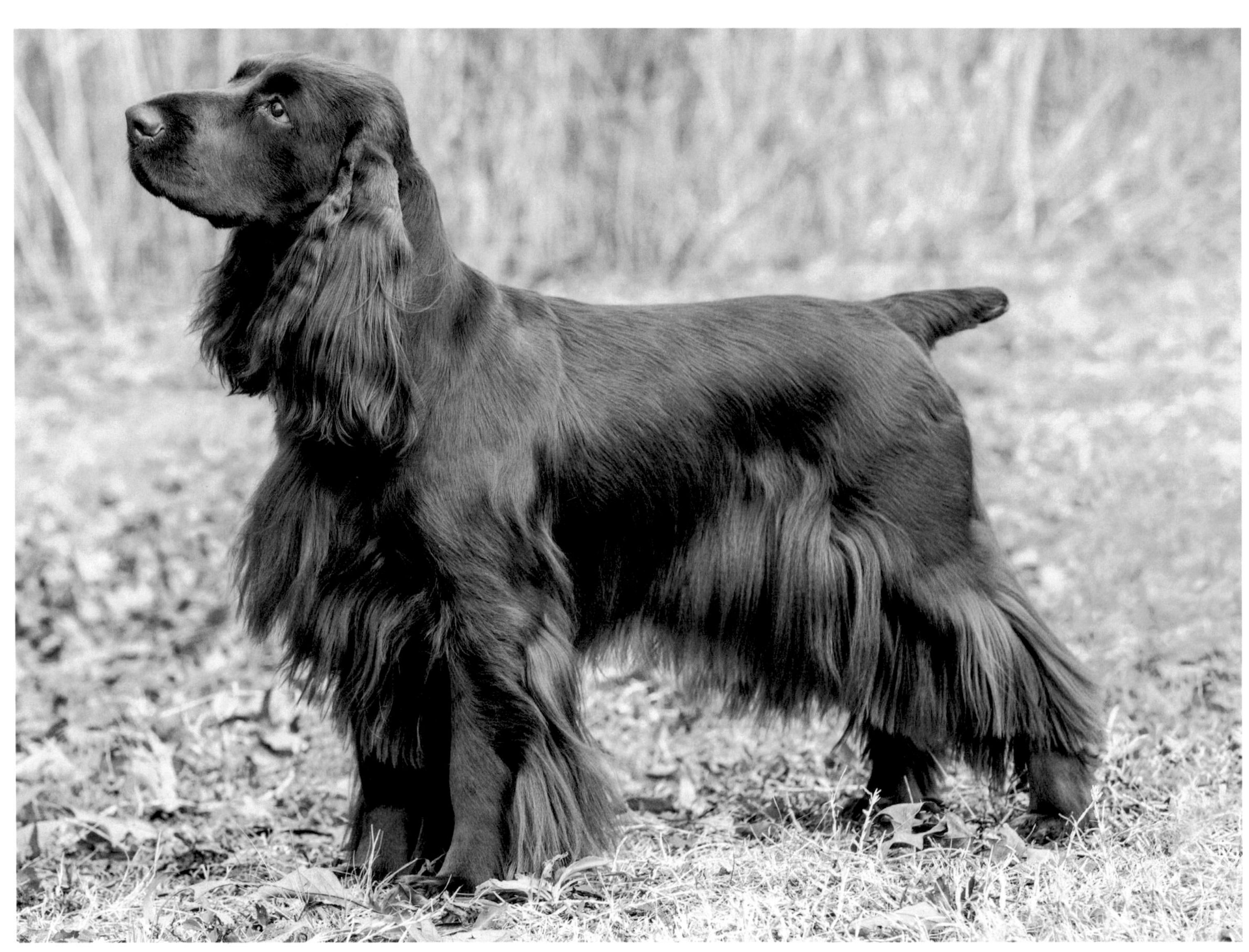

HISTORY

The Field Spaniel shares its early history with the English Cocker Spaniel, the only difference between the two breeds initially being one of size. The Field Spaniel was composed of those land spaniels weighing over 25 pounds. These larger Field Spaniels were derived from the Cocker, Sussex, and English Water Spaniels and were initially required to be black. After becoming recognized as a separate breed in the late 1800s, the Field Spaniel succumbed to breeding for exaggeration, and the repeated infusion of Sussex Spaniel blood resulted in dogs of excessive length, overly heavy bones, and short legs. The breed lost its usefulness as a hunter, and although it enjoyed a short vogue in the early 1900s, it ultimately teetered on the brink of extinction. Crosses to English Springer

ILLUSTRATED STANDARD

1 Moderate stop
2 Almond-shaped, medium-sized eyes
3 Distinct occiput
4 Low-set ears, moderately long and wide
5 Docked or undocked tail slanting downward when at rest
6 Little or no tuck-up
7 Large, round, webbed feet

Color: black, liver, golden liver; solid or bicolored; roaned or ticked in white areas; tan points allowed; white allowed on throat, chest, or brisket
DQ: none

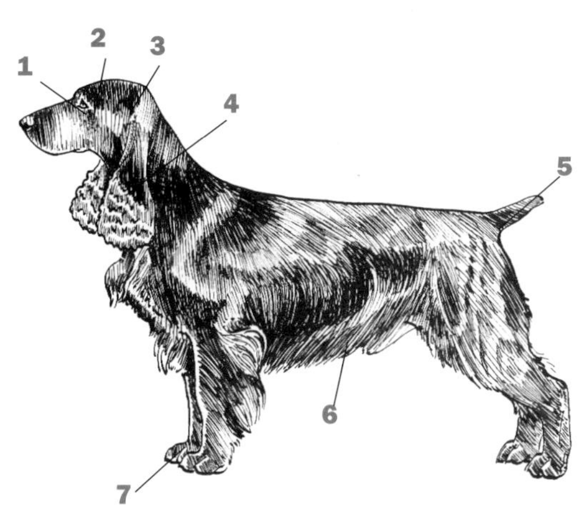

Spaniels were made in an effort to recreate the original Field Spaniel. The crosses were successful, and the modern Field Spaniel is not only a handsome replica of its former self but also an able hunter. All modern Field Spaniels can be traced back to four Field Spaniels from the 1950s: Ronayne Regal, Gormac Teal, Colombina of Teffont, and Elmbury Morwena of Rhiwlas. Despite the fact that Field Spaniels were being shown in America in the late 1800s, no champions were made up between 1916 and 1966; in fact, the breed was essentially extinct in America for much of that time. The breed was reintroduced into America in the late 1960s. The Field Spaniel remains among the rarest of breeds in America.

TEMPERAMENT

The Field Spaniel is happiest when it has a job to do. Although independent in nature, it is devoted, sensitive, and willing to please. Generally cheerful and affectionate, it is an excellent family companion as long as it is given regular exercise. The Field Spaniel is especially known for its docile nature. It is typical for a Field Spaniel to be somewhat reserved with strangers.

UPKEEP

The Field Spaniel needs daily exercise, and even though it is happiest when given the chance to run and explore, its needs can be met with a long walk on leash. Its coat needs brushing and combing once or twice weekly. The hair inside the ears and between the foot pads should be clipped. Straggling hairs should be scissored every few months, and some clipping and thinning is needed for show dogs. The ears should be checked and cleaned regularly. Some can be somewhat sloppy, and some snore.

HEALTH

- Major concerns: CHD
- Minor concerns: otitis externa, hypothyroidism
- Occasionally seen: heart murmur, patellar luxation, seizures
- Suggested tests: hip, eye, (elbow), (heart), (patella), thyroid
- Life span: 12–14 years

FORM AND FUNCTION

Somewhat longer than tall, solidly built with moderate bone, the Field Spaniel is a dog without exaggeration, a combination of beauty and utility. Its stride is long and low, with head held proudly and alertly and the tail wagging but not carried high. The Field Spaniel is built for both activity and stamina, enabling it to hunt in dense cover or water. It has a single coat, which is flat or slightly wavy and moderately long, giving it protection from thorns and water. The expression is grave and gentle.

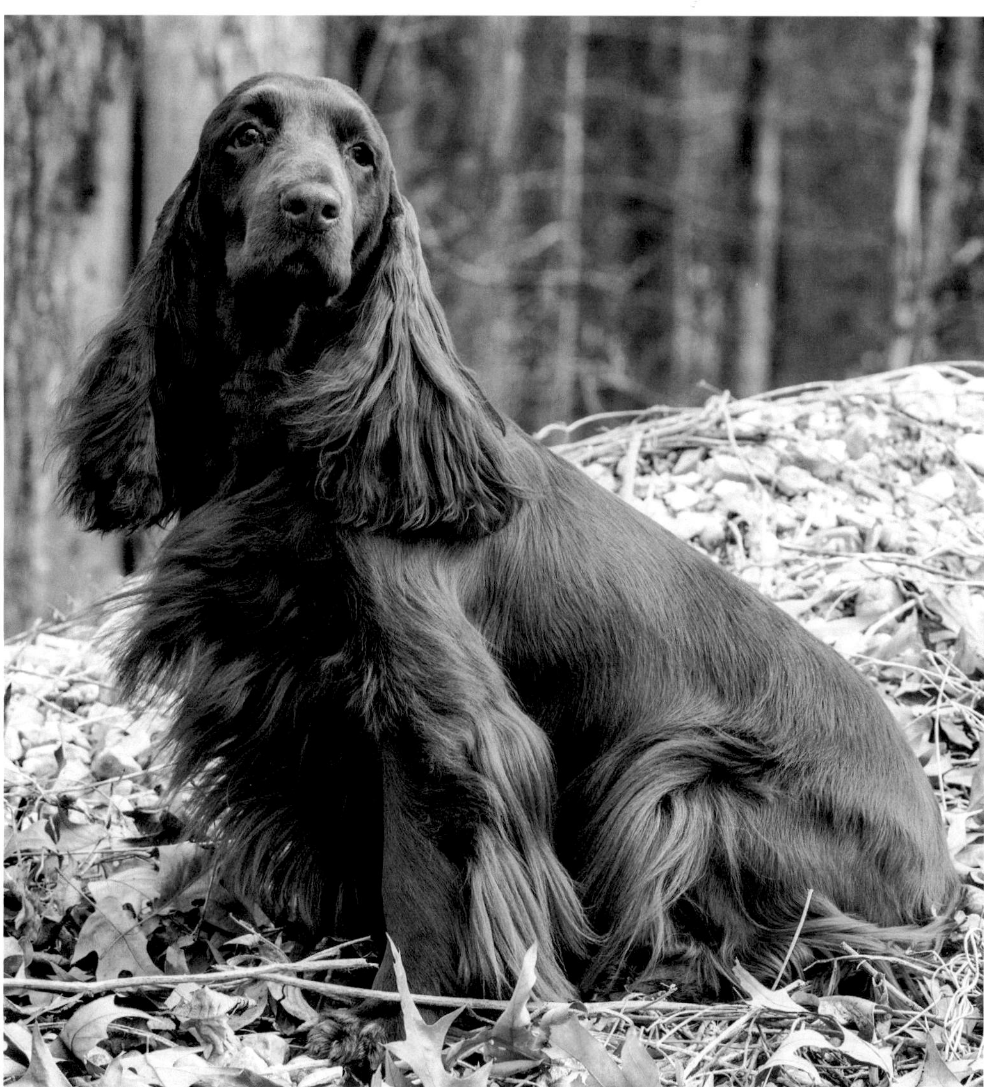

Irish Water Spaniel

AT A GLANCE

Energy level:	■■■■■	Watchdog ability:	■■■■
Exercise requirements:	■■■■■	Protection ability:	■■■
Playfulness:	■■■■■	Grooming requirements:	■■■
Affection level:	■■■	Cold tolerance:	■■■■
Friendliness toward dogs:	■■■	Heat tolerance:	■■■
Friendliness toward other pets:	■■■		
Friendliness toward strangers:	■■	WEIGHT: male: 55–65 lb; female: 45–58 lb	
Ease of training:	■■■■■	HEIGHT: male: 22–24″; female: 21–23″	

POPULARITY: Rare
FAMILY: Gundog, Spaniel
AREA OF ORIGIN: Ireland
DATE OF ORIGIN: 1800s
ORIGINAL FUNCTION: Water retrieving
TODAY'S FUNCTION: Water retrieving, retrieving field trials
OTHER NAME: None

HISTORY

The Irish Water Spaniel is one of the oldest and most distinctive spaniels. Dogs resembling them are depicted in manuscripts from 1,000 years ago. In the 1100s, mention is made of dogs called Shannon Spaniels, Rat-Tail Spaniels, Whip-Tail Spaniels, or Irish Water Spaniels. Continued references to the Irish Water Spaniel can be found from 1600 on. Around that time, the King of France is said to have been presented with an Irish Water Spaniel. Whether the breed was at one time found in different varieties or whether several similar breeds were its forebears is a matter of conjecture. What is agreed upon is that several similar spaniels existed in Ireland: the Northern Irish, Southern Irish, and Tweed Spaniels. The Southern Irish Spaniel, also called McCarthy's Breed, is

ILLUSTRATED STANDARD

1 Medium-sized, almond-shaped eyes, hazel in color
2 Topknot consisting of long, loose curls
3 Prominent occiput and gradual stop
4 Low-set, long ears
5 Topline level or slightly higher in rear
6 "Rat" tail, thick and covered with curls at base only, tapering to a fine point at end, carried nearly level with back
7 Large feet

Color: solid liver
DQ: none

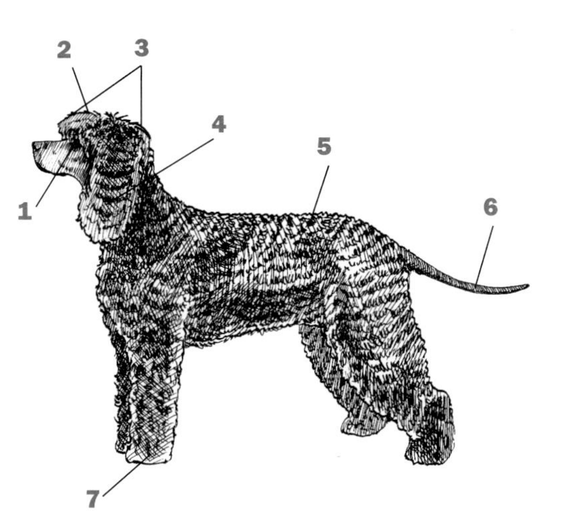

credited with being the eventual major forebear of today's dogs. In the mid 1800s, the appearance of the prolific sire Boatswain so influenced the breed that he is often credited as being the progenitor of the modern Irish Water Spaniel. The breed entered the show ring in both Britain and America by the late 1800s. In 1875, it was the third most popular sporting dog. Despite its enchantingly clownish appearance and adept water-retrieving ability, the Irish Water Spaniel lost popularity and is only rarely seen in the show ring or found as the family pet.

TEMPERAMENT

The Irish Water Spaniel goes at everything in life with gusto and enthusiasm. It loves to swim, run, hunt, and play and needs a lot of exercise. A clown at heart, it can be stubborn and independent, so it needs to be trained with patience, firmness, and a sense of humor. It tends to be reserved with strangers. It is generally good with children, though some can be timid.

UPKEEP

This active, athletic, inquisitive breed needs lots of mental and physical exertion to keep it from becoming frustrated or bored. An hour of free-running or strenuous playing a day is necessary to satisfy its needs. Obedience work can also be helpful in giving it the mental challenges it enjoys. The curly coat needs brushing and combing two to three times a week, plus scissoring every few months. Like all dogs, it loses its coat periodically; however, the hairs tend to become trapped in the other hairs rather than fall off. If not combed out, they will form mats and cords.

HEALTH

- Major concerns: CHD, otitis externa
- Minor concerns: distichiasis
- Occasionally seen: megaesophagus, hypothyroidism, elbow dysplasia, seizures, nail-bed disease
- Suggested tests: hip, elbow, eye, thyroid
- Life span: 10–12 years
- Note: May have adverse reactions to sulfa drugs or ivermectin

FORM AND FUNCTION

The Irish Water Spaniel is the tallest spaniel. However, it must never be so large that it can't be pulled into a boat! The body is of medium length, the whole dog being slightly rectangular in appearance. The general appearance suggests both dash and endurance. The gait is smooth and ground covering. The coat is one of the breed's distinctive features. The body is covered with a double coat consisting of crisp ringlets. This combination imparts water, weather, and thorn resistance to the dog, enabling it to hunt in the harshest of conditions. The Irish Water Spaniel's expression says it all: alert, intelligent, and quizzical.

Sussex Spaniel

AT A GLANCE

Energy level:	■ ■ ■	Watchdog ability:	■ ■ ■ ■
Exercise requirements:	■ ■ ■	Protection ability:	■ ■ ■
Playfulness:	■ ■ ■	Grooming requirements:	■ ■ ■
Affection level:	■ ■ ■ ■	Cold tolerance:	■ ■ ■
Friendliness toward dogs:	■ ■ ■	Heat tolerance:	■ ■ ■
Friendliness toward other pets:	■ ■ ■ ■		
Friendliness toward strangers:	■ ■ ■	WEIGHT: 35–45 lb	
Ease of training:	■ ■	HEIGHT: 13–15″	

POPULARITY: Very Rare
FAMILY: Gundog, Spaniel
AREA OF ORIGIN: England
DATE OF ORIGIN: 1800s
ORIGINAL FUNCTION: Small game tracking and flushing
TODAY'S FUNCTION: Bird flushing and retrieving
OTHER NAME: None

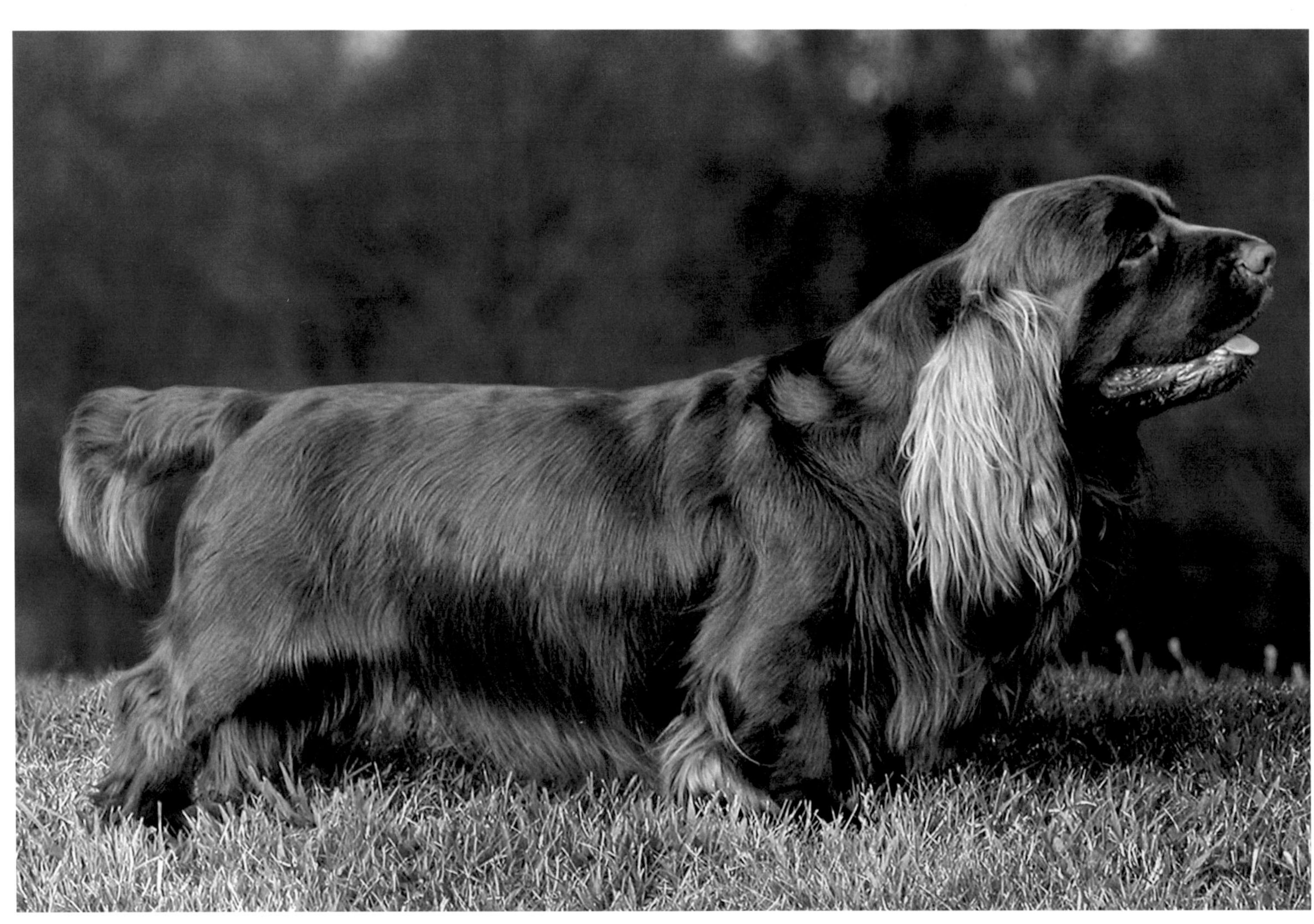

HISTORY

The "Spaniels of Sussex" are mentioned in a sporting publication of 1820 as good working dogs. The name was adopted from Sussex, England, the home of the first important kennel (established in 1795) of these small land spaniels. The breed soon became popular among the estates around Sussex County. They were adept as upland shooting dogs, slow working but with a good nose and apt to give tongue when on scent. This latter trait hurt the breed at field trials in the early 1900s, when quiet hunters were preferred. In addition, American hunters usually preferred a faster hunter. Although one of the first ten AKC-recognized breeds and among the earliest breeds to compete at dog shows, the Sussex has never been a particularly popular or competitive show dog. Perhaps because of these reasons, the Sussex Spaniel has been perilously close to extinction throughout most of the twentieth century. At times the breed has had so few individuals that inbreeding had to be practiced to a greater

ILLUSTRATED STANDARD

1 Somewhat pendulous lips
2 Eyes soft and languishing, fairly large, hazel colored
3 Rather short neck
4 Large, low-set ears
5 Level topline
6 Tail docked from 5 to 7"
7 Large, round feet, with long feathering

Color: rich golden liver
DQ: none

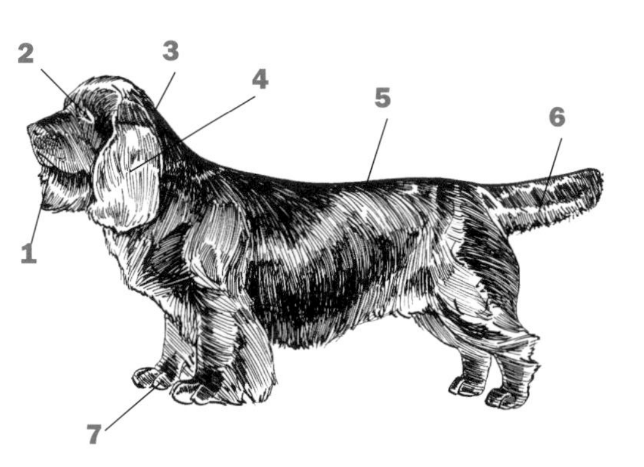

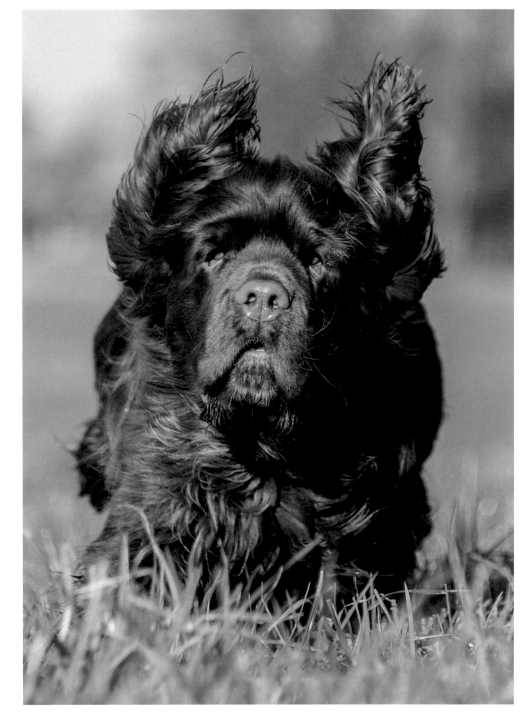

extent than otherwise desirable. In 1954, a cross was made with a Clumber Spaniel in an effort to expand the gene pool. The Sussex gene pool remains limited because the breed is still among the rarest of AKC breeds.

TEMPERAMENT
The Sussex Spaniel is more laid back than other spaniels. This makes it well suited for city life, but it still appreciates the chance to take to the wild and hunt up birds. It may be noisier than other spaniels when hunting, which has made it less popular with hunters. If left alone while other activities are ongoing, it may bark or howl. At home it is calm, steady, and easygoing. Its somber expression is misleading because it is quite cheerful.

UPKEEP
The Sussex needs daily exercise, but its needs can be met with a good walk on lead or a short romp in the yard. Given the chance, it will appreciate a longer foray into the field. The coat needs brushing and combing two to three times a week.

HEALTH
- Major concerns: CHD, intervertebral disk disease
- Minor concerns: otitis externa, heart murmurs, enlarged heart
- Occasionally seen: PDP1
- Suggested tests: hip, cardiac, (PDP1)
- Life span: 11–13 years

FORM AND FUNCTION
The long, low, "rectangular" body, coupled with a muscular and rather massive physique, allows the Sussex to penetrate dense cover when hunting. Its movement is deliberate and rolling because of its short legs and comparatively wide body, a gait that emphasizes power over speed. The abundant body coat is flat or slightly wavy, giving protection from thorns. A distinctive feature is the long feather between the toes, which should be long enough to cover the toenails. The expression is somber and serious, even frowning, but the wagging tail belies its true nature. The Sussex tends to bark when hunting, which helps the hunter locate it in thick cover.

Welsh Springer Spaniel

AT A GLANCE

Energy level:	■ ■ ■
Exercise requirements:	■ ■ ■
Playfulness:	■ ■ ■
Affection level:	■ ■ ■ ■
Friendliness toward dogs:	■ ■ ■
Friendliness toward other pets:	■ ■ ■
Friendliness toward strangers:	■ ■
Ease of training:	■ ■ ■

Watchdog ability:	■ ■ ■ ■
Protection ability:	■ ■
Grooming requirements:	■ ■ ■
Cold tolerance:	■ ■ ■
Heat tolerance:	■ ■ ■

WEIGHT: 35–50 lb*
HEIGHT: male: 18–19″; female: 17–18″

POPULARITY: Uncommon
FAMILY: Gundog, Spaniel
AREA OF ORIGIN: Wales
DATE OF ORIGIN: 1600s
ORIGINAL FUNCTION: Bird flushing and retrieving
TODAY'S FUNCTION: Bird flushing and retrieving
OTHER NAME: None

HISTORY

A dog identified as a Welsh Springer Spaniel is mentioned in some of the earliest records of the Laws of Wales dating around 1300. Whether this dog is the forebear of today's Welsh Springer is in dispute, however. Other evidence indicates the possibility that the Welsh Springer either developed alongside the English Springer or resulted from crosses of English Springers to Clumber Spaniels. Although land spaniels were used in Wales for some time before the Welsh Springer emerged as a recognized breed, the early dogs were probably not a uniform lot. At the first dog shows in England, English and Welsh Springers were shown together as one breed because the only difference at that time was in their color. The Welsh grew in popularity, and the breed came to America and was recognized by the

ILLUSTRATED STANDARD

1 Oval eyes
2 Slightly domed skull with moderate stop
3 Low-set, somewhat short ears
4 Prominent chest
5 Level topline
6 Docked tail carried near horizontal
7 Round feet

Color: rich red and white
DQ: none

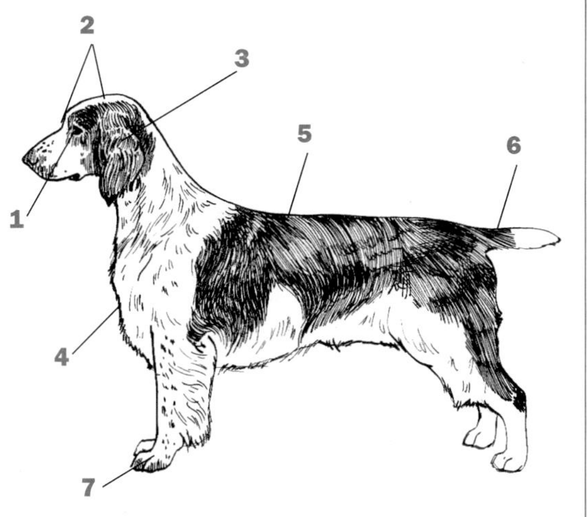

FORM AND FUNCTION

The Welsh Springer Spaniel is a hunting dog and should be in hard muscular condition. It is in no way a breed of exaggeration. It is very slightly longer than tall, compact, and possessing substance without coarseness. Its strides are powerful and ground covering. The coat is flat and straight, dense enough to protect it from water, weather, and thorns but not so excessive as to be a hindrance in the dog's work as a flushing spaniel. The expression is soft.

AKC in 1906. But the breed failed to gain the support it needed, and by the end of World War II it may have totally disappeared from America. New imports and, luckily, new supporters, arrived and the Welsh has since enjoyed a steady, if modest, popularity. Not as flashy in the show ring as the English Springer, the Welsh makes up for it in the field. It is an all-purpose, all-terrain hunter with a keen nose that can flush and retrieve over land and water.

TEMPERAMENT

Less exuberant that the English Springer, the Welsh Springer Spaniel is steady and easygoing. It still needs plenty of hard exercise, however, as it loves to hunt for birds. It is extremely devoted to its family, but it is independent in nature. It is reserved with strangers; some may even be timid. A sensitive breed, it requires ample socialization.

UPKEEP

The Welsh needs daily exercise, which can be met with long walks on leash combined with strenuous games in the yard. It especially likes jaunts afield and makes a good hiking companion. The coat needs brushing once or twice weekly and also needs occasional scissoring to neaten stragglers.

HEALTH

- Major concerns: CHD
- Minor concerns: glaucoma, otitis externa, epilepsy
- Occasionally seen: cataract, hypothyroidism, elbow dysplasia
- Suggested tests: hip, eye, thyroid, elbow
- Life span: 12–15 years

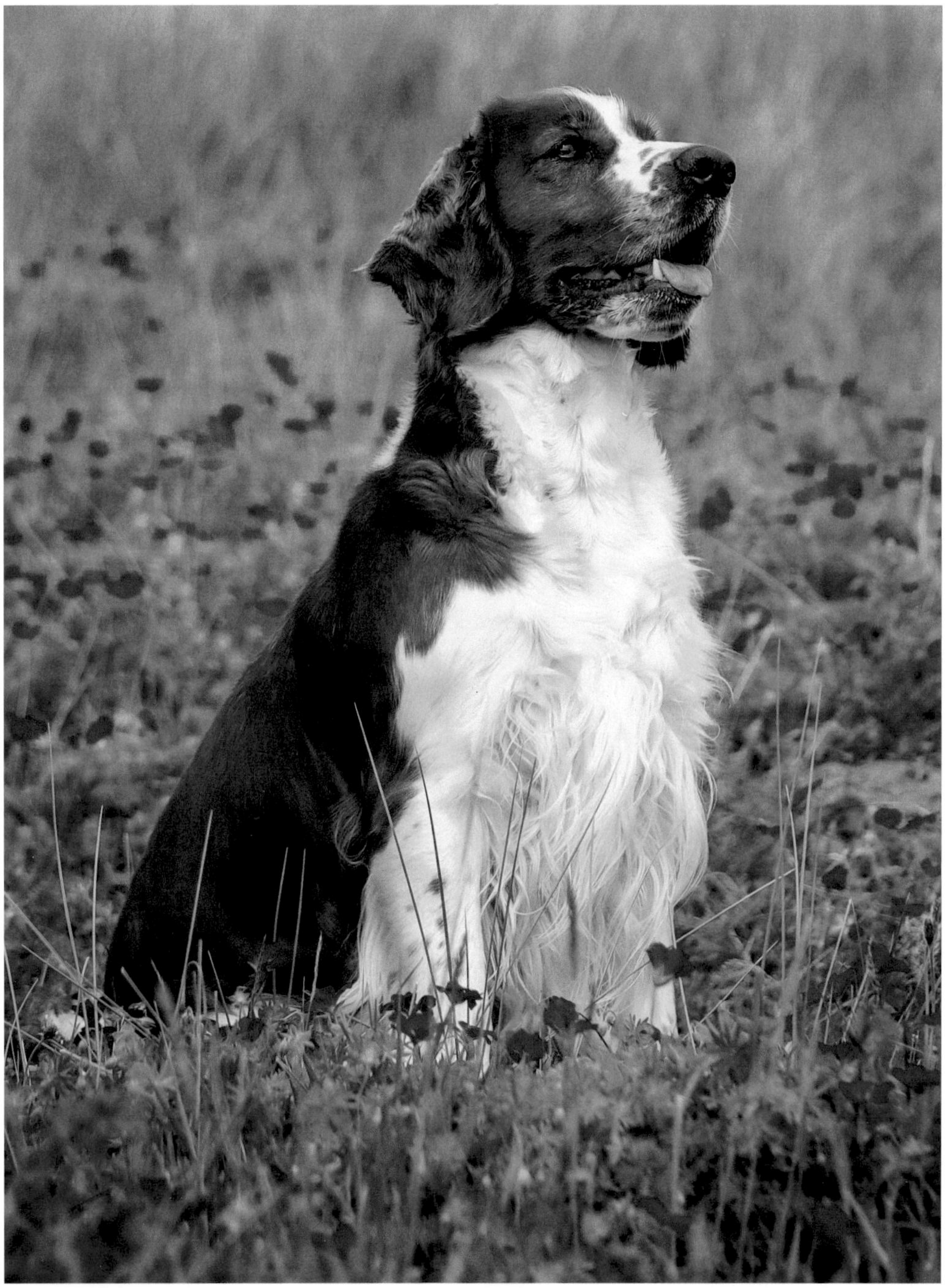

Spinone Italiano

AT A GLANCE

Energy level:	■■■
Exercise requirements:	■■■
Playfulness:	■■■
Affection level:	■■■■
Friendliness toward dogs:	■■■
Friendliness toward other pets:	■■■■
Friendliness toward strangers:	■■■■
Ease of training:	■■■
Watchdog ability:	■■■■
Protection ability:	■
Grooming requirements:	■■
Cold tolerance:	■■■
Heat tolerance:	■■■

WEIGHT: male: 71–82 lb; female: 62–71 lb*
HEIGHT: male: 23–27″; female: 22–25″

POPULARITY: Uncommon
FAMILY: Gundog, Pointer
AREA OF ORIGIN: Italy
DATE OF ORIGIN: 1200s
ORIGINAL FUNCTION: Pointing and retrieving
TODAY'S FUNCTION: Pointing and retrieving
OTHER NAME: Italian Spinone, Italian Griffon

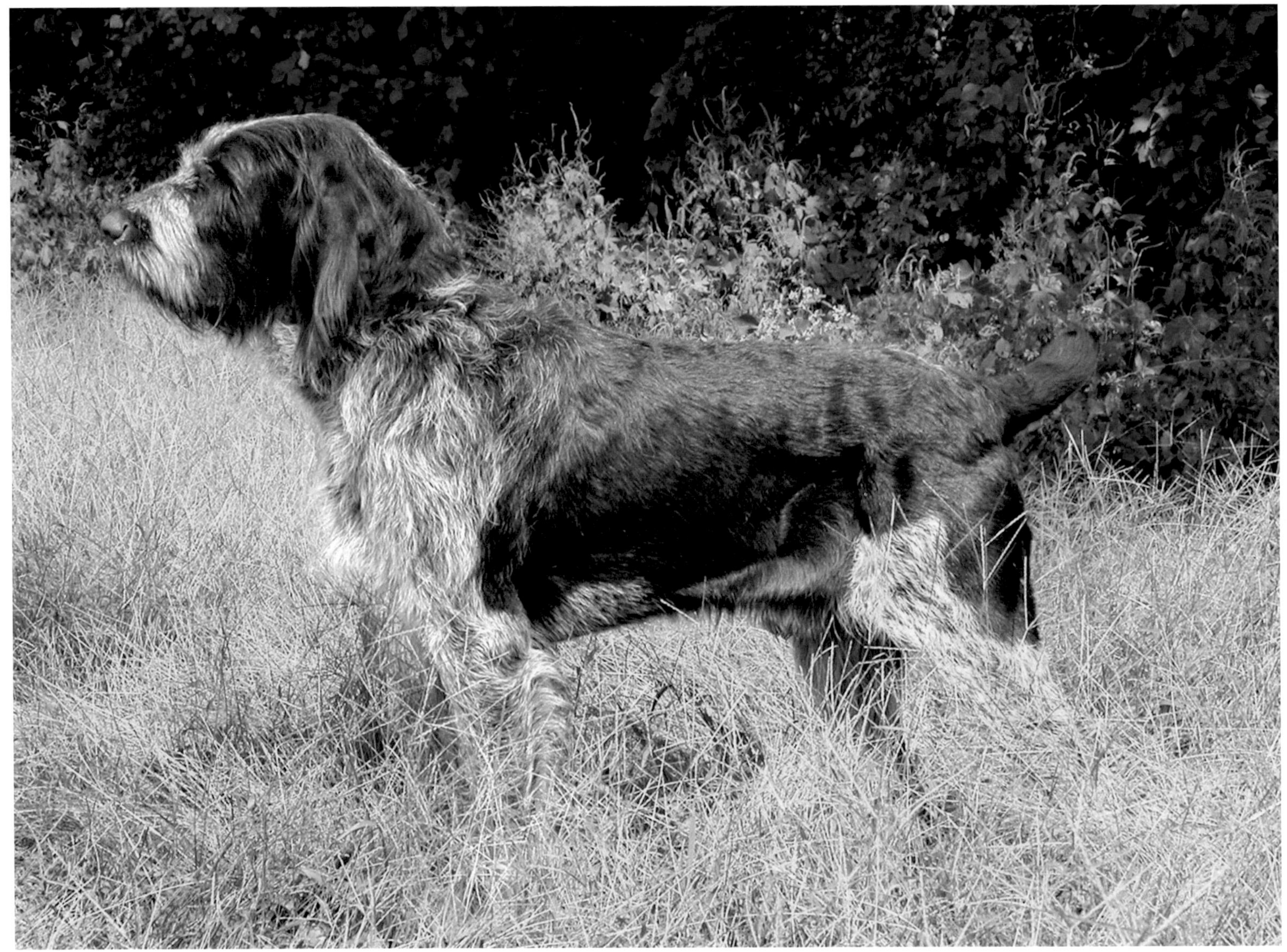

HISTORY

The Spinone is one of the earliest breeds developed as a pointing dog, with evidence of wirehaired pointing dogs dating as far back as 500 B.C. Dogs resembling the Spinone can be found in artwork of fifteenth- and sixteenth-century Italy. Still, its exact origin remains a mystery, although some believe it arose from Celtic wirehaired stock, whereas others place its origins with Greek traders who brought it to Italy during the times of the Roman Empire. Unfortunately, few records remain of the breed's subsequent development, even though present day Spinoni trace back principally to Italy's Piedmont region. It proved itself adept at penetrating thorny cover and finding feathered or fur game. During World War II, the Spinone further distinguished itself by tracking German patrols. The

ILLUSTRATED STANDARD

1. Muzzle long and square, with bridge straight or slightly Roman (preferred)
2. Eyes large, almost round, and ochre colored
3. Ears almost triangular
4. Well-arched loin
5. Tail carried down or horizontal; docked to 5½ to 8"
6. Large, rounded feet

Color: all white or white with orange or chestnut markings; orange or brown roan with or without larger markings
DQ: none

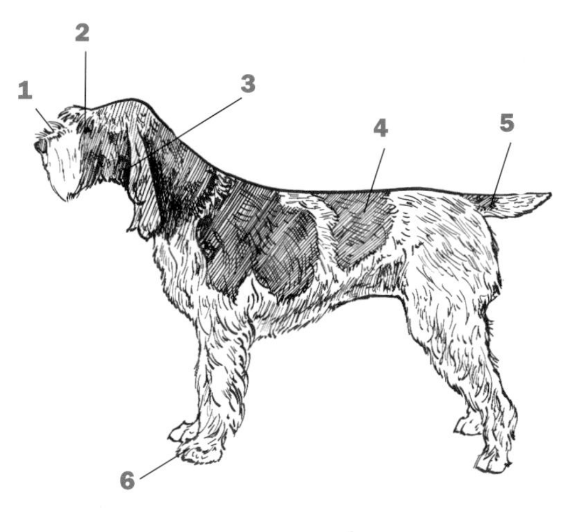

end of the war found the breed in trouble, however, because its numbers had been decimated and many of the remaining dogs crossed with other breeds. The Spinone was in danger of being lost. In the 1950s, breeders began a concerted effort to reconstruct the Spinone Italiano. Its hunting abilities are well worth the effort. This is a dog that can point, set, and retrieve, aided by a good nose and good sense. It is noted for hunting at a fast trot in a diagonal pattern that keeps it fairly close to the hunter and is classified as a versatile hunting breed. It is now a popular dog in Italy and some other European countries, but it has been slower to attract attention in America. The Spinone Italiano gained AKC status in 2000. The word *Spinone* is derived from *pino*, an Italian thorn bush through which these tough-skinned dogs could hunt in search of the small game often hiding within. The plural form is Spinoni (Spi-no-ni); the singular is Spinone (Spi-no-nay).

TEMPERAMENT

This is a devoted and gentle dog, very willing to please. It is affectionate and gets along well with other dogs and pets and children. It is also courageous. The Spinone is calmer and easier going than most pointing breeds.

UPKEEP

Like all sporting dogs, the Spinone needs daily exercise. This can take the form of a long walk or good run off leash. Coat care consists of weekly brushing, plus occasional hand-stripping to neaten the face and feet.

HEALTH

- Major concerns: CHD
- Minor concerns: ectropion, gastric torsion, otitis externa, cerebellar ataxia
- Occasionally seen: elbow dysplasia, allergies
- Suggested tests: hip, (eye), (ataxia), elbow
- Life span: 12–14 years

FORM AND FUNCTION

The Spinone Italiano has a hound look about it, with a fairly long head and muzzle, large, dropped ears, and somewhat pendulous lips. It is a strong, muscular dog, able to trot at fast pace all day and then retrieve over water or land. Its dense wiry coat allows it to hunt under any conditions. The coat is generally single, consisting of rough, dry, thick hair about 1.5 to 2.5" in length. Longer hair garnishing the lips and eyebrows adds further protection in addition to adding to its intelligent and gentle expression.

Vizsla

AT A GLANCE

Energy level:	■■■
Exercise requirements:	■■■
Playfulness:	■■■■
Affection level:	■■■■■
Friendliness toward dogs:	■■■
Friendliness toward other pets:	■■■■
Friendliness toward strangers:	■■■■■
Ease of training:	■■■

Watchdog ability:	■■■■
Protection ability:	■
Grooming requirements:	■
Cold tolerance:	■■
Heat tolerance:	■■■

WEIGHT: 45–65 lb*
HEIGHT: male: 22–24″; female: 21–23″

POPULARITY: Popular
FAMILY: Gundog, Pointer, Versatile Hunting Dog
AREA OF ORIGIN: Hungary
DATE OF ORIGIN: Middle Ages
ORIGINAL FUNCTION: Pointing, falconry, trailing
TODAY'S FUNCTION: Pointing, pointing field trials
OTHER NAME: Hungarian Vizsla, Magyar Vizsla, Hungarian Pointer, Drotszoru Magyar Vizsla

HISTORY

The Vizsla's forebears may have included breeds that the Magyars collected as they swarmed across Europe before settling in Hungary over a thousand years ago. Writings on falconry from the Middle Ages describe dogs of Vizsla type. The Hungarian plains were rich in game, and hunters wanted a fast but close-working dog that could not only point and retrieve birds but trail mammals over thick ground cover. The breed was unquestionably established by the eighteenth century, having found special favor with barons and warlords of the time. By the end of the nineteenth century, however, the breed had greatly declined in numbers. It was revived through the discovery and careful breeding of about a dozen good specimens. World War II spread the Vizsla through-

ILLUSTRATED STANDARD

1 Lean head with moderate stop
2 Eye color blends with coat color
3 Low-set, long ears
4 Tail docked one third off, carried near horizontal
5 Cat feet

Color: solid golden rust
DQ: completely black nose; white anywhere but on toes or forechest; long coat; male over 25.5" or under 20.5", or female over 24.5" or under 19.5"

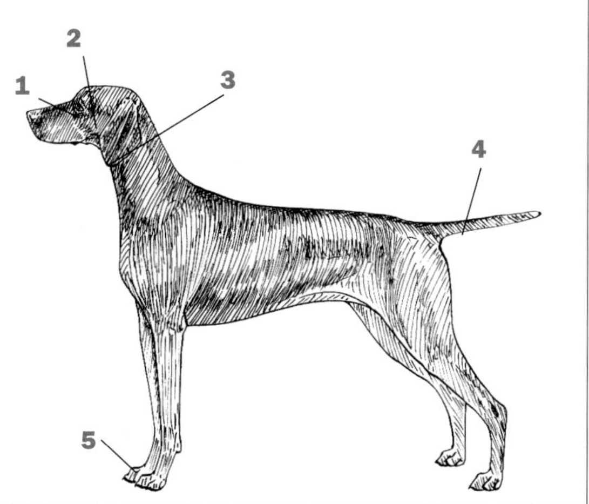

out the world. Hungarians fleeing Russian occupation took their pointing dogs to various other countries, including America, where their handsome appearance and exceptional hunting abilities were soon appreciated. AKC recognition came in 1960. Once again, the Viszla quickly gained admirers, and the breed is now regularly seen in the field, show ring, and home. It is also sometimes called the Hungarian Vizsla or Hungarian Pointer.

TEMPERAMENT
Bred to be a close-working gundog, the Viszla has the energy to range all day. It is a true hunter at heart, a talented pointer, and always on the lookout for bird scent. It can become frustrated and destructive if not given adequate exercise. Most can be stubborn, some can be timid, and others can be overly excitable. It is gentle, affectionate, and sensitive, and can be protective. The Vizsla makes a good companion for an active owner who spends a lot of time outdoors.

UPKEEP
The Vizsla needs a lot of strenuous exercise every day. This is an active breed that cannot be expected to meet its energy requirements with a short walk or within a small yard. It needs to be jogged or allowed to run in a large enclosed area. Otherwise, its needs are minimal. Its coat requires little care except an occasional brushing to remove dead hair.

HEALTH
- Major concerns: epilepsy
- Minor concerns: CHD, lymphosarcoma
- Occasionally seen: PRA, dwarfism, tricuspid valve dysplasia, persistent right aortic arch, hypothyroidism, vWD
- Suggested tests: hip, thyroid, eye, (cardiac), thyroid, (vWD)
- Life span: 10–14 years

FORM AND FUNCTION
The Vizsla is lightly built but muscular, giving it speed and endurance in the field. Its gait is light, graceful, smooth, and ground covering. Its short smooth coat is dense, providing some protection from the elements. The golden rust color is a hallmark of the breed.

Weimaraner

AT A GLANCE

Energy level:	■ ■ ■ ■ ■	Watchdog ability:	■ ■ ■ ■ ■	POPULARITY: Popular
Exercise requirements:	■ ■ ■ ■	Protection ability:	■ ■ ■ ■	FAMILY: Gundog, Pointer, Versatile Hunting Dog
Playfulness:	■ ■ ■ ■	Grooming requirements:	■	AREA OF ORIGIN: Germany
Affection level:	■ ■ ■	Cold tolerance:	■ ■	DATE OF ORIGIN: 1800s
Friendliness toward dogs:	■ ■	Heat tolerance:	■ ■ ■	ORIGINAL FUNCTION: Large game trailing
Friendliness toward other pets:	■ ■			TODAY'S FUNCTION: Pointing, pointing field trials
Friendliness toward strangers:	■ ■	WEIGHT: 55–90 lb*		
Ease of training:	■ ■ ■ ■	HEIGHT: male: 25–27"; female: 23–25"		OTHER NAME: Weimaraner Vorstehund

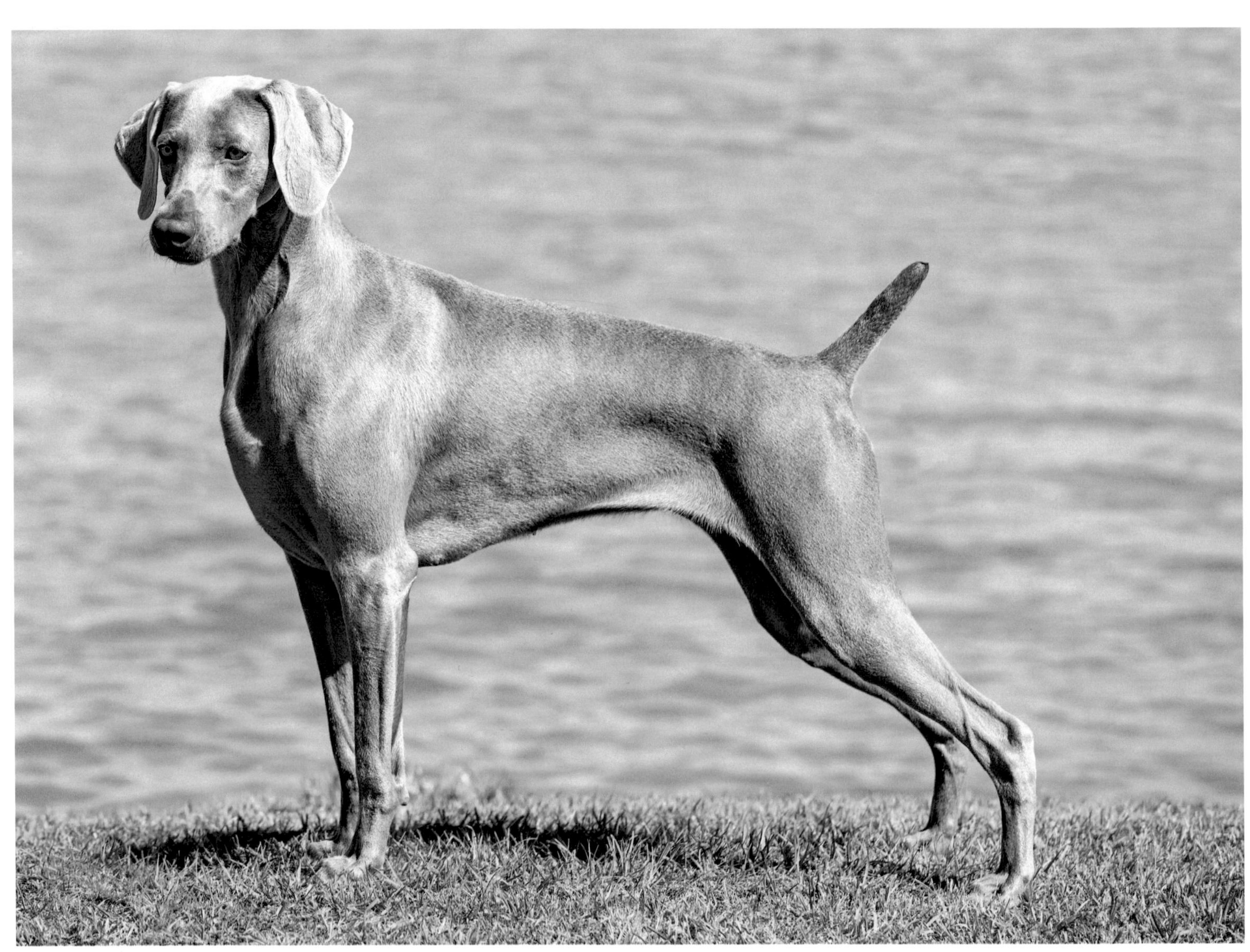

HISTORY

Germany has always been a country rich in wildlife, and German dog breeds have gained the reputation as some of the best in the world. The Weimaraner was produced in the nineteenth century by a concerted effort to create the ideal all-around gundog that could hunt game of all sizes, including deer and bear. This effort was sponsored by the court of Weimer, and the breed was initially known as the Weimar Pointer. Some of the breed's forebears include the Bloodhound, Red Schweisshund, and early pointing breeds. The origin of the Weimaraner's distinctive gray color is unknown, but it was an early feature of the breed. The breed's progress was strictly overseen by the German Weimaraner Club. Dogs could not be sold to nonmembers, and membership

ILLUSTRATED STANDARD

1 Nose gray
2 Eyes shaded light amber, gray, or blue-gray
3 Prominent occipit
4 High-set, long ears
5 Topline slopes slightly to rear
6 Tail docked to 6"
7 Webbed feet

Color: mouse-gray to silver-gray
DQ: deviation in height of more than 1" from standard in either way; distinctly long, blue, or black coat

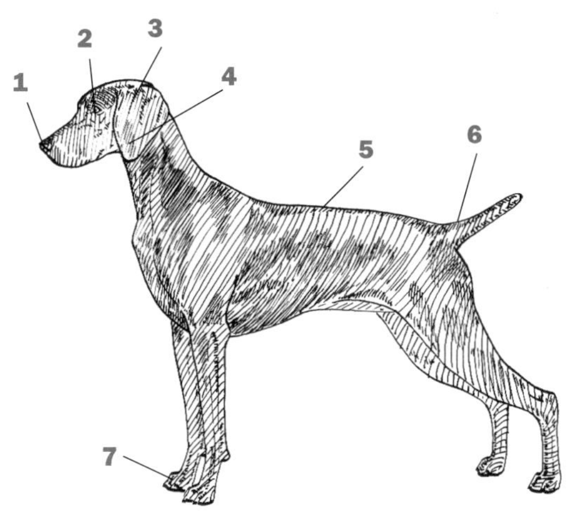

was hard to obtain. Dogs from nonapproved breedings could not be registered, and poor specimens had to be destroyed. Only when an American gained entry to the club and was allowed to take two dogs back to America in 1929 did the Weimaraner leave its native land. Early American Weimaraners performed so extraordinarily in obedience competitions that they aroused great interest. As more enthusiasts were attracted to the breed, they discovered its great worth as a hunting companion. AKC recognition came in 1943. The breed's beauty and versatility as personal gundog, pet, and competition dog have earned it a steady following.

TEMPERAMENT

The Weimaraner is bold and rambunctious, sometimes too much so for small children. It loves to run and hunt and can become frustrated and destructive if kept penned up. The Weimaraner may not be good with small pets unless raised with them. It can be stubborn or headstrong but learns easily. It functions best with an active owner who enjoys outdoor activities and wants a fun-loving companion. Breeders describe them as "needy" and "in your face," demanding attention.

UPKEEP

Daily strenuous exertion is a must for the Weimaraner. This is not a breed for city life unless its owner is a jogger. Even then, it needs to stretch its legs, run, and explore in a large, safe area. Coat care is minimal: occasional brushing to remove dead hair.

HEALTH

- Major concerns: gastric torsion
- Minor concerns: spinal dysraphism, CHD, entropion, distichiasis, vWD, hemophilia A, hypertrophic osteodystrophy*
- Occasionally seen: ununited anconeal process, eversion of nictitating membrane, PRA, dwarfism, tricuspid valve dysplasia, persistent right aortic arch, hypothyroidism
- Suggested tests: hip, eye, thyroid, (vWD)
- Life span: 10–13 years

FORM AND FUNCTION

The Weimaraner is built to hunt with great speed and endurance and combines grace, stamina, raciness, and an alert demeanor. It has fine aristocratic features, with a kind expression. The gait is smooth and effortless. The short sleek coat is noted for its unique gray color.

*To avoid this autoimmune reaction, it is best to avoid combination vaccines.

Wirehaired Pointing Griffon

AT A GLANCE

Energy level:	■■■■
Exercise requirements:	■■■■
Playfulness:	■■■
Affection level:	■■■
Friendliness toward dogs:	■■■
Friendliness toward other pets:	■■■
Friendliness toward strangers:	■■■
Ease of training:	■■■

Watchdog ability:	■■■■■
Protection ability:	■■■
Grooming requirements:	■■■
Cold tolerance:	■■■
Heat tolerance:	■■

WEIGHT: 50–60 lb*
HEIGHT: male: 22–24″; female: 20–22″

POPULARITY: Somewhat popular
FAMILY: Gundog, Pointer, Versatile Hunting Dog
AREA OF ORIGIN: France
DATE OF ORIGIN: 1800s
ORIGINAL FUNCTION: Pointing and retrieving
TODAY'S FUNCTION: Pointing and retrieving, pointing field trials
OTHER NAME: Korthals Griffon, Pointing Wirehaired Griffon, Griffon D'Arrêt a Poil Dur

HISTORY

Unlike the development of most breeds, most of the development of the Wirehaired Pointing Griffon was deliberate and fairly well documented, beginning in the middle 1800s with the creation of the Cherville Griffon, which was subsequently crossed with the setter and pointer. It was Edward Korthals of Holland, however, who is credited with developing and refining the breed. In fact, the Griffon is still known as the Korthals Griffon throughout most of the world. He began his mission in 1874, crossing twenty dogs representing seven breeds (griffons, spaniels, water spaniels, German and French pointers, and setter). Korthals traveled extensively in France and popularized his new breed wherever he went, whether it was a field activity, bench show, or business

ILLUSTRATED STANDARD

1 Eyes large and rounded, in all shades of yellow and brown
2 Nose brown
3 Abundant mustache and eyebrows
4 High-set, medium-sized ears
5 Topline slopes slightly to rear
6 Tail docked to two-thirds to one-half length, carried straight or slightly raised
7 Round, webbed feet

Color: preferably steel gray with brown markings, also chestnut brown, or roan, white and brown; less desirable is solid brown, solid white, or white and orange
DQ: nose any color but brown; black coat

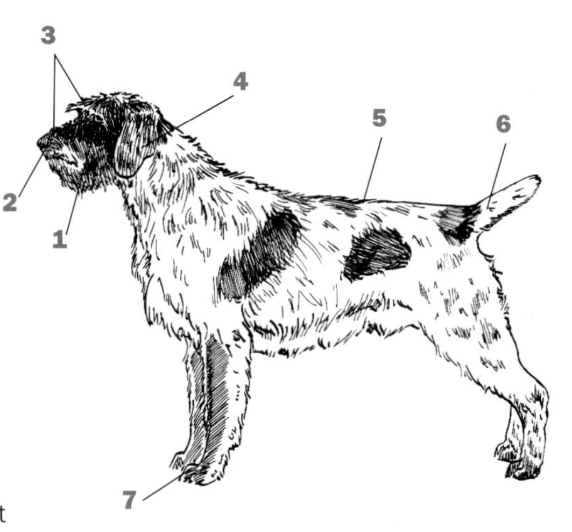

meeting. Through his French connections, his new breed became adopted in France, where it gained a reputation as a deliberate, careful hunter with a good nose. It was in France that the breed found a stronghold, causing people to consider it as a French breed despite its Dutch roots. By 1887, the breed type was stable, and a breed standard was published. The first show classes for the breed were offered in 1888 in England, although at that time it was referred to as a Russian Setter or Retriever (apparently any well-furred dog was assumed to be of Siberian origin). In fact, the first Griffon registered in America was registered as a Russian Setter in 1887. Its popularity grew steadily, only to be halted by the Second World War. After the war, its reputation as an ideal dog for the walking hunter again gained it new popularity, but the initiation of competitive field trials, in which faster-paced breeds dominated, caused many competitive hunters to turn away from the Griffon. Despite its low numbers, the Wirehaired Pointing Griffon has loyal followers who value its excellent abilities not only as a pointer and retriever but also as a versatile and loyal companion. In fact, it is often called "the supreme gundog."

TEMPERAMENT

The Wirehaired Pointing Griffon is a skilled field dog, pointing and retrieving with a deliberate style, generally staying within the hunter's gun range. It combines independent action with the ability to be directed by the hunter. It is an equally adept family pet, absolutely devoted, willing to please, amiable, and often, comical. It is generally friendly toward strangers, other dogs, and pets.

UPKEEP

The Wirehaired Pointing Griffon needs daily exertion, either in the form of jogging, games, or a run in the field. It particularly enjoys swimming. Its harsh coat needs combing or brushing once or twice a week, plus hand-stripping to remove dead hair twice a year. Its ears need regular cleaning and plucking of hair within the canal in order to avoid ear problems.

HEALTH

- Major concerns: none
- Minor concerns: CHD, otitis externa, entropion, ectropion
- Occasionally seen: elbow dysplasia
- Suggested tests: hip, eye, elbow
- Life span: 12–14 years

FORM AND FUNCTION

This strong breed can cope with any terrain. It should be slightly longer than tall, of medium substance. It functions as both a retriever and pointer, and its size and conformation reflects a compromise between the requirements of these jobs. Its gait is efficient and tireless, with low, catlike strides. The coat is of medium length, straight and wiry, with a fine, downy, thick undercoat. The combination provides protection in the swampy country in which it was developed, as well as insulation from cold and water. The abundant facial furnishings contribute to its friendly expression.

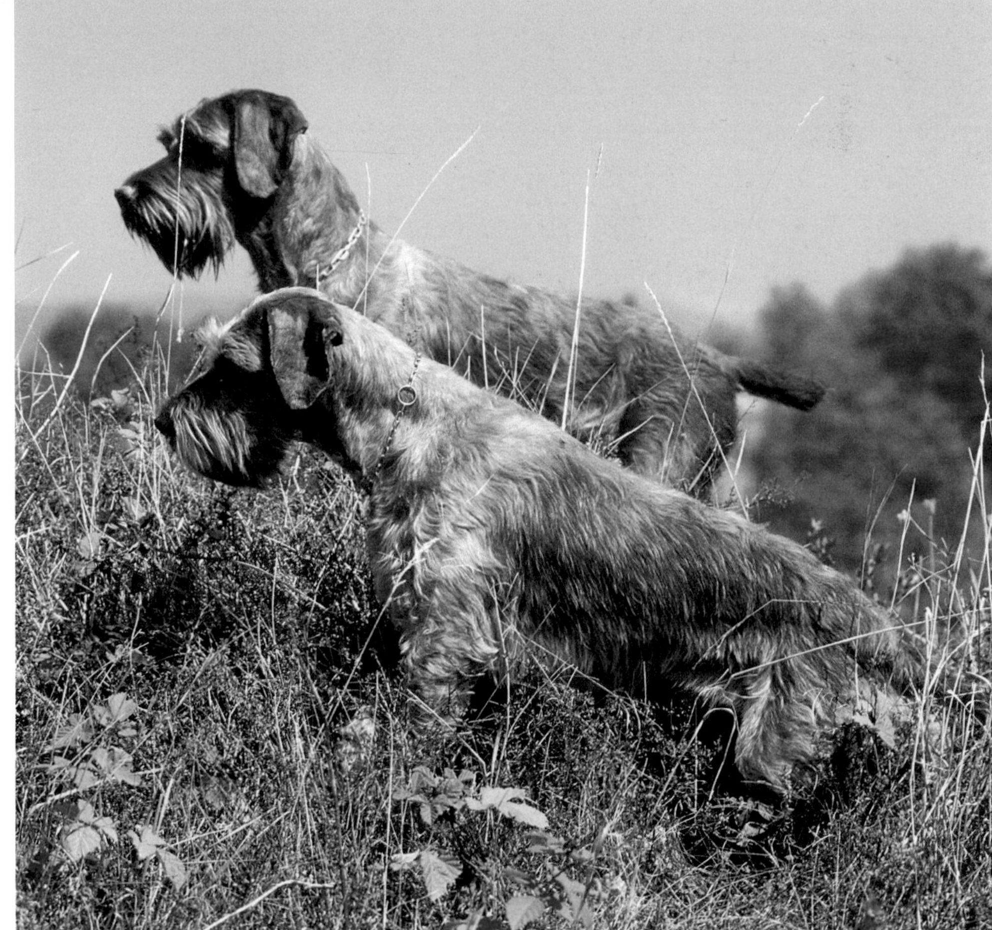

Wirehaired Vizsla

AT A GLANCE

Energy level:	■■■■	Watchdog ability:	■■■■
Exercise requirements:	■■■■	Protection ability:	■
Playfulness:	■■■■	Grooming requirements:	■■■
Affection level:	■■■■■	Cold tolerance:	■■■
Friendliness toward dogs:	■■■	Heat tolerance:	■■■
Friendliness toward other pets:	■■■		
Friendliness toward strangers:	■■■	WEIGHT: 40–55 lb	
Ease of training:	■■■	HEIGHT: male: 23–25″; female: 21.5–23″	

POPULARITY: Rare
FAMILY: Gundog, Pointer, Versatile Hunting Dog
AREA OF ORIGIN: Hungary
DATE OF ORIGIN: 1900s
ORIGINAL FUNCTION: General hunting
TODAY'S FUNCTION: Hunting, field trials
OTHER NAME: None

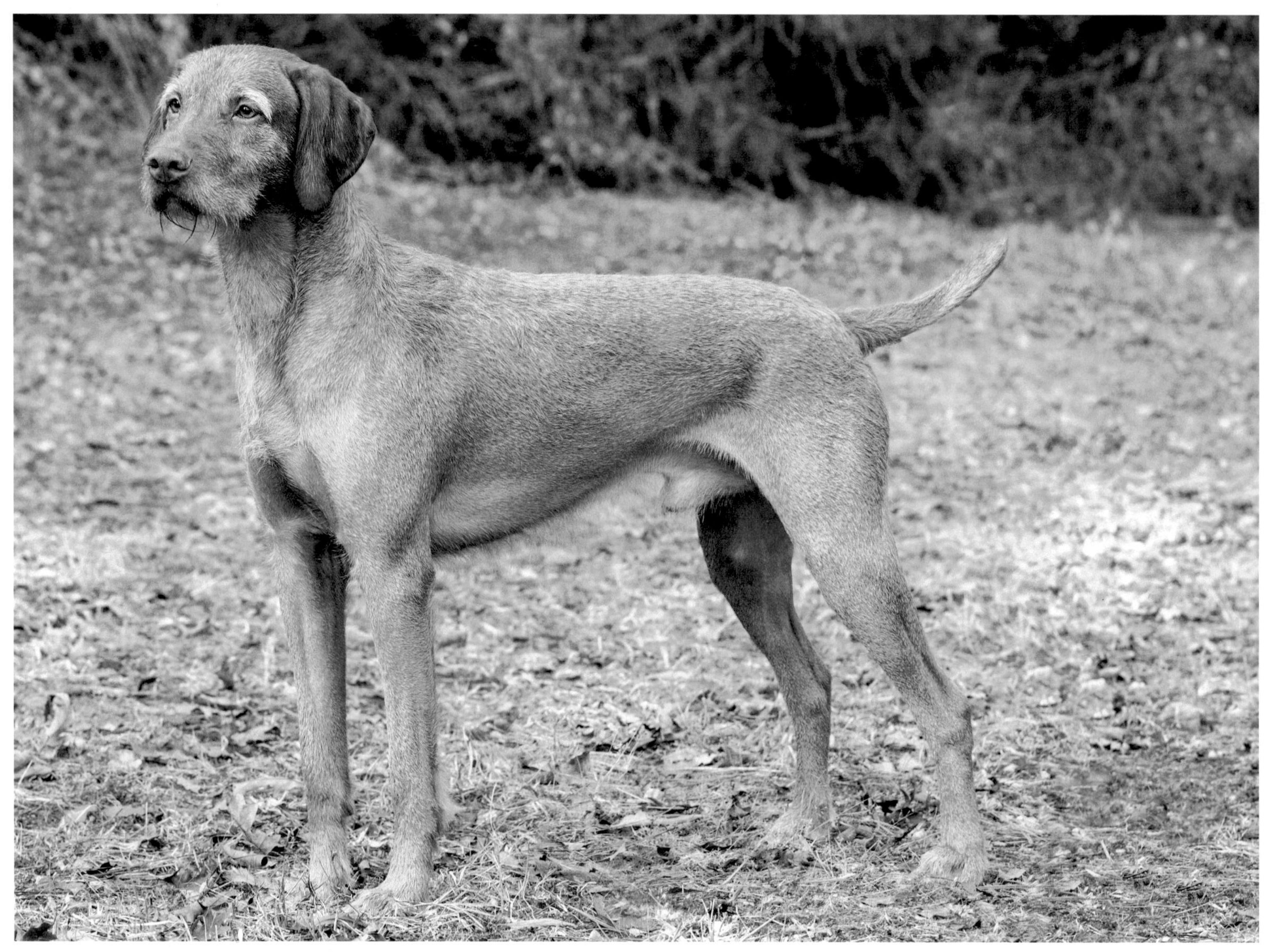

HISTORY

In the 1930s, several Hungarian hunters and falconers wanted to create a Vizsla with a slightly sturdier build and a coat better suited to extreme winter weather, icy water, and rough undergrowth. With permission from the Hungarian Vizsla Klub, two experienced breeders crossed two Vizsla females with a solid brown German Wirehaired Pointer. After three generations, the results were promising enough that the club gave the go-ahead to continue with the project. By 1944, the Vizsla Klub listed 60 wirehaired Vizslas. Almost all the dogs were lost during World War II, but breeding continued on a small scale, with some anecdotal evidence that the Wirehaired Pointing Griffon, Pudelpointer, Irish Setter, and maybe even Bloodhound were integrated into the scheme. The breed grew slowly

ILLUSTRATED STANDARD

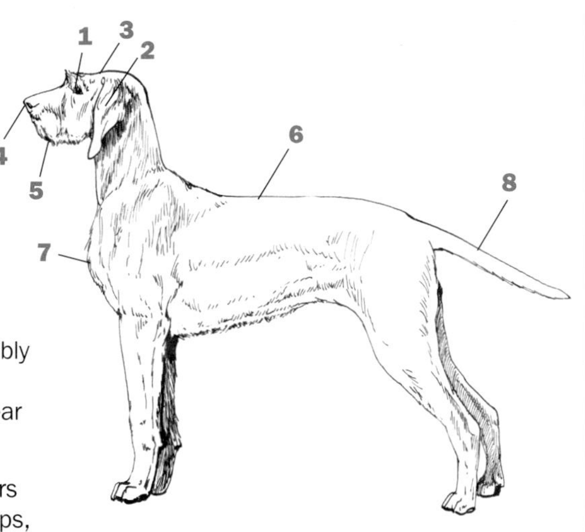

1 Slightly oval, medium-sized eyes
2 Ears set at medium height, moderate length, ending in rounded V-shape
3 Slightly domed skull
4 Nose color blends with coat color
5 Bearded lips
6 Straight topline
7 Well-developed forechest
8 Tail set just below croup level; preferably docked by one-quarter; if natural, reaches to hock; carried near horizontal when moving

Color: golden rust in varying shades, ears may be slightly darker; eyes, eye-rims, lips, nose, and toenails blend with the coat color
DQ: males over 26" or under 22"; females over 24" or under 20.5"; black on nose; under or overshot; more than two missing teeth; rear dewclaws; white anywhere but toes, forechest, and throat; more than 2" of white on forechest or throat

HEALTH

- Major concerns: CHD
- Minor concerns: none
- Occasionally seen: allergies, epilepsy, urinary stones, distichiasis
- Suggested tests: hip, eye
- Life span: 9–13 years

FORM AND FUNCTION

The Wirehaired Vizsla is a medium-sized, versatile hunting dog with an excellent nose for hunting and tracking furred and feathered creatures on land and in water. It is slightly longer than tall, with sufficient bone and substance. Its gait is powerful yet graceful, with far reaching drive enabling it to cover any terrain encountered by the walking hunter. The weather resistant coat is close lying, about 1 inch long, with a dense undercoat and wiry outer coat. It has pronounced eyebrows and a harsh beard, about 1 inch long, which gives it expressiveness.

following the war, but received Fèdèration Cynologique Internationale (FCI) recognition in 1966. Most owners were hunters, so the Hungarian Vizsla Klub held hunting tests to showcase their talents to other hunters. The first Wirehaired Vizslas came to Canada in the 1970s and to the United States in 1973. They were called Uplanders after the breed's origin in the uplands of northern Hungary. Their promoters formed an Uplander club, but the AKC declined to acknowledge them, so these dogs left no impact on today's Wirehaired Vizsla. The Canadian Kennel Club recognized the breed in 1986, the North American Versatile Hunting Dog Association in 1986, the UKC in 2006, and the AKC in 2014.

TEMPERAMENT

The Wirehaired Vizsla is bold, lively, playful, and affectionate. It is a devoted companion and a talented hunter. It can be reserved toward strangers, but it is generally good with other dogs and pets. It is eager to please and learns quickly, but can be stubborn if force methods are used. They make excellent watchdogs and fairly good protection dogs.

UPKEEP

This is an energetic dog that loves to run and explore and, mostly, hunt. It is an excellent hiking companion, strong swimmer, and good jogger. It needs the chance to run every day or to have a long walk or play session. Given adequate exercise, it is an excellent housedog. The coat is easy to care for, requiring minimal hand stripping and brushing. They are low shedders.

One of the oldest groups of dogs, hounds aid humans by pursuing and catching their quarry. Sighthounds pursue by sight and include the fast running dogs of greyhound build, whereas scenthounds pursue by scent and include the more solidly built dogs of general coonhound build. Some breeds hunt by both sight and scent, and a few breeds don't seem like hounds at all. Again, all hound breeds have in common the independent pursuit of mammalian quarry. As such, they traditionally could not wait for the hunter's direction; they led the way.

THE HOUND GROUP

Afghan Hound

AT A GLANCE

Energy level:	■■	Watchdog ability:	■■■	POPULARITY: Somewhat uncommon
Exercise requirements:	■■■	Protection ability:	■	FAMILY: Sighthound
Playfulness:	■■■	Grooming requirements:	■■■■	AREA OF ORIGIN: Afghanistan
Affection level:	■	Cold tolerance:	■■■	DATE OF ORIGIN: Ancient times
Friendliness toward dogs:	■■■	Heat tolerance:	■■■	ORIGINAL FUNCTION: Coursing hare and gazelle
Friendliness toward other pets:	■■■			
Friendliness toward strangers:	■	WEIGHT: male: 60 lb; female: 50 lb		TODAY'S FUNCTION: Lure coursing
Ease of training:	■■	HEIGHT: male: 27″; female: 25″(±1 inch)		OTHER NAME: Tazi, Baluchi Hound

HISTORY

With roots dating to the Egyptian pharaohs, the Afghan Hound is an ancient breed derived from the group of Middle Eastern sighthounds. Despite such illustrious roots, most of the Afghan Hound's development is the result of its use by nomadic tribes as a coursing hound capable of providing hare and gazelle meat for the pot. The dogs often hunted with the aid of falcons, which were trained to swoop at the quarry. Generations of hunting in the harsh mountainous terrain of Afghanistan produced a fast dog that also had a good deal of stamina, but most of all, had incredible leaping ability and nimbleness. Its long coat protected it from the cold climate. These dogs remained isolated for centuries, hidden in the impenetrable Afghanistan Mountains. The first Afghan Hound came to

ILLUSTRATED STANDARD

1 Long, refined head
2 Almond-shaped eyes
3 Topknot of long, silky hair
4 Long ears
5 Short-haired saddle
6 Pronounced hipbones
7 Ring on the end of tail
8 Large feet

Color: all colors permissible except spotted
DQ: none

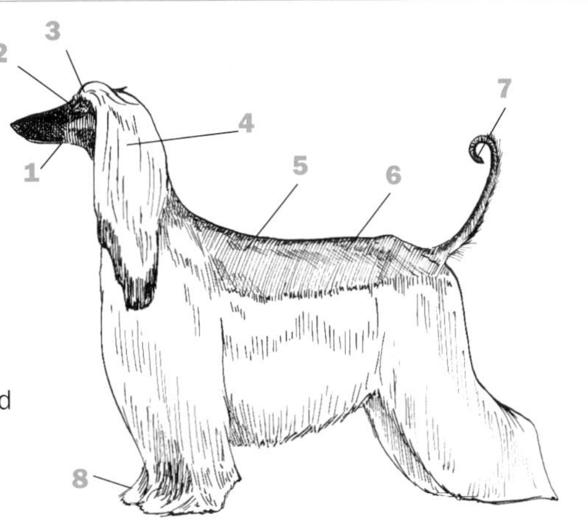

England in the early 1900s; at that time these dogs were called Persian Greyhounds or Barukhzy Hounds. These dogs were a diverse lot so a standard of perfection—modeled on Zardin, a particularly striking dog—that described the more elegant, racy dog of today was created. Popularity grew slowly, with the dog appealing mostly to the glamour set. Popularity in the show ring was faster coming, with the Afghan quickly becoming one of the most competitive and glamorous dogs in the rings. In the 1970s the Afghan became a fad breed with the public, but it has since dwindled in popularity.

TEMPERAMENT

Despite its glamorous reputation, the Afghan Hound is a hunter at heart, bred to chase down game over rugged terrain. While it maintains its regal bearings inside, it needs a daily chance to stretch its legs in a safe area. Its worst trait is a reluctance to come when called. It will chase small animals outside; inside, it will coexist peacefully. Though gentle with children, it may not be playful and interactive enough with them. Described by some as "catlike," it is independent yet sensitive, and not overly demonstrative. It is reserved with strangers; some can be timid. It has a gay, clownish side.

UPKEEP

The Afghan needs daily exertion, either in the form of a long walk followed by a short sprint, or preferably, a chance to run full speed in a safe enclosed area. It needs a soft bed and is best suited as a housedog with outdoor access. It is naturally thin and bony. The coat requires some commitment, especially when shedding the puppy coat; most adult coats need brushing or combing every two to three days. Weekly bathing helps prevent matting.

HEALTH

- Major concerns: none
- Minor concerns: cataract
- Occasionally seen: necrotic myelopathy, CHD, hypothyroidism
- Suggested tests: eye, hip, thyroidism
- Life span: 12–14 years
- Note: sensitive to barbiturate anesthesia; prone to tail injuries

FORM AND FUNCTION

The Afghan is built along greyhound-like lines, enabling it to execute a double-suspension gallop and run down fleet game. The comparatively short back and steep pelvis helped it to leap great heights and to turn almost in place, essential attributes for coursing in rocky mountainous terrain. The large feet gave it better foothold and were more resistant to injury on rough ground. The silky coat protected the dog from cold nights at high altitudes. The Afghan appears dignified and aloof, with an exotic expression and proud carriage. The gait shows great elasticity and spring, and the dog moves with head and tail high.

American English Coonhound

AT A GLANCE

Energy level:	■■■	Watchdog ability:	■■■	POPULARITY: Rare
Exercise requirements:	■■■	Protection ability:	■■	FAMILY: Scenthound
Playfulness:	■■■	Grooming requirements:	■	AREA OF ORIGIN: United States
Affection level:	■■■	Cold tolerance:	■■■	DATE OF ORIGIN: 1800s
Friendliness toward dogs:	■■■■	Heat tolerance:	■■■	ORIGINAL FUNCTION: Racoon trailing and treeing
Friendliness toward other pets:	■■■			TODAY'S FUNCTION: Racoon trailing and treeing
Friendliness toward strangers:	■■■	WEIGHT: 45–65 lb		OTHER NAME: English Coonhound, Redtick Coonhound
Ease of training:	■	HEIGHT: male: 24–26″; female: 23–25″		

HISTORY

In colors of red, white, and blue, the American English Coonhound is as all-American as you can get--except, of course, for the English part. Created from English hunting hounds brought to America during the seventeenth and eighteenth centuries, the breed's first American incarnation was known as the Virginia Hound. Selective breeding created a dog better suited to the tangled terrain of the southeastern United States and for hunting a variety of mammals including fox, raccoon, and sometimes, opossum, boar, and cougar. In 1905, the UKC recognized the breed as the English Fox and Coonhound. The name was eventually shortened to English Coonhound, which is still its name with the UKC. When the AKC recognized them in 2011 they took the name from the parent club,

ILLUSTRATED STANDARD

1 Wide-set, dark brown eyes; no drooping lids
2 Square muzzle; flews cover lower jaw
3 Prominent stop
4 Low-set, fine, soft ears, reaching almost to nose
5 Very slightly domed, broad skull
6 Hips slightly higher than withers
7 Tail set and carried high but not hooked over back; slight brush
8 Round, catlike feet

Color: red and white ticked, blue and white ticked, tri-colored with ticking, red and white, white and black

DQ: undershot; overshot; tri-colored with no ticking; solid color with less than 10 percent ticking; any brindle color

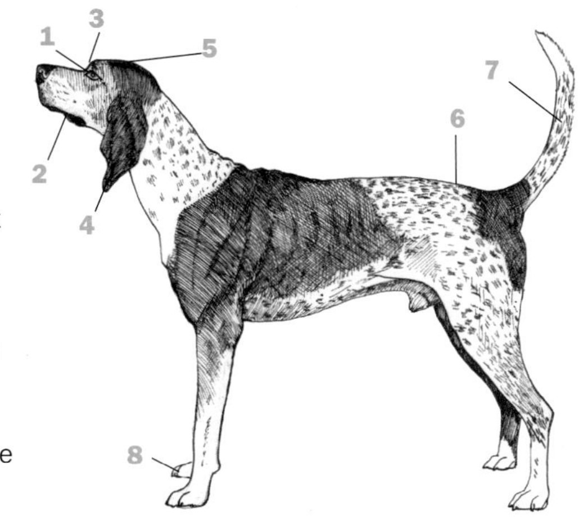

HEALTH

- Major concerns: none
- Minor concerns: none
- Occasionally seen: CHD, ear infections
- Suggested tests: (hip)
- Life span: 11 to 13 years

FORM AND FUNCTION

The American English Coonhound combines speed with endurance, and as such has a moderate build with a strong but racy body. It is almost square proportioned, being just slightly longer than tall. The coat is hard, which provides protection from heavy brush and harsh elements. The muzzle is fairly broad, providing plenty of room for olfactory organs. Flews and hanging ears may help sweep and trap odor molecules. The trot is effortless, with good reach and drive, giving the impression of great endurance. The voice is a strong loud bawl that can be heard from great distances.

the American English Coonhound Association. Nobody objected to the Americanization, because by that time they were true American citizens. To add to the confusion, many people call them Redtick Coonhounds, because most have the red ticked pattern—although they also come in other combinations of red, blue, and white. The Bluetick and Treeing Walker Coonhounds were initially part of the same breed until the mid-1940s. Although most American English are red ticked, some are still tri-colored or blue ticked like their Bluetick and Walker relatives. The breed embodies the American work—and play—ethic. Its primary role has always been that of a first-rate hunting hound. Known for its speed, endurance, and melodious voice, top hunters command top dollar.

TEMPERAMENT

Cheerful, alert, affectionate, strong-willed, fun-loving, and mischievous, they enjoy outwitting owners by sniffing out trouble. Hunting is their first love. They are independent and apt to follow their nose in pursuit of a scent trail. They tend to be laid-back at home, eager to earn a treat, and reluctant to challenge authority but are easily distracted by scents when training. They enjoy the company of other dogs and get along well with everyone, even small animals if they're raised with them. They are adequate watchdogs.

UPKEEP

Although fairly quiet inside, this is a dog that lives for the outdoors. It needs to take in new smells and have the chance to investigate scents every day. A good daily jog will satisfy its exercise requirements. Inside, food must be kept well out of reach. Coat care consists of occasional brushing. Their loud bay is freely given.

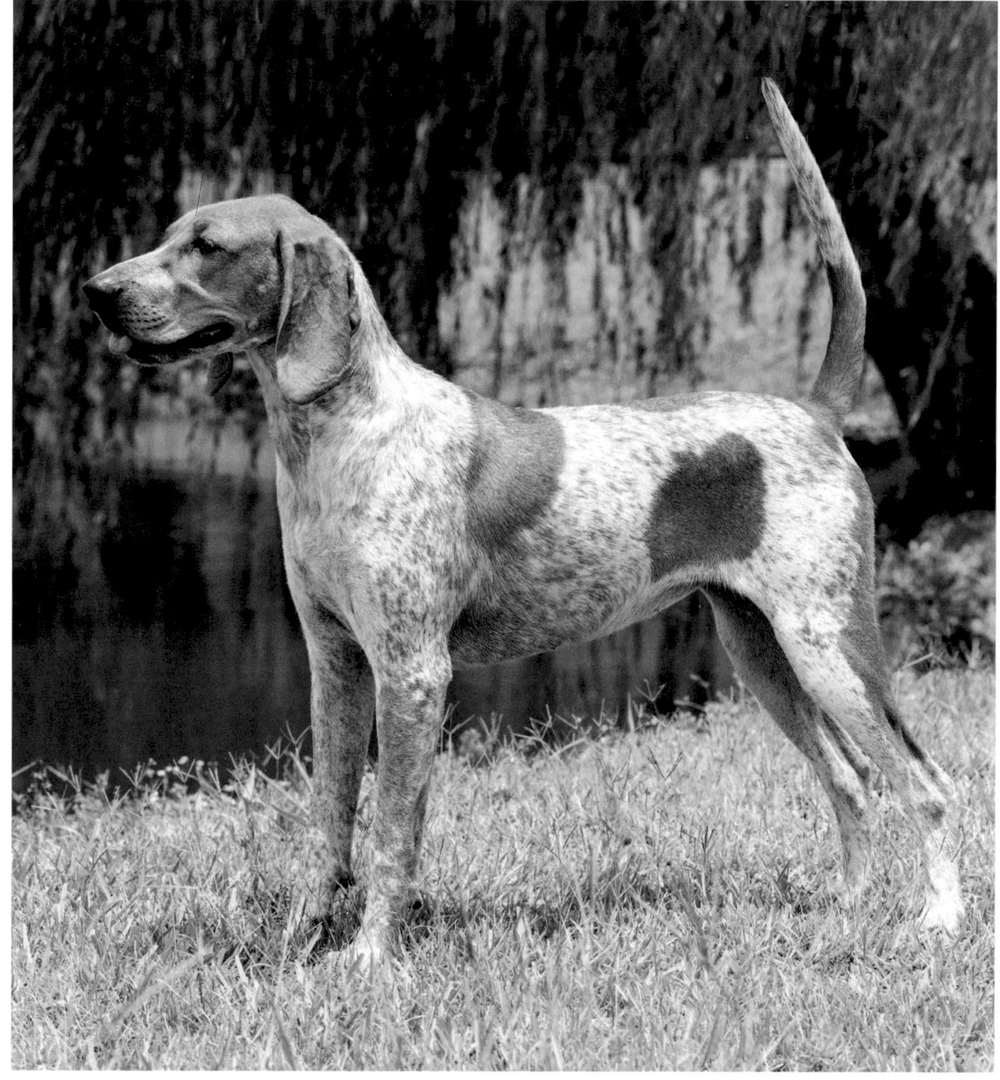

Basenji

AT A GLANCE

Energy level:	■ ■ ■ ■
Exercise requirements:	■ ■ ■
Playfulness:	■ ■ ■
Affection level:	■ ■ ■
Friendliness toward dogs:	■ ■
Friendliness toward other pets:	■
Friendliness toward strangers:	■ ■ ■
Ease of training:	■ ■

Watchdog ability:	■ ■ ■ ■ ■
Protection ability:	■
Grooming requirements:	■
Cold tolerance:	■
Heat tolerance:	■ ■ ■

WEIGHT: male: 24 lb; female: 22 lb
HEIGHT: male: 17″; female: 16″

POPULARITY: Somewhat uncommon
FAMILY: Sighthound, Primitive
AREA OF ORIGIN: Central Africa (Zaire and the Congo)
DATE OF ORIGIN: Ancient Times
ORIGINAL FUNCTION: Hunting small game
TODAY'S FUNCTION: Lure coursing
OTHER NAME: Congo Dog, Congo Terrier

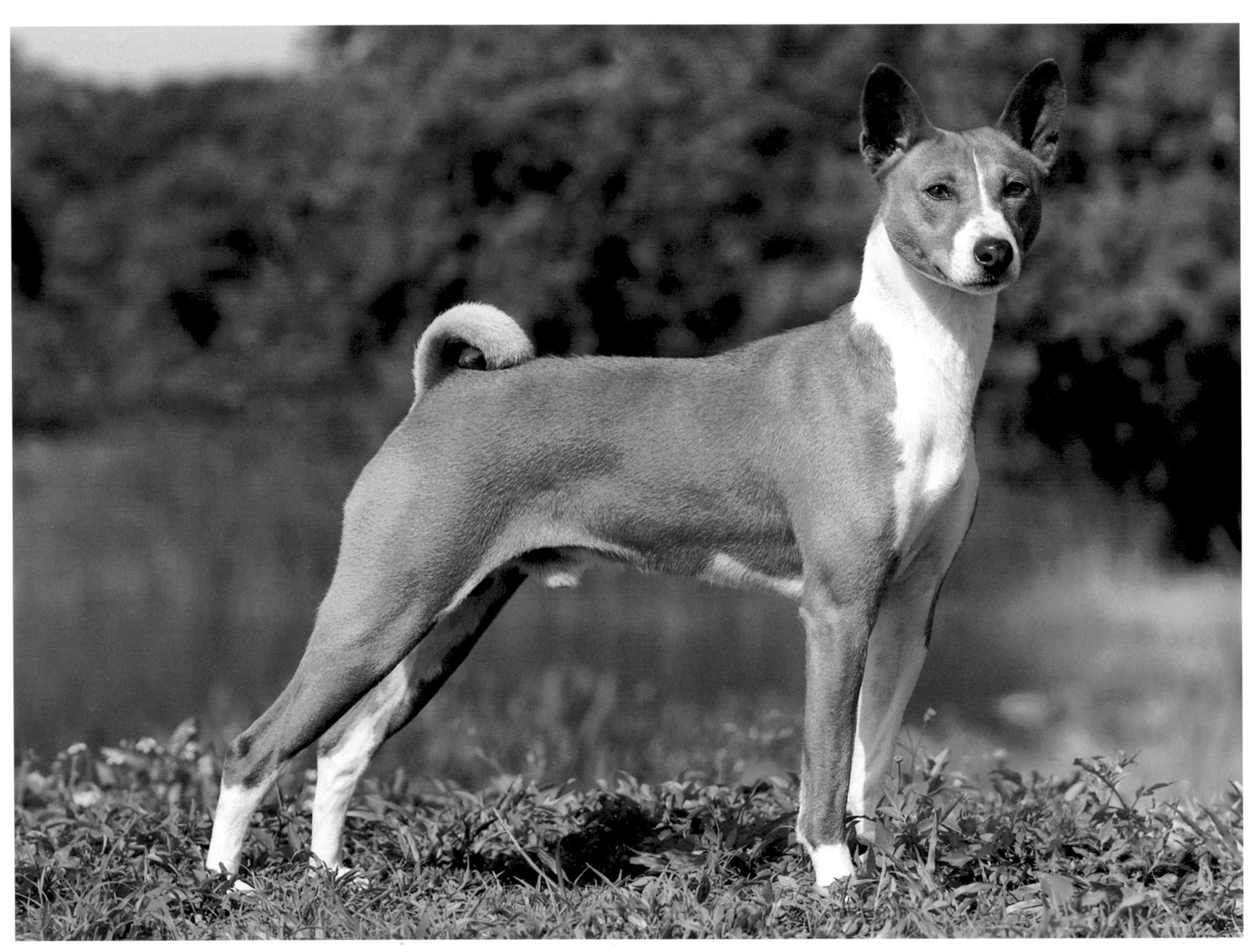

HISTORY

The Basenji is among the most primitive of breeds, discovered in the African Congo with Pygmy hunters. Early explorers called the dogs after the tribes that owned them or the area in which they were found, such as Zande dogs or Congo terriers. The native tribes used the dogs (which often wore a large bell) as pack hunters, driving game into nets. Early attempts to bring the dogs to England in the late 1800s and early 1900s were unsuccessful because they all succumbed to distemper. In the 1930s, a few dogs were successfully brought back to England and became the foundation (along with subsequent imports from the Congo and Sudan) of the breed outside of Africa. The name "Basenji," meaning "bush thing," was chosen. The early imports attracted much attention,

ILLUSTRATED STANDARD

1 Almond-shaped eyes
2 Fine, profuse wrinkles on forehead, visible when ears are erect
3 Small, erect ears
4 Short back
5 Tail bends acutely forward and lies well curled over to either side
6 Small oval feet

Color: red, black, black and tan, or brindle, all with white feet, chest and tail tips; white legs, blaze, and collar optional
DQ: none

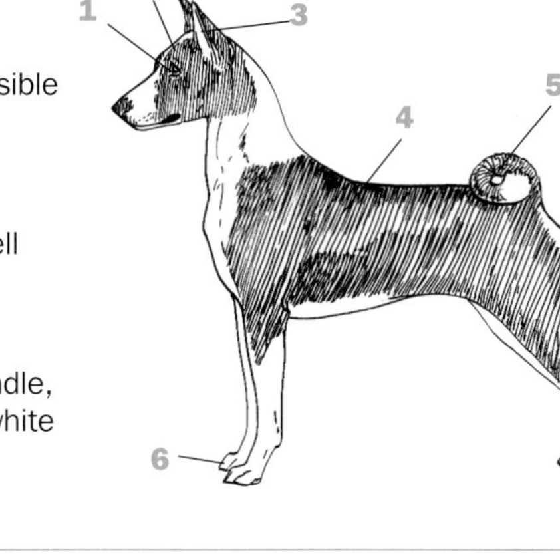

and soon after dogs were brought to America. The breed's popularity as both a pet and show dog grew modestly but steadily. In the 1950s, a surge of popularity occurred as a result of a book and movie featuring a Basenji. The 1980s saw two important but controversial events for the Basenji in America. First, several Basenjis were brought from Africa in an attempt to widen the gene pool and combat some widespread hereditary health problems; some of these introduced the previously unrecognized brindle color into the breed. Second, the Basenji was recognized by the American Sighthound Field Association as a sighthound and allowed to compete in lure-coursing trials. Its body structure and hunting style had previously been deemed too un-sighthound-like. The Basenji has always been hard to categorize. It retains several primitive characteristics, most notably its lack of barking ability and its yearly, rather than twice yearly, estrus cycle.

TEMPERAMENT

Some consider the Basenji to have terrier-like mannerisms because it is feisty for a hound. More often it is considered catlike in mannerisms: clever, inquisitive, stubborn, independent, and reserved. Its hunting roots are very evident, as it loves to chase and trail. It needs regular mental and physical stimulation lest it become frustrated and destructive. Basenjis may be barkless, but they are not mute. They do make a sort of yodel, howl, and shriek—and occasionally bark, but just one or two "fox barks" at a time. It gets along fairly well with other dogs, but often poorly with other Basenjis.

UPKEEP

The Basenji is an active dog that needs daily mental and physical exercise. Its needs can be met by a long walk followed by a vigorous game or by free-running in a safe enclosed area. Coat care is minimal, consisting of only occasional brushing to remove dead hair.

HEALTH

- Major concerns: Fanconi syndrome, PRA, Basenji enteropathy
- Minor concerns: PPM, PK, hypothyroidism, umbilical hernia
- Occasionally seen: CHD, patellar luxation, corneal dystrophy
- Suggested tests: eye, thyroid, hip, Fanconi, DNA for PK, DNA for PRA
- Life span: 12–14 years

FORM AND FUNCTION

The Basenji is square-proportioned and high on leg. It is far more slightly built and longer legged than most other primitive breeds, giving it a good amount of speed and the ability to perform the double-suspension gallop. Its erect ears help it locate prey in thick bush and may act as heat dissipaters. Its short coat also aids in dealing with the hot climate of Africa.

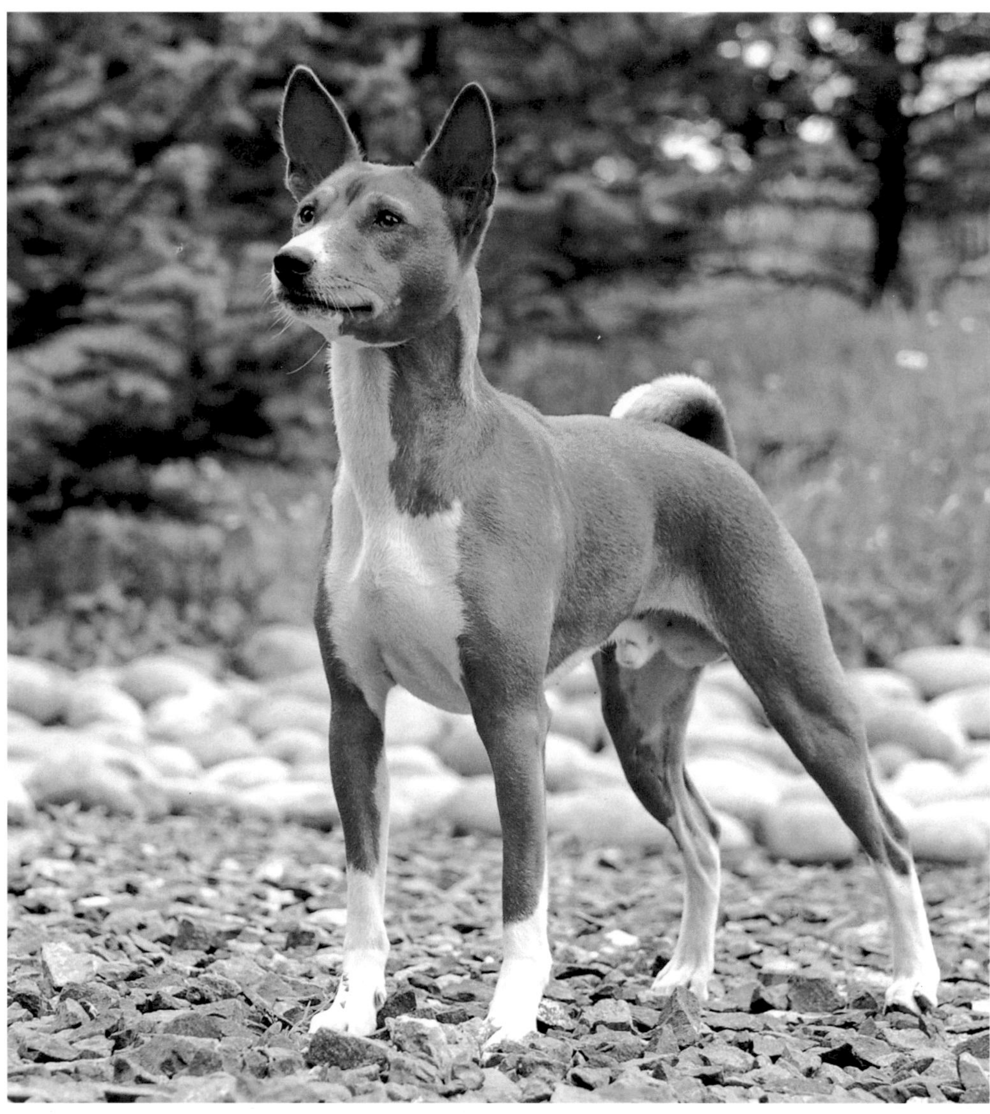

Basset Hound

AT A GLANCE

Energy level:	■ ■	Watchdog ability:	■ ■ ■	POPULARITY: Popular
Exercise requirements:	■ ■	Protection ability:	■	FAMILY: Scenthound
Playfulness:	■ ■	Grooming requirements:	■ ■	AREA OF ORIGIN: France
Affection level:	■ ■ ■ ■	Cold tolerance:	■ ■ ■	DATE OF ORIGIN: 1500s
Friendliness toward dogs:	■ ■ ■	Heat tolerance:	■ ■ ■	ORIGINAL FUNCTION: Trailing rabbits and hare
Friendliness toward other pets:	■ ■ ■			TODAY'S FUNCTION: Trailing rabbits and hare, field trials, Basset field trials
Friendliness toward strangers:	■ ■ ■	WEIGHT: 40–60 lb*		OTHER NAME: None
Ease of training:	■ ■	HEIGHT: preferably not over 14″		

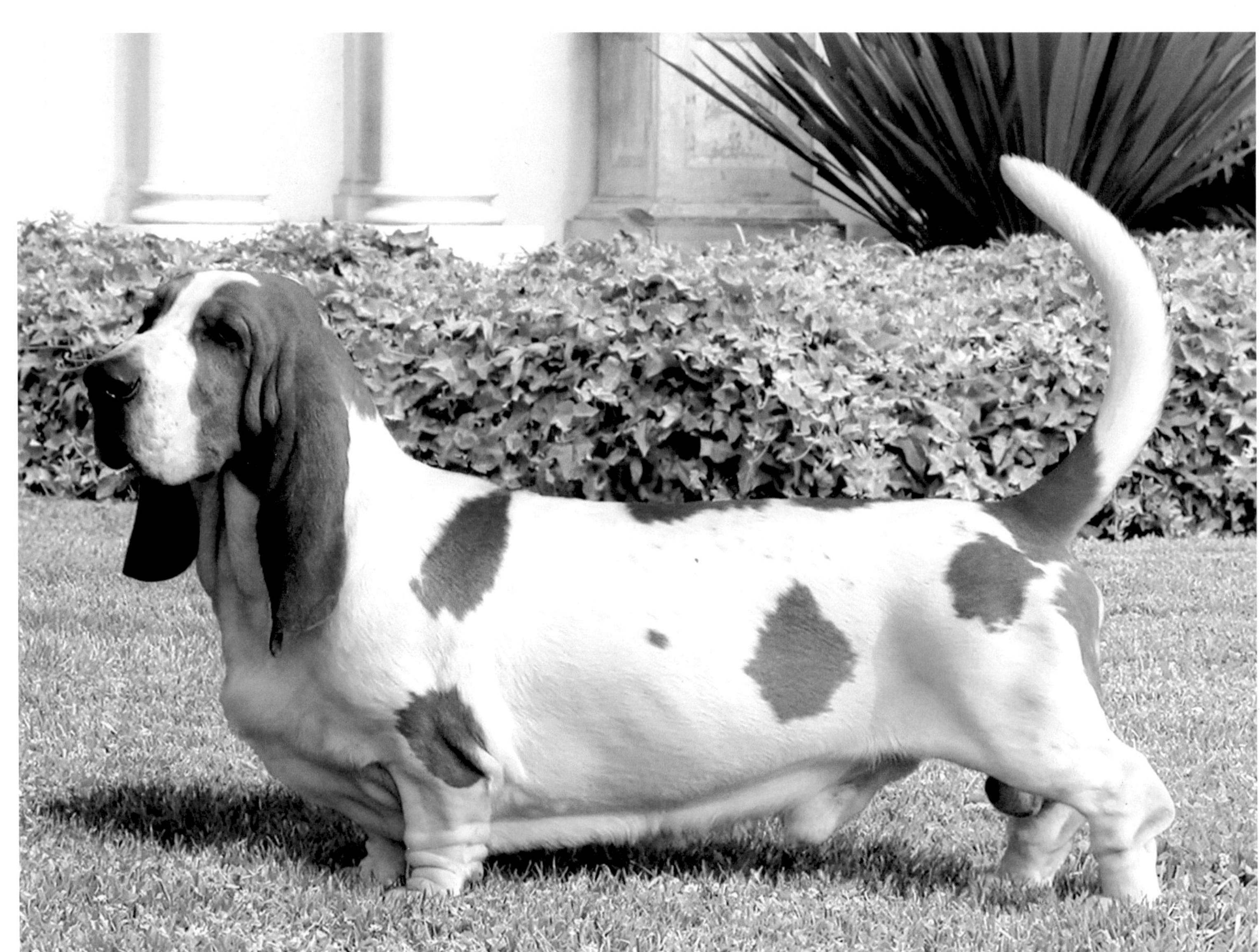

HISTORY

The first mention of the "Basset" dog is found in a sixteenth-century text about badger hunting. Dwarfed short-legged specimens occur in many breeds and have been known since ancient times, but it is difficult to know at what point such dogs were purposefully bred and which ones led to the present Basset Hound. There is, in fact, evidence that dwarfed hounds existed alongside full-sized hounds as long ago as the fifth century A.D. in France. The word Basset is derived from the French bas meaning low thing or dwarf, so that definitive evidence of the breed may be hard to follow. Short-legged dogs were used by the pre-Revolutionary French for hunting at a slower pace, but most of these dogs were dispersed, and their fates undocumented, during the French Revolution.

ILLUSTRATED STANDARD

1 Pendulous lips with hanging flews
2 Soft, sad eyes, showing prominent haw
3 Loose skin falling in distinct wrinkles over the brow when the head is lowered
4 Skull domed with prominent occiput
5 Extremely long, low-set ears
6 Straight topline
7 Tail slightly curved and carried gaily
8 Massive, round feet
9 Short, powerful forelegs with wrinkled skin

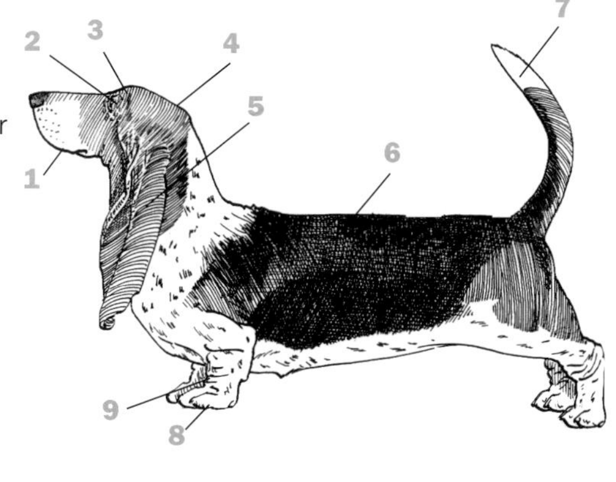

Color: any recognized hound color
DQ: over 15" in height; knuckled over forelegs; distinctly long coat

The history becomes clearer after the Revolution, when greater numbers of commoners took up hunting, often aided by guns. They needed a dog that they could follow on foot, but that still had great scenting ability and strong heavy bone—in essence, a short-legged version of the pack hounds popular with the aristocracy. Because the Basset could not pursue its quarry at speed, the quarry was less likely to be on the run and thus presented an easier target for the gunman. The dogs would hunt all mammals but were especially suited for rabbits and hares. Four different versions of short-legged hounds were created, with the Basset Artesien Normand most closely resembling today's Basset. In the late 1800s (and again in 1930), crosses with Bloodhounds were made to increase size; the results were then tempered with subsequent crosses to the Artesien Normand. The first Bassets were brought to England and America in the late 1800s, and interest in the breed grew gradually. In 1885, the Basset Hound became one of the first breeds to be AKC recognized. By the mid 1900s, the Basset's droll expression had won it a place in advertising and entertainment and in many new pet owner's hearts.

TEMPERAMENT

The Basset Hound is among the most good natured and easygoing of breeds. It is amiable with dogs, other pets, and children, although children must be cautioned not to put strain on its back with their games. It is calm inside, but it needs regular exercise in order to keep fit. It prefers to investigate slowly, and loves to sniff and trail. It is a talented and determined tracker, not easily dissuaded from its course. Because of this, it may get on a trail and follow it until it becomes lost. It tends to be stubborn and slow moving. It has a loud bay that it uses when excited on the trail.

UPKEEP

The Basset needs mild daily exercise, which can be satisfied by walking on leash or playing in the yard. The coat needs only minimal grooming, but the face may need regular cleaning around the mouth and wrinkles to combat odor. Bassets tend to drool.

HEALTH

- Major concerns: OCD, elbow dysplasia, thrombopathy, entropion, ectropion, otitis externa, glaucoma, gastric torsion, CHD
- Minor concerns: patellar luxation, vWD
- Occasionally seen: none
- Suggested tests: eye, hip, (vWD), (elbow), (platelets)
- Life span: 8–12 years
- Note: Obesity is a problem in the breed, especially because it contributes to back problems.

FORM AND FUNCTION

The Basset's long, heavy body and short legs make it easy to follow on foot, and give it an edge in dense cover. The Basset Hound has heavier bone, in proportion to its total size, than any other breed. Its thick, tight coat protects it from brambles without becoming caught in them. It is speculated that the long ears may stir up ground scent, and the wrinkles trap the scent around the face. The large muzzle gives ample room for the olfactory apparatus. Such room would not be available in a miniature dog; only a large dog with shortened legs can combine the short height with large muzzle size. Its movement is smooth and powerful; it tends to move with nose to the ground.

Beagle

AT A GLANCE

Energy level:	■■■
Exercise requirements:	■■■
Playfulness:	■■■■
Affection level:	■■■■■
Friendliness toward dogs:	■■■■■
Friendliness toward other pets:	■■■■■
Friendliness toward strangers:	■■■■■
Ease of training:	■
Watchdog ability:	■■■■
Protection ability:	■
Grooming requirements:	■
Cold tolerance:	■■■
Heat tolerance:	■■■

WEIGHT: 18–30 lb*
HEIGHT: 13″ variety: not exceeding 13″
15″ variety: over 13″ but under 15″

POPULARITY: Most popular
FAMILY: Scenthound
AREA OF ORIGIN: England
DATE OF ORIGIN: 1300s
ORIGINAL FUNCTION: Trailing rabbits
TODAY'S FUNCTION: Trailing rabbits, field trials, contraband detection, Beagle field trials
OTHER NAME: English Beagle

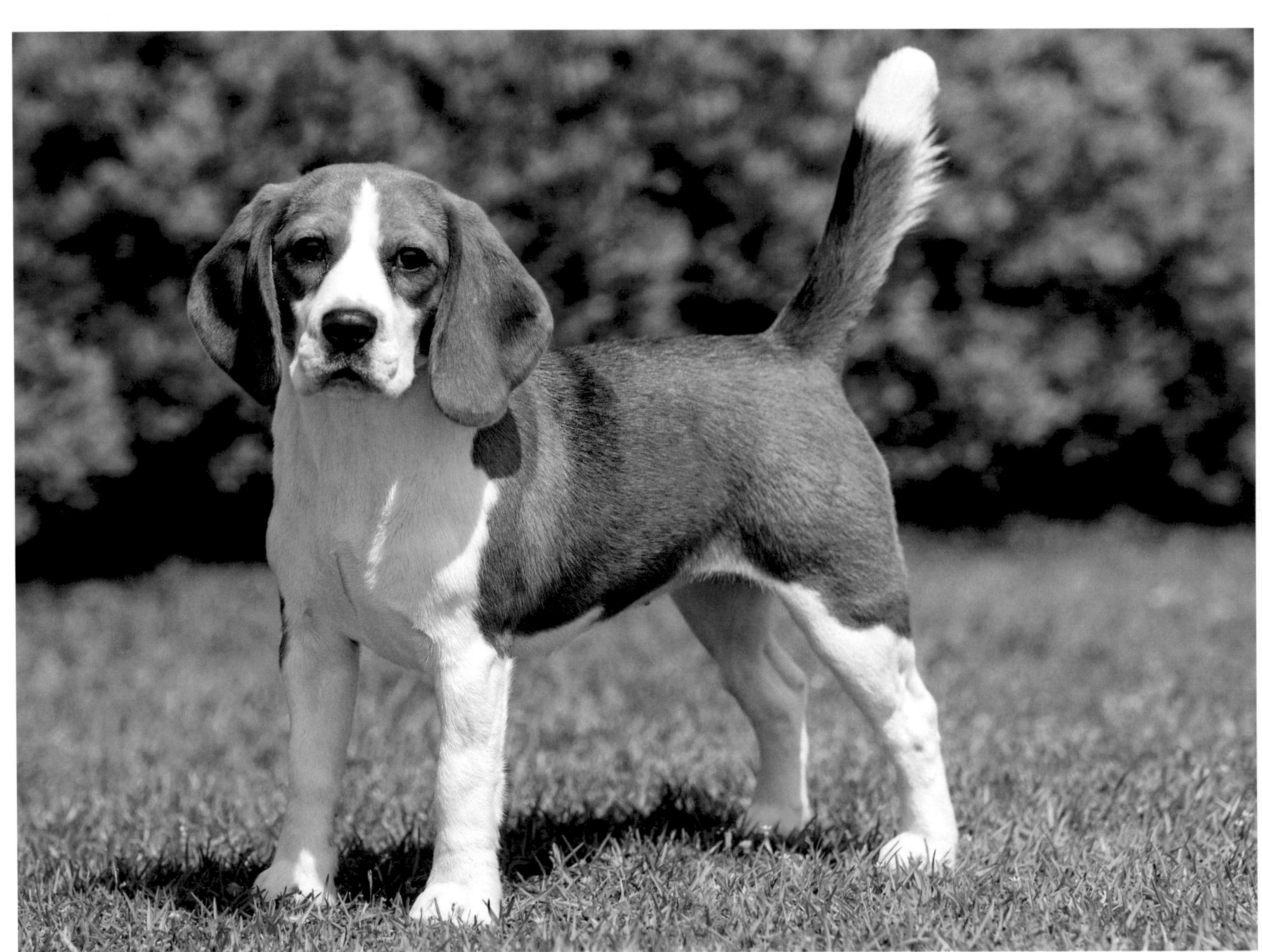

HISTORY

By the fourteenth century, hare-hunting had become a popular sport in England, and the dogs used were probably of Beagle type. The origin of the name Beagle may be from old French words meaning open throat in reference to the breed's melodious bay, or from the Celtic, old English, or old French words for small. The word Beagle was not used until 1475, however, but can then be found frequently in writings from the sixteenth century on. Hunters could follow these dogs on foot and could even carry one in a pocket if the need arose. By the 1800s, Beagles existed in several sizes, but the smaller "pocket-size" dogs were particularly popular. These dogs measured only about 9 inches and often needed the hunter's assistance in crossing rough fields. One of the special

ILLUSTRATED STANDARD

1 Square muzzle
2 Gentle, pleading expression
3 Stop moderately defined
4 Rounded ears
5 Short back
6 Slightly curved tail, carried gaily
7 Round feet

Color: any true hound color
DQ: taller than 15"

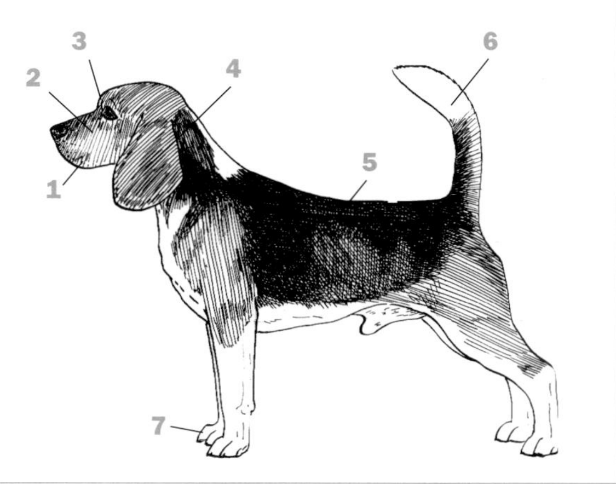

HEALTH

- Major concerns: intervertebral disk disease, CHD
- Minor concerns: glaucoma, epilepsy, CPRA, hypothyroidism, patellar luxation, chondrodysplasia, cherry eye, distichiasis, KCS
- Occasionally seen: deafness, hemophilia A, cataract, demodicosis, umbilical hernia, Musladin-Leuke Syndrome (MLS)
- Suggested tests: hip, eye, (thyroid), DNA for MLS
- Life span: 12–15 years

appeals of the smaller Beagles was that the hunt could be followed even by "ladies, the aged, or the infirm," as they slowly followed the winding path of the hare. The first mention of the Beagle in America was in 1642. Beagles were used in the South prior to the Civil War, but these dogs bore little resemblance to their English counterparts. After the war, English imports formed the basis of the modern American Beagle. By the end of the nineteenth century, Beagles were popular competitors in both field and conformation exhibitions. But the merry little scenthound did not stop there: it continued to become one of America's all-time favorite breeds, finding its special niche as family pet.

TEMPERAMENT

One of the most amiable hounds, the Beagle was bred as a pack hunter and needs companionship, whether human or canine. It loves to explore the outdoors and is an enthusiastic trailer. Given adequate exercise, it is a calm, tractable house pet. It is an excellent child's dog, gentle, incredibly tolerant, and always ready to join in a game or adventure. It is an independent breed, however, and may run off if a trail beckons. It barks and howls.

UPKEEP

The Beagle needs daily exercise, either a long walk on leash or a romp in a safe area. Coat care requires only occasional brushing and bathing.

FORM AND FUNCTION

The Beagle should look like a miniature Foxhound, solid for its size. The Beagle's moderate size enables it to be followed on foot. It can also be carried to the hunt, and once there, can scurry around in thick underbrush. Its close hard coat protects it from underbrush. Its moderate build enables it to nimbly traverse rough terrain. The Beagle's amiable personality allows it to get along with other dogs and to be a successful pack hunter. The Beagle is noted for its melodious bay, which helps hunters locate it from a distance. The deep muzzle allows more room for olfactory receptors, aiding the Beagle's uncanny sense of smell.

Black and Tan Coonhound

AT A GLANCE

Energy level:	■■	Watchdog ability:	■■■■
Exercise requirements:	■■■■	Protection ability:	■■■
Playfulness:	■■■	Grooming requirements:	■
Affection level:	■■■	Cold tolerance:	■■■
Friendliness toward dogs:	■■■	Heat tolerance:	■■■
Friendliness toward other pets:	■■■		
Friendliness toward strangers:	■■	WEIGHT: 55–75 lb*	
Ease of training:	■	HEIGHT: male: 25–27″; female: 23–25″	

POPULARITY: Uncommon
FAMILY: Scenthound
AREA OF ORIGIN: United States
DATE OF ORIGIN: 1700s
ORIGINAL FUNCTION: Hunting raccoons
TODAY'S FUNCTION: Hunting raccoons, nite hunts
OTHER NAME: American Black and Tan Coonhound

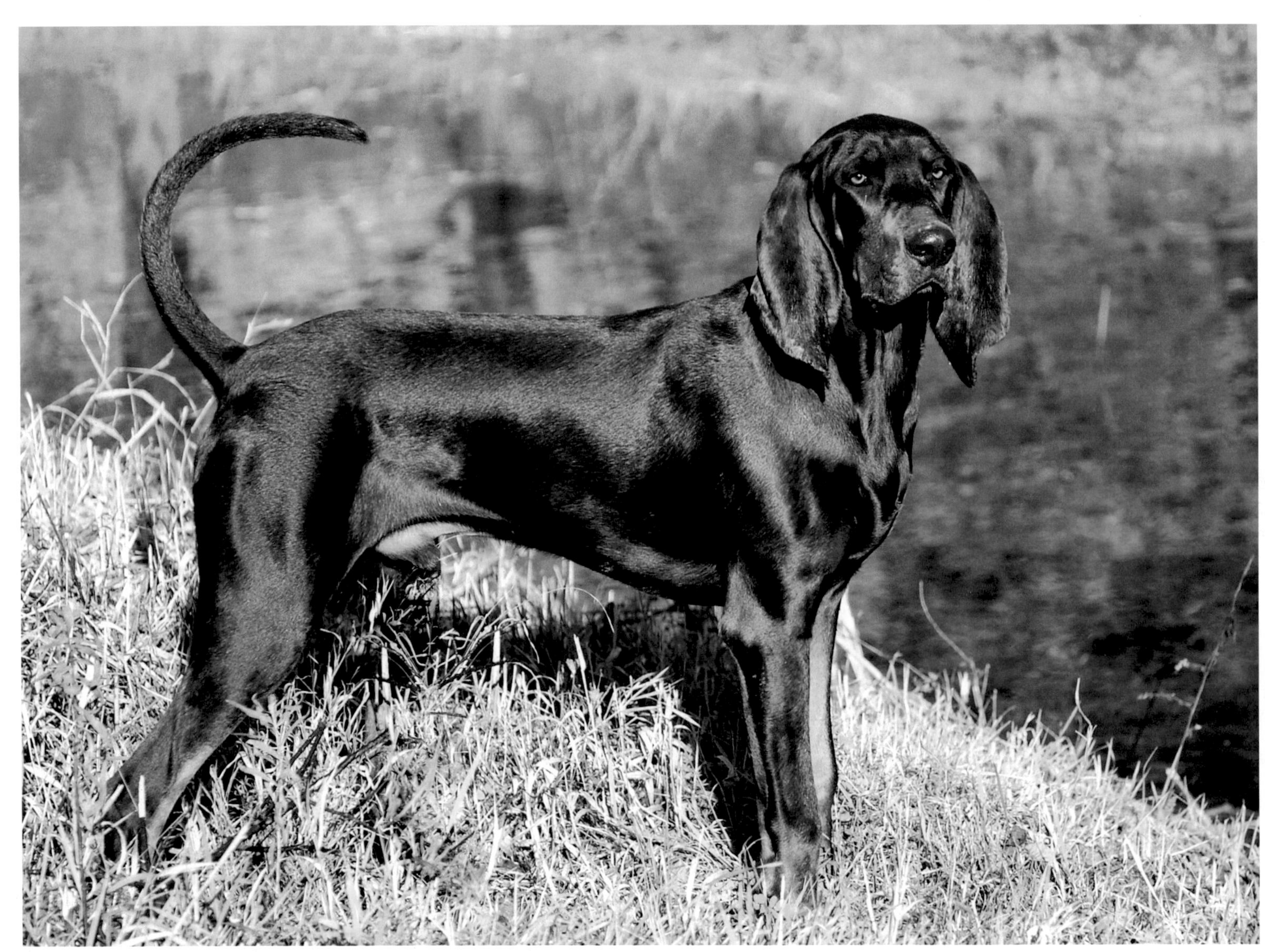

HISTORY

A true American breed, the Black and Tan Coonhound probably originated from crosses of the Bloodhound and the Foxhound, particularly the black and tan Virginia Foxhound. The Black and Tan Coonhound developed mostly in the Appalachian, Blue Ridge, Ozark, and Smokey Mountains, where these dogs were used to hunt raccoons and bears over fairly rugged terrain. They trailed in the fashion of their Bloodhound ancestors, with nose to ground but at a somewhat swifter pace. Although they will trail any mammal, they specialize in raccoons and opossums, often trailing at night. When the quarry is treed, the dogs bay until the hunter arrives and shoots the animal. The "American Black and Tan Fox and Coonhound" was the first coonhound breed recognized by

ILLUSTRATED STANDARD

1 Well-developed flews
2 Skin devoid of folds
3 Almost round eyes
4 Low-set, long ears hanging in folds
5 Tail carried high, nearly perpendicular to back

Color: black and tan
DQ: solid patch of white extending more than 1" in any direction

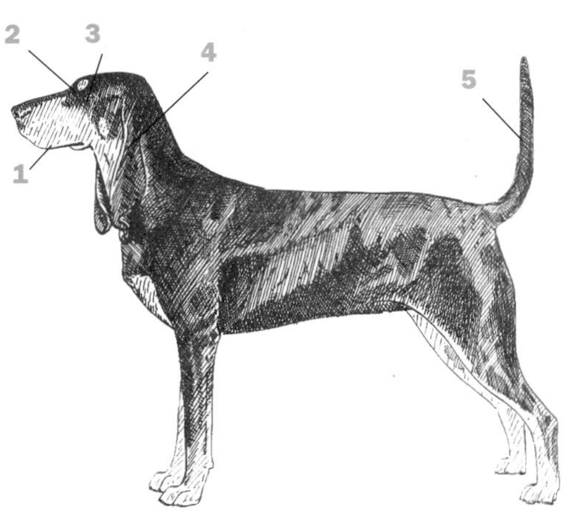

the UKC in 1900. The AKC recognized the breed in 1945—the only coonhound breed the AKC recognized for decades—but the Black and Tan has always been much more popular as a hunting dog than as a show dog or pet. Organized night hunts (called "nite hunts") are extremely competitive and popular, and the United Kennel Club holds many bench shows for coonhounds only, in which Black and Tan Coonhounds, Blue Tick Coonhounds, Redbone Coonhounds, English Coonhounds, Plott Hounds, and Treeing Walkers compete.

TEMPERAMENT

Not the prototypical housedog, the Black and Tan Coonhound, nonetheless, makes an exemplary pet. It is mellow, amiable, calm, and unobtrusive indoors. Outdoors, its strong hunting instincts take over, and it can be difficult, if not impossible, to turn from a track after it starts trailing. As befitting a dog with its heritage, it is strong, independent, and stubborn. It is gentle and tolerant with children, but it may be too independent to satisfy a playful child. It is reserved with strangers. It may bay and howl.

UPKEEP

The Black and Tan is a dog that can run for miles, although it is usually content with a moderate jog or long walk, with an occasional excursion into the field. It can wander if it catches a scent, so a safe area is mandatory. Its coat needs only occasional brushing. Most Coonhounds drool to some extent, and the face may need regular wiping. The ears should also be checked regularly.

HEALTH

- Major concerns: CHD
- Minor concerns: ectropion, hypothyroidism
- Occasionally seen: hemophilia B, elbow dysplasia
- Suggested tests: hip, (thyroid), eye, cardiac, (elbow)
- Life span: 10–12 years

FORM AND FUNCTION

The Black and Tan Coonhound's moderate build gives it a blend of strength, speed and agility. It is square or slightly longer than tall, with moderate bone. Its long ears may help stir up ground scents. Its deep muzzle allows room for olfactory apparatus. The deep voice enables the hunter to locate the dog when it has treed its quarry. Its hair is short but dense, providing an all-weather-protective coat. Its expression is alert, friendly, and eager. The stride is easy and graceful, with head and tail held high.

Bloodhound

AT A GLANCE

Energy level:	■ ■ ■
Exercise requirements:	■ ■ ■
Playfulness:	■
Affection level:	■ ■ ■ ■ ■
Friendliness toward dogs:	■ ■ ■
Friendliness toward other pets:	■ ■ ■ ■ ■
Friendliness toward strangers:	■ ■ ■
Ease of training:	■
Watchdog ability:	■ ■ ■ ■
Protection ability:	■
Grooming requirements:	■
Cold tolerance:	■ ■ ■
Heat tolerance:	■ ■

WEIGHT: male: average 90 lb, up to 110 lb; female: average 80 lb, up to 100 lb (Note: Most Bloodhounds are actually heavier than this)
HEIGHT: male: 25–27″; female: 23–25″

POPULARITY: Somewhat popular
FAMILY: Scenthound
AREA OF ORIGIN: Belgium, England
DATE OF ORIGIN: Middle Ages
ORIGINAL FUNCTION: Trailing
TODAY'S FUNCTION: Trailing humans, search and rescue
OTHER NAME: St. Hubert's Hound, Chien St. Hubert

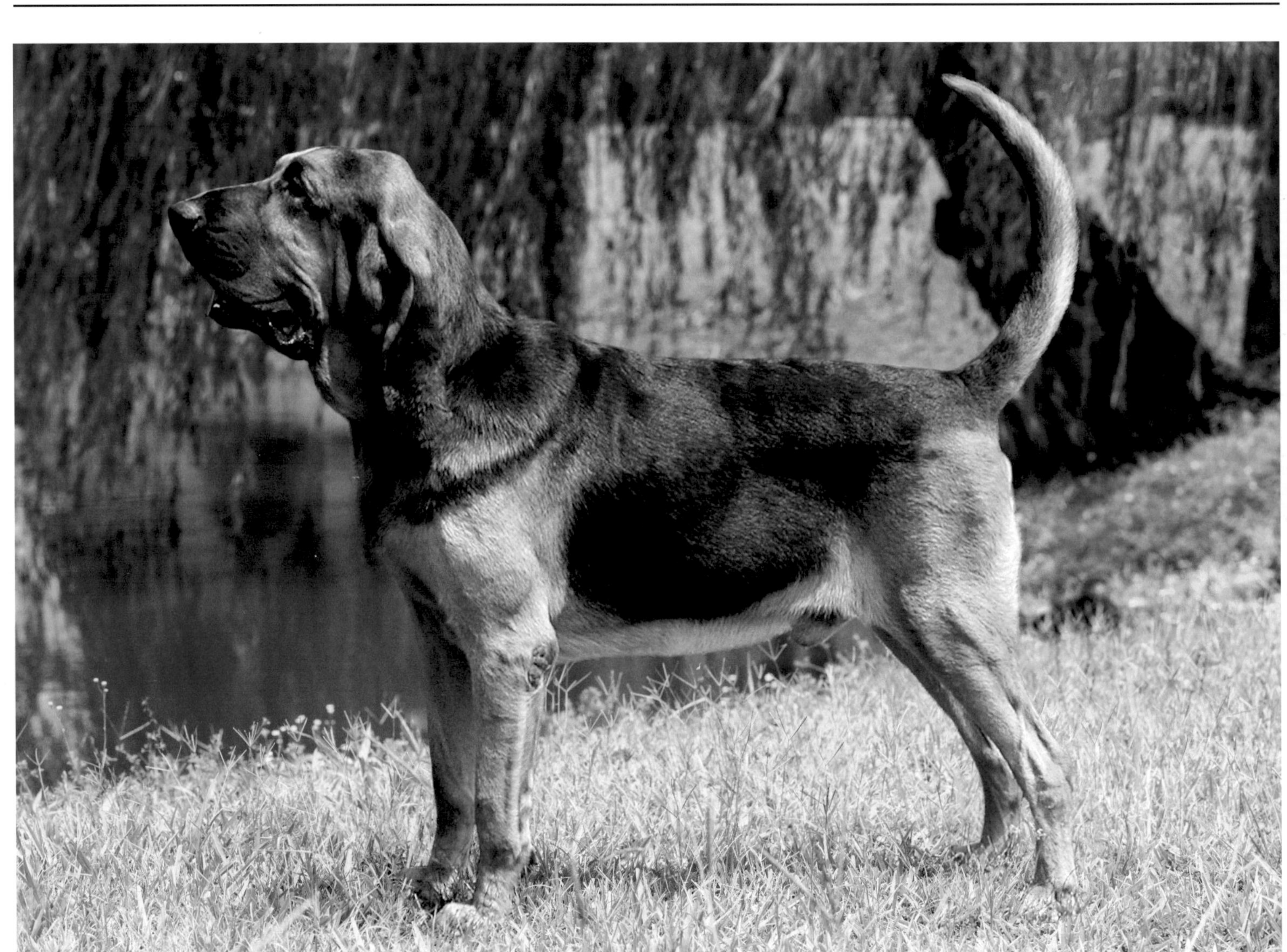

HISTORY

The quintessential scenthound, the Bloodhound traces its roots to ancient times. Their earliest ancestor may have been the black St. Huberts hound documented in Europe by the eighth century. William the Conqueror is credited with bringing these hounds to England in 1066. In the twelfth century, many Church dignitaries were interested in hunting with these dogs, and most monasteries kept carefully bred packs. So highly bred were these dogs that they came to be known as "blooded hounds," referring to their pure blood and noble breeding. Bloodhounds have been known in America since the mid 1800s. Even though they gained a reputation as slave trailers, many of those dogs were mixed scenthounds. The Bloodhound has since proved itself to be one of the

ILLUSTRATED STANDARD

1 Pendant folds of loose skin around neck and head
2 Deep hanging flews
3 Sunken diamond-shaped eyes
4 Proportionally long, narrow head
5 Pronounced occiput
6 Low-set, thin, extremely long ears
7 Long tapering tail, carried high
8 Deep keel

Color: black and tan, liver and tan, and red
DQ: none

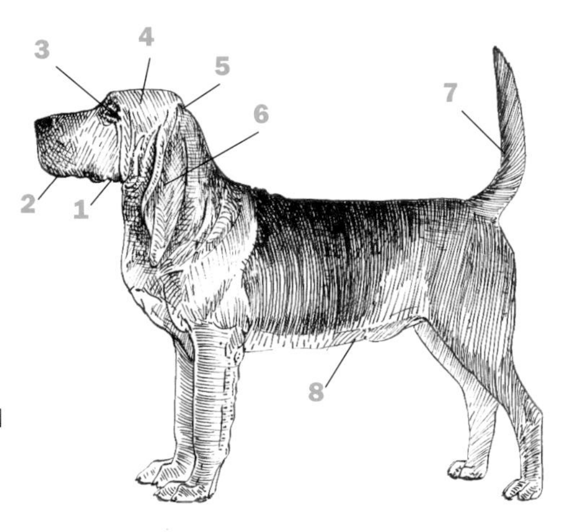

most useful of breeds, using its unrivaled sense of smell to trail lost persons and criminals alike. After the person is located, the Bloodhound's job is over because it is never inclined to attack. The Bloodhound holds many trailing records (for both length and age of trail), and at one time it was the only breed of dog whose identifications were accepted in a court of law. Ironically, the Bloodhound's name and bad press scared many people away from the breed because they believed stories that claimed the dogs trailed people out of a lust for blood. Nothing, of course, could be farther from the truth. The breed is well known to all but not particularly popular as a pet; it is a competitive show dog and unsurpassed working trailer, however.

TEMPERAMENT

For all its calm manners at home, the Bloodhound is a tireless trailer once on the track. It is tough, stubborn, and independent, yet it is so gentle and placid that it is extremely trustworthy around children—although it may not be playful enough for some children's needs. Nonetheless, it is not the lazy ol' hound dog portrayed in folklore but instead an active, playful companion. Although not the easiest breed to train for traditional obedience, it is exceptionally easy to train in tasks involving trailing. The Bloodhound is reserved with strangers.

UPKEEP

As a hunting hound, the Bloodhound needs a good deal of daily exercise. It was bred to trail through any hardship, and once on a trail it cannot be called off. It thus must be exercised in a safe area. The Bloodhound drools a lot, so its facial wrinkles require daily cleaning; the ear tips drag in food and must also be kept clean. The ear canals also need regular cleaning for good health. Coat care is minimal, requiring only occasional brushing or wiping. This is not the breed for people obsessed with cleanliness in the house!

HEALTH

- Major concerns: ectropion, entropion, gastric torsion, otitis externa, skin-fold dermatitis, CHD, elbow dysplasia
- Minor concerns: hypothyroidism
- Occasionally seen: degenerative myelopathy (DM)
- Suggested tests: hip, elbow, (eye), thyroid, cardiac, (DM)
- Life span: 7–10 years

FORM AND FUNCTION

The Bloodhound is a steadfast trailer, built for endurance rather than speed. The skin is thin and loose, falling in wrinkles around the head and throat. Its long ears are supposed to stir up scents as the ears rake along the ground, and its profuse wrinkles are said to trap the odors around the face, although neither of these assertions has ever been scientifically verified. Its dense short coat protects it from being caught in brambles. Its docile temperament makes it nonthreatening to the humans it is sometimes now called upon to trail. The gait is elastic and free, with the tail held high. The expression is noble and dignified.

Bluetick Coonhound

AT A GLANCE

Energy level:	■■■
Exercise requirements:	■■■
Playfulness:	■■■
Affection level:	■■■
Friendliness toward dogs:	■■■■
Friendliness toward other pets:	■■■
Friendliness toward strangers:	■■■
Ease of training:	■

Watchdog ability:	■■■
Protection ability:	■■
Grooming requirements:	■
Cold tolerance:	■■■
Heat tolerance:	■■■

WEIGHT: male: 55–80 lb; female: 45–65 lb
HEIGHT: male: 22–27″; female: 21–25″

POPULARITY: Uncommon
FAMILY: Scenthound
AREA OF ORIGIN: United States
DATE OF ORIGIN: 1800s
ORIGINAL FUNCTION: Trailing and treeing raccoon and other mammals
TODAY'S FUNCTION: Trailing and treeing raccoon and other mammals, nite hunts
OTHER NAME: None

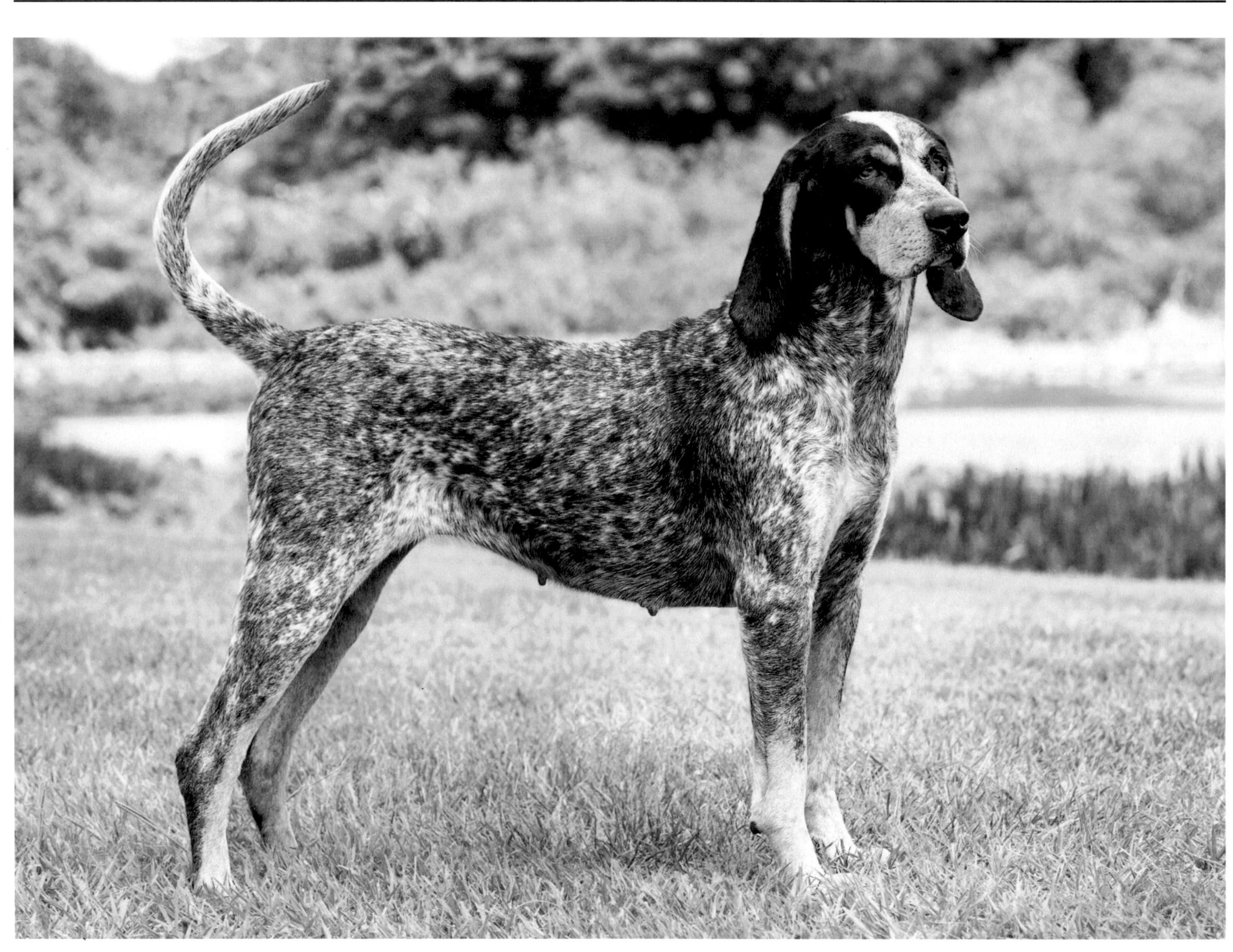

HISTORY

The Bluetick Coonhound shares its early history with the American English Coonhound. Its forbearers were English hunting hounds that came to America during the seventeenth and eighteenth centuries. Among the early breeders was George Washington, who combined English foxhounds with French hounds. Continued crosses to the slow-trailing but resolute French Grand Bleu de Gascogne produced larger dogs with black ticking and, more importantly, a slower hunting style with better ability to follow old ("cold") scent trails. Much of the breed's development took place in the Louisiana bayous and Tennessee Ozarks. The dogs were initially considered a subtype of English Coonhounds, which were recognized by the UKC in 1905. As the preference for English Coonhounds began to favor faster, hot-nosed dogs, breeders of the blue-ticked ones broke away from them, with UKC granting separate breed status in 1945. The Bluetick became a regular member of the AKC Hound Group in 2009. The breed has remained a favorite of hunters, with a reputation of staying on the toughest and most confusing trails and for its persistence when treeing. When on the trail the Bluetick has a strong bawl. Despite its name, it is also an adept hunter of opossum, bear, mountain lion, and wild boar.

TEMPERAMENT

Friendly, adventurous, independent, and strong-willed, the Bluetick is a generally laid-back but not overly obedient companion. Notorious counter surfers and escape artists, they like to follow their nose to food or quarry—and will pretend to be deaf to pleas to stop. Their easy going nature makes them a friend to all, enjoying the company of strangers, other dogs, and even other animals (if raised with them). They are adequate watchdogs. They enjoy baying—loudly—when excited.

UPKEEP

A hunter at heart, the Bluetick is happiest in the woods following a challenging trail. Even suburban Blueticks should have the chance to follow scent trails and to take in new scents regularly. More of an endurance runner than sprinter, the Bluetick needs a long walk or jog daily. The Bluetick is calm indoors as long as he gets a daily outing. Food must be kept well out of reach. Coat care consists of occasional brushing.

HEALTH

- Major concerns: none
- Minor concerns: none
- Occasionally seen: CHD, ear infections, lysosomal storage disease
- Suggested tests: (hip)
- Life span: 11 to 13 years

FORM AND FUNCTION

The Bluetick should have the appearance of a speedy and well-muscled hound. Although more strongly built than some other coonhounds, it should never be clumsy nor overly chunky in build. The legs are moderately angulated and well muscled, allowing for good speed, agility and endurance. The wide nostrils allow air and scent in, and the deep muzzle allows for more scenting receptor area. The coat is short and medium coarse, providing protection from brambles. In motion he carries his head and tail well up. The distinctive loud bawl allows the hunter to follow the dog from a distance and at night.

ILLUSTRATED STANDARD

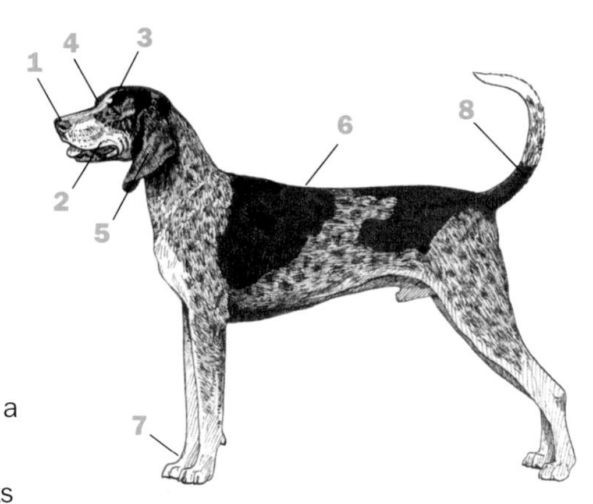

1. Large, black nose with wide nostrils
2. Long, broad, deep muzzle; flews cover lower jaw
3. Large, wide-set round eyes, dark brown in color
4. Prominent stop
5. Low-set ears, thin, tapering to a point, reaching well toward nose
6. Topline slopes downward slightly from withers to hips
7. Round, well-arched cat feet
8. Tail set on slightly low, carried high with a forward half-moon curve; without flag

Color: thickly mottled blue with black spots on back, ears, and sides (predominately black head and ears) with or without tan markings and red ticking on legs and feet
DQ: males under 22" or over 27"; females under 21" or over 25"; undershot or overshot; albinism

Borzoi

AT A GLANCE

Energy level:	■ ■
Exercise requirements:	■ ■ ■
Playfulness:	■ ■ ■
Affection level:	■ ■ ■
Friendliness toward dogs:	■ ■ ■
Friendliness toward other pets:	■ ■
Friendliness toward strangers:	■ ■
Ease of training:	■ ■

Watchdog ability:	■ ■
Protection ability:	■ ■ ■
Grooming requirements:	■ ■ ■
Cold tolerance:	■ ■ ■ ■
Heat tolerance:	■ ■

WEIGHT: male: 75–105 lb; female: 60–85 lb
HEIGHT: male: at least 28″ (30″ average*); female: at least 26″ (28″ average*)

POPULARITY: Somewhat uncommon
FAMILY: Sighthound
AREA OF ORIGIN: Russia
DATE OF ORIGIN: Middle Ages
ORIGINAL FUNCTION: Coursing wolves
TODAY'S FUNCTION: Lure coursing
OTHER NAME: Russian Wolfhound

HISTORY

The Borzoi (also known as the Russian Wolf-hound) was bred by the Russian aristocracy for hundreds of years. Coursing of hare for sport was known in Russia as early as the thirteenth century. In the fifteenth and sixteenth centuries, crosses of coursing hounds with bearhounds and with tall Russian sheepdogs were made to increase size and coat, both necessary for hunting wolves in the cold climate. The first standard was written in the 1600s in a book of Borzoi hunting rules. Perhaps no other breed has ever been the focus of hunting on such a grand scale. Hundreds of serfs worked in the upkeep of the hounds on huge estates; the hunts themselves were grand events. One account describes the hounds, horses, beaters, and hunters arriving in a train of

ILLUSTRATED STANDARD

1 Soft expression
2 Inclined to be Roman nosed
3 Scarcely perceptible stop
4 Long, narrow head, slightly domed skull
5 Small, folded ears
6 Gracefully curved topline
7 Long tail, carried low in a graceful curve
8 Deep, narrow chest
9 Hare feet

Color: any
DQ: none

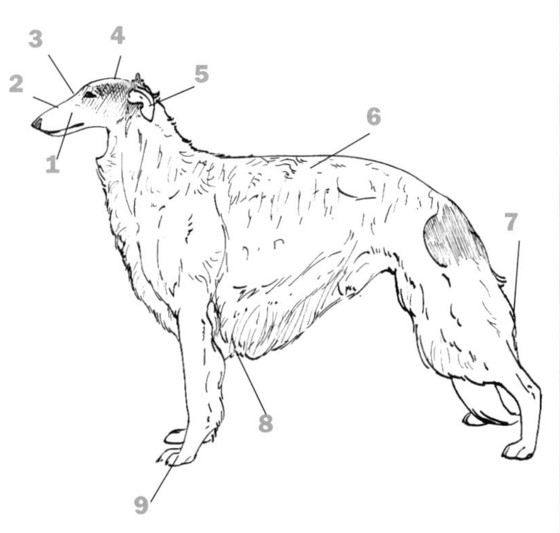

over 40 cars, with another train bringing the Grand Duke and other nobility. Over 100 Borzoi might partake in a hunt. Beaters and scenthounds initially trailed the wolf, followed by hunters on horseback. A pair or trio (consisting of two males and a female) of matched Borzoi was then unleashed when the wolf was sighted. The dogs would strike at the same time, forcing the wolf down and holding it until the hunter arrived to bind the wolf—and then, often, set it free. By the 1800s, seven distinct subtypes of Borzoi existed in Russia. Most present Borzoi descend from the Perchino type kept by the Grand Duke Nicolai Nicolayevitch, and many of the early American imports came directly from the Perchino kennels. The Russian Czar would often present Borzoi as gifts to visiting royalty. After the Russian Revolution, the days of the nobility were over, and many Borzoi were killed. The fate of the breed was left in the hands of foreign royalty who had been given Borzoi and of a few remaining Borzoi kennels. In America, the Borzoi soon gained the reputation as the ultimate glamour dog, often seen at the sides of movie stars. Although only enjoying modest popularity as a pet, the breed remains a popular show dog, coursing dog, and model.

TEMPERAMENT

A breed of quiet elegance, the Borzoi exemplifies the well-mannered house-dog indoors. Outdoors, it races with wild abandon, and it will chase any small animal that runs. It is independent but very sensitive. Although generally good with children, it may not be playful enough to satisfy some children. Some can be timid. It is reserved with strangers.

UPKEEP

The Borzoi needs the chance to exert itself daily. Although a long walk can satisfy most of its needs, it should be combined with a sprint in a large safe area. The coat, which is characteristically fuller on males, needs brushing or combing two or three times a week; at times it sheds a lot.

HEALTH

- Major concerns: gastric torsion
- Minor concerns: cardiomyopathy, hypothyroidism
- Occasionally seen: degenerative myelopathy (DM)
- Suggested tests: thyroid, cardiac, DM
- Life span: 10–12 years
- Note: sensitive to barbiturate anesthesia

FORM AND FUNCTION

The Borzoi is a running hound capable of hunting large, fierce game in a very cold climate. As such, it retains the greyhound build necessary for running at great speed, but it is larger and stronger than the greyhound. Its jaws should be strong enough to hold down a wolf. The long, silky coat, which can be either flat, wavy, or rather curly, provides protection against cold weather and snow. The Borzoi should possess elegance and grace, with flowing lines, whether standing or moving.

Cirneco dell'Etna

AT A GLANCE

Energy level:	■■■■	Watchdog ability:	■■■■
Exercise requirements:	■■■	Protection ability:	■
Playfulness:	■■■■	Grooming requirements:	■
Affection level:	■■■■	Cold tolerance:	■
Friendliness toward dogs:	■■■■■	Heat tolerance:	■■■■
Friendliness toward other pets:	■■■■		
Friendliness toward strangers:	■■■	WEIGHT: 18–26 lb*	
Ease of training:	■■■	HEIGHT: male: 18–19.5″; female: 17.5–19″	

POPULARITY: Very rare
FAMILY: Sighthound, Primitive
AREA OF ORIGIN: Italy
DATE OF ORIGIN: Ancient
ORIGINAL FUNCTION: Hunting
TODAY'S FUNCTION: Hunting, lure coursing
OTHER NAME: Sicilian Hound

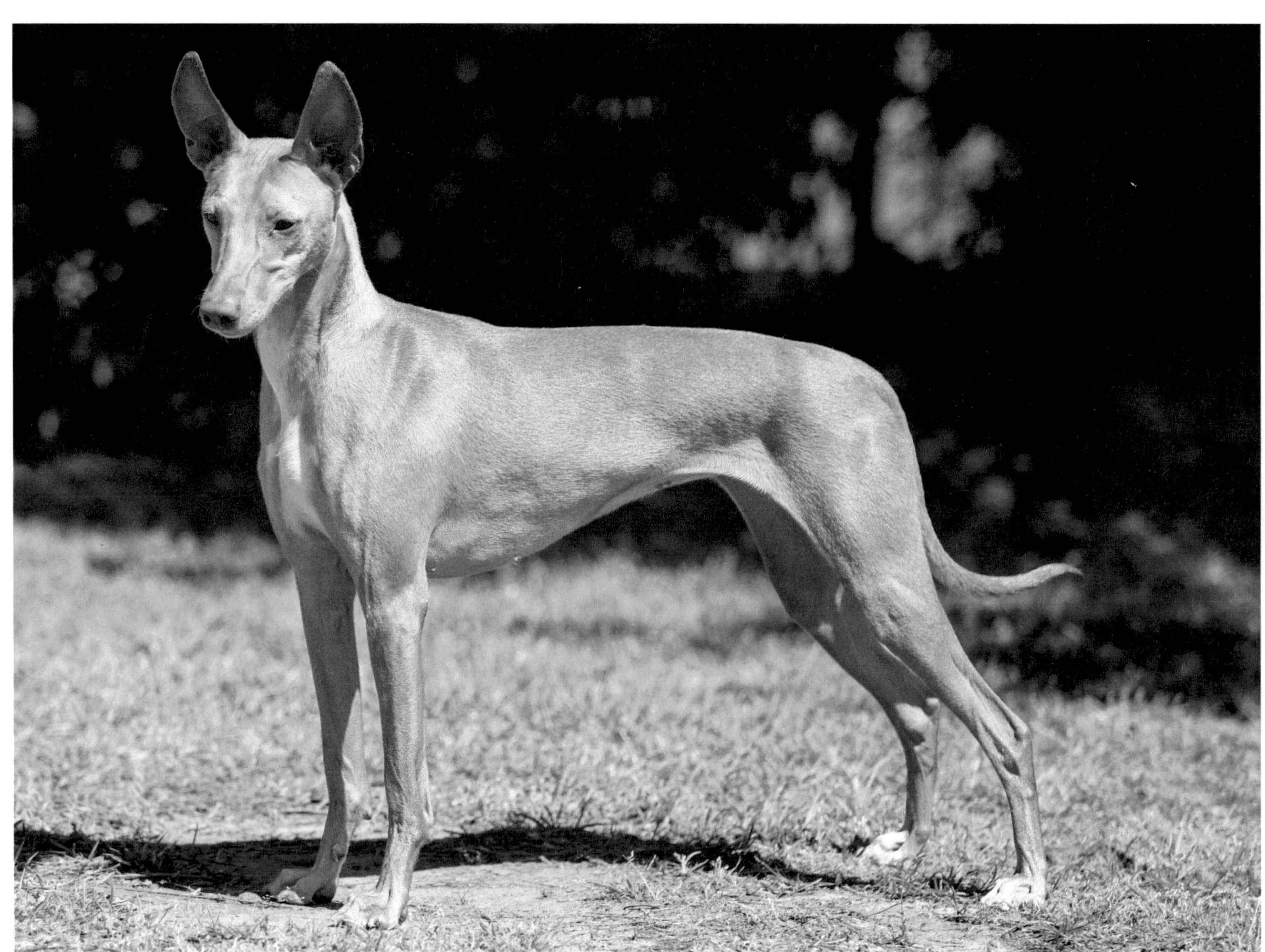

HISTORY

The Cirneco dell'Etna (pronounced 'cheer-NAY-co') traces back as much as 2,500 years ago on the island of Sicily, particularly in the area surrounding Mount Etna. The dogs hunted rabbits by scent and, to a lesser extinct, sight. They followed the rabbit to its warren and barked and dug at the opening. Traditionally, a ferret would then be sent in after the rabbit. The Cirneco can also point or chase the rabbit by sight if flushed. The Cirneco resembles a small Pharaoh Hound, and the two breeds are undoubtedly related. It's believed the Cirneco descends from the prick-eared, hound-type dogs of ancient Egypt that were spread by the seafaring Phoenicians. It's possible the dogs became smaller over time because of limited food and no need for big hunters in the area, which lacked

ILLUSTRATED STANDARD

1 Relatively small, oval, amber or ochre eyes
2 Triangular ears set very high and close together; parallel when alert
3 Slight stop.
4 Straight topline sloping from withers toward croup
5 Chest reaches to, or nearly to, the elbow without going beyond
6 Low set tail, reaching hock; carried high and curved when dog is in action
7 Slightly oval feet

Color: tan to dark chestnut
DQ: whitish or blue eye; overshot or undershot; hanging or bat ears; total depigmentation; brown or liver; brindle; black hairs, nails or mucous membranes; males under 17.5″ or over 20.5″; females under 16″ or over 19.5″

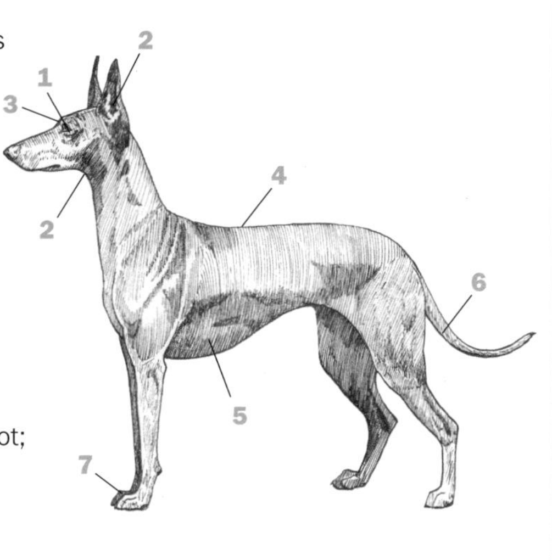

open spaces. Dogs resembling Cirnechi (plural form) are depicted on 5th to 3rd century B.C. coins from Segesta in Sicily. Legend has it that a thousand Cirnechi guarded an ancient temple dedicated to Adranos (fire god), and that the dogs could divinely discern—and attack—thieves and nonbelievers while guiding pilgrims to the temple. The breed was virtually unknown outside Sicily until 1932, when a visiting veterinarian published an article in an Italian hunting journal that outlined their poor outlook. The Baroness Agata Paternó Castello headed a group to revive the breed and worked diligently to do so until her death. In 1939, the Italian Kennel Club adopted a standard and recognized the breed. They came to America in 1996 and attracted more attention when they began lure coursing competitively in the late 1990s. In 2015, they were admitted into the AKC Hound Group where they are considered sighthounds.

TEMPERAMENT

The Cirneco is very affectionate, lively, and gentle. Although sighthound and primitive breeds are known for their independence, it is far less so than most. It's friendly to strangers and gets along well with kids, other dogs, and pets. It does like to hunt and can be led away by rabbit trails or fleeing wildlife. It tends to be a busy dog, always involved in some sort of project! In keeping with its hunting heritage, it is seldom deterred by obstacles in the way of anything it wants. It is an adequate watchdog and poor protection dog.

UPKEEP

The Cirneco is a family dog that should live indoors with its people. The Cirneco is very clean and enjoys creature comforts—they like warmth and dislike cold. They need a moderate jaunt around the neighborhood or a lively backyard game daily. They are not natural retrievers or swimmers but can be taught to do both. Coat care entails a quick weekly brushing.

HEALTH

- Major concerns: none
- Minor concerns: none
- Occasionally seen: none
- Suggested tests: none
- Life span: 12–14 years

FORM AND FUNCTION

The Cirneco is a medium-sized hunting breed that can hunt by scent, hearing, and sight. It has an elegant, strong build, lightly constructed with long limbs and a square outline. It is able to work over difficult terrain and survive under trying conditions. It has a springy trot without excessive extension. The coat is short and sleek. In personality it is strong, lively and independent; always alert.

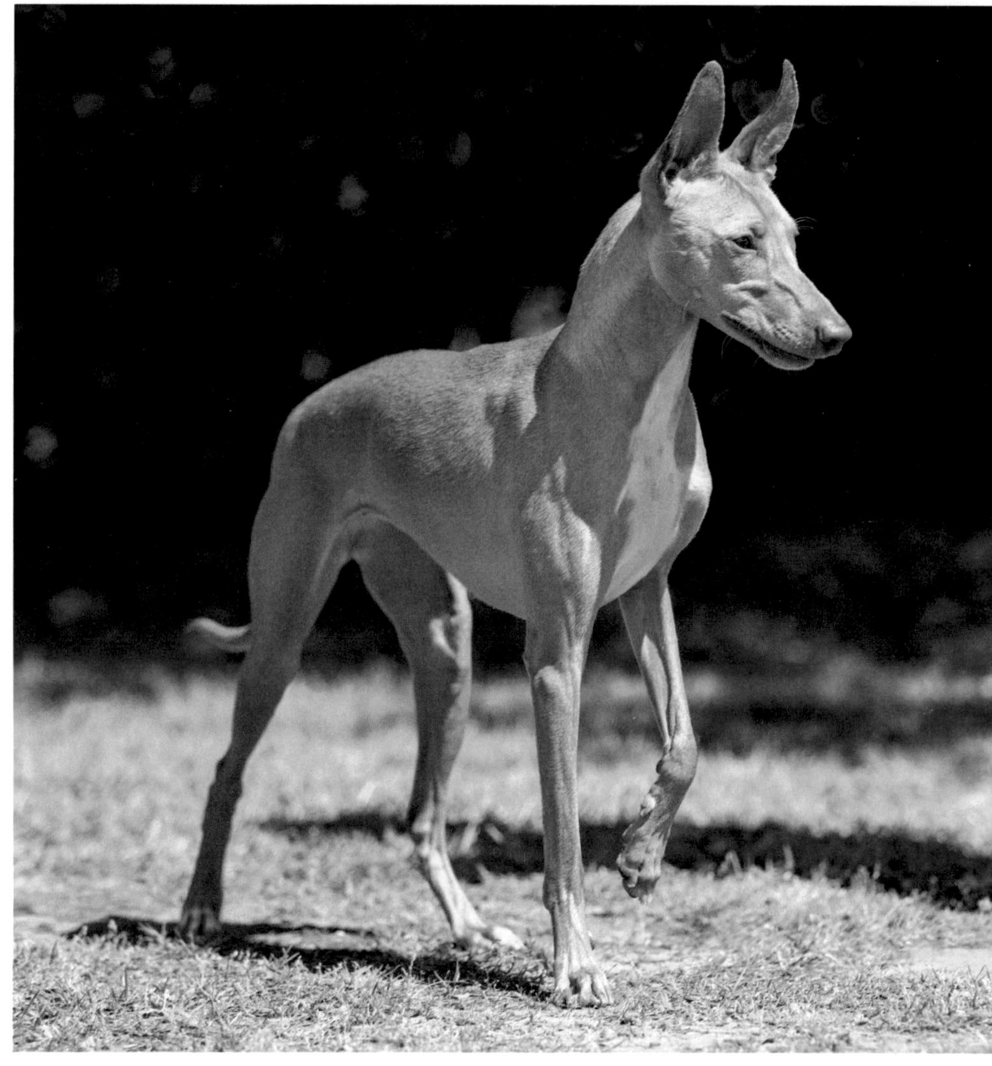

Dachshund

AT A GLANCE

Energy level:	■■■■
Exercise requirements:	■■
Playfulness:	■■■
Affection level:	■■■
Friendliness toward dogs:	■■■
Friendliness toward other pets:	■■
Friendliness toward strangers:	■
Ease of training:	■■
Watchdog ability:	■■■■■
Protection ability:	■■

Grooming requirements:	
Smooth:	■
Long:	■■
Wire:	■■■
Cold tolerance:	■■■
Heat tolerance:	■■■

WEIGHT: Miniature: 11 lb and under Standard: over 11 lb (usually 16–32 lb)
HEIGHT: Miniature: 5–6″; Standard: 8–9″*

POPULARITY: Very popular
FAMILY: Scenthound
AREA OF ORIGIN: Germany
DATE OF ORIGIN: 1500s
ORIGINAL FUNCTION: Flushing badgers
TODAY'S FUNCTION: Earthdog trials, Dachshund field trials
OTHER NAME: Teckel (Miniature: Zwergteckel)

HISTORY

Definitive evidence of the Dachshund as a breed isn't found until the sixteenth century, when reference was made to a "low crooked legged" dog called a Little Burrow Dog, Dacksel, or Badger Dog. The modern name "Dachshund" means simply badger (dachs) dog (hund) in German. These tenacious hunters would follow their quarry, enter its burrow, pull it out, and kill it. The Dachshund comes in three coat varieties and two sizes. The original Dachshunds were smooth coated and arose from crosses of the Bracke, a miniature French pointer, with the Pinscher, a vermin killer of terrier type. Some evidence exists of longer-haired Dachshund-like dogs in sixteenth-century woodcuts. It is also possible that smooth Dachshunds were later crossed with spaniels and the German

ILLUSTRATED STANDARD

1 Fine, slightly arched muzzle
2 Little perceptible stop
3 Almond-shaped eyes
4 High-set, rounded ears
5 Back straight and long
6 Tail set as a continuation of the topline
7 Legs short
8 Breastbone strongly prominent

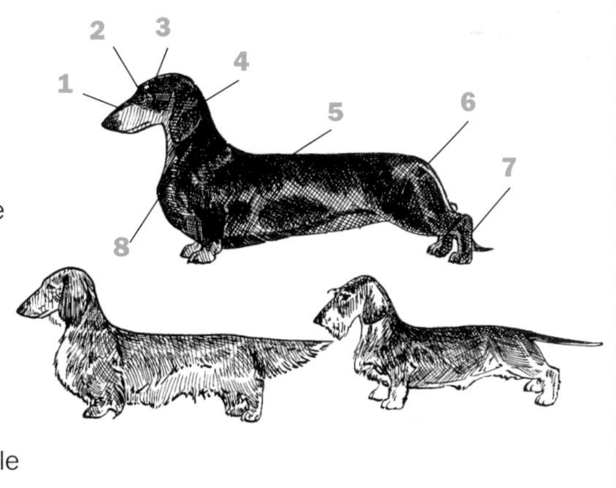

Color: solid red, sable, or cream; black and tan, chocolate and tan, wild boar and tan, gray and tan, or fawn and tan; single dapple (lighter color set on darker background, as in a merle); double dapple (white in addition to dapple); brindle
DQ: knuckled over

Stoberhund (a gundog) to produce the long-haired variety. Mention is made of wire-coated Dachshunds as early as 1797, but these dogs were not carefully bred and most modern wires were created around the end of the nineteenth century by crossing smooth Dachshunds with German Wire-haired Pinschers and the Dandie Dinmont Terrier. Each of these varieties was best suited for hunting under slightly different terrain and climatic conditions, but all were tough, strong dogs capable of dispatching badger, fox, and other small mammals. Before 1900, very small Dachshunds were kept for going to ground after small quarry, such as rabbits. Although some were simply runts, others were intentionally produced by crosses with toy terriers or pinschers. Most of the resulting miniatures lacked Dachshund type, however. By 1910, stricter criteria were adopted for type, and each coat type was crossed with different breeds to achieve the best results: smooths were bred with the Miniature Pinscher, longs with the Papillon, and wires with the Miniature Schnauzer. The Dachshund has since found its real niche as a family pet, steadily rising in popularity to hold a place as one of the most popular hounds in America.

TEMPERAMENT

The Dachshund is bold, curious, and always up for adventure. It likes to hunt and dig, tracking by scent and going to ground after game. It is independent but will join in its family's activities whenever given a chance. It is good with children in its own family, but some may snap at strange children. Most are reserved with strangers. Some bark. The longhaired variety may be quieter and less terrier-like; the wires may be more outgoing. Some miniatures are more prone to be timid.

UPKEEP

Although active, the Dachshund's exercise requirements can be met with moderate walks on leash and games in the yard. It is amenable to city life or apartment living, but it is still a hunter at heart and enjoys forays into the wilds. The smooth coat requires minimal grooming. The long coat requires brushing or combing once or twice weekly and occasional trimming of stray hairs. The wire coat requires brushing or combing about once a week, with occasional trimming of stray hairs and stripping to remove dead hair twice a year.

HEALTH

- Major concerns: intervertebral disk disease
- Minor concerns: KCS
- Occasionally seen: diabetes, seizures, patellar luxation, gastric torsion, Cushing's, deafness (in double dapples)
- Suggested tests: eye, knee
- Life span: 12–14 years
- Note: Obesity is a common problem. "Double dapples" (homozygous merles) are more likely to have visual and hearing problems.

FORM AND FUNCTION

The Dachshund's long low-slung body enables it to enter and move freely inside the confines of a den or tunnel, without sacrificing the necessary jaw and body strength to overcome its quarry. Its confidence, hunting instinct, keen nose, and loud voice also are of significant aid in hunting underground. Agility, freedom of movement, and endurance are necessary for the Dachshund's work, and its gait is fluid and smooth. The Dachshund has an energetic, pleasant expression. Each of the three coat varieties has special attributes: the smooth is short and shining, imparting some protection against the elements; the long hair is sleek, sometimes slightly wavy, providing somewhat more protection; the wire has tight, thick, and hard hair with a finer undercoat, providing maximal protection.

American Foxhound

AT A GLANCE

Energy level:	■■■■	Watchdog ability:	■■■■
Exercise requirements:	■■■■	Protection ability:	■
Playfulness:	■■■	Grooming requirements:	■
Affection level:	■■■	Cold tolerance:	■■■
Friendliness toward dogs:	■■■■■	Heat tolerance:	■■■
Friendliness toward other pets:	■■■■		
Friendliness toward strangers:	■■■■	WEIGHT: 40–65 lb*	
Ease of training:	■■	HEIGHT: male: 22–25″; female: 21–24″	

POPULARITY: Very rare
FAMILY: Scenthound
AREA OF ORIGIN: United States
DATE OF ORIGIN: 1600s
ORIGINAL FUNCTION: Trailing fox
TODAY'S FUNCTION: Trailing fox
OTHER NAME: None

HISTORY

This most American of breeds dates back to 1650, with the first record of fox-chasing hounds arriving from England. By the 1700s, riding to the hounds had become extremely popular with the upper class; even George Washington found it a favorite pastime. George Washington crossed descendents of these early foxhounds with French foxhounds the Marquis de Lafayette gave him, and these dogs are behind the American Foxhound. Imports from England, France, and Ireland helped further shape the breed. Foxhound pedigrees have been recorded in America since 1850. Around this same time, the sport spread to the southern United States, particularly the mountains of Kentucky and Tennessee, and hunters there preferred a faster dog with the ability to start, chase, and kill a fox

ILLUSTRATED STANDARD

1 Stop moderately defined
2 Head fairly long, broad backskull
3 Fairly low-set, broad ears
4 Loins broad and slightly arched
5 Tail carried gaily, but not over the back; slight brush
6 Rather narrow chest

Color: any
DQ: none

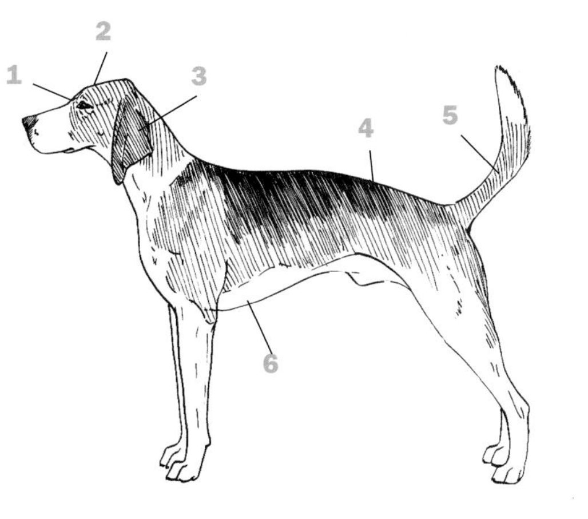

alone, and also to give chase to deer. The dogs became more streamlined than their English counterparts. The dogs further developed into different strains, the most popular being the Walker. This strain descends from a dog named Tennessee Lead, alleged to have been stolen from a deerchase by a dog trader, who subsequently sold him to George Washington Maupin. His breedings to this fast running foxhound produced some of the best running dogs seen to that time. Dogs from that strain were subsequently called Walker hounds. Other strains of foxhounds include Trigg, Goodman, July, Calhoun, and Hudspeth. These dogs eventually became specialized as either running hounds or show hounds, with the former being even further specialized as competitive field trial hounds and pack hounds. The pack type is generally considered the prototypical Foxhound. These dogs combine great speed, endurance, and jumping ability with a strong nose and willingness to give chase as a pack member. In 1886, the American Foxhound became one of the earliest breeds to be registered by the AKC, although registrations have never been particularly high. The low AKC registration numbers belie the Foxhound's popularity, however, because most Foxhounds are kept in large packs by hunters with little interest in AKC registration. Their dogs are instead registered with Foxhound specialty studbooks, most notably the International Foxhunter's Studbook, published by the Chase. The Foxhound can thus lay claim to being one of the most unpopular popular breeds in America.

TEMPERAMENT

Although by tradition the Foxhound is not a house pet, it is actually well mannered in the home. It gets along best with human or canine companionship. It is a tolerant, amiable, and gentle dog, even though it is not very demonstrative. Most are reserved with strangers. It is first and foremost a hunter, ever ready to hit the trail. It needs daily exercise in a safe area. Once on a scent, it will follow gleefully, heedless of commands. This is a dog that likes the outdoors; it is not a city dog. It bays.

UPKEEP

The Foxhound needs daily exercise, preferably in the form of a long walk or jog. If allowed to run off leash, it should only be in a safe enclosed area. The coat is easily maintained, requiring only occasional brushing to remove dead hair.

HEALTH

- Major concerns: none
- Minor concerns: none
- Occasionally seen: thrombopathy
- Suggested tests: (platelets)
- Life span: 11–13 years

FORM AND FUNCTION

The American Foxhound is slighter of bone and higher on leg that the English Foxhound, with more rear angulation and arch over the loin. These attributes give it greater speed and agility for hunting over rough terrain. It has a melodious voice when on the trail. The coat is hard and of medium length. The expression is gentle and pleading.

English Foxhound

AT A GLANCE

Energy level:	■■■■	Watchdog ability:	■■■■	POPULARITY: Very rare
Exercise requirements:	■■■■	Protection ability:	■	FAMILY: Scenthound
Playfulness:	■■■	Grooming requirements:	■	AREA OF ORIGIN: Great Britain
Affection level:	■■■	Cold tolerance:	■■■	DATE OF ORIGIN: 1700s
Friendliness toward dogs:	■■■■■	Heat tolerance:	■■■	ORIGINAL FUNCTION: Tailing Fox
Friendliness toward other pets:	■■■			TODAY'S FUNCTION: Trailing Fox
Friendliness toward strangers:	■■■■	WEIGHT: 55–75 lb*		OTHER NAME: Foxhound
Ease of training:	■■	HEIGHT: 23–27″*		

HISTORY

Careful pedigrees have been kept of English Foxhounds since the late 1700s—longer than for any other breed. Still, the exact origin of the breed is unknown. At the time of its inception, coursing the stag with Greyhounds was still the favored dog sport of the gentry. Around 1750, a few men envisioned hunting foxes with swift horses and hounds. The hounds would have to be able to track a faint scent while on the run and to maintain their chase for hours. Foxhunting gained its appeal as a pastime of the wealthy, and packs of hounds were tended to by Masters of Foxhounds, who looked to the care and breeding of the dogs. Riding to the hounds became an affair steeped in ceremony, with the actual killing of the fox anticlimatic. As the esthetic aspects of

ILLUSTRATED STANDARD

1 Pronounced brow
2 Low-set ears, often “rounded” (cut short)
3 Level topline
4 Tail carried gaily, but not over back; slight brush
5 Round feet
6 Forelegs strong and straight

Color: any good hound color
DQ: overshot or undershot

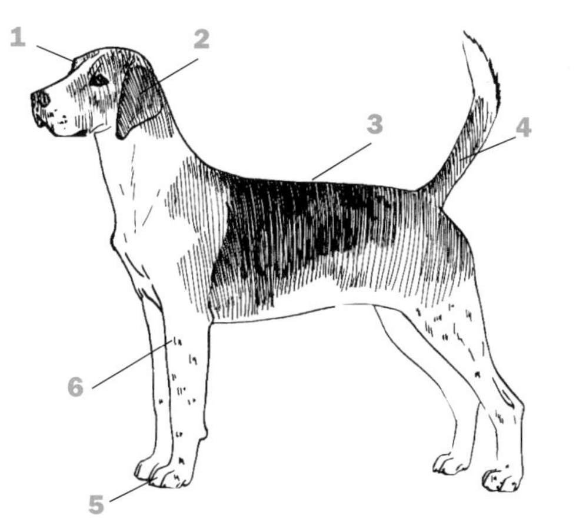

the hunt increased in significance, care was taken to produce dogs that looked good not only individually but also as a pack. Thus, pack members would usually share the same coat coloration, most often the black saddle over a tan body with white points. Foxhunting became so popular that by the late 1800s, 140 packs (each with about 50 hounds) were registered in England alone. Foxhounds came to America in the 1700s, although in time a good percentage of these dogs were bred with other dogs to produce the American Foxhound. The latter has since surpassed the English Foxhound in popularity in America, although neither is popular as a pet or show dog. The English Foxhound is still the first choice of hunters wishing a traditional outing on horseback, riding to the melodious bay of this most classic of breeds.

TEMPERAMENT

Traditionally a pack hound, the English Foxhound nonetheless makes a stately housedog, as long as it has human or canine companionship. It gets along well with horses, dogs, children, and other pets. It is an avid sniffer and trailer, however, and needs daily exercise in a safe area. It is a tolerant, amiable, and gentle dog even though it is not very demonstrative. Most are reserved with strangers. It is not well suited for city life. It bays.

UPKEEP

The Foxhound is an easygoing dog that nonetheless needs plenty of exercise. It is bred to run for miles, and it can make a good jogging companion on leash or a hiking companion in a safe area. The coat needs only occasional brushing.

HEALTH

- Major concerns: none
- Minor concerns: none
- Occasionally seen: CHD, renal disease
- Suggested tests: (hip)
- Life span: 10–13 years

FORM AND FUNCTION

The English Foxhound is of powerful build, with large bone. The size of bone at the ankle is considered especially important. This build, along with comparatively straight angulation of the stifles, favors stamina over speed. The rich, deep voice is prized for the hunt. Many English Foxhounds have “rounded” ears, in which about 1½" are surgically removed from the end of the ear.

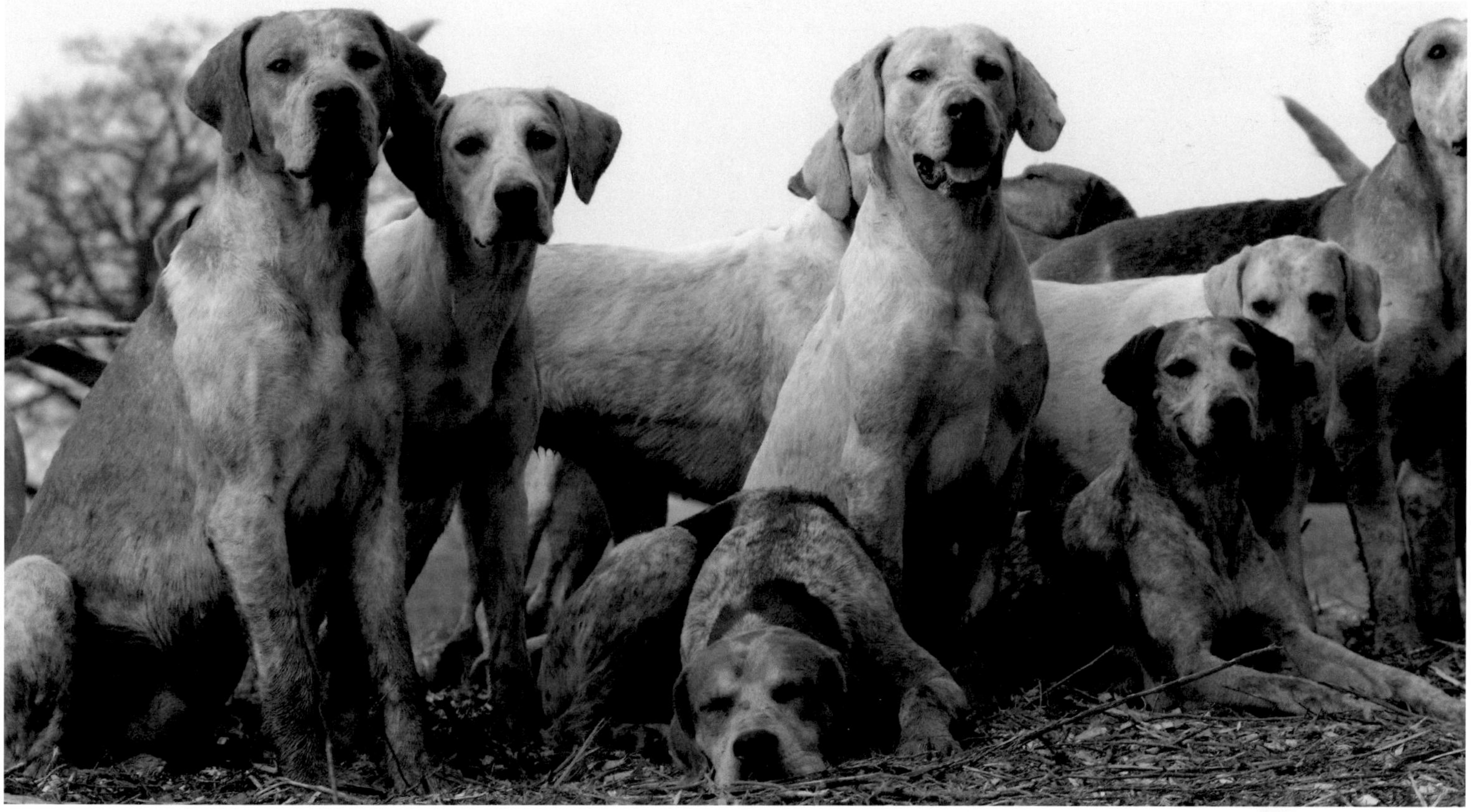

Greyhound

AT A GLANCE

Energy level:	■ ■	Watchdog ability:	■ ■	POPULARITY: Rare
Exercise requirements:	■ ■ ■	Protection ability:	■ ■	FAMILY: Sighthound
Playfulness:	■ ■ ■	Grooming requirements:	■	AREA OF ORIGIN: Great Britain
Affection level:	■ ■ ■	Cold tolerance:	■	DATE OF ORIGIN: Ancient times
Friendliness toward dogs:	■ ■ ■	Heat tolerance:	■ ■	ORIGINAL FUNCTION: Coursing hares
Friendliness toward other pets:	■ ■			TODAY'S FUNCTION: Racing, lure coursing, open-field coursing
Friendliness toward strangers:	■ ■ ■	WEIGHT: male: 65–70 lb; female: 60–65 lb		
Ease of training:	■ ■ ■	HEIGHT: male: 27–29″*; female: 26–28″*		OTHER NAME: None

HISTORY

One of the first types of dogs selectively bred by humans was the sighthound, a dog that could run after and catch game by outrunning it. The prototypical sighthound has always been the Greyhound. Greyhound-like dogs have been depicted since ancient Egyptian, Greek, and Roman times. The name Greyhound may come from Graius, meaning Greek, or from the Latin gradus, denoting high grade. By Saxon time, Greyhounds were well established in Britain and were valued by both commoners for their ability to put food on the table and by nobility for the sport of the chase. In 1014 the Forest Laws prohibited all but nobility from keeping Greyhounds near royal forests unless they had been "lamed"; these laws remained in effect for four hundred years. Even when they were repealed, Greyhounds

ILLUSTRATED STANDARD

1 Long, narrow head
2 Scarcely perceptible stop
3 Small, folded ears
4 Well-arched loins
5 Tail long, fine, and tapering
6 Deep chest
7 Hare feet

Color: immaterial (includes black, gray, red, fawn, either solid or brindled, either whole colored, or spotted)
DQ: none

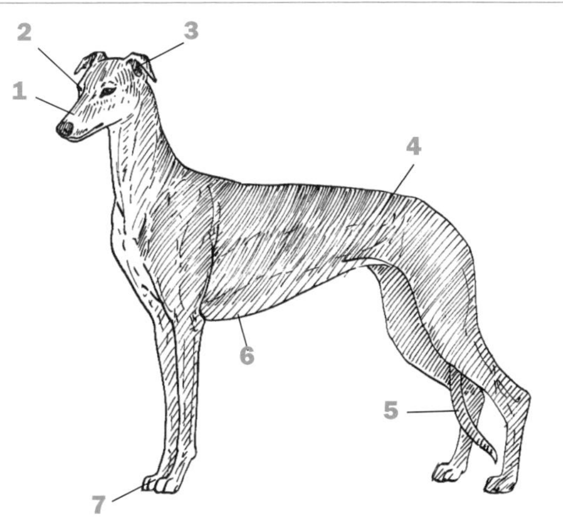

remained the dogs of nobility because with the growing importance of agriculture and domestic animal food sources, the running dog was not economically advantageous. Instead, Greyhounds were used for coursing hare for sport, and during the 1800s coursing became a consuming pastime of the upper class. Early American immigrants often brought Greyhounds with them to the New World; here they proved adept at coursing on the open plains. When coursing was made available to the masses by staging it first in closed parks and then on tracks after a mechanical lure, the Greyhound's fate was sealed. Track racing, which began in 1926, proved so popular that dogs were bred specifically for short bursts of speed, ultimately resulting in the fastest breed of dog. Greyhounds continued to compete at dog shows, which they had done since the 1870s. They were AKC recognized in 1885. The breed soon became divided into show and racing types, which were seldom interbred. In America, the Greyhound is one of the least popular breeds according to AKC registrations of show stock. The National Greyhound Association (NGA) registers many thousands of Greyhounds annually; however, recently retired racers from NGA stock have become popular as pets.

TEMPERAMENT

Known as "the world's fastest couch potato," the Greyhound is quiet, calm, and extremely well-mannered indoors. They are good with other dogs, and with other pets if raised with them; outdoors, they tend to chase any small thing that moves. They are reserved with strangers, very sensitive, and sometimes timid. Despite their independent nature, they are eager to please.

UPKEEP

The Greyhound needs daily exercise, but it is a sprinter, not an endurance runner. Its needs can thus be met with a chance to run, or by a longer walk on leash. It loves to run and chase outdoors, and can easily run into danger at great speed unless exercised in a safe area. Greyhounds relish creature comforts and must have soft bedding and warmth. The coat is extremely easy to care for, needing only occasional brushing to remove dead hair.

HEALTH

- Major concerns: osteosarcoma
- Minor concerns: esophageal achalasia, gastric torsion
- Occasionally seen: SAS, DCM, osteogenesis imperfecta
- Suggested tests: cardiac
- Life span: 10–13 years
- Note: Racing injuries, especially toe, hock, and muscle injuries, are common in retired NGA dogs. Both NGA and AKC Greyhounds are sensitive to barbiturate anesthesia and are prone to lacerations and tail-tip injuries.

FORM AND FUNCTION

The ultimate running dog, the Greyhound is built for speed. Its long legs and arched back enable it to contract and stretch maximally while executing the double-suspension gallop. It has tremendous muscle mass and light legs, further enhancing speed. The feet are long and narrow, giving maximum leverage. The long tail serves as a rudder and brake when running at high speed. The coat is short and smooth. Two types of Greyhounds are available: AKC (show) and NGA (racing). Retired NGA Greyhounds are smaller, sturdier, and faster than show dogs and may be more inclined to chase small animals.

Harrier

AT A GLANCE

Energy level:	■■■■	Watchdog ability:	■■■■■	POPULARITY: Very rare
Exercise requirements:	■■■■	Protection ability:	■	FAMILY: Scenthound
Playfulness:	■■■	Grooming requirements:	■	AREA OF ORIGIN: Great Britain
Affection level:	■■■	Cold tolerance:	■■■	DATE OF ORIGIN: Middle Ages
Friendliness toward dogs:	■■■■■	Heat tolerance:	■■■	ORIGINAL FUNCTION: Trailing hares
Friendliness toward other pets:	■■■			TODAY'S FUNCTION: Trailing hare and fox
Friendliness toward strangers:	■■■■	WEIGHT: male: 45–60 lb*; female: 35–45 lb*		OTHER NAME: None
Ease of training:	■■	HEIGHT: 19–21″		

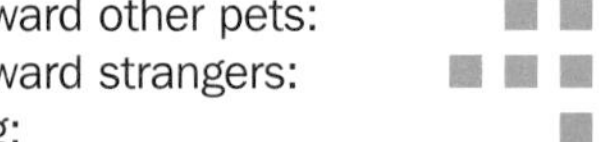

HISTORY

The word harier was Norman for dog or hound, so that it is difficult to unravel the ancient history of the Harrier from the history of hounds in general. Nonetheless, the Harrier may be one of the older scenthounds still in existence today, with references dating from thirteenth-century England. They probably stem from the long-extinct Talbot and St. Hubert hounds, and perhaps the Brachet and later, the French Basset. This lineage produced a dog that tracked hare by scent at a pace that enabled hunters to follow on foot. Thus, although Harrier packs were kept by the gentry, poorer hunters without horses could also hunt with Harriers, often combining the few dogs each individual had to form an impromptu pack. Smaller English Foxhounds may have been bred with

ILLUSTRATED STANDARD

1 Moderately defined stop
2 Low-set ears with round tips
3 Level topline
4 Long tail, carried gaily but not curled over back, with a brush
5 Cat feet
6 Inclined to knuckle over slightly

Color: any
DQ: none

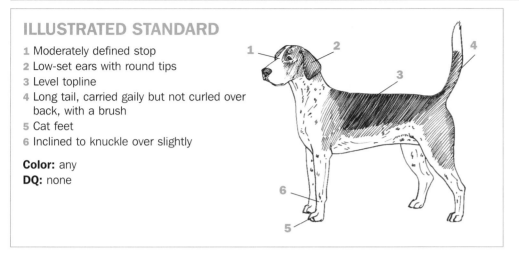

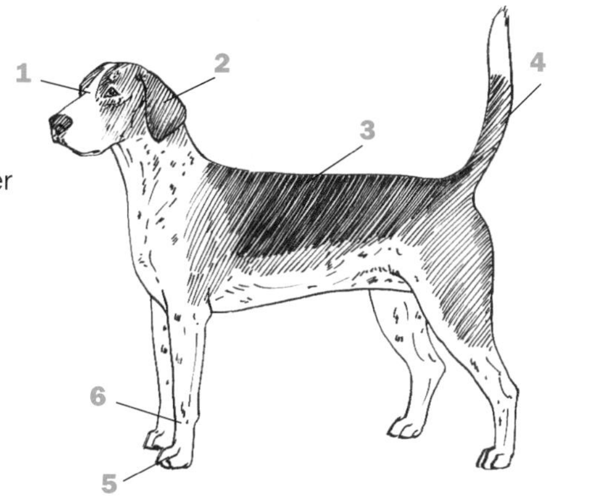

these dogs in the early 1800s to develop a longer legged, faster dog also capable of running with mounted hunters. The Harrier has been known in America since colonial times. Despite its classic proportions and handy size, it has never been popular as a show dog or pet.

TEMPERAMENT

The Harrier is somewhat more playful and outgoing than the Foxhound, but not as much as the Beagle. It is amiable, tolerant, and good with children. Its first love is for the hunt, and it loves to sniff and trail. It needs daily exercise in a safe area. Most are reserved with strangers. It tends to bay. Some may bay or bark if bored or lonely.

UPKEEP

The Harrier needs daily exercise, but its needs can be met with a long walk or jog and a vigorous game in the yard. The coat is easily cared for, needing only occasional brushing to remove dead hair. Harriers are very gregarious pack hounds and as such do not do well if left alone for long periods. Most are happiest with another dog to play with.

HEALTH

- Major concerns: CHD
- Minor concerns: none
- Occasionally seen: epilepsy, perianal fistula
- Suggested tests: hip, eye
- Life span: 12–14 years

FORM AND FUNCTION

The Harrier is a smaller version of the English Foxhound, more suited for hunting hares. It has large bone for its size, and is slightly longer than tall. It is a scenting pack hound and should be capable of running with other dogs, scenting its quarry, and hunting tirelessly over any terrain for long periods. It has a gentle expression when relaxed and alert when aroused. The coat is short and hard.

Ibizan Hound

AT A GLANCE

Energy level: ■■■
Exercise requirements: ■■■
Playfulness: ■■■
Affection level: ■■
Friendliness toward dogs: ■■■■
Friendliness toward other pets: ■■■
Friendliness toward strangers: ■■■
Ease of training: ■■

Watchdog ability: ■■■■
Protection ability: ■
Grooming requirements:
 Smooth: ■
 Wire: ■■■
Cold tolerance: ■■
Heat tolerance: ■■■

WEIGHT: male: 50 lb; female: 45 lb
HEIGHT: male: 23.5–27.5″; female: 22.5–26″

POPULARITY: Very rare
FAMILY: Sighthound
AREA OF ORIGIN: Ibiza (Balearic Islands)
DATE OF ORIGIN: Ancient times
ORIGINAL FUNCTION: Hunting rabbits
TODAY'S FUNCTION: Lure coursing, hunting rabbits
OTHER NAME: Podenco Ibicenco, Ca Eivissenc, Balearic Dog

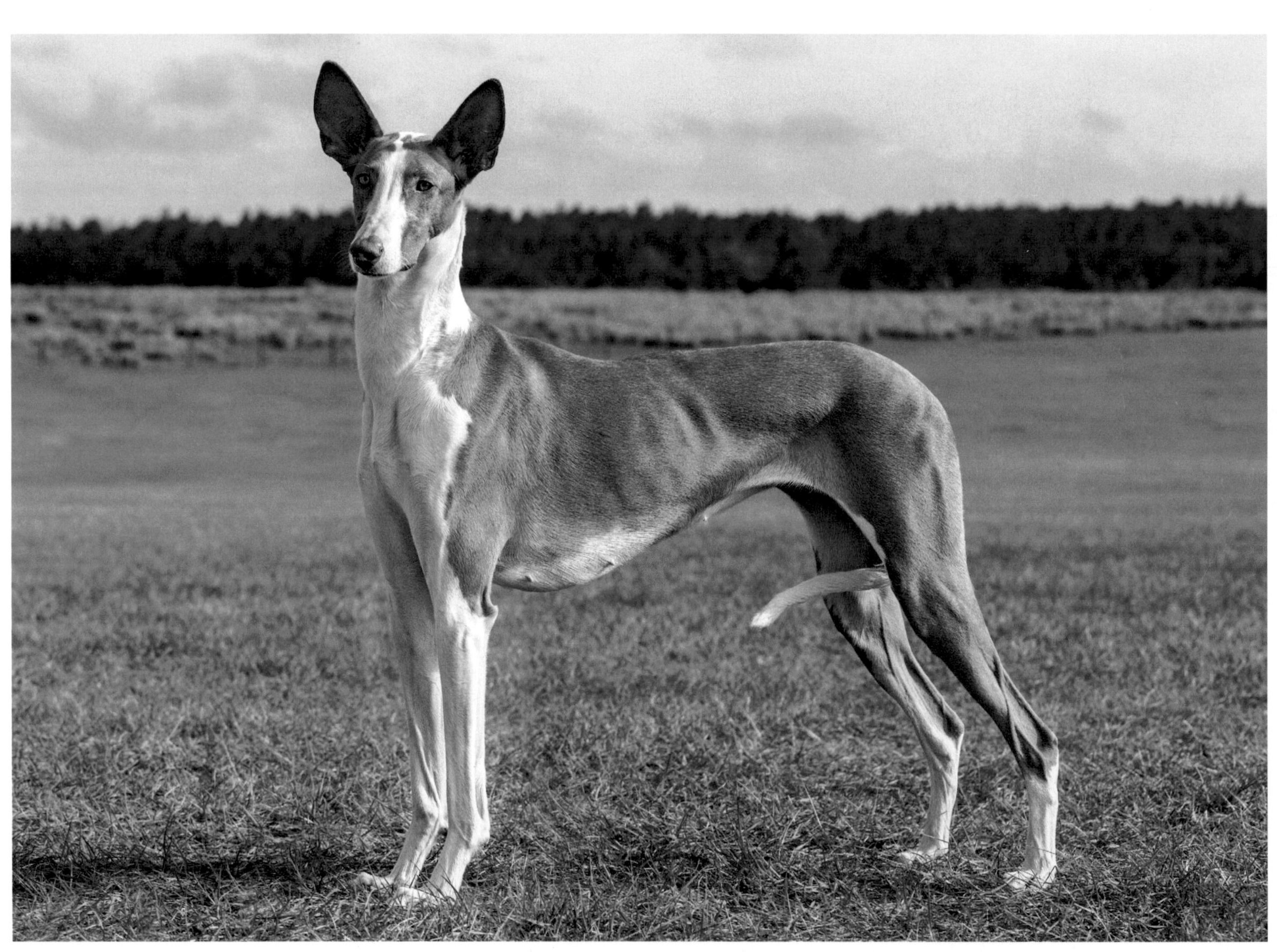

HISTORY

The Ibizan Hound probably shares the same roots as the Pharaoh Hound, bearing uncanny resemblance to the dogs depicted in Egyptian tombs and to the jackal god Anubis. Ancient Phoenician sea traders may have taken the dogs to the Balearic island of Ibiza, where they remained in relative seclusion. Ibiza saw many rulers through the ages, coming under the auspices of the Egyptians, Chaldeans, Carthaginians, Romans, Vandals, Arabs, and, most recently, Spanish. Spanish farmers on the island used them for hunting. With little outside influence, the dogs of Ibiza remain uncontaminated by crosses to other breeds. The hard conditions on the island imposed stringent selection by islanders because only the best rabbit hunters could be allowed to procreate or, for

ILLUSTRATED STANDARD

1 Rosy, flesh-colored nose
2 Long, narrow, cone-shaped head with prominent occiput, little-defined stop
3 Small, light eyes
4 Large, pointed ears, held erect when alert
5 Slightly arched loin
6 Tail set low and carried in a sickle, ring, or saber position
7 Brisket about 2½" above elbow
8 Rather upright upper arm, with elbow in front of deepest part of chest
9 Hare feet

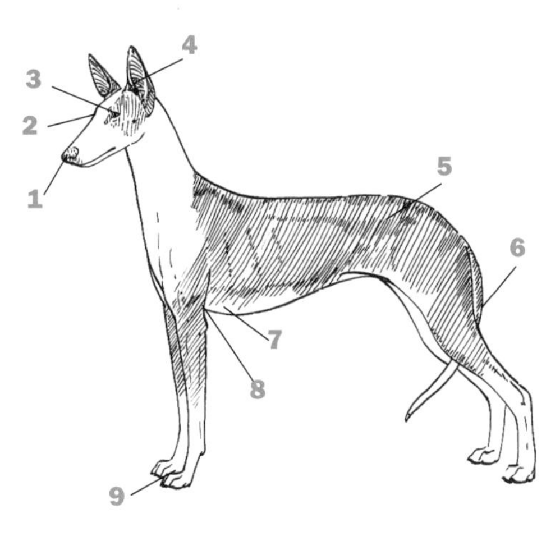

Color: white or red (from light yellowish red to deep red), solid, or in any combination
DQ: any color other than white or red

that matter, survive. These factors produced a hardy, true breeding dog little changed from its ancestral stock. The first Ibizan Hound came to America in the 1950s. The breed's striking appearance aroused much attention but has failed to attract a great number of pet owners. It gradually gained enough popularity to warrant AKC recognition in 1979, but the Ibizan Hound remains one of the rarer breeds.

TEMPERAMENT

The graceful Ibizan Hound retains great hunting instinct, using its acute senses of hearing and smell to locate small animals, and relishing the opportunity to chase anything that moves. Unlike most sighthounds, it barks when chasing. It is reserved with strangers; some can be timid. It is gentle, mild-mannered, even-tempered, and loyal, and makes a quiet house pet.

UPKEEP

As an independent and athletic dog, the Ibizan Hound needs daily exercise in a safe area. Ideal exercise allows the dog to stretch out at full speed, but its needs can also be met with long walks or jogs on leash, combined with an occasional chance to run full out. It is a skilled jumper, which should be taken into consideration when designing an enclosure. The smooth coat requires only occasional brushing, whereas the wire coat requires weekly brushing.

HEALTH

- Major concerns: none
- Minor concerns: seizures, allergies
- Occasionally seen: deafness, cataract, axonal dystrophy, retinal dysplasia
- Suggested tests: eye, (hip), (BAER), (thyroid)
- Life span: 12–14 years
- Note: sensitive to barbiturate anesthesia

FORM AND FUNCTION

The Ibizan should possess a deer-like elegance and expression, and its movement reflects these qualities. Its lithe build enables it to perform the double-suspension gallop with great speed, agility, and endurance. It is a superb jumper, able to spring to great heights from a standstill. It is racy, slightly longer than tall. With the exception of its large ears, it should not be exaggerated in any way. The trot is light and graceful. The coat can be hard, either short or wire, the latter from one to three inches in length.

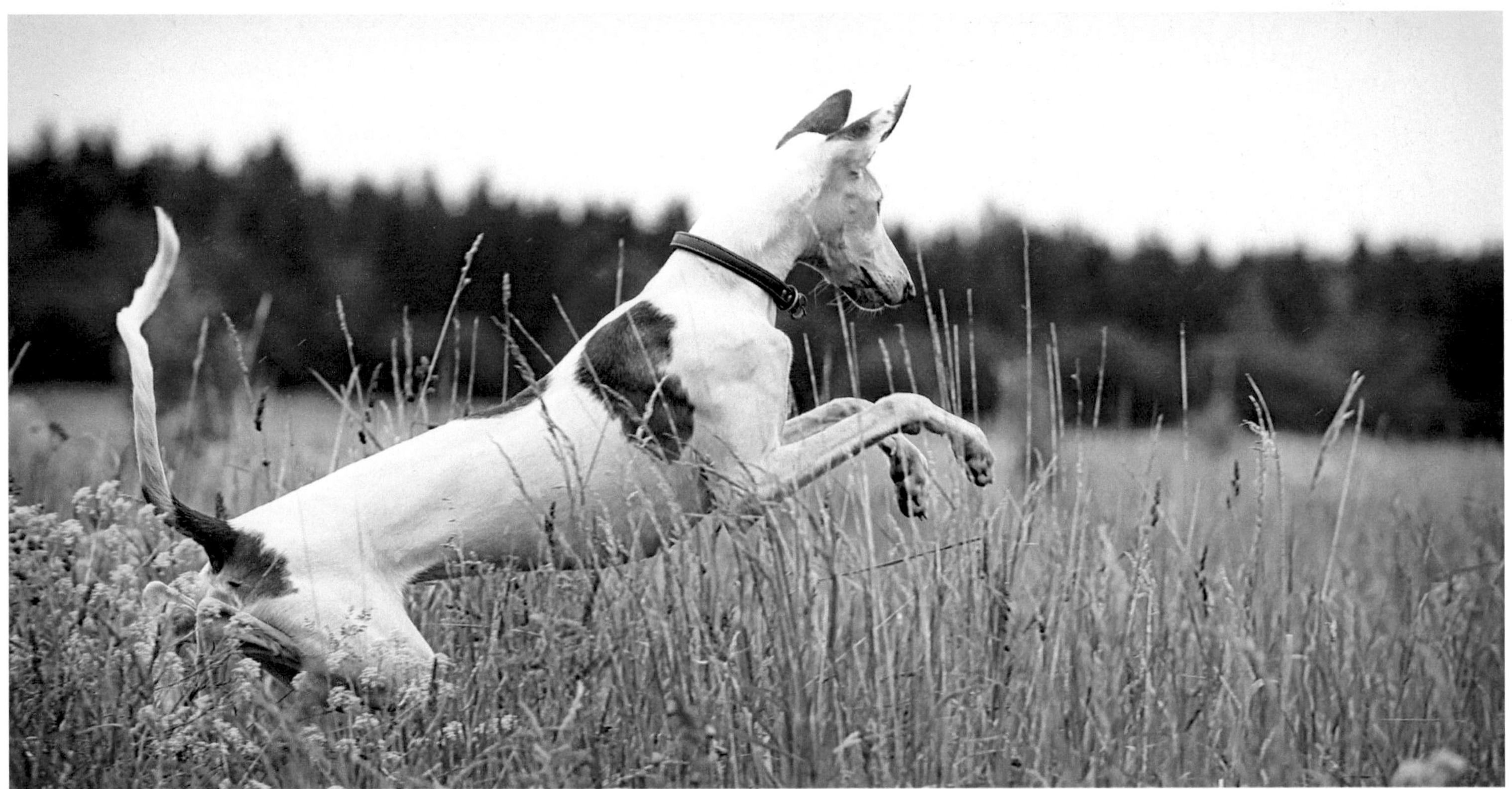

Irish Wolfhound

AT A GLANCE

Energy level:	■
Exercise requirements:	■ ■ ■
Playfulness:	■
Affection level:	■ ■ ■
Friendliness toward dogs:	■ ■ ■
Friendliness toward other pets:	■ ■ ■
Friendliness toward strangers:	■ ■ ■
Ease of training:	■ ■

Watchdog ability:	■ ■ ■
Protection ability:	■ ■
Grooming requirements:	■ ■ ■
Cold tolerance:	■ ■ ■ ■
Heat tolerance:	■

WEIGHT: male: at least 120 lb; female: at least 105 lb
HEIGHT: male: at least 32″; female: at least 30″

POPULARITY: Somewhat popular
FAMILY: Sighthound
AREA OF ORIGIN: Ireland
DATE OF ORIGIN: Ancient times
ORIGINAL FUNCTION: Coursing wolves
TODAY'S FUNCTION: Lure coursing
OTHER NAME: None

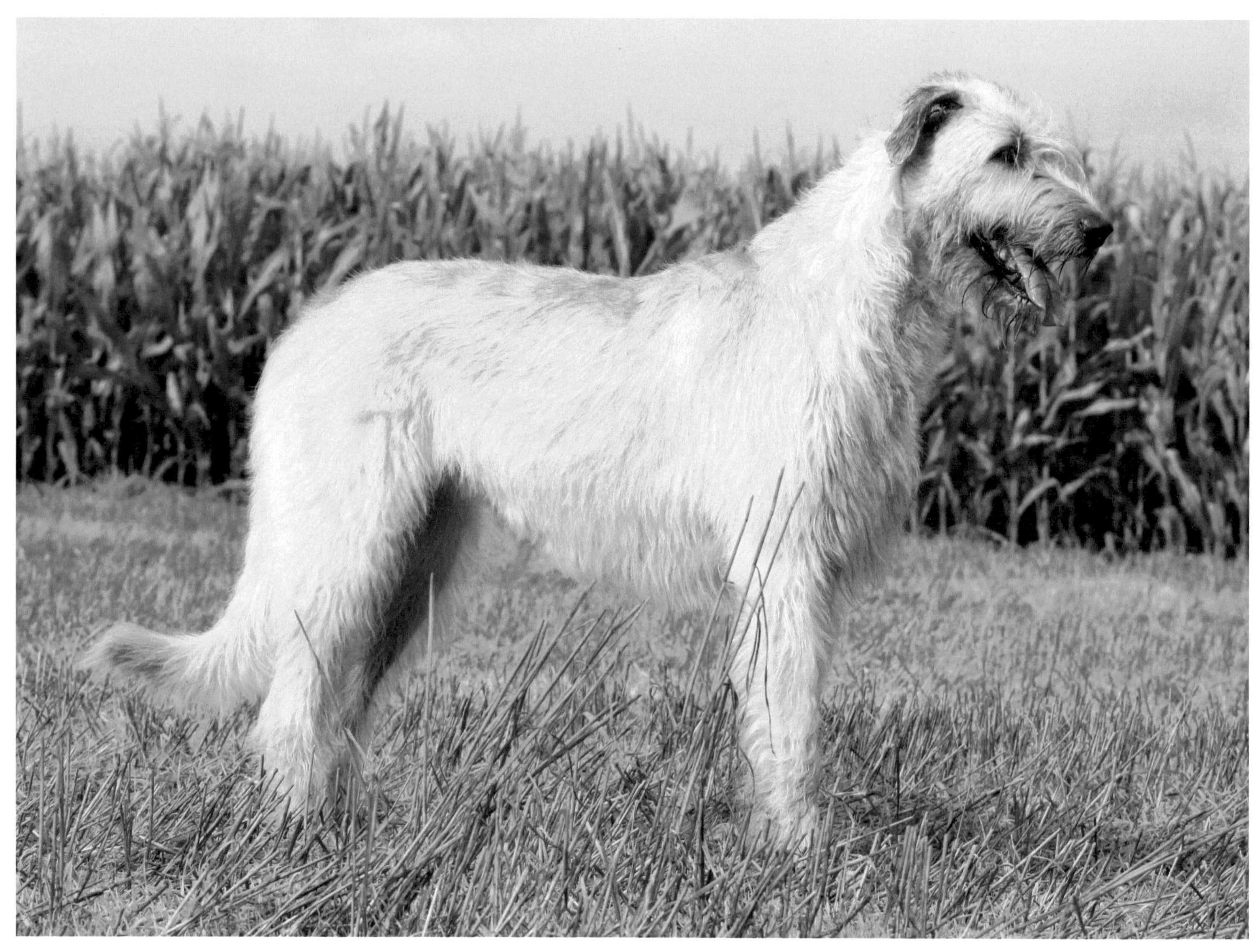

HISTORY

Dogs of great size are believed to have come to Ireland from Greece by 1500 B.C. In Ireland they became even more imposing, and gifts of these great dogs were made to Rome. The first definite mention of the Irish Wolfhound occurred in Rome in A.D. 391. The breed gained fame for its imposing stature and ability in fighting wild animals in arena sports. It was so acclaimed in Ireland that it became the subject of many legends recounting its valor in battle and chase. All large hounds were once known as *Cu*, a term implying bravery. The Irish name for the breed is Cu Faoil. Favored by Irish chieftains for the hunt, it gained its reputation as an unparalleled hunter of wolves and Irish elk. Illustrations of these dogs from the seventeenth century look very similar to modern Irish Wolfhounds. The impressive

ILLUSTRATED STANDARD

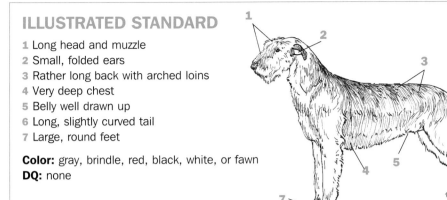

1 Long head and muzzle
2 Small, folded ears
3 Rather long back with arched loins
4 Very deep chest
5 Belly well drawn up
6 Long, slightly curved tail
7 Large, round feet

Color: gray, brindle, red, black, white, or fawn
DQ: none

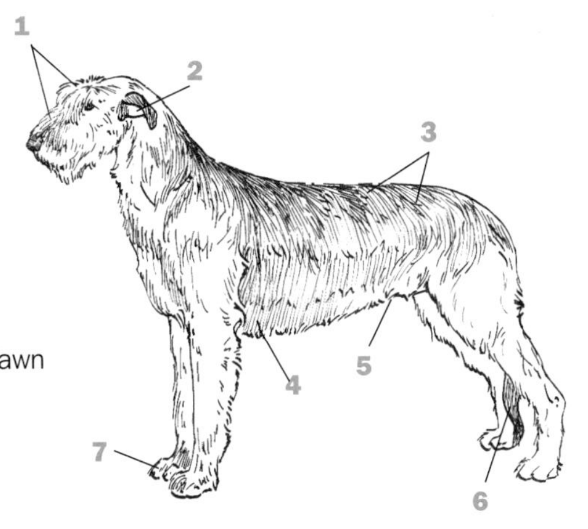

hounds (often seven at a time) were traditionally given to foreign nobility. This practice, along with the extinction of the wolf in Ireland in the eighteenth century, contributed to the decline of the breed's numbers. By the nineteenth century, Irish Wolfhounds were almost extinct in Ireland, and the famine of 1845 virtually decimated the breed. In 1869, Captain G. A. Graham determined to resurrect the Irish Wolfhound, a task he set about by crossing the few existing Wolfhounds—in particular one named Bran, thought to be the last true Wolfhound in Ireland—with such breeds as Scottish Deerhound as well as Great Dane, Borzoi, and even Tibetan Wolfdog. When first exhibited at a dog show in the 1870s, the reborn Wolfhound created a sensation—the same reaction it inspires to this day when first seen. Its commanding appearance draws many admirers, but its popularity is tempered by the practicalities of keeping such a large dog.

TEMPERAMENT

Known as the gentle giant, this is an apt description of this soft-natured, easygoing breed. It is calm around the house, sensitive, patient, easygoing, and sweet. Despite its great size, it is good with children, pets, and other dogs. It is friendly with strangers, and courageous when the need arises.

UPKEEP

The Irish Wolfhound enjoys a long walk and a chance to stretch its legs, so it needs daily exercise. At home it needs ample room to stretch out on a soft surface and should not be required to live in cramped quarters. It can develop calluses if allowed to lie on hard surfaces too often. Its coat needs to be brushed or combed once or twice weekly, plus occasional slight scissoring to neaten up straggly hairs. Dead hairs should be stripped twice a year.

HEALTH

- Major concerns: gastric torsion, elbow dysplasia, osteosarcoma
- Minor concerns: cardiomyopathy, OCD, osteosarcoma, CHD
- Occasionally seen: vWD, PRA, megaesophagus
- Suggested tests: hip, cardiac, eye, elbow
- Life span: 5–7 years
- Note: sensitive to barbiturate anesthesia; prone to tail-tip injuries

FORM AND FUNCTION

The tallest of the sighthounds, the Irish Wolfhound resembles a rough-coated Greyhound, although of more powerful build. Great size is especially valued in the breed. This combination of speed, power, and size enables the Irish Wolfhound to run down and overpower large prey. Despite its size, the breed should be gracefully built, its gait easy and active, its head held proudly. The rough coat, which provides protection against the cold and damp, as well as its opponents' teeth, is especially wiry and long over the eyes and under the jaw.

Norwegian Elkhound

AT A GLANCE

Energy level:	■■■■	Watchdog ability:	■■■	POPULARITY: Somewhat uncommon
Exercise requirements:	■■■	Protection ability:	■■	FAMILY: Spitz, Northern
Playfulness:	■■■■	Grooming requirements:	■■	AREA OF ORIGIN: Norway
Affection level:	■■■	Cold tolerance:	■■■■■	DATE OF ORIGIN: Ancient Times
Friendliness toward dogs:	■■	Heat tolerance:	■■	ORIGINAL FUNCTION: Hunting moose, bear, other big game
Friendliness toward other pets:	■■			
Friendliness toward strangers:	■■■■	WEIGHT: male: 55 lb; female: 48 lb		TODAY'S FUNCTION: Companion, moose hunting
Ease of training:	■■■	HEIGHT: male: 20.5″; female: 19.5″		OTHER NAME: Elkhound, Norsk Elghund

HISTORY

The Elkhound is an unusual hound because its roots lie in the spitz breeds, which it still closely resembles. Its placement in the Hound Group reflects partly the misinterpretation of its original "hund" name as "hound," but mostly because it is functionally a scenthound, using its tracking abilities to hunt moose and other large game. The Elkhound has served as a hunter, guardian, herder, and defender at least since the time of the Vikings. In a land of subzero temperatures, deep snow, thick forests, and rugged mountains, only the hardiest of breeds could evolve to perform the variety of jobs at which the Elkhound excels. Of all its roles, hunting the elk (actually, moose) is this breed's forte. Two hunting-style Elkhounds are used: the bandhund is attached by a long line to the hunter while

ILLUSTRATED STANDARD

1 Defined stop
2 Oval eyes
3 Wedge-shaped head, broad at ears
4 High-set, erect, fairly small ears with pointed tips
5 Tail tightly curved and carried over the centerline of the back
6 Small, oval feet

Color: gray, with lighter undercoat and undersides; muzzle, ears, and tail tip are black
DQ: an overall color other than gray

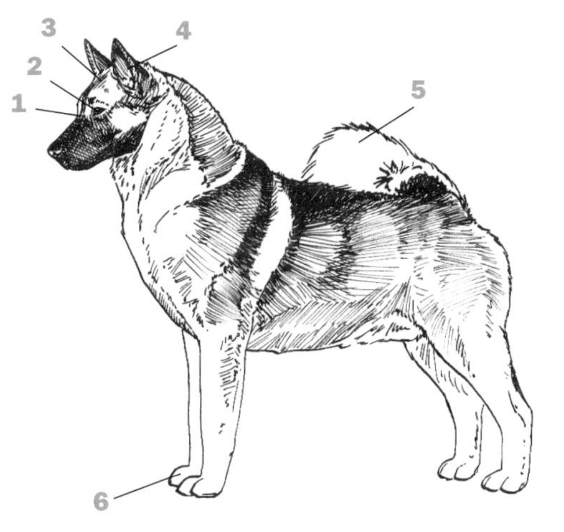

tracking the scent, as the loshund tracks ahead of the hunter until it confronts the quarry. Its goal is to hold the moose at bay, and it will hunt quietly if the moose begins to run away. If the moose stops, the dog begins barking furiously to alert the hunter. Nimbly jumping in and out toward the moose, it deftly avoids the swinging antlers. Either way, the Elkhound's job is not to kill the moose, but to locate it and hold it at bay until the hunter can shoot it. Although the breed had been carefully bred for centuries, only since the late 1800s were pedigrees kept and breeding according to standard performed. The breed has been exhibited in Scandinavian dog shows since that time and was brought to England and America shortly thereafter. The breed gained the American public's attention when President Hoover owned one, a gift from Norway in appreciation for his help in World War I. The AKC recognized the breed around 1930, and it has enjoyed moderate popularity since then. In Scandinavia, the Elkhound is still tested by grueling moose hunts that may entail an entire day of tracking.

TEMPERAMENT

The Norwegian Elkhound combines traits of hounds and spitz-like dogs, resulting in a breed that is bold, playful, independent, alert, and boisterous. This is a dog ready for adventure and happiest if that adventure takes place outdoors in cold weather. It needs daily exercise lest it become frustrated or even destructive. It is friendly with strangers but may quarrel with strange dogs. It tends to pull when on leash unless trained, and it does bark a lot.

UPKEEP

The Elkhound was developed to hunt all day under grueling conditions. It needs daily exertion in order to feel satisfied. This can be in the form of a good jog, very long walk, or invigorating play session. Its double coat needs brushing twice a week, and daily during main shedding season when it sheds a lot.

HEALTH

- Major concerns: CHD
- Minor concerns: hot spots, kidney disease (renal dysplasia), sebaceous cysts
- Occasionally seen: Fanconi syndrome, PRA, patellar luxation, intracutaneous cornifying epithelioma
- Suggested tests: hip, eye, (Fanconi), (knee), (PRA)
- Life span: 10–12 years

FORM AND FUNCTION

A typical northern spitz-like breed, the Norwegian Elkhound is square-proportioned, close coupled, with substantial bone, broad head, pricked ears, and tightly curled tail. It is constructed for agility and endurance, rather than speed, enabling it to trail for hours and then hold big game at bay by barking and dodging attack. Its trot is effortless. It has a thick, smooth-lying coat consisting of straight outer hairs and a wooly undercoat. This combination presents the best protection against cold and snow.

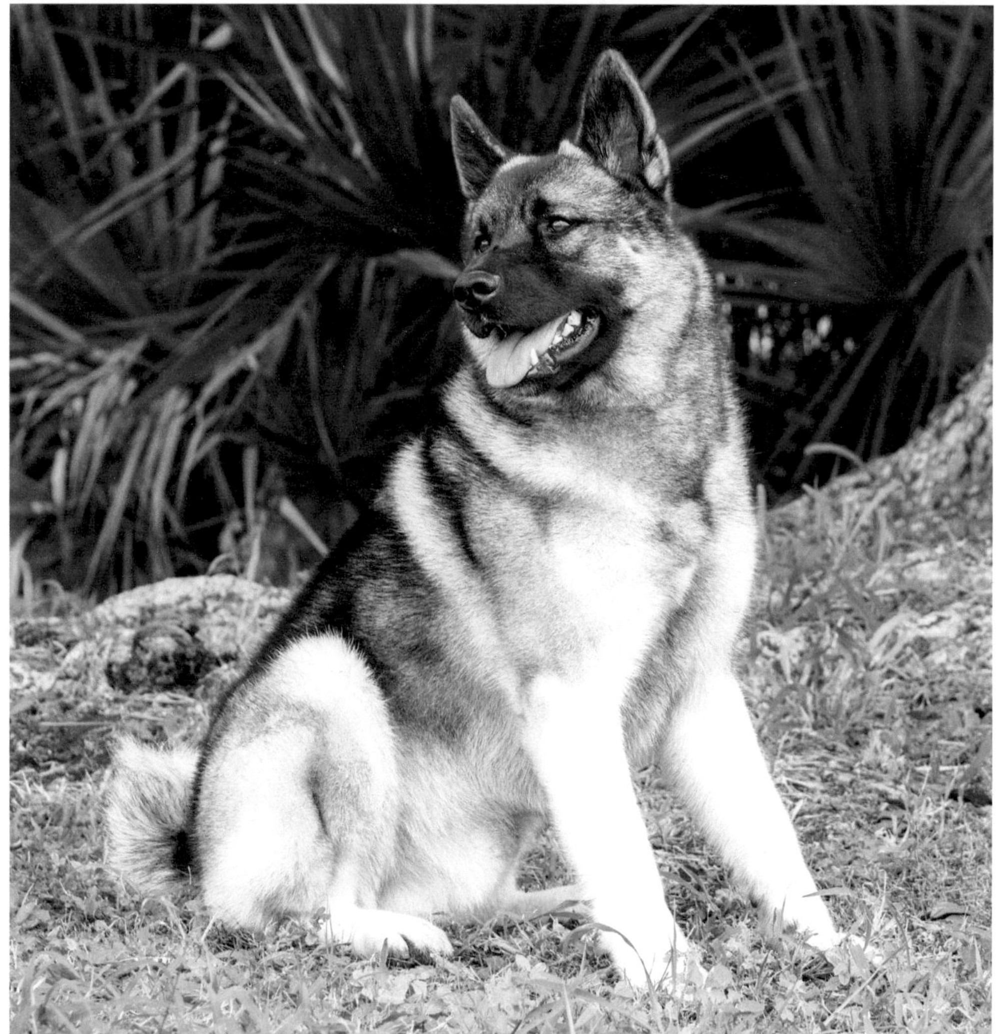

Otterhound

AT A GLANCE

Energy level:	■■	Watchdog ability:	■■■■	POPULARITY: Very rare
Exercise requirements:	■■■	Protection ability:	■	FAMILY: Scenthound
Playfulness:	■■■	Grooming requirements:	■■■	AREA OF ORIGIN: England
Affection level:	■■■■■	Cold tolerance:	■■■■	DATE OF ORIGIN: Ancient times
Friendliness toward dogs:	■■■	Heat tolerance:	■■	ORIGINAL FUNCTION: Hunting otters
Friendliness toward other pets:	■■■			TODAY'S FUNCTION: Companion
Friendliness toward strangers:	■■■■■	WEIGHT: male: 115 lb; female: 80 lb		OTHER NAME: None
Ease of training:	■■	HEIGHT: male: 27″; female: 24″		

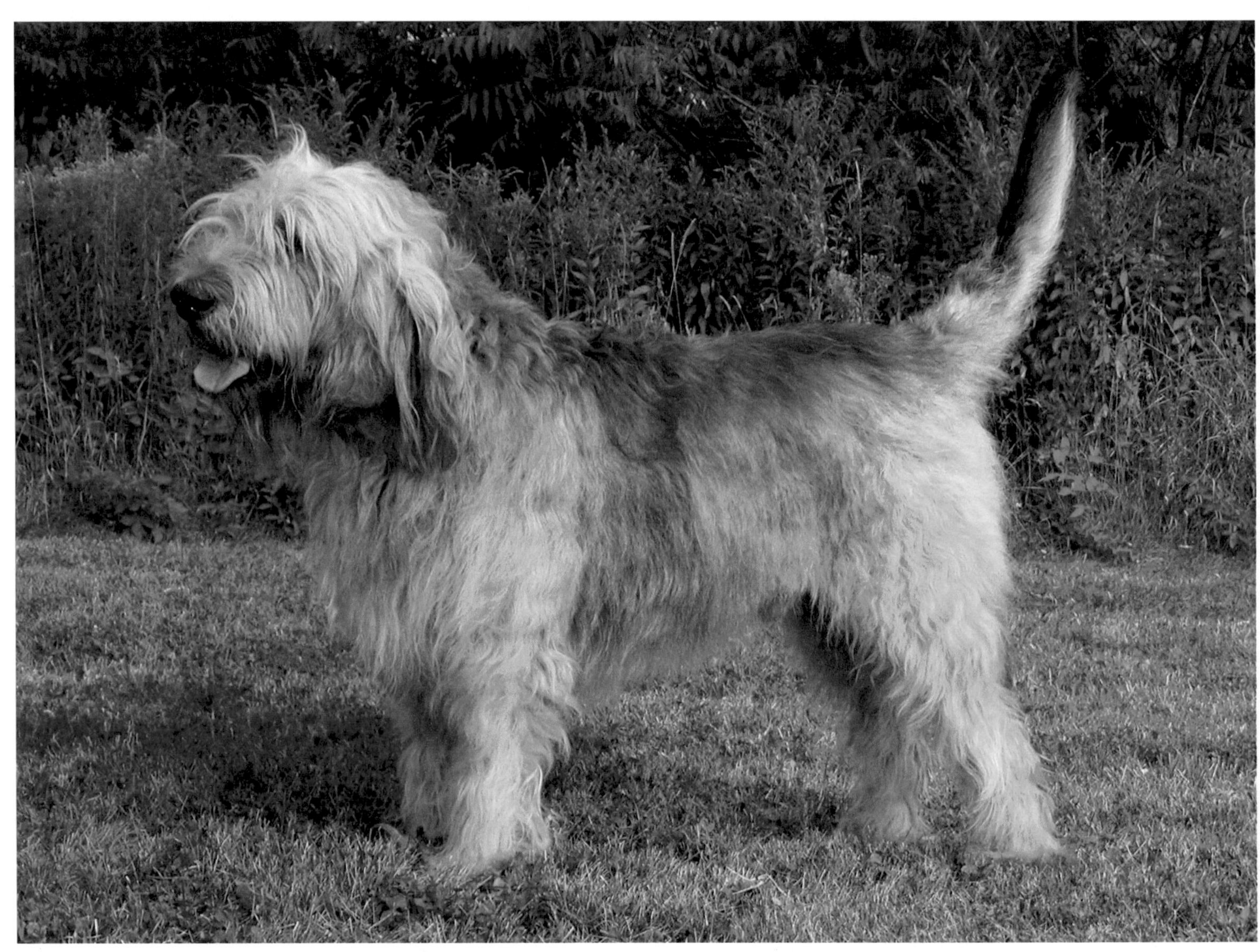

HISTORY

One of the most unusual members of the Hound Group is the Otterhound, a hardy, tousled scenthound of uncertain origin. The breed may have originated in France, and it closely resembles the old French Vendeen hound. Other breeds that may have played a part in its origin were the Welsh Harrier, Southern Hound (a foxhound-like breed), Bloodhound, or a type of water spaniel. Whatever the genetic makeup, the Otterhound came to fill a unique niche as a hunter of otters in England and is thus most associated with that country. King John kept the first documented packs of Otterhounds in 1212. The breed was useful for finding otters that were depleting fish in local streams. They would trail the otter to its den and bay when locating it. The hunters would then remove the Otterhounds

ILLUSTRATED STANDARD

1 Square muzzle with deep flews
2 Deep-set eyes
3 Large, fairly narrow head, well covered with hair
4 Long, pendulous, low-set ears
5 Tail carried saber fashion when moving
6 Large, webbed feet

Color: any
DQ: none

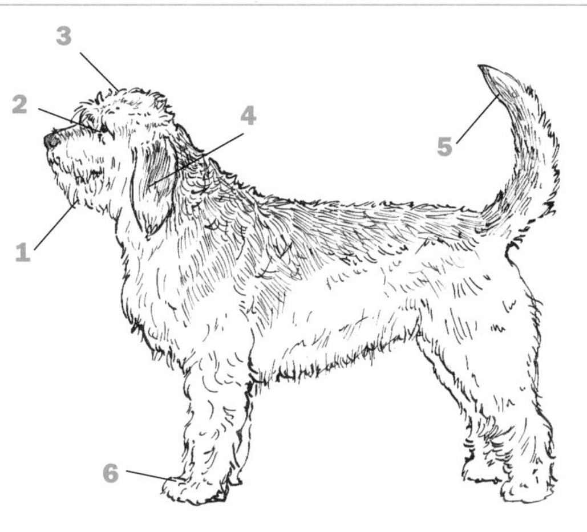

and send small terriers to dispatch the otter. Otterhunting was never among the most popular of sports, lacking the formal trappings of foxhunting and taking place under wet and uncomfortable conditions. Nonetheless, the sport reached its peak during the latter half of the nineteenth century, when over twenty packs were hunting in Britain, but it essentially died out after the Second World War. The first Otterhound came to America at the beginning of the twentieth century and was recognized by the AKC soon after. Otterhound aficionados have been especially adamant that the breed retain its functional characteristics, without succumbing to exaggerated grooming practices or the temptation to breed only for a competitive show dog. Even though this practice has maintained the true Otterhound type, the breed has never been especially popular as a show dog or pet. Despite the fact that the Otterhound is one of the most ancient of the English breeds, it is one of the rarest of English Kennel Club or AKC recognized breeds, verging perilously close to extinction.

TEMPERAMENT

As a packhound, the Otterhound is amiable with other dogs. As a hunter, it has an innate urge to follow the trails of mammals. Once on the trail, it is determined, single-minded, and nearly impossible to dissuade from its task. Even though the Otterhound's job was not to kill its quarry, it will nonetheless give chase to small animals. The Otterhound loves to hunt, sniff, trail, and, especially, swim. At home it is boisterous, amiable, and easygoing (although stubborn), affectionate with its family, and quite good with children. Because the Otterhound was never traditionally kept as a pet, it is not among the most responsive of breeds. However, the Otterhound is a low-key dog that can function as a quiet companion.

UPKEEP

The Otterhound needs daily exercise in a safe area or on a leash. It has a loud, melodious voice that carries for long distances. The Otterhound's coat requires only weekly brushing or combing. It may need its beard washed more frequently. Tidiness is not one of its virtues; the large, hairy feet tend to hold debris and mud, and the long hair around the mouth can hold water and food.

HEALTH

- Major concerns: CHD, gastric torsion
- Minor concerns: elbow dysplasia, CTP
- Occasionally seen: epilepsy, thrombopathy
- Suggested tests: hip, (elbow), DNA for thrombopathy
- Life span: 10–13 years

FORM AND FUNCTION

The Otterhound is a large dog with a somewhat stocky build, slightly longer than tall, not exaggerated in any way, enabling it to trot at a slow steady pace for long distances without tiring. Its coat, which consists of a rough, coarse outer coat combined with a soft wooly slightly oily undercoat, is essential for protecting it from brambles and cold water. It has a fairly large nose and muzzle, allowing ample room for olfactory receptors. Its large feet provide traction over rough and slippery terrain. This is a strong athletic breed that can withstand harsh weather and long strenuous hunts. Its expression is open and amiable, reflecting its temperament. The Otterhound is noted for its steadfast pursuit of its quarry despite the roughest of conditions. It has an acute sense of smell and can trail unerringly through running water and over all sorts of terrain.

Petit Basset Griffon Vendéen

AT A GLANCE

Energy level:	■■■■	Watchdog ability:	■■■■	POPULARITY: Rare
Exercise requirements:	■■■	Protection ability:	■	FAMILY: Scenthound
Playfulness:	■■■■	Grooming requirements:	■■	AREA OF ORIGIN: France
Affection level:	■■■■■	Cold tolerance:	■■■	DATE OF ORIGIN: 1700s
Friendliness toward dogs:	■■■■	Heat tolerance:	■■	ORIGINAL FUNCTION: Trailing hares
Friendliness toward other pets:	■■			TODAY'S FUNCTION: Companion
Friendliness toward strangers:	■■■■	WEIGHT: 25–35 lb*		OTHER NAME: Little Griffon Vendeen Basset
Ease of training:	■	HEIGHT: 13–15″		

HISTORY

The PBGV, as it is affectionately known, is a comparative newcomer to the AKC world, but it is an ancient breed with roots in sixteenth-century Europe. The long French name provides an accurate description of the breed: Petit (small) Basset (low) Griffon (rough-coated) Vendéen (its area of origin in France). This area, on the west coast of France, is filled with thick brambles, underbrush, and rocky terrain. Hunting in such terrain demanded a dog that had a coat that could withstand thorns and brambles, short legs that could enable it to wind its way through the underbrush in pursuit of rabbits, but nimbleness that allowed it to run over rocks and logs without tiring. Thus, the PBGV is more than a wire-coated Basset Hound, and more than a dwarf Grand Basset Griffon Vendéen

ILLUSTRATED STANDARD

1 Long beard and mustache
2 Large eyes surmounted by long eyebrows
3 Domed skull with well-defined occiput and stop
4 Proudly carried, long head
5 Low-set, long ears
6 Level back with slight arch over loin
7 Medium-length tail, carried proudly

Color: white with any combination of lemon, orange, tricolor, or grizzle markings
DQ: height over 15.5"

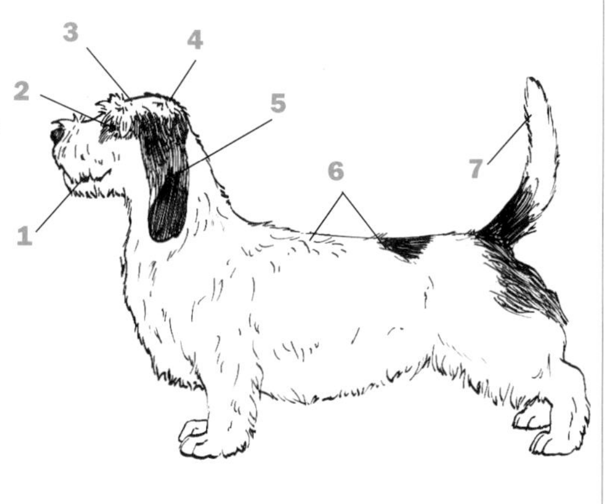

(a breed that resembles a slightly taller PBGV), even though it is closely related to both breeds. In England in the mid 1800s, the PBGV was shown with the Basset Hound as a wire-coated variety, but the PBGV is a longer legged, more nimble hound. In France, the Griffon Vendéen was considered to be one breed with two sizes until the 1950s. The two sizes were still interbred until the 1970s. The AKC recognized the PBGV in 1990, and since then the PBGV has attracted many new admirers because of its merry disposition and tousled carefree appearance.

TEMPERAMENT

Despite its appearance, the PBGV is not a Basset Hound in a wire coat. It is a merry, inquisitive, tough, busy dog, always on the lookout for excitement and fun. It loves to sniff, explore, trail, and dig, a true hunter at heart. Amiable and playful, it is good with children, other dogs, and most pets, and it is friendly toward strangers. It is stubborn and independent. It tends to dig and bark.

UPKEEP

The PBGV is not content to lie around. Its exercise requirements can be easily fulfilled, however, by a good walk on leash or a vigorous romp in the yard. The coat needs weekly brushing and occasional tidying of straggling hairs.

HEALTH

- Major concerns: none
- Minor concerns: otitis externa, CHD, PPM, some retinal and corneal conditions
- Occasionally seen: meningitis, patellar luxation, epilepsy, hypothyroidism, intervertebral disk disease
- Suggested tests: hip, eye
- Life span: 11–14 years

FORM AND FUNCTION

A correctly proportioned PBGV is about 50 percent longer than it is tall, enabling it to push its way through dense thickets. It has strong bone and surprising nimbleness. The gait is free, giving the appearance of a dog that is capable of a full day in the field. The tousled appearance results in part from its rough coat, with long facial furnishings. This, in combination with its thick shorter undercoat, gives the PBGV ample protection against brambles and the elements. Its expression—alert and friendly—reflects its nature.

Pharaoh Hound

AT A GLANCE

Energy level:	■■■	Watchdog ability:	■■■■	POPULARITY: Very rare
Exercise requirements:	■■■■	Protection ability:	■	FAMILY: Sighthound
Playfulness:	■■■	Grooming requirements:	■	AREA OF ORIGIN: Malta
Affection level:	■■■	Cold tolerance:	■■	DATE OF ORIGIN: Ancient Times
Friendliness toward dogs:	■■■■	Heat tolerance:	■■■	ORIGINAL FUNCTION: Hunting rabbits
Friendliness toward other pets:	■■			TODAY'S FUNCTION: Lure coursing
Friendliness toward strangers:	■■	WEIGHT: 45–55 lb*		OTHER NAME: Kelb-tal Fenek
Ease of training:	■■■	HEIGHT: male: 23–25″; female: 21–24″		

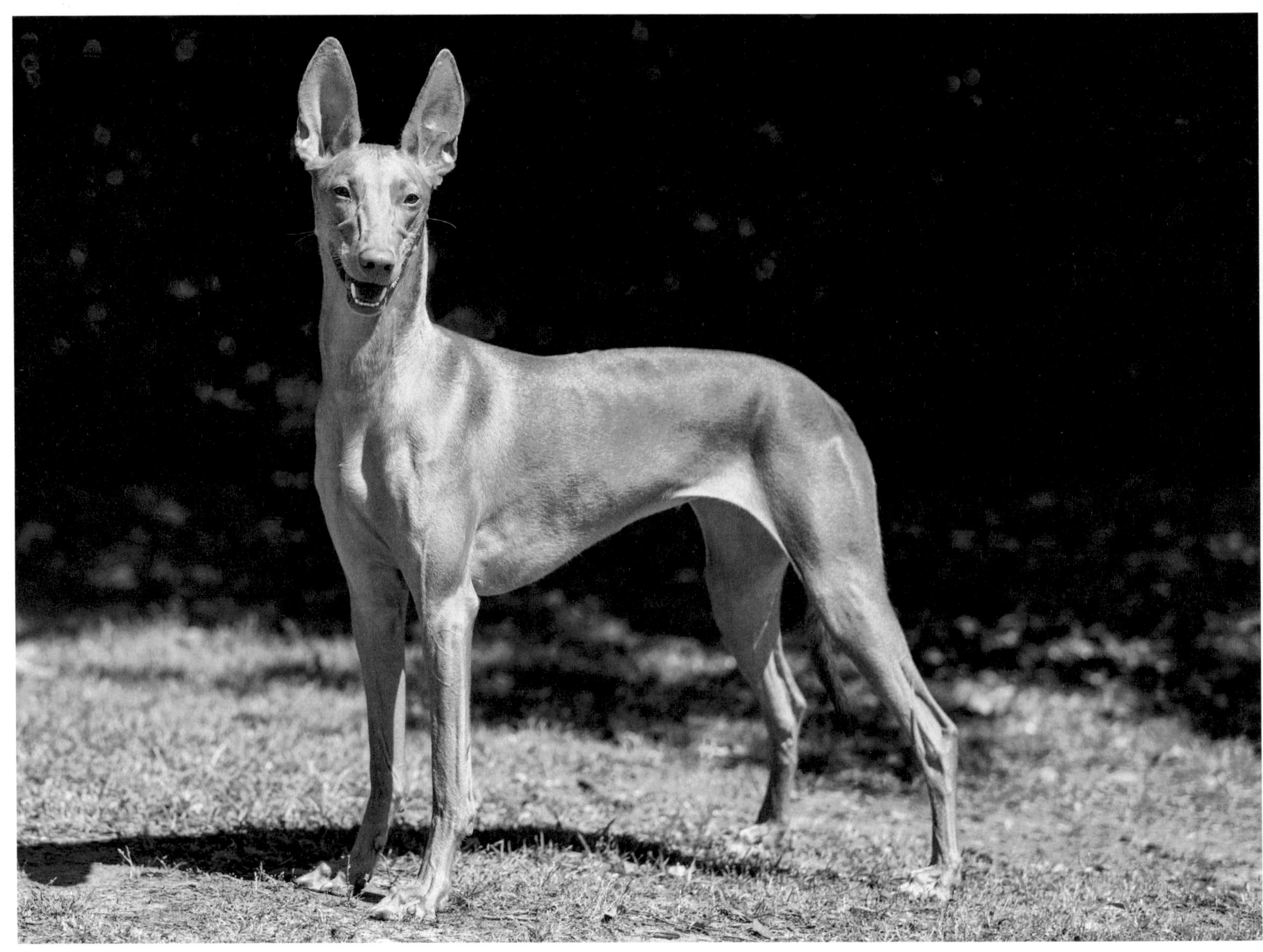

HISTORY

A hunting account from the XIX Egyptian dynasty supplies an apt description of the modern Pharaoh Hound: "The red, long-tailed dog goes at night into the stalls of the hills. He makes no delay in hunting, his face glows like a God and he delights to do his work." Even today, the Pharaoh Hound is noted for "blushing": the tendency of its nose and ears to flush with blood and "glow" when the dog is excited. The breed is one of several with a legitimate claim of most-ancient breed and appears to have changed little in the last 3,000 years. It bears an uncanny resemblance to the jackal god Anubis and to dogs depicted on the tombs of the Egyptian pharaohs, and later, dogs featured in ancient Greek art. Phoenician traders may have introduced the dogs from Greece and North Africa

ILLUSTRATED STANDARD

1 Flesh-covered nose
2 Amber-colored eyes
3 Slight stop
4 Long, chiseled head
5 Large ears, carried erect when alert
6 Whip-like tail

Color: tan or chestnut, with a white tail-tip desired

DQ: any solid white spot on the back of neck, shoulder, or any part of the back or sides

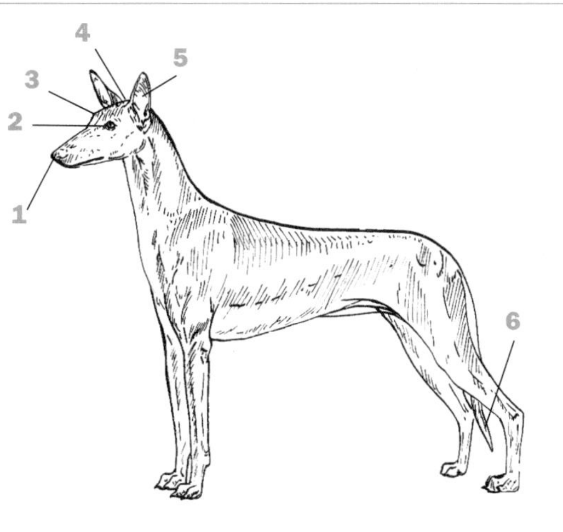

to the islands of Malta and Gozo, where they became essentially secluded from the rest of the world. Here they flourished as rabbit dogs, or Kelb-tal Fenek. Several hounds would be released (often at night) to find the scent of a rabbit; they would bark once the rabbit went to ground (usually in a stone wall or rocky crevice). A belled ferret would then be sent after the rabbit, and one hound would follow its progress by sound, until the rabbit was flushed and caught by the dog. The Pharaoh Hound is now the National Dog of Malta. In the 1960s, the breed was rediscovered and imported to England and later America. The AKC recognized it in 1983.

TEMPERAMENT

The svelte Pharaoh Hound is more than a gracious addition to the home (though it surely is that)—it is a keen hunter and an exuberant chaser. Although it is calm indoors, it loves to run. It is sensitive, loving, gentle, and good with children and other dogs, but it may chase strange animals. It tends to be reserved with strangers; some are even timid. It is independent but willing to please. The breed has the unique characteristic of "blushing" when excited, with the nose and ears turning a rosy color.

UPKEEP

The Pharaoh Hound relishes the opportunity to stretch its legs in a safe area, although it can manage with long daily walks on leash and occasional sprints. It needs soft bedding and warmth. Its coat is low maintenance, requiring only occasional brushing to remove dead hair.

HEALTH

- Major concerns: none
- Minor concerns: none
- Occasionally seen: patellar luxation, CHD, hypothyroidism
- Suggested tests: (hip, (knee), (thyroid)
- Life span: 11–14 years
- Note: sensitive to barbiturate anesthesia

FORM AND FUNCTION

Although considered a sighthound in America, the Pharaoh Hound hunts by both sight and scent—as well as hearing. It has an unexaggerated greyhound-like build, combining grace, power, and speed, enabling it to run nimbly along rocky walls and ground. It has a good nose. Its large, mobile ears help it follow animals underground. Slightly longer than tall, its gait is free and flowing, with head held high. The coat is short and glossy.

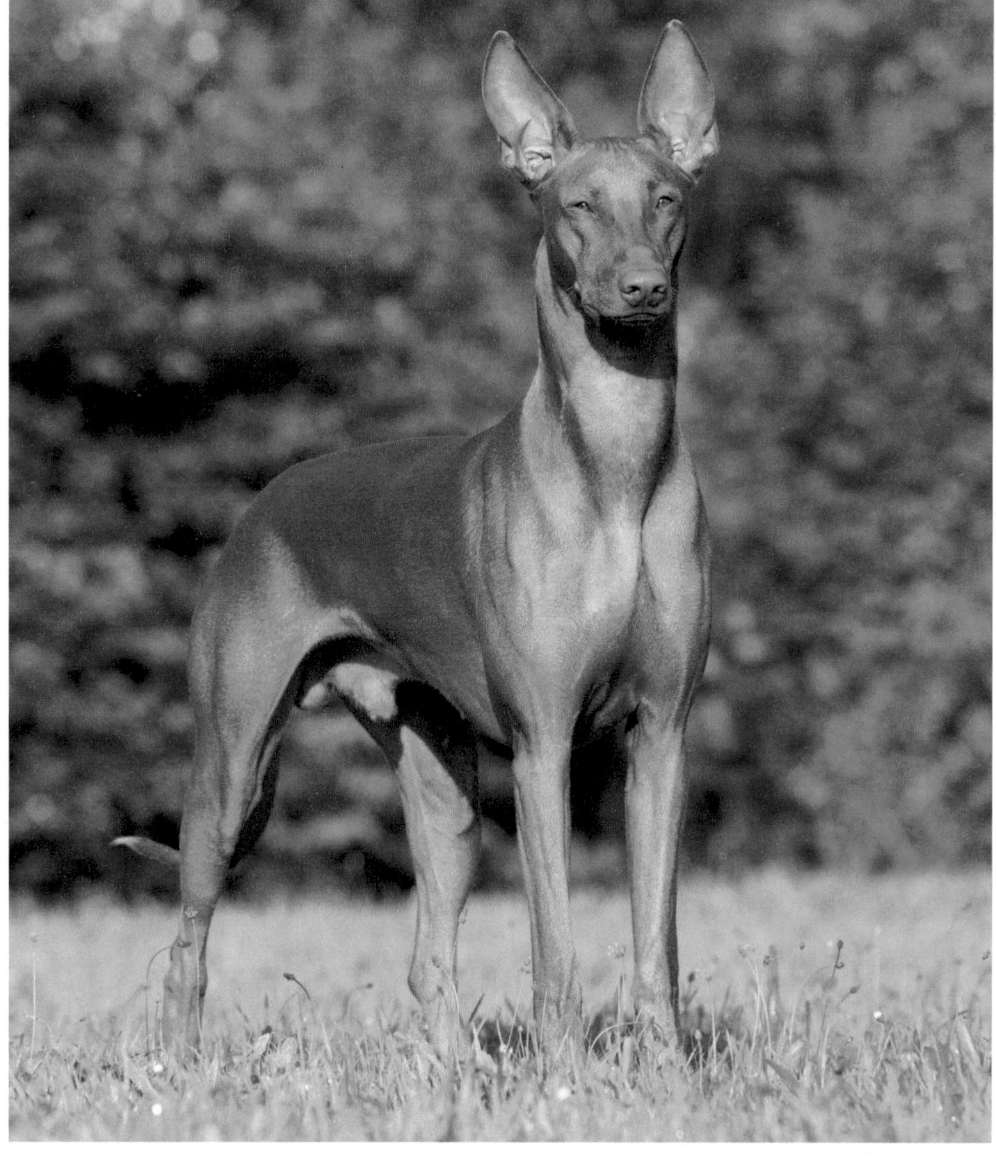

Plott

AT A GLANCE

Energy level:	■ ■ ■	Protection ability:	■ ■ ■ ■
Exercise requirements:	■ ■ ■	Grooming requirements:	■
Playfulness:	■ ■ ■	Cold tolerance:	■ ■ ■
Affection level:	■ ■ ■	Heat tolerance:	■ ■ ■
Friendliness toward dogs:	■ ■		
Friendliness toward other pets:	■ ■		
Friendliness toward strangers:	■ ■		
Ease of training:	■ ■		
Watchdog ability:	■ ■ ■ ■		

WEIGHT: male: 50–60 lb; female: 40–55 lb (UKC: male: 50–75 lb; female: 40–65 lb)
HEIGHT: male: 20–25″; female: 20–23″ (UKC: male: 22–27″; female: 21–25″)

POPULARITY: Rare
FAMILY: Scenthound
AREA OF ORIGIN: United States
DATE OF ORIGIN: 1750
ORIGINAL FUNCTION: Cold trailing, bear hunting
TODAY'S FUNCTION: Cold trailing; bear, boar, and raccoon hunting; nite hunts
OTHER NAME: Plott Hound

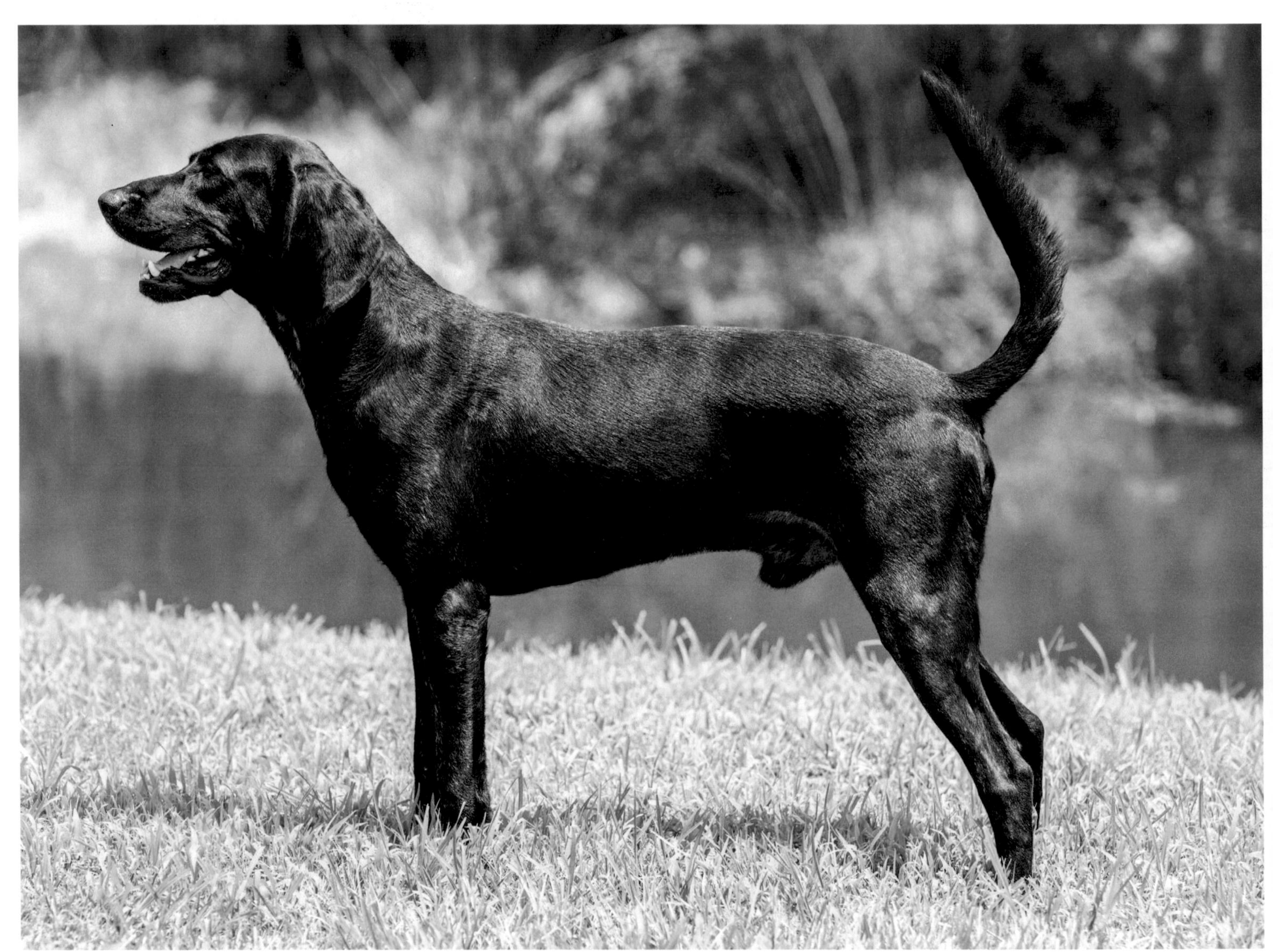

HISTORY

Now the official state dog of North Carolina, the Plott's roots spring from Germany, where Hanoverian Schweisshunds were valued for their ability to hunt wild boars and track wounded game even over week-old trails. In 1750, 16-year-old Joahnnes Georg Plott brought five of these dogs with him to his new home in the Great Smoky Mountains. Although there were no wild boars there at the time, the dogs and their descendents proved themselves to be great cold trailers of large animals, especially bear. They didn't just find bear, but could hold at bay or even bring down a 500-pound bear. The Plott family bred their line of cold-trailing brindle dogs for seven generations, the dogs distributing across the Smoky Mountains as their family grew. Other

ILLUSTRATED STANDARD

1 Eyes prominent, not drooping
2 Moderately high-set ears of medium length
3 Erect pasterns
4 Slightly higher at withers than at hips
5 Loin slightly arched
6 Cat feet
7 Rather long, saber-like tail

Color: any shade of brindle, including blue; solid black, brindle with black saddle, black with brindle trim, buckskin; some white permissible on chest or feet only.
DQ: length of ear extending beyond tip of nose or hanging bloodhound-like; splayed feet

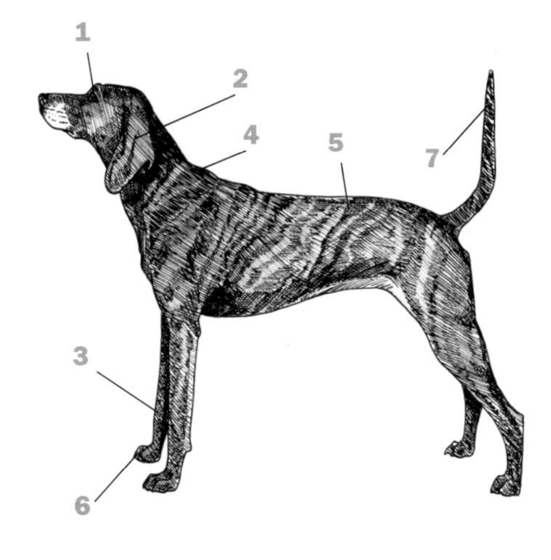

mountain men incorporated the Plott blood into their own lines of dogs, but stories disagree as to the extent, if any, other strains were introduced to the Plotts. Some maintain an early cross with a "leopard-spotted bear dog," and others claim crosses to cur dogs for better treeing ability. It was not until the early 1900s that documented crosses with other lines were made to improve the Plott strain. At that time Gola Ferguson crossed his Plotts with a strain of black-saddled hounds known as Blevins or Great Smokies, producing "Tige" and "Boss," two hounds of such talent that even the Plott family incorporated their blood back into their line. This introduced the black-saddled brindle pattern into the breed. Almost all Plotts can be traced back to one of these dogs. Although used primarily for bear, boar, and mountain lions, many Plotts were also adept at treeing raccoons, and coonhunters—far more populous than bear hunters—found them ideal for their needs. In 1946 the breed finally received the official name of Plott Hound when it was recognized by the UKC. It is the only UKC coonhound breed that doesn't trace back to foxhounds. In 1989 it was designated the official state dog of North Carolina. In 2006 the AKC admitted the Plott into the Hound Group.

TEMPERAMENT

Bred for generations as a bear and coon dog, the Plott's first nature is to sniff up a cold trail and follow it to the end. Yet the Plott makes the transition to family dog with ease, being eager to please and loyal. This is an extremely courageous breed, and, as befitting any good hound, it can be headstrong. Plotts can be wary of strangers, but generally warm up quickly. They are not as gregarious with other dogs as some hounds, and true to their bear hunting heritage, can be ferocious fighters if pushed. They may tree the family cat!

UPKEEP

Plotts are easy keepers, but must have a securely fenced yard. They need canine or human companionship, and an opportunity to hunt or at least go for some woodland hikes. They enjoy swimming. Coat care is minimal.

HEALTH

- Major concerns: none
- Minor concerns: none
- Occasionally seen: CHD
- Suggested tests: (hip)
- Life span: 11–13 years

FORM AND FUNCTION

The Plott is a no-frills dog built to follow cold trails at speed over rough terrain and through water in all weather, and to grapple with large animals, including bear, once cornered. It is streamlined and agile, yet powerful with great endurance. The hair is short to medium in length, fine to medium coarse in texture. When trailing, the Plott is bold and confident, not backing down from a challenge. Its voice is open and unrestricted, with a loud bugle-like chop or bawl.

Portuguese Podengo Pequeno

AT A GLANCE

Energy level:	■■■■
Exercise requirements:	■■■
Playfulness:	■■■■
Affection level:	■■■
Friendliness toward dogs:	■■■■■
Friendliness toward other pets:	■■■■
Friendliness toward strangers:	■■■■
Ease of training:	■■

Watchdog ability:	■■■■■
Protection ability:	■■
Grooming requirements:	■■
Cold tolerance:	■■■
Heat tolerance:	■■■■

WEIGHT: 9–13 lb
HEIGHT: 8–12″

POPULARITY: Very rare
FAMILY: Primitive
AREA OF ORIGIN: Portugal
DATE OF ORIGIN: Ancient
ORIGINAL FUNCTION: Hunting rabbits
TODAY'S FUNCTION: Hunting rabbits, lure coursing
OTHER NAME: Portuguese Warren Hound

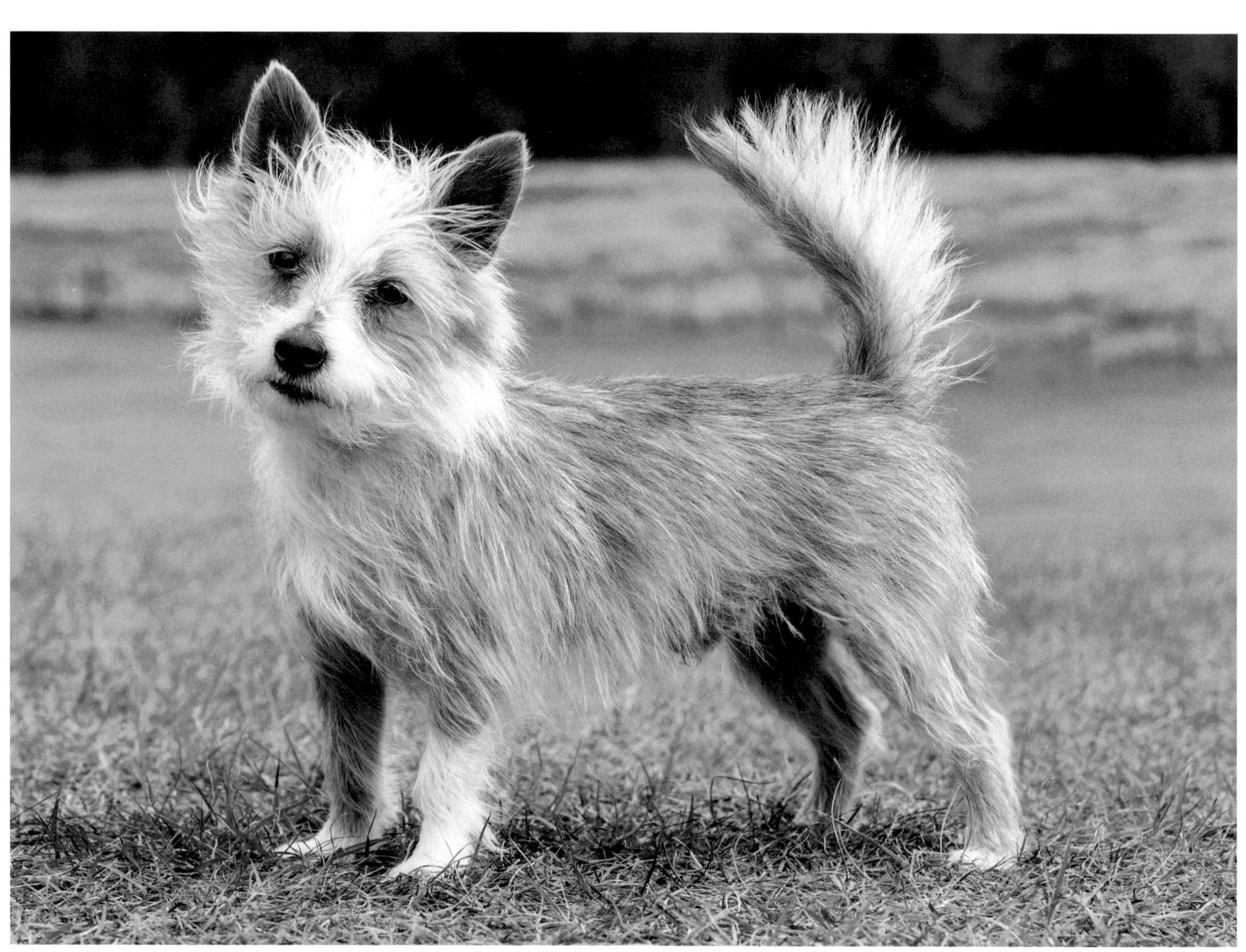

HISTORY

The Portuguese Podengo Pequeno (pronounced peh-KEN-oo) is the smallest of three Portuguese Podengo breeds, the other two being the Medio and Grande. Their ancestors were brought by the ancient Romans and Phoenicians to the Iberian Peninsula over 2,000 years ago. Different sized dogs gradually became specialized to hunt different sized prey, with the smallest dogs hunting rabbits for their peasant owners. Although the original dogs had smooth coats, ideal in Portugal's wet north, wiry coats flourished in hot, dry southern Portugal where brambles were particularly abundant. "Podengo" has been used at least since the 16th century to mean any pack hunting dog. The dogs hunt together using first their sense of scent, then hearing, to locate and flush rabbits

ILLUSTRATED STANDARD

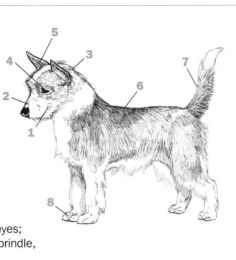

1 Wedge-shaped head
2 Pointed muzzle; shorter than backskull
3 Prominent occiput
4 Small, almond-shaped eyes
5 Ears obliquely set in line with eyes; pointed; longer than base width
6 Level topline
7 Tail medium, high-set, and of medium length, reaching hock; carried horizontal or above and curved when in motion
8 Oval feet

Color: yellow or fawn of any shade, either solid
DQ: aggressive or overly shy; different colored eyes; undershot or overshot; folded or hanging ears; brindle, black and tan, tricolor, or solid white

from crevices and dense undergrowth. They are said to use their hearing to hone in on game by calling to each other with a single yip (called the Maticar, or cry of the kill) as they surround it. Because the peasants often had only sticks, the dogs often had to chase, kill, and retrieve the rabbit as well. Podengos were also adept ratters, and they accompanied Portuguese ships to keep vermin down—possibly spreading them to other ports. The Podengo is one of the 10 National Dogs of Portugal and is the symbol of the Portuguese Kennel Club. It is considered an integral part of the Portuguese people's survival through the centuries and is still widely used for hunting today. The first smooth Pequeno came to the United States in 1995, and the first wire in 2001. It joined the AKC Hound Group in 2013, where it is labeled as a sighthound.

TEMPERAMENT

Pequenos are active, independent dogs that love to explore and hunt. While they are affectionate they are not lap dogs, preferring adventure to cuddling. As with most primitive breeds, they aren't great obedience dogs, but they do aim to please. They are friendly toward strangers, other dogs, and usually, other pets. They are good watchdogs but ineffective protectors.

UPKEEP

Podengos are active, little dogs and need a good walk or jog daily, plus a chance to run and explore weekly. Given adequate exercise they are good housedogs, but relaxation is not their favorite thing. They enjoy activities like agility and lure coursing. The Podengo should have a rustic look, so trimming isn't desired. Even the wire coat needs only weekly brushing. Long hairs around the eyes, particularly in the corners, should be gently plucked. Some breeders also suggest plucking any hair within the ears.

HEALTH

- Major concerns: none
- Minor concerns: none
- Occasionally seen: Legg Calves, patellar luxation
- Suggested tests: none
- Life span: 12–15 years

FORM AND FUNCTION

This is a breed of moderation, a rustic dog that should always look natural. It is small enough to push through brambles and flush rabbits, but it is not a go-to-ground breed. It hunts by scent first, hearing second, and sight third. The coat may be smooth, which is short and very dense; or wire, which is long and harsh but not as dense as the smooth coat. Neither has an undercoat. The Pequeno is 20 percent longer than tall. Its movement is light and agile.

Redbone Coonhound

AT A GLANCE

Energy level:	■■■	Watchdog ability:	■■■	POPULARITY: Rare
Exercise requirements:	■■■	Protection ability:	■■	FAMILY: Scenthound
Playfulness:	■■■	Grooming requirements:	■	AREA OF ORIGIN: United States
Affection level:	■■■■	Cold tolerance:	■■	DATE OF ORIGIN: 1800s
Friendliness toward dogs:	■■■■	Heat tolerance:	■■■	ORIGINAL FUNCTION: Racoon hunting
Friendliness toward other pets:	■■			TODAY'S FUNCTION: Racoon hunting, nite hunts
Friendliness toward strangers:	■■■	WEIGHT: 45–65 lb*		
Ease of training:	■■	HEIGHT: male: 22–27″; female: 21–26″		OTHER NAME: Redbone Hound

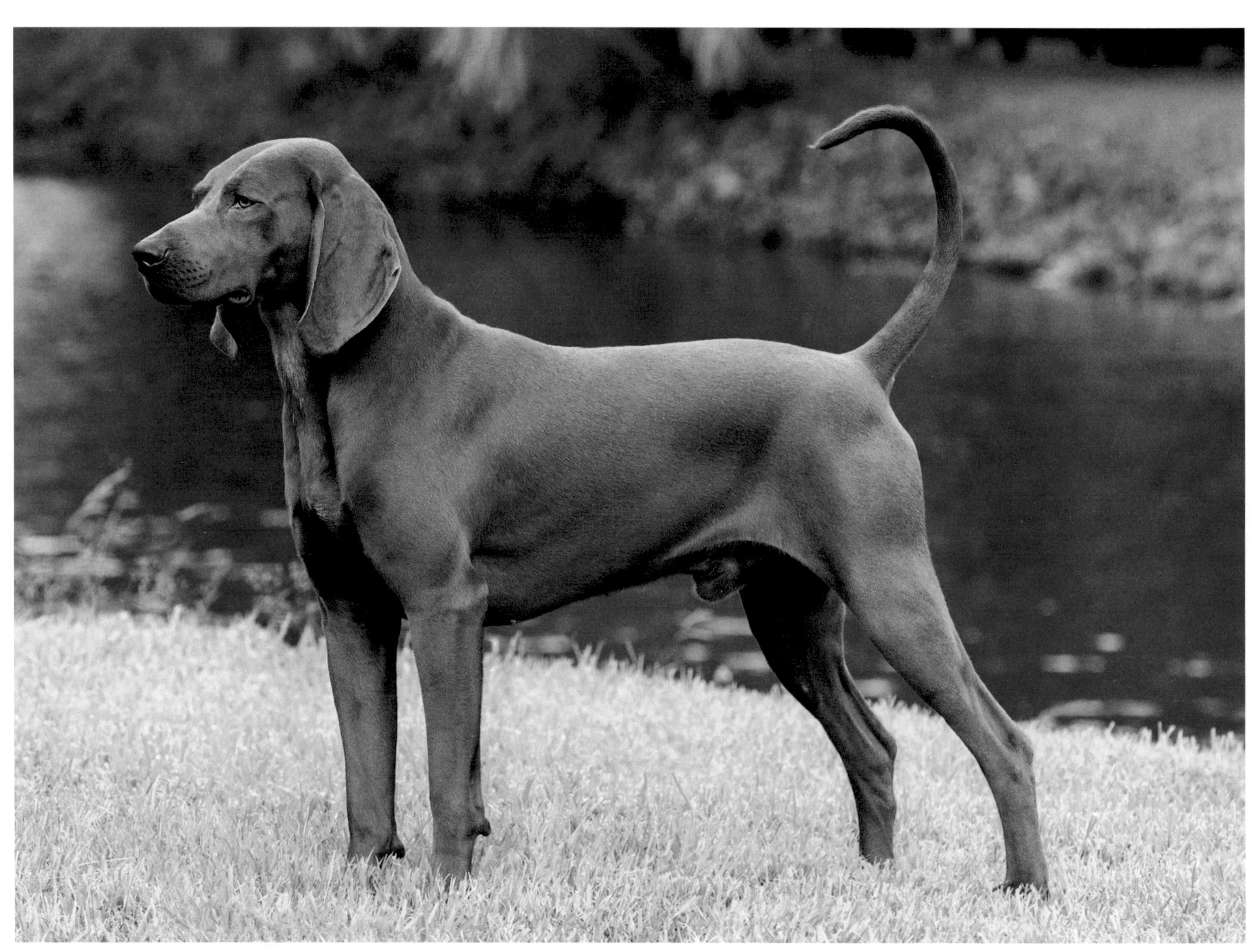

HISTORY

Like most coonhounds, the Redbone derives from foxhound ancestors. Scottish immigrants brought red foxhounds to America in the late 1700s, and they may have formed the basis of the breed. The breed's development was heavily influenced by George Birdsong, a hunter from Georgia, who began with a pack he obtained in the 1840s. As more coonhunters became interested in the breed, they set about to create a faster, hotter-nosed dog that was even quicker to locate and tree raccoons. They crossed the existing dogs with later imports of hot, swift Red Irish Foxhounds. These early dogs were sometimes called Saddlebacks because they tended to be red with black saddles. However, in an unusual choice of priorities for coonhunters, breeders emphasized color

ILLUSTRATED STANDARD

1 Pleading expression
2 Round eyes, not drooping
3 Fine, moderately low-set ears
4 Slightly taller at withers than at hips
5 Loin slightly arched
6 Medium-length saber-like tail
7 Straight pasterns
8 Cat feet

Color: solid red preferred; dark muzzle and small amount of white on brisket and feet permissible

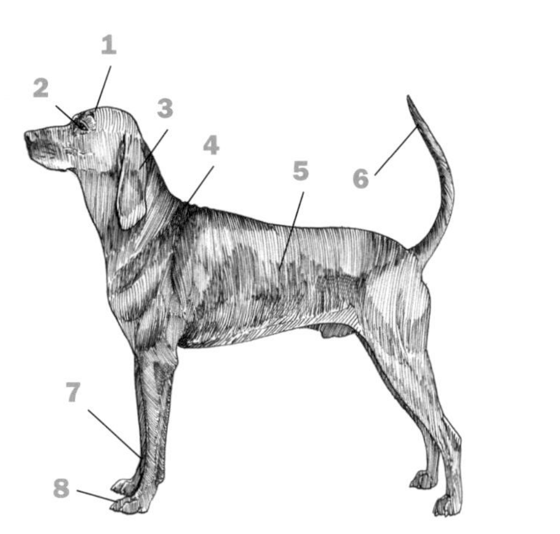

for several generations, preferring the solid-colored red dogs. The black saddle was bred out and the breed became known as Redbone Coonhounds, either in recognition of its color or after Peter Redbone, a Tennessee promoter of the breed. In 1902 the Redbone became the second coonhound breed recognized by the UKC. Over 100 years later, in 2010, it became a regular AKC breed. The Redbone remains a favorite of serious hunters who want a versatile hunter with uncanny treeing ability.

TEMPERAMENT

Redbones are generally easygoing, gentle dogs that don't let much bother them. They want to be with their people, but aren't clingy or "in your face." Redbones are eager to please but can become bored with formal training. They are active when on the hunt, but quiet inside. Their passion is hunting, and once the nose hits a scent they are oblivious to much else. Redbones get along well with people, children, and dogs, but may or may not do well with small pets.

UPKEEP

Because they are driven to follow their nose as fast as they can, care must be taken to exercise Redbones in safe, fenced areas. They do well with a daily walk or jog, and enjoy swimming. Although traditionally kept as an outdoor dog, Redbones are very family oriented and make good inside dogs. Some tend to drool. They have a loud, melodious voice when trailing or exited. Coat care consists of weekly brushing.

HEALTH

- Major concerns: none
- Minor concerns: none
- Occasionally seen: none
- Suggested tests: (hip)
- Life span: 12–14 years

FORM AND FUNCTION

The Redbone is a versatile hunter that specializes in treeing raccoons, but also excels in trailing and treeing bear, cougar, and bobcat. It's both fast and agile, able to tirelessly traverse swamplands through rocky hills, and even swim through water at a fast pace. It can follow a cold trail and has a sweet voice on the trail. The coat is short and smooth but coarse enough to provide protection.

Rhodesian Ridgeback

AT A GLANCE

Energy level:	■ ■ ■
Exercise requirements:	■ ■ ■
Playfulness:	■ ■ ■
Affection level:	■ ■ ■
Friendliness toward dogs:	■ ■
Friendliness toward other pets:	■ ■ ■
Friendliness toward strangers:	■
Ease of training:	■ ■ ■

Watchdog ability:	■ ■ ■ ■
Protection ability:	■ ■ ■ ■
Grooming requirements:	■
Cold tolerance:	■ ■ ■
Heat tolerance:	■ ■ ■

WEIGHT: male: 85 lb; female: 70 lb
HEIGHT: male: 25–27″; female: 24–26″

POPULARITY: Popular
FAMILY: Sighthound, Scenthound
AREA OF ORIGIN: South Africa
DATE OF ORIGIN: 1800s
ORIGINAL FUNCTION: Large game (including lion) hunting, guardian
TODAY'S FUNCTION: Lure coursing
OTHER NAME: African Lion Hound

HISTORY

When European Boer settlers arrived in South Africa in the sixteenth and seventeenth centuries, they brought with them such breeds as the Mastiff, Great Dane, Bloodhound, Pointer, Staghound, and Greyhound, among others. These settlers needed a dog that could withstand both hot and cold temperatures, limited water, and rough bush, while performing the duties of guard dog and hunting dog. By breeding their European dogs with native Hottentot tribal hunting dogs (which were distinguished by a ridge of hair growing in the opposite direction along the top of their back) they produced just such a dog. These dogs hunted by both sight and scent and were devoted protectors of the entire family. In the 1870s, several of these dogs were taken to Rhodesia to hunt lions, tracking them and then keep-

ILLUSTRATED STANDARD

1 Round eyes
2 Flat skull, rather broad between ears
3 High-set ears of medium size
4 Ridge on back extending from just behind shoulders to hips, with two symmetrical whorls at top
5 Tapering tail, carried with a slight curve
6 Feet compact

Color: light wheaten to red wheaten; nose can be black, brown, or liver
DQ: ridgelessness

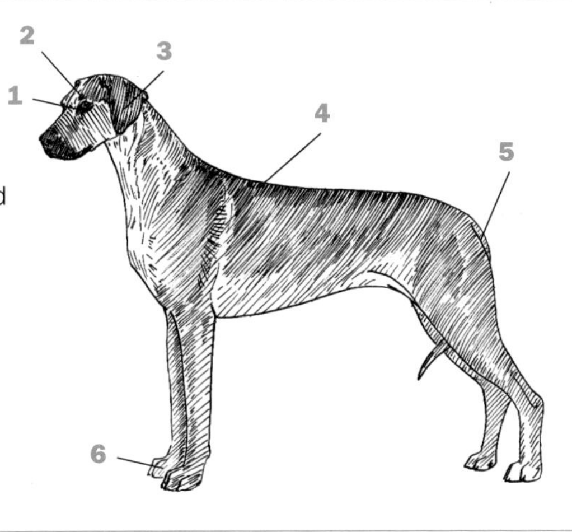

ing them at bay. The "lion dogs" were so successful that they soon became popular, their distinctive ridge becoming a trademark of quality. By the 1920s, so many different types of ridged Lion Dogs existed in Rhodesia that a meeting was held to elucidate the most desirable points of the breed, which became the basis for the current standard. Dogs meeting the standard criteria were known as Rhodesian Ridgebacks (the dogs' former designation as Lion Dogs was deemed to sound too savage). The breed was introduced into England in the 1930s and to America soon after. In both cases, it gained recognition in the 1950s and quickly attracted admirers. In the 1980s, the breed received recognition as a sighthound and became eligible to compete in sighthound field trials. Today it is among the more popular hounds, undoubtedly because it combines the abilities of hunter, protector, and companion in a sleek handsome body.

TEMPERAMENT

The Rhodesian Ridgeback is the Hound Group's answer to a somewhat protective dog. Not only is it a keen and versatile hunter, but it is a loyal guardian. It is good with children, especially protective of those in its family, but it is sometimes overly boisterous in play for small children. It is strong-willed and powerful; some can become domineering. It is reserved with strangers. It does well around other dogs, although males can have dominance disputes. Ridgebacks are good with cats if they are raised with them.

UPKEEP

The Ridgeback loves to run, and it needs daily mental and physical exercise to keep it from becoming bored. It can be a good jogging or hiking companion. Coat care is minimal, consisting only of occasional brushing to remove dead hair.

HEALTH

- Major concerns: none
- Minor concerns: CHD, hypothyroidism, elbow dysplasia
- Occasionally seen: deafness, dermoid sinus
- Suggested tests: hip, elbow, thyroid, dermoid sinus (as puppy)
- Life span: 10–12 years

FORM AND FUNCTION

Slightly longer than tall, the Ridgeback combines features of speed, power, and endurance. The Rhodesian Ridgeback must have an athletic build to enable it to bring down wounded game. This physique also allows them to succeed in current performance events. Its stride is efficient and long. The short glossy coat is adapted for living in hot climates. A distinctive feature is the clearly defined ridge, which should start with two identical whorls just behind the shoulders and taper to the prominence of the hipbones.

Saluki

AT A GLANCE

Energy level: ■■
Exercise requirements: ■■■
Playfulness: ■■■
Affection level: ■■■
Friendliness toward dogs: ■■■
Friendliness toward other pets: ■■■
Friendliness toward strangers: ■
Ease of training: ■■■
Watchdog ability: ■■■

Protection ability: ■■
Grooming requirements:
  Smooth: ■
  Feathered: ■■
Cold tolerance: ■■
Heat tolerance: ■■■

WEIGHT: 35–65 lb
HEIGHT: male: 23–28″; female: may be considerably smaller

POPULARITY: Uncommon
FAMILY: Sighthound
AREA OF ORIGIN: Middle East
DATE OF ORIGIN: Ancient times
ORIGINAL FUNCTION: Coursing hare and gazelles
TODAY'S FUNCTION: Lure coursing, open-field coursing
OTHER NAME: Gazelle Hound, Persian Greyhound, Tazi

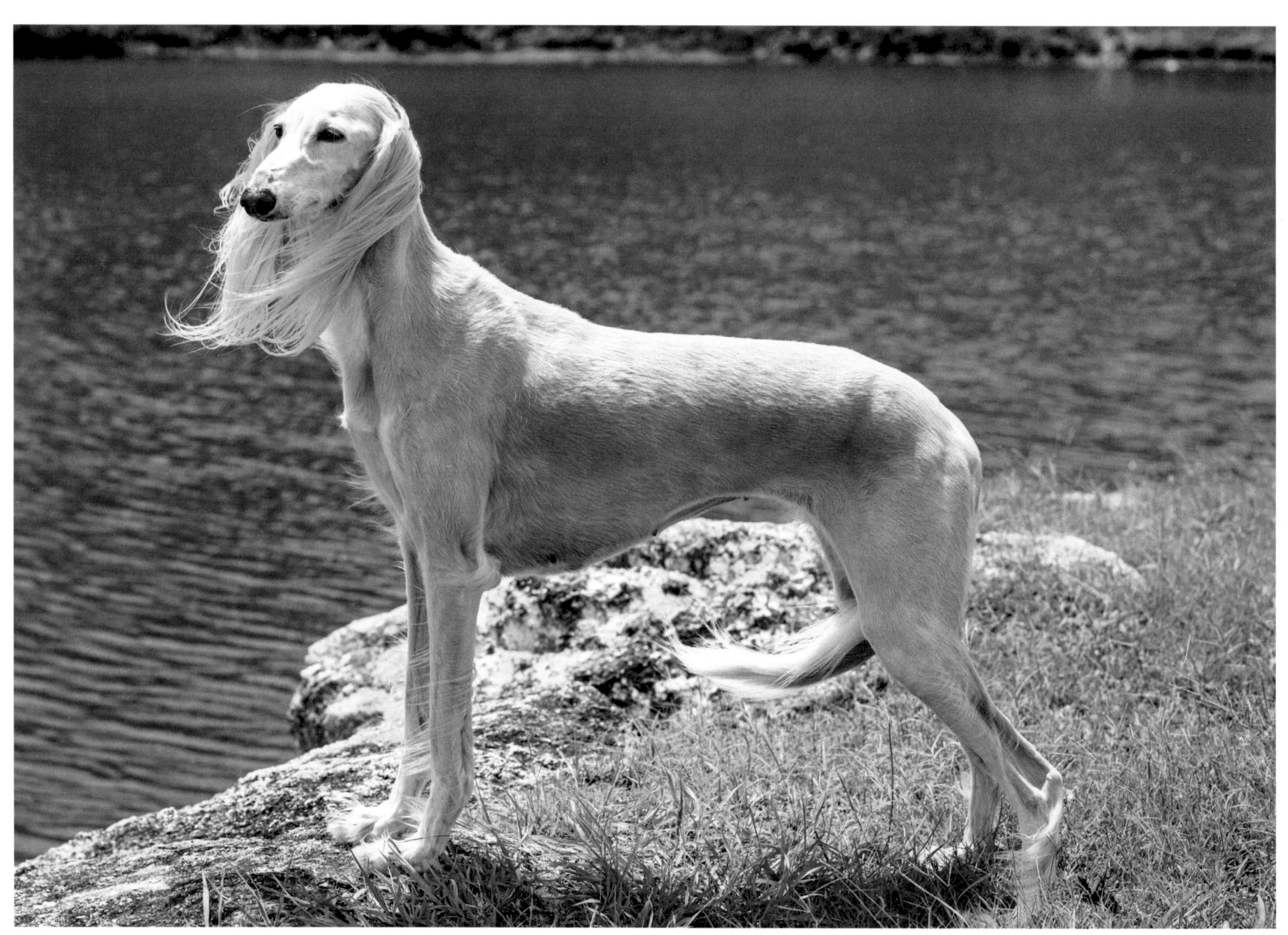

HISTORY

The Saluki is one of the most ancient breeds of domestic dog. Evidence of the Saluki can be found on Egyptian tombs dating several thousand years B.C. The name Saluki may come from the ancient civilization of Seleucia. Arab nomads used Salukis to run down gazelles, foxes, and hares in the desert, often with the aid of falcons. Although the Muslim religion considered the dog to be unclean, an exception was made for the Saluki, which was referred to as el hor, the noble one. As the provider of meat, the Saluki was allowed to sleep in the tents and enjoy the tender attention of its Bedouin master. Salukis were not allowed to breed with non-Salukis, accounting for their purity throughout the centuries. Because they ranged with their nomadic owners over a wide area of the Middle

ILLUSTRATED STANDARD

1 Stop not pronounced
2 Large, oval eyes
3 Long, narrow head, moderately wide backskull
4 Slightly arched loin
5 Long tail, well feathered underneath*
6 Deep, moderately narrow chest
7 Long toes, well feathered between them*
8 Long legs

Color: white, cream, fawn, golden, red, grizzle, black and tan, tricolor, or any of these on a white background
DQ: none

*no feathering appears in smooth variety

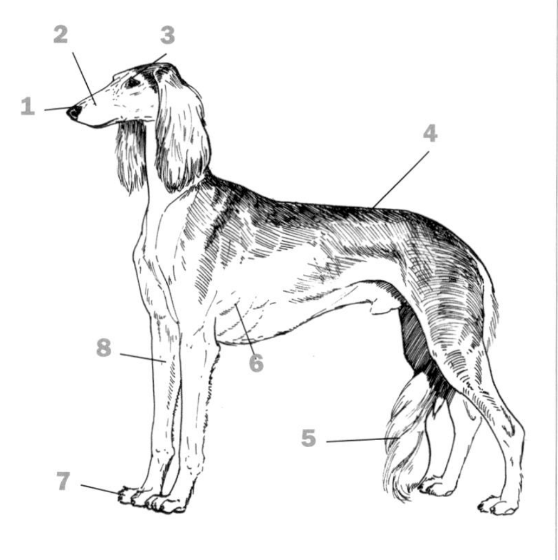

East, Salukis became widely distributed with great local variation, resulting in the breed's variability today. The Saluki came to the attention of the Western world around 1900 and was recognized by the AKC in 1928. Their numbers have decreased in the lands of their origin as a result of the advent of hunting with guns from jeeps and more recently, war. The Arabian Saluki Center in Dubai is working to protect the Saluki in its native lands. The primary role of the Saluki today is as an exotic companion and show dog, although many are still used for coursing and racing. They are one of the most successful breeds in open field coursing of jackrabbits.

TEMPERAMENT

The Saluki tends to be aloof and reserved with strangers. It is extremely devoted to its own family, but it is not particularly demonstrative. The Saluki is very gentle with children, but it may not be playful enough to satisfy most children. The Saluki is extremely sensitive and does not take to rough and tumble play or deal well with harsh corrections. Some can be shy. It is very quiet and sedate inside, seeking out a soft warm spot. Outside, it runs in great circles at tremendous speeds and will chase any small running animals or fast-moving objects. It may not come when called.

UPKEEP

Daily exercise is essential, preferably in the form of free-running in a safe enclosed area. Its needs can also be met with long leash walks or jogging. The Saluki must have a soft bed. A Saluki in proper weight is naturally thin, but many tend to be picky eaters, which can result in a very thin-looking dog. The smooth coat needs only occasional brushing to remove dead hair, but the longer feathering needs combing once or twice a week to prevent matting. Neutered or spayed feathered Salukis often grow a long coat over their entire body.

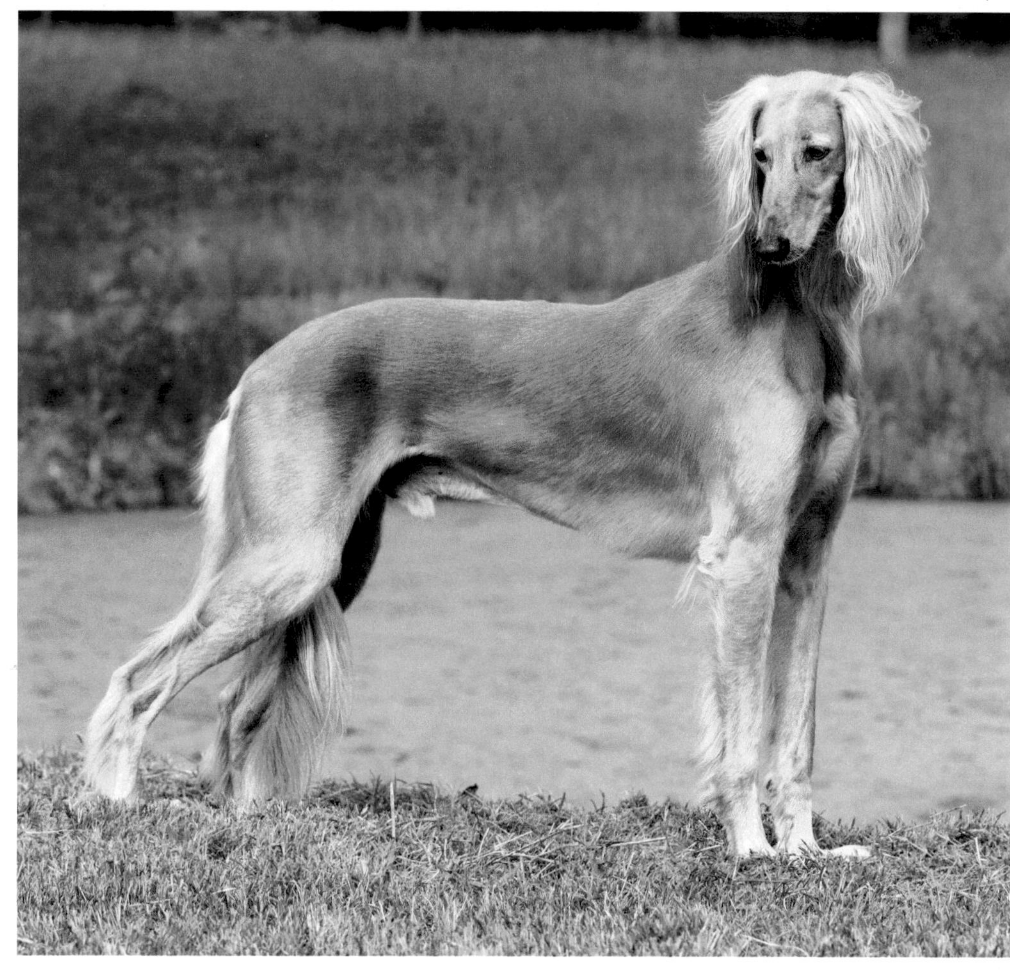

HEALTH

- Major concerns: hemangiosarcoma
- Minor concerns: cardiomyopathy
- Occasionally seen: hypothyroidism
- Suggested tests: cardiac, thyroid
- Life span: 12–14 years
- Note: sensitive to barbiturate anesthesia

FORM AND FUNCTION

The Saluki has a general greyhound-like build and should combine the aspects of grace, symmetry, great speed, and endurance coupled with strength to enable it to kill gazelle or other quarry over deep sand or rocky mountains. The expression should be dignified and gentle with deep, faithful, far-seeing eyes. Its movement is light. The coat is smooth and silky; the feathered variety has long hair on ears, tail, between its toes, and sometimes on the backs of its legs; the smooth variety has no long feathering. This breed has a wide range of equally acceptable types, reflecting the wide area over which it was developed.

Scottish Deerhound

AT A GLANCE

Energy level:	■ ■
Exercise requirements:	■ ■ ■
Playfulness:	■ ■
Affection level:	■ ■ ■
Friendliness toward dogs:	■ ■ ■ ■
Friendliness toward other pets:	■ ■ ■
Friendliness toward strangers:	■ ■ ■
Ease of training:	■ ■

Watchdog ability:	■
Protection ability:	■ ■
Grooming requirements:	■ ■ ■
Cold tolerance:	■ ■ ■
Heat tolerance:	■ ■

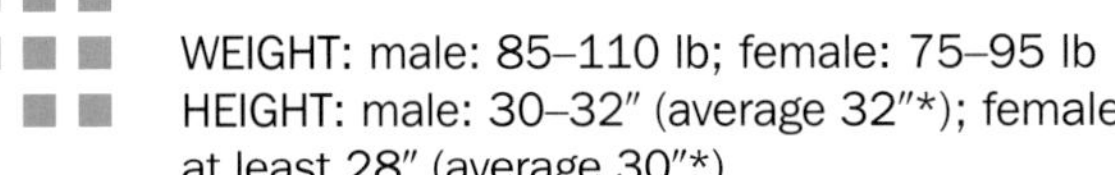

WEIGHT: male: 85–110 lb; female: 75–95 lb
HEIGHT: male: 30–32″ (average 32″*); female: at least 28″ (average 30″*)

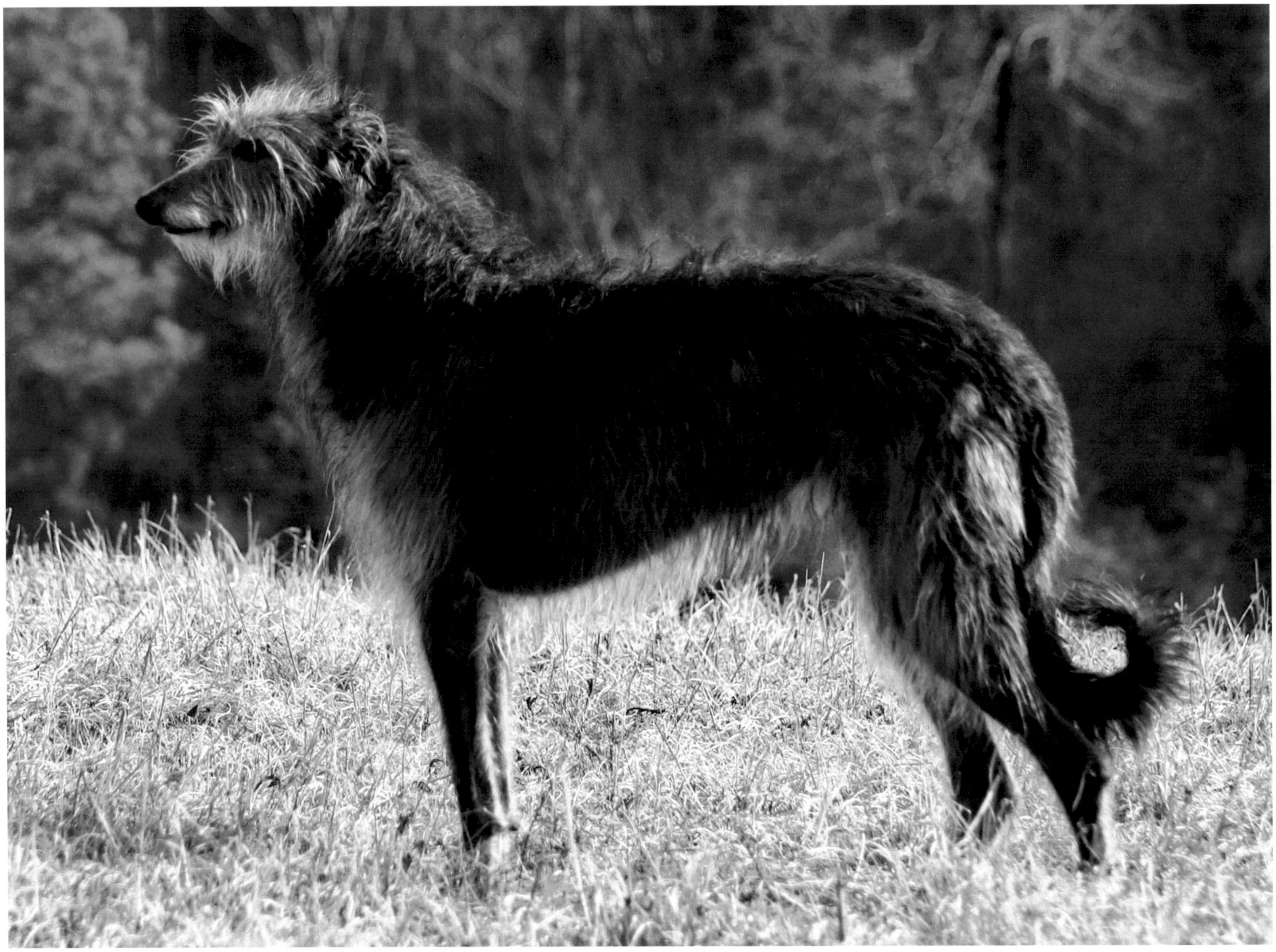

POPULARITY: Very rare
FAMILY: Sighthound
AREA OF ORIGIN: Scotland
DATE OF ORIGIN: Middle Ages
ORIGINAL FUNCTION: Coursing stag
TODAY'S FUNCTION: Lure coursing
OTHER NAME: Deerhound

HISTORY

Among the most aristocratic of breeds, the Scottish Deerhound has been valued by nobility for its prowess in running down deer at least since the sixteenth century. Confusion regarding names makes tracing its exact history before that time difficult, but it probably is a very ancient breed, deriving from ancestral Greyhound roots. Like its smooth-coated Greyhound relative, the rough-coated Deerhound could not be owned by anyone ranked lower than an Earl during the Age of Chivalry. As the stag population declined in England, the larger, rough-coated dogs suited for hunting stag became concentrated where the stag remained plentiful—namely, the Scottish Highlands—where they were valued and hoarded by Highland chieftains. This hoarding resulted in the

ILLUSTRATED STANDARD

1 Good mustache and beard of silky hair
2 Long head with flat skull
3 Small, folded ears, dark in color
4 Arched loin drooping to the tail
5 Wide, drooping hindquarters
6 Long, tapering tail
7 Deep chest
8 Compact feet

Color: all shades of gray and gray brindle, with dark blue-gray preferred; yellow, red, and fawn are permitted but not seen today
DQ: white blaze on head, or a white collar

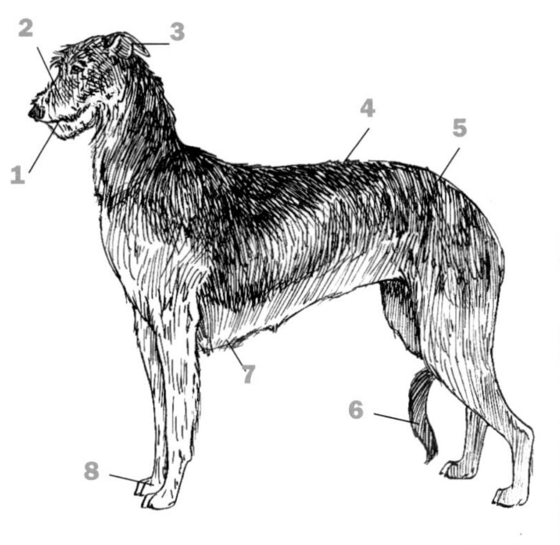

decline of the breed in the mid 1700s following the collapse of the clan system of Culloden. Further decline occurred with the advent of breech-loading rifles in the 1800s because hunting deer with guns supplanted coursing in popularity. By the mid 1800s, however, a concerted effort to restore the breed had proved successful, and although its numbers were never great, the quality of the dogs was high. The first Deerhound club was formed in England in the 1860s, around the same time the first Deerhounds were exhibited in dog shows. The First World War again decimated the breed's numbers because most of the dogs had been the property of a limited number of large estates, most of which did not survive the war intact. Since then, the Deerhound has remained low in number but high in quality, a classic in every sense.

TEMPERAMENT

The Scottish Deerhound is mellow, low-key, and easygoing, a gracious and well-mannered addition to the home. Outdoors, it loves to run and chase anything that moves. Indoors, it needs plenty of room to stretch on a soft surface. It is independent but willing to please; it is extremely sensitive. It is amiable toward but often reserved with strangers. It is good with children, other dogs, and usually other pets, although it may give chase to strange animals.

UPKEEP

The Deerhound needs a good amount of daily exercise, either a long walk or a romp in a safe area. Although physically suited to outdoor living in temperate or cool climates, it prefers to live inside with its family and needs human companionship. Regardless, it needs soft bedding to avoid callouses. The crisp coat needs combing one or two times weekly. Some scissoring is optional to neaten up straggling hair, plus minimal stripping around the face and ears.

HEALTH

- Major concerns: gastric torsion, cardiomyopathy, osteosarcoma
- Minor concerns: cystinuria, atopy (allergies)
- Occasionally seen: hypothyroidism, neck pain, factor VII deficiency
- Suggested tests: cardiac, (cystinuria), factor VII
- Life span: 7–9 years
- Note: sensitive to barbiturate anesthesia

FORM AND FUNCTION

The Scottish Deerhound has a body like that of a Greyhound but is of larger size and bone, enabling it to run at great speed using the double-suspension gallop without sacrificing strength and endurance. Its trotting gait is easy and true. The hair is harsh and crisp, about three to four inches long on the body, ideally close lying. Such a coat imparts a weather- (and dirt-) resistant quality, an essential asset in cold, damp climates.

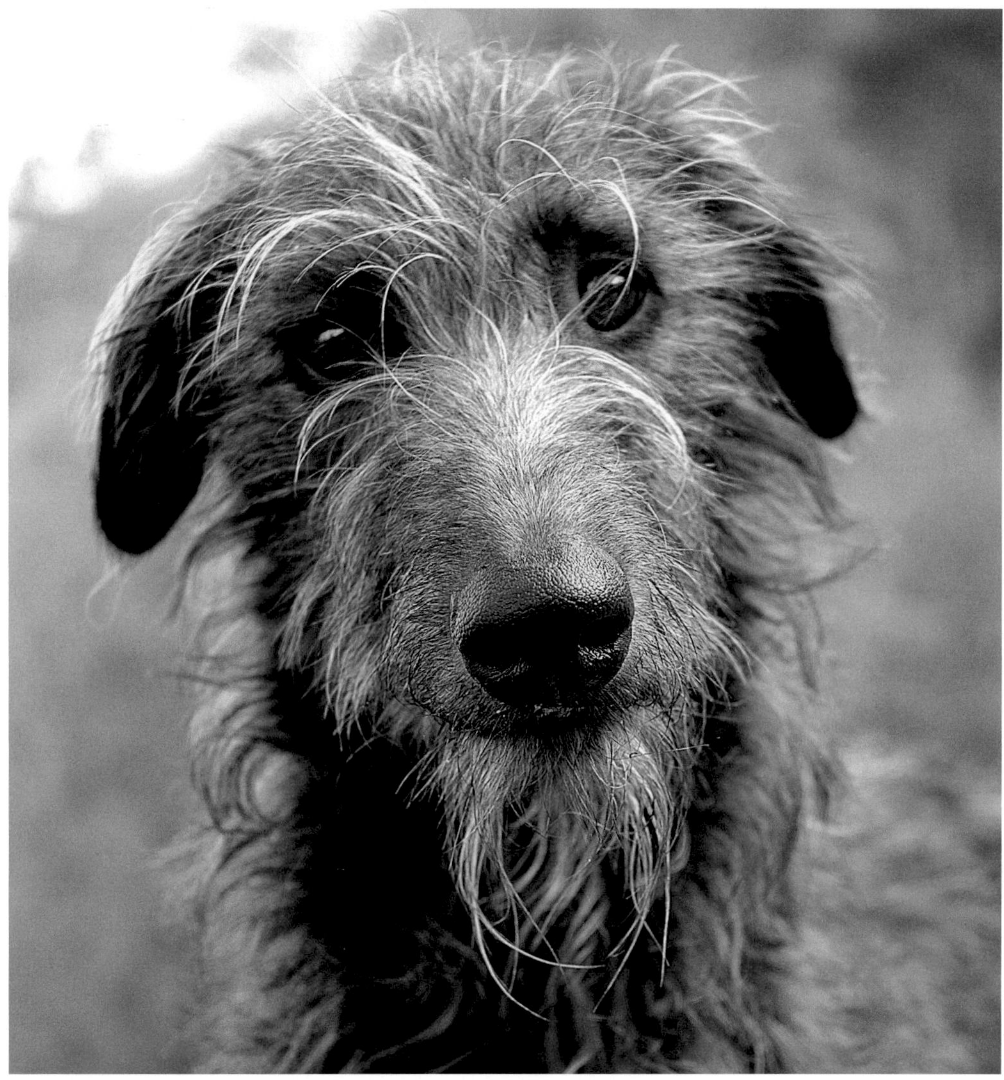

Treeing Walker Coonhound

AT A GLANCE

Energy level:	■■■■	Watchdog ability:	■■■■	POPULARITY: Uncommon
Exercise requirements:	■■■■	Protection ability:	■	FAMILY: Scenthound
Playfulness:	■■■	Grooming requirements:	■	AREA OF ORIGIN: United States
Affection level:	■■■	Cold tolerance:	■■■■	DATE OF ORIGIN: 1800s
Friendliness toward dogs:	■■■■■	Heat tolerance:	■■■	ORIGINAL FUNCTION: Fox hunting
Friendliness toward other pets:	■■■■			TODAY'S FUNCTION: Hunting racoon, bear, and other game; nite hunt competitions
Friendliness toward strangers:	■■■■	WEIGHT: 45–65 lb*		OTHER NAME: None
Ease of training:	■■	HEIGHT: male: 22–27″; female: 20–25″		

HISTORY

In the mid 1800s, Kentucky hunters used Virginia Hounds, descendants of English Foxhounds, to trail deer and gray fox, but these dogs were unsuccessful on the red foxes that began to appear in the region. Cousins John Walker and George Maupin were especially enthusiastic hunters and breeders. In 1850, Maupin was given a dog that a traveler had spotted in the lead of a pack chasing deer. The traveler stole the dog, later known as Tennessee Lead, and gave him to Maupin. Lead was great on red foxes and was bred to several local dogs. Later, his lines were crossed with imports from other states, even Europe, with Walker's sons taking over. By 1900, Walker hounds dominated fox hunting derbies. Walker hounds trailed foxes over ground, but hunters who wanted a dog that trailed quarry such as raccoons,

ILLUSTRATED STANDARD

1 Occipital bone prominent
2 Moderately low-set ears
3 Large eyes, set well apart; soft expression
4 Rather square, medium-length muzzle
5 Medium stop
6 Topline nearly level or sloping slightly from shoulder to rear
7 Tail set moderately high, carried well up and saber-like
8 Cat foot

Color: tri-colored (white, black, and tan) preferred
DQ: none

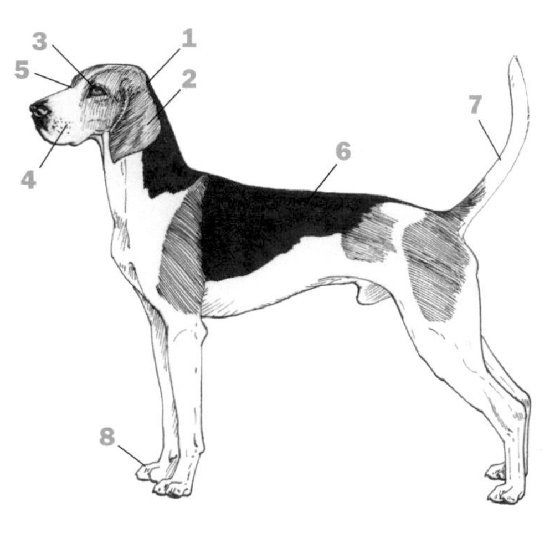

HEALTH

- Major concerns: none
- Minor concerns: none
- Occasionally seen: CHD
- Suggested tests: hip
- Life span: 12–13 years

FORM AND FUNCTION

Called "the people's choice" among coonhounds, the Treeing Walker is a moderately proportioned hound ideal for tracking and treeing raccoons over rough terrain with good speed and excellent endurance. The gait is smooth, effortless, and ground-covering, with good reach and drive. Its coat is short, hard, and close—dense enough to provide protection against brambles and weather. It has a clear, ringing bugle voice or a steady clear chop that changes when the dog is at the tree.

bobcats, and bears that treed needed a dog that checked trees for scent, and then treed the quarry. Crosses to treeing coonhounds probably achieved this, although even today the Treeing Walker is often described as a "trailing hound that trees" rather than a "treeing hound that trails." The Treeing Walker Coonhound was first registered with the UKC as part of the English Coonhound breed. Walker breeders eventually requested separate recognition, and in 1945 the breed was first registered as Walkers (Treeing) and then as Treeing Walkers. Known for its speed on the trail, this hot-nosed hunter is one of the most competitive in nite hunt competitions. The Treeing Walker Coonhound became a regular AKC breed in 2012.

TEMPERAMENT

The Treeing Walker Coonhound is a fairly energetic dog that loves to hunt and use its nose. It has a tendency to become oblivious to calls when it's on a trail. Although most Treeing Walkers are kept as hunting dogs, they make excellent companions and house dogs. They are loving and eager to please and get along well with everyone: strangers, dogs, and most other pets. They are not known for their obedience inclination. Their bark can be quite loud.

UPKEEP

Treeing Walkers need to get outside and stretch their legs, either with a long walk or jog or off-lead run in a safe area. They like to use their nose and enjoy tracking and nose work activities—and of course, hunting! The coat is basically wash and wear.

Whippet

AT A GLANCE

Energy level:	■ ■ ■	Watchdog ability:	■ ■ ■ ■	POPULARITY: Somewhat popular
Exercise requirements:	■ ■ ■	Protection ability:	■	FAMILY: Sighthound
Playfulness:	■ ■ ■	Grooming requirements:	■	AREA OF ORIGIN: England
Affection level:	■ ■ ■ ■	Cold tolerance:	■	DATE OF ORIGIN: 1700s
Friendliness toward dogs:	■ ■ ■ ■ ■	Heat tolerance:	■ ■ ■	ORIGINAL FUNCTION: Racing, rabbit coursing
Friendliness toward other pets:	■ ■ ■ ■			TODAY'S FUNCTION: Racing, lure coursing
Friendliness toward strangers:	■ ■ ■	WEIGHT: 20–40 lb*		OTHER NAME: None
Ease of training:	■ ■ ■	HEIGHT: male: 19–22"; female: 18–21"		

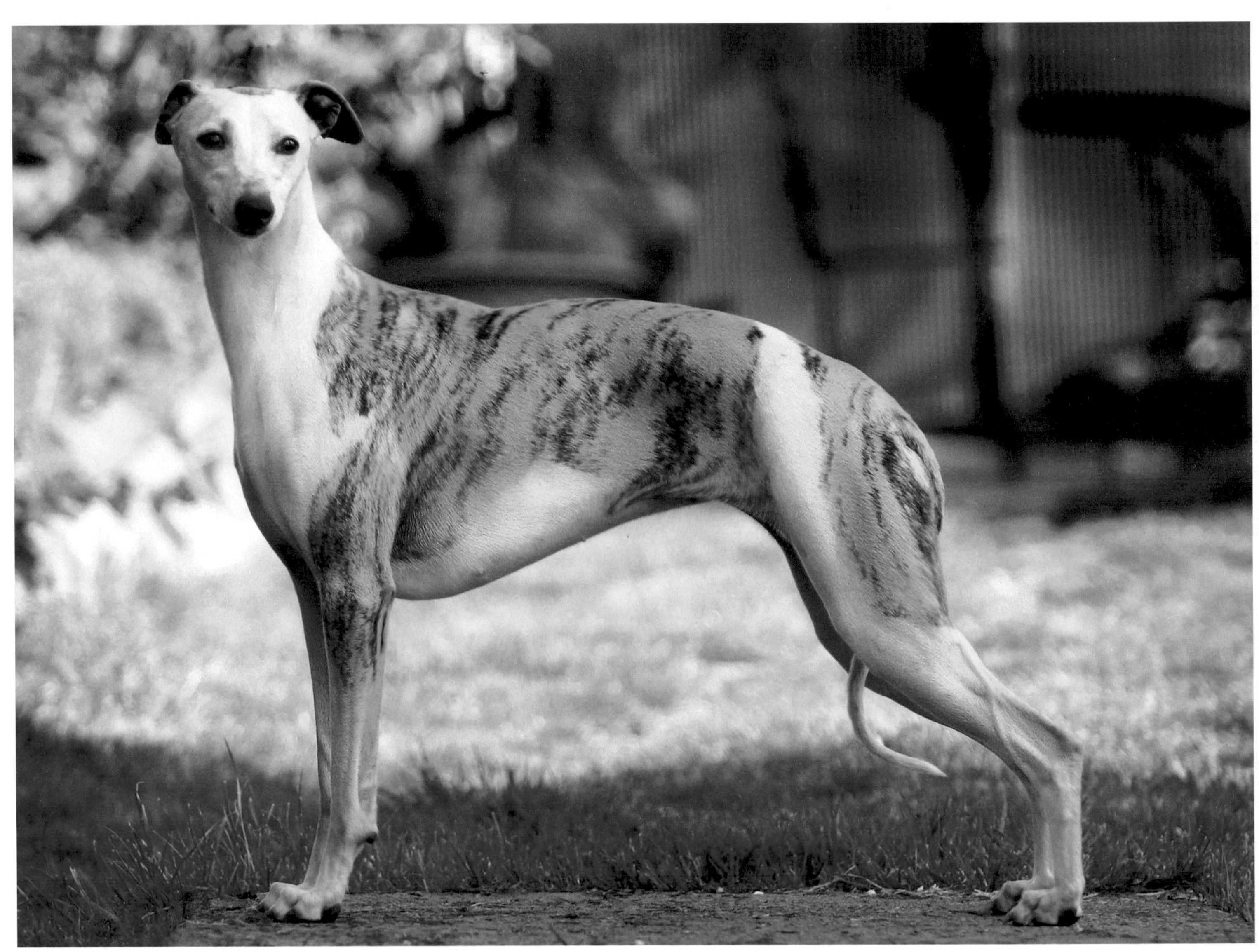

HISTORY

A medium-sized sighthound, the Whippet stems from Greyhound roots. The Whippet's progenitors may have come from crosses between small Greyhounds and even smaller dogs, to be used by peasants for poaching rabbits and other small game in the eighteenth century. The peasants also found entertainment in "snap dog" contests, in which bets were made on which dog could "snap up" as many rabbits as possible before they escaped from a circle. Crosses with ratting terriers were probably made to increase quickness and gameness. It was the advent of the Industrial Revolution, however, that spurred the development of the true Whippet breed. Masses of rural workers moved to industrialized areas, bringing with them their snap dogs and a need for entertainment. Without a supply

ILLUSTRATED STANDARD

1 Long, lean skull with scarcely perceptible stop
2 Small, folded ears
3 Gracefully arched loin
4 Long tail carried low
5 Deep chest with definite tuck-up
6 Hare feet

Color: immaterial
DQ: over ½" above or below stated height limits; blue or wall eyes; undershot, overshot ¼" or more; any coat other than short

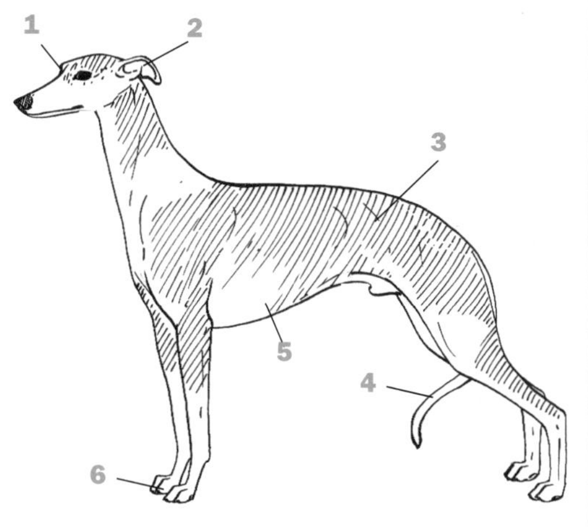

of rabbits, they found their dogs would just as readily race toward a waving rag. Rag racing became the sport of coal miners; in fact, the Whippet was dubbed the "poor man's race horse." A family's Whippet was not only an immense source of pride but sometimes also a source of extra income and procurer of food for the pot. As a valued family member, it shared the family rations and often, the children's beds, and came to be valued as a companion as well. Whippet racing is still popular today, but it never gained the commercial appeal of Greyhound racing and so remains strictly an amateur sport. After the Whippet was officially recognized as a breed in 1888, it began to be appreciated for its aesthetic appeal, and crosses with the Italian Greyhound further refined its appearance. The Whippet gained popularity only slowly, but its unequaled combination of lithe elegance and gracious companionship gradually created a devoted following. Today the Whippet is the most popular of the sighthounds and is highly valued as a show dog, lure-courser, racer, and family companion.

TEMPERAMENT

Perhaps the most demonstrative and obedient of the true sighthounds, the Whippet makes an ideal pet for people who want a quiet housedog and absolutely devoted companion. The Whippet is extremely gentle with children and can make an excellent companion for them. It is calm indoors but loves to run and play outdoors. It is extremely sensitive (both physically and mentally) and cannot take rough treatment or harsh corrections.

UPKEEP

The Whippet can make a good apartment dog if it is taken for a long walk or run daily. Grooming is minimal. The Whippet must have a warm, soft bed. It dislikes cold weather intensely. The hair is extremely short and fine, and the Whippet is virtually free of "doggy odor."

HEALTH

- Major concerns: none
- Minor concerns: none
- Occasionally seen: deafness, some eye defects
- Suggested tests: eye, cardiac, BAER
- Life span: 12–15 years
- Note: sensitive to barbiturate anesthesia; prone to lacerations

FORM AND FUNCTION

The Whippet is among the sleekest of dogs, with a curvaceous, streamlined silhouette, long legs, and a lean physique. The Whippet is the ultimate sprinter, unsurpassed by any other breed in its ability to accelerate to top speed and to twist and turn with unequaled agility. It is a lightweight version of the Greyhound, with an especially supple topline and powerful hindquarters enabling it to execute the double-suspension gallop at its most extreme. It is square or slightly longer than tall. The gait is low and free-moving. The expression is keen and alert.

Dogs in this group are those that put their bravery or brawn into the service of humans. They can be broadly divided into guarding or protecting breeds, sledding breeds, carting breeds, and rescue breeds. In general, the Working breeds are known for their intelligence, hardiness, and confidence.

THE WORKING GROUP

Akita

AT A GLANCE

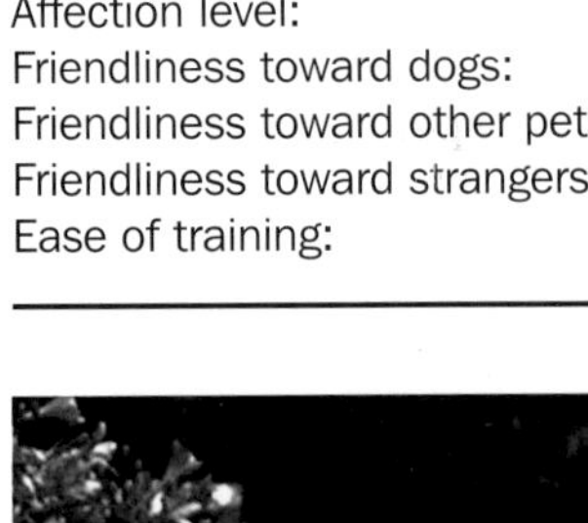

Energy level:	■ ■ ■
Exercise requirements:	■ ■ ■
Playfulness:	■ ■ ■
Affection level:	■ ■ ■
Friendliness toward dogs:	■
Friendliness toward other pets:	■ ■
Friendliness toward strangers:	■
Ease of training:	■ ■ ■

Watchdog ability:	■ ■ ■ ■ ■
Protection ability:	■ ■ ■ ■
Grooming requirements:	■ ■
Cold tolerance:	■ ■ ■ ■ ■
Heat tolerance:	■

WEIGHT: male: 85–115 lb*; female: 65–90 lb*
HEIGHT: male: 25–28″; female: 23–26″

POPULARITY: Popular
FAMILY: Northern
AREA OF ORIGIN: Japan
DATE OF ORIGIN: Unknown
ORIGINAL FUNCTION: Large game hunting, dog fighting, guardian
TODAY'S FUNCTION: Security
OTHER NAME: Akita Inu, Japanese Akita

HISTORY

The Akita is perhaps the most renowned and venerated of the native Japanese breeds. Although it bears a likeness to dogs from ancient Japanese tombs, the modern Akita is the result of a concerted nineteenth century effort to restore seven native Japanese dog breeds. The Akita, largest of these breeds, was restored using many breeds and mixed breeds used for fighting. Indigenous Odate dogs were also used as the best representatives of native Japanese animals. Over time, Japanese breeders selected against many traits descended from the fighting ancestors, including black mask, pinto pattern, and substantial size; whereas American breeders have perpetuated those traits. In 1918, the Akita-inu Hozankai Society of Japan was formed to preserve the original

ILLUSTRATED STANDARD

1 Stop well defined
2 Eyes small and triangular
3 Head forms a blunt triangle viewed from above
4 Ears erect and small; set follows the angle of the neck
5 Skull flat
6 Level back
7 Tail curled, large, full, set high and carried over back, or dipping below level of back
8 Cat feet

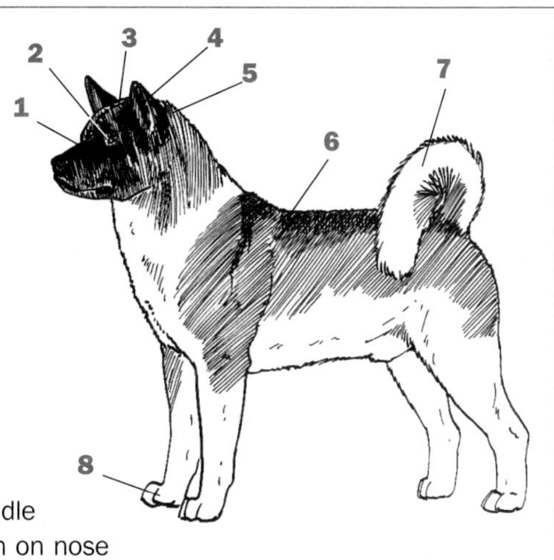

Color: any color, including white, pinto, or brindle
DQ: butterfly nose or total lack of pigmentation on nose (liver is permitted on white Akitas); drop or broken ears; noticeably undershot or overshot; sickle or uncurled tail; males under 25", females under 23"

Akita, and in 1931 the Akita was designated as one of Japan's natural monuments. The most honored Akita of all time was Hachiko, who greeted his master every evening at the train station to accompany him home. When his master died at work one day, Haichiko waited for him, and continued to return and wait for his master every day until he died nine years later on March 8, 1935. Today, a statue and annual ceremony pay homage to Haichiko's loyalty. The first Akita arrived in America in 1937, when Helen Keller returned from Japan with one. Following World War II, servicemen returned home with Akitas from Japan. The breed's popularity grew slowly until it received AKC recognition in 1972. Since then, it has steadily gained admirers and continues to grow in popularity. The Akita is now used as a guard and police dog in Japan.

TEMPERAMENT

As befitting its spitz-like heritage, the Akita is bold, independent, stubborn, and tenacious. Demonstrative to its family, it is utterly devoted and will protect family members. It is reserved with strangers and can be aggressive toward other dogs. It can be domineering. Though not the breed for everyone, in the right hands the Akita is an excellent companion.

UPKEEP

The Akita appreciates mental and physical exercise every day. It needs the chance to run in a safe area or on leash for a long jog. Given ample exercise and training, it can be a quiet and well-mannered house dog. The coat needs brushing about once a week to remove dead hair, much more often when shedding. They tend to be somewhat messy drinkers!

HEALTH

- Major concerns: CHD, PRA
- Minor concerns: elbow dysplasia, pemphigus, sebaceous adenitis, gastric torsion, cruciate ligament rupture, osteosarcoma, lymphosarcoma, hypothyroidism
- Occasionally seen: PRA, patellar luxation, VKH-like syndrome, entropion, epilepsy, cataract, polyneuropathy, renal cortical hypoplasia, microphthalmia
- Suggested tests: hip, (elbow), eye, thyroid
- Life span: 10–12 years
- Note: Akitas are especially sensitive to anemia from red blood cell damage caused by eating onions.

FORM AND FUNCTION

This is a large and powerful breed, with much substance and heavy bone; it is slightly longer than tall. The Akita's build reflects its original job of hunting big game through deep snow and rugged terrain. Its double coat consists of a dense undercoat and straight, harsh, outer coat standing off from the body, about 2 inches or less in length. Such a combination provides ample insulation from water and weather. The gait is brisk and powerful. The Akita is a versatile dog of large spitz type, able to perform as hunting companion and protector.

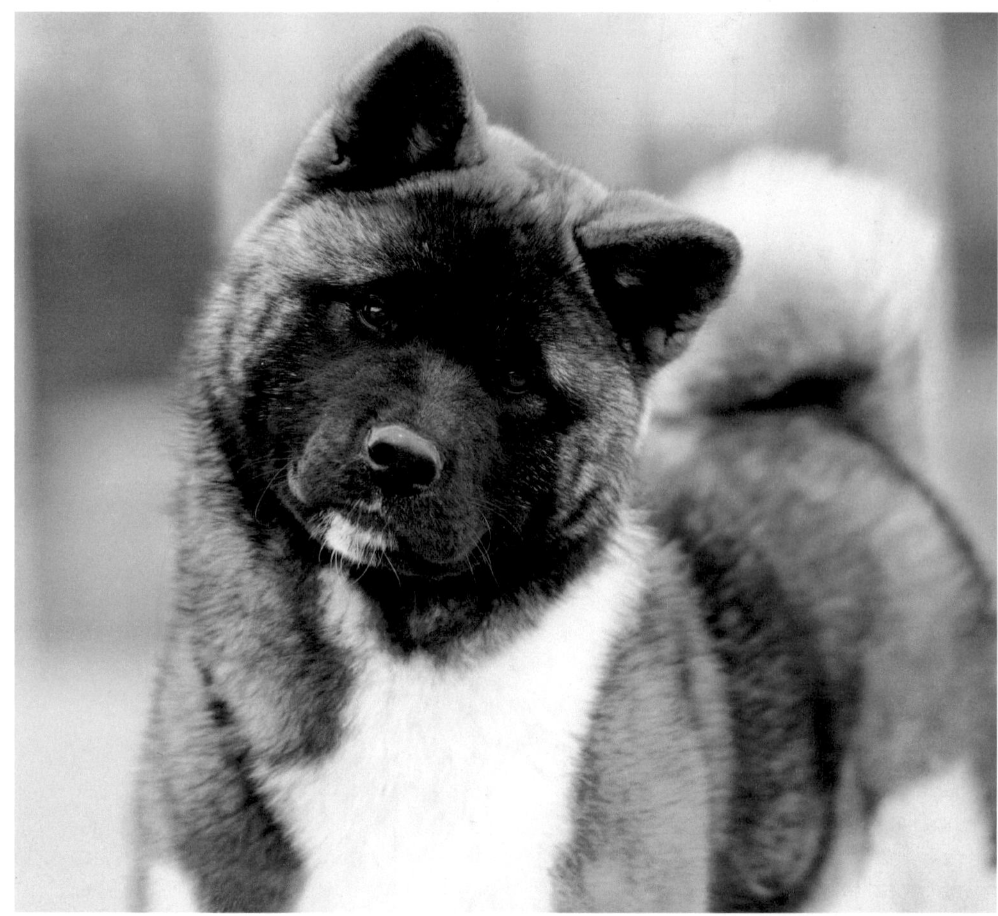

Alaskan Malamute

AT A GLANCE

Energy level:	■■■
Exercise requirements:	■■■■
Playfulness:	■■■
Affection level:	■■■■■
Friendliness toward dogs:	■
Friendliness toward other pets:	■
Friendliness toward strangers:	■■■■
Ease of training:	■

Watchdog ability:	■■■
Protection ability:	■■■
Grooming requirements:	■■■
Cold tolerance:	■■■■■
Heat tolerance:	■

WEIGHT: male: 85 lb; female: 75 lb
HEIGHT: male: 25″; female: 23″

POPULARITY: Somewhat popular
FAMILY: Spitz, Northern
AREA OF ORIGIN: Alaska
DATE OF ORIGIN: Ancient times
ORIGINAL FUNCTION: Heavy sled pulling, large game hunting
TODAY'S FUNCTION: Sled pulling
OTHER NAME: None

HISTORY

Like most of the dogs of the spitz family, the Alaskan Malamute evolved in the Arctic regions, shaped by the adverse climatic conditions. Its origin is unknown, but it was first described living among the native Inuit people known as the Mahlemuts, who lived along Norton Sound on Alaska's northwest coast. The word Mahlemut comes from Mahle, an Inuit tribe name, and mut, meaning village. The dogs served as hunting partners for big game (such as seals and polar bears), and hauled the heavy carcasses back home. These dogs were, of necessity, large and strong rather than fast, enabling one dog to do the work of many smaller dogs. They were an essential cog in these people's lives and were treated almost as one of the family, although they were never

ILLUSTRATED STANDARD

1 Muzzle large
2 Eyes almond-shaped, moderately large
3 Head broad and powerful
4 Ears medium-sized, triangular, slightly rounded at tips
5 Straight back
6 Tail carried over back
7 Large feet

Color: light gray through to black, with white shading and a white mask or cap; also shades of sable or red with shading, or all white
DQ: blue eyes

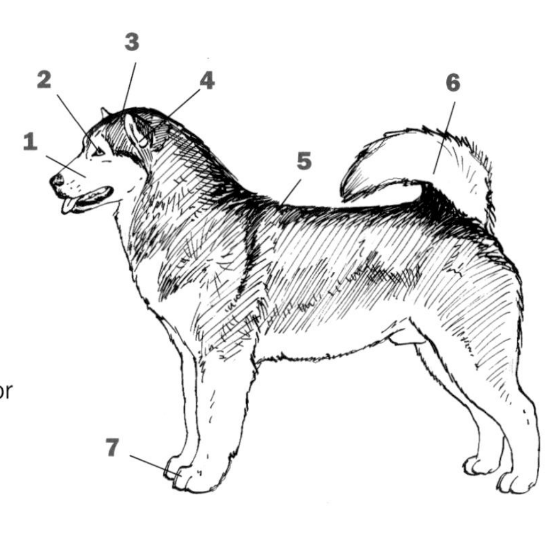

pampered as pets. The unforgiving environment meant that a less than optimal dog would probably not have been kept. When the first outside explorers came to the region in the 1700s, they were impressed not only by the hardy dog but also by their owners' obvious attachment to them. With the discovery of gold in 1896, a flood of outsiders came to Alaska; for entertainment, they staged weight-pulling contests and races among their dogs. The native breeds were interbred with each other and those brought by settlers, often in an attempt to create a faster racer or simply supply the vast numbers of dogs needed to supply the gold rush. The pure Malamute was in danger of being lost. In the 1920s, a New England dog racing enthusiast obtained some good specimens, and began to breed the traditional Malamutes. As the breed's reputation grew, some were chosen to help Admiral Byrd in his 1933 trek to the South Pole. During World War II, the Malamute was once again called into service, this time to serve as freight haulers, pack animals, and search-and-rescue dogs. In 1935, the breed received AKC recognition and began a new phase as an imposing show dog and loyal pet.

TEMPERAMENT

The Alaskan Malamute is powerful, independent, strong willed, and fun loving. Its idea of great fun is to pull a sled or cart, but it also loves to run and roam. It is family oriented, and as long as it is given daily exercise, it is well-mannered in the home. Without proper exercise, it can become frustrated and destructive. It is friendly and sociable toward people, but it may be aggressive to strange dogs, pets, or livestock. Some can be domineering. It tends to dig and howl.

UPKEEP

The Alaskan Malamute loves cold weather, and especially loves to haul a sled through the snow. It can run for miles and needs to have adequate exercise every day, either in the form of a long walk on leash or the opportunity to run or mush. It can live outdoors in temperate to cold climates, but it does better inside during warm weather. Its coat needs brushing once or twice a week, more when shedding.

HEALTH

- Major concerns: CHD, cataract
- Minor concerns: chondrodysplasia, hypothyroidism
- Occasionally seen: gastric torsion, hemeralopia, polyneuropathy, seizures
- Suggested tests: hip, eye, (thyroid), (elbow), chondrodysplasia, (polyneuropathy)
- Life span: 10–12 years

FORM AND FUNCTION

The Alaskan Malamute is a powerfully built dog of Nordic breed type, developed to haul heavy loads rather than race. It is slightly longer than it is tall. It is heavy boned and compact, designed for strength and endurance. Its gait is steady, balanced, and tireless. Its coat is thick and double, with a coarse outer coat and dense, wooly, oily undercoat, providing the ultimate in insulation. Although the eyes have a "wolf-like" appearance, the expression is soft.

Anatolian Shepherd

AT A GLANCE

Energy level:	■■
Exercise requirements:	■■■
Playfulness:	■■■
Affection level:	■■■
Friendliness toward dogs:	■
Friendliness toward other pets:	■■■
Friendliness toward strangers:	■
Ease of training:	■■■

Watchdog ability:	■■■■■
Protection ability:	■■■■■
Grooming requirements:	■■
Cold tolerance:	■■■■
Heat tolerance:	■■■

WEIGHT: male: 110–150 lb; female: 80–120 lb
HEIGHT: male: from 29″ up; female: from 27″ up

POPULARITY: Somewhat uncommon
FAMILY: Livestock Dog, Mastiff, Flock Guard
AREA OF ORIGIN: Turkey
DATE OF ORIGIN: Ancient times
ORIGINAL FUNCTION: Flock guard
TODAY'S FUNCTION: Flock guard, security
OTHER NAME: Coban Kopegi, Karabash Dog, Kangal Dog

HISTORY

The Anatolian Shepherd is an ancient guardian breed with a long working history. Its roots probably lie in the Tibetan Mastiff and Roman Mollosian war dogs that came to Turkey more than 4,000 years ago. Here they proved invaluable as staunch defenders of livestock against formidable predators, including wolves and bears. They accompanied the nomadic shepherds and became widespread over a large geographical region, accounting for the Anatolian's great variation in size, coat type, and color. Several traits that remained constant throughout all the breed, however, are loyalty, independence, and hardiness. The name Shepherd is a misnomer because the breed was never used as a herder. Its Turkish name, *koban kopegi*, means shepherd's dog. There is disagreement over whether the

ILLUSTRATED STANDARD

1 Dewlap not excessive
2 Eyes almond-shaped
3 V-shaped ears with rounded apex
4 Gradual arch over loin
5 Tail long, high-set, with a curl in the end; carried in a wheel when alert
6 Double dewclaws optional on rear feet
7 Oval feet

Color: any, most common is fawn with black mask
DQ: blue eyes or eyes of two different colors; erect ears; overshot; undershot; or wry bite

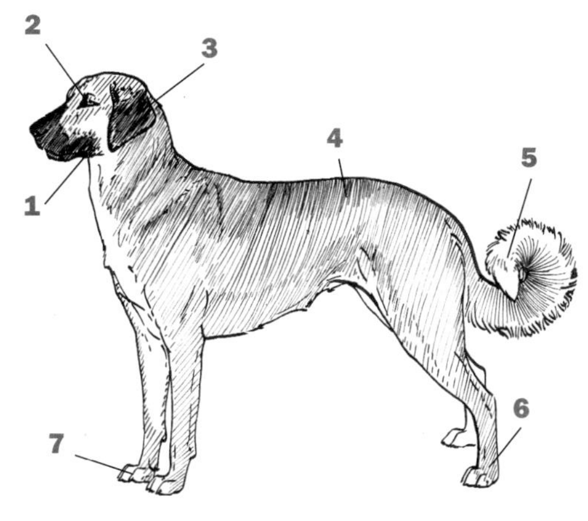

Anatolian is a separate breed from the Kangal (or Karabash) dog. The first of the breed did not come to America until the 1950s, where although it proved itself as an effective livestock guard against coyotes and other predators, it remained unknown to most dog fanciers. Only in the late 1970s and 1980s did the Anatolian Shepherd begin to be more widely appreciated, still valued for its utilitarian, rather than cosmetic, attributes. Pet owners desiring a loyal and effective guardian began to acquire the breed. In 1996, the Anatolian Shepherd was accepted in the AKC Working Group; Anatolian fanciers are adamant about retaining the dog's working instincts above all else. Anatolians are used for cheetah conservation in Africa by protecting livestock from cheetahs.

TEMPERAMENT

This is a serious dog, devoted to its family and its duty as family protector. At the same time, it is laid back and easygoing, never on the lookout for trouble. It is suspicious of strangers and is territorial. It is good with children, but it may not be playful enough to satisfy children's desires. As a serious watch dog, it tends to bark a lot when its suspicions are aroused.

UPKEEP

The Anatolian Shepherd needs a chance to exercise every day, either with a long walk or brisk run. It can live outside in temperate to cool climates but needs to socialize with its family. Coat care is minimal, consisting only of a weekly brushing to remove dead hair.

HEALTH

- Major concerns: CHD
- Minor concerns: entropion
- Occasionally seen: elbow dysplasia
- Suggested tests: hip, elbow
- Life span: 10–13 years
- Note: sensitive to barbiturate anesthesia

FORM AND FUNCTION

The Anatolian is built tough to do a tough job. It is a large, powerful, rugged dog, having both great agility and endurance. It has good bone and a large head. Its gait is powerful, smooth, and fluid. Its coat consists of a thick undercoat and an outer coat that ranges from short (about 1 inch) to rough (about 4 inches), slightly longer around the neck and mane. The expression is intelligent, and the general impression is one of a bold yet calm protector.

Bernese Mountain Dog

AT A GLANCE

Energy level:	■■	Watchdog ability:	■■■	POPULARITY: Popular
Exercise requirements:	■■■	Protection ability:	■■	FAMILY: Livestock Dog, Mountain Dog, Mastiff
Playfulness:	■■	Grooming requirements:	■■■	AREA OF ORIGIN: Switzerland
Affection level:	■■■	Cold tolerance:	■■■■■	DATE OF ORIGIN: Ancient times
Friendliness toward dogs:	■■■	Heat tolerance:	■	ORIGINAL FUNCTION: Draft
Friendliness toward other pets:	■■■■			TODAY'S FUNCTION: Draft, herding
Friendliness toward strangers:	■■■	WEIGHT: male: 90–120 lb; female: 70–100 lb*		OTHER NAME: Berner Sennenhund, Bernese Cattle Dog
Ease of training:	■■■■	HEIGHT: male: 25–27.5″; female: 23–26″		

HISTORY

The most well known of the Sennehunde, or Swiss mountain dogs, the Bernese is distinguished by being the only one to have a fairly long, silky coat. The origin of the breed is speculative at best. Some experts believe its history traces to the Roman invasion of Switzerland, when the Roman mastiffs were crossed with native flock-guarding dogs. This cross produced a strong dog that was able to withstand the Alpine weather and that could serve as draft dog, flock guard, drover, herder, and general farm dog. Despite their utility, little attempt was made to perpetuate them as a breed purposefully. By the late 1800s, the breed was in danger of being lost. At that time, Professor Albert Heim initiated a study of Swiss dogs that led to the identification of the Bernese Mountain Dog as one of the

ILLUSTRATED STANDARD

1 Well-defined stop
2 Skull flat
3 Ears medium-sized, triangular with rounded tips, hanging close to head
4 Level topline with broad back
5 Tail bushy, carried low
6 Feet round

Color: tricolored; black with tan markings and white flashings
DQ: blue eyes, any ground color other than black

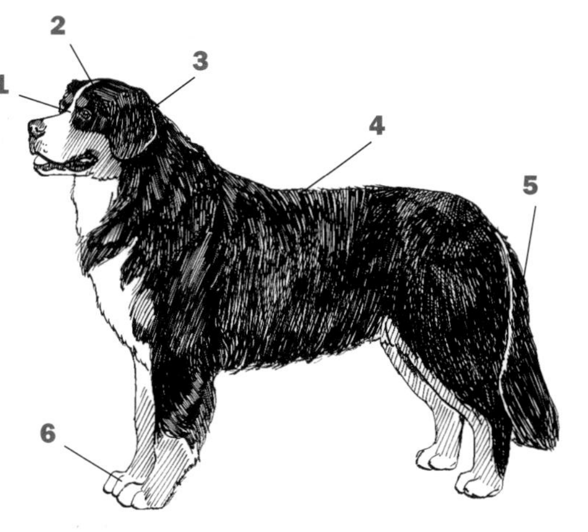

existing types. These dogs were found only in the valleys of the lower Alps. Through Dr. Heim's efforts, these dogs were promoted throughout Switzerland and even Europe. The finest specimens came to be found in the Durrbach area, at one time giving the breed the name Durrbachler. With the breed's spread, the name was changed to Bernese Mountain Dog. The first Bernese came to America in 1926; official AKC recognition was granted in 1937.

TEMPERAMENT

The Bernese Mountain Dog is an easy-going, calm family companion (that is, after it leaves its adolescent stage). It is sensitive, loyal, and extremely devoted. It is gentle with children and often reserved with strangers. It generally gets along well with other dogs and pets. They do not do well isolated from family activities.

UPKEEP

This dog enjoys the outdoors, especially in cold weather. It needs daily but moderate exercise, either a good hike or walk on leash. It enjoys pulling. Its coat needs brushing one or two times weekly, much more often when shedding. The Bernese life span is described by a Swiss expression: "Three years a young dog, three years a good dog, and three years an old dog. All else is a gift from God."

HEALTH

- Major concerns: CHD, elbow dysplasia, mast cell tumor, gastric torsion
- Minor concerns: cataract, entropion, ectropion, SAS
- Occasionally seen: hypomyelination, allergies, vWD, hepatocerebellar degeneration, hypothyroidism, PRA
- Suggested tests: hip, elbow, eye, cardiac, DNA for vWD
- Life span: 6–9 years
- Note: Extra care must be taken to avoid heat stroke.

FORM AND FUNCTION

The Bernese Mountain Dog is slightly longer than tall, though appearing square. It is a sturdy, large, hardy dog capable of both draft and droving work. This requires a combination of strength, speed, and agility. Its natural working gait is a slow trot, but with good reach and drive. Its thick coat is moderately long, and slightly wavy or straight, providing insulation from the cold. The expression is gentle, and the color is striking.

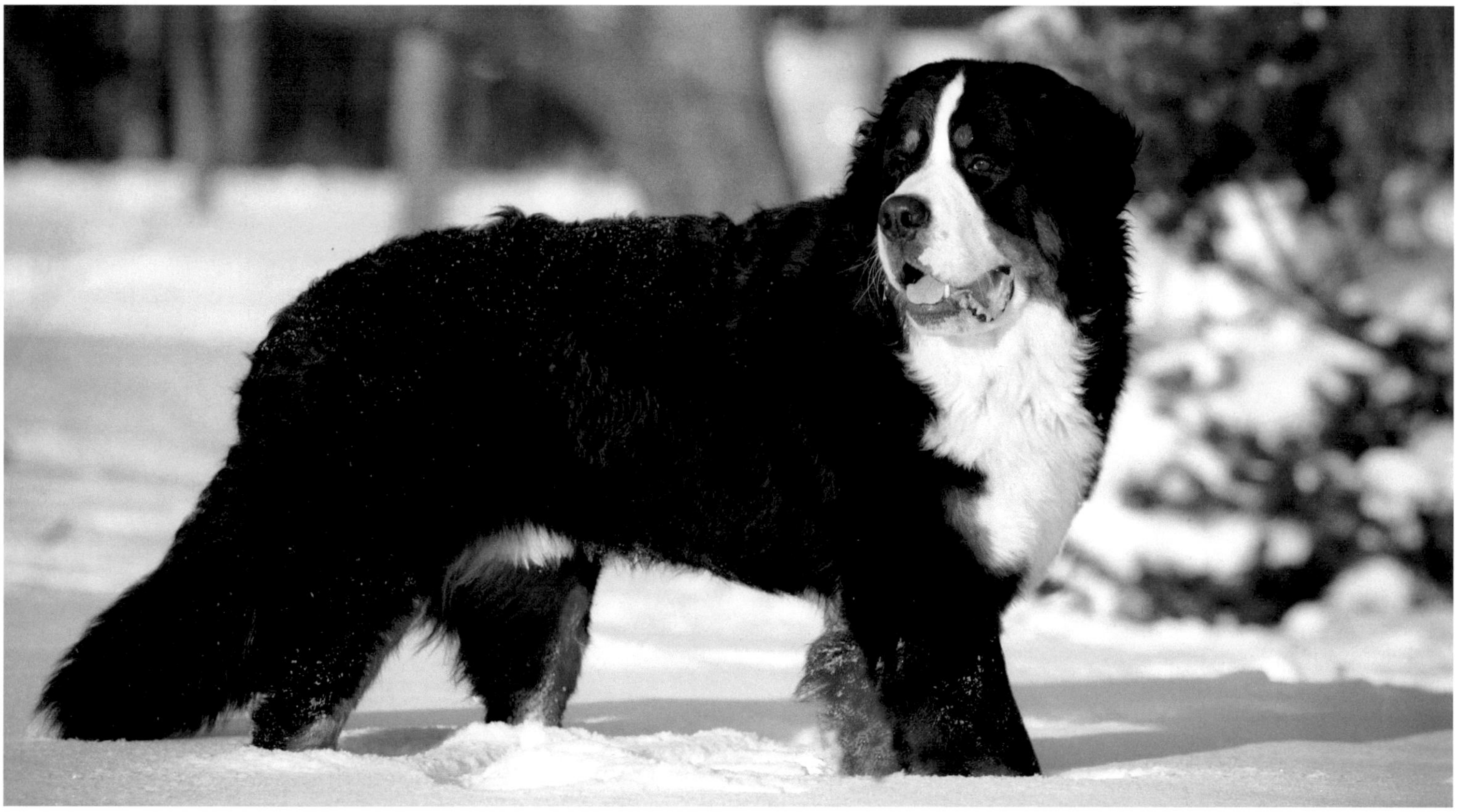

Black Russian Terrier

AT A GLANCE

Energy level:	■■
Exercise requirements:	■■■
Playfulness:	■■
Affection level:	■■■■
Friendliness toward dogs:	■■■
Friendliness toward other pets:	■■■■
Friendliness toward strangers:	■
Ease of training:	■■■

Watchdog ability:	■■■■■
Protection ability:	■■■■■
Grooming requirements:	■■■
Cold tolerance:	■■■■
Heat tolerance:	■■

WEIGHT: 80–145 lb*
HEIGHT: male: 27–30″; female: 26–29″

POPULARITY: Uncommon
FAMILY: Schnauzer
AREA OF ORIGIN: Soviet Union
DATE OF ORIGIN: 1950s
ORIGINAL FUNCTION: Military
TODAY'S FUNCTION: Personal protection, search and rescue
OTHER NAME: Chornyi, Terrier Noir Russem, Russian Black Terrier, Schwarzer Russicher Terrier, Tchiorny Terrier, Svart Terrier, Mustaterrieri

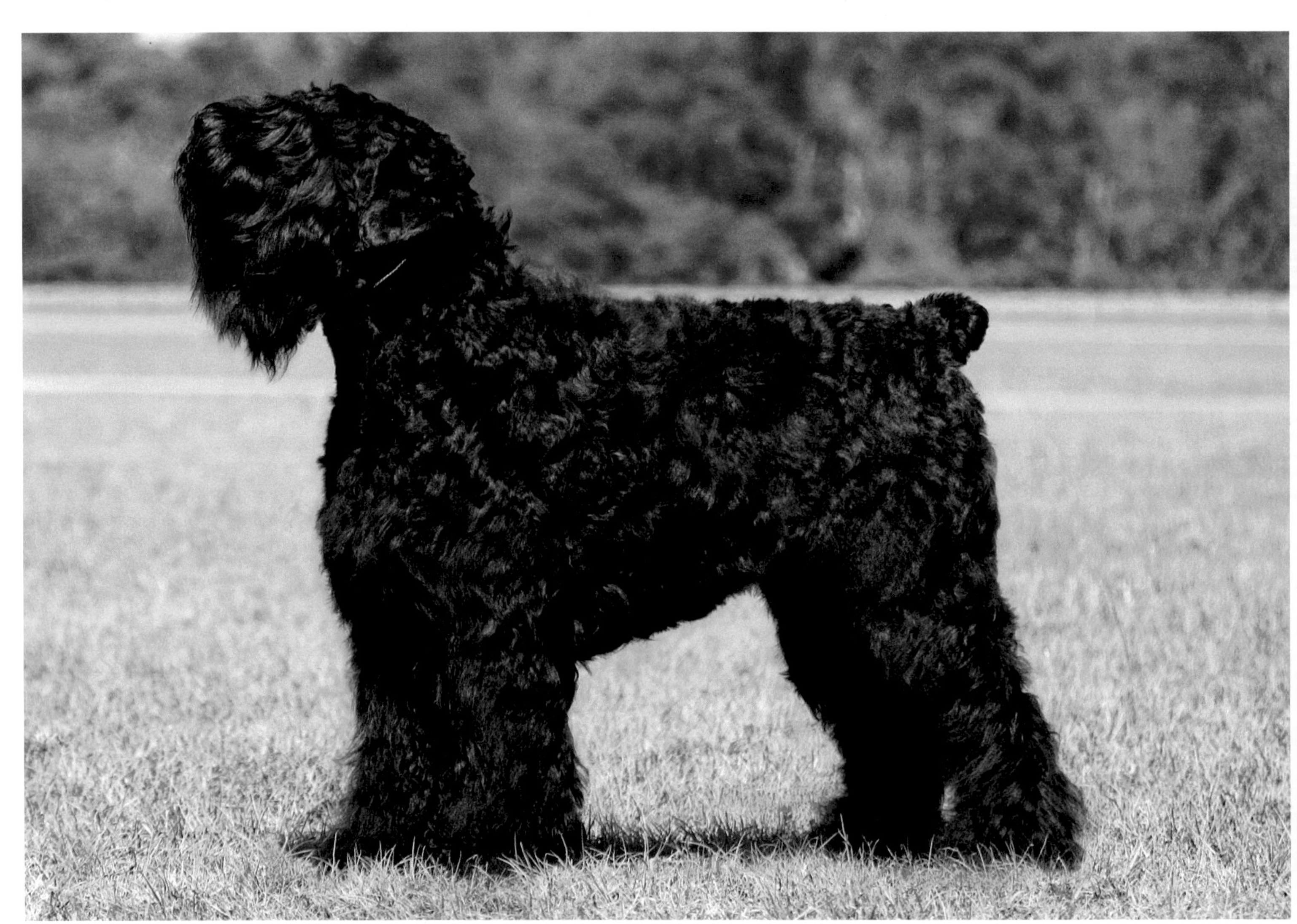

HISTORY

In the 1940s the Soviets faced the task of populating their military with suitable working dogs. With a dearth of qualified canines, they imported breeds from their occupied countries, mainly German breeds, into their state Red Star kennels. The most impressive of their imports was a Giant Schnauzer named Roy, born in 1947. Roy was bred extensively with females from various breeds, with the most successful coming from Airedale Terrier, Rottweiler, and Moscow Water Dog crosses. They were all black, and were distinguished from the others as the "Black Terrier" group. The best were bred among themselves, and by 1957 second- and third-generation dogs were presented to the public and the first puppies went to family breeding situations to continue the project. The main criteria were working

ILLUSTRATED STANDARD

1 Powerful head
2 Dark, oval eyes
3 High-set, triangular ears, rather small
4 Straight, level topline
5 Thick, high-set tail, docked to 3 to 5 vertebra
6 Large, round feet

Color: black or black with a few gray hairs
DQ: height under 26″; nose other than black; undershot or overshot bite; any color other than black

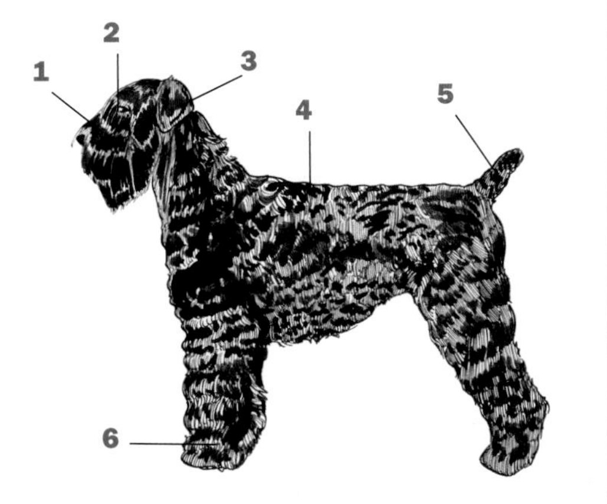

ability and versatility, but care was also taken to improve conformation. Besides sharing border guard duty with soldiers, military tasks included detecting mines and explosives, transporting supplies, pulling sledges, and finding wounded soldiers, all done independently and in the harshest of climates. Black Russian Terriers served in military operations in Afghanistan and Bosnia. In 1968 a breed standard was registered with the international FCI, which officially recognized the breed in 1984. As BRT breeders emigrated to other countries, the dogs' value as companions became more obvious, and their popularity spread. In 2001 the AKC admitted the breed into its Miscellaneous class, and in 2004 it became a regular member of the Working Group.

TEMPERAMENT

Calm, confident, and courageous sums up the Black Russian Terrier. Reserved with strangers, BRTs are very attached to and protective of their family. They are fast learners, but also independent thinkers, and they can be stubborn if pushed to do something they don't want to do. BRTs are affectionate and social. They tend to stick close to their people, even inside the house. They are gentle and playful with children. They may not be good with strange or dominant dogs, but are fine with other pets and smaller canine housemates.

UPKEEP

BRTs need social interaction as well as mental and physical exercise. Obedience or agility training is helpful in channeling the breed's need for work. They are quiet inside. They do not bark frivolously. The BRT doesn't shed much, but its coat needs thorough combing once or twice a week, and it needs trimming every six to eight weeks. A show trim is carefully done to show off the dog's conformation without giving it a sculpted look. The coat should appear tousled.

HEALTH

- Major concerns: CHD, elbow dysplasia
- Minor concerns: hyperuricosuria (HU)
- Occasionally seen: PRA, JLPP
- Suggested tests: hip, elbow, eye, cardiac, HU, (JLPP)
- Life span: 10–11 years

FORM AND FUNCTION

The Black Russian Terrier must be strong of body and mind to perform its duties as a reliable guard and military dog. This is a large-boned and well-muscled dog, capable of pulling a heavy load yet having the agility to traverse rocky terrain or overtake an adversary. The head and neck are powerful. A reliable intelligent temperament is essential in a dog that also has strong protective instincts; courage is also a must.The weatherproof outer coat repels water while the undercoat insulates the dog from the cold. Length of coat should vary from 1.5" to 4" with longer coats detracting from the dog's working ability.

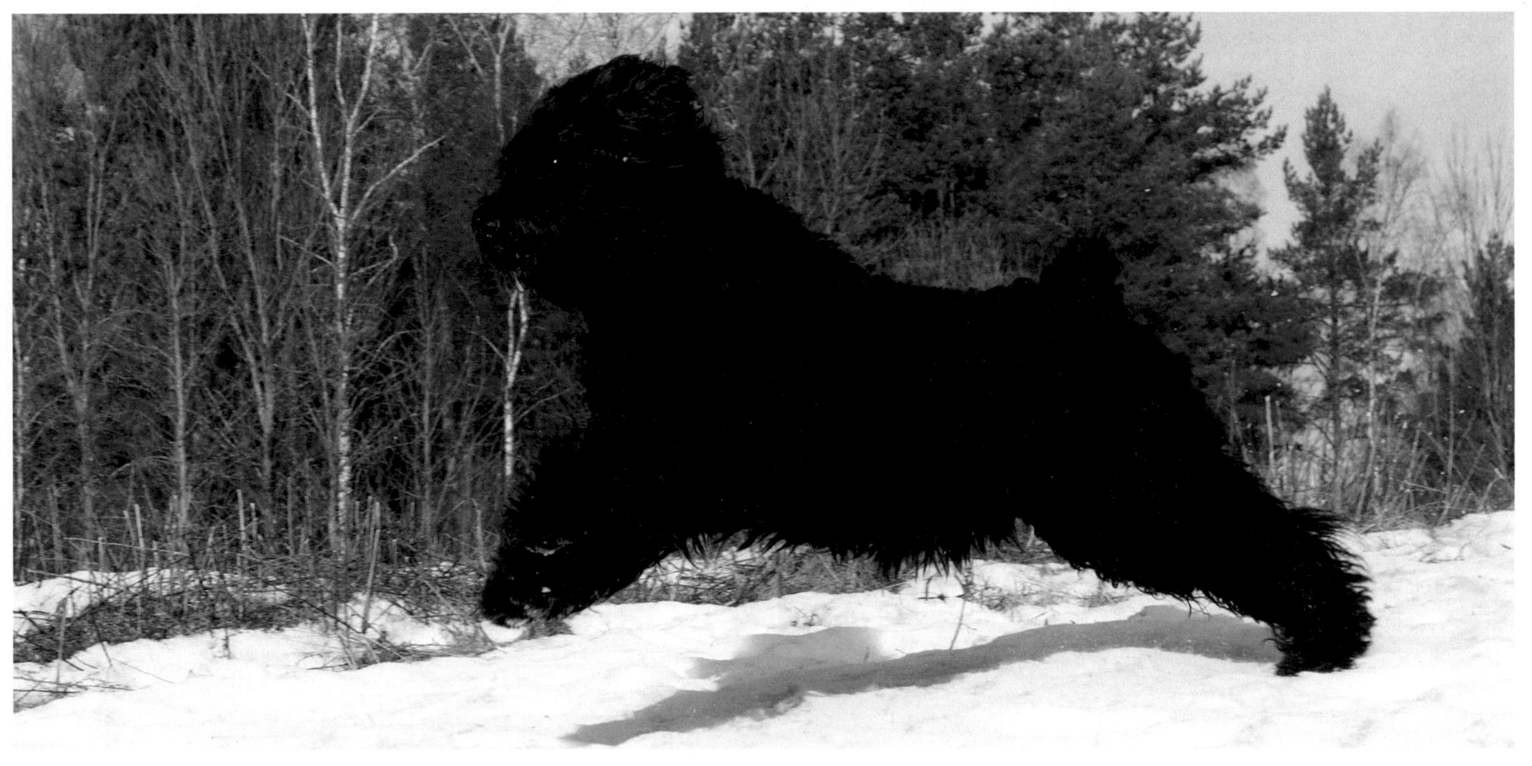

Boerboel

AT A GLANCE

Energy level:	■■■	Watchdog ability:	■■■■■	POPULARITY: Very rare
Exercise requirements:	■■■	Protection ability:	■■■■■	FAMILY: Mastiff
Playfulness:	■■	Grooming requirements:	■	AREA OF ORIGIN: South Africa
Affection level:	■■■	Cold tolerance:	■■■	DATE OF ORIGIN: 1800s
Friendliness toward dogs:	■	Heat tolerance:	■■■	ORIGINAL FUNCTION: Farm guardian
Friendliness toward other pets:	■■			TODAY'S FUNCTION: Guardian
Friendliness toward strangers:	■	WEIGHT: male: 140–180 lb; female: 100–130 lb		OTHER NAME: None
Ease of training:	■■	HEIGHT: male: 24–27″; female: 22–25″		

HISTORY

When Jan van Riebeeck and company arrived in South Africa in 1652 to establish a trading post (Cape Town) for the Dutch East India Company, they brought their Bullenbijters with them for protection. Subsequent colonists also brought large protective dogs. More Bulldog and Mastiff breeds arrived with British settlers in the 1800s. These dogs all interbred and were further dispersed northward during the Great Trek beginning in 1838. They were likely also crossed with native African dogs, and the Rhodesian Ridgeback may have even played a role. The name Boerboel (pronounced BUR-bul) means "farmer's dog." The boers (Dutch/Afrikaans for "farmers") used the dogs for protection from dangerous animals and humans in the sparsely populated land, often keeping

ILLUSTRATED STANDARD

1. Deep, square, muscular head with flat skull
2. Muzzle is just over 1/3 of total head length
3. Loose fleshy upper lip; moderately tight lower lip without excessive jowls
4. Tight eyelids
5. Medium-sized, V-shaped ears
6. Level topline with broad back
7. Thick, high-set tail, docked at the third or fourth caudal vertebrae; natural tail reaches hocks
8. Large, round feet

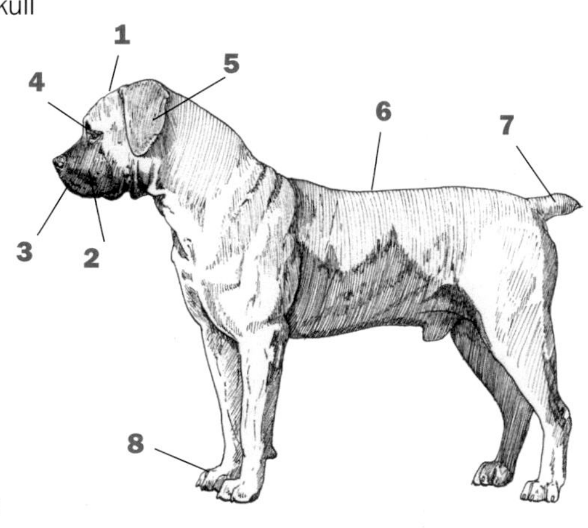

Color: All shades of brown, red, or fawn; brindle; limited clear white patches on the legs and forechest permissible; black mask preferred; dark skin

DQ: blue eyes; entropion or ectropion; undershot greater than ¼″ or overshot bite; wry mouth; prick ears; black (without a trace of brindle), black with white markings, or blue; more than 33 percent white; ticking or spots within areas of white; long coat; nose any color other than black

large numbers of them around the farm. During the day, the dogs would disperse to different duties—guarding groups of livestock, controlling oxen, or accompanying the farmer. A single Boerbel could kill a leopard (but they could not, as some claim, kill a lion alone). Tail docking is said to have originated to prevent baboons from grabbing the dog by the tail. In 1938, the diamond mining company De Beers imported Bullmastiffs to guard their South African mines, and these dogs were subsequently integrated into the Boerboel gene pool. In the early 1980s, two fanciers searched Africa for authentic Boerboel dogs, eventually locating 250 and selecting 72 for registration. The breed has since spread throughout the world but has been banned in at least one country as a fighting dog. It was recognized as a member of the AKC Working group in 2015.

TEMPERAMENT

The Boerboel is a confident dog known for being protective of both property and people. It is a strong-willed working dog with an intelligent nature, thus, this is not a dog for a novice owner. They tend to be aloof with strangers but are extremely affectionate with those they know. The Boerboel requires proper, ongoing training and socialization from an early age to prevent aggression and other negative behavior issues from forming.

UPKEEP

Boerboels need a medium level of activity. A long walk or short jogging venture will usually satisfy their exercise needs. This is not a good breed for dog parks. They enjoy challenging sports such as tracking. Coat care is minimal, consisting of an occasional bath or brushing. They do well outside in temperate climates.

HEALTH

- Major concerns: CHD, elbow dysplasia
- Minor concerns: entropion, ectropion
- Occasionally seen: epilepsy
- Suggested tests: hip, eye, heart
- Life span: 8–12 years

FORM AND FUNCTION

The Boerboel is a large, muscular dog showing strength and agility in motion. As a dog bred to protect people and livestock, it needed to be strong enough to overpower and nimble enough to avoid a wide variety of dangerous African animals. It also needed to be intelligent enough to recognize danger, courageous enough to face it, and cautious enough to stay clear. The jaws are particularly strong. The coat is short but dense. The skin is thick and loose for added protection. It is well pigmented to protect against the African sun. The dog is slightly longer than tall, with powerful free-flowing movement.

Boxer

AT A GLANCE

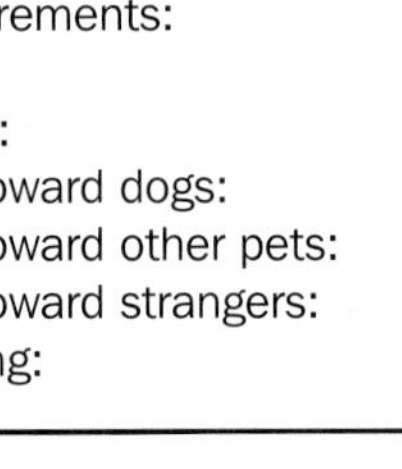

Energy level:	■ ■ ■ ■ ■	Watchdog ability:	■ ■ ■	POPULARITY: Most popular
Exercise requirements:	■ ■ ■	Protection ability:	■ ■ ■ ■ ■	FAMILY: Livestock Dog, Mastiff, Bull
Playfulness:	■ ■ ■ ■ ■	Grooming requirements:	■	AREA OF ORIGIN: Germany
Affection level:	■ ■ ■ ■ ■	Cold tolerance:	■ ■	DATE OF ORIGIN: 1800s
Friendliness toward dogs:	■ ■ ■	Heat tolerance:	■	ORIGINAL FUNCTION: Bullbaiting, guardian
Friendliness toward other pets:	■ ■ ■			TODAY'S FUNCTION: Guardian
Friendliness toward strangers:	■ ■ ■	WEIGHT: male: 65–80 lb; female: 50–65 lb*		OTHER NAME: None
Ease of training:	■ ■ ■	HEIGHT: male: 22.5–25″; female: 21–23.5″		

HISTORY

The Boxer derives from two central European breeds of dog that no longer exist: the larger Danziger Bullenbeiser and smaller Brabenter Bullenbeiser. *Bullenbeiser* means bull-biter, and these dogs were used to chase large game (wild boar, deer, and small bear) through the forest, hanging onto it until the hunter arrived to kill it. This required a strong but agile dog with a broad powerful jaw and a recessed nose to enable the dog to breathe while its jaws were clamped onto an animal. Similar attributes were required of dogs used in bull baiting, a popular sport in many European countries. In England, the Bulldog was the favored breed for the sport, whereas in Germany large mastiff-type dogs were used. Around the 1830s, German hunters began a

ILLUSTRATED STANDARD

1 Broad, blunt muzzle
2 Undershot bite
3 Shallow wrinkles on forehead when alert
4 Distinct stop
5 Slightly arched skull
6 Ears cropped long and tapering
7 Slightly sloping topline
8 Tail set high, docked, and carried upward
9 Stomach slightly tucked up

Color: fawn and brindle, both with or without white flashing and black mask

DQ: any color other than fawn or brindle; white markings exceeding one third of entire coat

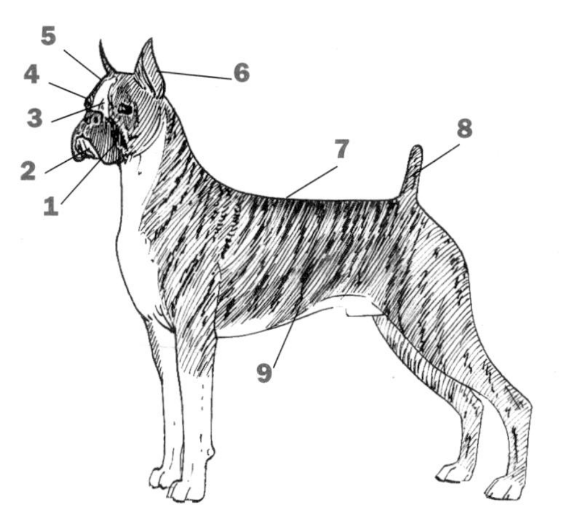

concerted effort to create a new breed, crossing their Bullenbeisers with mastiff-type dogs for size, terriers for tenacity, and, finally, Bulldogs. The result was a tough agile dog with a streamlined body and strong grip. When bull baiting was outlawed, the dogs were mostly used as butcher's dogs in Germany, controlling cattle in slaughteryards. By 1895, an entirely new breed, the Boxer, had been established. Although the exact origin of the name Boxer is obscure, it may have been derived from the German *Boxl*, as they were called in the slaughterhouses. The Boxer was one of the first breeds to be employed as a police and military dog in Germany. By 1900, the breed had become established as a general utility dog, family pet, and even show dog. The AKC recognized the breed soon after, but only in the 1940s did the breed begin its steady rise to the top of the popularity charts, eventually peaking as the fourth most popular breed in America.

TEMPERAMENT

The Boxer is playful, exuberant, inquisitive, attentive, demonstrative, devoted, and outgoing; it is a perfect companion for an active family. It can be stubborn, but it is sensitive and responsive to commands. It may be aggressive toward strange dogs, but it is generally good with other household dogs and pets.

UPKEEP

The Boxer needs daily mental and physical exertion. It likes to run, but its exercise needs can also be met with a good jog or long walk on leash. It does not do well in hot weather and is generally unsuited to live outdoors. Some snore. Its coat needs only occasional brushing to remove dead hair.

HEALTH

- Major concerns: boxer cardiomyopathy, SAS, CHD
- Minor concerns: gastric torsion, hypothyroidism, corneal erosion, colitis
- Occasionally seen: brain tumors, degenerative myelopathy
- Suggested tests: thyroid, hip, cardiac (Holter monitoring)
- Life span: 8–10 years
- Note: Sensitive to heat. White boxers may be deaf. The drug acepromazine can cause severe reactions.

FORM AND FUNCTION

The Boxer is exemplary in its combination of stylish elegance with strength and agility. It is square-proportioned with good substance and musculature. Its stride is free and ground covering, with proud carriage. Its head is distinctive, with a broad, blunt muzzle and alert expression. Its coat is short and shiny. It is perfectly suited to serve as a working watchdog.

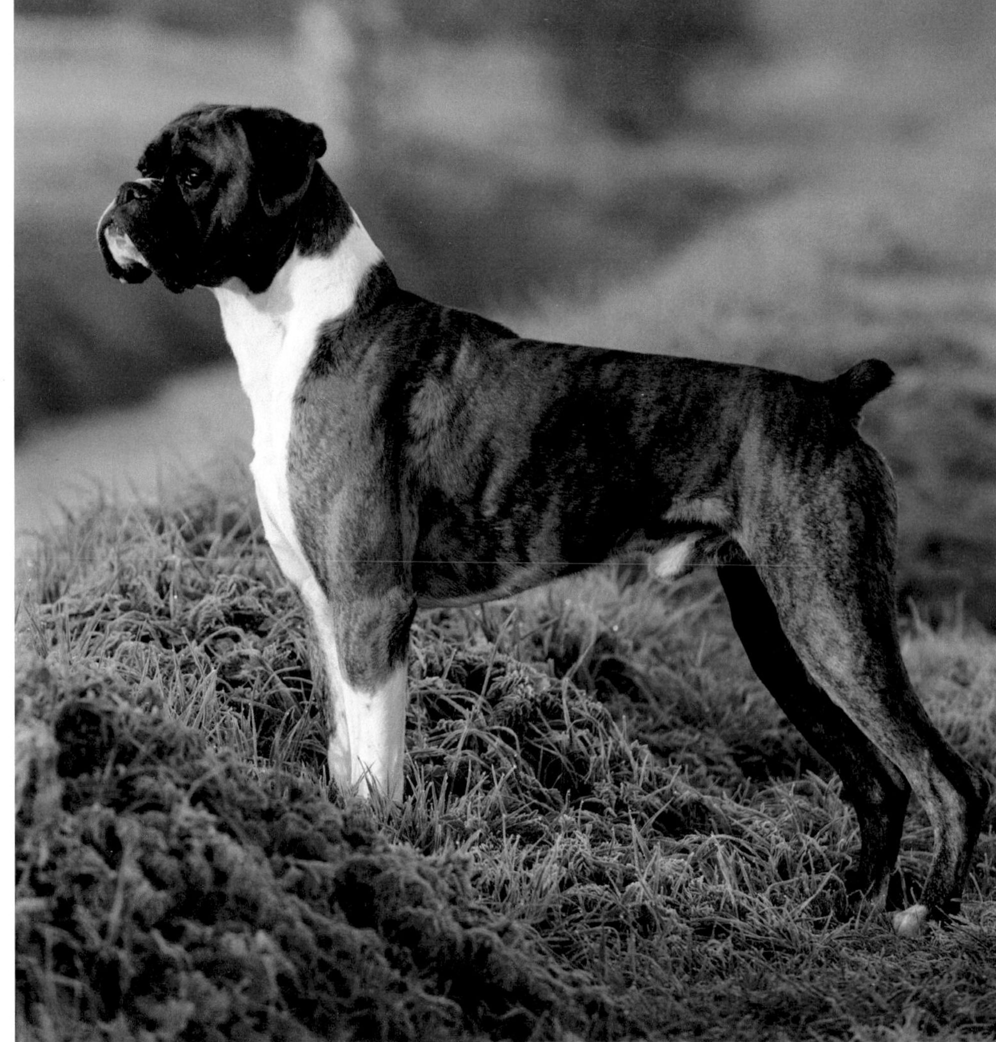

Bullmastiff

AT A GLANCE

Energy level: ■
Exercise requirements: ■■
Playfulness: ■
Affection level: ■■■
Friendliness toward dogs: ■■
Friendliness toward other pets: ■■■■
Friendliness toward strangers: ■
Ease of training: ■

Watchdog ability: ■■■■■
Protection ability: ■■■■■
Grooming requirements: ■
Cold tolerance: ■■■
Heat tolerance: ■

WEIGHT: male: 110–130 lb; female: 100–120 lb
HEIGHT: male: 25–27″; female: 24–26″

POPULARITY: Popular
FAMILY: Mastiff, Bull
AREA OF ORIGIN: England
DATE OF ORIGIN: 1800s
ORIGINAL FUNCTION: Estate guardian
TODAY'S FUNCTION: Companion
OTHER NAME: None

HISTORY

Although the Mastiff is one of Britain's oldest breeds, its immediate descendant, the Bullmastiff, is probably a fairly recent development. It is true that occasional references to the Bullmastiff, or crosses of the Mastiff and Bulldog, can be found as early as 1791; however, no evidence exists that these strains were bred on. The documented history of the Bullmastiff begins near the end of the nineteenth century, when poaching game from the large estates had become such a problem that the gamekeepers' lives were endangered. They needed a tough courageous dog that could wait silently as a poacher and his dog approached, attack on command, and subdue but not maul the poacher. The Mastiff was not fast enough, and the Bulldog was not large enough, so they crossed the breeds in an

ILLUSTRATED STANDARD

1 Muzzle broad, dark preferred
2 Stop moderate
3 Eyes medium size
4 Skull large, with fair amount of wrinkle when alert
5 V-shaped ears carried close to cheeks
6 Topline straight and level
7 Tail set high, not carried over back

Color: red, fawn, or brindle
DQ: none

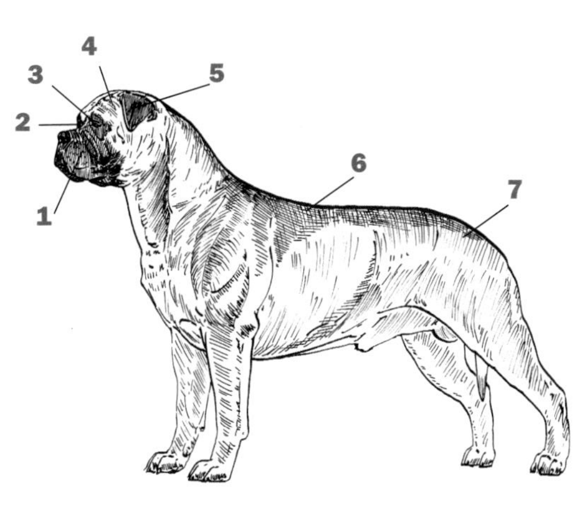

attempt to create their perfect dog; the aptly named "Gamekeeper's Night Dog." The preferred color was dark brindle, as it faded into the night. As the breed's reputation grew, however, many estate owners chose the dogs as estate sentries and preferred the lighter fawns, especially those with black masks, a coloration reminiscent of their Mastiff ancestry. Breeders began to aim for a pure-breeding strain rather than relying upon repeating crosses between the Mastiff and Bulldog. They worked for an ideal animal that appeared to be 60 percent Mastiff and 40 percent Bulldog. By 1924, the breed was deemed to be pure and was recognized by the English Kennel Club. AKC recognition followed in 1933.

TEMPERAMENT

The Bullmastiff is gentle and quiet, a devoted companion and guardian. It is not easily roused, but once threatened it is fearless. It is stubborn and cannot easily be goaded into action against its will. Some can be aggressive toward strange dogs. Males especially tend to not tolerate other males. They are good with children, but should be raised with them. The Bullmastiff needs a firm but loving home. It is not for fragile or timid owners.

UPKEEP

The Bullmastiff is a big dog and needs daily exercise to stay in shape. Its needs are moderate, however, and can be met with walks on leash and short romps. It does not do well in hot, humid weather and generally should be kept as an indoor dog. It needs a soft bed and plenty of room to stretch out. It drools; some snore. Coat care is minimal.

HEALTH

- Major concerns: gastric torsion, CHD, elbow dysplasia
- Minor concerns: entropion
- Occasionally seen: hemangiosarcoma, osteosarcoma, lymphosarcoma, mast cell tumors, cardiomyopathy, SAS, hypothyroidism
- Suggested tests: hip, elbow, eye, cardiac, thyroid
- Life span: 8–10 years

FORM AND FUNCTION

This nearly square breed should be powerful and active, a combination of strength, endurance, and alertness. It should appear to be 60 percent Mastiff and 40 percent Bulldog. Its gait is smooth and powerful, but its angulation is moderate. Its coat is short and dense, and its expression keen and alert. These attributes allowed the Bullmastiff to both overtake and over-power intruders.

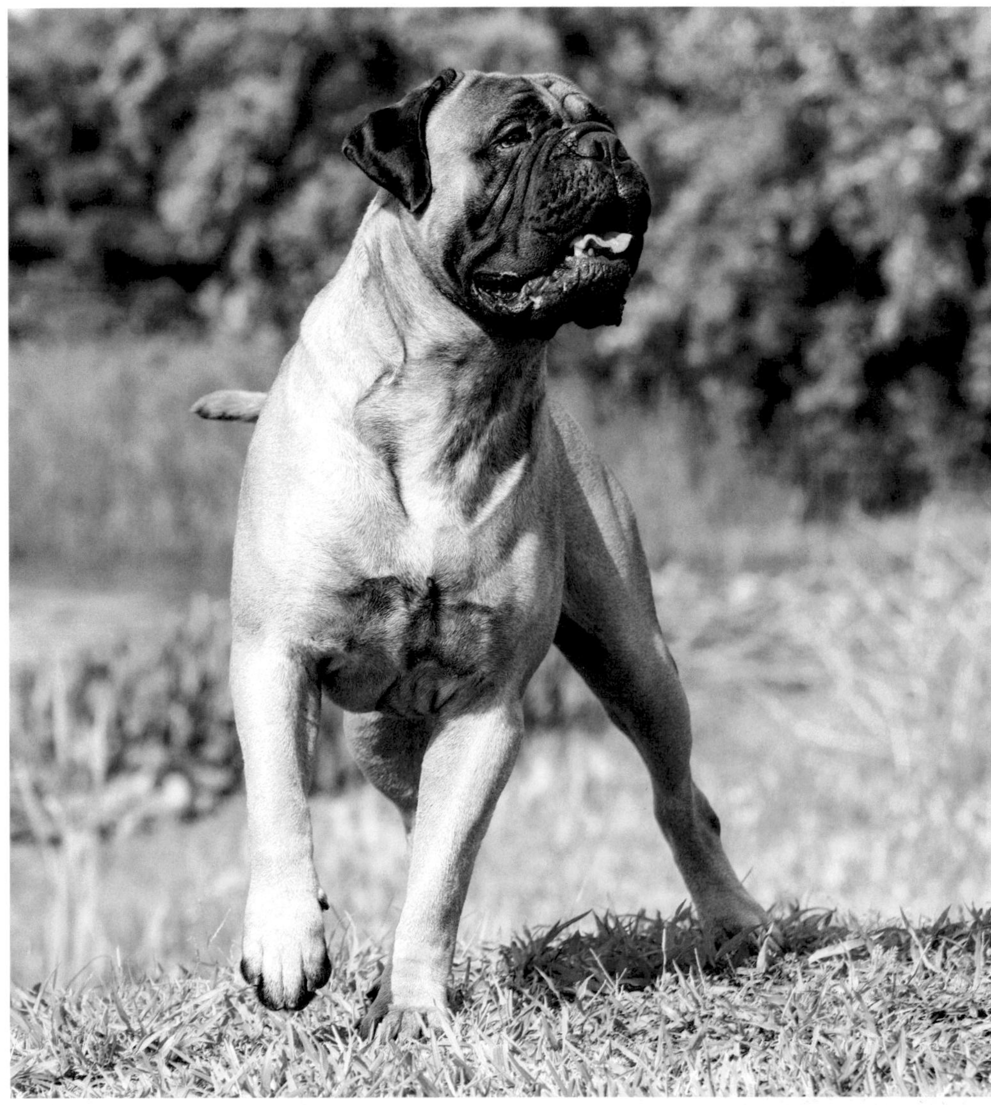

Cane Corso

AT A GLANCE

Energy level:	■■■
Exercise requirements:	■■■
Playfulness:	■■
Affection level:	■■■■
Friendliness toward dogs:	■■
Friendliness toward other pets:	■■
Friendliness toward strangers:	■■
Ease of training:	■■■

Watchdog ability:	■■■■■
Protection ability:	■■■■■
Grooming requirements:	■
Cold tolerance:	■■■
Heat tolerance:	■■■

WEIGHT: 90–130 lb*
HEIGHT: male: 25–27.5″; female: 23.5–26″

POPULARITY: Somewhat popular
FAMILY: Mastiff
AREA OF ORIGIN: Italy
DATE OF ORIGIN: Middle Ages
ORIGINAL FUNCTION: Guardian, hunting, herding
TODAY'S FUNCTION: Guardian
OTHER NAME: None

HISTORY

The Cane Corso is the more streamlined of the two Italian breeds descending from the ancient Roman molossian war dogs, the heavier version being the Neapolitan Mastiff. While the Neo evolved as a dedicated guard dog, the Corso became a versatile farm dog. Cane Corso (pronounced KAHN-nay Corso) comes from the word for *catch dog*, a dog used to overpower large prey. The name was used to describe these dogs as early as the twelfth century. After the fall of the Roman Empire Corsos were used to guard farms, hunt tough prey like wild boar, and control livestock. The dogs were chained during the day in the area they needed to guard to protect visitors and to prevent fighting among them; they were let loose to guard flocks against wolves. The dogs also subdued sows,

ILLUSTRATED STANDARD

1 Large, wide, mastiff-like head; skull is as wide as long
2 Well-defined stop
3 Medium-sized, almond-shaped eyes
4 Ears triangular, cropped or uncropped
5 Muzzle about 1/3 length of head
6 Level back
7 Thick tail, reaching just to hock or docked at fourth vertebrae
8 Round feet

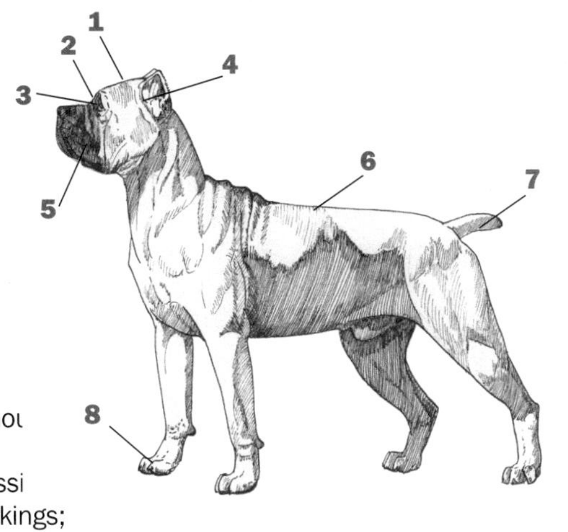

Color: black, gray, fawn or red, with or withou solid red and fawn have a black mask
DQ: blue or yellow eyes; more than two missi undershot more than 1/4"; tan pattern markings; knotted, deviated, or atrophied natural tail

boars, and bulls, and were sometimes used in bull baiting. They worked with other dogs to hunt wild boar, badger, and porcupine, by either holding the cornered animal until the hunter could dispatch it or pulling it from its den. They even rounded up and controlled sheep, goats, and semi-wild cattle. With the onset of modern times, jobs for Corsos declined; then World War I and especially World War II decimated the Corso population in southern Italy. By the 1970s, only a few Corsos survived with peasants spread throughout the countryside. In 1973, two eminent dog fanciers located, collected, and bred surviving specimens, and a decade later a breed club was formed. By 1996, the Cane Corso was recognized by the Fédération Cynologique Internationale. The first documented litter of Corsos was imported to the United States in 1988. The AKC granted the breed full recognition in 2010.

TEMPERAMENT

The Cane Corso is utterly devoted to its family and tends to stick close to them at all times. They are alert watchdogs and dedicated protection dogs. They are eager to please and fairly easy to train, but because some can be domineering, they are not a breed for a novice owner. They are suspicious of strangers and if not extensively socialized can be overly cautious or even aggressive. Most, but not all, get along well with dogs of the opposite sex and with other animals. However, they are not a good candidate for dog parks.

UPKEEP

Corsos tend to be quiet indoors but do need a moderate amount of exercise daily. A long jog or a couple of high-energy play sessions such as tugging, fetching, or swimming are fine. This is not a good breed for dog parks. They thrive on mental stimulation, and they especially enjoy herding and other dog sports that combine mental and physical challenges. Coat care is minimal.

HEALTH

- Major concerns: CHD
- Minor concerns: elbow dysplasia, cardiac problems
- Occasionally seen: entropion, ectropion, gastric torsion
- Suggested tests: hip, elbow, eye, heart
- Life span: 10-11 years

FORM AND FUNCTION

This is a medium to large size mastiff-like dog—sturdy, muscular, large-boned, and athletic. It is both strong and agile enough to bring down wild boar and control unruly bulls, so it should be neither overly bulky nor racy. It is longer than tall. The gait is effortless and powerful. The coat is short, stiff, and dense. The Cane Corso projects confidence and power, a capable protector of property and family.

Chinook

AT A GLANCE

Energy level:	■■■	Watchdog ability:	■■■	POPULARITY: Very rare
Exercise requirements:	■■■	Protection ability:	■■	FAMILY: Northern
Playfulness:	■■■	Grooming requirements:	■■■	AREA OF ORIGIN: United States
Affection level:	■■■■	Cold tolerance:	■■■■■	DATE OF ORIGIN: 1900s
Friendliness toward dogs:	■■■■	Heat tolerance:	■■	ORIGINAL FUNCTION: Sledding
Friendliness toward other pets:	■■■■			TODAY'S FUNCTION: Sledding
Friendliness toward strangers:	■■	WEIGHT: male: 60–90 lb; female: 50–65 lb*		OTHER NAME: None
Ease of training:	■■■	HEIGHT: male: 24–26″; female: 22–24″		

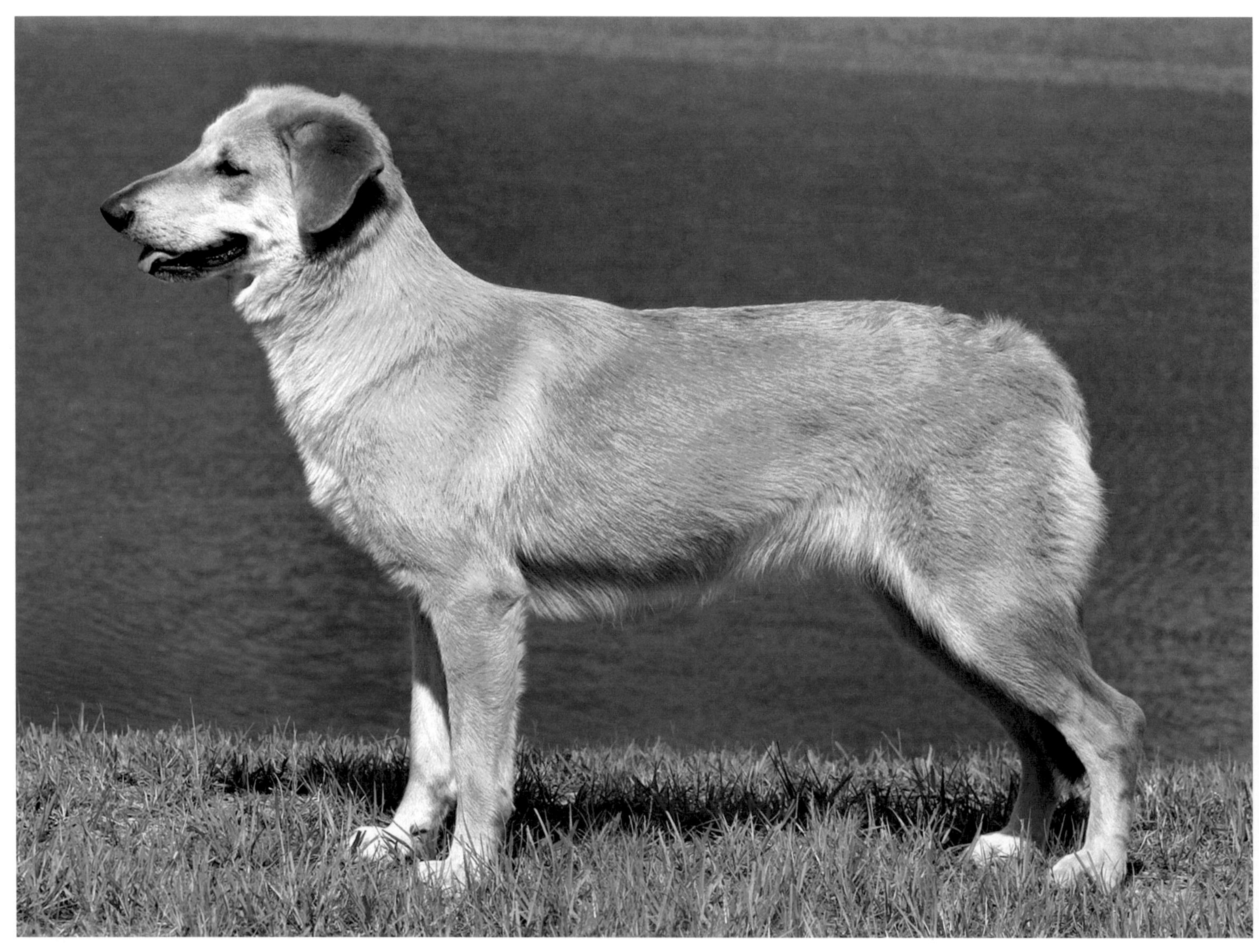

HISTORY

The Chinook is largely the creation of one man, Arthur Walden of New Hampshire, who had experience as a musher in the Yukon. In 1917, he bred a large, tawny, mastiff-type farm dog to Admiral Peary's Greenland husky lead dog, Polaris, to produce three puppies (Rikki, Tikki, and Tavi). Walden renamed one Chinook, and this dog became a prized lead dog. Walden and Chinook brought the sport of sled dog racing to New England. Chinook was bred to Belgian and German Shepherd working dogs, Canadian Eskimo Dogs, and possibly others. His offspring were named Chinooks in his honor. At almost age 12, the original Chinook and 15 other Chinook dogs were part of Admiral Byrd's 1929 Antarctic expedition. Byrd described them as the backbone of the expedition. Unfortunately,

ILLUSTRATED STANDARD

1 Broad, wedge-shaped head; slightly rounded cheeks
2 Medium-sized, almond-shaped eyes, preferably surrounded by dark markings
3 High-set, medium-sized, V-shaped ears either drop, prick, or propeller
4 Moderate stop
5 Straight level back
6 Prominent prosternum
7 Fringed saber tail reaching hock
8 Oval, webbed feet

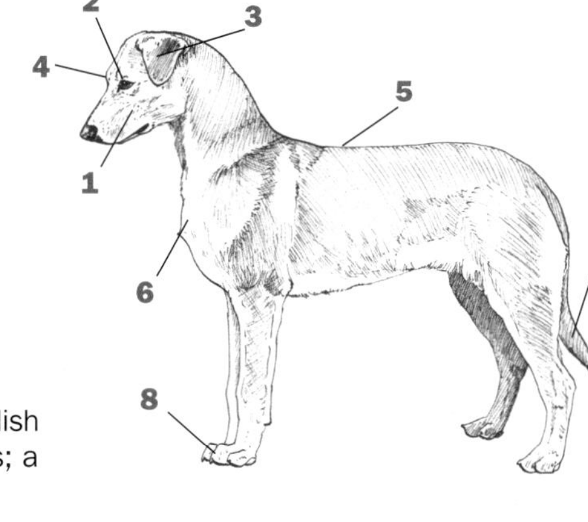

Color: tawny, from pale honey to deep reddish gold, preferably with darker muzzle and ears; a black apostrophe-shaped mark at the inner corner of each eye is desirable
DQ: any eye color other than brown; any color other than tawny

Chinook died while there. The Chinook Trail in New Hampshire was renamed to honor Chinook. Walden subsequently passed on his kennel to another breeder, who did not continue the line. Instead, current Chinooks descend from three dogs—Jock, Hootchinoo, and Zembla—who were placed before the Antarctica expedition. Eventually, these dogs were passed to another breeder, who sold only males or spayed females so nobody else was able to breed them. After his death in 1965, another breeder continued. In 1965, the *Guinness Book of World Records* listed them as the rarest dog, with only 125 specimens. By 1981, only 11 breedable Chinooks remained. Several breeders fought to save the breed, crossing dogs with other Chinook foundation breeds and working to raise awareness of the breed. The UKC recognized the breed in 1991. In 2009, the Chinook became the state dog of New Hampshire. The breed entered the AKC Working Group in 2013.

TEMPERAMENT

Chinooks are calm, gentle, affectionate, and biddable. Unlike most sledding breeds, they tend to be reliable off lead. They are good with children, other dogs, and pets. However, some males can be aggressive toward other male dogs. Most are reserved toward strangers, and some can be shy. They are generally quiet, so are only adequate watchdogs and are poor protection dogs. Although not big barkers, they can be vocal and often talk or whine when excited.

UPKEEP

Chinooks enjoy the company of their family, so although they could physically live outside they do much better inside. They tend to be mellow but need a long walk daily with chances to run off lead throughout the week. They are not natural retrievers. The coat requires weekly brushing but daily brushing during shedding seasons, as shedding can be heavy.

HEALTH

- Major concerns: none
- Minor concerns: seizures, CHD, cryptorchidism
- Occasionally seen: cataract
- Suggested tests: hip, eye
- Life span: 11–14 years

FORM AND FUNCTION

The Chinook was developed as a drafting and racing sled dog, combining the power of freight-hauling breeds with the speed of the lighter racing sled dogs. It has a moderate, athletic build, slightly longer than tall. The bone is moderate, with males noticeably more masculine than females. The coat is close-fitting but thick and double, providing insulation without overheating. The gait appears tireless with good reach and drive. The Chinook exemplifies a sound, northern athlete in grace, muscle tone, movement, and carriage.

Doberman Pinscher

AT A GLANCE

Energy level:	■■■■
Exercise requirements:	■■■
Playfulness:	■■■
Affection level:	■■■
Friendliness toward dogs:	■■
Friendliness toward other pets:	■■■
Friendliness toward strangers:	■
Ease of training:	■■■■■
Watchdog ability:	■■■■■
Protection ability:	■■■■■
Grooming requirements:	■
Cold tolerance:	■■■
Heat tolerance:	■■■

WEIGHT: 65–90 lb*
HEIGHT: male: 26–28″; female: 24–26″

POPULARITY: Very popular
FAMILY: Mastiff
AREA OF ORIGIN: Germany
DATE OF ORIGIN: 1800s
ORIGINAL FUNCTION: Guardian
TODAY'S FUNCTION: Security, police, military, Schutzhund, agility
OTHER NAME: Dobermann

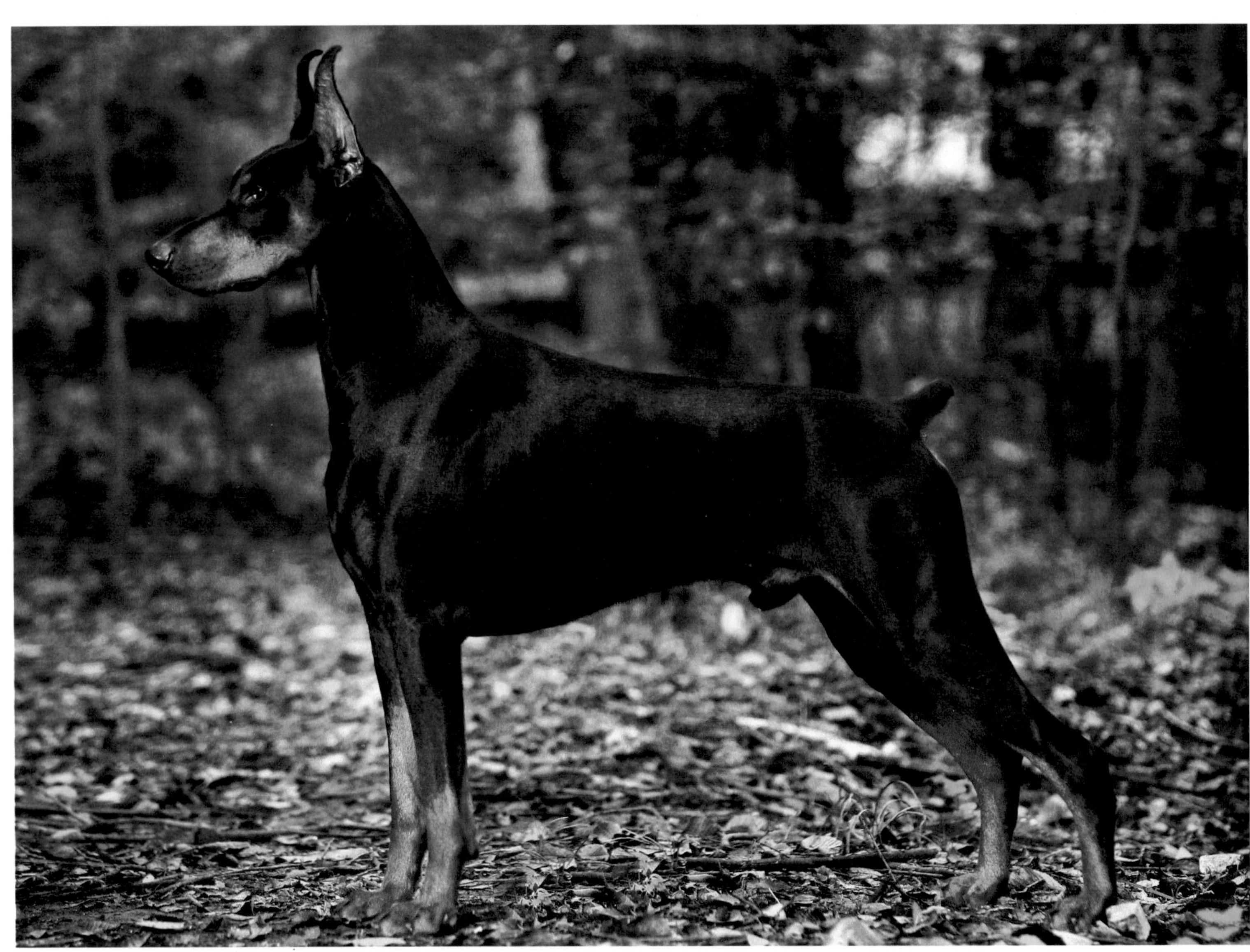

HISTORY

Few people can claim to have had so great an impact upon the dog world as Louis Dobermann of Thuringen, Germany. Herr Doberman was a door-to-door tax collector who needed a watchful guard dog to accompany him on his rounds. In the late 1800s he set about to create an alert streamlined guard dog, most likely by crossing the old German Shepherd and German Pinscher, with later crosses to the Black and Tan Manchester Terrier, Greyhound, and Weimaraner. He soon obtained the prototype of the breed that now bears his name. The original Dobermans were still somewhat heavy boned and round-headed; subsequent breeders selected for a more racy-looking dog. The breed evolved in remarkable time; by 1899 the first breed club was formed. The breed

ILLUSTRATED STANDARD

1 Head long and dry, resembling a blunt wedge from front and side
2 Almond-shaped eyes
3 Skull flat
4 Ears normally cropped and carried erect*
5 Tail docked near second joint, carried slightly above horizontal
6 Stomach well tucked up
7 Feet catlike

Color: black, red, blue, and fawn, all with tan markings
DQ: overshot more than 3⁄16″; undershot more than 1⁄8″; four or more missing teeth; dog of non-allowed color

*Ears may be uncropped.

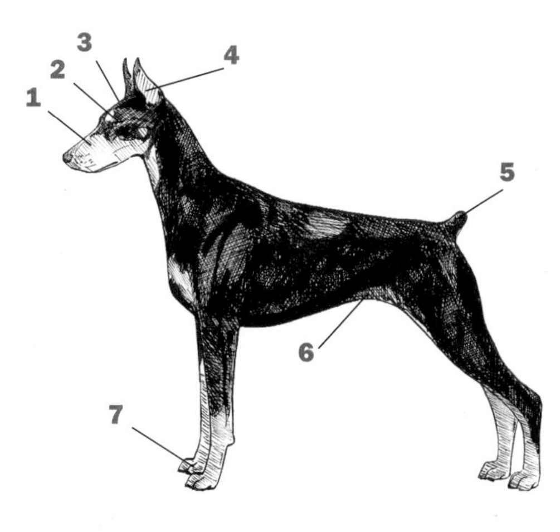

continued to attract acclaim, and the first Doberman arrived in America in 1908. It soon found favor throughout Europe and America as a police and guard dog, and later as a war dog. Its prowess in these areas soon brought more admirers, and the Doberman quickly became a valued family protector. Its chiseled silhouette and fearless alert demeanor has made the Doberman a top contender as a show dog. As its fame grew, many families grew to appreciate the breed as a family pet, and the Doberman eventually rose to be the second most popular breed in America in 1977. Unfortunately, the media cast the Dobe in the role of a vicious breed and its reputation unfairly suffered. During this same time period, albinistic white Dobermans emerged. In an effort to decrease the chance of producing these dogs, the Doberman Pinscher Club of America convinced the AKC to tag the registration numbers of dogs with the likelihood of carrying the albino gene with the letter Z (a DNA test is now available).

TEMPERAMENT

The Doberman Pinscher is an intelligent capable guardian, ever on the alert and ready to protect its family or home. It is also a loyal and adventurous companion. It likes to be mentally challenged, and is a gifted obedience, agility, and Schutzhund pupil. It is sensitive, and very responsive to its owner's wishes, though some can be domineering. It is generally reserved with strangers. It can be aggressive with strange dogs.

UPKEEP

This is an active breed that needs daily mental and physical exercise lest it become frustrated or destructive. Its exercise requirements can be met with a long jog or walk on leash, or a strenuous run in a safe area. Coat care is minimal.

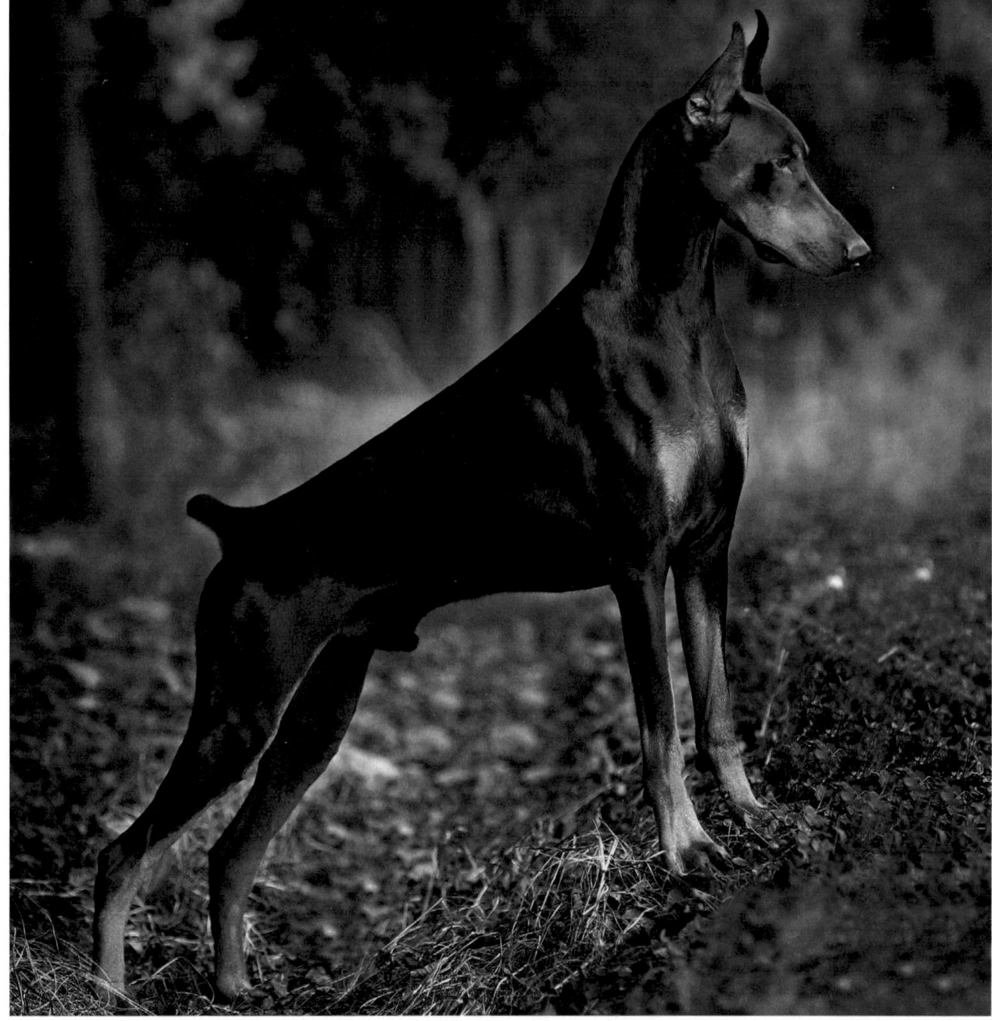

HEALTH

- Major concerns: CVI (wobbler's syndrome), cardiomyopathy
- Minor concerns: vWD, demodicosis, osteosarcoma, gastric torsion, CHD
- Occasionally seen: albinism, hypothyroidism, PRA, narcolepsy
- Suggested tests: cardiac (Holter monitor), hip, eye, DNA for vWD, thyroid
- Life span: 10–12 years
- Note: Blue Dobermans sometimes have hair loss; "white" Dobermans are albinos and are light-sensitive

FORM AND FUNCTION

The Doberman is compactly built, muscular, powerful, and square-proportioned. It combines elegance and strength, speed and endurance. Its carriage is proud and alert, and its gait is free and vigorous. Its coat is short, smooth, and hard, showing off the exceptionally clean-cut lines of this athletic breed.

Dogue de Bordeaux

AT A GLANCE

Energy level:	■■
Exercise requirements:	■■
Playfulness:	■■
Affection level:	■■■■
Friendliness toward dogs:	■
Friendliness toward other pets:	■■■
Friendliness toward strangers:	■■
Ease of training:	■■

Watchdog ability:	■■■■■
Protection ability:	■■■■■
Grooming requirements:	■■
Cold tolerance:	■■■
Heat tolerance:	■

WEIGHT: male: at least 110 lb; female: at least 99 lb
HEIGHT: male: 23.5–27″; female: 23–26″

POPULARITY: Somewhat popular
FAMILY: Mastiff
AREA OF ORIGIN: France
DATE OF ORIGIN: Middle Ages
ORIGINAL FUNCTION: Guardian, hunting, herding
TODAY'S FUNCTION: Guardian
OTHER NAME: French Mastiff, Bordeaux Mastiff, Bordeaux Bulldog

HISTORY

It's difficult to unravel the Dogue de Bordeaux's origin from that of other Mastiff and Bulldog breeds. It probably predates the Bullmastiff, and possibly even the Bulldog, or it may come down from the Bulldog or the Tibetan Mastiff. It may descend from a now extinct breed, such as the ancient Roman molosser or the ancient French Dogue de Bordeaux of Aquitaine. It's likely the breeds were interbred so that their histories are forever intertwined. But it's generally thought that the breed (or a strain resembling it) existed in southern France as early as the 14th century. Early Dogues de Bordeaux were classified into three types (Parisian, Toulouse, and Bordeaux) depending on the region and job, and they came in several colors. They had cropped ears, as did all fighting dogs. Aside from

ILLUSTRATED STANDARD

1. Large, angular, broad head; rather short
2. Oval eyes, set wide apart
3. Small fairly high-set ear, which should fall back but not hang limply
4. Deep wrinkles on either side of median groove
5. Rather short, broad, thick muzzle; foreface slightly concave
6. Nose color matches mask (black, brown, or if no mask, reddish)
7. Well defined dewlap
8. Tail very thick at base, reaching just to hock

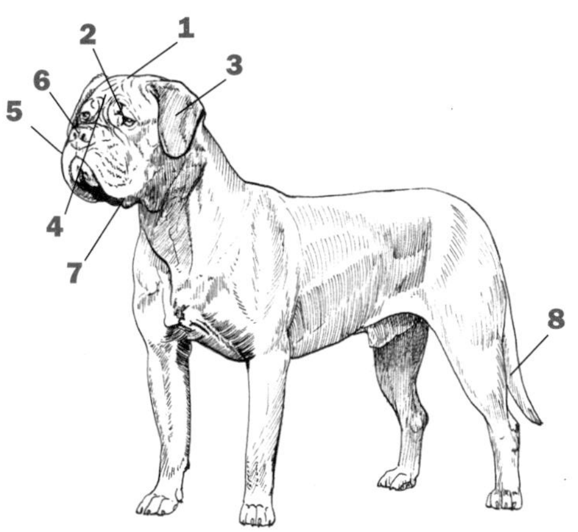

Color: all shades of fawn, with or without a black or brown mask

DQ: mouth not undershot; wry jaw; atrophied, knotted, or laterally deviated or twisted tail; white on head or body; any coat color but fawn

fighting, Dogues were used to bait bulls and bears; control cattle; and guard property and people, particularly the rich. During the French Revolution, many perished with their wealthy owners. The first use of the name Dogue de Bordeaux was in 1863, following the exhibition of one at the first dog show. The first breed standard was published in 1896. Emphasis was placed on the pink nose, light eyes, and red mask to distinguish it from those with recent Mastiff crosses. The breed suffered setbacks after both world wars, but in the 1960s breeders began a concerted effort to revive it. A 1982 article in a dog magazine introduced the breed to American fanciers, and the 1989 movie *Turner and Hooch* introduced the breed to the American public (although few knew its name). The breed gradually gained followers, and it entered the AKC Working Group in 2008.

TEMPERAMENT

The Dogue de Bordeaux is extremely devoted and loyal. It tends to stay close to its chosen person or family at all times. They are vigilant watchdogs and dedicated protection dogs. They are eager to please but are not particularly good at obedience unless it's worth their while. Although males can be aggressive toward other dogs, most are pretty mellow unless provoked. They get along well with other pets.

UPKEEP

Dogues need a chance to stroll around the block and stretch their legs every day, but they don't need to go jogging or have marathon fetch sessions. They tend to be quiet indoors. Their size and strength can present challenges to people with small quarters or minimal strength. Coat care is minimal. Drooling is abundant and may be intolerable to those who are house proud or those who don't like their clothes adorned with glistening streaks.

HEALTH

- Major concerns: CHD, elbow dysplasia
- Minor concerns: brachycephalic syndrome, ectropion, entropion
- Occasionally seen: aortic stenosis, DCM
- Suggested tests: hip, elbow, eye, heart
- Life span: 5–8 years

FORM AND FUNCTION

The Dogue de Bordeaux is a typical brachycephalic molossoid type, with a short, broad skull, massive head, and powerful physique. The body is slightly longer than tall, and the distance from the chest to the ground is slightly less than the depth of the chest. The massive head, serious expression, stocky and athletic build, and self-assured attitude make an imposing picture. The coat is fine, with thick and fairly loose fitting skin, aiding the dog if it is grasped by an adversary. The gait is free with good reach and drive.

German Pinscher

AT A GLANCE

Energy level: ■■■■
Exercise requirements: ■■■
Playfulness: ■■■■
Affection level: ■■■■
Friendliness toward dogs: ■■
Friendliness toward other pets: ■
Friendliness toward strangers: ■■
Ease of training: ■■■

Watchdog ability: ■■■■■
Protection ability: ■■■
Grooming requirements: ■
Cold tolerance: ■
Heat tolerance: ■■■■

WEIGHT: 25–35 lb*
HEIGHT: 17–20″

POPULARITY: Rare
FAMILY: Pinscher
AREA OF ORIGIN: Germany
DATE OF ORIGIN: 1600s
ORIGINAL FUNCTION: Ratting
TODAY'S FUNCTION: Watchdog, companionship
OTHER NAME: None

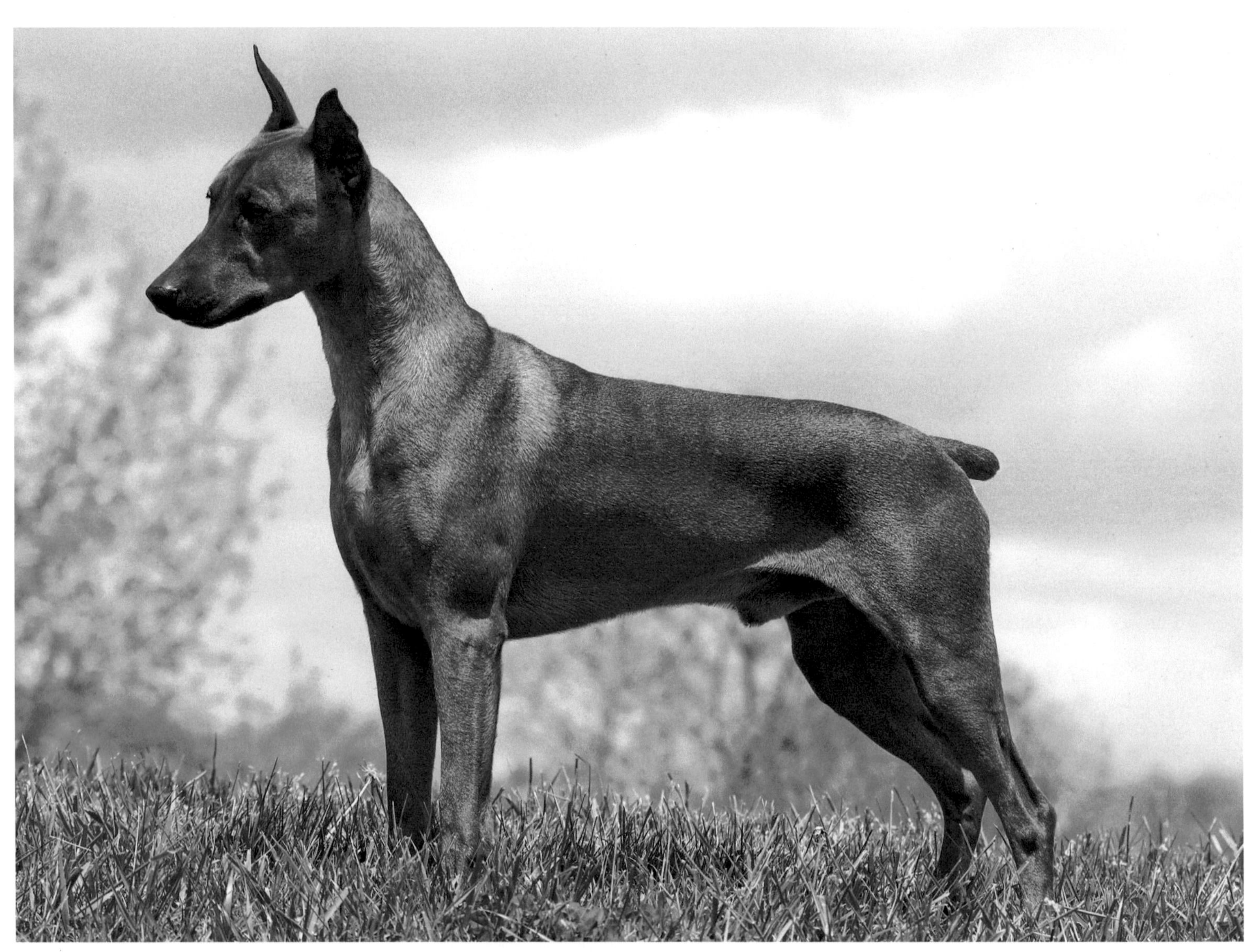

HISTORY

The progenitor of better-known Pinscher breeds, the German Pinscher is an old breed that can trace back to the German Bibarhund of the seventh century and the Tanner of the fourteenth century. In the 1600s dogs with this ancestry or type were mixed with Black and Tan Terriers, creating the Rattenfanger, a versatile working ratter and watchdog. The Rattenfanger became the Pinscher, and it remained a hard working dog for several centuries, especially valued for its rodent-catching ability around the stables. With the advent of dog shows in the late 1800s, interest in the Pinscher grew. The first Pinscher breed standard was drawn up in 1884. The breed didn't garner immediate favor with dog fanciers and numbers fell. An effort to count, register, and exhibit Pinschers was

ILLUSTRATED STANDARD

1 Oval eyes, not bulging
2 High-set ears, carried erect if cropped; if uncropped, either small and erect or V-shaped and folded
3 Tail carried above the horizontal and customarily docked between the second and third vertebra.
4 Pasterns almost perpendicular to ground
5 Feet short and round

Color: isabella (fawn) to red to stag red; black and tan, blue and tan.
DQ: dog of non-allowed color

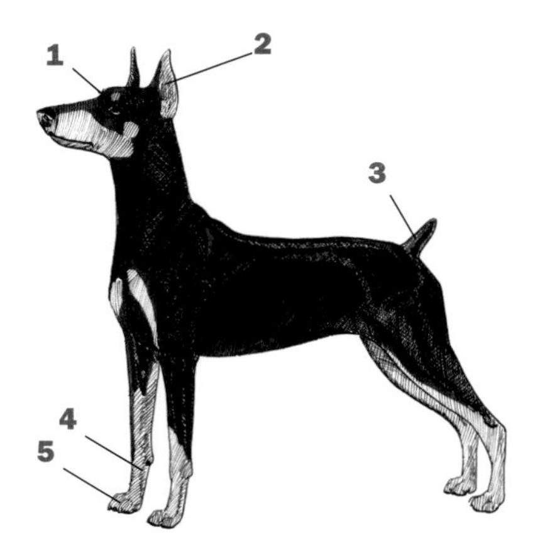

HEALTH

- Major concerns: none
- Minor concerns: none
- Occasionally seen: vWD, cataract, CHD
- Suggested tests: hip, eye, DNA for vWD
- Life span: 12–15 years

FORM AND FUNCTION

The German Pinscher is a medium-sized dog with a muscular square build. It is light enough to be extremely agile and solid enough to be strong. It can hunt all day, aided by extremely sensitive senses. If it turns up a rodent, it can catch and dispatch it. If it turns up an unwelcome human, it can sound the alert and adamantly encourage the person to leave. The German Pinscher has found a new niche as a companion and watchdog of ideal size and loyal temperament.

thwarted by the world wars. After World War II the breed was on the verge of extinction. Between 1949 and 1958 not a single Pinscher litter was registered in West Germany. Now the Pinscher had to rely on its descendent, the Miniature Pinscher, for survival. Four oversize Miniature Pinschers were selected and registered in 1958 by the Pinscher-Schnauzer Klub in West Germany. A Pinscher female was smuggled from East Germany, where Pinschers still existed, and bred to three different MinPin males. Almost all current German Pinschers descend from these five dogs. German Pinschers began their presence in America in the late 1970s. In 2001 the AKC admitted the German Pinscher into its Miscellaneous class, and in 2003 it became a bonafide member of the Working Group.

TEMPERAMENT

Vivacious, tenacious, and courageous, the German Pinscher is a lively self-appointed property patroller. Ever alert, the German Pinscher does not bark frivolously, but does sound the alert to intruders. A quick learner, the German Pinscher is nonetheless not inclined to obey unless there's a good reason to do so. The breed is playful and affectionate, and good with considerate children. It can be wary of strangers. German Pinschers may argue over which of them gets to be boss, and they may not be good with small pets—especially rodents!

UPKEEP

German Pinschers like to be in the thick of things and do not appreciate being left outside alone or relegated to a kennel. This is a high-energy dog that is easily bored and frustrated if not given a way to stimulate its mind and exercise its body. Grooming is wash and wear; only occasional brushing is required.

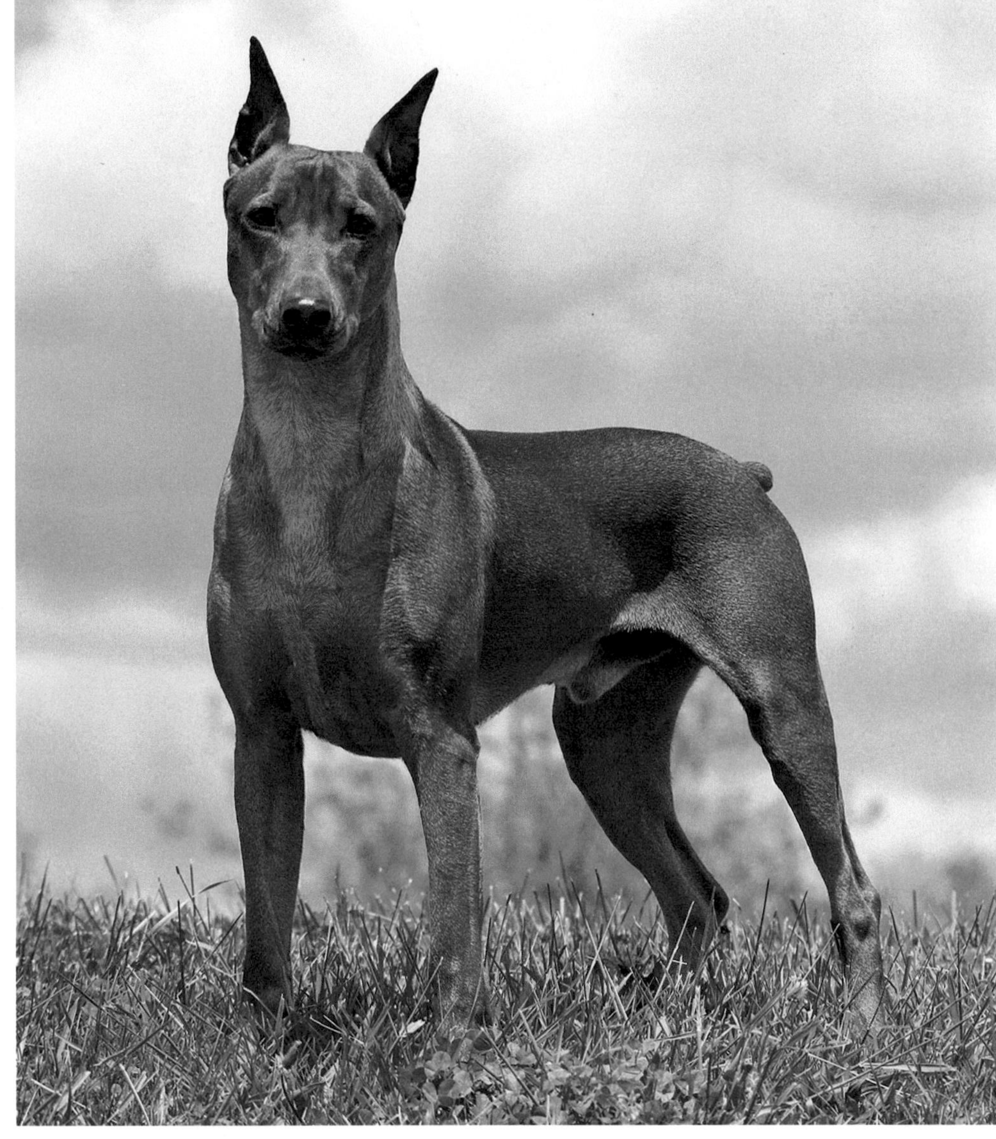

Giant Schnauzer

AT A GLANCE

Energy level: ■■■
Exercise requirements: ■■■■
Playfulness: ■■■■
Affection level: ■
Friendliness toward dogs: ■
Friendliness toward other pets: ■■
Friendliness toward strangers: ■
Ease of training: ■■■

Watchdog ability: ■■■■■
Protection ability: ■■■■■
Grooming requirements: ■■■
Cold tolerance: ■■■
Heat tolerance: ■■■

WEIGHT: 65–90 lb*
HEIGHT: male: 25.5–27.5″; female: 23.5–25.5″

POPULARITY: Somewhat uncommon
FAMILY: Livestock Dog, Herding, Schnauzer
AREA OF ORIGIN: Germany
DATE OF ORIGIN: Middle Ages
ORIGINAL FUNCTION: Cattle herding, guardian
TODAY'S FUNCTION: Security, police, Schutzhund
OTHER NAME: Riesenschnauzer

HISTORY

The Giant Schnauzer originated in the countryside of Bavaria and Wurrtemburg. Cattlemen there were impressed by the smaller Standard Schnauzer, and sought to emulate it on a larger scale that would be suitable for driving cattle. It is likely, though not documented, that they crossed the Standard Schnauzer with their larger smooth-coated cattle-driving dogs in an attempt to create a wire-haired drover. Later crosses with rough-coated Sheepdogs and the Great Dane and Bouvier des Flandres probably occurred, and even crosses with the black Poodle, Wolf Spitz, and Wirehaired Pinscher have been suggested. The result was a weather-resistant, smart-looking dog capable of handling cattle, then known as the Munchener. They later became more popular as butcher's or stockyard dogs,

ILLUSTRATED STANDARD

1 Rectangular head
2 Oval, deep-set eyes
3 Ears may be cropped or uncropped; when uncropped, ears are V-shaped
4 Short, straight back
5 Tail docked to second or third joint, carried high
6 Cat feet

Color: solid black or pepper and salt
DQ: overshot or undershot; markings other than specified

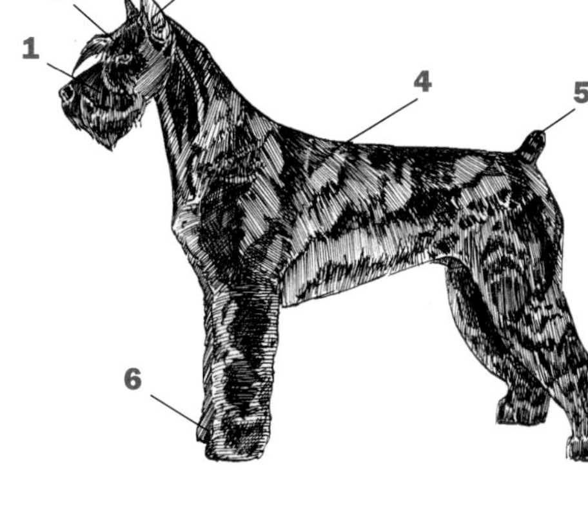

FORM AND FUNCTION

This is a larger, more powerful version of the Standard Schnauzer. Its body is strong, compact, and nearly square, combining great power with agility. The stride is free and vigorous, with good reach and drive. Its double coat consists of a soft undercoat and a harsh, wiry, dense outer coat, a combination that enables it to withstand harsh, alpine conditions. Its hallmark harsh beard and eyebrows, coupled with its smart outline, make a striking figure. The combination of rugged build, reliable temperament, and weather-resistant coat make for a powerful and versatile worker.

and even later, brewery guard dogs. The dogs maintained a low profile, with little exposure until just before World War I, when it was suggested that they could be trained as police dogs. They excelled at their new assignment but have not been well accepted outside of Germany in that capacity. They have gained more headway as a pet in recent years, however, and now enjoy modest popularity in America.

TEMPERAMENT

The playful, rambunctious Giant Schnauzer may be too boisterous for small children, even though it is otherwise very good with children in its own family. It is bold and protective of its family and reserved with strangers. It may be aggressive toward other dogs. This intelligent and exuberant breed is a good choice for an active person wanting a partner in adventure, although at times the Giant may try to be the leader.

UPKEEP

The Giant Schnauzer needs daily exercise and daily fun. Its exercise requirements can be met with vigorous games and long hikes or walks. Its harsh coat needs combing once or twice weekly, plus shaping two to four times yearly. Shaping is best done by professional scissoring and hand-stripping, but clipping is acceptable for pets.

HEALTH

- Major concerns: CHD
- Minor concerns: OCD, gastric torsion, hypothyroidism
- Occasionally seen: PRA, cataract
- Suggested tests: hip, thyroid, eye
- Life span: 10–12 years

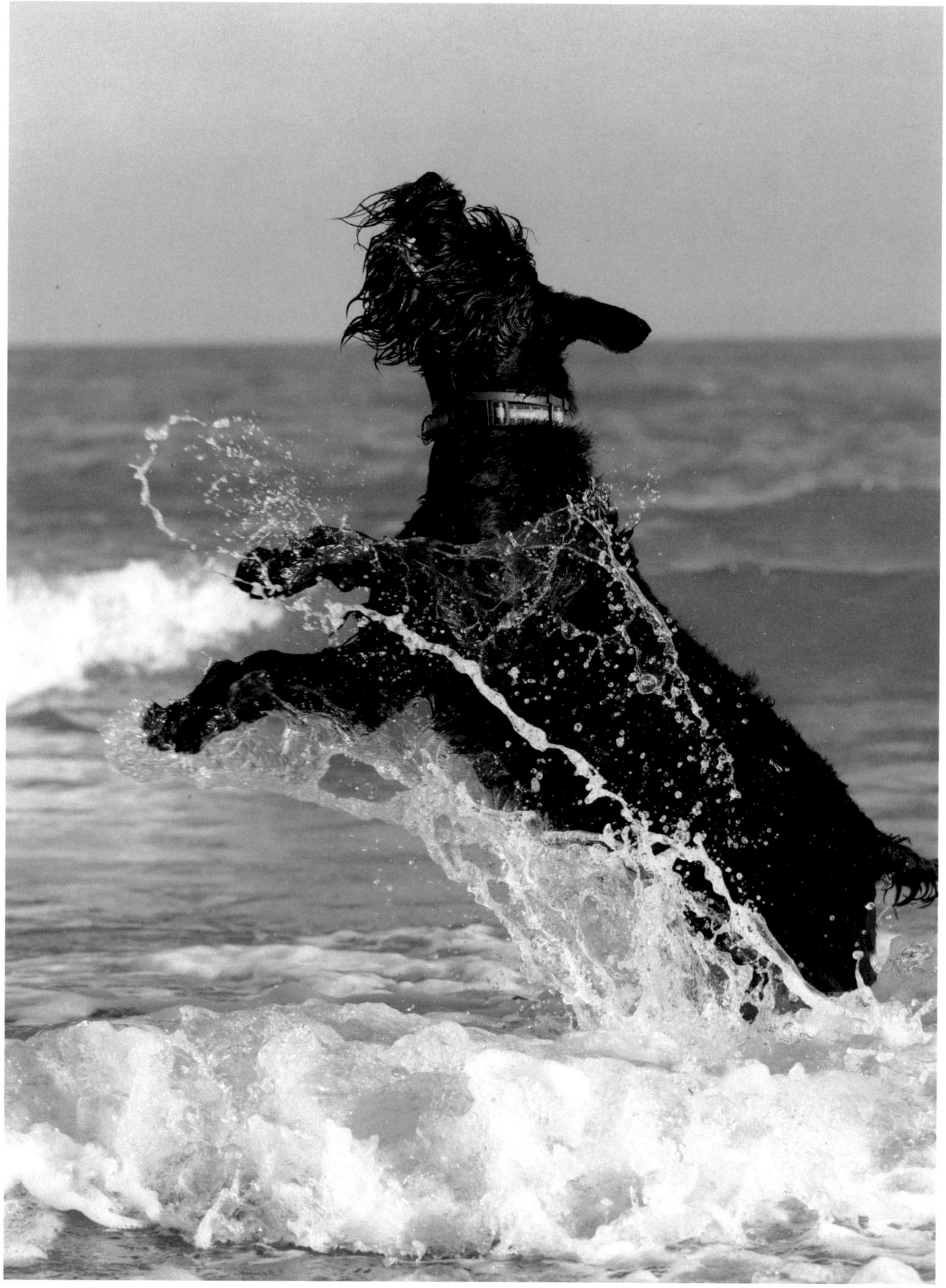

Great Dane

AT A GLANCE

Energy level:	■■
Exercise requirements:	■■
Playfulness:	■■
Affection level:	■■■■
Friendliness toward dogs:	■■
Friendliness toward other pets:	■■
Friendliness toward strangers:	■■■■
Ease of training:	■■■
Watchdog ability:	■■■■
Protection ability:	■■■
Grooming requirements:	■
Cold tolerance:	■■
Heat tolerance:	■■

WEIGHT: male: 130–180 lb*; female: 110–150 lb*
HEIGHT: male at least 30″*, preferably 32″ or more (Note: most 32–35″*); female: at least 28″, preferably 30″ or more (Note: most 31–33″*)

POPULARITY: Very popular
FAMILY: Mastiff
AREA OF ORIGIN: Germany
DATE OF ORIGIN: Middle Ages
ORIGINAL FUNCTION: Guardian, hunting large game
TODAY'S FUNCTION: Companion
OTHER NAME: Deutsche Dogge, German Mastiff

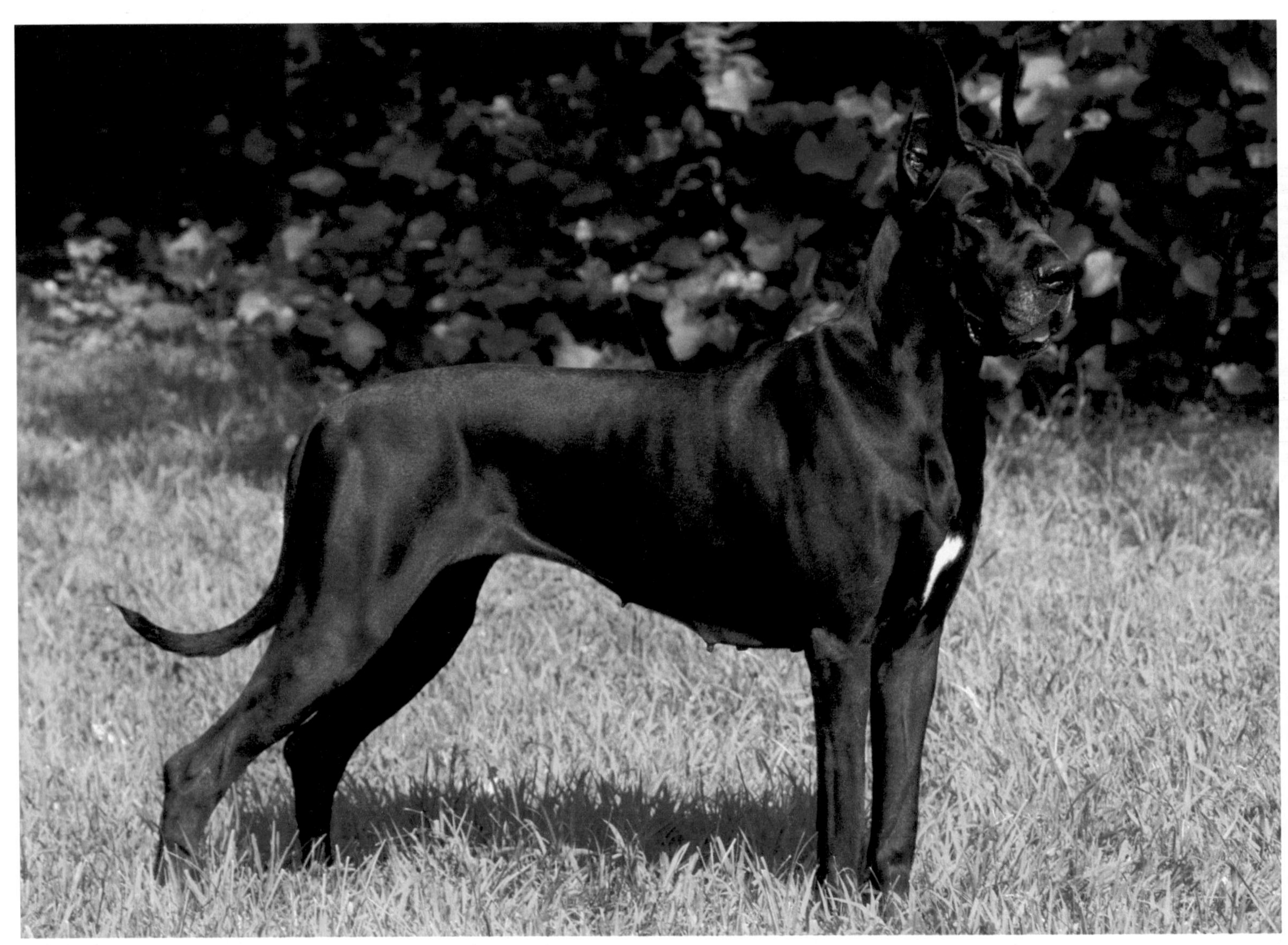

HISTORY

Dubbed the "Apollo of Dogs," the Great Dane is probably the product of the ancient Molossus war dog and the Greyhound. With these ancestors, its ability as a fearless big game hunter seemed only natural. By the fourteenth century, these dogs were proving themselves as able hunters in Germany, combining speed, stamina, strength, and courage in order to bring down the tough wild boar. The dogs became popular with the landed gentry not only because of their hunting ability but also because of their imposing yet graceful appearance. These noble dogs made gracious additions to any estate. British familiar with the breed first referred to them as German Boarhounds. Exactly when and why the breed was later dubbed the Great Dane is a mystery because, although undeniably great, it is

ILLUSTRATED STANDARD

1 Square jaw with deep muzzle
2 Almond-shaped, medium-sized eyes
3 Head long and rectangular, stop pronounced
4 Ears medium size; if cropped, carried uniformly erect
5 Short level back
6 Tail set high, not carried over level of back
7 Well-defined tuck-up
8 Round feet

Color: brindle, black-masked fawn, blue, black, harlequin (white with irregular black patches), or mantle (black with white collar, muzzle, chest, and tail tip)

DQ: under minimum height; split nose; docked tail; any color other than those specified

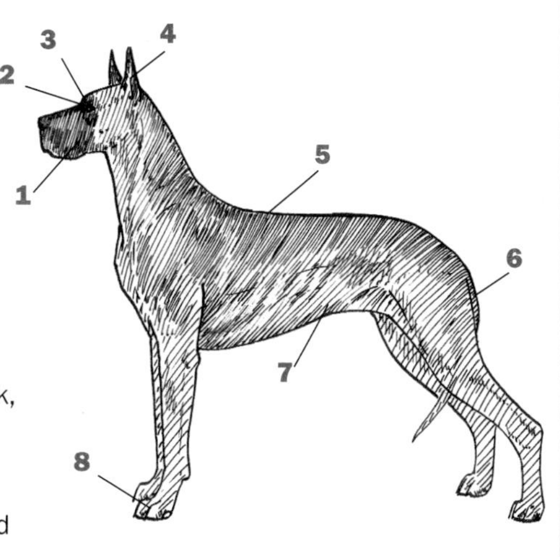

not Danish. It is a German breed, and in 1876, the breed was declared Germany's National Dog. In 1880 German authorities declared the dog should be called the Deutsche Dogge, the name by which it still goes in Germany. The English paid no heed, and the old name stuck for the English-speaking world. By the late 1800s, the Great Dane had come to America. It quickly attracted attention, as it does to this very day. The breed has since achieved great popularity in spite of some of the challenges owning a giant dog entails. The record of world's tallest dog has been held by several Great Danes.

TEMPERAMENT

The Great Dane is spirited, courageous, friendly, and dependable. It is generally good with children (although its friendly overtures may overwhelm a small child) and usually friendly toward other household dogs and pets, but like all large dogs should be supervised. With training, it makes a pleasant, well-mannered family companion.

UPKEEP

The Great Dane needs daily moderate exercise. Its needs can be met with a good walk or romp. It needs soft bedding and sufficient room to stretch out when sleeping. Some tend to drool. Coat care is minimal.

HEALTH

- Major concerns: gastric torsion, cardiomyopathy, osteosarcoma
- Minor concerns: CHD, CVI (Wobbler's syndrome), OCD, HOD, hypothyroidism
- Occasionally seen: vWD, cataract, entropion
- Tests: cardiac, hip, eye, thyroid, cardiac
- Life span: 7–10 years
- Note: Danes are usually bred within three separate color families: fawn and brindle; harlequin and mantle; and black and blue. Because dogs from the color families are seldom interbred, each color family tends to have different characteristics and health concerns.

FORM AND FUNCTION

This regal breed combines great size and power with elegance. It is square proportioned and well balanced. Its gait is strong and powerful with long, easy strides. These attributes are necessary in a dog required to overtake and then overpower relatively swift but formidable quarry. Its coat is short, thick, and glossy. The Great Dane is most noteworthy for its majestic carriage and appearance—the Apollo of Dogs.

Great Pyrenees

AT A GLANCE

Energy level: ■
Exercise requirements: ■■■
Playfulness: ■■
Affection level: ■■■
Friendliness toward dogs: ■■
Friendliness toward other pets: ■■■
Friendliness toward strangers: ■■
Ease of training: ■

Watchdog ability: ■■■■■
Protection ability: ■■■■
Grooming requirements: ■■■
Cold tolerance: ■■■■■
Heat tolerance: ■

WEIGHT: male: 115 lb; female: 85–90 lb
HEIGHT: male: 27–32″; female: 25–29″

POPULARITY: Somewhat popular
FAMILY: Livestock Dog, Flockguard
AREA OF ORIGIN: France
DATE OF ORIGIN: Ancient times
ORIGINAL FUNCTION: Sheep guardian
TODAY'S FUNCTION: Companion, livestock guardian
OTHER NAME: Pyrenean Mountain Dog, Chien des Pyrenees, Chien de Montagne des Pyrenees

HISTORY

The Great Pyrenees is a very old breed that probably descended from the first flock guardian dogs, which were large white dogs that existed in Asia Minor about 10,000 B.C. When nomadic shepherds brought their sheep to the Pyrenees Mountains around 3000 B.C, their flock guarding dogs came with them, forming the basis of the Great Pyrenees. These dogs excelled as livestock guardians for several centuries. In medieval France, the Pyrenees became a formidable fortress guard, and eventually a band of these imposing dogs was the pride of many large chateaus. In the late 1600s, the breed caught the eye of French nobility, and for a brief time they were in great demand in the court of Louis XIV. In fact, in 1675 the Great Pyrenees was decreed the "Royal Dog of France" by Louis XIV.

ILLUSTRATED STANDARD

1 Eyes medium-sized, almond-shaped
2 Head wedge-shaped, not heavy, slightly rounded crown
3 Ears small to medium, V-shaped with rounded tips
4 Tail well plumed
5 Rear feet tend to toe out
6 Double dewclaws on each hind leg
7 Round feet

Color: white or white with markings of gray, badger, reddish brown, or tan
DQ: none

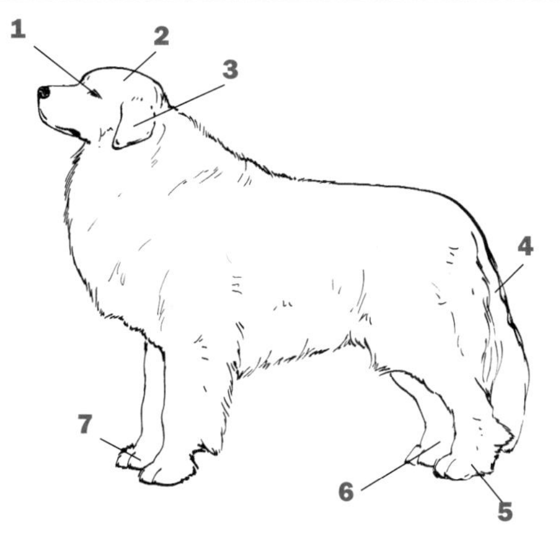

Around the same time Great Pyrenees came to Newfoundland, where they may have played a role in the development of the Newfoundland breed, but it did not itself continue as a pure breed. The first documented Pyrenees came to America with General Lafayette in 1824. By the 1900s, the breed had disappeared from French court life, and the remaining dogs were those found still working in the isolated countryside. Many of the poorer puppies were sold to tourists who brought them back to England and other countries. These dogs bore little resemblance to the magnificent Pyrenees that had once been so admired, however. Interest in the breed declined in England, but fortunately the breed still existed in sufficient numbers and quality in its native mountain land that later fanciers were able to obtain good breeding stock. These dogs served as the foundation of the modern Pyrenees. Serious importation of the breed to America occurred in the 1930s, and by 1933 the Great Pyrenees received AKC recognition. It attracted great attention as well as new owners, and today the Great Pyrenees enjoys moderate popularity. It has earned a reputation as a reliable livestock guardian in service in much of the United States.

TEMPERAMENT

The Great Pyrenees is a capable and imposing guardian, devoted to its family and somewhat wary of strangers—human or canine. When not provoked, it is calm, well-mannered, and somewhat serious. It is very gentle with its family and children. It has an independent, somewhat stubborn, nature, and may try to dominate a less secure owner. They are not good off leash and may wander away. The Great Pyrenees tends to bark a lot.

UPKEEP

The Great Pyrenees needs daily exercise to stay in shape, though its needs are not excessive. A moderate walk will usually suffice. It enjoys hiking, especially in cold weather and snow. It does not do well in hot weather. Its coat needs brushing once or twice weekly, daily when shedding. It may drool at times, and it tends to be a messy drinker.

HEALTH

- Major concerns: CHD, patellar luxation
- Minor concerns: entropion, OCD, skin problems, osteosarcoma, cataract, chondrodysplasia (dwarfism), panosteitis
- Occasionally seen: gastric torsion, otitis externa, spinal muscular atrophy
- Suggested tests: hip, knee, (eye)
- Life span: 10–12 years

FORM AND FUNCTION

Elegant, imposing, and majestic, the Great Pyrenees is a large dog of medium substance that is slightly longer than tall. Its thick coat gives the impression of heavier bone and stature. This breed was developed to guard flocks on steep mountain slopes and so must combine strength with agility. It moves smoothly, with good reach and drive. The weather-resistant double coat consists of a dense, wooly undercoat and a long, flat, coarse outer coat, imparting great insulation from the Pyrenean cold. Its expression is elegant and contemplative.

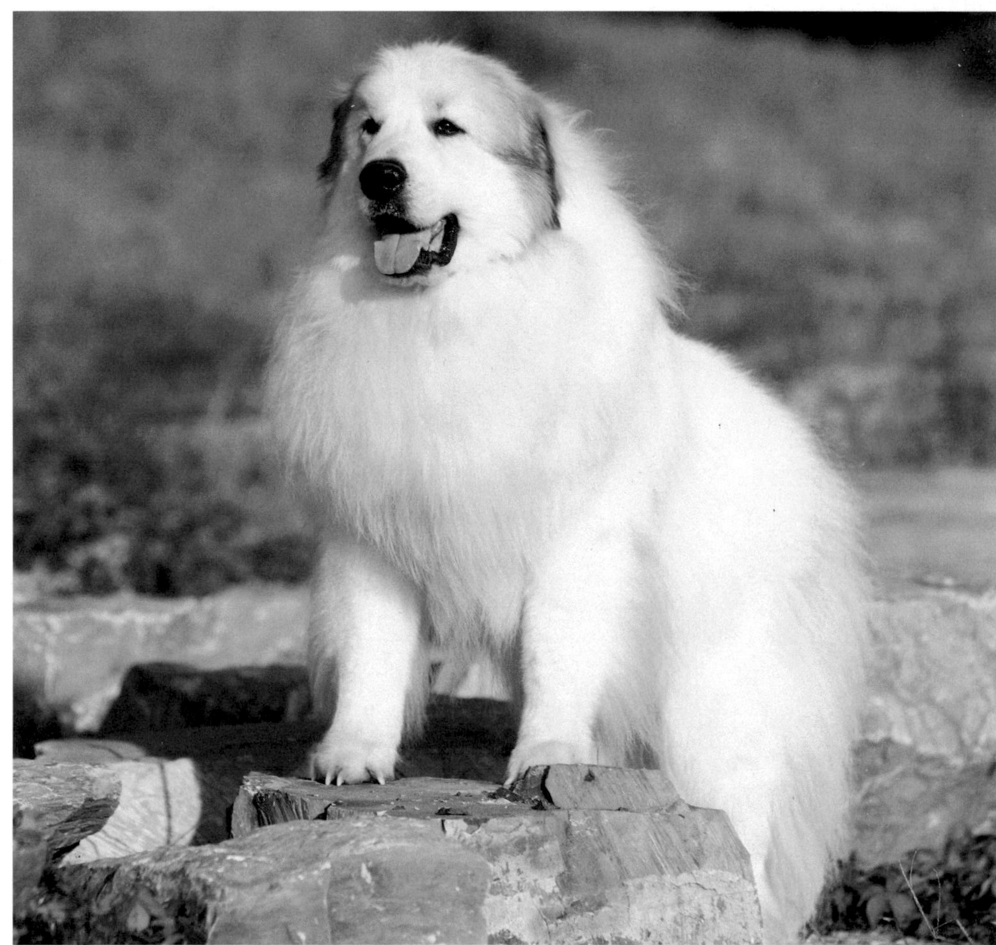

Greater Swiss Mountain Dog

AT A GLANCE

Energy level:	■■
Exercise requirements:	■■■
Playfulness:	■■
Affection level:	■■■
Friendliness toward dogs:	■■■
Friendliness toward other pets:	■■■■
Friendliness toward strangers:	■■
Ease of training:	■■■■
Watchdog ability:	■■■■
Protection ability:	■■■
Grooming requirements:	■
Cold tolerance:	■■■■
Heat tolerance:	■■

WEIGHT: male: 105–140 lb; female: 85–110 lb*
HEIGHT: male: 25.5–28.5″; female: 23.5–27″

POPULARITY: Somewhat uncommon
FAMILY: Livestock Dog, Mastiff
AREA OF ORIGIN: Switzerland
DATE OF ORIGIN: Ancient times
ORIGINAL FUNCTION: Draft dog, guardian
TODAY'S FUNCTION: Companion, herding
OTHER NAME: Grosser Schweizer Sennenhund, Great Swiss Cattle Dog

HISTORY

The Greater Swiss Mountain Dog is the oldest and largest of four varieties of Sennenhunde, or Swiss Mountain Dogs, the other three being the Appenzeller, Entlebucher, and Bernese. The breeds share a common heritage, probably derived from the Mastiff or Molossian dogs of the Romans. These dogs were probably introduced when the Romans crossed through Switzerland. Another theory is that the Phoenicians brought them to Spain around 1100 B.C. Whatever their origin, they spread over Europe and interbred with native dogs, eventually developing along independent lines in isolated communities. They shared the same working ethic, dividing their duties between acting as guardian of livestock and home, herder, and draft dog. Many came to be known as Metzgerhunde, or

ILLUSTRATED STANDARD

1 Eyes medium-sized, almond-shaped
2 Skull flat and broad
3 Ears set high, triangular with rounded tip
4 Topline level
5 Tail carried down in repose, raised when excited
6 Round feet

Color: black and rust, with white feet, chest, tail tip, muzzle, blaze, and possibly collar; rust color present on legs between white and black

DQ: any color other than black, tan, and white tricolor; blue eye color

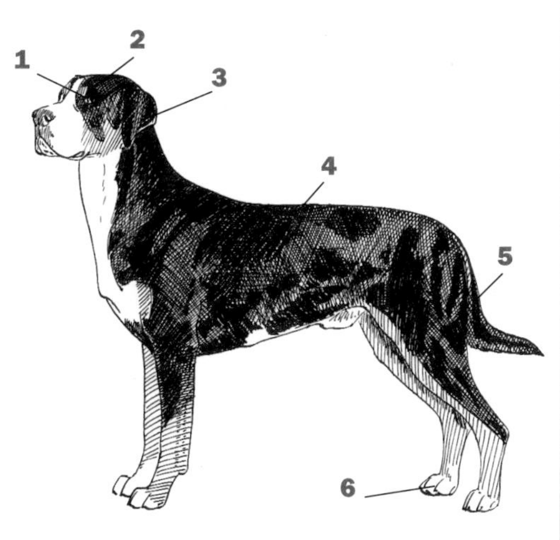

butcher's dogs. Until the late 1800s, all these dogs, which share a common coat color pattern, were generally assumed to be of one breed or type. Only when Professor A. Heim endeavored to study the native Swiss mountain breeds seriously did he discern consistent differences that allowed them to be categorized as four distinct breeds. The year 1908 can be regarded as the birth date of the Greater Swiss; in this year Professor Heim spotted a magnificent short-haired dog entered in a Bernese Mountain Dog contest. He considered the dog a separate breed, and dubbed it the Greater Swiss because of its resemblance to the sturdy Swiss butcher's dogs he had also seen. The breed grew very slowly in popularity, additionally thwarted by two world wars. Only in 1968 did the Greater Swiss come to America, with the first litter born in 1970. In 1985 the breed was admitted into the AKC Miscellaneous class, achieving full recognition in 1995.

TEMPERAMENT

The Greater Swiss Mountain Dog is a sensitive, loyal, and extremely devoted family companion. It is calm and easy-going, very gentle with children as well as other pets. It is territorial, alert, bold, and vigilant.

UPKEEP

As befitting of a dog with working roots, this breed likes the outdoors, especially in cold weather. It needs daily exercise, either a good long walk or vigorous romp. It especially enjoys pulling. Its coat needs brushing once weekly, more often when shedding.

HEALTH

- Major concerns: CHD
- Minor concerns: panosteitis, shoulder OCD, distichiasis, gastric torsion, splenic torsion, seizures, female urinary incontinence
- Occasionally seen: none
- Suggested tests: elbow, eye, (shoulder), hip
- Life span: 10–12 years

FORM AND FUNCTION

This is a strong draft breed. It is large and powerful, slightly longer than tall. Its movement displays good reach and drive. Its double coat consists of a thick undercoat and dense outer coat, about 1 to 1¾ inches long. Its expression is gentle and animated.

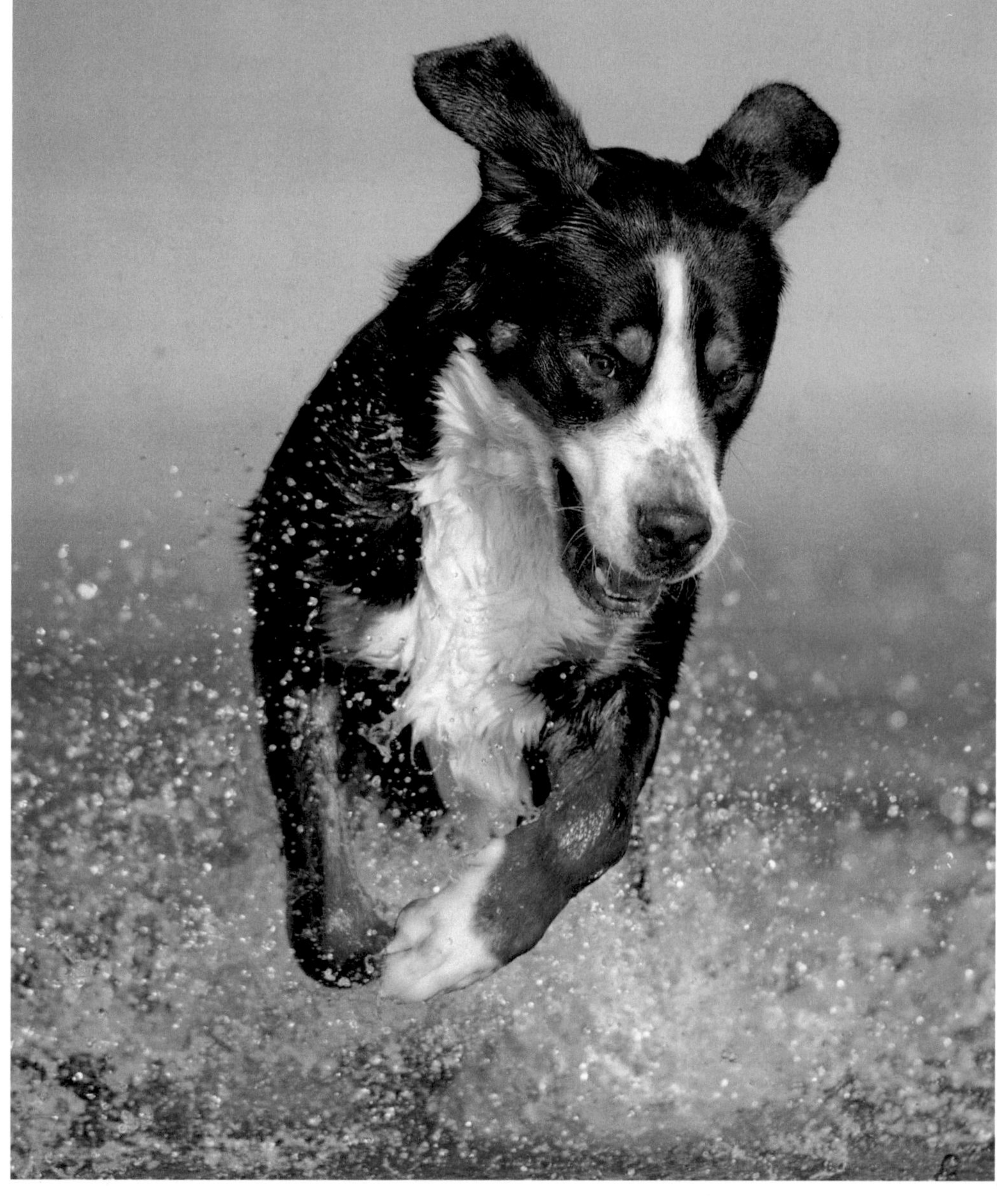

Komondor

AT A GLANCE

Energy level:	■■■	Watchdog ability:	■■■■■	POPULARITY: Very rare
Exercise requirements:	■■■	Protection ability:	■■■■■	FAMILY: Livestock Dog, Flockguard
Playfulness:	■■■	Grooming requirements:	■■■	AREA OF ORIGIN: Hungary
Affection level:	■■■■	Cold tolerance:	■■■■	DATE OF ORIGIN: Ancient times
Friendliness toward dogs:	■	Heat tolerance:	■■	ORIGINAL FUNCTION: Sheep Guardian
Friendliness toward other pets:	■■■■			TODAY'S FUNCTION: Sheep Guardian
Friendliness toward strangers:	■	WEIGHT: male: avg. 80 lb; female: avg. 70 lb*		OTHER NAME: None
Ease of training:	■■■	HEIGHT: male 27.5″ +; female: 25.5″ +		

HISTORY

When the Huns came to Hungary, they brought with them the large, long-legged, Russian Owtcharka, which became the progenitor of the Komondor (plural: Komondorok). These dogs bore a close resemblance to the Magyar sheep known as Racka, which had a proud "dog-like" carriage and masses of curly wool. Thus, the dogs easily intermingled with the sheep and at first glance appeared to be one of the flock. Greatly valued by the Magyar shepherds, the Komondorok were not allowed to interbreed with other breeds. The earliest documentation of the breed dates back to 1555, although the breed is certain to have existed long before then. The Komondor earned its keep by guarding the flocks against marauding animals. So effective was it that some claim it is responsible for

ILLUSTRATED STANDARD

1 Eyes medium-sized and almond-shaped
2 Wide skull and muzzle
3 Ears hanging, elongated triangular shape
4 Back level
5 Tail continues the rumpline, reaches to hocks with slight curve at end; carried low
6 Feet strong, rather large

Color: white

DQ: blue eyes; flesh-colored nose; three or more missing teeth; short, smooth hair on both head and legs; failure of coat to cord by 2 years of age; color other than white (puppies can have a small amount of cream or buff)

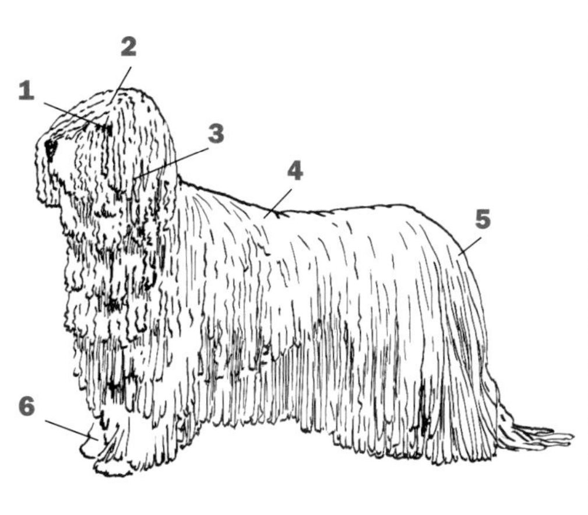

wiping out the wolf in Hungary. The Komondor was still used as a guard into the twentieth century. The first Komondor came to America in 1933, and the AKC recognized the breed in 1937. World War II almost decimated the breed in Europe, but through the concerted efforts of breeders, the Komondor was saved. Although one of the most impressive dogs to ever grace the show ring, the difficulty of preparing its coat has usually dictated that none but the very finest be shown. As a result, the Komondor remains an uncommon breed everywhere but in its native Hungary. Recent attempts to use the breed as a guardian of flocks in the western United States have yielded promising results, attracting the attention of a new generation of shepherds.

TEMPERAMENT

Bred as an independent protector of livestock, the Komondor is true to its heritage. It is an independent thinker and can be stubborn or domineering. It is not for meek owners who can be dominated; socialization is essential. It is reserved with strangers and possibly aggressive toward strange dogs. It is good with other pets and especially livestock. In fact, it is happiest when it has something or someone to watch over. Although usually calm and quiet, it is utterly fearless when the need arises. As a natural guardian, it is protective of children in its own family, but it may at times misunderstand rough and tumble games of visiting children.

UPKEEP

The Komondor needs daily exercise in the form of long walks or short romps. Swimming is not a good idea because of the time it takes the coat to dry. It may also be difficult to keep the coat clean in some areas. This breed does not like warm weather. The Komondor is non-shedding but not carefree. Its cords must be regularly separated or they will look like flat mats, and its coat tends to hold dirt; bathing is time-consuming and drying takes as much as a day. Care of the coat in non-show dogs is far less extensive. Pets can be clipped but then lose part of the breed's unique appeal. It may take a dog up to two years of age before cords form.

HEALTH

- Major concerns: CHD, gastric torsion
- Minor concerns: otitis externa, hot spots
- Occasionally seen: entropion
- Suggested tests: hip, eye
- Life span: 10–12 years

FORM AND FUNCTION

The Komondor is a large, muscular dog, with plenty of bone and substance; it is slightly longer than tall. Its gait is light and leisurely, with long strides. Its hallmark coat is double, consisting of a dense wooly undercoat and a coarser outer coat that is wavy or curly. The undercoat is trapped in the outer coat so that it forms strong, felty, tassel-like cords. This coat helped protect the dog from the elements as well as the teeth of tough adversaries. It also helped the dog to blend in with its flock.

Kuvasz

AT A GLANCE

Energy level:	■■■	Watchdog ability:	■■■■■	POPULARITY: Very rare
Exercise requirements:	■■■■	Protection ability:	■■■■■	FAMILY: Livestock Dog, Flockguard
Playfulness:	■■■	Grooming requirements:	■■■	AREA OF ORIGIN: Hungary
Affection level:	■	Cold tolerance:	■■■■	DATE OF ORIGIN: Middle Ages
Friendliness toward dogs:	■	Heat tolerance:	■■	ORIGINAL FUNCTION: Guardian, hunting large game
Friendliness toward other pets:	■■■■			
Friendliness toward strangers:	■	WEIGHT: male: 100–115 lb; female: 70–90 lb		TODAY'S FUNCTION: Sheep guardian, guardian
Ease of training:	■	HEIGHT: male: 28–30″; female: 26–28″		OTHER NAME: Hungarian Kuvasz

HISTORY

Although considered a Hungarian breed, the Kuvasz probably descends from giant dogs of Tibet. It came to Hungary from Tibet by way of Turkey. Nor is its name Hungarian, but probably a corruption of the Turkish kawasz, meaning armed guard of the nobility. At one time only those nobility in favor with the royal family were allowed to keep one. This is a very old breed; in the latter fifteenth century, the Kuvasz was held in highest esteem. Breedings were carefully planned and recorded, and the dogs were a fixture of most large Hungarian estates. They served as both guard and hunting dog, capable of defending the estate against marauders and of pulling down large game such as bear and wolf. King Matthias I was a special patron of the breed, keeping a large kennel and

ILLUSTRATED STANDARD

1 Eyes almond-shaped
2 Skull elongated but not pointed
3 V-shaped ears, tip slightly rounded
4 Back straight and broad
5 Stomach well tucked up
6 Cat feet

Color: white
DQ: overshot or undershot bite; males smaller than 26″ or females smaller than 24″; any color other than white

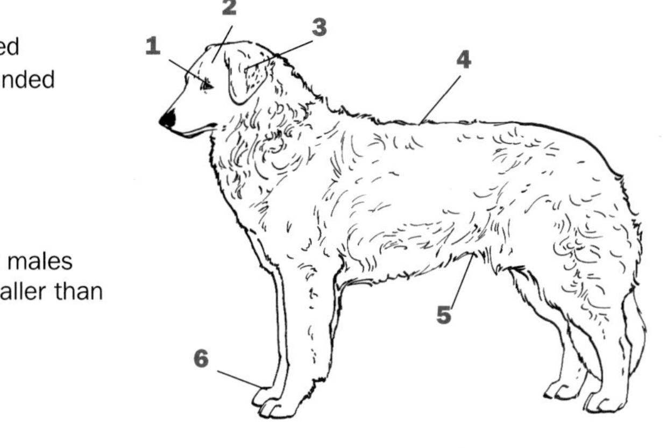

HEALTH

- Major concerns: CHD, OCD
- Minor concerns: hypothyroidism
- Occasionally seen: panosteitis, HOD
- Suggested tests: hip, elbow, thyroid
- Life span: 9–12 years

FORM AND FUNCTION

The Kuvasz is a large dog, slightly longer than tall, with medium bone. It is not bulky, but instead it is light footed, with a free, easy gait. The breed's combination of power and agility stems from its versatile roots as a guardian, hunter, and herder. Its double coat is medium coarse, ranging from wavy to straight.

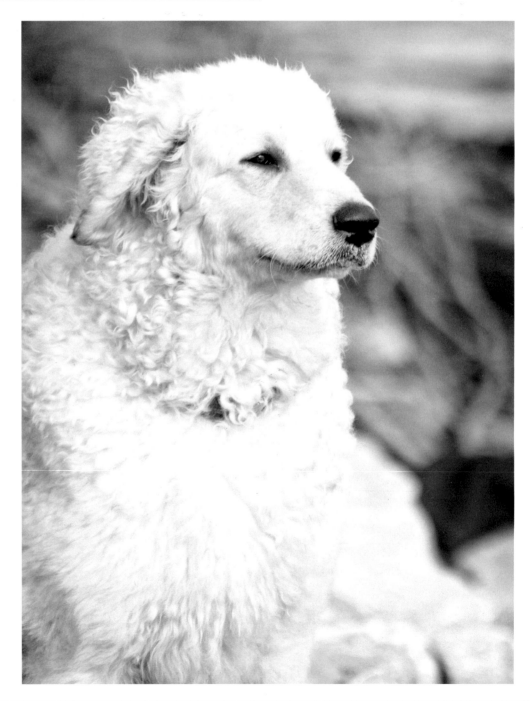

doing much to improve the quality of the breed. In the succeeding centuries, the Kuvasz gradually came into the hands of commoners, who found them to be capable livestock dogs. During this period, the name was corrupted to its present spelling, which ironically, translates as mongrel. Incidentally, the plural form of Kuvasz is Kuvaszok. The breed seriously declined as a result of two world wars, but German stock formed a basis for the breed to continue through these hard times. Some dogs had also been imported to America in the 1930s. The AKC recognized the Kuvasz in 1935.

TEMPERAMENT

Despite its sweet looks, the Kuvasz is a tough protector, fearlessly defending its family or home. It is gentle with and protective of children in its own family, but it may misinterpret a child's rough and tumble games with other children as attacks on its child. It is reserved with strangers and may be aggressive toward strange dogs; however, it tends to be very gentle with other pets and livestock. It is devoted and loyal but not very demonstrative. Some can be domineering.

UPKEEP

The Kuvasz needs daily exercise and enjoys a long walk or good run in a safe area. It especially enjoys cold weather. It does best when allowed access to both house and yard. Its coat needs brushing one or two times weekly, more during heavy shedding periods.

Leonberger

AT A GLANCE

Energy level:	■■	Watchdog ability:	■■■■■	POPULARITY: Uncommon
Exercise requirements:	■■■	Protection ability:	■■■■	FAMILY: Mastiff
Playfulness:	■■■	Grooming requirements:	■■■■	AREA OF ORIGIN: Germany
Affection level:	■■■■	Cold tolerance:	■■■■■	DATE OF ORIGIN: 1900s
Friendliness toward dogs:	■■■	Heat tolerance:	■■	ORIGINAL FUNCTION: Multipurpose farm dog, draft
Friendliness toward other pets:	■■■■			
Friendliness toward strangers:	■■■■	WEIGHT: male: 130–170 lb; female: 100–130 lb*		TODAY'S FUNCTION: Draft, water rescue
Ease of training:	■■■■	HEIGHT: male: 28–31.5″; female: 25.5–29.5″		OTHER NAME: None

HISTORY

Leonbergers come from the German town of Leonberg, where they were supposedly bred beginning in the 1830s to resemble the lion on the town crest. The town's mayor, Heinreich Essig, was a dog breeder and is said to have crossed a Landseer Newfoundland with a "Barry" (precursor to the Saint Bernard), and then a Great Pyrenees. This claim is disputed, however, as there are also descriptions of very Leonberger-like dogs in Austria as long ago as 1585. Further, modern geneticists say more breeds than those three would be needed to produce the traits seen in early Leos. Regardless, Essig was a talented promoter, and he placed his dogs with the celebrities of the day including several royal families. Regular folk also appreciated the breed as all-purpose farm dogs, watchdogs, and draft dogs. In the

ILLUSTRATED STANDARD

1. Medium-sized eyes, oval to almond-shaped
2. Medium-sized ears, hanging flat and close
3. Moderately defined stop
4. Level back; rump not higher than withers
5. Pronounced prosternum
6. Tail hangs at least to hock; carried no higher than back level
7. Rounded feet
8. Rear dewclaws may be present

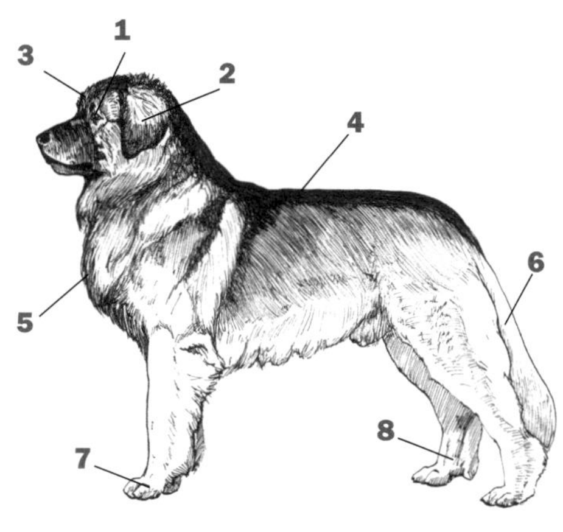

Color: lion-yellow, golden to red, red-brown, or sand colored and all their combinations, with a black mask; all colors may have black tips of various length

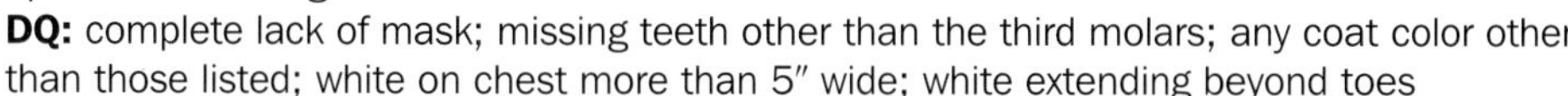

DQ: complete lack of mask; missing teeth other than the third molars; any coat color other than those listed; white on chest more than 5″ wide; white extending beyond toes

second half of the nineteenth century, the breed became very popular and commanded huge prices, largely because the breed's creator gave them to nobility to create a fad for them. During World War I, Leonbergers pulled ammunition carts. Only five Leos survived that war. Only eight Leos survived World War II. All modern Leonbergers trace to these dogs, following a concerted effort by a group of German breeders to rescue them in 1945. Now the breed is fairly popular in Europe, though still uncommon in America. The first Leo came to America in 1971. The AKC recognized the breed in 2010, and it has surged in popularity since. Leos have served as water rescue dogs, leaping from helicopters to reach drowning people.

TEMPERAMENT

The Leo is a devoted and trustworthy companion, even-tempered, and very affectionate. They are eager to please and fairly easy to train. They are friendly to strangers but also protective of their owners. They are generally good with other pets and dogs, although some can be domineering toward other dogs. Quiet and calm indoors, they are nonetheless good watchdogs.

UPKEEP

Leos are more athletic and agile than many of the giant breeds, but they are not good jogging dogs. They enjoy a daily walk or romp and even longer hikes. They also are good at pulling carts, swimming, and search and rescue. The thick coat requires brushing several times a week and daily during shedding seasons. They enjoy cold weather.

HEALTH

- Major concerns: CHD
- Minor concerns: elbow dysplasia, gastric torsion, osteosarcoma
- Occasionally seen: entropion, ectropion, polyneuropathy
- Suggested tests: hip, eye, DNA for polyneuropathy
- Life span: 8–11 years

FORM AND FUNCTION

The Leonberger is a large, muscular working dog, well suited for its original purpose of family dog, farm dog, and draft dog. It is strong and powerful, with medium to heavy bone. It is slightly longer than tall. The males, in particular, carry a lion-like mane on the neck and chest, but all have a double coat. The coat is medium to long on the body. The outer coat is medium-soft to coarse and lies flat and is mostly straight. The undercoat is soft and dense. The outline of the body is always recognizable. The Leonberger is light on its feet and graceful in motion. It has an effortless, powerful, ground-covering gait with good reach and strong drive. An even, confident temperament along with obedience and vigilance is essential in its role as a family companion.

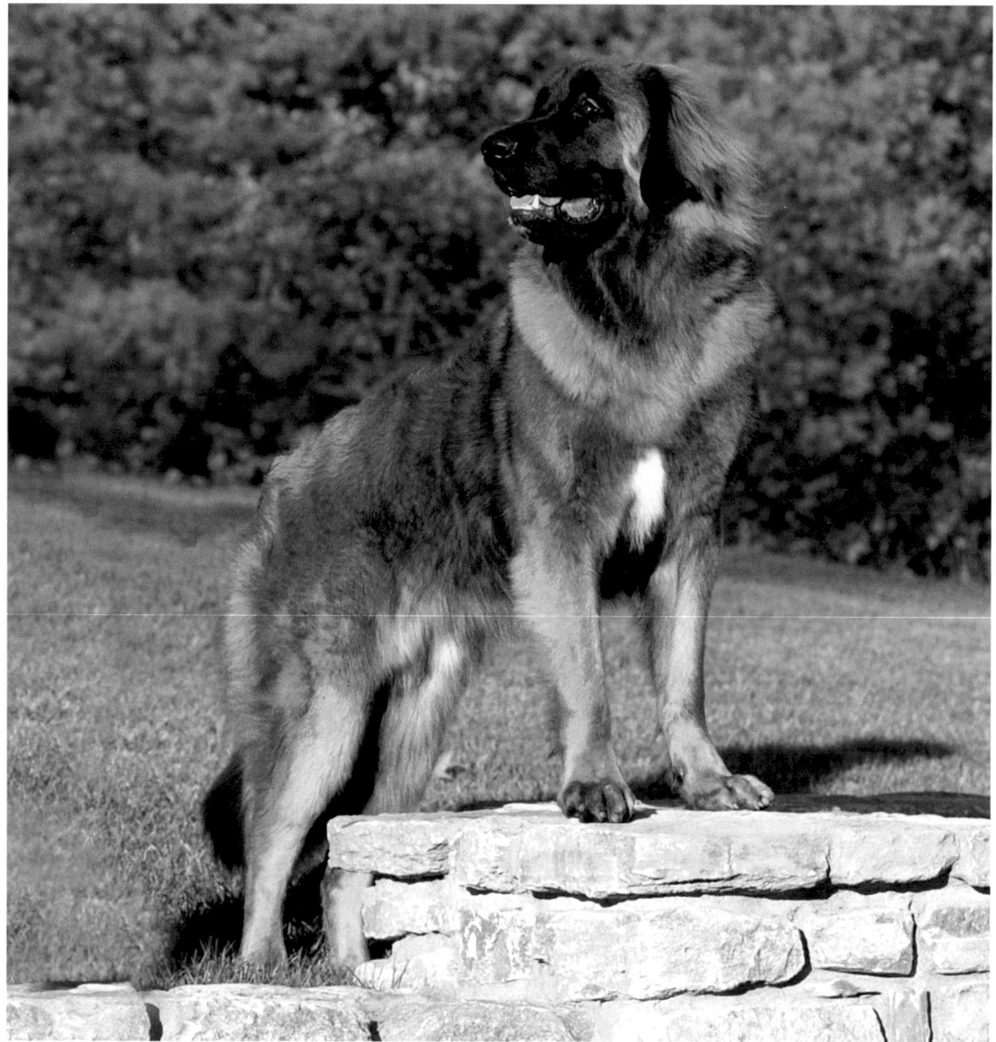

Mastiff

AT A GLANCE

Energy level:	■
Exercise requirements:	■■
Playfulness:	■
Affection level:	■■■■
Friendliness toward dogs:	■■■
Friendliness toward other pets:	■■■■
Friendliness toward strangers:	■■
Ease of training:	■■■

Watchdog ability:	■■■■■
Protection ability:	■■■■
Grooming requirements:	■
Cold tolerance:	■■■
Heat tolerance:	■■

WEIGHT: 175–190 lb*
HEIGHT: male min. 30″; female: min. 27.5″

POPULARITY: Popular
FAMILY: Livestock Dog, Sheepdog, Mastiff
AREA OF ORIGIN: England
DATE OF ORIGIN: Ancient times
ORIGINAL FUNCTION: Guardian
TODAY'S FUNCTION: Guardian
OTHER NAME: English Mastiff

HISTORY

The Mastiff is the prototypical breed of the ancient mastiff group of dogs. The confusion between the Mastiff breed and the mastiff family makes it very difficult to trace the history of the breed. Even though the mastiff family is one of the oldest and most influential in dogdom, the breed is undoubtedly of more recent, though still ancient, origin. By the time of Caesar, mastiffs were used as war dogs and gladiators. In medieval times, they were used as guard dogs and hunting dogs and became so widespread as to become commonplace. Kubla Khan is said to have kept 5,000 Mastiffs for hunting in the 1200s. Mastiffs later stepped into the arena of dog fighting, bull baiting, and bear baiting. Even when these cruel sports were banned in England in 1835, they continued to be popular

ILLUSTRATED STANDARD

1 Muzzle short and broad
2 Eyes set wide
3 Head massive, good breadth
4 Ears proportionally small, V-shaped with rounded ends
5 Level topline
6 Tail set high, never carried over back
7 Large cat feet

Color: fawn, apricot, or brindle, all with dark muzzle, ears and nose
DQ: none

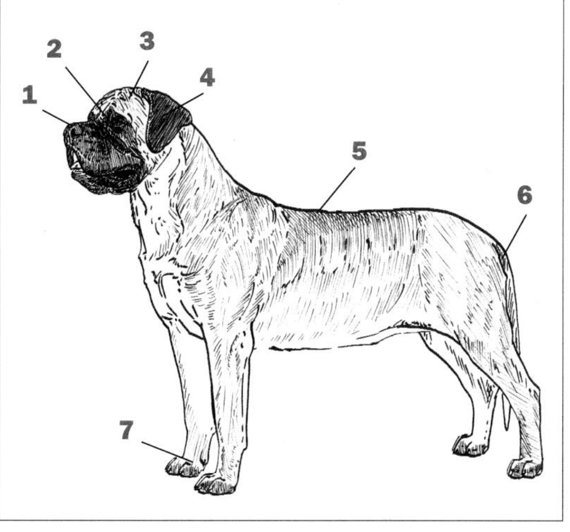

events. The modern Mastiff descends not only from these pit dogs but also from more noble lines, being descendants of one of the most famous Mastiffs of all time: the Mastiff of Sir Peers Legh. When Sir Legh was wounded in the battle of Agincourt, his Mastiff stood over him and protected him for many hours through the battle. Although he later died, the Mastiff returned to Legh's home and was the foundation of the Lyme Hall Mastiffs. Five centuries later the Lyme Hall Mastiffs figured prominently in founding the modern breed. Some evidence exists that the Mastiff came to America on the Mayflower, but the breed's documented entry to America did not occur until the late 1800s. The breed was nearly decimated in England by World War II, but sufficient numbers had been brought to America by that time to keep the breed going. Since that time, it has gradually risen in popularity.

TEMPERAMENT

The Mastiff is innately good natured, calm, easygoing, and surprisingly gentle. It is a well-mannered house pet but needs sufficient room to stretch out. This is an extremely loyal breed, and though not excessively demonstrative, it is devoted to its family and good with children.

UPKEEP

The adult Mastiff needs daily moderate exercise, consisting of either a good walk or game. It does not enjoy hot weather. It tends to drool. Coat care is minimal.

HEALTH

- Major concerns: CHD, gastric torsion
- Minor concerns: elbow dysplasia, osteosarcoma, cystinuria
- Occasionally seen: cardiomyopathy, allergies, vaginal hyperplasia, cruciate ligament rupture, hypothyroidism, OCD, entropion, PRA, PPM
- Suggested tests: hip, elbow, eye, cardiac, (cystinuria), thyroid, DNA for PRA
- Lifespan: 9–11 years
- Note: obesity can be a problem

FORM AND FUNCTION

The massive Mastiff is heavy boned and with a powerful musculature, being slightly longer than tall. It combines great strength with endurance. Its power and strength are evident in its gait, which should have good reach and drive. The double coat consists of a dense undercoat and a straight, coarse, outer coat of moderately short length. The expression is alert but kindly. The overall impression should be one of grandeur and dignity.

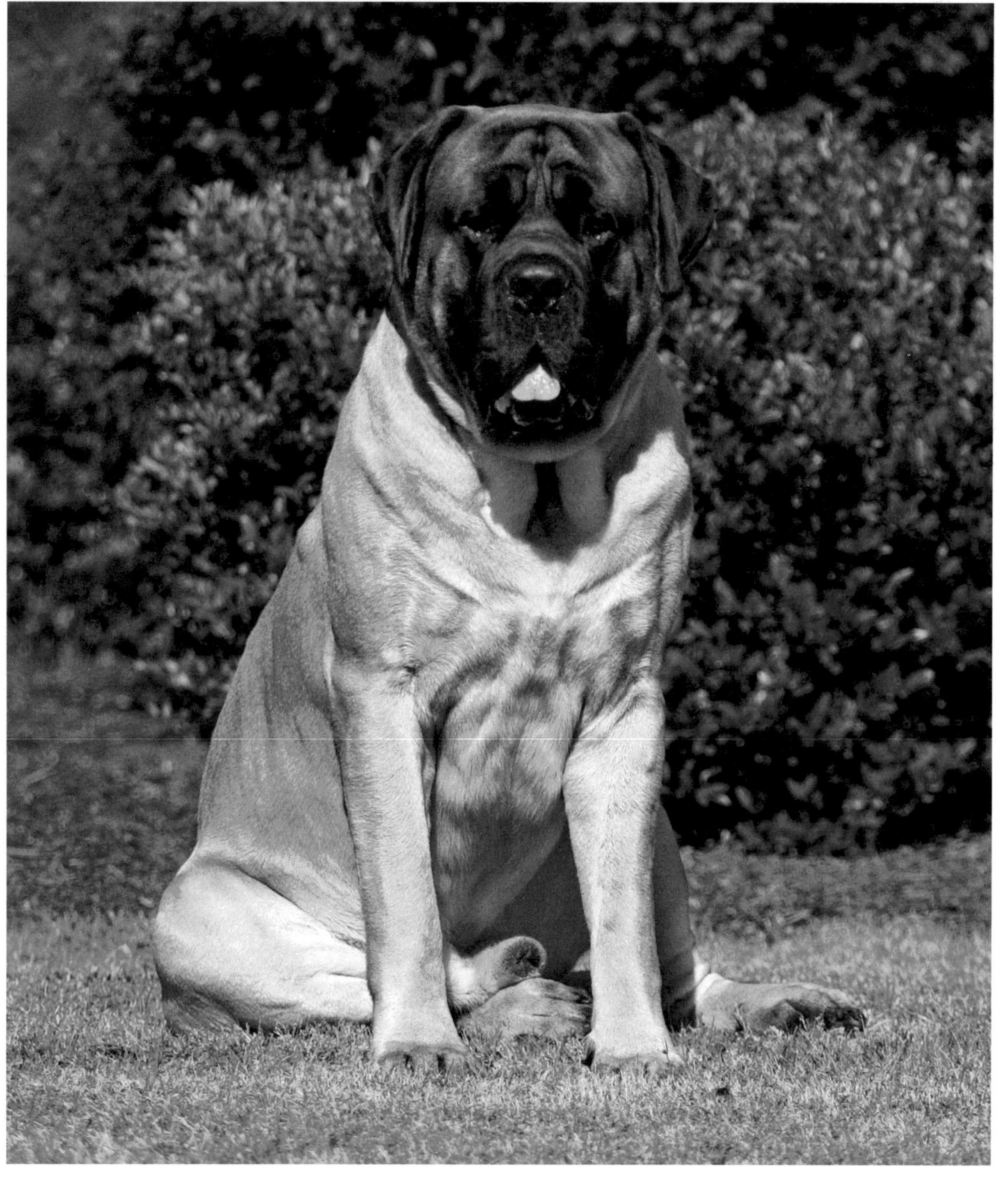

Neapolitan Mastiff

AT A GLANCE

Energy level:	■■
Exercise requirements:	■
Playfulness:	■
Affection level:	■■■■
Friendliness toward dogs:	■
Friendliness toward other pets:	■■
Friendliness toward strangers:	■
Ease of training:	■■

Watchdog ability:	■■■■■
Protection ability:	■■■■■
Grooming requirements:	■■
Cold tolerance:	■■■■
Heat tolerance:	■

WEIGHT: male: 150 lb; female: 110 lb; greater weight is usual
HEIGHT: male: 26–31″; female: 24–29″

POPULARITY: Uncommon
FAMILY: Mastiff
AREA OF ORIGIN: Italy
DATE OF ORIGIN: Ancient times
ORIGINAL FUNCTION: Guardian
TODAY'S FUNCTION: Guardian, companion
OTHER NAME: Mastino Napoletano

HISTORY

Heavy-bodied dogs with powerful grips have been known since ancient times, tracing to the giant war dogs of the Middle East and Asia. They were used to control livestock, guard homes, or even fight men, lions, and elephants in battle. Around 330 B.C. Alexander the Great dispersed some native giant Macedonian war dogs in the lands he conquered, and crossed some with shorthaired dogs from India. The resulting Molossus became the progenitor of many modern breeds. When the Romans took over Greece they also took their Molossus dogs. In 55 B.C. the Romans invaded Britain, where they admired and appropriated fierce British mastiff dogs that fought valiantly in defending Britain. These British mastiffs were even better gladiators than the Molossus dogs, but when bred together

ILLUSTRATED STANDARD

1 Extensive wrinkling
2 Pendulous lips, ample dewlap
3 Deep-set eyes, almost hidden under drooping upper lid; lower lids droop exposing haw
4 Very defined stop
5 Ears cropped or uncropped
6 Level topline
7 Tail docked by one third
8 Little or no tuck-up
9 Round feet

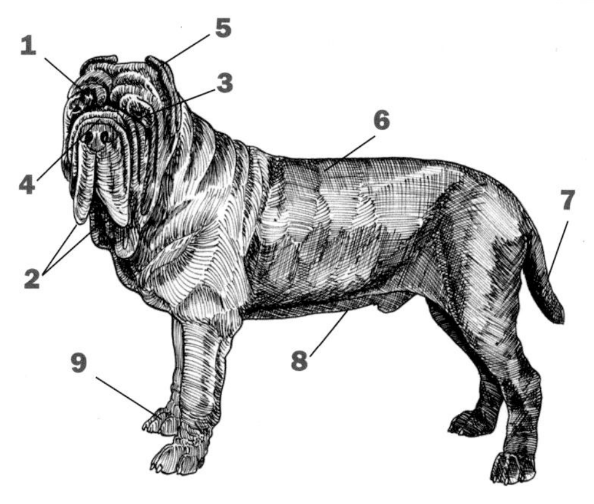

Color: gray, black, mahogany, tawny, with or without tan brindling; white allowed on underside, chest, throat, toes, and backs of pasterns

DQ: absence of massiveness; absence of wrinkles and folds; absence of dewlap; tail shorter than one third length; white markings other than those allowed

they produced an unsurpassed strain of giant gladiators and war dogs. These dogs, called "mastini" (Italian for mastiffs), were dispersed further. In the Neapolitan area in the south of Italy, they were perfected over the next centuries for guarding estates and homes. Still, the breed remained virtually unknown to the rest of the world until a chance sighting at a Naples dog show in 1946. Piere Scanziani recognized the dog and solicited other fanciers to help rescue the breed from obscurity. They drew up a standard and petitioned the Italian kennel club and the FCI to recognize them under the name Mastino Napoletano. Although a few specimens may have come to America with Italian immigrants, only in the 1970s has the breed been documented in the United States. They immediately elicited great interest and a breed club was formed around 1973. An initial standard was approved by the AKC in 1996, and they entered the AKC Working Group in 2004.

TEMPERAMENT

The Neapolitan Mastiff was bred for centuries to guard its family. As such, it is incredibly loyal and devoted to its family, watchful and suspicious of strangers, and tolerant of acquaintances. It is a stay-at-home-type dog. Although it is loving toward children, its sheer size can make accidents possible. It may not get along well with other dogs, especially domineering-type dogs. Because of its size, it should be carefully socialized at an early age.

UPKEEP

Neos don't need a lot of exercise, but they do need a lot of living space. They enjoy the outdoors but do not tolerate warm weather well. As with any giant breed, food, boarding, and even veterinary bills can be higher. They drool and can leave a trail of food and water leading from their bowls. This is not a breed for obsessive house cleaners!

HEALTH

- Major concerns: CHD, cardiomyopathy, demodicosis
- Minor concerns: cherry eye, elbow dysplasia
- Occasionally seen: none
- Suggested tests: hip, elbow, cardiac, eye
- Life span: 8–10 years (larger individuals tend to live toward the shorter end of the range)
- Note: breeding often requires artificial insemination and Caesarean delivery

FORM AND FUNCTION

With its massive size made even more imposing by its abundant loose skin and dewlap, the Neapolitan Mastiff may have the most alarming appearance of any dog, and some say this look was purposefully bred in order to scare away intruders without the dog having to act. However, when forced to act, the Neo can spring into action with surprising speed. Its massive muscular body can knock down almost any intruder. Its huge head with short, powerful jaws and large teeth can crush or hold an opponent. The skin is tough and hanging, adding to the imposing impression of size as well as formidable expression.

Newfoundland

AT A GLANCE

Energy level:	■■
Exercise requirements:	■■
Playfulness:	■■■
Affection level:	■■■■■
Friendliness toward dogs:	■■■■
Friendliness toward other pets:	■■■■■
Friendliness toward strangers:	■■■■■
Ease of training:	■■■

Watchdog ability:	■■■
Protection ability:	■■■■
Grooming requirements:	■■■
Cold tolerance:	■■■■■
Heat tolerance:	■

WEIGHT: male: 130–150 lb; female: 100–120 lb
HEIGHT: male 28″ average; female: 26″ average

POPULARITY: Popular
FAMILY: Livestock Dog, Mastiff, Water Dog
AREA OF ORIGIN: Canada
DATE OF ORIGIN: 1700s
ORIGINAL FUNCTION: All-purpose water dog and fishing aid, draft
TODAY'S FUNCTION: Water rescue
OTHER NAME: None

HISTORY

As its name suggests, the Newfoundland was developed on the coast of Newfoundland. Here the agreement about its origin ceases. Although it ultimately traces back to the Tibetan Mastiff, no actual record exists of Tibetan Mastiffs being brought to Newfoundland. Some authorities believe that it descends from the Tibetan Mastiff by way of the Great Pyrenees. In 1662, the first permanent colony at Roougnoust was settled, complete with Great Pyrenees dogs. These dogs were crossed with black English retrievers belonging to English settlers. Some Husky blood may also have been introduced. Whatever the ingredients, the result was a massive water-loving, cold-resistant dog found in either solid black or black and white coloration. The latter "Landseer"

ILLUSTRATED STANDARD

1 Broad skull
2 Eyes relatively small and deep-set
3 Proud head carriage
4 Ears relatively small, triangular with rounded tips
5 Tail held down when relaxed; never carried over the back
6 Cat feet, webbed

Color: solid black, brown, or gray, may have white on chin, chest, toes, and tail tip; or white base color with black markings ("Landseer")
DQ: any colors not specified

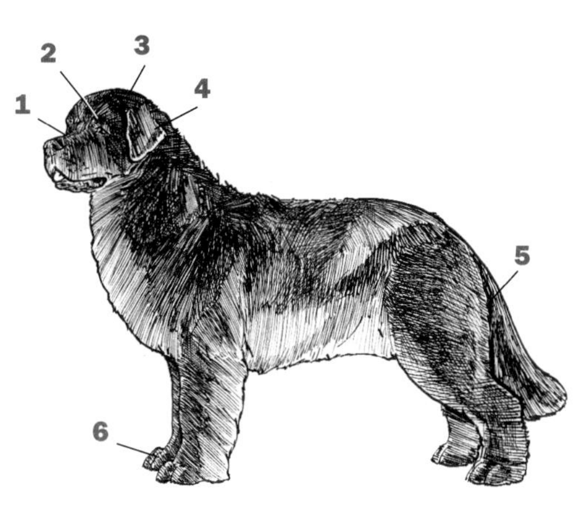

Newfoundland was only identified in 1779. The Newfoundland name predates it only by a few years, named after an individual dog called Newfoundland. The Newfoundland distinguished itself as an all-purpose water dog, hauling heavy fishing nets through the cold water and saving many people from watery graves. Its work didn't stop on dry land; here it served as a draft dog and pack animal. European visitors were so impressed that they returned to Europe with many specimens, and it is here that the breed first entered the show ring. The export of dogs from Newfoundland, along with laws forbidding ownership of more than one dog, drove the breed's numbers down in its place of origin. The breed's stronghold switched to England, and American fanciers resorted to replenishing their stock with English dogs. After World War II, the tables turned, and American Newfoundlands were responsible for reviving the decimated English stock. Recovery in both countries is now complete, and the Newfoundland is one of the more popular of the giant breeds of dogs. Although the solid black color is most identified with the breed, the black and white Newfoundlands (dubbed Landseers after the well-known artist who first portrayed them) are also popular.

TEMPERAMENT

The most important single characteristic of the Newfoundland is sweetness of temperament. The Newfoundland is calm, patient, easygoing, gentle, and amiable—a friend to all. If its family is threatened, however, the Newfoundland can act protectively.

UPKEEP

This easygoing dog needs daily exercise to stay fit, either in the form of a moderate walk or short romp. It loves to swim and pull, especially in cold weather. Some breeders contend that Landseers tend to be more active than solids. It does not do well in hot weather. Its coat needs combing twice weekly, more when shedding. Newfs do drool and also tend to be messy drinkers.

HEALTH

- Major concerns: SAS, cystinuria, elbow dysplasia, CHD, gastric torsion
- Minor concerns: OCD, entropion, ectropion, vWD, cataract, cruciate ligament rupture
- Occasionally seen: epilepsy, vWD
- Suggested tests: hip, elbow, cardiac, vWD, cystinuria
- Life span: 8–10 years
- Note: Newfoundlands do not tolerate heat well; some are sensitive to anesthesia.

FORM AND FUNCTION

The Newfoundland is a large, heavily boned, powerful dog, strong enough to pull a drowning man from rough seas and imposing enough to make an effective guard dog. It is slightly longer than it is tall. Its gait gives the impression of effortless power, with good reach and drive. Its double coat consists of a soft, dense undercoat and a coarse, moderately long and straight outer coat. Its soft expression reflects its benevolent and dignified temperament.

Portuguese Water Dog

AT A GLANCE

Energy level:	■■■■	Watchdog ability:	■■■■	POPULARITY: Somewhat popular	
Exercise requirements:	■■■■	Protection ability:	■■■	FAMILY: Water Dog	
Playfulness:	■■■■	Grooming requirements:	■■■■■	AREA OF ORIGIN: Portugal	
Affection level:	■■■■	Cold tolerance:	■■■	DATE OF ORIGIN: Middle Ages	
Friendliness toward dogs:	■■■	Heat tolerance:	■■■	ORIGINAL FUNCTION: Fishing aid	
Friendliness toward other pets:	■■■■			TODAY'S FUNCTION: Water rescue	
Friendliness toward strangers:	■■■	WEIGHT: male: 42–60 lb; female: 35–50 lb		OTHER NAME: Cao de Agua	
Ease of training:	■■■	HEIGHT: male 20–23″; female: 17–21″			

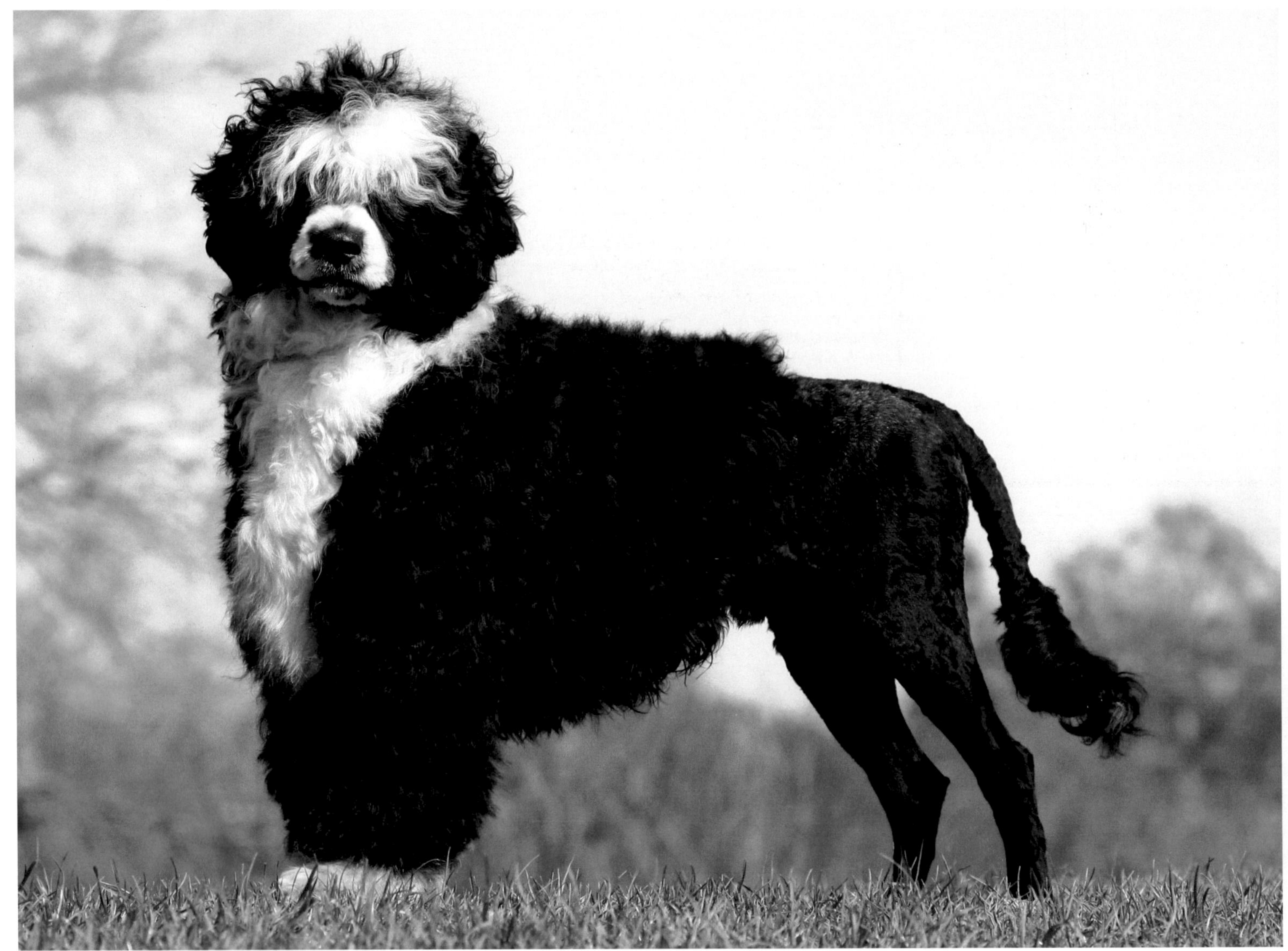

HISTORY

The consummate water working dog, the Portuguese Water Dog probably shares some of its ancestry with the Poodle. Their ancestors were herding dogs from the central Asian steppes, either brought to Portugal by way of the Visigoths in the fifth century or by way of the Berbers and then Moors in the eighth century. Once in Portugal, it distinguished itself through its affinity for water, eventually herding fish into nets, retrieving lost nets or equipment, and serving as a boat-to-boat or boat-to-shore courier. Later the dogs were part of trawler crews fishing the waters from Portugal to Iceland. The breed is known in its native land as Cao de Agua (pronounced Kown-d'Ahgwa), which means dog of water. It comes in a long-haired variety known as the *Cao de Agua de Pelo Ondulado* and

ILLUSTRATED STANDARD

1 Stop well defined
2 Eyes roundish, medium size
3 Large head
4 Ears set high, heart shaped
5 Topline level
6 When at attention, the tail is held in a ring, the front of which should not reach forward of the loin
7 Feet round and rather flat, with webbed toes; central pad very thick

Color: black, white, brown, or combinations of black or brown with white
DQ: none

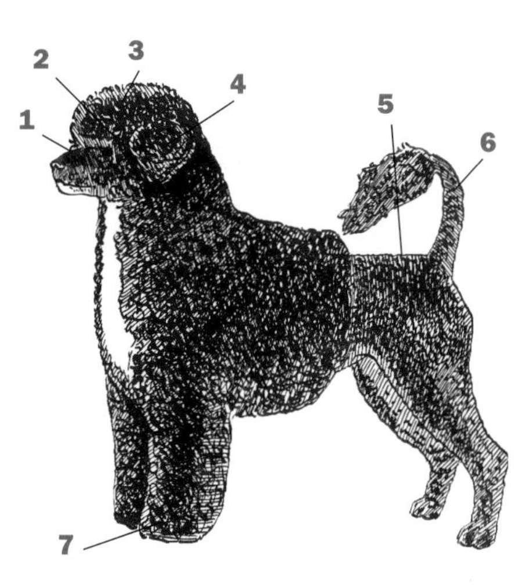

a curly-coated variety known as the *Cao de Agua de Pelo Encaradolado*. With the demise of traditional fishing methods, the Portuguese fishermen and their dogs began to disappear from the coast in the early twentieth century. The breed was saved largely through the attempts of one man, Dr. Vasco Bensuade, a wealthy shipping magnate. He promoted the breed, and through his efforts, the breed club was reorganized, a standard was written, and the first dogs were exhibited in the show ring. After a brief appearance in England in the 1950s, the breed virtually died out there. Around this time, the first PWDs came to America, where they slowly gained a following. After they were officially AKC recognized in 1984, their popularity grew more rapidly, and the breed is now proving itself as a family companion.

TEMPERAMENT

The gregarious Portuguese Water Dog is a fun-loving, family-loving, water-loving dog. It is good with children, other dogs, and pets. It is sensitive and responds well to direction. It is a good breed for an active person wanting an adventurous, affectionate, biddable partner.

UPKEEP

This is an active breed needing daily physical and mental exercise, preferably involving swimming and retrieving. Otherwise, it needs a long walk or jog or a vigorous romp. The coat needs combing every other day, plus monthly clipping or scissoring.

HEALTH

- Major concerns: PRA
- Minor concerns: GM1 storage disease, distichiasis, Addison's, CHD, juvenile cardiomyopathy, hair loss (follicular dysplasia)
- Occasionally seen: irritable bowel syndrome, seizures
- Suggested tests: eye, hip, DNA for GM1, DNA for PRA, (cardiac)
- Life span: 10–14 years

FORM AND FUNCTION

The Portuguese Water Dog is a robust dog of medium build, slightly longer than it is tall. It is strong and well muscled, able to work both in and out of the water for long periods. It has a profuse single coat, either wavy or curly. Two clips are acceptable: the lion clip, in which the muzzle and middle part, up to the tail tip, are clipped, and the retriever clip, in which the entire coat is scissored to about 1 inch in length, with tail tip again left full length. The Water Dog's expression is steady, penetrating, and attentive, reflecting its spirited disposition.

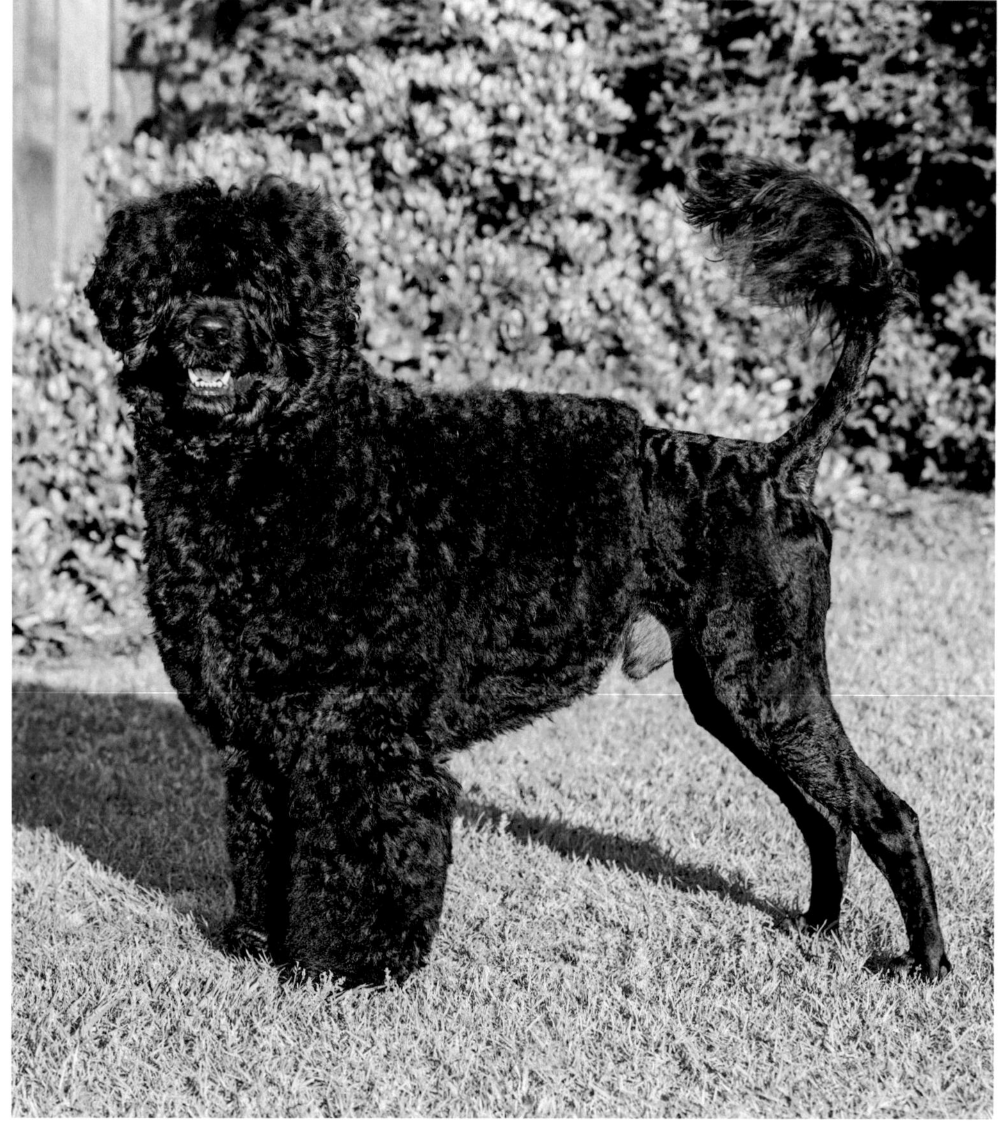

Rottweiler

AT A GLANCE

Energy level:	■ ■ ■
Exercise requirements:	■ ■ ■
Playfulness:	■ ■
Affection level:	■ ■
Friendliness toward dogs:	■
Friendliness toward other pets:	■ ■
Friendliness toward strangers:	■
Ease of training:	■ ■ ■

Watchdog ability:	■ ■ ■ ■ ■
Protection ability:	■ ■ ■ ■ ■
Grooming requirements:	■
Cold tolerance:	■ ■ ■
Heat tolerance:	■ ■

WEIGHT: male: 85–135 lb; female: 80–100 lb*
HEIGHT: male: 24–27″; female: 22–25″

POPULARITY: Most popular
FAMILY: Livestock Dog, Mastiff
AREA OF ORIGIN: Germany
DATE OF ORIGIN: Ancient times
ORIGINAL FUNCTION: Cattle drover, guardian, draft
TODAY'S FUNCTION: Security, herding trials, Schutzhund, carting
OTHER NAME: None

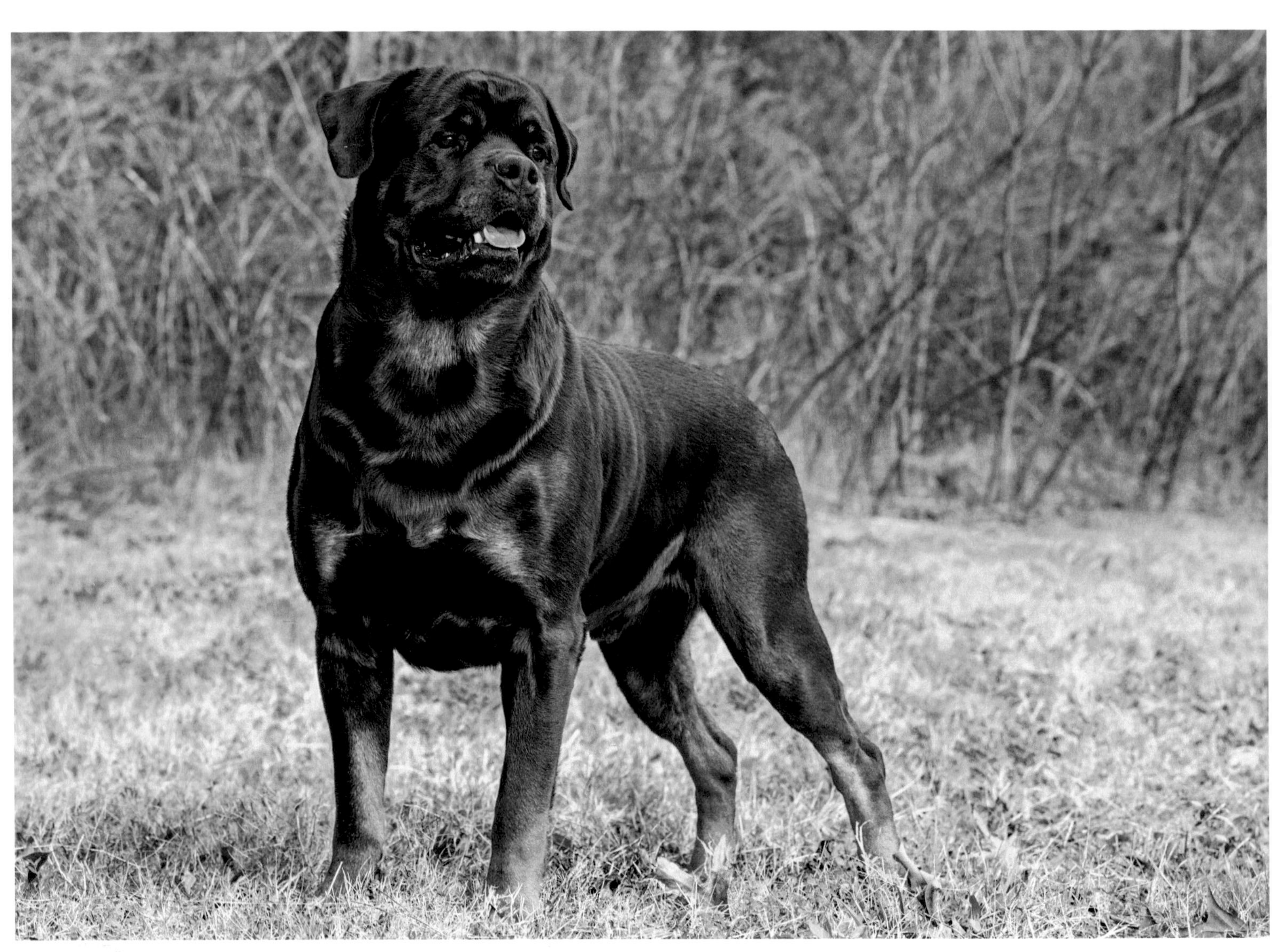

HISTORY

The Rottweiler's ancestors were probably Roman drover dogs, responsible for driving and guarding herds of cattle as they accompanied Roman troops on long marches. At least one of these marches led to southern Germany, where some of the people and their dogs settled. Throughout the succeeding centuries, the dogs continued to play a vital role as cattle drovers as well as bear hunters around what was to become the town of Rottweil (which is derived from red tile, denoting the red tile roof of the Roman baths that had been unearthed there in the eighth century). The dogs almost certainly mixed with various Sennehund (Mountain Dog) strains. Rottweil prospered and became a center of cattle commerce. Their dogs drove and guarded cattle and guarded the money earned by the cattle sales. With

ILLUSTRATED STANDARD

1 Head broad
2 Ears medium-sized, triangular, pendant
3 Back level
4 Tail docked short, leaving one or two tail vertebrae; carried slightly above horizontal when dog is moving

Color: black with tan markings
DQ: entropion or ectropion; overshot or undershot; two or more missing teeth; long coat; any base color other than black, absence of all markings; a dog that attacks any person in the ring

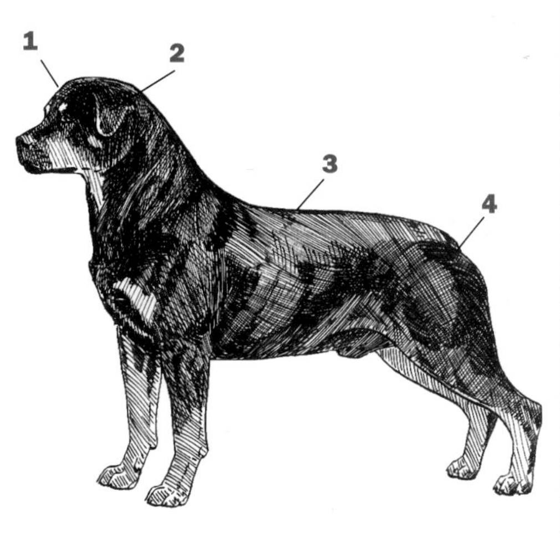

the advent of trains, cattle driving was outlawed, so the Rottweiler found a new job as a butcher's dog and draft dog. So evolved the Rottweiler metzgerhund (butcher dog), an integral component in the town's industry until the mid nineteenth century. The Rottweiler was also used as a draft dog, but it was replaced by donkeys. With little need for this once vital breed, the Rottweiler fell into such decline that it was nearly lost. In 1905 there was only one female Rottweiler in Rottweil. With the realization that the breed was teetering near extinction, dog fanciers formed a club in 1901 and set about to revive it. Even though the 1901 club was short-lived, it did formulate a breed standard. Two subsequent clubs were formed in 1907, one of which promoted the breed as a police dog. The two clubs merged in 1921. The breed continued to grow, and by 1931 had arrived in America and gained AKC recognition. It has since been used as a police, military, guard, and even mountain rescue dog. The Rottweiler recovered from its brush with extinction to work its way to the second most popular breed in America by the early 1990s. Its popularity has since slightly waned and it is finding itself in homes better suited to its needs.

TEMPERAMENT

Confident, bold, alert, and imposing, the Rottweiler is a popular choice for its protection abilities. As befitting its self-assured nature, it tends to be headstrong and stubborn. It is reserved, often guarded, toward strangers. It may be overly protective if it perceives that its family is being threatened. This is a powerful breed that needs socialization, consistent training, and daily exercise.

UPKEEP

The Rottweiler needs daily physical and mental activity, either in the form of long walks or jogs, or a vigorous game in a safe area, as well as obedience lessons. It enjoys cold weather and may become overheated in hot weather. Coat care is minimal, consisting only of occasional brushing to remove dead hair.

HEALTH

- Major concerns: CHD, elbow dysplasia, SAS, osteosarcoma
- Minor concerns: gastric torsion, hypothyroidism, allergies
- Occasionally seen: PRA, cataract, seizures, vWD, panosteitis, entropion, ectropion
- Suggested tests: hip, elbow, cardiac, eye, (vWD)
- Life span: 8–11 years

FORM AND FUNCTION

The Rottweiler is a medium large breed, slightly longer than it is tall, and robust with a powerful, substantial build. It combines the abilities necessary to drive cattle for long distances as well as serve as a formidable guard dog, jobs that entail great strength, agility, and endurance. Its trot is sure and powerful, with strong reach and drive. Its coat is straight, coarse, and dense. The jaws are wide and deep for strength; the muzzle is short enough for strength but long enough for proper breathing and cooling. Its expression reflects the Rottweiler at its best; noble, alert, and self-assured.

Saint Bernard

AT A GLANCE

Energy level:	■■
Exercise requirements:	■■
Playfulness:	■■■
Affection level:	■■■■
Friendliness toward dogs:	■■
Friendliness toward other pets:	■■■■
Friendliness toward strangers:	■■■
Ease of training:	■■■
Watchdog ability:	■■
Protection ability:	■
Grooming requirements:	
Smooth	■■
Long	■■■
Cold tolerance:	■■■■■
Heat tolerance:	■

WEIGHT: 120–200 lb*
HEIGHT: male: min. 27.5″; female: 25.5″

POPULARITY: Somewhat popular
FAMILY: Mastiff
AREA OF ORIGIN: Switzerland
DATE OF ORIGIN: Middle Ages
ORIGINAL FUNCTION: Draft, search and rescue
TODAY'S FUNCTION: Companion
OTHER NAME: St Bernhardshund, Alpine Mastiff

HISTORY

The Saint Bernard probably has its roots in the Roman Molossian dogs, but it wasn't until between 1660 and 1670 that the breed developed into the magnificent dog responsible for saving so many lives. Around this time, the first of these large dogs arrived at the St. Bernard Hospice, a refuge for travelers crossing between Switzerland and Italy. The Saint Bernards originally came to help pull carts and turn spits and may have also functioned as watchdogs or companions, but the monks soon found them invaluable pathfinders through the deep snow. The dogs were adept at locating lost travelers. When a dog found a person, it would lick the person's face and lie beside him, thus reviving and warming the person. The dogs continued to serve in this invaluable role for three centuries, saving over 2,000 lives.

ILLUSTRATED STANDARD

1 Flews of upper jaw are well developed
2 Muzzle short and deep
3 Lower eyelids usually do not close completely but form an angular wrinkle
4 Skin wrinkled on forehead
5 Head powerful with massive skull
6 Ears rather high-set, in shape of a rounded triangle
7 Straight back
8 Tail carried fairly low
9 Broad feet

Color: white with red, red or brindle with white; white must appear on chest, feet, tail tip, noseband, and collar (or spot on nape); may have dark mask and ears
DQ: none

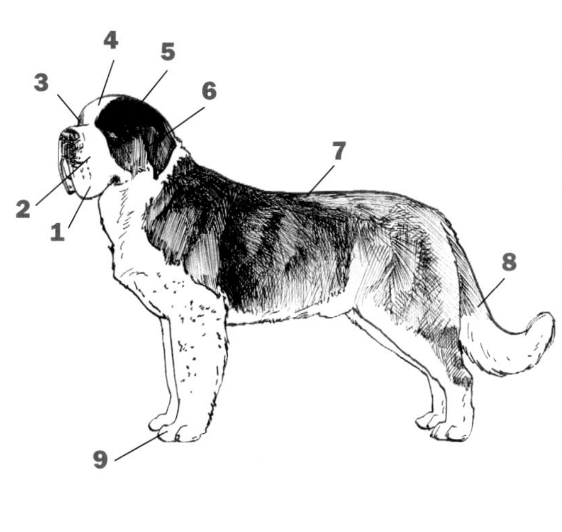

The most famous of all Saint Bernards was Barry, who was credited with saving 40 lives. Before Barry's death, the dogs were known by several names, including Hospice Dogs, but by the time he died he was of such fame that the dogs were called Barryhund in his honor. In the early 1800s many of the dogs were lost to severe weather, disease, and inbreeding. Some of the remaining dogs were crossed with Newfoundlands in 1830. As a result, the first long-coated dogs of Saint Bernard type appeared. Although it seemed that long hair would help a dog in the cold snow, in fact it hindered them as the ice clung to the coat. Thus, these long-haired dogs were not kept for rescue work. The first Saints came to England around 1810, referred to by many different names, among them Sacred Dog. By 1865, the name Saint Bernard was in common use, and it became the official name in 1880. Around this time, the breed caught the eye of American fanciers. By 1900, the Saint Bernard was the most popular AKC breed. Although it has since vacillated in popularity, it is always one of the most popular of the giant breeds.

TEMPERAMENT

The calm, easygoing, low-energy Saint Bernard is gentle and patient around children, although it is not particularly playful. Most get along with other family dogs. It's not a big barker, but its bark is loud. It is devoted to its family and is willing to please, although at its own pace. It can be stubborn.

UPKEEP

The Saint Bernard needs daily exercise in order to stay fit. Its requirements can be met with moderate walks and short runs, however. It enjoys cold weather and does not do well in heat. Its coat, whether long or short, needs weekly brushing, more so when shedding. All Saints drool.

HEALTH

- Major concerns: CHD, gastric torsion, entropion, ectropion, elbow dysplasia, osteosarcoma
- Minor concerns: OCD, diabetes, seizures, heart conditions, cardiomyopathy, CVI, hot spots
- Occasionally seen: distichiasis
- Suggested tests: hip, elbow, cardiac, eye
- Life span: 8–10 years
- Note: The Saint Bernard does not tolerate heat well.

FORM AND FUNCTION

The imposing Saint Bernard is powerful and proportionately tall. It is strong and well-muscled, necessary qualities in a dog that must trek through deep snow for miles. Its coat comes in two types: smooth, in which the short hair is very dense and tough, and long, in which the medium length hair is straight to slightly wavy. The expression should appear intelligent.

Samoyed

AT A GLANCE

Energy level: ■■■
Exercise requirements: ■■■
Playfulness: ■■■■
Affection level: ■■■■
Friendliness toward dogs: ■■■
Friendliness toward other pets: ■■■■■
Friendliness toward strangers: ■■■■
Ease of training: ■■

Watchdog ability: ■■■■■
Protection ability: ■
Grooming requirements: ■■■
Cold tolerance: ■■■■■
Heat tolerance: ■

WEIGHT: male: 45–65 lb; female: 35–50 lb*
HEIGHT: male: 21–23.5″; female: 19–21″

POPULARITY: Somewhat popular
FAMILY: Northern
AREA OF ORIGIN: Russia (Siberia)
DATE OF ORIGIN: Ancient times
ORIGINAL FUNCTION: Herding reindeer, guardian, draft
TODAY'S FUNCTION: Sled pulling, herding trials
OTHER NAME: Samoyedskaya

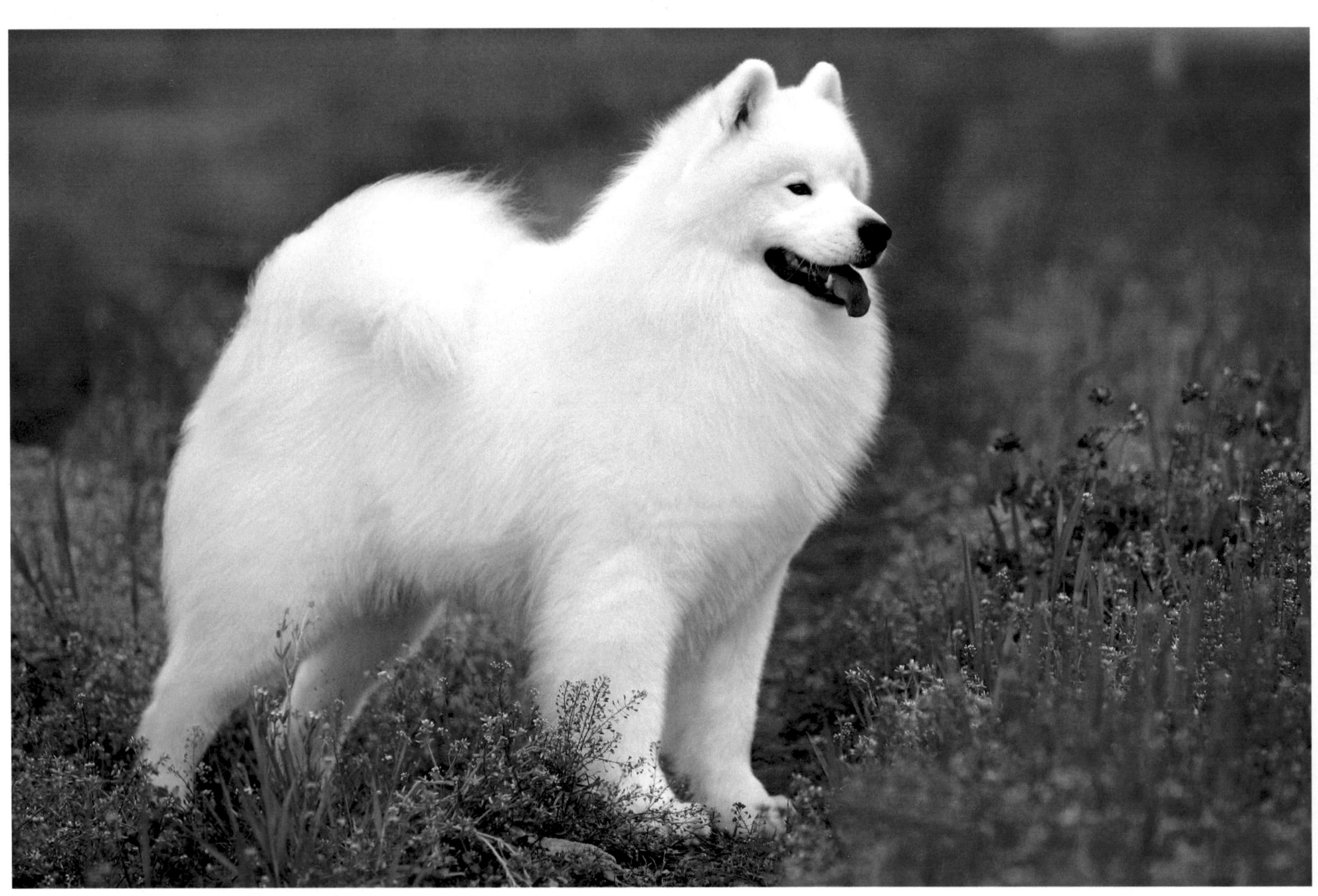

HISTORY

The nomadic Samoyed people, for whom the Samoyed dog is named, came to northwestern Siberia from central Asia. They depended upon herds of reindeer for food, and had to keep on the move in order that the reindeer could find sufficient food for themselves. They also depended upon strong hardy spitz dogs to herd the reindeer and to guard them against the fierce predators of the Arctic. They occasionally helped to hunt bears and tow boats and sledges. These dogs lived as part of the family in the hide tents of their people, where one of their "jobs" was to keep the children warm in bed. The first Samoyeds came to England in the late 1800s, but not all these early imports were the pure white the breed is known for today. One of these dogs was presented to Queen Alexandria, who did much to promote the breed. Descendants of the queen's dogs can still be found in modern pedigrees. In 1906, the first Samoyed came to America, originally a gift of Russia's Grand Duke Nicholas. Meanwhile, the breed was becoming a popular sled dog because it was more tractable than other sledding breeds. In the early 1900s, Samoyeds formed part of the sled teams on the expeditions to Antarctica and shared in the triumph of reaching the South Pole. The breed's

ILLUSTRATED STANDARD

1 Lips slightly curved up at corners of mouth
2 Skull wedge-shaped, broad
3 Ears erect, triangular with slightly rounded tips, well covered inside with hair
4 Neck carried proudly erect
5 Tail profusely covered with hair and carried over the back or side when alert
6 Loins slightly arched
7 Large, long hare feet, slightly spread with hair between toes

Color: white, white and biscuit, cream, or all biscuit
DQ: any color other than specified, blue eyes

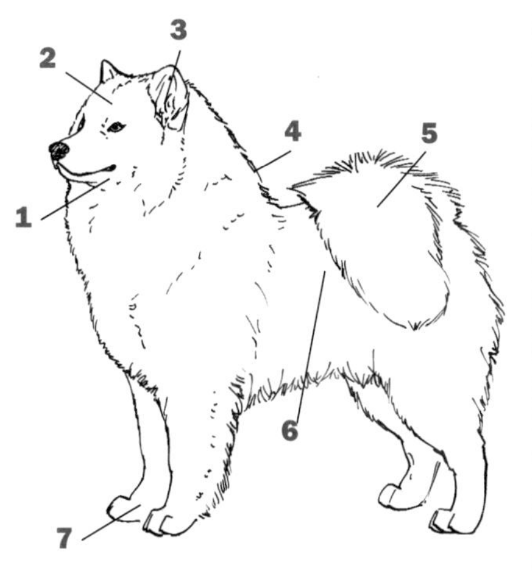

FORM AND FUNCTION

The Samoyed combines strength, agility, dignity, and grace in a general spitz outline. Slightly longer than it is tall, it is nonetheless compact. It has a strong, muscular body that is able to combine power, speed, agility, and endurance. It has a quick, agile stride with good reach and drive. Its double coat is heavy and weather resistant. The undercoat is soft and thick, whereas the outer coat is straight and harsh, standing straight out from the body, and glistening with a silver sheen. The expression is animated, with the characteristic "Samoyed smile" created by the upcurved corners of the mouth.

exploits, combined with its glistening good looks, soon won the public's attention in America, and its popularity has grown tremendously since the Second World War. Although the once nomadic Samoyed people have long since settled in one place, the breed they created has journeyed around the world.

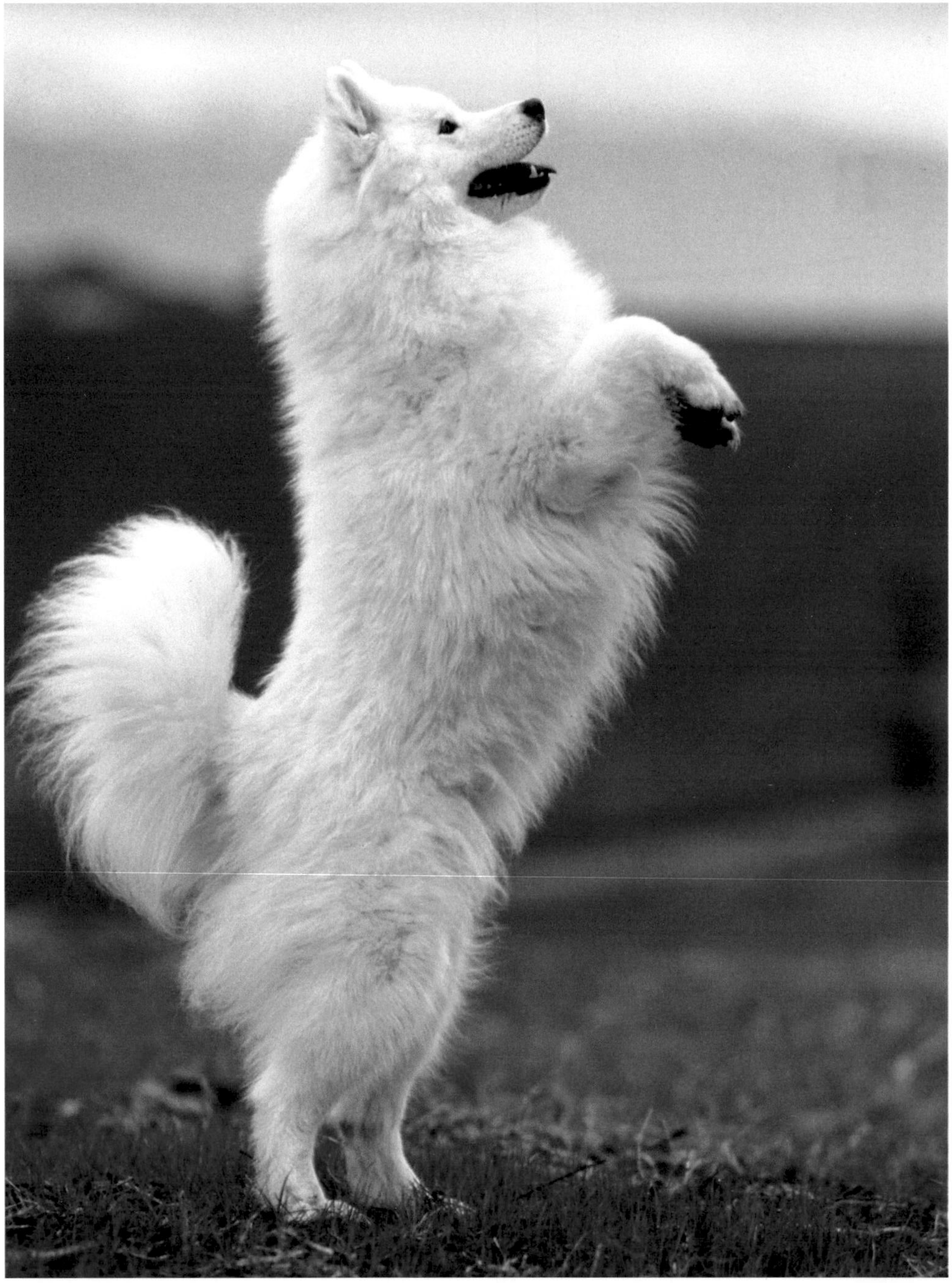

TEMPERAMENT

Gentle and playful, the Samoyed makes a good companion for a child or person of any age. It is a closely bonded family dog. It is amiable with strangers, other pets, and usually, other dogs. It is calm indoors, but this clever, sometimes mischievous breed needs daily physical and mental exercise. If allowed to become bored, it will dig and bark. It is independent and often stubborn, but it is willing to please and is responsive to its owner's wishes. It may tend to herd children.

UPKEEP

The Samoyed is active and needs a good workout every day, either in the form of a long walk or jog or a vigorous play session. It likes to pull and herd, and it loves cold weather. Its thick coat needs brushing and combing two to three times a week, daily when shedding.

HEALTH

- Major concerns: CHD
- Minor concerns: gastric torsion, cataract, hypothyroidism
- Occasionally seen: PRA, diabetes, RD/OSD, PDA
- Suggested tests: hip, eye, DNA for PRA, DNA for RD/OSD, cardiac
- Life span: 10–12 years

Siberian Husky

AT A GLANCE

Energy level:	■■■
Exercise requirements:	■■■■
Playfulness:	■■■■
Affection level:	■■■■
Friendliness toward dogs:	■■■
Friendliness toward other pets:	■■■
Friendliness toward strangers:	■■■■■
Ease of training:	■

Watchdog ability:	■■■
Protection ability:	■
Grooming requirements:	■■■
Cold tolerance:	■■■■■
Heat tolerance:	■

WEIGHT: male: 45–60 lb; female: 35–50 lb
HEIGHT: male: 21–23.5″; female: 20–22″

POPULARITY: Very popular
FAMILY: Northern
AREA OF ORIGIN: Russia (Siberia)
DATE OF ORIGIN: Ancient times
ORIGINAL FUNCTION: Sled pulling
TODAY'S FUNCTION: Sled racing
OTHER NAME: Arctic Husky

HISTORY

The Chukchi people of northeast Asia developed the breed now known as the Siberian Husky. Its ancestry is unknown, but it is of obvious spitz stock, evolved over hundreds of years as a sledge dog for these nomadic people. During the Alaskan gold rush, dogs became a vital part of life in the Arctic regions, and dog racing became a favorite source of entertainment. The All-Alaska sweepstakes race, covering 408 miles between Nome and Candle, was especially popular, and in 1909 the first team of these Chukchi huskies brought over from Siberia was entered. Smaller and more docile than most of the other competitors, they aroused little admiration, with the exception of one racer who was so impressed he imported seventy to train for the 1910 race. His three teams placed first,

ILLUSTRATED STANDARD

1 Eyes almond-shaped; brown, blue, or any combination
2 Ears erect, well furred, slightly rounded tips
3 Skull slightly rounded
4 Neck carried proudly erect and arched
5 Topline level
6 Well-furred tail of fox brush shape, carried in a sickle curve
7 Feet oval, medium-sized, well furred between toes and pads

Color: all colors from black to pure white
DQ: males over 23.5″ or females over 22″

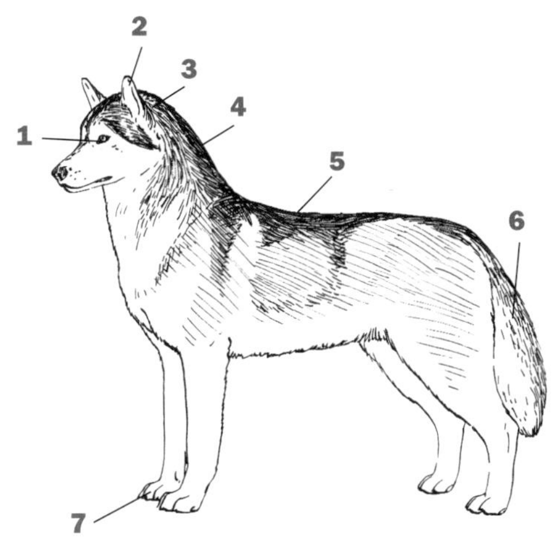

second, and fourth and so set the stage for the Siberian Husky's unrivaled dominance in this race. Throughout the rest of the year, the dogs earned their keep as utilitarian sledders, but it was in 1925 that they gained their greatest acclaim. Teams of Huskies raced 340 miles with life-saving serum for diphtheria stricken Nome and were credited with saving the town. A statue in their honor stands in Central Park. The first Siberian Huskies came to Canada, and then the United States, at around this time. The AKC recognized the breed in 1930. During World War II, many Siberians served in the U.S. Army's Search and Rescue teams, further capturing the public's admiration. The breed's popularity continued to grow until it was cherished as much for a family pet as for a racing sled dog or show dog. It remains one of the most popular of the Arctic breeds.

TEMPERAMENT

Fun-loving, adventurous, alert, independent, clever, stubborn, mischievous, and obstinate all describe the Siberian Husky. This breed loves to run and will roam if given the chance. It may be aggressive toward strange dogs, but it is generally good with other household dogs. In fact, it is a very social dog that must have human or canine companionship. It may chase strange cats or livestock. Some howl, dig, and chew.

UPKEEP

This is an active dog, bred to run tirelessly for miles. It needs ample daily exercise, either in the form of a long jog or a long run off-leash in a safe area. It also loves to pull and enjoys cold weather. Its coat needs brushing one or two times a week, daily during periods of heaviest shedding.

HEALTH

- Major concerns: none
- Minor concerns: PRA, cataract, corneal dystrophy, hypothyroidism
- Occasionally seen: CHD
- Suggested tests: eye, (thyroid), hip
- Life span: 11–13 years

FORM AND FUNCTION

The Siberian Husky combines power, speed, and endurance, enabling it to carry a light load at moderate speed over a great distance. It is moderately compact, slightly longer than it is tall, and of definite Northern heritage. It is quick and light on its feet, with a smooth and effortless stride exhibiting both good reach and drive. It has a double coat of medium length, with a soft, dense undercoat and straight, somewhat flat-lying outer coat. Its expression is keen but friendly, interested, and even mischievous.

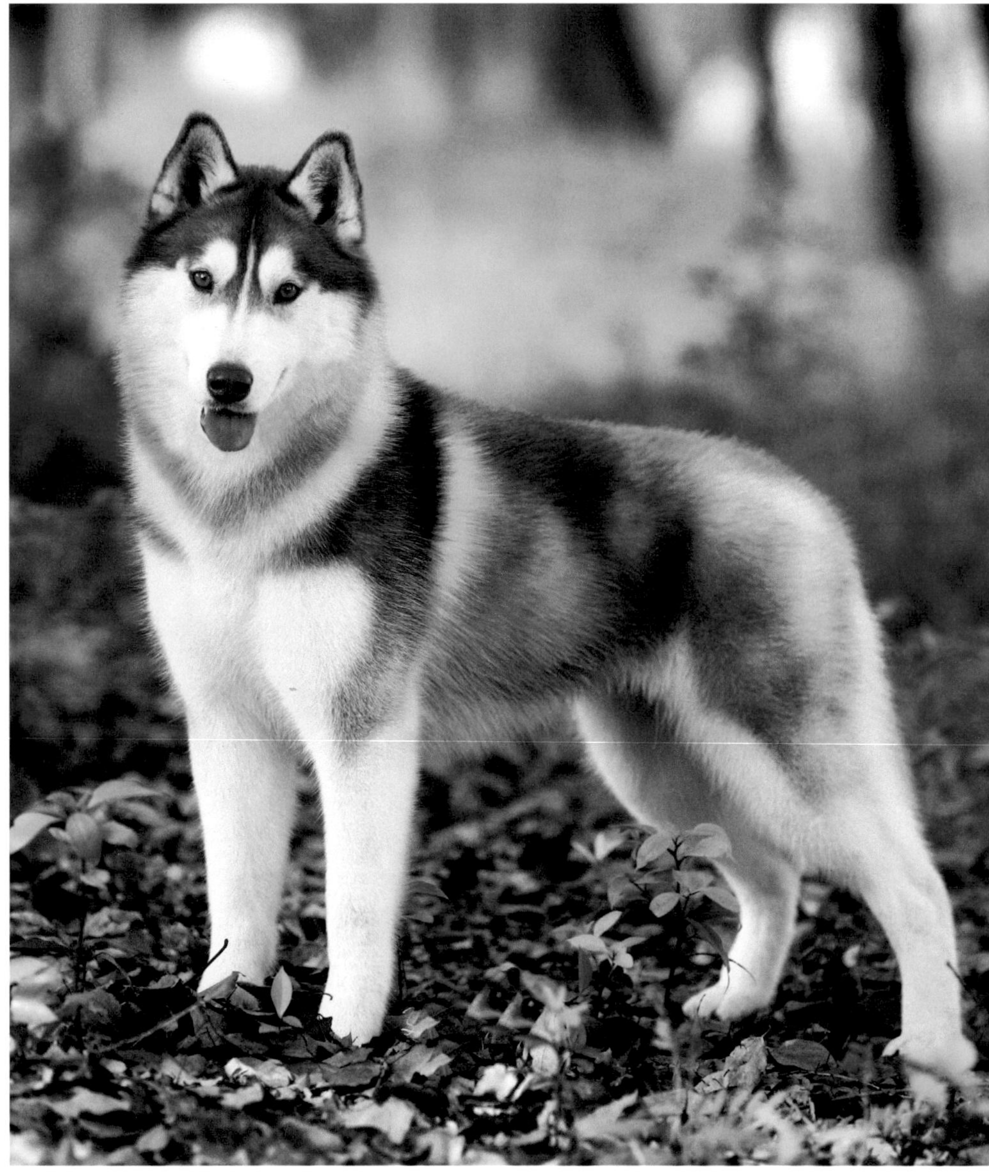

Standard Schnauzer

AT A GLANCE

Energy level:	■■■■
Exercise requirements:	■■■
Playfulness:	■■■
Affection level:	■■
Friendliness toward dogs:	■■
Friendliness toward other pets:	■■■
Friendliness toward strangers:	■
Ease of training:	■■■

Watchdog ability:	■■■■■
Protection ability:	■■■■■
Grooming requirements:	■■■■
Cold tolerance:	■■■
Heat tolerance:	■■■

WEIGHT: male: 40–45 lb; female: 35–40 lb*
HEIGHT: male: 18.5–19.5″; female: 17.5–18.5″

POPULARITY: Somewhat uncommon
FAMILY: Schnauzer, Livestock Guard, Terrier
AREA OF ORIGIN: Germany
DATE OF ORIGIN: Middle Ages
ORIGINAL FUNCTION: Ratting, guardian
TODAY'S FUNCTION: Companion
OTHER NAME: Mittelschnauzer

HISTORY

The Standard Schnauzer is the prototypical Schnauzer, the oldest of the three breeds. Definite evidence of the breed exists as early as the fourteenth century; even then, it was appreciated as a household pet and hunting companion. The breed is a fortuitous blend of terrier, working, and hunting stock, most likely derived from crossing Wire-Haired Pinschers with black German Poodles and gray wolf spitz. The result was a hardy rat catcher that also functioned as a capable guard dog. By the beginning of the twentieth century, they were the most popular dogs for guarding farmers' carts at the marketplace while the farmers were elsewhere. The first Schnauzers entered the show ring as Wirehaired Pinschers at an 1879 German show. Their smart looks quickly enam-

ILLUSTRATED STANDARD

1 Expression alert and spirited
2 Eyes oval with long eyebrows, which should not impair vision
3 Head strong, rectangular, and long
4 Ears set high; carried erect if cropped; V-shaped and mobile so they break at skull level if uncropped
5 Topline slopes slightly down
6 Tail carried erect and docked from 1 to 2″
7 Feet small, round, compact

Color: pepper and salt or pure black
DQ: males under 18″ or over 20″; females under 17″ or over 19″

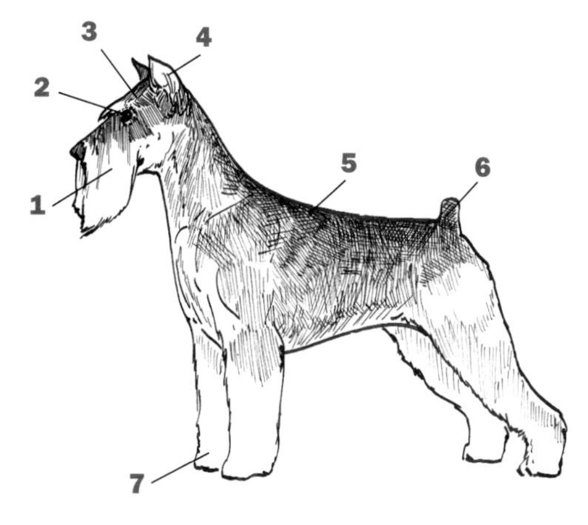

HEALTH

- Major concerns: none
- Minor concerns: CHD, follicular dermatitis
- Occasionally seen: cataract
- Suggested tests: hip, eye
- Life span: 12–14 years

FORM AND FUNCTION

This is a robust, sturdily built, heavy-set dog of square proportion. It is both strong and agile, enabling it to perform as both a guard and ratter. Its stride is quick, powerful, and ground covering. Its coat is hard, wiry, and thick, with soft undercoat. Its hallmark whiskers, mustache, and eyebrows add to its alert, spirited expression.

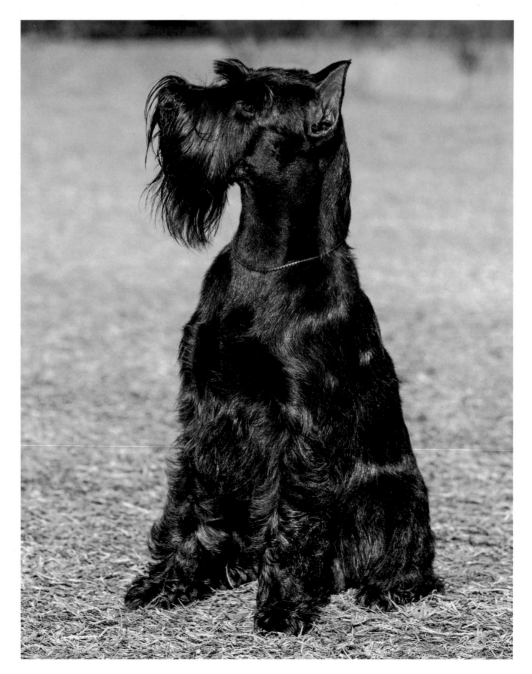

ored them to the dog fanciers, and they became very popular as show dogs by 1900. Although the first Schnauzers came to America by this time, they were slower to catch on with American dog fanciers. The breed was initially classified as a terrier, but it was later reclassified as a working dog. Their alert and intelligent nature gained them a role as dispatch carrier and aide during World War I. Like the larger Giant Schnauzer, the Standard Schnauzer was also used in police work. Only after World War II did it gain more public attention; even so, it has not achieved the popularity of the other Schnauzers.

TEMPERAMENT

Bold and lively, the Standard Schnauzer is a fun-loving companion and guardian. It is clever and headstrong, and unless given daily physical and mental exercise, it can be mischievous. It does best with a firm, patient owner. It is a devoted family dog and very reliable with children. It is good with family pets, but it can be aggressive toward strange dogs, animals, or rodents. It is reserved with strangers, sometimes acting suspicious and protective.

UPKEEP

The Standard Schnauzer needs daily exertion, either a long walk on leash, a vigorous game, or an off-lead outing in a safe area. Its harsh coat needs combing twice weekly, plus professional scissoring and shaping four times yearly. Shaping is done by clipping for pets and stripping for show dogs.

Tibetan Mastiff

AT A GLANCE

Energy level:	■■	Watchdog ability:	■■■■■	POPULARITY: Uncommon
Exercise requirements:	■■	Protection ability:	■■■■■	FAMILY: Mastiff
Playfulness:	■■■	Grooming requirements:	■■■	AREA OF ORIGIN: Tibet
Affection level:	■■■■	Cold tolerance:	■■■■■	DATE OF ORIGIN: Ancient
Friendliness toward dogs:	■■■	Heat tolerance:	■■	ORIGINAL FUNCTION: Guardian
Friendliness toward other pets:	■■■			TODAY'S FUNCTION: Guardian, companion
Friendliness toward strangers:	■■	WEIGHT: male: 90–150 lb +; female: 80–110 lb*		OTHER NAME: Do-Khyi
Ease of training:	■■	HEIGHT: male: 26″; female: 24″ minimum		

HISTORY

Among the most ancient and influential of breeds, the Tibetan Mastiff's origins have long been lost. Archeological evidence of massive dogs dating to 1100 B.C. can be found in China; such dogs may have traveled with Attila the Hun and Genghis Khan, providing root stock for mastiffs in Central Asia. Those on the Himalayan plateaus developed into camp guardians of nomadic herdsmen. Their nomadic lifestyle furthered their distribution, but the high mountains separating plateaus and valleys created isolated populations. Thus, a wide range of dogs emerged, with hardiness and guarding ability guiding selection. Besides guarding the campsites, dogs were used to guard villages and monasteries. Village sentries were usually chained to gates and rooftops by day and allowed to roam at night. The breed remained largely

ILLUSTRATED STANDARD

1 Strongly defined stop
2 Broad, heavy head; some wrinkling from eyes to mouth corner; moderate flews
3 Deep-set, almond-shaped eyes
4 Medium-sized, V-shaped ears, set high and hanging close to the head
5 Topline straight and level
6 Pronounced tuck-up
7 Medium to long tail, set high and curled over
8 Fairly large, compact cat feet; single or double dewclaws may be present on rear feet

Color: black, brown, and gray, all with or without tan markings; various shades of gold; white markings on breast and feet acceptable.

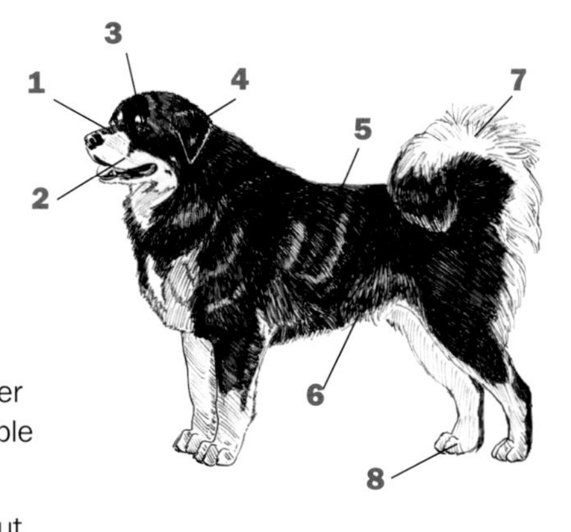

unknown outside its native Tibet until 1847, when the Viceroy of India sent a large dog from Tibet named Siring to Queen Victoria; it gained greater exposure when two dogs imported by the Prince of Wales were exhibited at a dog show in 1874. Imports remained at a trickle, and only in 1931 did the Tibetan Breeds Association in England develop a breed standard. With few dogs outside their native country, the breed's future was threatened when China invaded Tibet in the 1950s, displacing the native dogs. Survival depended on fleeing to neighboring countries or retreating to isolated mountain villages. The Dalai Lama sent two dogs to President Eisenhower, but they soon disappeared into obscurity. Only in the 1970s did stock from Nepal and India arrive to found breeding programs in America. The imports came from a wide genetic base, accounting for the natural variation in size and style in the breed today. The Tibetan Mastiff is now mostly a companion and family guardian, although some are used as livestock protectors. In 2005 this ancient breed began a new chapter as it entered the AKC Miscellaneous class.

TEMPERAMENT

As befitting their long past as a solitary sentry and protector, Tibetan Mastiffs are independent, strong willed, and territorial. They are aloof toward strangers but devoted to their family. Proper socialization is essential so that they will accept strangers and not become overly suspicious. They are gentle and patient with their children, but may guard their home against visiting children who may appear to be threatening the family children. They are generally good with other dogs and are rarely dog aggressive. (In Tibet, they were often kept with Lhasa Apsos.) Most Tibetan Mastiffs are good with other animals.

UPKEEP

The Tibetan Mastiff tends to be calm indoors and moderately active outside. A long daily leash walk along with access to an outdoor yard should meet its needs. Grooming consists of brushing a few times a week (daily during shedding), paying special attention to the longer hair of the britches, tail, and ruff. They like cold temperatures and are not suited for hot, humid climates. They like to bark loudly at night. Females have only one estrus each year.

HEALTH

- Major concerns: CHD, elbow dysplasia
- Minor concerns: hypothyroidism
- Occasionally seen: entropion, seizures, canine inherited demyelinative neuropathy
- Suggested tests: hip, thyroid, eye, (elbow)
- Life span: 11–14 years

FORM AND FUNCTION

A powerful, heavy, but athletic dog, the Tibetan Mastiff is built to combine strength and agility. Its body is slightly longer than it is tall. Its walk is slow and deliberate, while its trot is powerful and light-footed. The whole appearance is impressive, with a solemn but kindly expression. The coat, which is noticeably heavier in males than in females, is thick and fairly long, especially around the neck and shoulders. The tail is densely coated and the hind legs well feathered on the upper parts. The hair is coarse, straight, and hard, standing off from the body. It carries a heavy undercoat in cold weather but little undercoat in warm weather. This combination of coat types allows the Tibetan Mastiff to endure the extremes of Tibetan weather.

THE TERRIER GROUP

Terriers have the proclivity to kill rodents and vermin, often by digging or going to ground after them. The word *terrier*, in fact, refers to earth or *terra*. The vermin-catching terriers are roughly divided into long-legged and short-legged breeds. Other terriers descend from bull-baiting dogs crossed with terriers. They were used to fight one another. Terriers tend to be independent, adventurous, cocky, and sometimes scrappy.

Airedale Terrier

AT A GLANCE

Energy level:	■ ■ ■ ■	Watchdog ability:	■ ■ ■ ■
Exercise requirements:	■ ■ ■	Protection ability:	■ ■ ■ ■
Playfulness:	■ ■ ■ ■	Grooming requirements:	■ ■ ■ ■
Affection level:	■ ■ ■	Cold tolerance:	■ ■ ■
Friendliness toward dogs:	■	Heat tolerance:	■ ■ ■
Friendliness toward other pets:	■ ■		
Friendliness toward strangers:	■ ■ ■	WEIGHT: about 55 lb*	
Ease of training:	■ ■ ■	HEIGHT: male: 23″; female: slightly less	

POPULARITY: Somewhat popular
FAMILY: Terrier
AREA OF ORIGIN: England
DATE OF ORIGIN: 1800s
ORIGINAL FUNCTION: Versatile hunter: badger and otter hunting, bird flushing and retrieving
TODAY'S FUNCTION: Guardian, police dog
OTHER NAME: Waterside Terrier, Bingley Terrier

HISTORY

Known as the King of Terriers, the Airedale is the tallest terrier. Like many terriers, it counts the old English, or Black and Tan, Terrier as one of its primary progenitors. These medium-sized dogs were prized by Yorkshire hunters (and poachers) for hunting a variety of game from water rat to fox. The dogs could also find and retrieve birds. Around the mid 1800s, some of these terriers around the River Aire in South Yorkshire were crossed with Otterhounds in order to improve their hunting ability around water, as well as their scenting ability. The result was a dog adept at otter hunting, originally called the Bingley or Waterside Terrier but recognized as the Airedale Terrier in 1878. As it entered the world of the show dog, crosses to the Irish and Bull Terriers were made in

ILLUSTRATED STANDARD

1 Skull long and flat
2 Eyes small
3 Stop hardly visible
4 V-shaped ears with fold above the level of the skull
5 Back short and level
6 Tail set and carried high, of fair length
7 Feet small and round

Color: tan with black or grizzle saddle
DQ: none

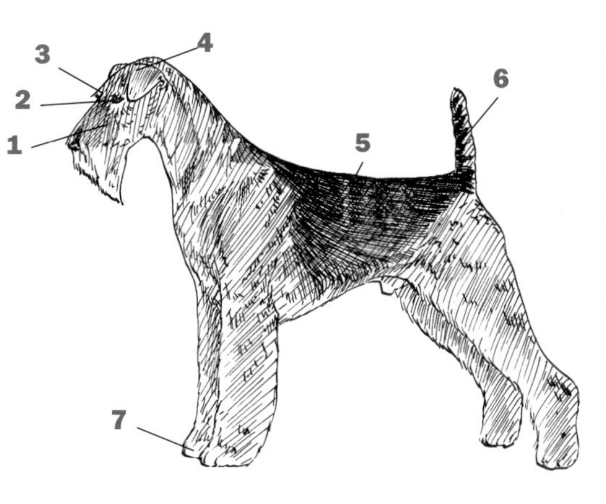

order to breed away from some of the remnants of the Otterhound cross that were now considered less than beautiful. By 1900, the patriarch of the breed, Champion Master Briar, was gaining renown, and his offspring carried on his influence in America. The Airedale's size and gameness continued to win it worldwide fame as a hunter, even proving itself as a big game hunter. Its smart looks and manners won it a place as a police dog and family pet, both roles it still enjoys. After World War I, however, its popularity declined, and today its reputation is greater than its numbers.

TEMPERAMENT

Among the most versatile of terriers, the Airedale is bold, playful, and adventurous; it is a lively yet protective companion. It is intelligent, but often stubborn and headstrong. Some can be domineering, but most are biddable, reliable, and responsive to their owner's wishes. It makes a good housedog as long as it gets daily mental and physical exercise. It likes to be the head dog and may not do well when another dog challenges that position, although they usually get along well with smaller dogs.

UPKEEP

This is an active breed that needs a chance to get vigorous exercise every day. Its needs can be met with a long walk, a strenuous game, or a chance to hunt and romp in a safe area. Its wire coat needs combing twice weekly, plus scissoring and shaping (clipping for pets, and hand stripping for show dogs) every one to two months. Clipping will layer the texture and color. Ears often need "glueing" as puppies in order to ensure proper shape as adults.

HEALTH

- Major concerns: CHD
- Minor concerns: gastric torsion, hypothyroidism
- Occasionally seen: colonic disease
- Suggested tests: hip, thyroid
- Life span: 10–13 years

FORM AND FUNCTION

The Airedale Terrier is a neat, upstanding, long-legged terrier, not exaggerated in any way. It has strong round bone and combines strength and agility, enabling it to hunt tough game. Its jaws are strong and punishing. Its gait is free. The coat is hard, dense, and wiry; it lies straight and close, with some hair crinkling or waving.

American Staffordshire Terrier

AT A GLANCE

Energy level:	■■■
Exercise requirements:	■■■
Playfulness:	■■■
Affection level:	■■■
Friendliness toward dogs:	■
Friendliness toward other pets:	■
Friendliness toward strangers:	■■■
Ease of training:	■■■■

Watchdog ability:	■■■■■
Protection ability:	■■■■■
Grooming requirements:	■
Cold tolerance:	■■■
Heat tolerance:	■■■

WEIGHT: 57–67 lb*
HEIGHT: male: 18–19″; female: 17–18″

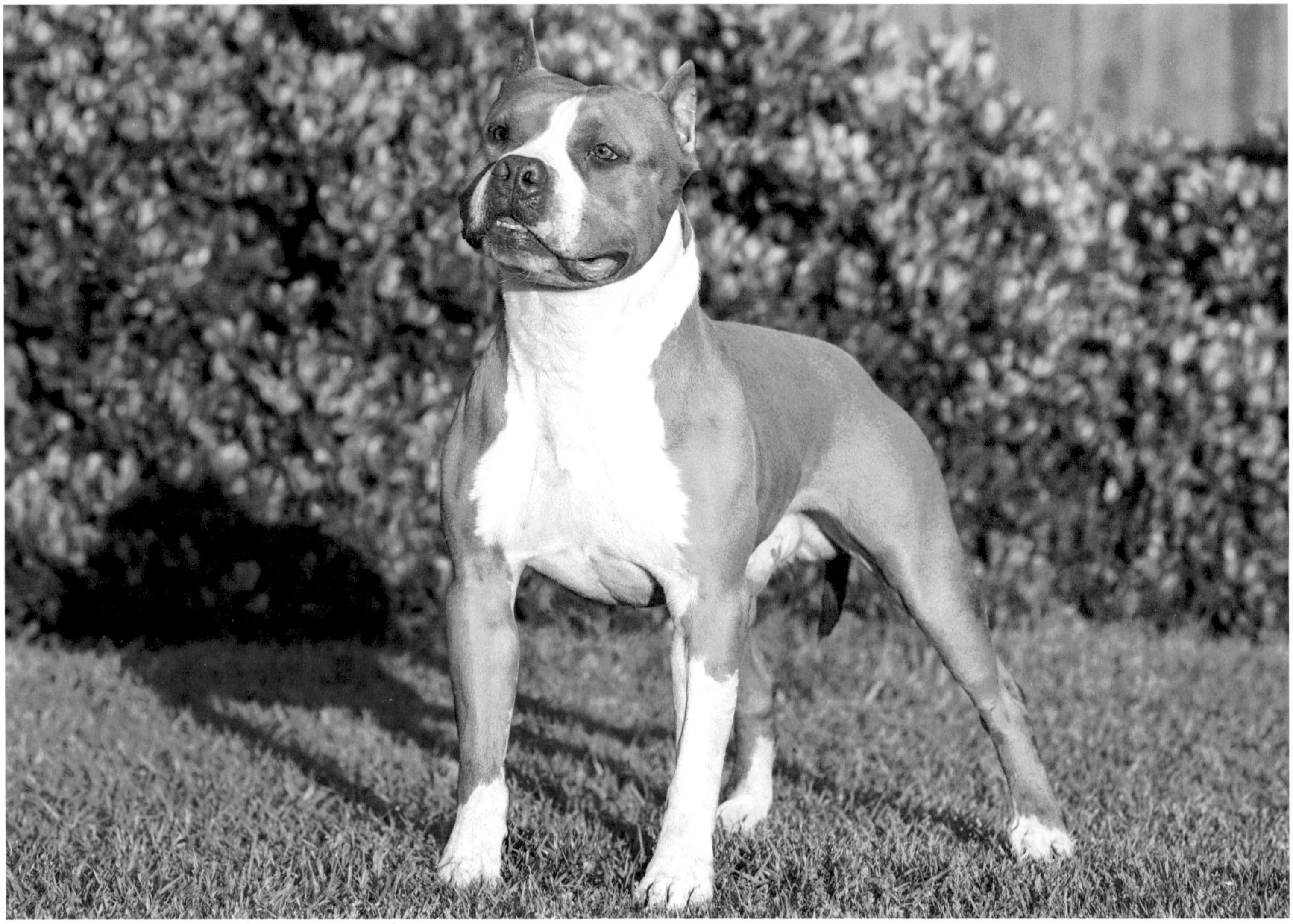

POPULARITY: Somewhat uncommon
FAMILY: Terrier, Mastiff, Bull
AREA OF ORIGIN: United States
DATE OF ORIGIN: 1800s
ORIGINAL FUNCTION: Bullbaiting, dog fighting
TODAY'S FUNCTION: Companion
OTHER NAME: American Pit Bull Terrier

HISTORY

The American Staffordshire Terrier and the Staffordshire Bull Terrier descended from the same lines. The prototype originally sprang from crossing the old type of Bulldog with some old terrier types, probably the English Smooth Terrier. The result was aptly called the Bull and Terrier, later to be dubbed the Staffordshire Bull Terrier. The dogs gained fame among fanciers of dog fighting, a popular sport despite its having been declared illegal. Their fighting ability gained them passage to America in the late 1800s, where they dominated the fighting "pits." Here they became known as the Pit Bull Terrier, American Bull Terrier, and even Yankee Terrier. Americans favored a slightly bigger dog than the English preferred, and with time the two strains diverged. In 1936, the AKC recognized the breed as the Staffordshire Terrier (the name was changed in 1972 to American Staffordshire Terrier). Docility and tractability have always been vital traits in a powerful dog that must be handled even in the midst of a dog fight;

ILLUSTRATED STANDARD

1 Ears set high, cropped or uncropped (preferred); uncropped ears short and held half rose or prick
2 Head broad, pronounced cheek muscles, distinct stop
3 Back fairly short, sloping slightly to rear
4 Tail short but not docked
5 Forelegs set wide, straight

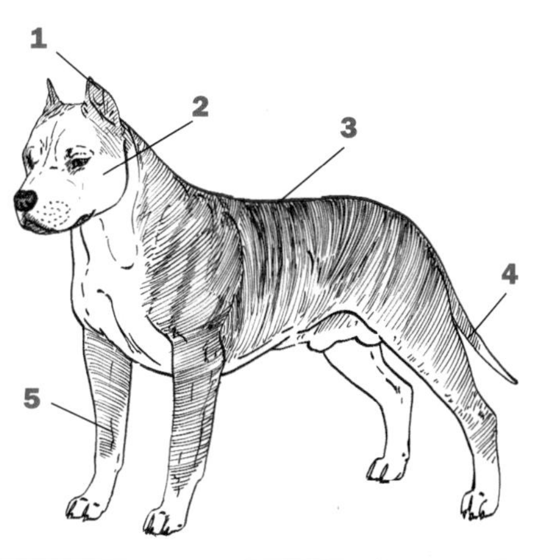

Color: any solid or partial color, but more than 80 percent white, black and tan, or liver are less preferred
DQ: none

therefore, the Am Staff evolved to have a sweet and trustworthy disposition around people. Unfortunately, this game dog has too often appealed to people seeking it for its fighting rather than its loving abilities. Often in the midst of controversy, beginning in the 1980s, it sometimes found itself the target of breed-specific laws aimed at banning or controlling certain types of dogs. Despite this, the Am Staff is currently enjoying one of its most popular periods among people wanting a people- and fun-loving dog.

TEMPERAMENT

Typically docile and playful with its family, the American Staffordshire Terrier is also generally friendly toward strangers as long as its owners are present. It is generally very good with children. It is a protective breed and can be aggressive toward other dogs—especially those that challenge it. It is stubborn, tenacious, and fearless. For all of its tough persona, the most important thing in life to this breed is its owner's fond attention.

UPKEEP

The Staff needs a daily outlet for its energy, preferably in the form of a long walk on leash or a vigorous game in the yard. Coat care is minimal. As one of the breeds popularly considered a "pit bull," public acceptance may sometimes be low.

HEALTH

- Major concerns: CHD, cerebellar ataxia, PRA
- Minor concerns: elbow dysplasia, heart disease, hypothyroidism
- Occasionally seen: cruciate ligament rupture, allergies, hypothyroidism
- Suggested tests: hip, cardiac, (elbow), thyroid, eye, DNA for ataxia
- Life span: 12–14 years
- Note: CHD seldom causes problems or symptoms in this breed.

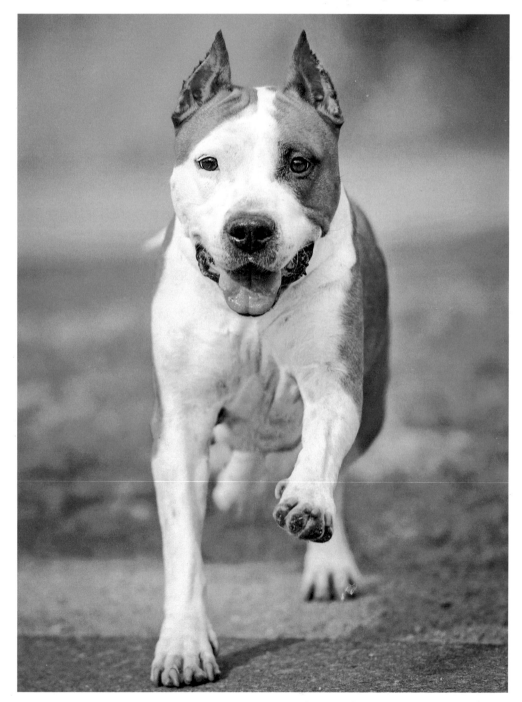

FORM AND FUNCTION

This stocky dog should be muscular, giving the impression not only of great strength for its size but also of grace and agility. Its gait is springy. Its low center of gravity helped it stay on its feet in a fight, and its nimbleness helped it avoid its opponent's teeth. Its own jaws are strong with great power. Its coat is short, close, and glossy.

Australian Terrier

AT A GLANCE

Energy level:	■■■	Watchdog ability:	■■■■■	POPULARITY: Rare
Exercise requirements:	■■■	Protection ability:	■	FAMILY: Terrier
Playfulness:	■■■	Grooming requirements:	■■■	AREA OF ORIGIN: Australia
Affection level:	■■■	Cold tolerance:	■■■	DATE OF ORIGIN: 1900s
Friendliness toward dogs:	■■■	Heat tolerance:	■■■	ORIGINAL FUNCTION: Killing small vermin
Friendliness toward other pets:	■■■			TODAY'S FUNCTION: Earthdog trials
Friendliness toward strangers:	■■	WEIGHT: 12–14 lb*		OTHER NAME: None
Ease of training:	■■	HEIGHT: 10–11″		

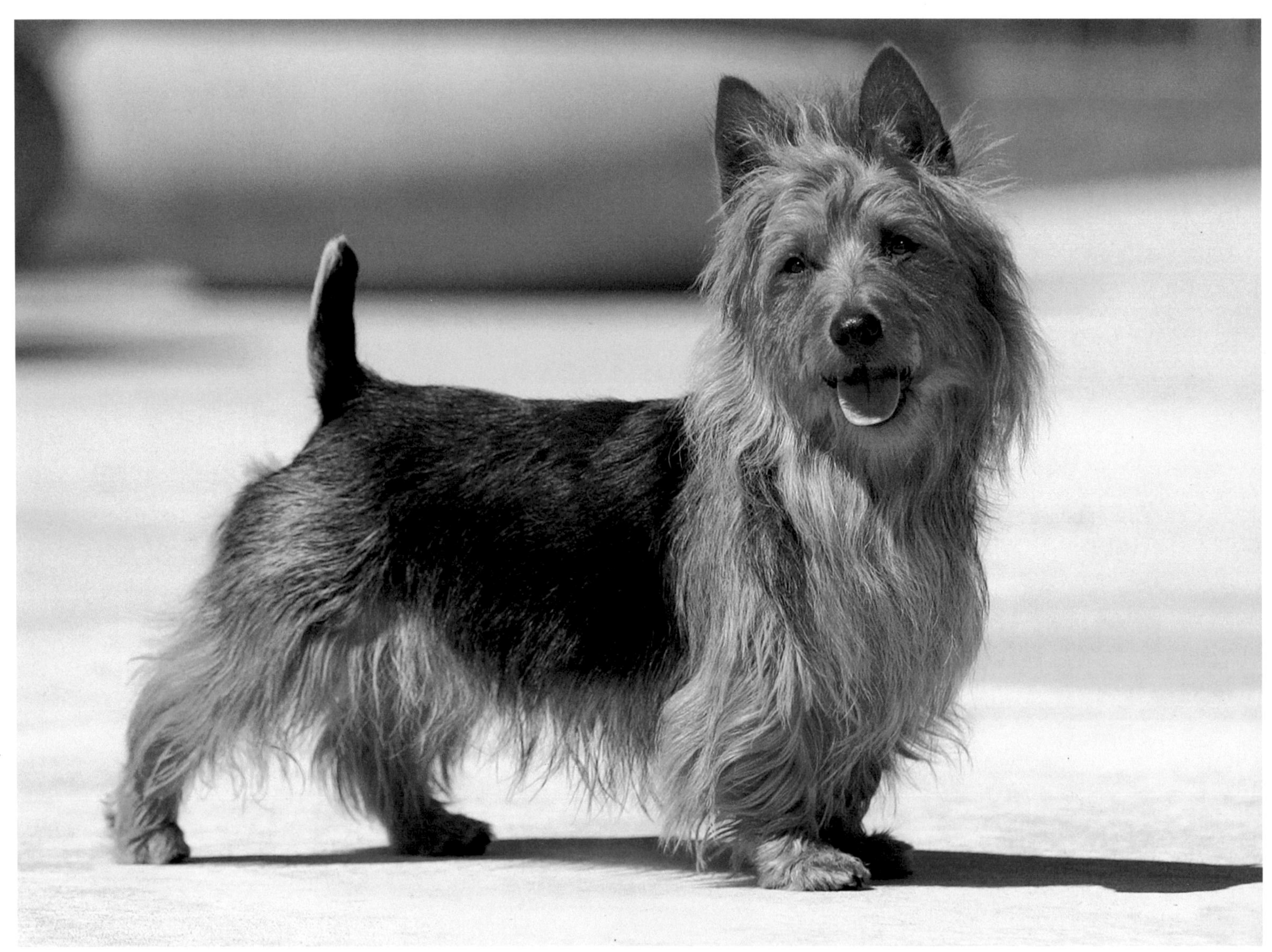

HISTORY

The national terrier of Australia, this is one of the smallest of the working terriers. It was born in Tasmania, from various European breeds, and shares much of its background with the Silky Terrier. In Tasmania, the Rough Coated Terrier was an all-purpose companion, killing vermin and snakes, controlling livestock, and sounding the alarm at intruders. A cornucopia of breeds was crossed with this root stock, among them the precursors of the Skye, Dandie Dinmont, Scotch, Yorkshire, and Manchester Terriers. The result was a dog that was both useful and striking in appearance. The first of the breed was shown in the late 1800s as a "broken-coated terrier of blackish blue sheen." The name was soon changed to the Blue and Tan, the Toy, then the Blue Terrier, then in 1900 the Rough-Coated

ILLUSTRATED STANDARD

1 Eyes small and oval
2 Head long and strong
3 Ears small, erect, and pointed
4 Topline level
5 Tail set high and carried at twelve or one o'clock, docked leaving just less than one half*
6 Small cat feet

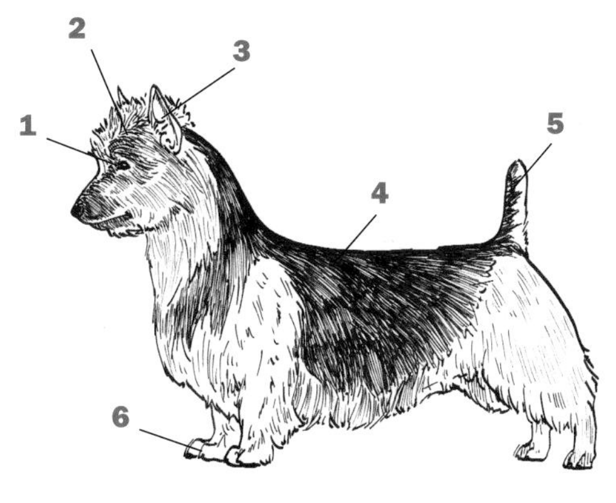

Color: blue and tan, solid sandy, and solid red
DQ: none

*Docking is optional.

Terrier, Blue and Tan. Although mainly known for its blue and tan coloration, a red or sandy color was also found among the early representatives of the breed. Soon after the breed had made its way to British show rings and homes, and by 1925 it had come to America. It received AKC recognition in 1960.

TEMPERAMENT
One of the quieter terriers, the Aussie is nonetheless a plucky, tough character, ready to go after a rodent when the chance arises. It is fun loving and adventurous, and needs daily exercise to keep it from becoming frustrated. It is clever and generally eager to please, making it one of the more obedient terriers. It gets along fairly well with other dogs and household pets. It is reserved with strangers. Reflecting its earth dog heritage, it does like to dig.

UPKEEP
This is an active breed that needs a good outing every day, either a moderate walk, a rollicking game, or an off-lead run in a safe area. Its wire coat needs weekly combing plus twice yearly stripping of dead hairs (regular plucking of dead hairs will keep the coat in optimal condition year round). Some trimming around the feet will add to a tidy look.

HEALTH
- Major concerns: none
- Minor concerns: patellar luxation, diabetes
- Occasionally seen: Legg-Perthes, seizures, cruciate ligament rupture
- Suggested tests: (eye), knee, thyroid
- Life span: 12–14 years

FORM AND FUNCTION
The Australian Terrier is small, sturdy, and medium boned; it is long in proportion to height. This is a working terrier that should exhibit a ground-covering gait and hard condition. Its weatherproof coat is made up of a short, soft undercoat and a harsh, straight, outer coat, about 2.5 inches long, shorter on the tail and lower legs. It sports a ruff around the neck and a topknot of longer hair adds to its keen, intelligent expression.

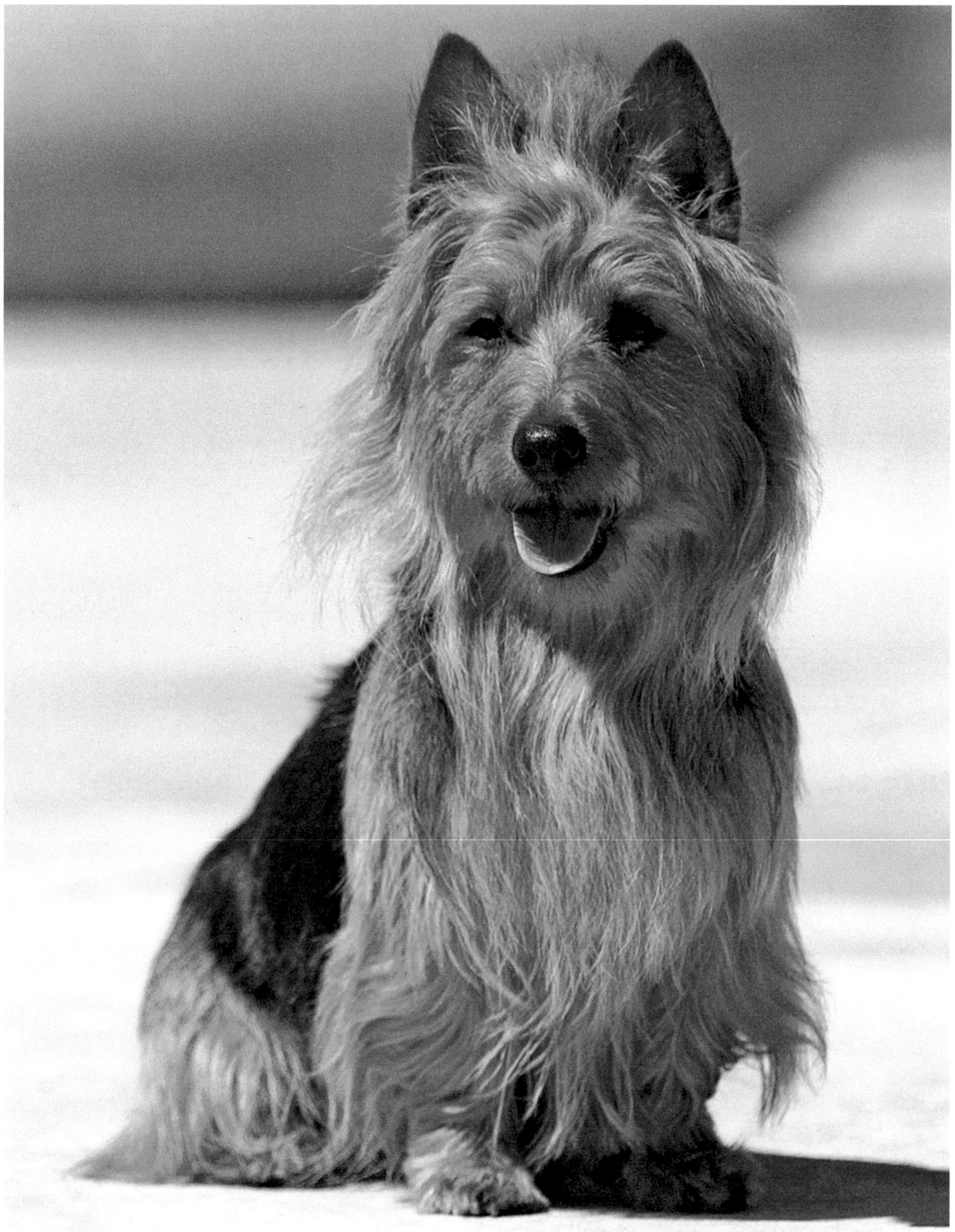

Bedlington Terrier

AT A GLANCE

Energy level:	■■■	Watchdog ability:	■■■■■	POPULARITY: Rare
Exercise requirements:	■■■	Protection ability:	■	FAMILY: Terrier
Playfulness:	■■■	Grooming requirements:	■■■■■	AREA OF ORIGIN: England
Affection level:	■■■	Cold tolerance:	■■■	DATE OF ORIGIN: 1800s
Friendliness toward dogs:	■■■	Heat tolerance:	■■■	ORIGINAL FUNCTION: Killing rat, badger, and other vermin
Friendliness toward other pets:	■■			
Friendliness toward strangers:	■■■■	WEIGHT: 17–23 lb		TODAY'S FUNCTION: Earthdog trials
Ease of training:	■■	HEIGHT: male: 16.5″; female: 15.5″		OTHER NAME: Rothbury Terrier

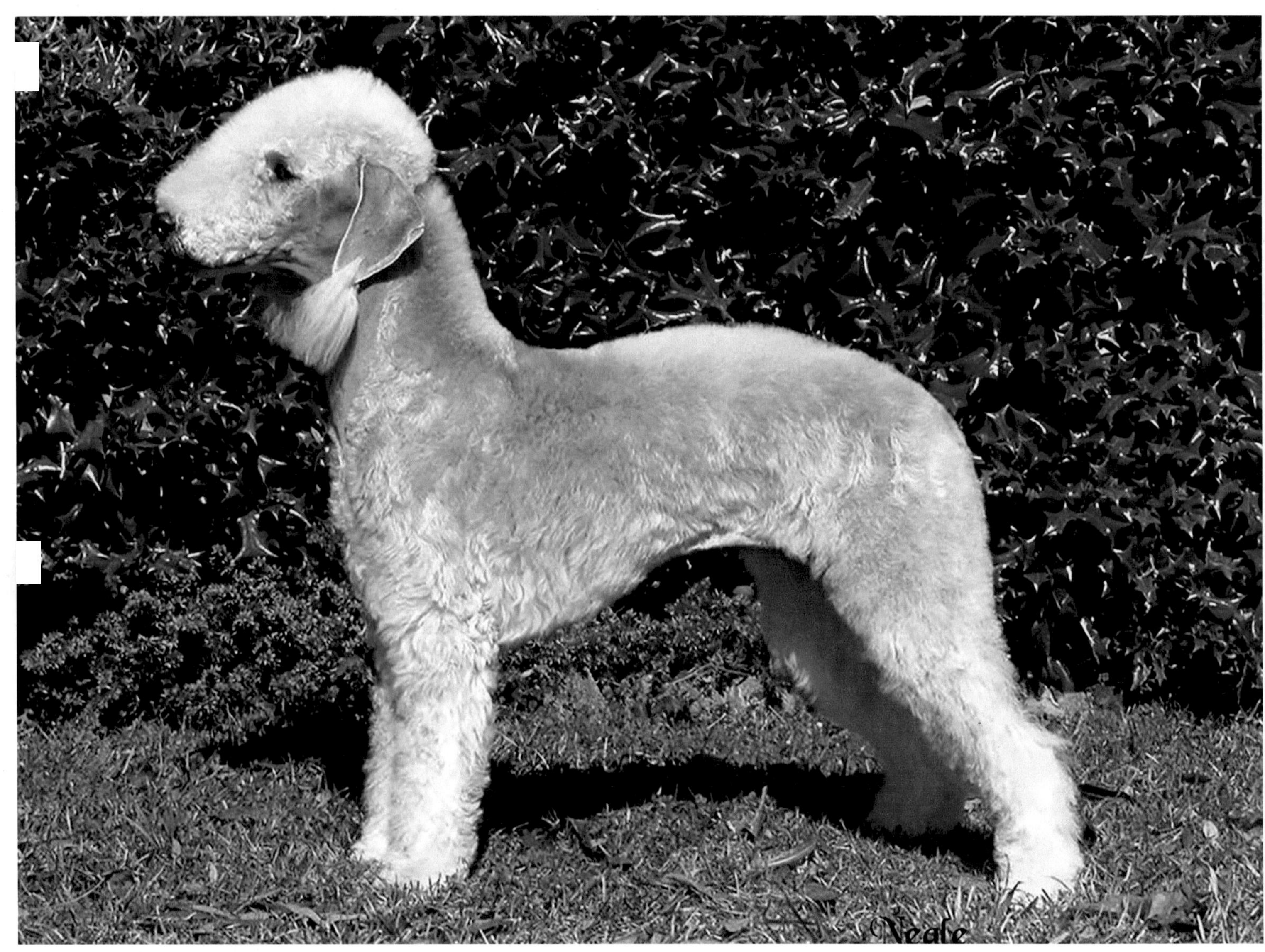

HISTORY

One of the most unusual members of the terrier group is the Bedlington Terrier. It is an English product, hailing from the Hanny Hills of Northumberland. Its exact origin is obscure, but in the late eighteenth century a strain of game terriers was developed that became known as Rothbury Terriers. In 1825, Joseph Ainsley of the town of Bedlington bred two of his Rothbury Terriers and christened their offspring a Bedlington Terrier. Occasional crosses to other breeds arguably included the Whippet (for speed) and Dandie Dinmont Terrier (for coat), but no documented evidence of such crosses exist, and some breed historians assert that such crosses were never made. Whatever the process, the result was an agile game terrier that was effective on badger, fox, otter, rats, and even rabbits. By the late

ILLUSTRATED STANDARD

1 Eyes almond-shaped
2 Skull narrow, deep, and rounded
3 No stop
4 Profuse topknot
5 Ears triangular with rounded tips, hanging, set low, with a silky tassel at tip
6 Back has arch over loin
7 Good tuck-up
8 Hare feet

Color: blue, sandy, and liver, each with or without tan points; Bedlington pups are born dark, and lighten to adult color by about one year of age
DQ: none

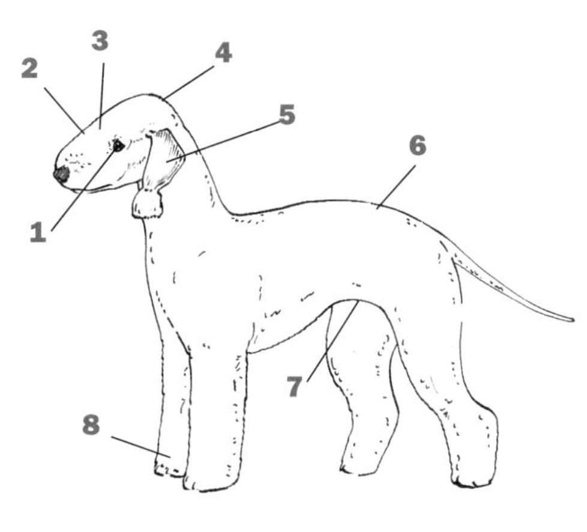

1800s, the breed had stepped into the show ring as well as into the homes of the more elite. At one time the liver color was more popular, although the blue has since passed it in popularity. The Bedlington's lamb-like appearance draws many admirers, but the emphasis on show trimming eventually dampened the breed's popularity as a show dog. With more easily available grooming tools and instructions, the Bedlington has regained much of its popularity with the public.

TEMPERAMENT

The Bedlington is among the softer terriers, not only in looks and feel but in temperament. It is companionable, demonstrative, and loyal. It enjoys its creature comforts and is a fairly quiet housedog. Even though it will seldom initiate a fight, it will not allow itself to be intimidated by other dogs and can be a scrappy fighter when pushed. It will give chase to small animals outdoors, but it can usually coexist with them indoors.

UPKEEP

The Bedlington needs daily exercise in a safe place; it loves to run and chase. Its needs can be met with a good long walk or vigorous romp. Its coat needs combing once or twice weekly, plus scissoring to shape the coat every other month. Hair that is shed tends to cling to the other hair rather than shedding.

HEALTH

- Major concerns: copper toxicosis
- Minor concerns: retinal dysplasia, renal cortical hypoplasia, distichiasis
- Occasionally seen: patellar luxation
- Suggested tests: DNA for copper toxicosis, liver biopsy, eye, knee
- Life span: 12–14 years

FORM AND FUNCTION

This graceful, lithe dog has a distinctive silhouette. Its arched loin and racy outline give it great speed and agility. A wolf in lamb's clothing, the Bedlington is unrivaled in its ability to chase and fight agile but tough quarry. Its gait is light and springy. Its coat is a mixture of hard and soft hair standing off the skin, affording good protection as well as outstanding appearance.

Border Terrier

AT A GLANCE

Energy level:	■■■
Exercise requirements:	■■■
Playfulness:	■■■
Affection level:	■■■
Friendliness toward dogs:	■■■
Friendliness toward other pets:	■■
Friendliness toward strangers:	■■■
Ease of training:	■■■■

Watchdog ability:	■■■■
Protection ability:	■
Grooming requirements:	■■■
Cold tolerance:	■■■
Heat tolerance:	■■■

WEIGHT: male: 13–15.5 lb; female: 11.5–14 lb
HEIGHT: 10–11"*

POPULARITY: Somewhat uncommon
FAMILY: Terrier
AREA OF ORIGIN: Border of Scotland and England
DATE OF ORIGIN: 1700s
ORIGINAL FUNCTION: Fox bolting, ratting
TODAY'S FUNCTION: Earthdog trials
OTHER NAME: None

HISTORY

Perhaps the oldest of Britain's terriers, the Border Terrier originated around the Cheviot Hills forming the border country between Scotland and England. The dog originated to chase and bolt (or remain underground and bark at) the fox that were considered a nuisance to farmers. The smallest of the long-legged terriers, the Border Terrier had to be fast enough to keep up with a horse yet small enough to go in after the fox once it had gone to ground. The first evidence of these dogs dates from the eighteenth century. Its progenitors are unknown, although it is probably related to the Dandie Dinmont and possibly Bedlington Terriers. The breed was once known as the Coquetdale Terrier or Redesdale Terrier, but the name Border Terrier, taken from the Border Hunt, was adopted in 1870. By this time, the breed

ILLUSTRATED STANDARD

1 Muzzle short, darker colored, and with a few short whiskers
2 Eyes medium-sized
3 Head similar to an otter
4 Small, V-shaped ears, dropping forward
5 Tail moderately short, carried gaily when alert
6 Feet small

Color: red, grizzle and tan, blue and tan, or wheaten
DQ: none

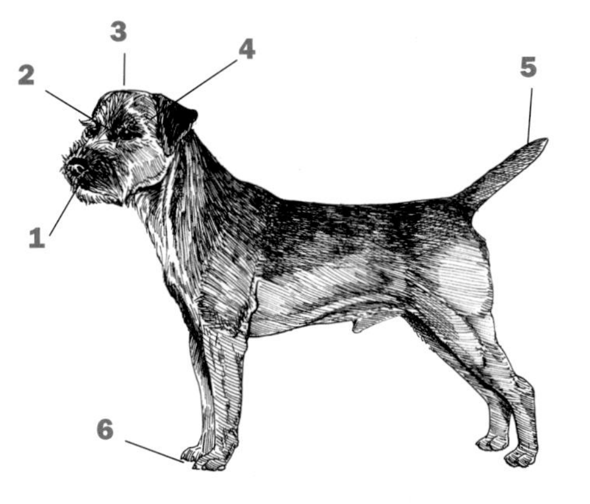

had risen from its utilitarian roots to take a valued place alongside the Foxhounds in the gentry's elegant foxhunts. The Border Hunt had a long association with these game yet amiable terriers whose job it was to dispatch the fox. The first Border Terrier was shown in the 1870s. The breed was recognized by the AKC in 1930. Less flashy than many other terriers, the Border continued to be better appreciated by patrons of the hunt than of the show ring. Unlike many terriers, the breed has changed very little since it was recognized. In recent years, it has experienced a rise in popularity and is fast becoming a fairly popular pet and successful show dog. It is especially popular in the United Kingdon, where it is among the ten most popular breeds.

TEMPERAMENT

One of the few terriers bred to run with the pack, the Border is one of the most amiable and tractable of the group. It is inquisitive, busy, friendly, and biddable. It does like to hunt and can be independent, ingredients that make for a dog that may tend to roam if given the chance. It is generally good with other dogs and cats, but not with rodents. It is very good with children and makes a good companion for people of all ages. It digs, and some bark. Some are talented escape artists.

UPKEEP

The Border likes activity and needs either a good walk on leash, a vigorous game session, or an off-lead expedition in a safe area every day. Its harsh coat needs brushing weekly, plus stripping of dead hairs about four times yearly to maintain its clean outline.

HEALTH

- Major concerns: none
- Minor concerns: patellar luxation
- Occasionally seen: CHD, heart defects
- Suggested tests: hip, cardiac, knee, (eye)
- Life span: 12–15 years

FORM AND FUNCTION

The Border Terrier is of medium bone, slightly taller than long. Its long legs impart the speed, agility, and endurance necessary to follow a horse over all sorts of terrain, whereas its fairly narrow body allows it to squeeze through narrow passages in pursuit of a fox. Its gait displays good length of stride. Its coat consists of a short, dense undercoat covered by a very wiry, straight, somewhat broken outer coat, which should conform to the body. Its hide is very thick and loose fitting, affording protection from the bites of its quarry. The Border is known for its distinctive otter head, and its alert expression matches its alert demeanor.

Bull Terrier

AT A GLANCE

Energy level:	■ ■ ■ ■
Exercise requirements:	■ ■ ■
Playfulness:	■ ■ ■ ■ ■
Affection level:	■ ■ ■
Friendliness toward dogs:	■
Friendliness toward other pets:	■ ■ ■
Friendliness toward strangers:	■ ■ ■
Ease of training:	■

Watchdog ability:	■ ■ ■ ■ ■
Protection ability:	■ ■ ■ ■
Grooming requirements:	■
Cold tolerance:	■ ■ ■
Heat tolerance:	■ ■ ■

WEIGHT: male: 60–70 lb; female: 50–60 lb*
HEIGHT: 21–22″*

POPULARITY: Somewhat popular
FAMILY: Terrier, Mastiff, Bull
AREA OF ORIGIN: England
DATE OF ORIGIN: 1800s
ORIGINAL FUNCTION: Companion
TODAY'S FUNCTION: Companion
OTHER NAME: English Bull Terrier

HISTORY

Bull baiting and dog fighting were long considered great entertainment by many Europeans, and patrons were constantly trying crosses to achieve the ultimate fighting dog. Around 1835, a cross between a Bulldog and the old English Terrier produced a particularly adept pit dog known as the Bull and Terrier. A later cross to the Spanish Pointer added needed size, and the result was a tenacious, strong, yet agile dog that came to dominate the pits. As interest in the exhibition of dogs grew in England, little attention was paid to these dogs so long associated with the lower echelons of society. With the abolition of dog fighting, however, some Bull Terrier patrons turned to this new venue to compete with their dogs, and they began to breed for appearance. Around 1860 James

ILLUSTRATED STANDARD

1 Head long, strong, and deep, curving from skull to nose; oval outline viewed face on
2 Eyes small, triangular, deep-set, and placed close together
3 Ears small, erect, close set
4 Short strong back
5 Tail short, carried horizontally
6 Cat feet
7 Big boned but not coarse

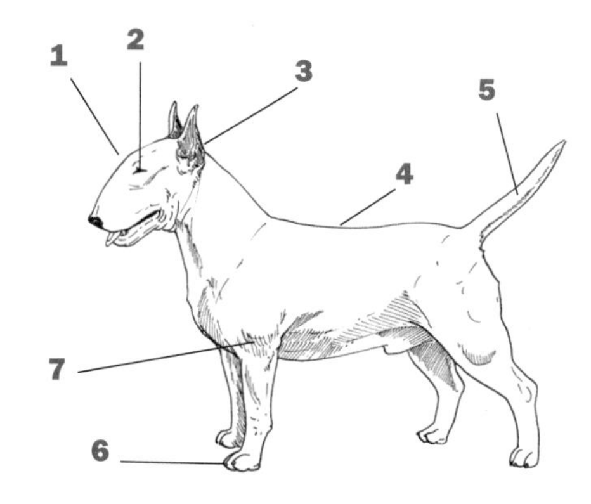

Color: white variety: white, with markings on head permissible; colored variety: any color other than white, or any color with white markings; brindle preferred

DQ: blue eyes; in colored variety, any dog predominantly white

Hinks crossed the Bull and Terrier with the White English Terrier and the Dalmatian, producing an all-white strain he called Bull Terriers. The new all-white strain immediately succeeded in the ring and captured the attention of the public; they became a fashionable companion for young gentlemen who wanted a good-looking masculine dog at their sides. The dogs gained the reputation for defending themselves, but not provoking a fight, and were thus dubbed "the white cavalier." The dogs gradually became more streamlined, and the Bull Terrier's distinctive head evolved. Around 1900, crosses with Staffordshire Bull Terriers reintroduced color into the breed. It was not well accepted at first, but it finally gained equal status as a separate AKC variety in 1936. The white variety still continues as the more popular variety, but both colors have enjoyed great popularity as show dogs and pets. Their comical nature and expression wins them many friends, and they have proven to be very successful in movies and advertising.

TEMPERAMENT

Exuberant, comical, playful, assertive, and very mischievous describes the Bull Terrier. It is an imaginative breed that often sees things its own way and is stubborn to the end. For all its tough bravado, this is an extremely sweet-natured, affectionate, and devoted breed, but some can be aggressive with other dogs and small animals. They are prone to compulsive behaviors such as tail-chasing or dot staring.

UPKEEP

The Bull Terrier needs to be entertained, either with a good exercise session or mental stimulation every day—preferably both. This is an active breed that enjoys a good run, but it is best to run it only in a safe area. Coat care is minimal.

HEALTH

- Major concerns: deafness (in whites), kidney problems (hereditary nephritis and renal dysplasia)
- Minor concerns: heart problems (SAS, mitral stenosis), compulsive behavior, allergies
- Occasionally seen: patellar luxation
- Suggested tests: hearing (whites), UP:UC ratio for kidney function, cardiac, knee
- Life span: 11–14 years

FORM AND FUNCTION

The Bull Terrier is the cavalier gladiator—a good looking tough character. It is strongly built and muscular, longer than it is tall. Its muscle mass combined with its relatively low center of gravity make it difficult for opponents to knock it off its feet. Its distinctive head not only shows off its keen and determined expression, but also its great jaw strength. Its gait is smooth and easy. Its skin is tight, and its coat short, flat, and harsh.

Cairn Terrier

AT A GLANCE

Energy level:	■■■■	Watchdog ability:	■■■■■	POPULARITY: Somewhat popular
Exercise requirements:	■■■	Protection ability:	■	FAMILY: Terrier
Playfulness:	■■■	Grooming requirements:	■■■	AREA OF ORIGIN: Scotland
Affection level:	■■■	Cold tolerance:	■■■	DATE OF ORIGIN: Middle Ages
Friendliness toward dogs:	■■■	Heat tolerance:	■■■	ORIGINAL FUNCTION: Killing vermin
Friendliness toward other pets:	■			TODAY'S FUNCTION: Earthdog trials
Friendliness toward strangers:	■	WEIGHT: male: 14 lb; female: 13 lb		OTHER NAME: None
Ease of training:	■	HEIGHT: male: 10″; female: 9.5″		

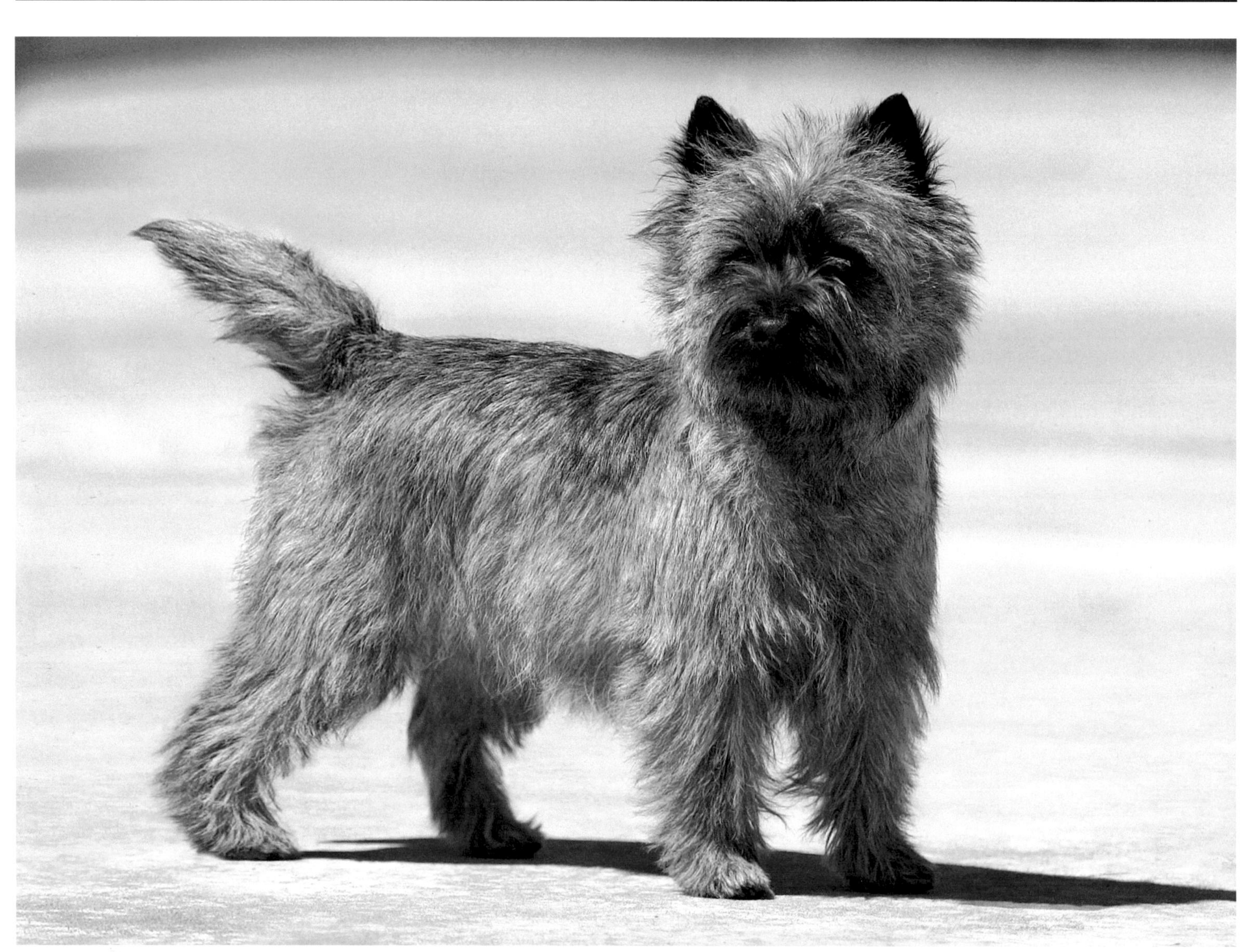

HISTORY

One of a family of short-legged terriers developed on the Scottish Isle of Skye, the Cairn Terrier probably still resembles the ancestral form to a greater degree than others descended from the same stock. These dogs seem to have existed since the fifteenth century and were used to hunt fox, badger, and otter. The dogs were adept at bolting otters from the cairns (piles of stone that served as landmarks or memorials). The dogs came in a variety of colors, ranging from white to gray to red, and were all considered Scotch Terriers when they began to enter the show ring. In 1873, they were divided into Dandie Dinmont and Skye Terriers, with the Cairn in the latter group. This group was later again divided into Skye and Hard-haired Terriers in 1881, and the Hard-haired Terriers eventually separated

ILLUSTRATED STANDARD

1 Eyes sunken, with shaggy eyebrows
2 Skull broad, well-defined stop
3 Ears small, pointed, erect, set wide
4 Level back of medium length
5 Tail carried gaily but not curled over back

Color: any color but white; dark ears, muzzle, tail tip desired
DQ: none

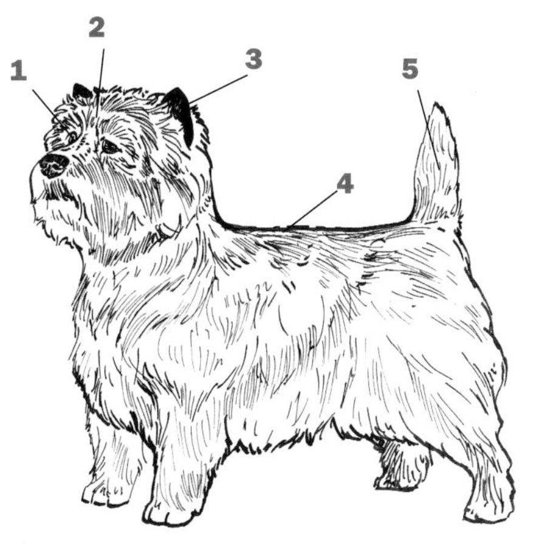

into Scotch, West Highland White, and the breed eventually known as the Cairn. At one time, the Cairn was called the Short-haired Skye, then the Cairn Terrier or Skye, and finally, around 1912, the Cairn Terrier. Some of the most influential early Cairns were all white, but white, as well as crossing to West Highland Whites, was banned by the 1920s. The breed became quite popular in England, and fairly popular in America, gaining its greatest fame as the dog playing Toto in the *Wizard of Oz*. As one of the more natural and less sculpted terriers, the breed is highly regarded by those who appreciate a working terrier. Perhaps the motto of the British breed club sums it up best: "The best little pal in the world."

TEMPERAMENT

The Cairn is the essence of terrier; plucky, spirited, bold, inquisitive, hardy, clever, stubborn, and scrappy. It is responsive to its owner's wishes, however, and tries to please; in fact, it is surprisingly sensitive. This breed can be a good house pet as long as it is given daily physical and mental exercise in a safe area. It enjoys playing with children and is tough enough to withstand some roughhousing. It can be aggressive with other dogs and chases small animals; it loves to sniff, explore, and hunt. It digs; some bark.

UPKEEP

Despite its small size, the Cairn needs outdoor exercise every day, either a moderate walk on leash, a fun game in the yard, or an excursion in a safe area. Its wire coat needs combing once weekly, plus stripping of dead hair at least twice yearly.

HEALTH

- Major concerns: none
- Minor concerns: portacaval shunt, glaucoma (in association with or without ocular melanosis), CMO
- Occasionally seen: GCL, patellar luxation, congenital heart defects
- Suggested tests: GCL, knee, eye, cardiac
- Life span: 12–14 years

FORM AND FUNCTION

This is a working terrier, and it should be hardy, game, and active. It is short-legged, and longer than it is tall, but not as low to the ground as the Sealyham or Scottish Terriers. Its build enables it to fit into close quarters in pursuit of its quarry. Its head is shorter and wider than any other terrier, giving it good jaw strength. Its weather-resistant coat consists of a soft, close undercoat and a profuse, harsh outer coat. Furnishing around the face adds to its somewhat foxy expression.

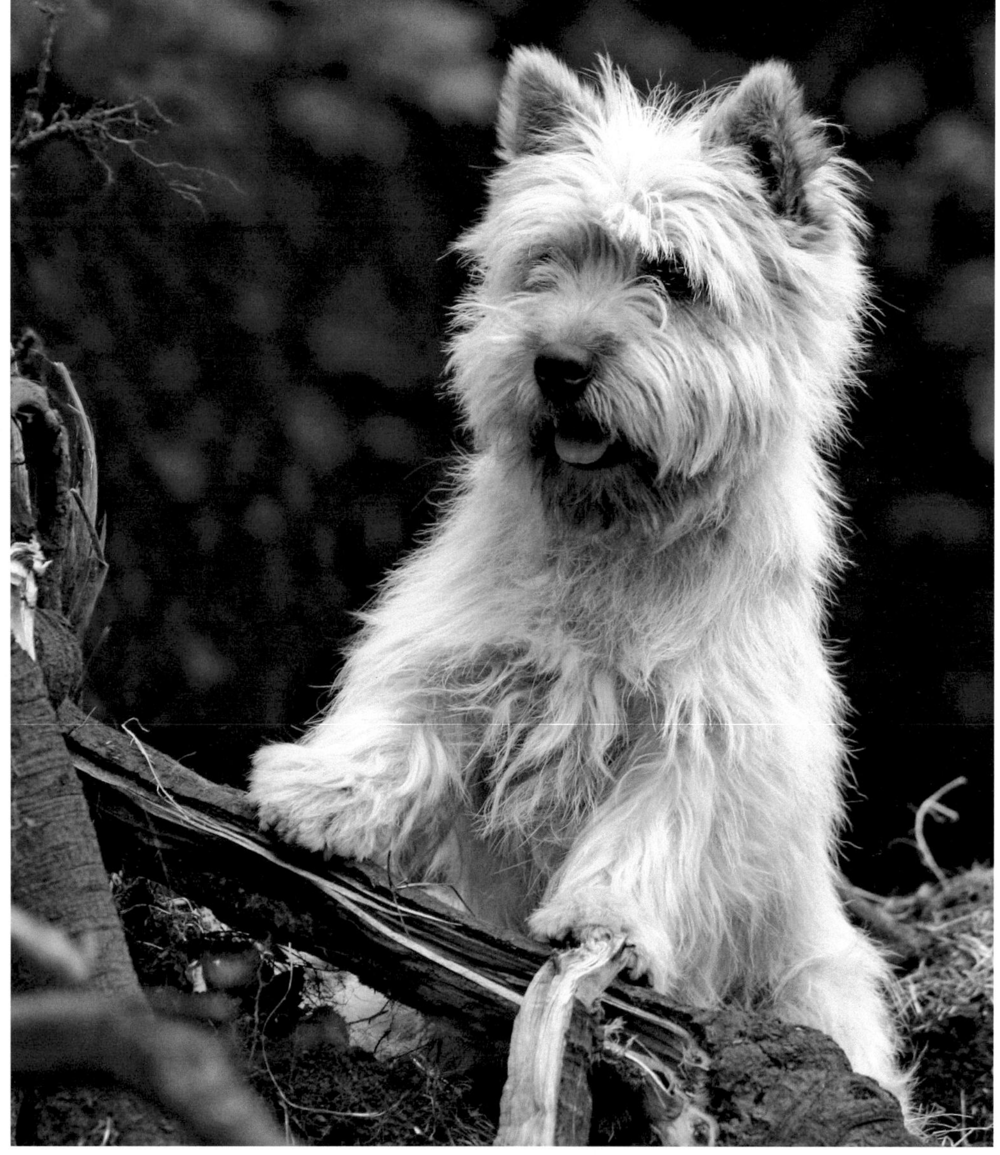

Cesky Terrier

AT A GLANCE

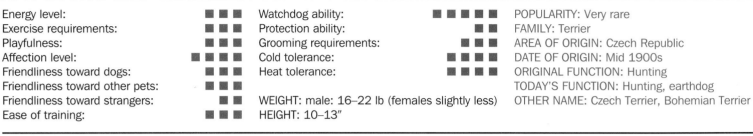

Energy level:	■■■	Watchdog ability:	■■■■■	POPULARITY: Very rare
Exercise requirements:	■■■	Protection ability:	■■	FAMILY: Terrier
Playfulness:	■■■	Grooming requirements:	■■■	AREA OF ORIGIN: Czech Republic
Affection level:	■■■■	Cold tolerance:	■■■■	DATE OF ORIGIN: Mid 1900s
Friendliness toward dogs:	■■■	Heat tolerance:	■■■■	ORIGINAL FUNCTION: Hunting
Friendliness toward other pets:	■■■			TODAY'S FUNCTION: Hunting, earthdog
Friendliness toward strangers:	■■	WEIGHT: male: 16–22 lb (females slightly less)		OTHER NAME: Czech Terrier, Bohemian Terrier
Ease of training:	■■■	HEIGHT: 10–13″		

HISTORY

The Cesky (pronounced CHESS-key) Terrier is one of the few breeds that can trace it roots back to its exact beginnings, and whose origin rests almost entirely in the hands of one man. Frantisek Horak was a Czechoslovakian accountant, technician, and hunter who purchased his first Scottish Terrier in 1932 to hunt hare, fox, and red deer. Although he bred a successful line of hunting Scotties, he was unhappy they didn't do well in packs, and he also wanted a dog less inclined to get stuck in burrows. In 1940, he added a Sealyham Terrier to his group, believing they were easier to control and better in groups. He eventually crossed the two breeds, making meticulous notes of the progeny and subsequent generations. His goal was to produce not only a good hunter that got along in packs, but an

ILLUSTRATED STANDARD

1. Medium-sized, almond-shaped eyes; slightly deep set
2. Medium-sized, triangular ears, set high
3. Long, blunt, wedge-shaped head; slight but definite stop
4. Topline rising slightly toward rear
5. Tail around 7 to 8″ and set low; curled, squirrel tail penalized
6. Short, straight front legs
7. Large, well-arched feet

Color: in mature dogs, any shade of grey from charcoal to platinum; or coffee brown
DQ: none

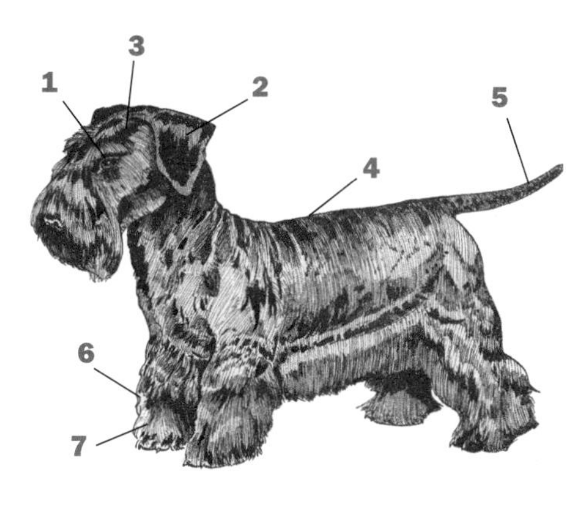

easy to care for family dog. In 1963, his work was rewarded when the Federation Cynologique Internationale (FCI) recognized the Cesky Terrier. In that same year, several were exported to various European countries. The first Cesky came to the United States in the 1980s. In 2002, the American Cesky Terrier Fanciers Association was formed. Other terrier lovers noticed them as they competed in Earthdog trials. They entered the Miscellaneous Class in 2008 and the AKC Terrier Group in 2011.

TEMPERAMENT

The Cesky Terrier is one of the more mellow terriers, surprisingly calm and nonaggressive. Both traits were very important to the breed's originator, who wanted a dog that could run with the pack without squabbling and that could also be an indoor family dog when not hunting. They tend to be loyal to their family and reserved with strangers. The chance to hunt, either following a scent trail or going underground, will bring them to life. They get along well with other dogs and are generally quiet.

UPKEEP

The Cesky tends to be quiet indoors but needs a moderate amount of exercise daily—a brisk walk around the neighborhood or a high-energy play session such as tugging or chasing are ideal. They also need mental stimulation and enjoy challenging dog sports like agility. Unlike most terriers, their coat is not stripped, but clipped, which makes coat care much simpler. The body and tail are clipped every 6 to 8 weeks. The longer hair on the lower body, legs, and face should be combed every few days.

HEALTH

- Major concerns: none
- Minor concerns: hip dysplasia, patellar luxation, lens luxation, heart murmurs
- Occasionally seen: none
- Suggested tests: hips, knees, CERF, cardiac
- Life span: 10–14 years

FORM AND FUNCTION

The Cesky Terrier was purposefully developed as a hunting terrier that could follow all sizes of game by scent and follow smaller game to ground. It resembles both of its ancestral breeds, the Scottish and Sealyham Terriers. It is about one and half times longer than tall, with a topline that rises slightly higher over the loin and rump. The body is lean and movement powerful. The coat is long, soft, and silky. In adults, it is in all shades of gray, but puppies are born black. Unlike most terriers, the Cesky can work in packs without aggression.

Dandie Dinmont Terrier

AT A GLANCE

Energy level:	■■■
Exercise requirements:	■■■
Playfulness:	■■■
Affection level:	■■■
Friendliness toward dogs:	■■■
Friendliness toward other pets:	■■■
Friendliness toward strangers:	■
Ease of training:	■■
Watchdog ability:	■■■■
Protection ability:	■
Grooming requirements:	■■■
Cold tolerance:	■■■
Heat tolerance:	■■■

WEIGHT: 18–24 lb
HEIGHT: 8–11″

POPULARITY: Very rare
FAMILY: Terrier
AREA OF ORIGIN: Border of Scotland and England
DATE OF ORIGIN: 1700s
ORIGINAL FUNCTION: Otter and badger hunting
TODAY'S FUNCTION: Earthdog trials
OTHER NAME: None

HISTORY

The Dandie Dinmont Terrier stands out as a most unusual terrier in appearance, yet its roots are as quintessentially terrier as any. It first appeared as a distinct type of terrier in the eighteenth century around the border country of Scotland and England. Here they were owned by farmers and gypsies and valued for drawing and killing otters, badgers, and foxes. At one time, they were known as Catcleugh, Hindlee, or Pepper and Mustard terriers. The most well known of these dogs were owned by James Davidson, who named almost all his dogs either Pepper or Mustard along with some identifying adjective. Davidson and his dogs are believed by some to have been the models for Sir Walter Scott's characters of Dandie Dinmont and his dogs in his novel *Guy Mannering*,

ILLUSTRATED STANDARD

1 Large, round eyes
2 Head is covered with soft, silky hair
3 Ears set low, hanging
4 Topline is low at withers, arching over the loin
5 Tail is long, carried a little above the level of the body, with a curve
6 Hindlegs slightly longer than forelegs
7 Round feet

Color: pepper (all shades of gray and silver) or mustard (all shades of brown and fawn); Dandie Dinmont puppies are much darker than adults
DQ: none

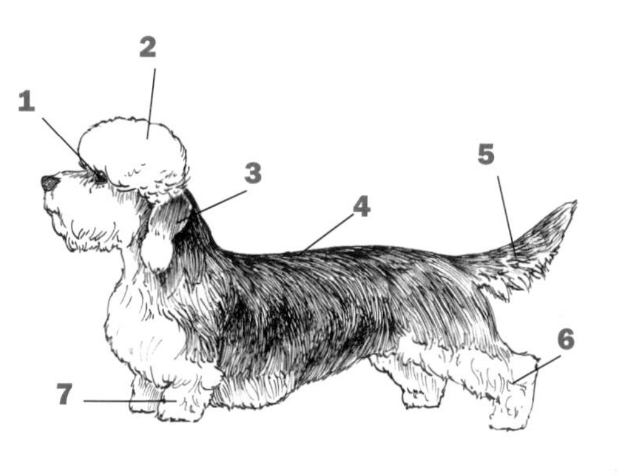

published in 1814. The dogs became known as Dandie Dinmont's Terriers. A letter written by James Davidson proclaimed that all Dandies descended from two of his dogs named Tarr and Pepper. At one time the breed was included in the general family of Scotch Terriers, which encompassed several short-legged terriers now recognized as distinct breeds. The Dandie was recognized separately from this group in 1873. The Dandie Dinmont has never been extremely popular, and remains one of the lesser-known terriers. An old Scottish saying says, "A Dandie looks at you as though he's forgotten more than you ever knew."

TEMPERAMENT

The Dandie Dinmont is no "dandified" dog; it is rough and tumble and ready for the hunt. Yet it functions well as a dignified house pet, affectionate but not doting. It is a loyal companion suitable for people of all ages, but it does need daily exercise to keep it from becoming frustrated. It is intelligent and very independent. It tends to be reserved with strangers and aggressive toward strange dogs. Some dig.

UPKEEP

The Dandie enjoys the chance to hunt around and explore in a safe area and needs a moderate walk to stay in condition. Its coat needs combing twice weekly, plus regular scissoring and shaping. Shaping for show dogs is done on an almost continual (but light) basis; that for pets can be done by stripping or clipping about four times a year. When clipped, the coat will lose its characteristic texture and color.

HEALTH

- Major concerns: none
- Minor concerns: intervertebral disk disease, glaucoma
- Occasionally seen: none
- Suggested tests: eye
- Life span: 11–13 years

FORM AND FUNCTION

Unlike the prototypical terrier, the Dandie is made up of a series of curves, ending in a scimitar-shaped tail of moderate length. The Dandie is almost twice as long as tall, constructed to go to ground after tough quarry. Its hind legs are definitely longer than its front legs. Its gait is free and easy. It has a distinctive coat made up of about two-thirds hardish (not wiry) hair and one-third soft hair, about 2 inches in length. The head is covered with soft, silky hair, lending to the appearance of a large head. The topknot also enhances the expression, which is determined, dignified, soft, and wise. Tassels on the ear tips of the same texture and color as the topknot enhance the look.

Fox Terrier (Smooth)

AT A GLANCE

Energy level:	■■■■
Exercise requirements:	■■■
Playfulness:	■■■■
Affection level:	■■■■
Friendliness toward dogs:	■■■
Friendliness toward other pets:	■■
Friendliness toward strangers:	■■■■
Ease of training:	■■■■

Watchdog ability:	■■■■■
Protection ability:	■
Grooming requirements:	■
Cold tolerance:	■■■
Heat tolerance:	■■■

WEIGHT: male: 17–19 lb; female: 15–17 lb
HEIGHT: male: should not exceed 15.5″; female: smaller

POPULARITY: Uncommon
FAMILY: Terrier
AREA OF ORIGIN: England
DATE OF ORIGIN: 1700s
ORIGINAL FUNCTION: Vermin hunting, fox bolting
TODAY'S FUNCTION: Earthdog trials
OTHER NAME: None

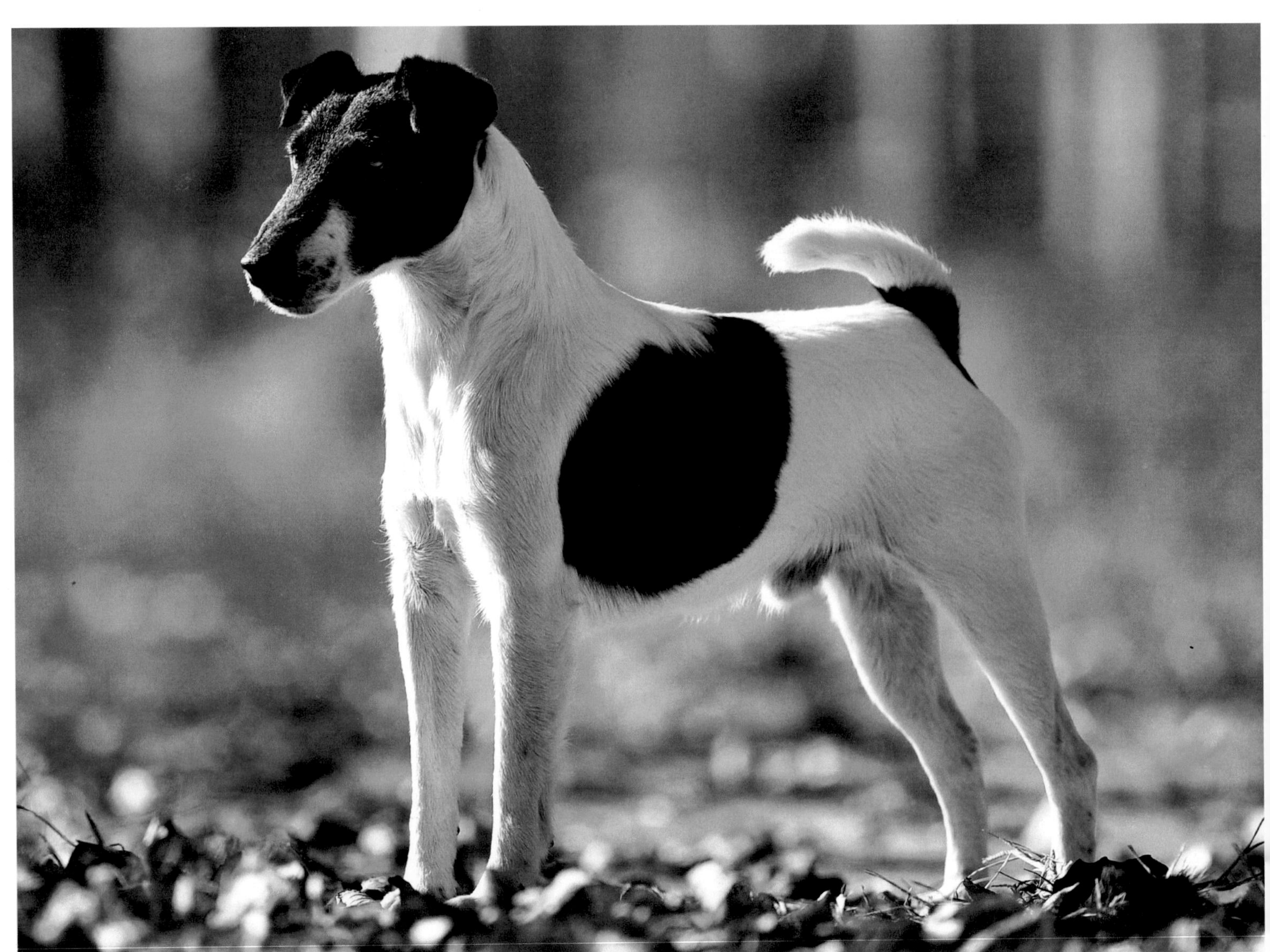

HISTORY

The Smooth Fox Terrier's ancestors are not documented, but the breed was certainly known by 1800 and was already popular before the advent of dog shows. It accompanied Foxhound packs and dislodged foxes that had taken cover. Predominantly white dogs were preferred because they could be more easily distinguished from the quarry in dim lighting. Some speculation exists that the Smooth and Wire Fox Terriers arose from distinct backgrounds, with the Smooth descending from the smooth-coated Black and Tan, the Bull Terrier, and even the Greyhound and Beagle. The Smooth Fox Terriers were among the first breeds to enter the show ring, classified initially with the Sporting breeds. The two varieties were interbred extensively at one time, but the practice

ILLUSTRATED STANDARD

1. Skull flat and moderately narrow, head 7–7.25" long
2. Rather small, deep-set, round eyes
3. Small, V-shaped ears, dropping forward with fold above skull level
4. Tail set high and carried gaily, but not over back or curled; about one fourth docked off
5. Feet round and compact

Color: white should predominate (brindle, red, or liver markings are objectionable)
DQ: ears prick, tulip, or rose; nose white, cherry or considerably spotted with white or cherry; much undershot or overshot

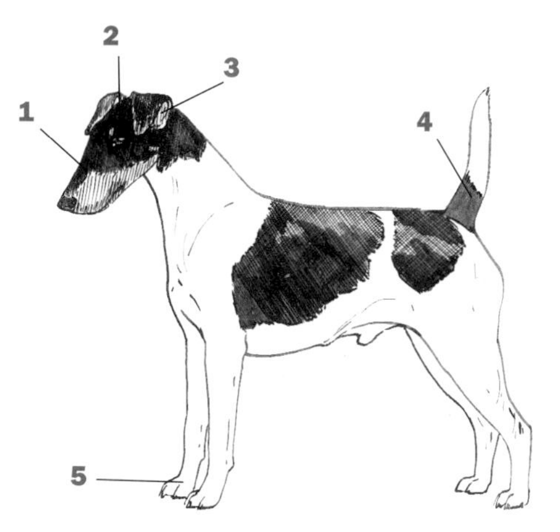

gradually declined. Because the two breeds had long since ceased to be crossed by the latter part of the 1900s, the AKC divided them into separate breeds in 1985.

TEMPERAMENT
Energetic, inquisitive, bold, feisty, playful, mischievous, independent, and adventurous describe the Fox Terrier. This breed lives to run, chase, and explore. It is usually fairly reserved with strangers. It tends to bark and dig.

UPKEEP
The Smooth Fox Terrier is energetic and cannot be ignored. As an active dog, it will do much to exercise itself given the room. It enjoys a vigorous game or walk, as well as an off-lead outing in a safe area. Smooth coat care consists of weekly brushing to remove shedding hair. In fact, the Smooths shed more than the Wires. Some training of the ears may be necessary as puppies for proper adult shape to develop.

HEALTH
- Major concerns: none
- Minor concerns: lens luxation, distichiasis, cataract, Legg–Perthes
- Occasionally seen: deafness, patellar luxation
- Suggested tests: (eye), knee, cardiac
- Life span: 10–13 years

FORM AND FUNCTION
The Smooth Fox Terrier is square proportioned, standing over a lot of ground but with a short back. Its conformation combines speed, endurance, and power, enabling it to gallop and stay with the horses and hounds during the hunt and to follow a fox up a narrow passage. The gait while trotting gets most of its propulsion from the rear quarters. The expression, like the attitude, is keen; the carriage is alert and expectant. The coat is flat, hard, and dense, also with a short, fine undercoat.

Fox Terrier (Wire)

AT A GLANCE

Energy level:	■■■■
Exercise requirements:	■■■
Playfulness:	■■■■
Affection level:	■■■■
Friendliness toward dogs:	■
Friendliness toward other pets:	■■
Friendliness toward strangers:	■■■■
Ease of training:	■■■■

Watchdog ability:	■■■■■
Protection ability:	■
Grooming requirements:	■■■■
Cold tolerance:	■■■
Heat tolerance:	■■■

WEIGHT: male: 17–19 lb; female: 15–17 lb
HEIGHT: male: should not exceed 15.5″; female: smaller

POPULARITY: Somewhat uncommon
FAMILY: Terrier
AREA OF ORIGIN: England
DATE OF ORIGIN: 1800s
ORIGINAL FUNCTION: Vermin hunting, fox bolting
TODAY'S FUNCTION: Earthdog trials
OTHER NAME: None

HISTORY

The ultimate show dog, the Wire Fox Terrier has its roots as an effective hunting dog. Its forebears were adept at bolting and perhaps dispatching game, especially fox, that had gone to ground. Some speculation exists that the Smooth and Wire Fox Terriers arose from distinct backgrounds, with the Wire descending from the rough-coated Black and Tan Terrier of Wales. The Wire entered the show ring about 15 to 20 years after the Smooth made its debut. The two varieties were interbred extensively at one time, mainly with the objective of improving the Wire variety by decreasing its size, increasing the amount of white on its coat, and imparting a sleeker outline. This objective was met quite early. Wire Fox Terriers became extremely popular in the years following World War II. In

ILLUSTRATED STANDARD

1 Rather small, deep-set, and round eyes
2 Skull flat and moderately narrow, head 7–7.25" long
3 Small, V-shaped ears, dropping forward with fold above skull level
4 Tail set high and carried gaily, but not over back or curled; about one fourth docked off
5 Feet round and compact

Color: white should predominate (brindle, red, or liver markings are objectionable)
DQ: ears prick, tulip, or rose; nose white, cherry or considerably spotted with white or cherry; much undershot or overshot

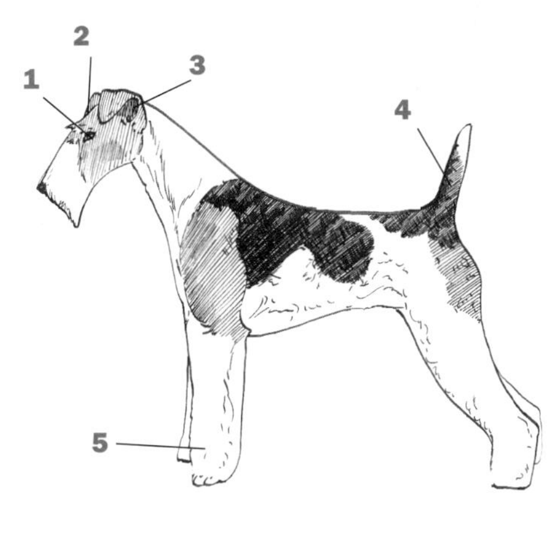

1985, 100 years after the establishment of the American Fox Terrier Club, the AKC divided the Fox Terrier into two separate breeds. That century had seen many triumphs for the breed both as a show dog and a pet; the split into two varieties seemed a logical step because they were no longer interbred.

TEMPERAMENT

A true "live-wire," the Wire Fox Terrier is always up for adventure. This breed lives to play, explore, run, hunt, and chase. It can be mischievous and independent and may dig and bark. It is usually fairly reserved with strangers. The Wire has a reputation for being somewhat scrappier with other dogs when compared to the Smooth.

UPKEEP

The Fox Terrier must have daily exercise. It will do much to exercise itself given the room, but it profits from a good walk on leash, a vigorous play session, or an off-lead outing in a safe area. The Wire's coat needs combing two or three times weekly, plus shaping every three months. Shaping for pets is by clipping, and for show dogs, by stripping. Clipping softens the coat and dulls the color. Some training of the ears may be necessary as puppies for proper adult shape to develop.

HEALTH

- Major concerns: none
- Minor concerns: lens luxation, distichiasis, cataract, Legg–Perthes
- Occasionally seen: deafness, patellar luxation
- Suggested tests: (eye), cardiac, knee
- Life span: 10–13 years

FORM AND FUNCTION

The Wire Fox Terrier is short backed and square proportioned, but at the same time standing over a lot of ground. Its conformation combines speed, endurance, and power, enabling it to gallop and stay with the horses and hounds during the hunt and to follow a fox up a narrow passage. The gait while trotting gets most of its propulsion from the rear quarters. The expression, like the attitude, is keen; the carriage is alert and expectant. The coat is dense, wiry, broken, and twisted, almost appearing like coconut matting, with a short, fine undercoat. The outer coat may be crinkled, but it should not be curly.

Glen of Imaal Terrier

AT A GLANCE

Energy level:	■■■
Exercise requirements:	■■■
Playfulness:	■■■■■
Affection level:	■■■■
Friendliness toward dogs:	■■
Friendliness toward other pets:	■■■
Friendliness toward strangers:	■■■
Ease of training:	■■■

Watchdog ability:	■■
Protection ability:	■■
Grooming requirements:	■■
Cold tolerance:	■■■
Heat tolerance:	■■

WEIGHT: male: about 35 lb; female: less (actually this is a thin working weight; most are heavier)
HEIGHT: 12.5–14″

POPULARITY: Very rare
FAMILY: Terrier
AREA OF ORIGIN: Ireland
DATE OF ORIGIN: Unknown; possibly 1600s
ORIGINAL FUNCTION: All-around farm dog, vermin hunting, turnspit dog
TODAY'S FUNCTION: Companion, earthdog, farm dog
OTHER NAME: Irish Glen of Imaal Terrier

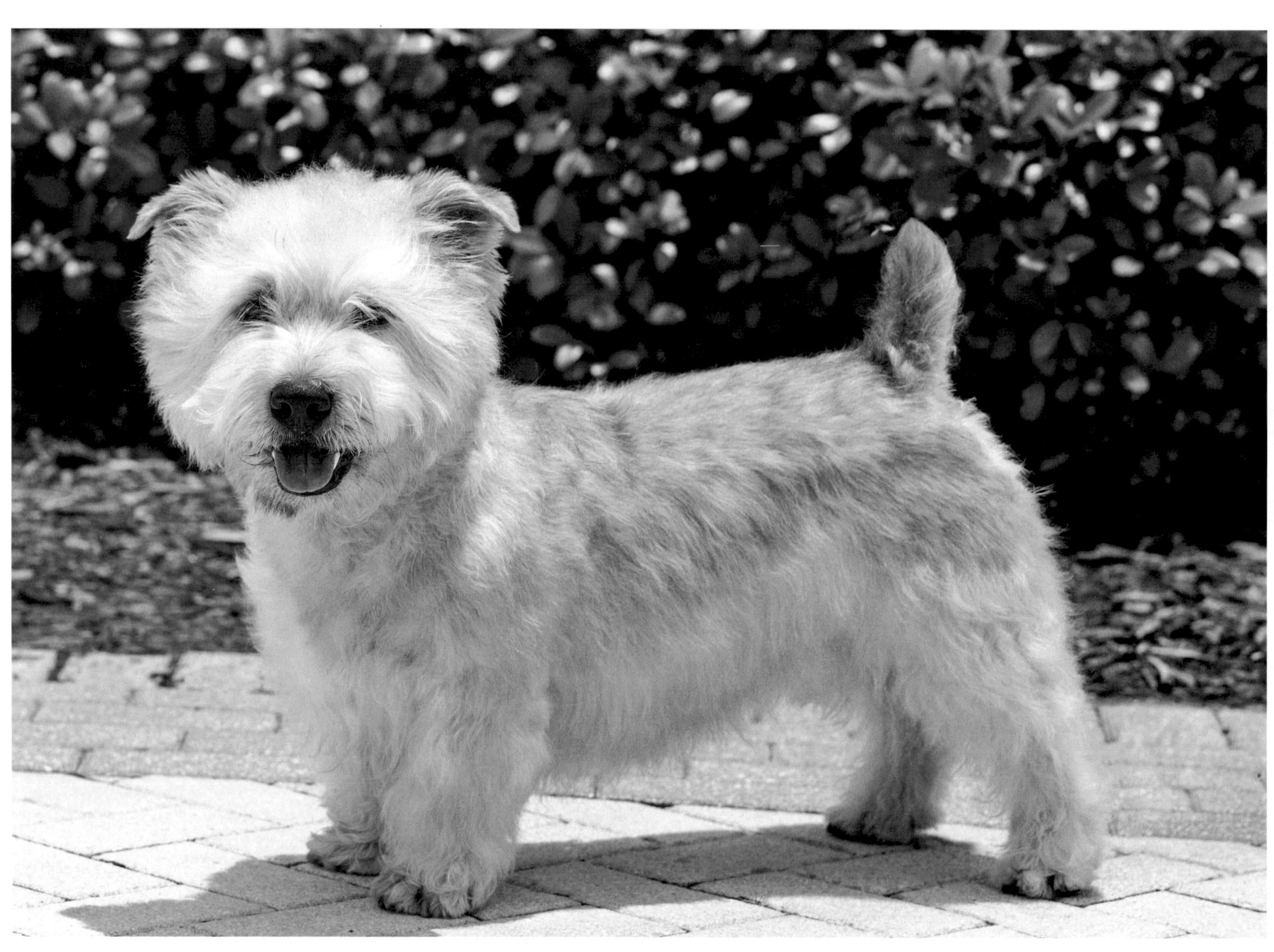

HISTORY

Ireland is a land known for its lush vistas, but not all of Ireland is cloaked in emerald. The Glen area, in County Wicklow, is a bleak land strewn with rocks in which people toil to make a meager living. But Ireland is also a land known for its terriers and its leprechauns, and the Glen area has its own special magical terrier: the Glen of Imaal Terrier. In this harsh land, a dog had to earn its keep. The plucky terriers did so by tackling rats, badgers, and foxes, entertaining the men by fighting in the pits by night, and working for the women as turnspit dogs by day. Here was a dog with courage to face off against a badger underground and the stamina to run for mile after mile in a turnspit of a hot kitchen. On top of that, the Glen of Imaal Terrier had a sparkling personality that made it part of the

ILLUSTRATED STANDARD

1 Powerful head
2 Round eyes
3 Pronounced stop
4 Rose or half-prick ears
5 Topline straight, slightly rising to loin
6 Tail docked to about half length, carried gaily
7 Forelegs short, bowed, and well-boned
8 Forefeet turned out slightly

Color: wheaten, blue, or brindle
DQ: none

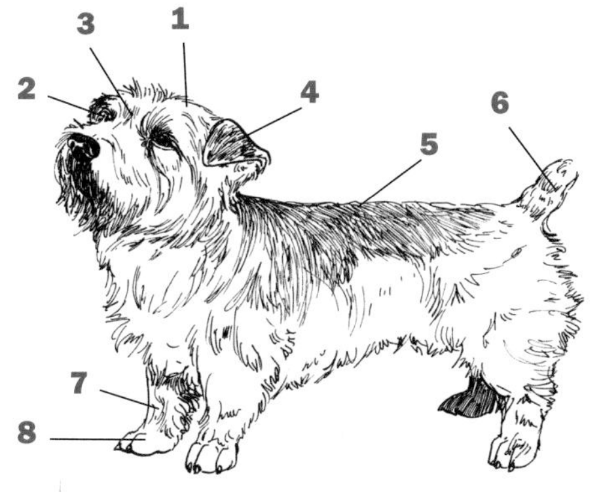

family. Some say only a leprechaun could emerge from such a past with such a rosy attitude. Very few turnspit breeds survived into the twentieth century, partly because they weren't deemed illustrious or intriguing enough to preserve or develop through dog shows. The Glen of Imaal Terrier was largely bypassed in the rush to promote new breeds, allowing it to retain its natural traits rather than evolve into a fashion plate. In 1934 it became one of the first terrier breeds recognized by the Irish Kennel Club. Most Glen shows required a working certificate in which the dog had to follow and extricate a badger in a maze of tunnels, keeping quiet all the while. It wasn't until the 1980s that a concerted effort was made to foster the breed in America. The Glen of Imaal Terrier Club of America was formed in 1986, and the AKC admitted the breed to the Miscellaneous class in 2001. It became a full-fledged member of the Terrier Group in 2004.

TEMPERAMENT

A big dog on short legs, the Glen is a dog of big ideas that's never short of ways to achieve them. This is a spirited, inquisitive, courageous breed, always ready for a game or a hunt. Less excitable than most terriers, it is nonetheless an active dog. However, once given its daily dose of activity, it is content to snuggle by your side. At home the Glen is good-natured and gentle with family members; with its childlike exuberance, it especially enjoys the companionship of children. Some Glens can be dog aggressive. Glens learn quickly but may not always do what you ask. They are not inclined to bark much.

UPKEEP

The Glen is large enough to take part in almost any family activity, and small enough to take almost anywhere. It deals well with inclement weather, but is not a fan of hot weather. The Glen tends to stay around on walks, but because it tends to be fearless in the face of oncoming automobiles or threatening dogs, and loves a good hunt on fresh scent or a good chase, it should not be allowed off lead unsupervised. Glens are not usually great swimmers, and shouldn't be allowed near deep water until you know they can swim. The coat needs stripping a few times a year, but is otherwise easily maintained.

HEALTH

- Major concerns: PRA
- Minor concerns: CHD
- Occasionally seen: elbow dysplasia, cone-rod dystrophy (CRD)
- Suggested tests: eye, hip, elbow, DNA for CRD
- Life span: 10–14 years

FORM AND FUNCTION

Longer than tall, the Glen's short, bowed front legs, well-muscled loin, rising topline, and strong rear allow it to dig and then get adequate leverage to back out of a hole dragging a struggling badger that might weigh more than the Glen itself. The medium-length coat is harsh with a soft undercoat, and is less prone to mat or catch burrs than a longer, softer coat. The strong tail provides a sturdy handle for pulling the Glen from a hole. Unlike most terriers, barking while working is discouraged. This is a working terrier that has not sacrificed form for fashion.

Irish Terrier

AT A GLANCE

Energy level:	■■■
Exercise requirements:	■■■
Playfulness:	■■■■■
Affection level:	■■
Friendliness toward dogs:	■
Friendliness toward other pets:	■
Friendliness toward strangers:	■■
Ease of training:	■

Watchdog ability:	■■■■■
Protection ability:	■■■■
Grooming requirements:	■■■■
Cold tolerance:	■■■
Heat tolerance:	■■■

WEIGHT: male: 27 lb; female: 25 lb (ideally)
HEIGHT: about 18″

POPULARITY: Uncommon
FAMILY: Terrier
AREA OF ORIGIN: Ireland
DATE OF ORIGIN: 1700s
ORIGINAL FUNCTION: Hunting fox, otter, and other vermin
TODAY'S FUNCTION: Vermin hunting
OTHER NAME: Irish Red Terrier

HISTORY

The quintessential long-legged terrier, the Irish Terrier is also one of the oldest terrier breeds. Its creation is not documented, but it may have descended from the old Black and Tan Terrier and a larger but racier solid wheaten-colored terrier, both of which were found in Ireland and used for hunting fox, otter, and vermin. Its similarity to the Irish Wolfhound has led to conjecture that it may have descended at least in part from that breed. The Irish Terrier is the raciest member of the Terrier Group, with a longer body and longer legs than the other terriers. Early Irish Terriers came in a variety of colors, including black and tan, gray, and brindle; only near the end of the nineteenth century did the solid red color become a fixture of the breed. The first Irish Terrier was shown in 1875. By

ILLUSTRATED STANDARD

1 Head long and fairly narrow
2 Eyes small, with intense expression
3 Small, V-shaped ears, dropping forward with fold above skull level
4 Body moderately long
5 Tail set high but not curled; about one fourth docked off
6 Feet rounded

Color: red, golden red, red wheaten, or wheaten
DQ: none

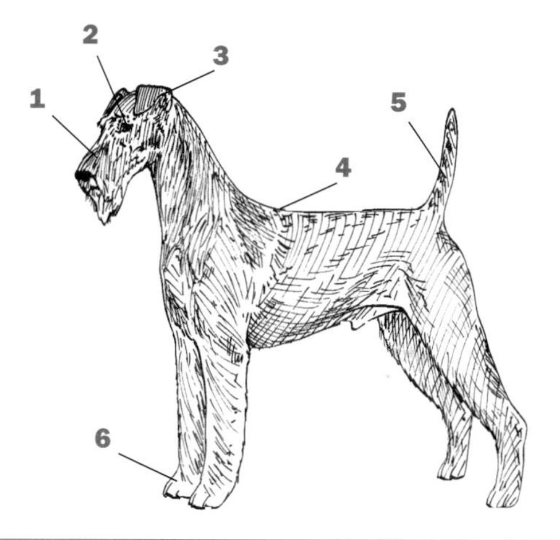

the 1880s, the breed was the fourth most popular in England. At that time, it was fashionable to crop the ears of many terriers, but in 1889 the Irish Terrier Club of England banned ear cropping in the breed. The ruling was to have far-reaching implications for all dogs because it instigated the debate about ear cropping and eventually led to the abolition of cropped ears in all breeds shown in England. The breed also became quite popular in America, ranking thirteenth of all breeds in the late 1920s. It was a dominant force in the show rings of the day. In World War I, the breed proved its mettle by serving as a messenger and sentinel. With such an auspicious beginning, the Irish Terrier seemed certain to remain one of the most popular terriers, but it didn't. Today the Irish is one of the rarer terriers, an uncommon sight in either the show ring or home.

TEMPERAMENT

Called the daredevil of dogdom, the Irish Terrier is brash, bold, assertive, playful, inquisitive, independent, strong-willed, and ever ready for action and adventure. It is usually aggressive toward other dogs and small animals and tends to be reserved with strangers. It likes to chase and run and hunt and explore; it needs daily physical and mental exercise in a safe area. Given sufficient exercise, it is surprisingly well-mannered and dignified indoors. It is a loyal and entertaining companion.

UPKEEP

This is a dog with an active mind and body. It needs daily entertainment and exercise. It makes a good walking and jogging companion, as well as hiking or hunting partner. Its needs can also be met with a rigorous play session. Its wire coat needs combing one or two times weekly, plus scissoring and shaping (clipping for pets and stripping for show dogs) two to four times yearly. Clipping softens the coat and dulls the color. Some training of the ears is necessary to ensure proper adult shape.

HEALTH

- Major concerns: none
- Minor concerns: urinary stones
- Occasionally seen: cataract, hypothyroidism
- Suggested tests: none
- Life span: 12–15 years

FORM AND FUNCTION

The Irish Terrier has a graceful, racy outline, with a moderately long body. It should not have the short back characteristic of so many of the long legged terriers. It is sturdy and strong in substance, but it is also active and lithe in movement. This is an all-round terrier that must combine speed, endurance, agility, and power to perform a great variety of jobs. Its broken coat is dense and wiry, never so long as to obscure the body shape. Its expression, like its nature, is intense.

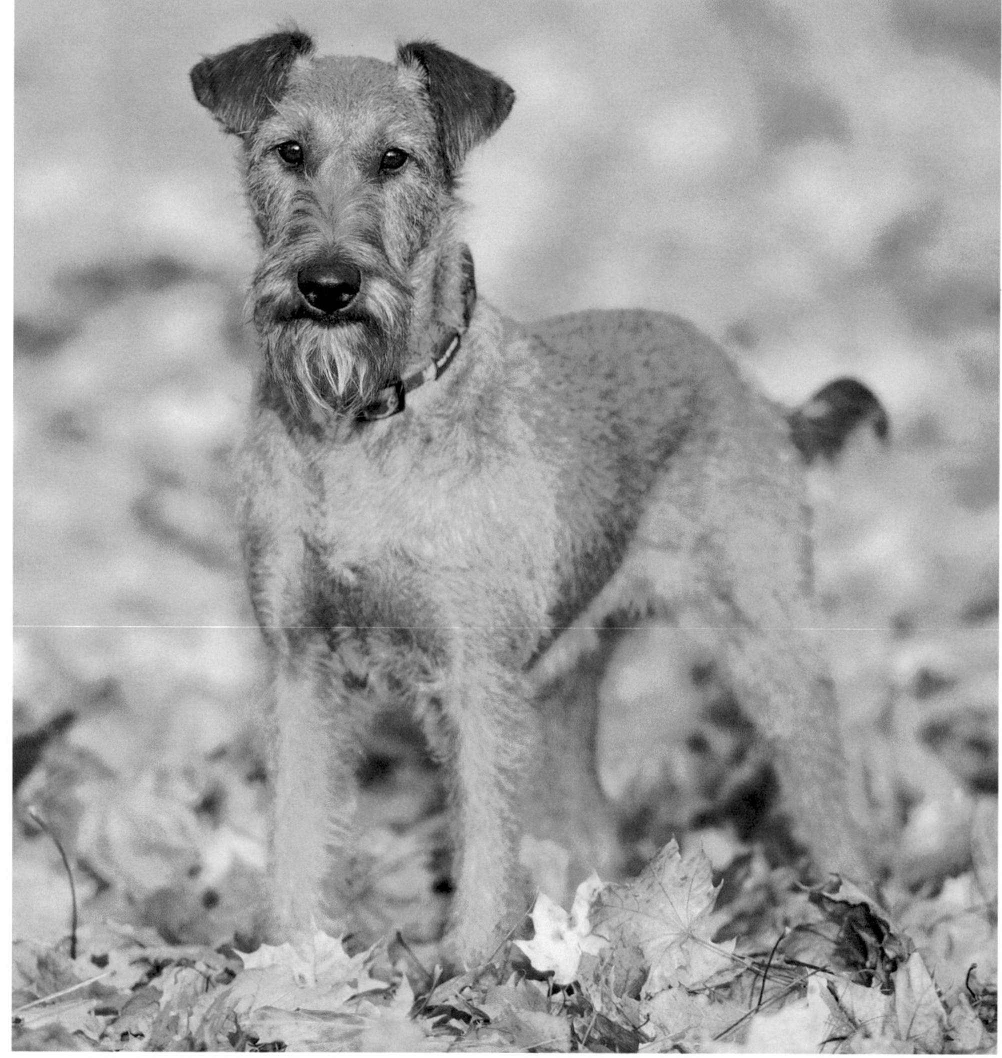

Kerry Blue Terrier

AT A GLANCE

Energy level:	■■■
Exercise requirements:	■■■
Playfulness:	■■■■
Affection level:	■■■
Friendliness toward dogs:	■
Friendliness toward other pets:	■
Friendliness toward strangers:	■■■
Ease of training:	■■■

Watchdog ability:	■■■■■
Protection ability:	■■■■
Grooming requirements:	■■■■■
Cold tolerance:	■■■
Heat tolerance:	■■■

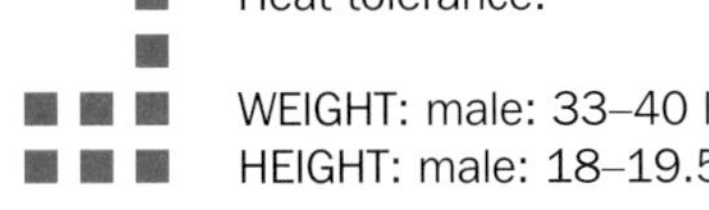

WEIGHT: male: 33–40 lb; female: less
HEIGHT: male: 18–19.5″; female: 17.5–19″

POPULARITY: Uncommon
FAMILY: Terrier
AREA OF ORIGIN: Ireland
DATE OF ORIGIN: 1700s
ORIGINAL FUNCTION: Versatile farm dog
TODAY'S FUNCTION: Herding
OTHER NAME: Irish Blue Terrier

HISTORY

The Kerry Blue originated in the south and west of Ireland, first gaining notice in the Ring of Kerry. Here the dog had been known for at least a century as a versatile farm dog, hunting vermin, small game, and birds; retrieving over land and water; and herding sheep and cattle. How such a talented and attractive dog should have remained unknown outside of Ireland for so long is a mystery, but it only came on the English and American show scenes around the 1920s. It received AKC recognition in 1924. Early specimens were somewhat disheveled, but as more grooming became accepted, the breed caught on and became a popular show dog. Once groomed, the Kerry Blue is one of the most striking of all dogs. It has the peculiarity of being born black, the blue coloration not appearing

ILLUSTRATED STANDARD

1 Head long
2 Eyes small, keen expression
3 Small, V-shaped ears, dropping forward with fold above skull level
4 Back short and straight
5 Tail set high, carried gaily erect and straight
6 Feet fairly round and moderately small

Color: any shade of blue-gray in mature (over 18 months) dog; immature dogs may be very dark blue or have tinges of brown
DQ: solid black; dewclaws on hind legs

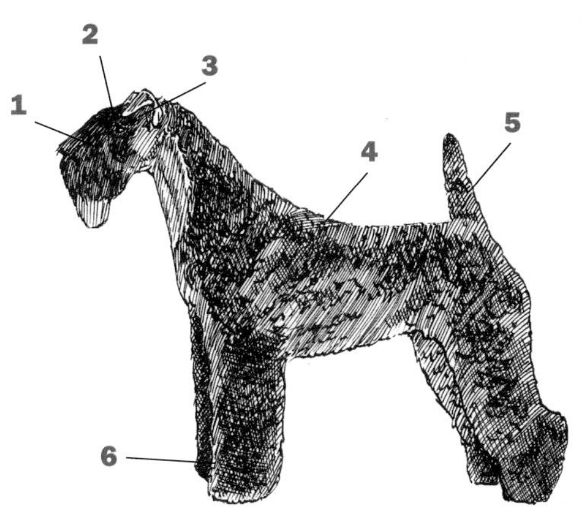

until between 9 months and 2 years of age. It remains a versatile dog, adding police work and trailing to its list of talents. Despite this, it enjoys only modest popularity as a pet.

TEMPERAMENT

A versatile terrier, the Kerry Blue's personality is many faceted. It can guard, hunt, herd, or just be a fun-loving companion. It needs daily mental and physical activity in a safe area. It loves to run, chase, hunt, explore, play, and dig. Indoors, it is well mannered. It can be protective toward strangers yet greet verified friends with great enthusiasm. It is apt to be aggressive toward other dogs and small animals. It is clever and independent, often stubborn. Some tend to bark.

UPKEEP

The Kerry Blue needs a good amount of exercise, but its needs can be met with either a long walk on leash, a vigorous play session, or a chance to explore off-leash in a safe area. Its coat needs combing about twice a week, more often if around twigs and leaves. Its coat needs combing about twice a week, plus scissoring and coat shaping every month. Its ears need to be trained when developing to ensure proper shape.

HEALTH

- Major concerns: cerebellar abiotrophy
- Minor concerns: cataract, spiculosis, hair follicle tumors, entropion, KCS, CHD, otitis externa
- Occasionally seen: retinal folds, clotting factor XI deficiency, vWD, degenerative myelopathy (DM)
- Suggested tests: eye, hip, (vWD), (factor XI), (DM)
- Life span: 12–15 years

FORM AND FUNCTION

This versatile breed has the build of a dog able to perform a variety of tasks, all requiring athletic ability. It can run, herd, trail, retrieve, swim, and dispatch vermin—the ideal all around farm companion. In keeping with this, it is not exaggerated in build. It is an upstanding, long-legged terrier with a short back, displaying strong bones and muscle. Its coat is soft, dense, and wavy, and of a distinctive blue-gray color.

Lakeland Terrier

AT A GLANCE

Energy level:	■■■■	Watchdog ability:	■■■■■	POPULARITY: Rare
Exercise requirements:	■■■	Protection ability:	■	FAMILY: Terrier
Playfulness:	■■■■■	Grooming requirements:	■■■■	AREA OF ORIGIN: England
Affection level:	■■■	Cold tolerance:	■■■	DATE OF ORIGIN: 1700s
Friendliness toward dogs:	■	Heat tolerance:	■■■	ORIGINAL FUNCTION: Vermin hunting
Friendliness toward other pets:	■			TODAY'S FUNCTION: Earthdog trials
Friendliness toward strangers:	■	WEIGHT: about 17 lb		OTHER NAME: None
Ease of training:	■	HEIGHT: male: 14.5″; female: 13.5″		

HISTORY

The first Lakeland Terriers were kept by farmers who took them along with small packs of hounds in order to kill the foxes that were a problem in the area. The dogs were extremely game and were also used on otter and vermin with great success. Although its background is not documented, it shares common ancestors with the Border Terrier, Bedlington Terrier, and Fox Terrier. As fox hunting became valued more for its sporting aspect, the terriers became more fashionable as a part of the fox hunt. Those dogs from the English Lake region gained a reputation as particularly game dogs, although at that time they were identified as Patterdale, Fell, and Elterwater Terriers, all of which came from the Lakeland region. Only in 1921 were they recognized as Lakeland Terriers, although Cumberland is consid-

ILLUSTRATED STANDARD

1 Head appears rectangular from all angles
2 Eyes moderately small and oval
3 Stop barely perceptible
4 Small, V-shaped ears, dropping forward with fold above skull level
5 Topline short and level
6 Tail set high, carried upright with a slight curve forward; docked to about same height as occiput
7 Feet round

Color: solid (blue, black, liver, red, or wheaten); or wheaten or golden tan with a saddle of blue, black, liver or grizzle
DQ: teeth overshot or undershot

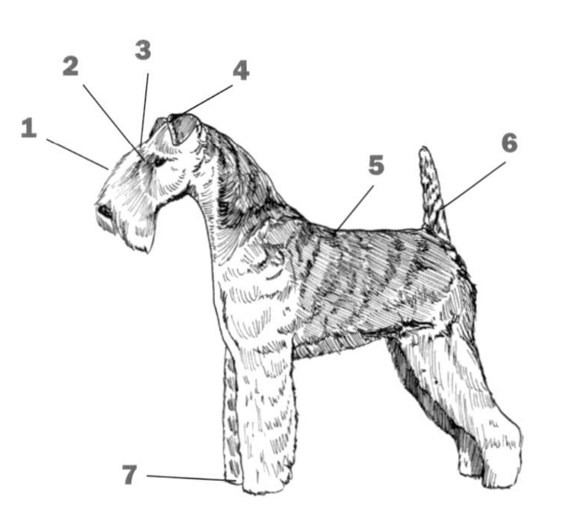

ered the exact birthplace of the breed. The breed was accepted for AKC registration in 1934. Since then, the Lakeland Terrier has been a prominent contender in the show ring, combining dapper good looks with unsurpassed showmanship. Its popularity as a pet, however, has remained moderate.

TEMPERAMENT

The spunky Lakeland makes the most of every day, always busy investigating, playing, and, if it really gets its wish, hunting, running, and chasing. Given daily exercise in a safe area, it settles down in the home and makes an entertaining and endearing house pet. It is reserved with strangers and usually aggressive toward other dogs and small animals. Clever, independent, and stubborn, it can be mischievous. It is nonetheless sensitive and must be trained with patience as well as a sense of humor.

UPKEEP

This is an active breed that needs daily entertainment or it will make it for itself. A moderate walk on leash or a hardy game in the yard can usually satisfy its needs, but it also enjoys the chance to explore off-leash in a safe area. Its wire coat needs combing one or two times weekly, plus scissoring and shaping (clipping for pets and stripping for show dogs) four times yearly. Clipping softens the coat and lightens the color.

HEALTH

- Major concerns: none
- Minor concerns: lens luxation, distichiasis
- Occasionally seen: Legg–Perthes, vWD
- Suggested tests: eye, (vWD)
- Life span: 12–16 years

FORM AND FUNCTION

The Lakeland Terrier is a rather small dog of short-backed, square proportion with a sturdy, workmanlike build. Its legs are fairly long, enabling it to run at good speed and traverse the rugged shale terrain of its native mountain countryside. Its gait is smooth and ground covering, with good reach and drive. Its body is deep and narrow, allowing it to squeeze through small passages after its quarry. Its expression reflects its mood, ranging from intense to gay or impish. Its double coat consists of a soft undercoat and a hard, wiry outer coat.

Manchester Terrier

AT A GLANCE

Energy level:	■ ■ ■ ■	Watchdog ability:	■ ■ ■ ■ ■	POPULARITY: Uncommon
Exercise requirements:	■ ■ ■	Protection ability:	■	FAMILY: Terrier
Playfulness:	■ ■ ■ ■	Grooming requirements:	■	AREA OF ORIGIN: England
Affection level:	■ ■ ■ ■	Cold tolerance:	■	DATE OF ORIGIN: 1500s
Friendliness toward dogs:	■ ■ ■	Heat tolerance:	■ ■ ■ ■	ORIGINAL FUNCTION: Ratting, rabbit hunting
Friendliness toward other pets:	■			TODAY'S FUNCTION: Earthdog trials
Friendliness toward strangers:	■	WEIGHT: standard: over 12 lb to 22 lb		OTHER NAME: Black and Tan Terrier
Ease of training:	■ ■	toy: under 12 lb		
		HEIGHT: 15–16"*		

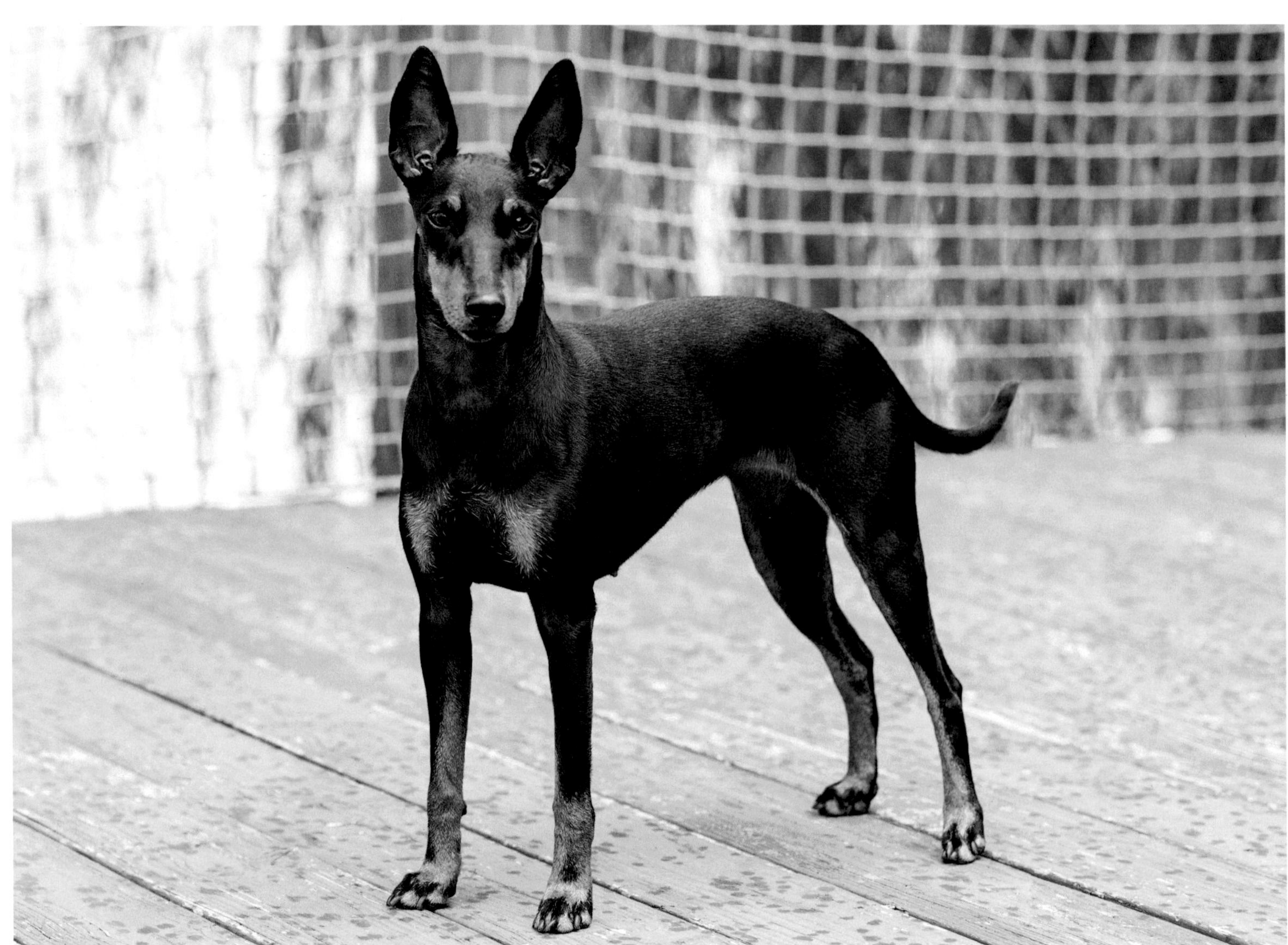

HISTORY

One of the most popular and accomplished terriers of early England was the Black and Tan Terrier, mentioned as early as the sixteenth century. The Black and Tan was a skilled dispatcher of rats, either along the watercourses or in the pits. With the advent of industrialization, sport of the working class in England's towns centered around rat killing with Black and Tans and dog racing with Whippets. It was only a matter of time before the two breeds were crossed, and this was done by John Hulme of Manchester, with the goal of creating a dog that could excel in both arenas. The result was a refined black and tan terrier with a slightly arched back. Similar crosses had almost certainly been made in other regions because other dogs resembling this new strain were not

ILLUSTRATED STANDARD

1 Head resembles a blunted wedge in profile and from front
2 Small, almond-shaped eyes
3 Naturally erect, button, or cropped ear
4 Slight arch over loin
5 Tapered tail carried in a slight upward curve
6 Tucked up abdomen

Color: black and tan, with a black "thumbprint" patch on the front of each foreleg and "pencil marks" on the top of each toe
DQ: patch of white over ½″ at its longest dimension; any color other than black and tan; weight over 22 lb; (in Toy variety only: cropped or cut ears)

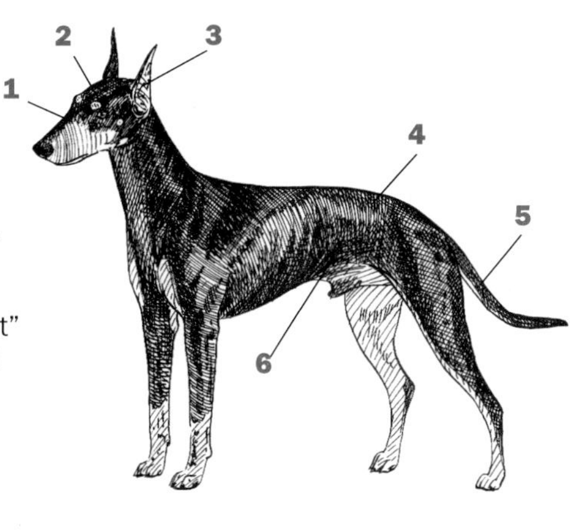

uncommon, but the breed's popularity centered around Manchester. In 1860, the breed was formally dubbed the Manchester Terrier. The name did not catch on, however, and it was dropped in favor of Black and Tan Terrier, only to be revived in 1923. The breed has always had a large size range, and until 1959 Standard and Toy Manchesters were shown as two separate breeds, although interbreeding was allowed. In 1959, they were reclassified as one breed with two varieties, legitimizing the practice of interbreeding. Besides size, the only difference in the two varieties is in whether cropping is allowed (it is allowed in the Standard variety only).

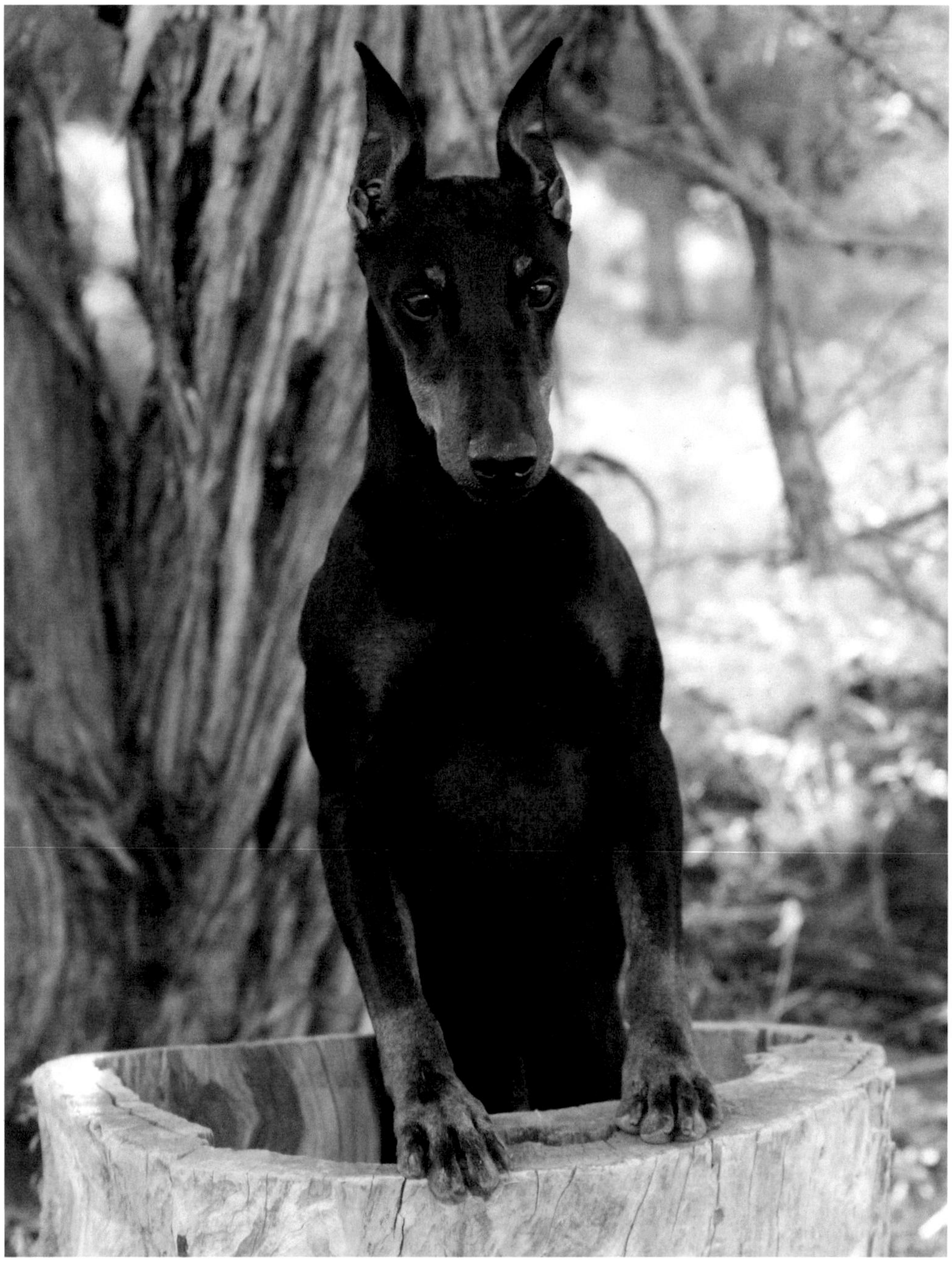

TEMPERAMENT

The Manchester Terrier has been described as "catlike," being impeccably clean, independent, reserved with strangers, yet sensitive. It is more responsive than many terriers and is generally a well-mannered housedog. It is devoted to its family, and enjoys napping at its special person's side. Otherwise, it is busy, ever nosing around for adventure or a game. Some tend to dig.

UPKEEP

This alert and active breed can have its exercise needs met with a moderate walk on leash, good romp in the yard, or off-lead foray in a safe area. It likes a warm, soft bed. Coat care is minimal.

HEALTH

- Major concerns: none
- Minor concerns: cardiomyopathy, vWD, hypothyroidism
- Occasionally seen: Legg-Perthes, patellar luxation, deafness, PRA
- Suggested tests: eye, thyroid, DNA for vWD
- Life span: 15–16 years

FORM AND FUNCTION

The Manchester Terrier is perhaps the sleekest and raciest of all terriers, with a smooth, compact, muscular body, slightly longer than tall, and a slightly arched topline. The combination of power and agility enables the breed to course and kill small game and vermin. Its gait is free and effortless, not hackney. Its expression is keen and alert, and its coat is smooth and glossy.

Miniature Bull Terrier

AT A GLANCE

Energy level:	■■■■
Exercise requirements:	■■■
Playfulness:	■■■■■
Affection level:	■■
Friendliness toward dogs:	■■
Friendliness toward other pets:	■■■
Friendliness toward strangers:	■■■
Ease of training:	■

Watchdog ability:	■■■■■
Protection ability:	■■■
Grooming requirements:	■
Cold tolerance:	■■■
Heat tolerance:	■■■

WEIGHT: 25–33 lb*
HEIGHT: 10–14″

POPULARITY: Uncommon
FAMILY: Terrier, Mastiff, Bull
AREA OF ORIGIN: England
DATE OF ORIGIN: 1800s
ORIGINAL FUNCTION: Companion
TODAY'S FUNCTION: Earthdog trials
OTHER NAME: None

HISTORY

The Miniature Bull Terrier comes directly from the Bull Terrier and so shares the breed's early history. In the early days of the Bull Terrier, the standards allowed for a great range of weights, reflecting the great range in size of the Bull Terrier's ancestors: the Bulldog, White English Terrier, and Black and Tan Terrier. Smaller Bull Terriers have long been a part of the breed, with specimens weighing as little as 4 pounds being recorded early on. These smallest white Bull Terriers were at one time called Coverwood Terriers after the kennel that produced them. These tiny toys tended to have poor type and interest waned in them. Better type was found in slightly larger specimens, the miniatures rather than toys. By 1939, the Miniature Bull Terrier was recognized by

ILLUSTRATED STANDARD

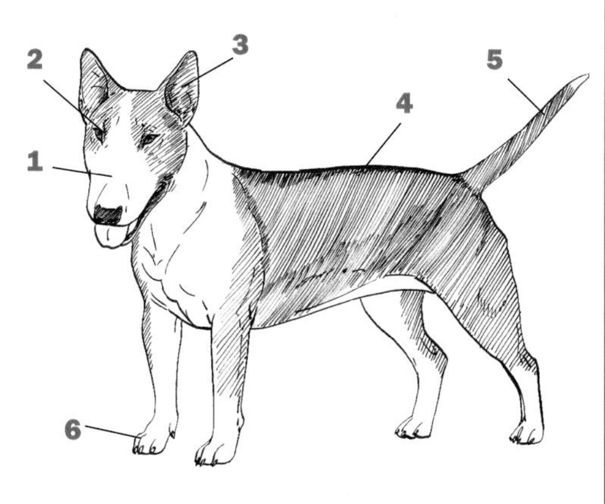

1 Long, strong, deep head, curving from skull to nose; oval outline viewed face on
2 Eyes small, triangular, deep-set, and placed close together
3 Ears small, erect, close set
4 Short strong back, slight arch over loin
5 Tail short, carried horizontally
6 Cat feet

Color: for white: pure white; for colored: any color to predominate
DQ: none

the English Kennel Club, yet this recognition as a separate breed proved to be a problem. As a separate breed, the Miniature could no longer be interbred with standard-sized Bull Terriers, and there were so few Miniatures that considerable inbreeding resulted. The breed never gained popular attention and grew only slowly. In 1991 it was recognized by the AKC. Still an uncommon breed, it is bound to increase in popularity as a true miniature version of the popular Bull Terrier.

TEMPERAMENT

Very much like the larger Bull Terrier, the Mini is comical, lively, playful, and mischievous. Despite its smaller size, it is not a lap dog. It is every bit as tough as the larger version and apt to want to prove itself even more. It is a sweet clown, devoted but not fawning. It is stubborn and independent and needs to be trained with a firm yet gentle hand—and a good sense of humor. It likes to play and investigate. It likes to dig, and it needs ample exercise.

UPKEEP

The Mini's exercise needs are daily, but not excessive. It needs either a moderate walk or a romp in a safe area. It can do well as an apartment or city dog. Coat care is minimal.

HEALTH

- Major concerns: deafness (whites)
- Minor concerns: glaucoma, lens luxation
- Occasionally seen: kidney disease
- Suggested tests: hearing (whites), eye, cardiac, kidney
- Life span: 11–14 years

FORM AND FUNCTION

This is a strongly built, square-proportioned dog, big boned but not coarse. It should reflect those attributes that made the standard-sized Bull Terrier a formidable foe in the fighting ring with its sturdy bone and muscle and strong jaws. Its gait is free and easy. Its skin is tight and its coat is short, flat, and harsh. It wears a keen and determined expression on its characteristic clown face.

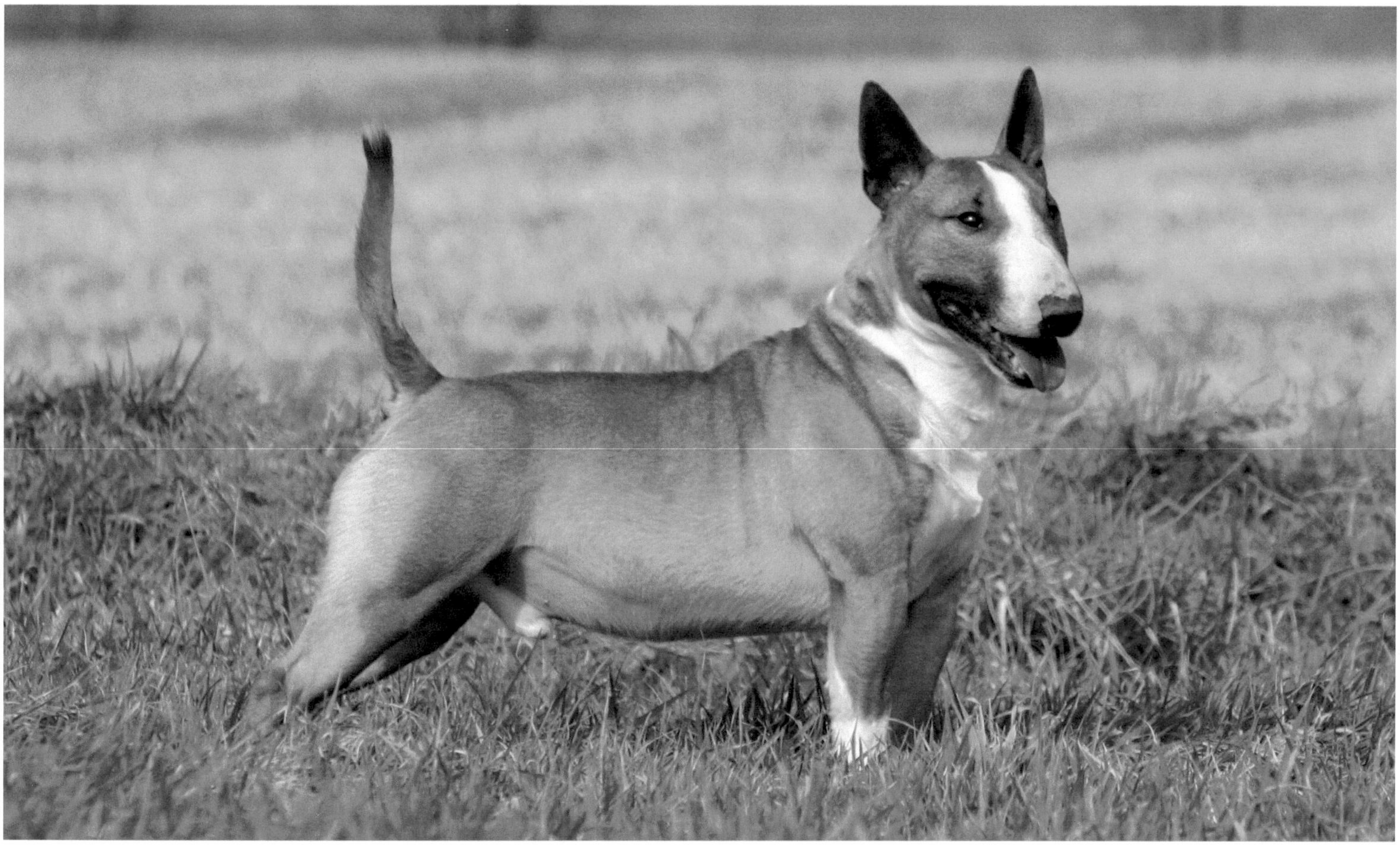

Miniature Schnauzer

AT A GLANCE

Energy level:	■■■	Watchdog ability:	■■■■■	POPULARITY: Very popular
Exercise requirements:	■■■	Protection ability:	■	FAMILY: Schnauzer
Playfulness:	■■■■	Grooming requirements:	■■■	AREA OF ORIGIN: Germany
Affection level:	■■■■	Cold tolerance:	■■■	DATE OF ORIGIN: 1800s
Friendliness toward dogs:	■■■	Heat tolerance:	■■■	ORIGINAL FUNCTION: Ratting
Friendliness toward other pets:	■■■			TODAY'S FUNCTION: Earthdog trials
Friendliness toward strangers:	■■■	WEIGHT: 13–15 lb*		OTHER NAME: Zwergschnauzer
Ease of training:	■■■	HEIGHT: 12–14″		

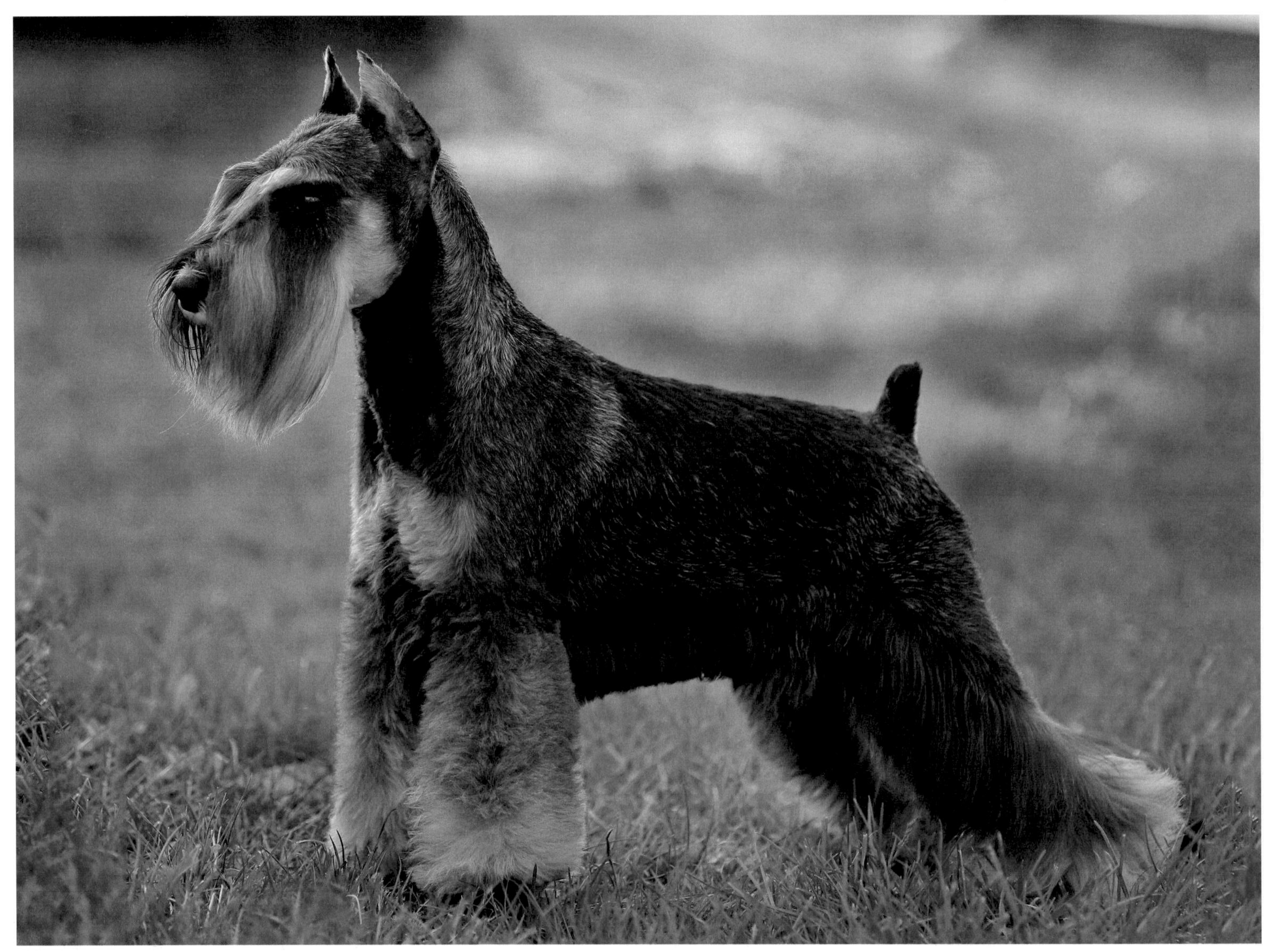

HISTORY

The smallest and most popular of the Schnauzers, the Miniature Schnauzer was developed in the late 1800s as a small farm dog and ratter in Germany. In fact, the Miniature Schnauzer is the only terrier not originating from European Isle stock. It was derived from crossing the Standard Schnauzer with the Affenpinscher (and possibly Poodle) to produce a smaller dog more adept at ratting. All the Schnauzers get their name from one individual dog named Schnauzer who was exhibited around 1879—an apt name, since Schnauzer means small beard. The first recorded Miniature Schnauzer was in 1888. The Miniature Schnauzer was exhibited as a breed distinct from the Standard Schnauzer by 1899 in Germany. The AKC recognized the Standard Schnauzer in

ILLUSTRATED STANDARD

1 Head strong, rectangular, and long
2 Eyes small, oval, and deep-set
3 Ears set high; carried erect and pointed if cropped; if uncropped, small and V-shaped, folding close to the skull
4 Topline straight, slopes slightly down
5 Tail set high and carried erect, docked just long enough to be visible over backline
6 Cat feet

Color: salt and pepper, black and silver, or black
DQ: under 12″ or over 14″; white except for small white spot permitted on chest of black dogs (white not to be confused with silver white under throat and chest)

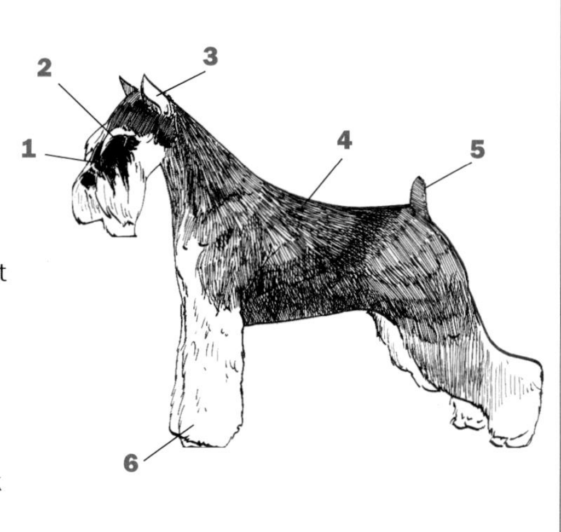

HEALTH

- Major concerns: urolithiasis, PRA
- Minor concerns: Schnauzer comedo syndrome, vWD, myotonia congenita, allergies
- Occasionally seen: cataract, retinal dysplasia, mycobacterium avian infection
- Suggested tests: eye; DNA tests for: type A PRA, vWD, and myotonia congenita, cardiac
- Life span: 12–14 years

FORM AND FUNCTION

The Miniature Schnauzer is a robust, sturdily built terrier of nearly square proportion. It was developed as a ratter and is quick and tough. Its gait displays good reach and drive. Its coat is double, with a close undercoat, and hard, wiry, outer coat which is longer on the legs, muzzle, and eyebrows. Its facial furnishings add to its keen expression.

1904. The AKC recognized the Miniature (once called Wirehaired Pinscher) in 1926. Most Miniature Schnauzers today trace back to Champion Dorem Display, born in 1945, who won Best in Show at the Westminster dog show. The Miniature is the only Schnauzer to remain in the Terrier Group in America. In England it joins the other Schnauzers in the Utility Group. The Miniature Schnauzer came to America long after its Standard and Giant counterparts, but in the years after World War II, it far outpaced them in popularity, eventually rising to become the third most popular breed in America at one time. It remains as a perennial favorite, a smart looking and acting alert family pet and competitive show dog.

TEMPERAMENT

The Miniature Schnauzer deserves its place as one of the most popular terrier pets. It is playful, inquisitive, alert, spunky, and companionable. It is a well-mannered housedog that also enjoys being in the middle of activities. It is less domineering than the larger Schnauzers and less dog-aggressive than most terriers. It is also better with other animals than most terriers, although it will gladly give chase. It is clever and can be stubborn, but it is generally biddable. It enjoys children. Some may bark a lot.

UPKEEP

This energetic breed can have its exercise requirements met with a moderate walk on leash or a good game in the yard. Its wire coat needs combing once or twice weekly, plus scissoring and shaping (clipping for pets and stripping for show dogs) every couple of months. Clipping softens the coat texture.

Norfolk Terrier

AT A GLANCE

Energy level:	■■■■	Watchdog ability:	■■■■■	POPULARITY: Uncommon
Exercise requirements:	■■■	Protection ability:	■	FAMILY: Terrier
Playfulness:	■■■	Grooming requirements:	■■■	AREA OF ORIGIN: England
Affection level:	■	Cold tolerance:	■■■	DATE OF ORIGIN: 1800s
Friendliness toward dogs:	■■■	Heat tolerance:	■■■	ORIGINAL FUNCTION: Ratting, fox bolting
Friendliness toward other pets:	■■■			TODAY'S FUNCTION: Earthdog trials
Friendliness toward strangers:	■■■	WEIGHT: 11–12 lb		OTHER NAME: None
Ease of training:	■■	HEIGHT: 9–10″		

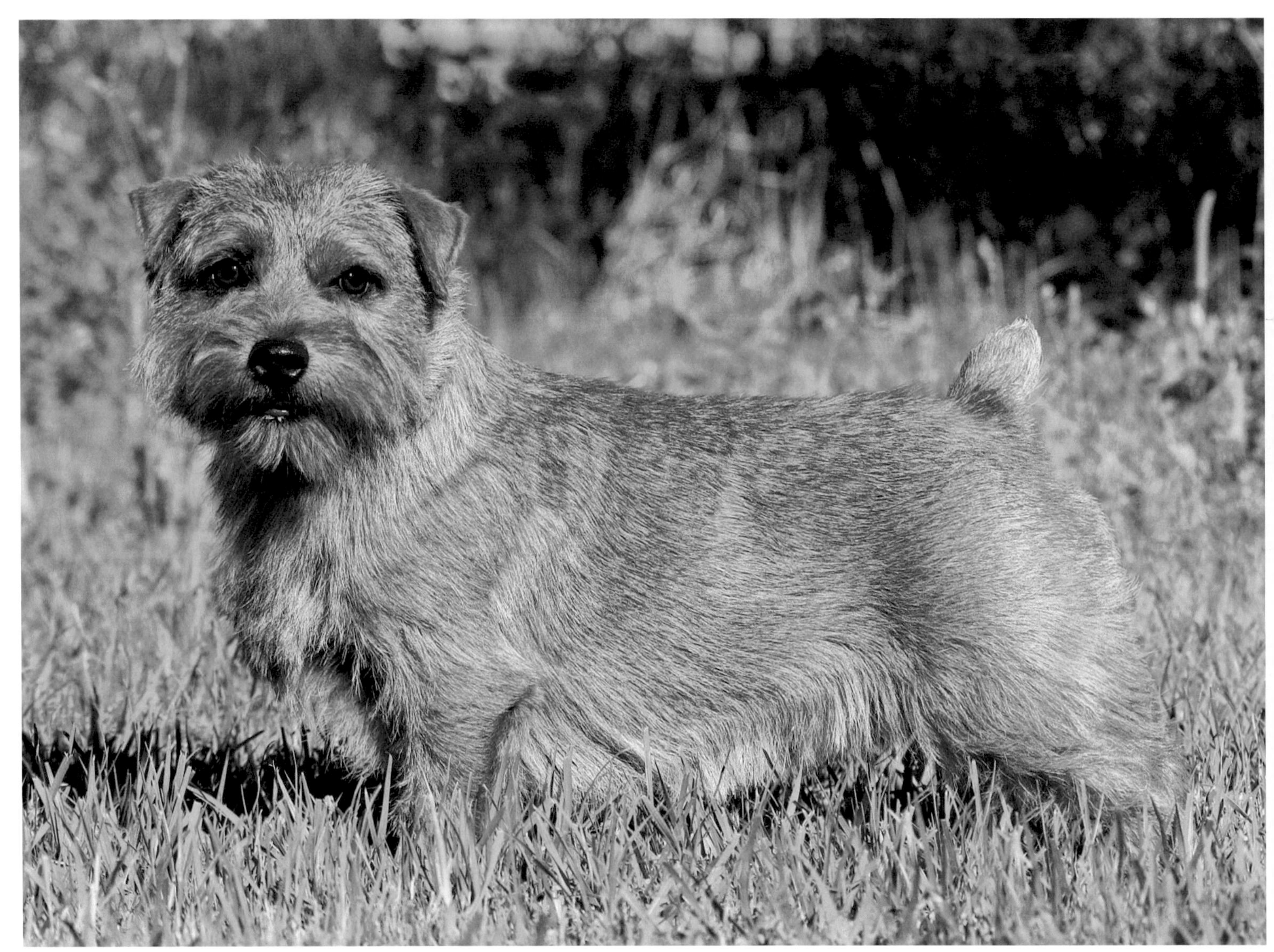

HISTORY

The Norfolk Terrier shares an identical early history with the Norwich Terrier. During the development of these breeds, both prick and drop ears were seen, and neither could lay claim to being more authentic or original than the other.

In the 1930s, soon after their entry into the show rings, breeders found that crossing the two types of ear carriage resulted in uncertain ear carriage in the offspring, so they began avoiding crossing the two ear types. The prick-eared type were more numerous; in fact, the drop-eared type almost vanished during World War II. The drop-eared strain owes its existence to the single-handed and determined efforts of Miss Macfie of the Colansays. In the 1940s, breeders came to her to renew breeding the drop-eared type of Norwich, and they soon caught

ILLUSTRATED STANDARD

1 Small, oval eyes
2 Skull wide, slightly rounded
3 V-shaped ears, tips slightly rounded, dropped with a break at skull level
4 Topline level
5 Tail medium docked, set on high
6 Feet round

Color: all shades of red, wheaten, black and tan, or grizzle
DQ: none

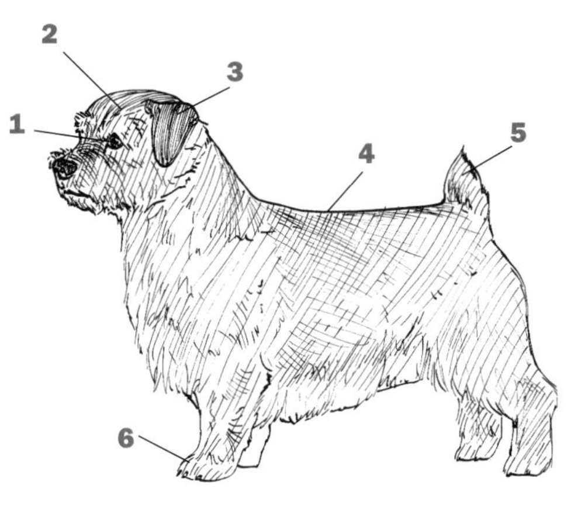

up with the prick-eared type in popularity, although not in show awards.

Eventually, amid some controversy, the breed was officially changed from one breed with two varieties to two separate breeds. This happened in 1964 in England and in 1979 in the United States.

TEMPERAMENT

Feisty, bold, inquisitive, game, scrappy, stubborn, and independent, the Norfolk is all terrier. It has been called a "demon" in the field, and it loves to hunt, dig, and investigate. It must be exercised in a safe area. It is clever and amiable but strong willed.

UPKEEP

The Norfolk Terrier needs an exercise outing every day, either a short to moderate walk or a lively and boisterous play session. It especially likes to hunt and investigate, but it must do so in a safe area. It does best as a housedog with access to a yard. Its wire coat needs combing once or twice weekly, plus stripping of dead hairs three to four times yearly.

HEALTH

- Major concerns: CHD
- Minor concerns: allergies
- Occasionally seen: patellar luxation
- Suggested tests: hip, knee, cardiac
- Life span: 13–15 years

FORM AND FUNCTION

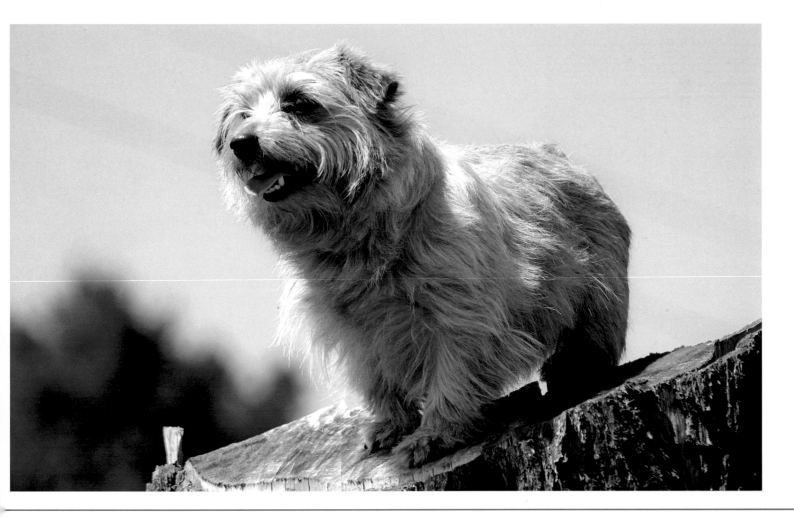

Unlike the Norwich Terrier, the Norfolk is slightly longer than it is tall. Like the Norwich, it is a formidable adversary to vermin and fox and can bolt and dispatch its quarry working alone or with a pack. It is small, short-legged, and compact, with good bone and substance. Its gait is low and driving. Its double coat is weather resistant, with the outer coat consisting of hard, wiry, straight hair about 1.5 to 2 inches long, with a longer ruff. It wears a keen, intelligent expression.

Norwich Terrier

AT A GLANCE

Energy level:	■■■■	Watchdog ability:	■■■■■	POPULARITY: Somewhat uncommon
Exercise requirements:	■■■	Protection ability:	■	FAMILY: Terrier
Playfulness:	■■■	Grooming requirements:	■■■	AREA OF ORIGIN: England
Affection level:	■■■■	Cold tolerance:	■■■	DATE OF ORIGIN: 1800s
Friendliness toward dogs:	■■■	Heat tolerance:	■■■	ORIGINAL FUNCTION: Ratting, fox bolting
Friendliness toward other pets:	■■■			TODAY'S FUNCTION: Earthdog trials
Friendliness toward strangers:	■■■	WEIGHT: approx. 12 lb		OTHER NAME: None
Ease of training:	■■■	HEIGHT: less than 10″		

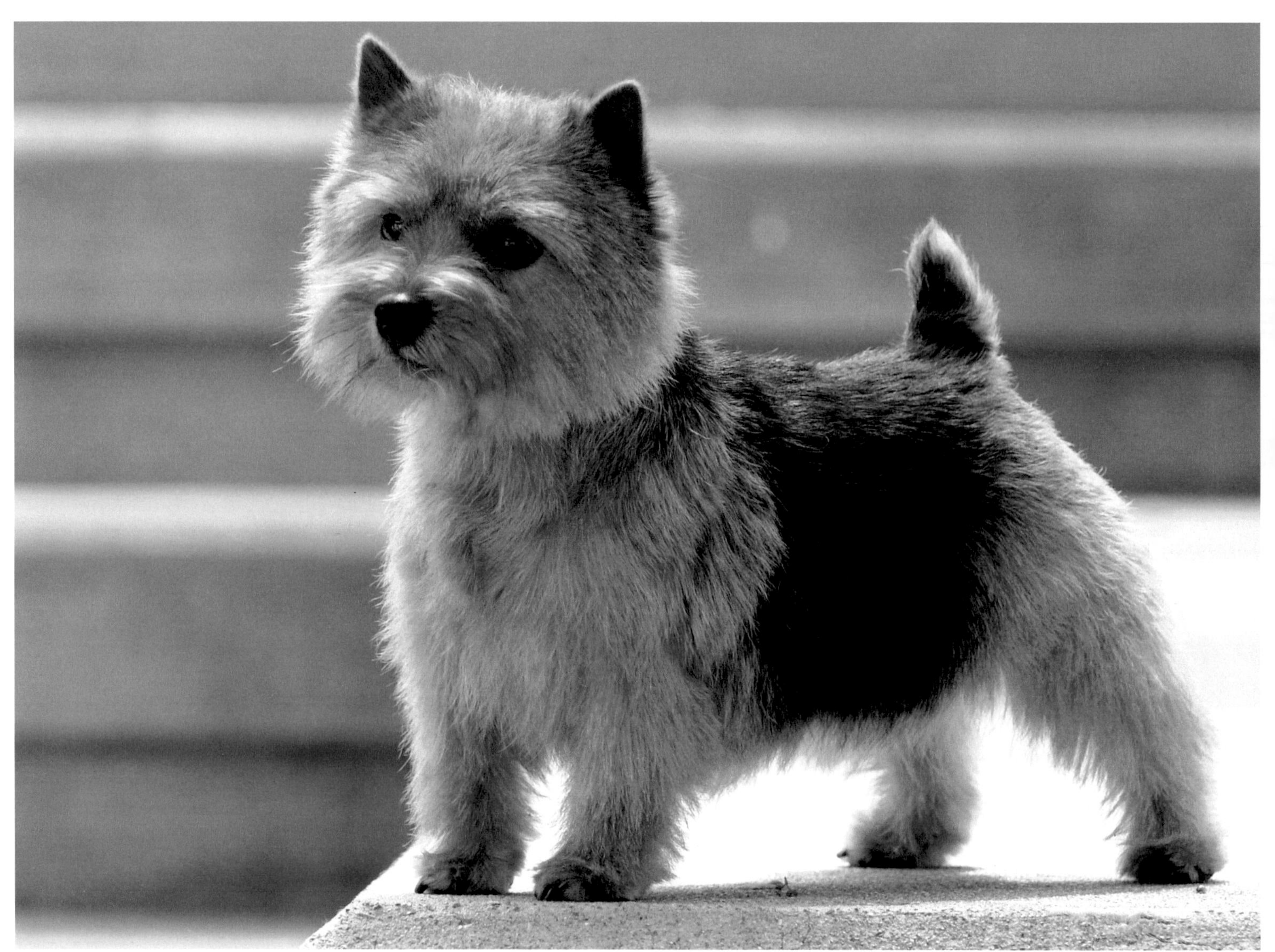

HISTORY

Short-legged ratting terriers have long been valued in England, but only in the 1880s did the breed that would eventually become both the Norwich and Norfolk Terriers emerge from obscurity. At that time, owning one of these small ratters became a fad among Cambridge University students. The little terriers became known as CanTab, and later Trumpington, Terriers. Around 1900, a Trumpington Terrier named Rags came to a stable near Norwich and gained notoriety as a ratter as well as sire. He sired countless offspring and is the patriarch of the modern Norwich. One of his sons came to America and proved to be an amiable ambassador for the breed. To this day, many people still refer to the Norwich as the "Jones" Terrier, after this dog's owner. The "Jones" Terrier was

ILLUSTRATED STANDARD

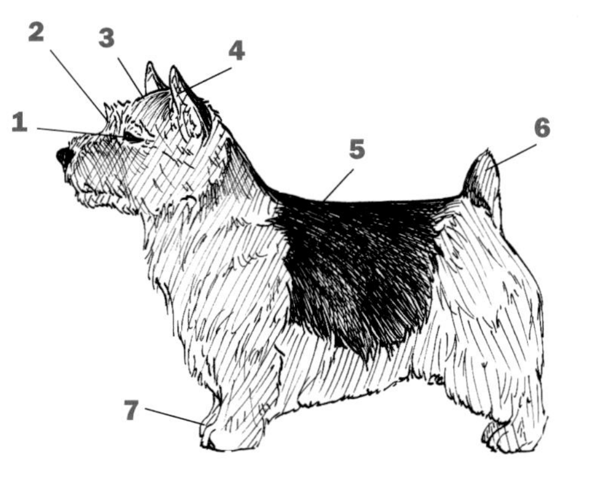

1 Small, oval eyes
2 Well-defined stop
3 Skull broad and slightly rounded
4 Medium-sized ears, erect with pointed tips
5 Topline level
6 Tail medium docked, carried erect
7 Feet round

Color: all shades of red, wheaten, black and tan, or grizzle
DQ: none

FORM AND FUNCTION

This spirited dog, one of the smallest of the working terriers, is sturdy and stocky, of square proportion. Its small size is an asset when following vermin or fox down tight passageways. Its teeth are large, to aid in dispatching its quarry. It shows great power in its movement. The tail should be long enough to grasp firmly, so that the dog can be pulled from a hole. The double coat has a hard, wiry, and straight outer coat that lies close to the body and is thicker around the mane for protection. The dog bears a slightly foxy expression.

incorporated into various foxhound hunt packs. The AKC recognized the breed in 1936. At that time the breed had both prick and drop ears, but in 1979 the dropped-eared variety was recognized as a separate breed, the Norfolk Terrier. Although lacking the flash of its long-legged competitors in the Terrier group, the Norwich has proven itself as formidable a competitor in the show ring as it ever was in the field. Despite its show ring success, however, it enjoys only moderate popularity as a pet.

TEMPERAMENT

The Norwich Terrier, like the Norfolk, is a true terrier at heart, always ready for adventure and excitement. It is a hunter and may chase small animals. It is a pert, independent, amusing—but sometimes challenging—companion, best suited for people with a sense of adventure and humor.

UPKEEP

The Norwich needs to stretch its legs with a good walk or short run every day. It especially likes combining a run with a chance to explore, but any such off-leash expeditions must be done only in a safe area. Its wiry coat needs combing one to two times weekly, plus stripping of dead hairs three to four times a year.

HEALTH

- Major concerns: CHD
- Minor concerns: allergies, seizures
- Occasionally seen: patellar luxation, cheyletiella mites, deafness, cataract
- Suggested tests: hip, knee, eye
- Life span: 13–15 years

Parson Russell Terrier

AT A GLANCE

Energy level:	■ ■ ■ ■ ■
Exercise requirements:	■ ■ ■ ■
Playfulness:	■ ■ ■ ■ ■
Affection level:	■ ■ ■
Friendliness toward dogs:	■ ■
Friendliness toward other pets:	■
Friendliness toward strangers:	■ ■ ■
Ease of training:	■ ■ ■

Watchdog ability:	■ ■ ■ ■ ■
Protection ability:	■ ■
Grooming requirements:	
Smooth:	■
Broken:	■ ■ ■
Cold tolerance:	■ ■ ■
Heat tolerance:	■ ■ ■

WEIGHT: 13–17 lb
HEIGHT: 12–14″

POPULARITY: Uncommon
FAMILY: Terrier
AREA OF ORIGIN: England
DATE OF ORIGIN: 1800s
ORIGINAL FUNCTION: Fox bolting
TODAY'S FUNCTION: Earthdog trials
OTHER NAME: Parson Jack Russell Terrier, Jack Russell Terrier

HISTORY

Parson Russell Terriers descend in most part from a dog named Trump, which was obtained by the Parson John Russell of Devonshire, England, in the mid 1800s. John Russell was a fox-hunting enthusiast, and he sought to develop a line of terriers that could keep up with the horses and bolt and dispatch fox. His line was so successful that it eventually carried his name. Although John Russell became extremely active in the English Kennel Club, for some reason he declined to show his own breed in conformation shows. Parson Russell Terrier aficionados followed his example, proving their dogs' mettle in the field rather than the show ring. This tradition holds true even today. After heated debates in which most fanciers objected to AKC recognition, the breed was nonetheless admit-

ILLUSTRATED STANDARD

1 Almond-shaped eyes
2 Skull flat
3 Button ears; small V-shaped drop ear carried forward with the tip pointing toward the eye
4 Topline straight, with loin slightly arched
5 Tail set high and carried gaily; docked so tip is about level with skull
6 Cat feet

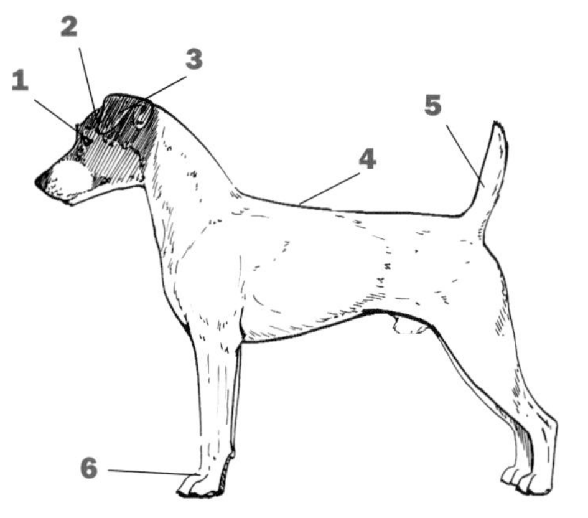

Color: predominantly white with tan, black, or brown markings, or a combination
DQ: under 12″ or over 15″ tall; prick ears; liver nose; four or more missing teeth; overshot, undershot, or wry mouth; brindle markings; overt aggression toward dogs or humans

ted into the Terrier Group in 1998. In England, it was admitted into conformation classes as the Parson Jack Russell Terrier in 1991. Jack Russells have long been popular with horse owners and are frequently seen around stables, but the type of terrier more often seen there has short legs and a long body. The term Parson was added to distinguish the traditional long-legged terrier. In 2003 the AKC-recognized dogs had their name changed from Jack Russell Terrier to Parson Russell Terrier. The PRT has become a popular media dog, and its exposure caused great interest in the breed from pet owners. As a result, its numbers are growing at an alarming rate. As irresistibly cute as this irascible scamp may be, it is definitely not a breed for everyone.

TEMPERAMENT

This is a dog that thrives on action and adventure. In the process, it often finds itself in the middle of trouble. It is a true hunter at heart and will explore, wander, chase, and dig when it gets a chance. It is very playful and intelligent. It gets along well with children and strangers. It can be scrappy with strange dogs, but is better than many terriers. It does well with horses, but it may chase cats and is not good with rodents. It may tend to bark and dig. It makes an ideal companion for an active person with a good sense of humor who wants a lot of entertainment—and mischief—in one dog.

UPKEEP

The Parson Russell needs a lot of mental and physical stimulation every day. It is not a dog that can sit around inside. It needs a long walk or strenuous game every day, plus a short training session. It enjoys the chance to explore on its own, but it must do so only in a safe area because it tends to go off in search of trouble, and some go down holes and must be dug out! Coat care for the smooth type consists only of weekly brushing to remove dead hair; for the broken coat it also consists of occasional hand stripping.

HEALTH

- Major concerns: none
- Minor concerns: lens luxation, patellar luxation
- Occasionally seen: glaucoma, ataxia, compulsive behavior, Legg–Perthes, deafness
- Suggested tests: eye, knee, hearing
- Life span: 13–15 years

FORM AND FUNCTION

The Parson is slightly taller than it is long, of medium bone. Its long legs enable it to keep up with the horses and hounds during a long fox hunt. Its slender build allows it to fit into small passageways in pursuit of its quarry. Spanning is a critical part of judging the Parson. The chest behind the elbows must be easily spanned by average-size hands, such that the thumbs should meet at the spine and the fingers under the chest. Its gait is free and lively, with good reach and drive. Its coat can be either smooth or broken, both coarse and weatherproof with short, dense undercoat. The outer coat of the smooth is flat and hard; that of the broken is harsh, straight, tight, and close lying, with no sculpted furnishings. The PRT's expression is keen and full of life.

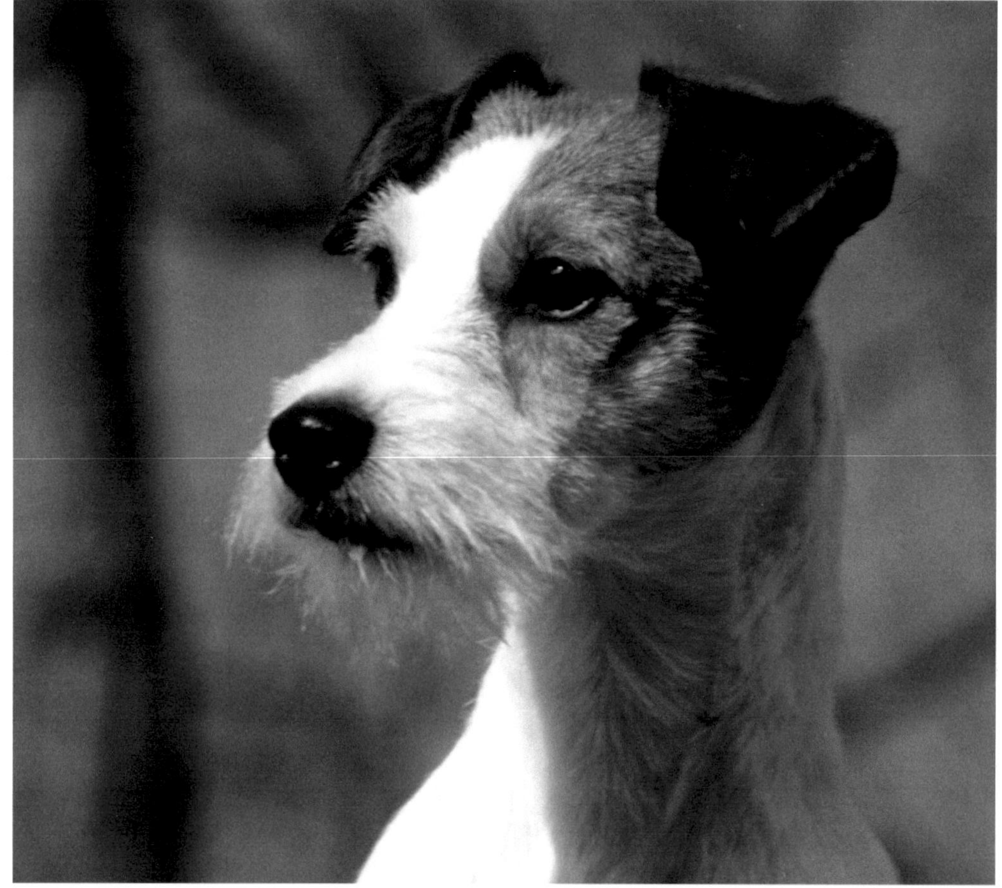

Rat Terrier

AT A GLANCE

Energy level:	■■■■	Watchdog ability:	■■■■■	POPULARITY: Uncommon
Exercise requirements:	■■■	Protection ability:	■■	FAMILY: Terrier
Playfulness:	■■■■■	Grooming requirements:	■	AREA OF ORIGIN: United States
Affection level:	■■■■	Cold tolerance:	■■	DATE OF ORIGIN: 1800s
Friendliness toward dogs:	■■■	Heat tolerance:	■■■■	ORIGINAL FUNCTION: Ratting
Friendliness toward other pets:	■■■			TODAY'S FUNCTION: Earthdog trials
Friendliness toward strangers:	■■	WEIGHT: 8–25 lb*		OTHER NAME: None
Ease of training:	■■■■	HEIGHT: miniature: 10–13″ ;standard: 13–18″		

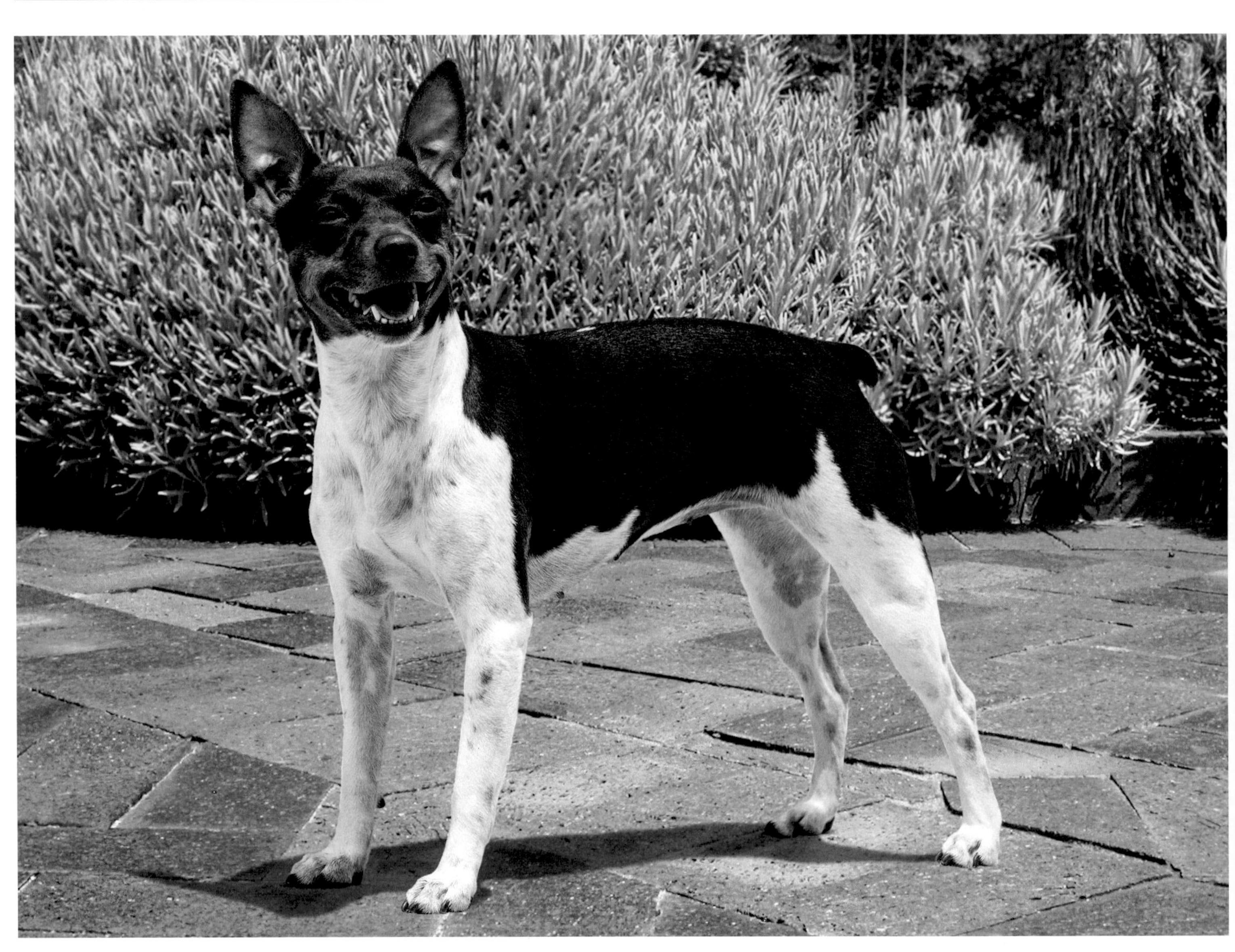

HISTORY

The Rat Terrier's ancestors probably included Manchester Terriers, Smooth Fox Terriers, Old English White Terriers, and Bull Terriers, among others. Working class British immigrants brought mixes of these breeds to America in the late 1800s. Rat Terriers were used for both vermin control and for rat pit contests, where men bet on how many rats in a pit a dog could kill in a certain time period. A Rat Terrier holds the rat killing record of 2,501 rats in a seven hour period in an infested barn. Rat Terriers were popular farm dogs by the early 1900s--they were probably among the most popular dogs in America. President Theodore Roosevelt even kept some in the White House. The Teddy Roosevelt Terrier is a short-legged offshoot of the Rat Terrier. In the early 1900s, Midwestern farmers

ILLUSTRATED STANDARD

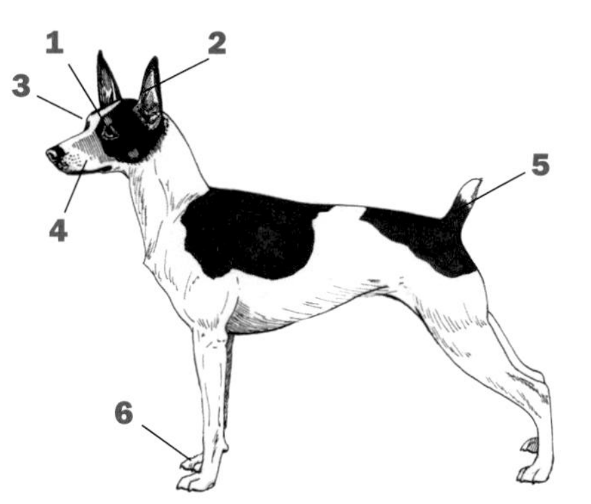

1 Oval eyes, not large, set wide
2 V-shaped ears, either erect, semi-erect and tipped, or button, but should match
3 Moderate but distinct stop
4 Muzzle slightly shorter than skull
5 Tails usually docked between the second and third joint; or can be natural, either bobtail or long, reaching hock joint; carried from just below horizontal to almost erect
6 Oval feet

Color: white with patches of one or more color, which may be almost any color but brindle or merle
DQ: dog over 6 months old less that 10" or over 18" in height; any blue in eyes; cropped ears; hairlessness; kinked coat; lack of white, or white measuring less than 1" at its widest point; brindle or merle

crossed their ratters with Whippets and Italian Greyhounds to increase speed so they could better catch jackrabbits that were eating the crops. In the South, they were crossed with Beagles for better pack drive and scenting ability. The Rat Terrier was traditionally considered a strain, rather than a breed, so crossing to other breeds and mixes was always permissible—much like modern-day feist dogs, small terriers used to catch squirrels. Because of this, and because they were used to hunt game of varied size, Rat Terrier size varies. With the advent of pesticides in the 1950s, the terrier's popularity as a working vermin hunter declined, but the breed persisted because of its companionship attributes. The UKC recognized the Rat Terrier in 1999; and the AKC in 2013.

TEMPERAMENT
The Rat Terrier is a loyal and energetic companion, very playful, and always on a quest for fun and adventure. It's eager to please and learns quickly but does have a stubborn streak and is easily bored and distracted. It is somewhat reserved with strangers. The hound in its background makes it friendlier toward other dogs compared to most terriers, and most get along well—but they won't back down from a challenge and can scrap with much larger dogs. It is good with cats if raised with them, but rats are ill-advised. Most are not excessive barkers.

UPKEEP
This is a very active and playful dog. A daily walk around the block, coupled with several play sessions will help meet its exercise needs. Indoor games and tricks can provide mental exercise on inclement days. With exercise, it is a calm housedog. Its thin coat and small size makes it vulnerable to chilling. Coat care is minimal.

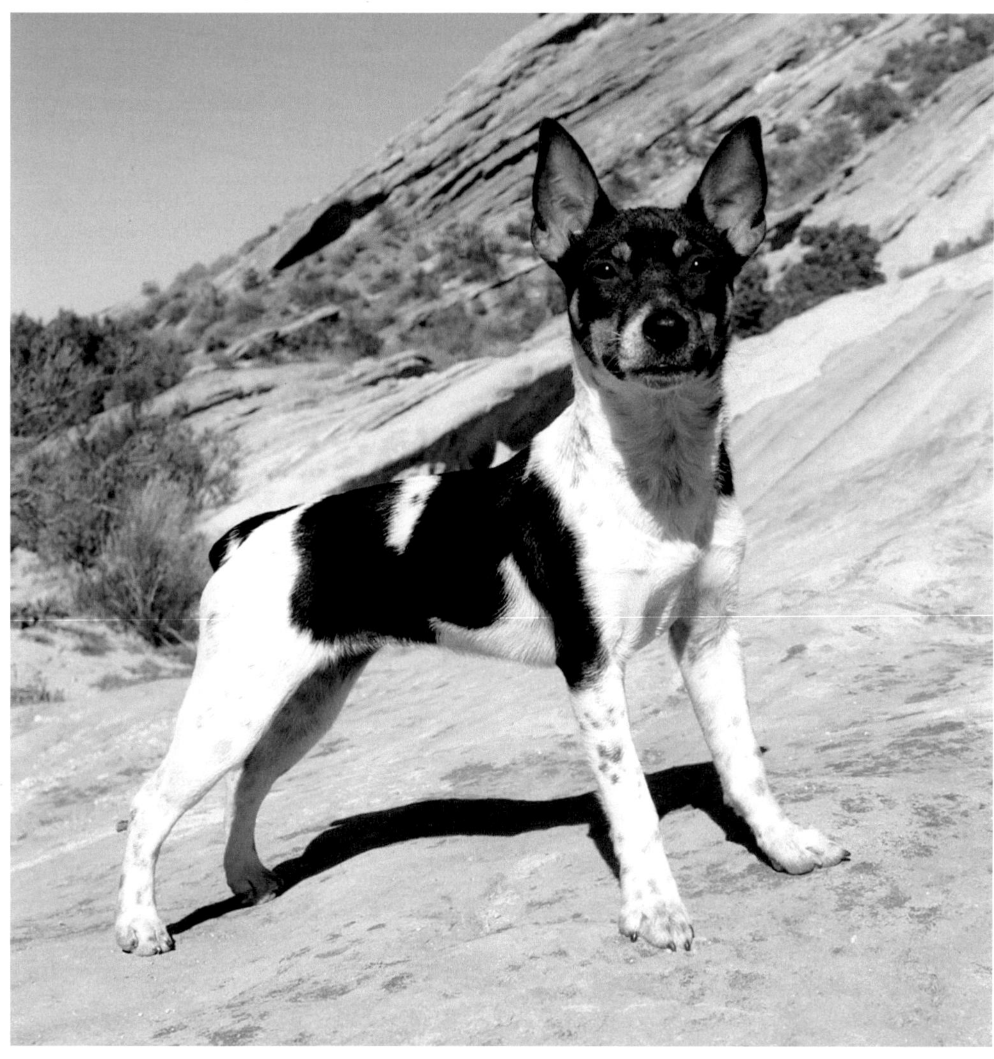

HEALTH
- Major concerns: none
- Minor concerns: allergies, patellar luxation
- Occasionally seen: none
- Suggested tests: knee
- Life span: 12–15 years

FORM AND FUNCTION
The Rat Terrier is a multipurpose companion dog capable of hunting rodents and vermin above and below ground, and coursing small game. It should be sturdy and compact but also elegant. The Rat Terrier should be neither rangy, fine boned, and toyish; nor bulky and coarse. There are two size divisions, but both are slightly longer than tall (but not short-legged) with moderate bone. The coat is short and smooth. Note that the American Hairless Terrier is derived from Rat Terriers with a hairless mutation, so hairless Rat Terriers are disqualified. The trot has good reach and drive.

Russell Terrier

AT A GLANCE

Energy level:	■ ■ ■ ■ ■	Watchdog ability:	■ ■ ■ ■ ■	POPULARITY: Uncommon
Exercise requirements:	■ ■ ■ ■	Protection ability:	■ ■	FAMILY: Terrier
Playfulness:	■ ■ ■ ■ ■	Grooming requirements:	■	AREA OF ORIGIN: England and Australia
Affection level:	■ ■ ■ ■	Cold tolerance:	■ ■	DATE OF ORIGIN: 1800s
Friendliness toward dogs:	■ ■ ■	Heat tolerance:	■ ■ ■ ■	ORIGINAL FUNCTION: Fox bolting
Friendliness toward other pets:	■ ■ ■			TODAY'S FUNCTION: Earthdog trials
Friendliness toward strangers:	■ ■ ■	WEIGHT: 14–18 lb		OTHER NAME: None
Ease of training:	■ ■ ■ ■	HEIGHT: 10–12″		

HISTORY

The Russell Terrier shares a good deal of history with the Parson Russell Terrier. They originated with the Parson John ("Jack") Russell in England in the mid 1800s, and were both called Jack Russell Terriers. Eventually, both longer-legged and shorter-legged Jack Russells had strong advocates in England, America, and Australia. The taller version (now the Parson Russell Terrier) was better suited for running with the pack and bolting foxes, while the shorter version was more easily transported in terrier bags on horseback and could go to ground in smaller dens and work amid more brambles. The Russell Terrier is not to be confused with the colloquially named Puddin' Jack Russell, which is a very short-legged version with crooked front legs and pointed ears. Instead, Russell Terriers

ILLUSTRATED STANDARD

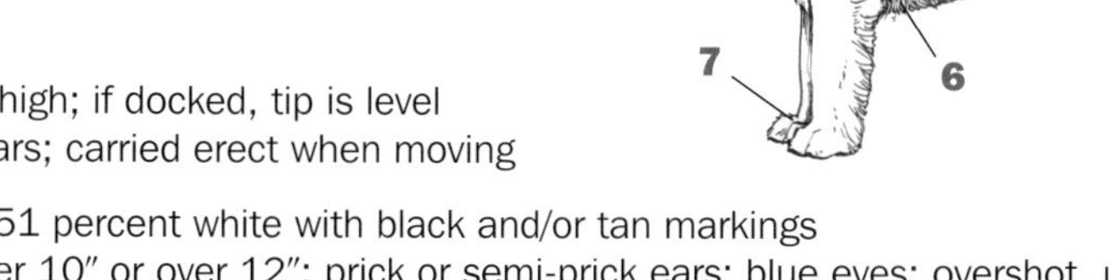

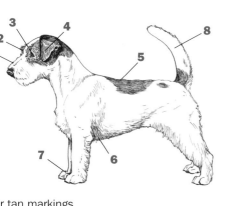

1 Muzzle slightly shorter than skull
2 Well-defined stop
3 Almond-shaped eyes
4 Small, V-shaped button or drop ears
5 Level topline
6 Brisket never below elbow; chest small enough to be spanned by average-sized hands
7 Oval feet
8 Tail set fairly high; if docked, tip is level with top of ears; carried erect when moving

Color: at least 51 percent white with black and/or tan markings
DQ: height under 10″ or over 12″; prick or semi-prick ears; blue eyes; overshot, undershot, wry mouth; nose any color other than black; less than 51 percent white; brindle coloring; any color other than black or a shade of tan

as a breed were developed in Australia. Even in Australia, the short-legged version was initially recognized as the Jack Russell Terrier in 1972; but this was also the name given to the longer-legged dogs in America and England. The AKC eventually changed the name of the long-legged version to Parson Russell Terrier. The shorter-legged version still had an identity crisis, but eventually was renamed the Russell Terrier to prevent confusion. The UKC recognized the breed in 2001; and the AKC in 2012. The Russell Terrier is considered by many to be the ultimate working earth terrier.

TEMPERAMENT

The Russell Terrier is an energetic and fun-loving companion as well as an intense hunter. It is inquisitive and adventurous and relishes challenging games. It learns quickly but bores easily. It is bold and fearless, but not quarrelsome. They are fairly outgoing to strangers. Some can be feisty with other dogs, but most get along fine. They also get along with other pets as long as they're raised with them. They are affectionate and devoted to their people. Some can bark a lot, but not as much as many other terriers.

UPKEEP

This dog needs a lot of activity to satisfy its racing mind. It likes to scurry around the yard, walk around the block, or go for hikes—but beware, it can take off in search of underground animals. It enjoys indoor games and makes a great housedog given enough exercise. Coat care is minimal—occasional brushing plus some stripping for the wirier coats.

HEALTH

- Major concerns: none
- Minor concerns: lens luxation, patellar luxation
- Occasionally seen: ataxia, deafness
- Suggested tests: eye, knee, hearing
- Life span: 13–15 years

FORM AND FUNCTION

The Russell Terrier is a strong, active, lithe dog with a small chest, short legs, and flexible body of moderate length. It has a good nose, strong voice, and fearless nature. It is rectangular in profile. These traits make it an ideal working terrier, unequaled in ability to bolt a fox or traverse tight tunnels. It is highly animated and confident. The coat may be smooth, broken, or rough, all with an undercoat and a harsh weatherproof outer coat. The smooth coat is dense and coarse. The rough coat is dense and harsh. The broken coat is between the two, usually with facial furnishings and a slight ridge on the back.

Scottish Terrier

AT A GLANCE

Energy level:	■■■	Watchdog ability:	■■■■■	POPULARITY: Somewhat popular
Exercise requirements:	■■■	Protection ability:	■■	FAMILY: Terrier
Playfulness:	■■■	Grooming requirements:	■■■	AREA OF ORIGIN: Scotland
Affection level:	■■■	Cold tolerance:	■■■	DATE OF ORIGIN: 1800s
Friendliness toward dogs:	■■■	Heat tolerance:	■	ORIGINAL FUNCTION: Vermin hunting
Friendliness toward other pets:	■■■			TODAY'S FUNCTION: Earthdog trials
Friendliness toward strangers:	■■■	WEIGHT: male: 19–22 lb; female: 18–21 lb		OTHER NAME: Aberdeen Terrier
Ease of training:	■	HEIGHT: about 10″		

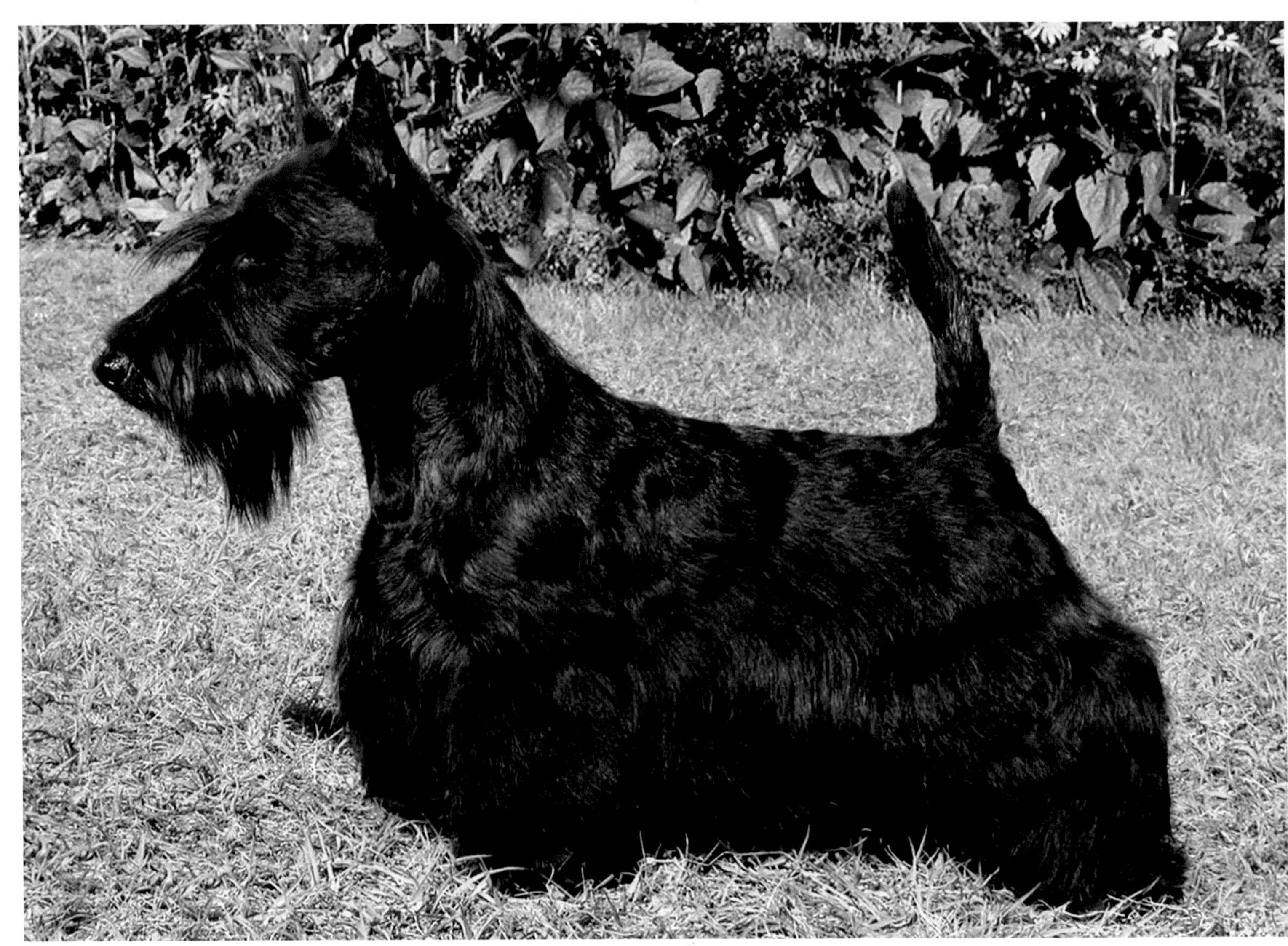

HISTORY

Great confusion exists about the background of the Scottish Terrier, stemming from the early custom of calling all terriers from Scotland Scottish or Scotch Terriers. To further confuse matters, the present Scottish Terrier was once grouped with Skye Terriers, in reference not to the modern Skye Terrier but of a large group of terriers from the Isle of Skye. Whatever the origin, the early Scottish Terriers were definitely a hardy lot of Highlanders, used for going to ground in pursuit of their prey. Only in the late 1800s can the Scottish Terrier's history be confidently documented. Of the several short-legged harsh-coated terriers, the dog now known as the Scottish Terrier was most favored in the Aberdeen area, and so for a time it was called the Aberdeen Terrier. By the 1870s, the situation had become so confusing that a series of protests were made, ultimately leading to a detailed

ILLUSTRATED STANDARD

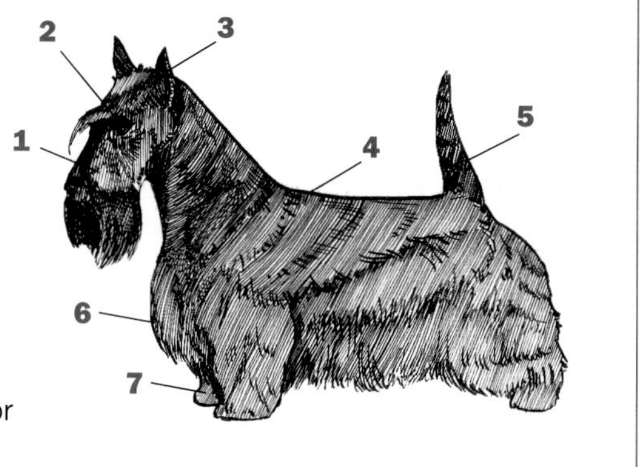

1 Long skull, of medium width
2 Small, almond-shaped eyes
3 Small, prick ears, pointed
4 Level topline
5 Uncut tail, about 7″ long, carried with a slight curve but not over the back
6 Forechest extends well in front of legs
7 Legs, short and heavy boned

Color: black, wheaten, or brindle of any color
DQ: none

FORM AND FUNCTION

The Scottish Terrier is a short-legged, compact, relatively heavy boned dog, giving the impression of great power in a small package. This combination is essential in a dog that must meet tough adversaries in tight spaces. Its coat is a combination of dense undercoat and extremely hardy and wiry outer coat, about 2 inches in length. The distinctive eyebrows and beard add to its expression, which is keen and sharp.

description of how the true Scottish Terrier should appear. Around 1880, the first breed standard was put forth. The first Scotty came to America in 1883. It gradually gained popularity until World War II, after which its popularity soared. The most well-known Scotty in America was Fala, Franklin Roosevelt's dog, who was his constant companion in life and buried at his side in death. The Scottish Terrier remains a fixture of the Terrier Group, always a contender in the show ring and a favorite in the home.

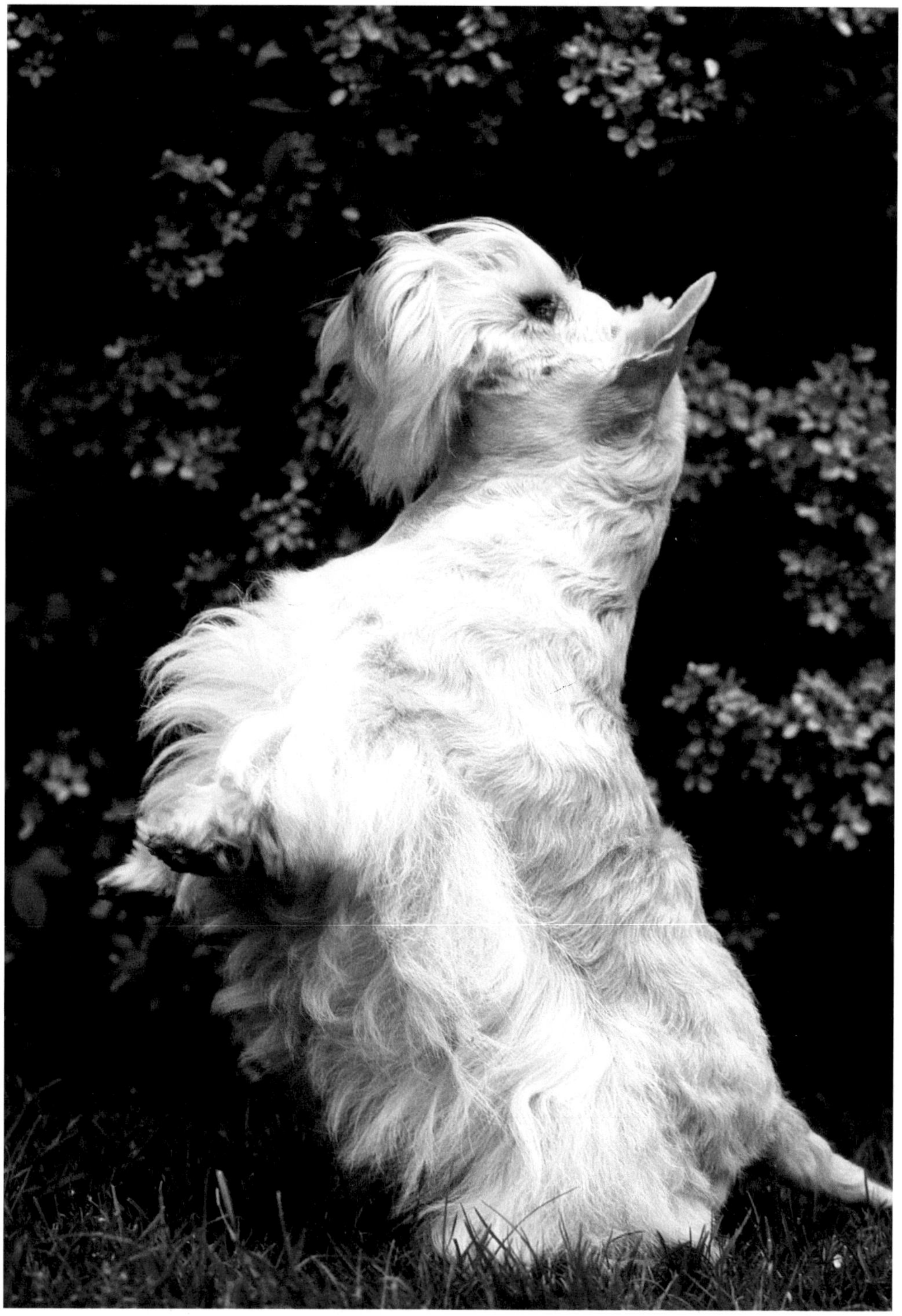

TEMPERAMENT

Nicknamed The Diehard in reference to its rugged character, the Scottish Terrier is a tough, smart, determined character, ready for action. It is fearless and feisty and may be aggressive toward other dogs and animals. It is reserved, but friendly, with strangers, and devoted to its family. Although independent and stubborn, it is sensitive. Left alone, it tends to dig and bark.

UPKEEP

This is a dog on the lookout for adventure, and it needs some excitement and exercise in its life every day. This can take the form of a moderate walk on leash, a boisterous game, or an off-leash exploration in a safe area. Its wire coat needs combing two to three times weekly, plus shaping every three months. Shaping for pets is by clipping, and for show dogs by stripping.

HEALTH

- Major concerns: vWD, CMO
- Minor concerns: Scotty cramp, cerebellar abiotrophy, patellar luxation
- Occasionally seen: bladder cancer
- Suggested tests: DNA for vWD, knee
- Life span: 11–13 years

Sealyham Terrier

AT A GLANCE

Energy level:	■■	Watchdog ability:	■■■■	POPULARITY: Very rare
Exercise requirements:	■■	Protection ability:	■	FAMILY: Terrier
Playfulness:	■■	Grooming requirements:	■■■■	AREA OF ORIGIN: Wales
Affection level:	■■■	Cold tolerance:	■■■	DATE OF ORIGIN: 1800s
Friendliness toward dogs:	■■■	Heat tolerance:	■■■	ORIGINAL FUNCTION: Badger, otter, and fox hunting
Friendliness toward other pets:	■■■			
Friendliness toward strangers:	■■■	WEIGHT: male: 23–24 lb; female: slightly less		TODAY'S FUNCTION: Earthdog trials
Ease of training:	■	HEIGHT: approx. 10.5″		OTHER NAME: None

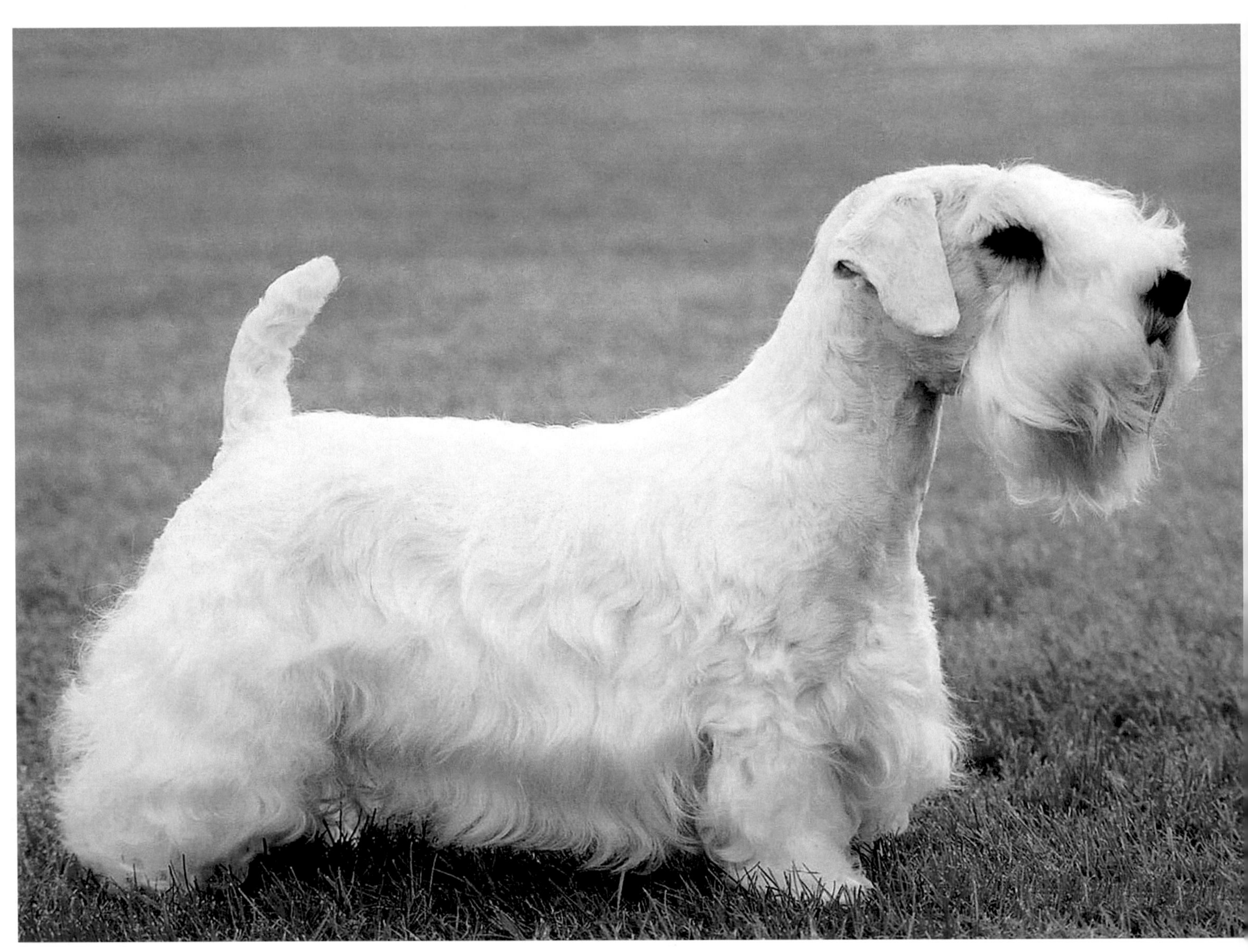

HISTORY

Although some evidence exists of a small, white, long-backed terrier imported into Wales in the fifteenth century, the documented history of the Sealyham begins only in the mid 1800s. The only reason the earlier observation receives some credence is that the originator of the breed, Captain John Edwardes of Sealyham House in Pembrokeshire, was a descendant of the family said to have imported the particular dog centuries earlier. Regardless, Captain Edwardes worked from 1850 to 1891 to develop the breed now known as the Sealyham Terrier. The breeds that went into its makeup are a mystery; some suggest that the Dandie Dinmont Terrier, Wire Fox Terrier, English White Terrier, and Pembroke Welsh Corgi may have played a role. Whatever

ILLUSTRATED STANDARD

1 Medium-sized, oval, deep-set eyes
2 Long, broad, powerful head
3 Ears folded level with top of head, rounded tips
4 Topline level
5 Tail docked, carried upright; set high
6 Feet large and round

Color: all white, or with lemon, tan, or badger markings
DQ: none

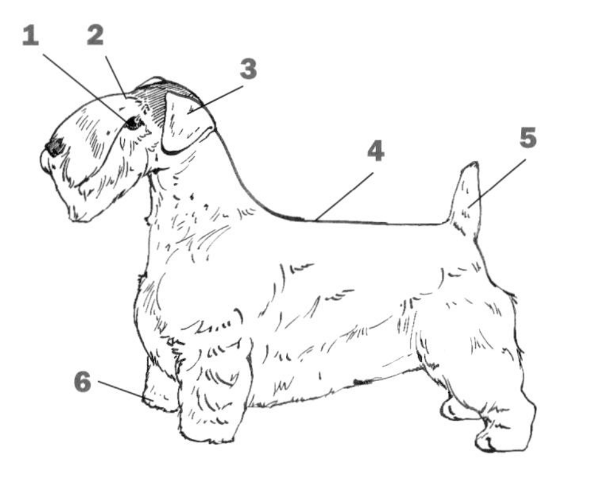

the ingredients, the result was a plucky terrier that soon gained notoriety for its ability to face badgers, otters, and foxes. Its smart appearance made it a dog show natural, and it first entered the show ring in 1903. The AKC recognized the Sealyham in 1911. Demand for these terriers quickly grew, especially because they were still exceptional hunting dogs as well as extremely competitive show dogs and status symbols. Today the breed's popularity has waned somewhat, but the Sealyham still retains its dual abilities to excel in both ring and field.

TEMPERAMENT

One of the calmer terriers, the Sealyham is nonetheless ready for action, always happy to investigate, dig, or give chase. It is friendly, playful, and generally outgoing. The Sealy is reserved with strangers, but devoted to its family. It is stubborn, independent, and can dig if bored.

UPKEEP

The Sealyham's exercise needs are not too demanding, consisting of a short to moderate walk or game session every day. If allowed off leash, it should be in a safe area because it may tend to follow its nose. This breed is suited for apartment life, preferably with yard access. Its wire coat needs combing two to three times weekly, plus shaping every three months. Shaping for pets is by clipping, and for show dogs by stripping. Dirt shows up on their white coats!

HEALTH

- Major concerns: none
- Minor concerns: retinal dysplasia, lens luxation
- Occasionally seen: deafness
- Suggested tests: eye
- Life span: 11–13 years

FORM AND FUNCTION

The Sealyham Terrier is a short-legged terrier, slightly longer than it is tall. Its body is strong, short-coupled, and substantial, allowing for plenty of flexibility. This combination of short legs with a strong and flexible body allows the Sealyham to maneuver in tight quarters. Its weather-resistant coat consists of a soft, dense undercoat and a hard, wiry outer coat. This is a keen, alert, and determined breed and should look the part.

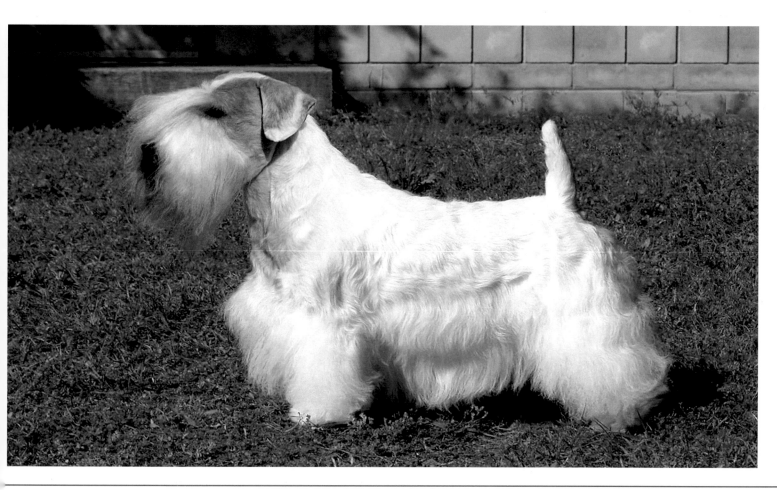

Skye Terrier

AT A GLANCE

Energy level:	■■	Watchdog ability:	■■■■■	POPULARITY: Very rare
Exercise requirements:	■■	Protection ability:	■	FAMILY: Terrier
Playfulness:	■■■	Grooming requirements:	■■■	AREA OF ORIGIN: Scotland
Affection level:	■■■■	Cold tolerance:	■■■■	DATE OF ORIGIN: 1500s
Friendliness toward dogs:	■	Heat tolerance:	■■	ORIGINAL FUNCTION: Fox and otter hunting
Friendliness toward other pets:	■			TODAY'S FUNCTION: Earthdog trials
Friendliness toward strangers:	■	WEIGHT: male: 35–40 lb*; female: 25–30 lb*		OTHER NAME: None
Ease of training:	■■■	HEIGHT: male: 10″*; female: 9.5″ (overall average 10–11″*)		

HISTORY

Scotland has long been a stronghold of small plucky terriers, and the Skye Terrier is among the oldest of them. They developed along the west coastal area, where they hunted fox and otter from among the rocky cairns. The purest of these dogs were found on the Isle of Skye, and the dogs were thus dubbed Skye Terriers. It was first described in the sixteenth century, when it was already noteworthy for its long coat. Some confusion exists in tracing its history because, for a time, several different breeds were grouped under the name Skye Terrier. The true Skye Terrier became prominent in 1840 when Queen Victoria fancied the breed, keeping both drop- and prick-eared dogs. This enhanced its popularity both in high society and among commoners, and the Skye

ILLUSTRATED STANDARD

1 Medium-sized, close-set eyes
2 Head long and powerful
3 Ears, if prick: placed high, held erect; if drop: larger and set lower
4 Topline level
5 Tail long, well-feathered, preferably carried no higher than backline
6 Large hare feet

Color: black, blue, gray, silver, fawn, or cream, preferably with black ears, muzzle, and tail tip; adult color may not be present until 18 months
DQ: dudley; flesh colored; or brown nose

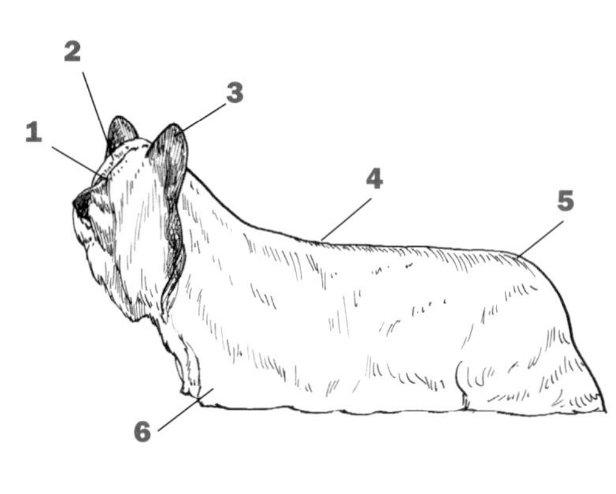

soon came to America. The AKC recognized the breed in 1887, and it quickly rose to the top of the show scene. Despite this strong start and the breed's distinctive appearance, its popularity has waned, and it is now among the least known terriers. The most famous Skye of all time was Greyfriar's Bobby, who slept on his master's grave for 14 years until his own death; he continues his vigil still, being buried where he waited next to his master. A statue commemorates this most loyal of dogs.

TEMPERAMENT

The Skye Terrier's soft look belies its tough nature. It is a fearless and a deadly rodent hunter. It is also a mild-mannered house pet, one of the few terriers calm enough to live in the city. It still needs daily exercise in a safe area or on leash, however. It is sensitive yet stubborn. The Skye is affectionate with its family but cautious with strangers. It gets along fairly well with other dogs in the same household but may not mingle well with strange dogs. It is extremely courageous and game and makes a good watchdog.

UPKEEP

This is a hunting dog at heart and enjoys a daily outing, exploring in a safe area. It also needs a short to moderate walk to stay in shape. Regular combing (about twice a week) is all that is needed to keep the Skye looking good. An occasional bath will not soften the coat too much, as is often the case with other terriers. The hair around the eyes and mouth may need extra cleaning.

HEALTH

- Major concerns: none
- Minor concerns: premature closure of distal radius, intervertebral disk disease
- Occasionally seen: copper toxicosis
- Suggested tests: none
- Life span: 12–14 years

FORM AND FUNCTION

The Skye Terrier is a stylish and elegant dog that is, first of all, a working terrier. It is solidly built, with substantial bone, and twice as long as it is tall. The Skye's short legs enable it to go to ground in pursuit of fox and badger, and the long back imparts flexibility within a confined space. Its strong jaws further aid it in dispatching its prey. Its movement is free and effortless. The hard outer coat and close undercoat afford protection from the teeth of its quarry as well as harsh weather. The outer coat lies straight and flat, 5.5 inches or more in length. The hair covers its forehead and eyes for protection from brush and aggressive quarry.

Soft Coated Wheaten Terrier

AT A GLANCE

Energy level:	■■■	Watchdog ability:	■■■■	POPULARITY: Somewhat popular
Exercise requirements:	■■■	Protection ability:	■■	FAMILY: Terrier
Playfulness:	■■■■	Grooming requirements:	■■■■	AREA OF ORIGIN: Ireland
Affection level:	■■■■■	Cold tolerance:	■■■	DATE OF ORIGIN: 1700s
Friendliness toward dogs:	■■■	Heat tolerance:	■	ORIGINAL FUNCTION: Vermin hunting, herding, guardian
Friendliness toward other pets:	■■■			
Friendliness toward strangers:	■■■■	WEIGHT: male: 35–40 lb; female: 30–35 lb		TODAY'S FUNCTION: Companion
Ease of training:	■■■	HEIGHT: male: 18–19″; female: 17–18″		OTHER NAME: None

HISTORY

One of only three large terriers of Ireland, the Soft Coated Wheaten Terrier originated as an all-around farm dog, perhaps serving in this function for hundreds of years. Besides the ever-essential terrier function of extinguishing vermin, it also helped round up stock and guard the homestead. It was later even known to be trained as a gundog. Its early history is largely undocumented; however, it is mentioned as a progenitor of the Kerry Blue Terrier. The Wheaten was a comparative latecomer to the show scene. Only in 1937 was it granted breed status in Ireland. For many years, an Irish Championship required that a dog not only prove itself in the ring but also in the field over badger, rat, and rabbit. The English Kennel Club recognized the breed in 1943, and

ILLUSTRATED STANDARD

1 Medium-sized, slightly almond-shaped eyes
2 Head appears rectangular, powerful
3 Ears fairly small, breaking level with skull
4 Back strong and level
5 Tail docked, carried gaily but not over back
6 Feet round

Color: any shade of wheaten
DQ: none

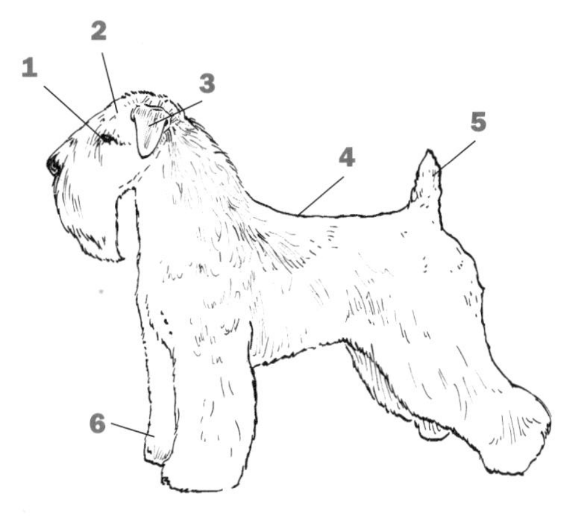

in 1946 the first Wheaten came to America. The breed did not instantly catch the public's attention, but instead it took its time building a firm basis of support. In 1973 the AKC granted recognition. The Soft Coated Wheaten Terrier has remained a breed of only moderate popularity.

TEMPERAMENT

The Wheaten makes a playful companion at home and a fun-loving partner in the field. It is affectionate, congenial, and much gentler than most terriers. It is generally responsive to its owner's wishes but can be headstrong at times. It is good and patient with children (although some may be overly boisterous with small children) and usually very friendly with other household dogs and pets. It may dig or jump. It is one of the quietest terriers, barking only for real alarms.

UPKEEP

This is an athletic dog that needs a good daily workout, either in the form of a moderate to long walk or an invigorating game in the yard. It should be allowed loose only in a safe area because it still loves to hunt and chase. Its long coat needs brushing or combing every two days. As a nonshedding dog, loose hair becomes entangled in the coat and will mat if not combed out. Bathing and trimming every other month is necessary to maintain the desirable coat and silhouette; pets can be better managed if their coats are clipped to about 3 inches, but then they lose the breed's typical outline.

HEALTH

- Major concerns: protein losing diseases (PLE and PLN)
- Minor concerns: renal dysplasia, Addison's
- Occasionally seen: PRA, CHD
- Suggested tests: blood and urine protein screens, eye, hip
- Life span: 12–14 years

FORM AND FUNCTION

The Soft Coated Wheaten Terrier is an all-around dog, square-proportioned, graceful, and strong, not exaggerated in any way. It is large enough to function as a general farm worker yet agile enough to perform its job as vermin exterminator. Its gait is free and lively with good reach and drive; the tail held erect. Its abundant, soft, single coat distinguishes it from all other terriers. The wavy coat is not evident in youngsters. It is long and silky with a gentle wave. The overall appearance is one of grace and strength in an alert and happy dog.

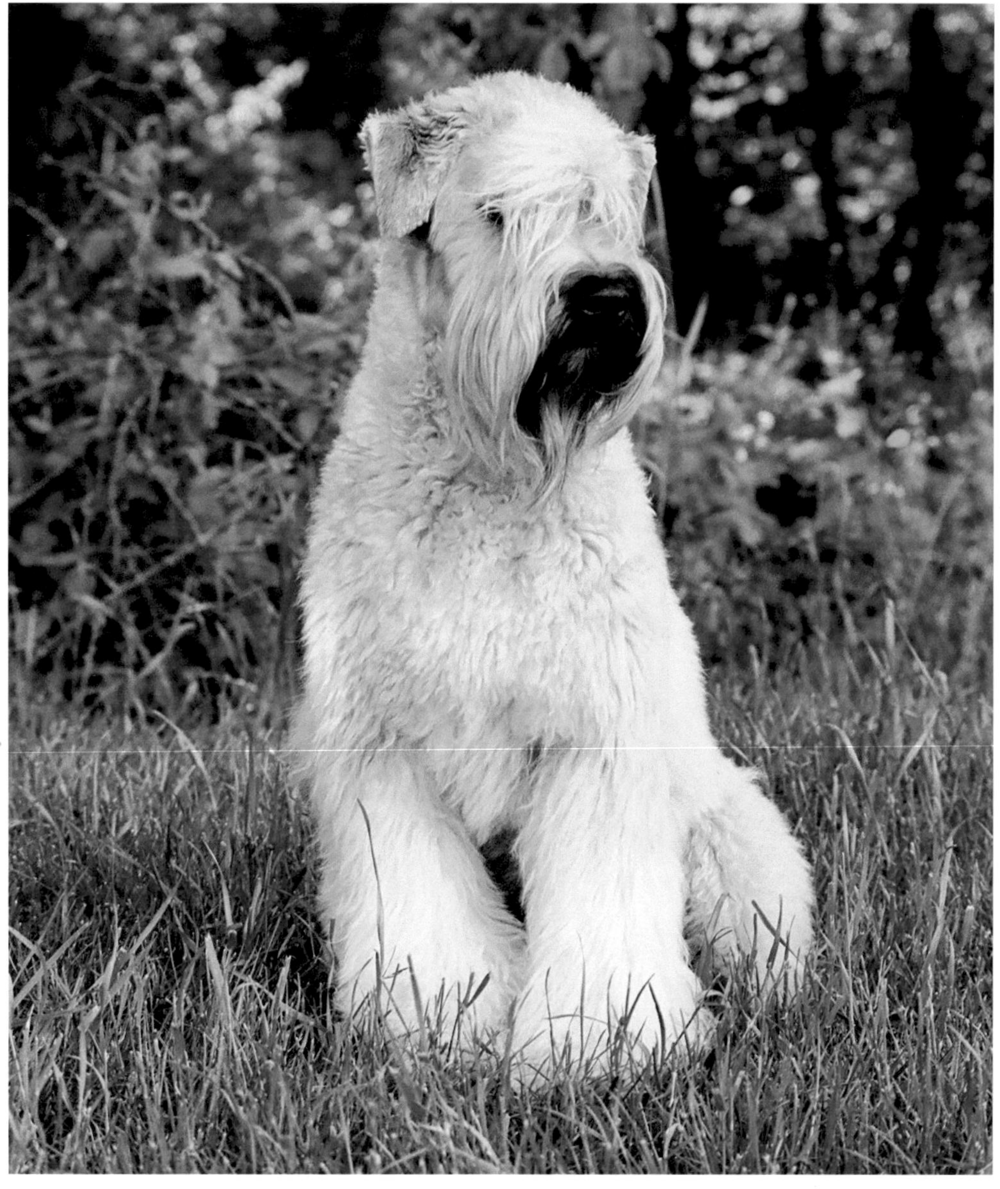

Staffordshire Bull Terrier

AT A GLANCE

Energy level: ■■■
Exercise requirements: ■■■
Playfulness: ■■■■■
Affection level: ■■■■
Friendliness toward dogs: ■■
Friendliness toward other pets: ■■■
Friendliness toward strangers: ■■■
Ease of training: ■■■

Watchdog ability: ■■■
Protection ability: ■■■
Grooming requirements: ■
Cold tolerance: ■■
Heat tolerance: ■■

WEIGHT: male: 28–38 lb; female: 24–34 lb
HEIGHT: male: 14–16″

POPULARITY: Somewhat uncommon
FAMILY: Terrier, Mastiff, Bull
AREA OF ORIGIN: England
DATE OF ORIGIN: 1800s
ORIGINAL FUNCTION: Dog fighting
TODAY'S FUNCTION: Companion
OTHER NAME: None

HISTORY

In the early 1800s, the sport of rat killing had become quite popular among the working classes. Bull baiting, which had been popular in earlier times, did not lend itself to the cities, and fanciers of the rat pit became increasingly enamored of dog fighting as a more exciting alternative to rat killing. In their efforts to produce a fearless, quick, strong contender for the dog pit, they crossed the Bulldog of the time with the Black and Tan Terrier, thus producing the Bull and Terrier. Selective breeding resulted in a small nimble dog with incredibly strong jaws. It also produced a dog that was specifically not aggressive toward people because it had to be handled safely when it was at its most aroused state. By the time dog fighting was banned in England, these dogs had so endeared

ILLUSTRATED STANDARD

1 Medium-sized, round eyes
2 Distinct stop, short foreface
3 Head short, deep, broad skull, pronounced cheek muscles
4 Ears rose or half prick, not large
5 Level topline
6 Tail medium length, carried low
7 Wide front

Color: red, fawn, white, black, or blue, solid or with white; any shade of brindle or brindle with white
DQ: black and tan or liver color

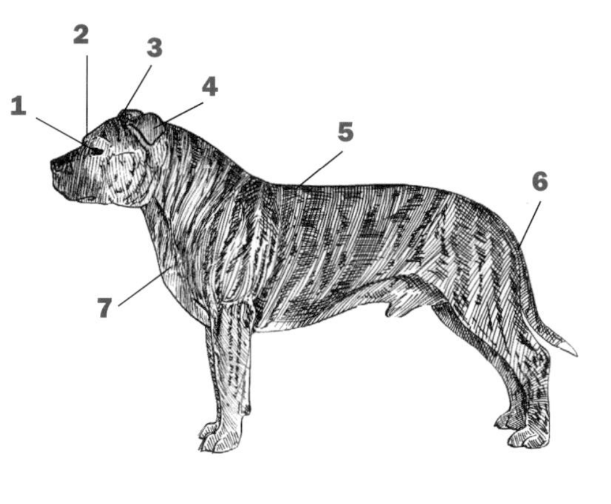

themselves to their fans that they continued to have a loyal following. Although some fanciers continued to fight them in clandestine gatherings, true aficionados sought a legal venue of competition and found their answer in the show ring. Concerted efforts to produce a dog more amenable to the ring and attractive as a pet finally resulted in the breed's recognition by the English Kennel Club in 1935, but it was not until 1974 that the AKC confirmed similar status. Although the breed's reputation as a combatant may have dogged it into the present, those who live with one know it as a lover, not a fighter.

TEMPERAMENT
The Staffordshire Bull Terrier is a fun-loving character that loves playing with its family and friends. It is typically playful, companionable, amiable, docile, and generally responsive to its owner's wishes. Its love of a good game is rivaled only by its need for human companionship. It is also characteristically friendly toward strangers. Some can be strong willed. Although it doesn't usually look for a fight, it is fearless and tenacious. It may not do well around strange dogs or sometimes even household dogs that challenge it. It is generally very good with children; although usually gentle, some can be rambunctious. In the United Kingdom the Stafford is known as the Nanny Dog, in reference to its eagerness and ability to assume the role of a child's nursemaid.

UPKEEP
This is an athletic breed that needs a good walk on leash every day. It also enjoys a good game in the yard or a run in a safe area. Most Staffords are poor swimmers. Coat care is minimal.

HEALTH
- Major concerns: CHD
- Minor concerns: none
- Occasionally seen: cataract, L2 HGA
- Suggested tests: hip, eye, DNA for L2 HGA, DNA for cataract
- Life span: 12–14 years
- Note: CHD seldom causes problems or symptoms.

FORM AND FUNCTION
The Stafford is slightly longer than it is tall, and relatively wide, giving it a low center of gravity and firm stance. Its small size imparts a surprising agility, while its heavy musculature provides great strength. The wide head provides ample room for attachment of jaw muscles. Its gait should be powerful and agile. Its coat is smooth, short, and close.

Welsh Terrier

AT A GLANCE

Energy level: ■■■
Exercise requirements: ■■■
Playfulness: ■■■
Affection level: ■■■
Friendliness toward dogs: ■■■
Friendliness toward other pets: ■
Friendliness toward strangers: ■
Ease of training: ■

Watchdog ability: ■■■■■
Protection ability: ■
Grooming requirements: ■■■■
Cold tolerance: ■■■
Heat tolerance: ■■■

WEIGHT: 20 lb
HEIGHT: male: 15–15.5″; female: smaller

POPULARITY: Uncommon
FAMILY: Terrier
AREA OF ORIGIN: Wales
DATE OF ORIGIN: 1700s
ORIGINAL FUNCTION: Otter, fox, badger, and rat hunting
TODAY'S FUNCTION: Earthdog trials
OTHER NAME: None

HISTORY

One of only two terriers native to Wales, the Welsh Terrier probably descended from the old Black and Tan Rough Terrier that was popular in Britain in the eighteenth and nineteenth centuries. By the late 1700s, a distinctive strain—known as Ynysfor—was running with Otterhounds in North Wales. At the same time, a similar dog, the "Old English Broken Haired" Terrier, was being bred in northern England. The two strains were so similar that when they began to be shown, the same dog could compete successfully as either breed, and they were classified together. Eventually, they all became known as Welsh Terriers, regardless of their origin. After all, both strains had shared similar backgrounds and were used to hunt otter, fox, and badger. In 1886, the English Kennel Club recognized

ILLUSTRATED STANDARD

1 Head rectangular
2 Small, almond-shaped eyes
3 Small, V-shaped ears, folding just above level of skull
4 Level topline
5 Tail carried upright, docked to level of occiput
6 Small cat feet

Color: deep tan with black or grizzle jacket
DQ: none

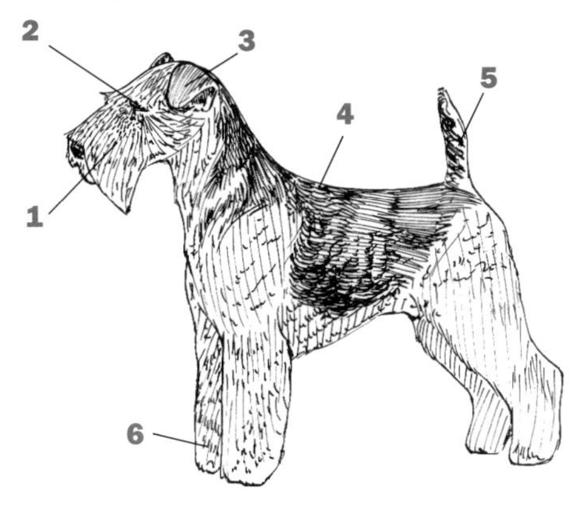

the breed. The early dogs were too rough to be competitive in the show ring, and breeders sought to improve the Welsh's lines not only by selective breeding but also with crosses to the racier Wire Fox Terrier. The result was a dog that in some ways resembles a miniature Airedale Terrier. It became a competitive show dog, but for some reason it has never attained the heights of show ring success that similar small, long-legged terriers have achieved.

TEMPERAMENT

The Welsh, although more mild-mannered than many terriers, is still playful and mischievous enough to provide plenty of entertainment and challenges, yet it is calm enough to be a reliable house pet. It is independent, inquisitive, and sensitive, reserved with strangers, and possibly scrappy with other dogs and pets. It needs daily exercise in a safe area. Unquestioning obedience is not its forte. It tends to dig and bark.

UPKEEP

The Welsh Terrier needs a moderate walk on leash every day or an invigorating play session. If allowed to run off leash, it should be in a safe area because it tends to hunt. The coat does not shed. Its wiry jacket needs combing two to three times weekly, plus shaping every three months. Shaping for pets is by clipping, and for show dogs is by stripping. Clipping softens the coat texture and alters the color. The ears of puppies may need to be trained in order to ensure proper adult shape.

HEALTH

- Major concerns: none
- Minor concerns: lens luxation, glaucoma
- Occasionally seen: allergies, seizures
- Suggested tests: eye
- Life span: 12–14 years

FORM AND FUNCTION

This is a square-proportioned, compact, sturdy dog of medium size, capable of running at good speed for long distances and then bolting or dispatching its quarry. Its gait is free and effortless, with good reach and drive. The large teeth are set in powerful vise-like jaws for gripping and killing tough quarry. Its coat is double, with a short, soft undercoat for insultion and a hard, dense, wiry outer coat for protection. The expression and demeanor are confident and alert.

West Highland White Terrier

AT A GLANCE

Energy level:	■■■■	Watchdog ability:	■■■■	POPULARITY: Popular
Exercise requirements:	■■■	Protection ability:	■	FAMILY: Terrier
Playfulness:	■■■	Grooming requirements:	■■■■	AREA OF ORIGIN: Scotland
Affection level:	■■■■■	Cold tolerance:	■■■	DATE OF ORIGIN: 1800s
Friendliness toward dogs:	■■■	Heat tolerance:	■■■	ORIGINAL FUNCTION: Fox, badger, and vermin hunting
Friendliness toward other pets:	■■■			
Friendliness toward strangers:	■■■■	WEIGHT: male: 15–21 lb*		TODAY'S FUNCTION: Earthdog trials
Ease of training:	■■■■	HEIGHT: male: 11″; female: 10″		OTHER NAME: Poltalloch Terrier

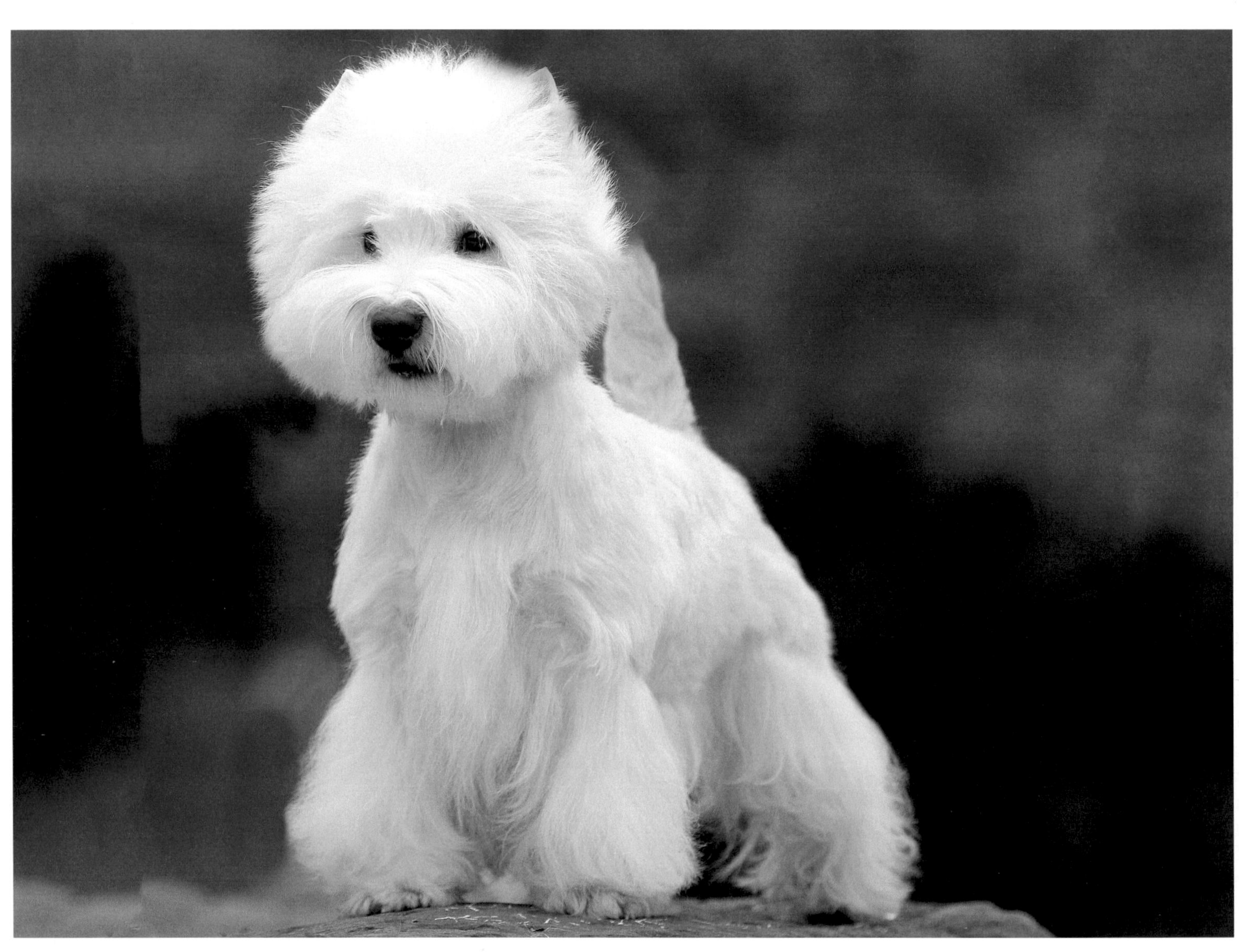

HISTORY

The West Highland White Terrier shares its roots with the other terriers of Scotland, proving itself on fox, badger, and various vermin. At one time the Westie, Skye, Cairn, and Scottish Terriers were all considered one breed with considerable diversity. Selective breeding based on such qualities as coat type or color could have produced distinctive strains that would have been easily maintained in the relative isolation of the various parts of the Scottish mainland and the western islands of the country. The Westie first gained attention in 1907 as the Poltalloch Terrier, named for the home of Col. E.D. Malcolm, who had been breeding the short-legged white terriers for many years. The breed has gone under several different names, including Roseneath, Poltalloch, White Scottish, Little Skye, and Cairn. In fact, the

ILLUSTRATED STANDARD

1 Muzzle blunt
2 Medium-sized, almond-shaped eyes
3 Stop defined
4 Head appears round
5 Small, erect, pointed ears
6 Relatively short, carrot-shaped tail, carried gaily but not over back
7 Feet round

Color: white
DQ: none

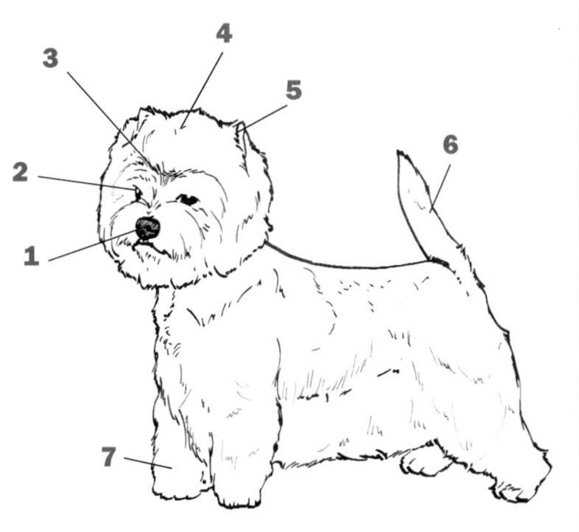

FORM AND FUNCTION

The Westie is compact and short coupled. It must be small enough to fit between rocks in a narrow passageway that was the typical fox den in its area of origin. These passages were often so narrow that the dog could not turn around. Short legs aided in maneuverability in the cramped passages. It had to have formidable teeth and jaws in order to face a fox in closed quarters. The harsh double coat, especially the hard, straight outer coat, provided protection from the fox's teeth, especially around the head, as well as from the elements. The tail needed to be sufficiently long to provide a handhold by which the dog could be pulled from shallow holes.

AKC first registered it as the Roseneath Terrier in 1908, but the name was changed to West Highland White Terrier in 1909. Since that date it has made quite a name for itself, establishing itself as one of the most competitive terriers in the show ring and one of the most popular terriers in the home.

TEMPERAMENT

The busy Westie is happy, curious, and always in the thick of things. It is affectionate and demanding, one of the friendliest terriers. It is not friendly, however, toward small animals. It enjoys a daily romp in a safe area or a walk on lead, as well as playtime at home. It is independent and somewhat stubborn. It can be vocal and can dig.

UPKEEP

The Westie enjoys the outdoors, but it can also function as an indoor dog if taken for regular exercise. It needs either a short to moderate walk on leash or a good game in the yard every day. Its wire coat needs combing two or three times weekly, plus shaping every three months. Shaping for pets is by clipping, and for show dogs is by stripping. In some areas, it may be difficult to keep the coat white.

HEALTH

- Major concerns: globoid cell leukodystrophy, Legg–Perthes, CMO, skin disease
- Minor concerns: copper toxicosis, cataract, patellar luxation, KCS
- Occasionally seen: deafness
- Suggested tests: hip, knee, eye
- Life span: 12–14 years

These breeds are the miniature versions of the dog world. Many of them are quite ancient, attesting to the value people have long placed in dogs for the sake of companionship and adornment. It is difficult to ascribe behavioral characteristics to the entire group because many of these dogs are basically miniaturized versions of dogs from other groups, although several others are of such ancient origin that they cannot be traced to their larger ancestors. They are the products of generations of selection for companionship.

THE TOY GROUP

Affenpinscher

AT A GLANCE

Energy level:	■■■■	Watchdog ability:	■■■■■
Exercise requirements:	■■■	Protection ability:	■
Playfulness:	■■■■	Grooming requirements:	■■■■
Affection level:	■■■■	Cold tolerance:	■■
Friendliness toward dogs:	■■■	Heat tolerance:	■■
Friendliness toward other pets:	■■■		
Friendliness toward strangers:	■■■	WEIGHT: 7–9 lb*	
Ease of training:	■■■	HEIGHT: 9.5–11.5″	

POPULARITY: Rare
FAMILY: Pinscher
AREA OF ORIGIN: Germany
DATE OF ORIGIN: 1600s
ORIGINAL FUNCTION: Small vermin hunting, lapdog
TODAY'S FUNCTION: Companion
OTHER NAME: None

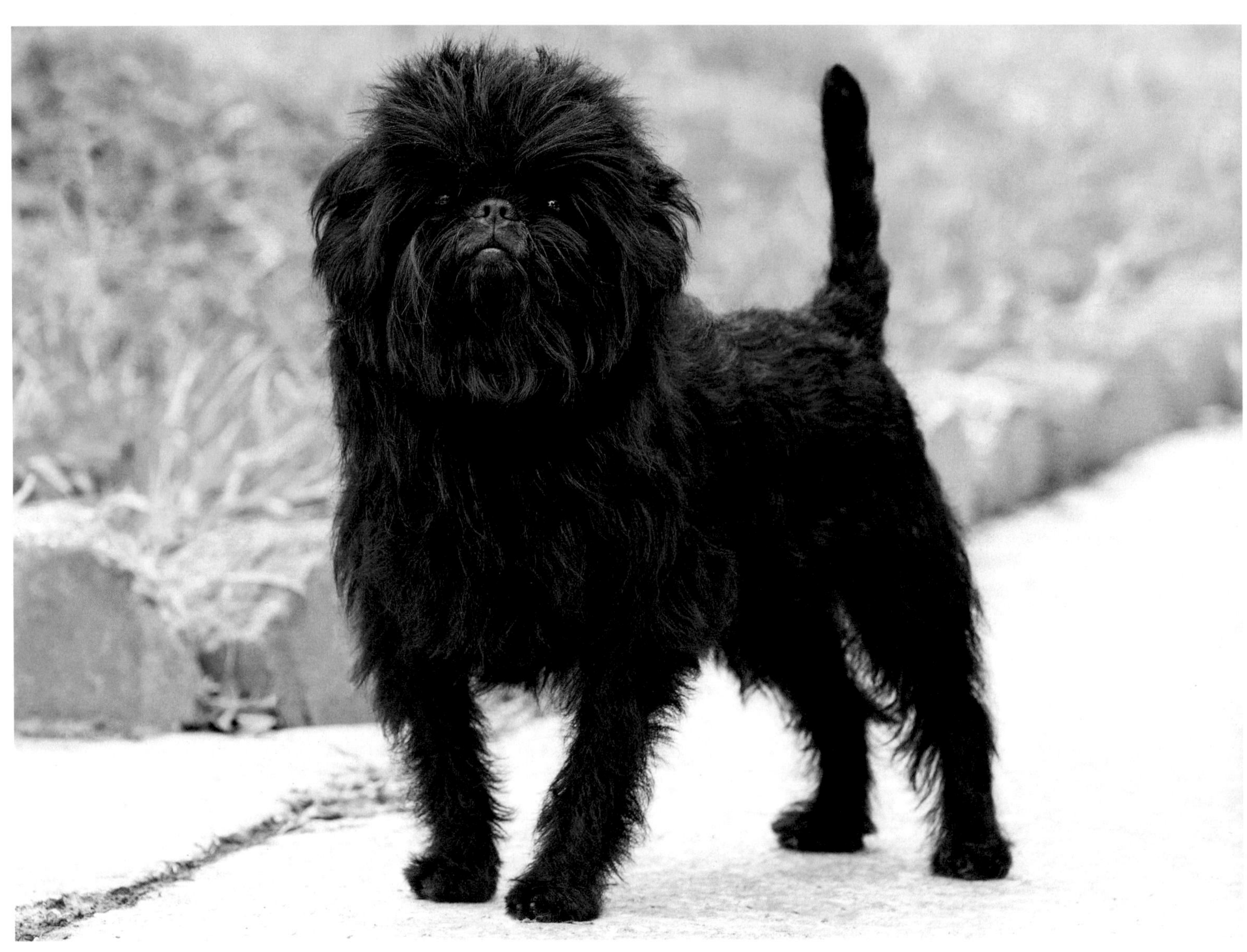

HISTORY

The Affenpinscher's name describes it well: Affen meaning monkey and Pinscher meaning terrier. In France the Affenpinscher is known as the "diablotin moustachu"—moustached little devil, which also aptly describes it! As one of the oldest toy breeds, the Affenpinscher's origins are obscure. Paintings by the old Dutch Masters from the fifteenth century often included dogs resembling Affenpinschers, but more definite evidence of the breed is absent. Small terriers adept at dispatching rats were abundant in central Europe by the seventeenth century. In Germany, they were used to rid stables and kitchens of rodents. Even smaller versions of these dogs were preferred for lady's lap dogs, able to kill mice in the home, warm their mistress' lap, and amuse the entire house-

ILLUSTRATED STANDARD

1 Slightly undershot bite; level acceptable
2 Short muzzle
3 Domed skull, well-defined stop
4 Ears either cropped to a point and erect, or uncropped and erect, semi-erect, or drop
5 Topline straight and level
6 Tail natural or docked 1–2″ long, carried erect
7 Small round feet

Color: black, gray, silver, red, black and tan, or beige; with or without black mask
DQ: none

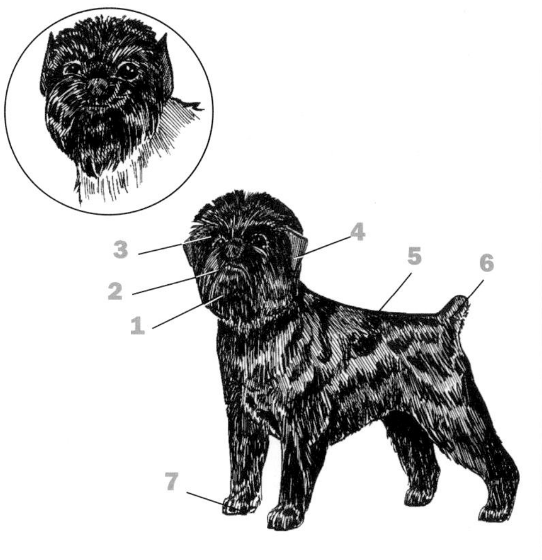

hold with their antics. This small version eventually became the Affenpinscher, which was later refined by occasional crosses with the Pug, German Pinscher, and German Silky Pinscher. The Affenpinscher in turn became the progenitor of other wire-coated toys, most notably the Brussels Griffon. The breed was most popular in Germany, which can lay claim as its homeland. In 1936 the AKC recognized the Affenpinscher, but World War II slowed any momentum in popularity the breed had gained. Since then, the breed has remained extremely rare even in America and Germany, its comparative strongholds.

TEMPERAMENT

The Affenpinscher lives up to its name monkey terrier in both looks and actions. It is a terrier at heart, busy, inquisitive, bold, and stubborn, but it also loves to monkey around, being playful and mischievous. It tends to bark and even climb. Unlike most terriers, it is fairly good with other dogs and pets. This little dog is best with a family that likes entertainment and has a very good sense of humor.

UPKEEP

Although an energetic and active dog, the exercise needs of the Affenpinscher can be met with vigorous indoor games or romps in the yard, or with short walks on leash. Its harsh coat needs combing two or three times weekly, plus shaping every three months. Shaping for pets is by clipping, whereas show dogs require stripping.

HEALTH

- Major concerns: none
- Minor concerns: patellar luxation, corneal ulcers
- Occasionally seen: PDA, open fontanel, respiratory difficulties, Legg-Perthes
- Suggested tests: knee, eye
- Life span: 12–14 years

FORM AND FUNCTION

The Affenpinscher is square-proportioned, compact and sturdy, with medium bone. It is a smaller version of a working terrier, and as such is not a delicate dog. This is an active, tough dog that is agile enough to catch and dispatch rats and mice. The gait is light, sound, and confident. The Affenpinscher has a monkey-like facial expression with long eyebrows and beard, which lends it an air of comic seriousness. Its rough coat is about 1 inch long on the body, somewhat longer on the head, neck, chest, stomach and legs. This coat type provided protection from vermin and harsh conditions.

Brussels Griffon

AT A GLANCE

Energy level:	■■■■
Exercise requirements:	■■
Playfulness:	■■■■
Affection level:	■■■■
Friendliness toward dogs:	■■■
Friendliness toward other pets:	■■■
Friendliness toward strangers:	■■
Ease of training:	■■■

Watchdog ability:	■■■■■
Protection ability:	■
Grooming requirements:	
Smooth:	■
Rough:	■■■■
Cold tolerance:	■■
Heat tolerance:	■

WEIGHT: 8–10 lb
HEIGHT: 9–11″*

POPULARITY: Somewhat uncommon
FAMILY: Pinscher
AREA OF ORIGIN: Belgium
DATE OF ORIGIN: 1800s
ORIGINAL FUNCTION: Small vermin hunting, companion
TODAY'S FUNCTION: Companion
OTHER NAME: Griffon Belge, Griffon Bruxellois, Belgian Griffon

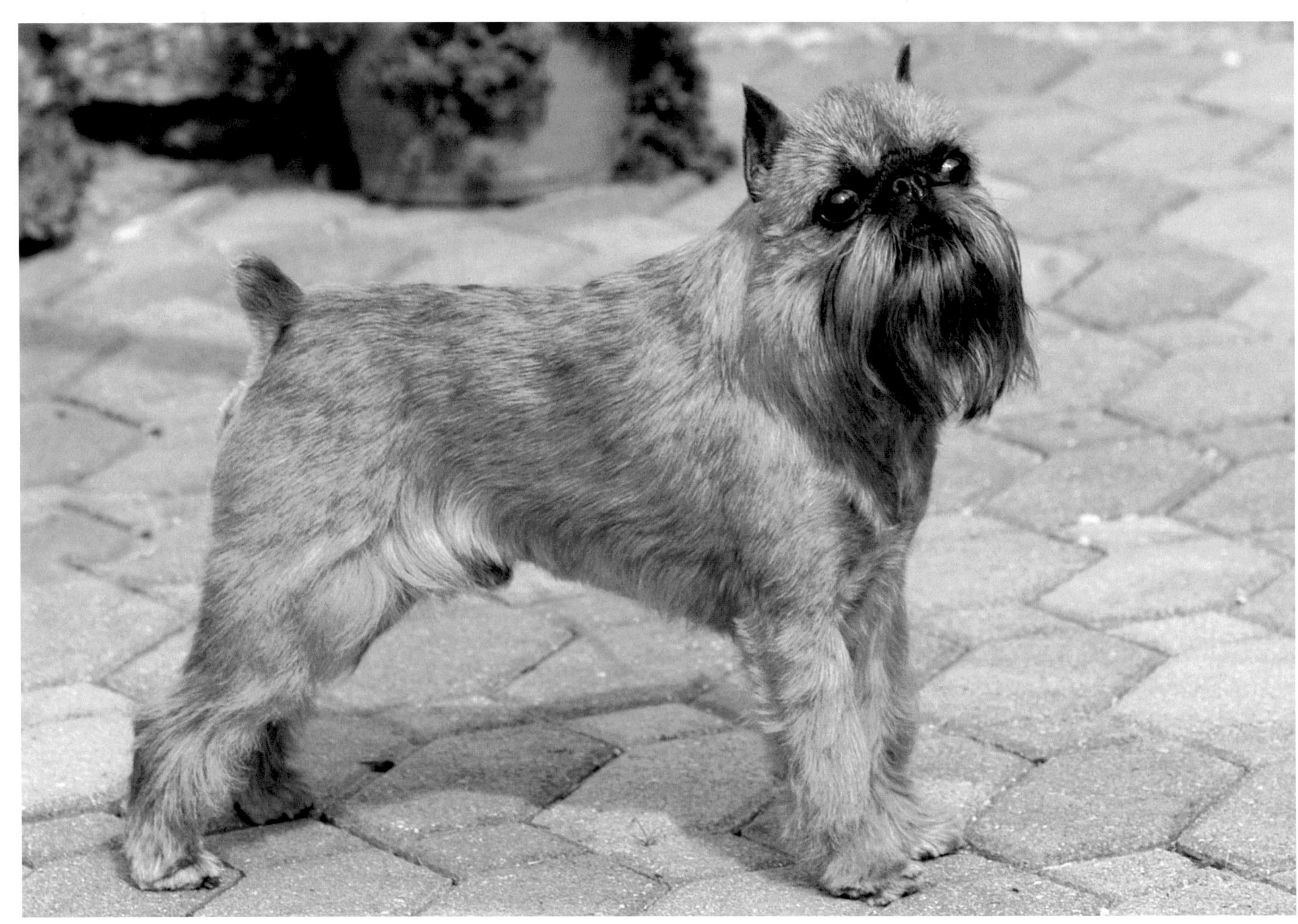

HISTORY

A product of Belgium, the Brussels Griffon's forebears were probably the Affenpinscher and a Belgian street dog, the Griffon d'Ecurie (Stable Griffon). The breed gained favor as a guard of cabs in Brussels, where its cocky but comic demeanor was probably more effective at attracting riders than dissuading robbers. In the late 1800s, this mixture was then crossed with the Pug, at that time extremely popular in neighboring Holland. The Pug crosses account for the brachycephalic head type and for the smooth-coated individuals of the breed, known then (and still in some countries) as the Petit Brabancon. Although the smooths were initially destroyed (after all, griffon means wiry), they were soon after accepted. By 1880, the breed was sufficiently established to be recognized

ILLUSTRATED STANDARD

1 Undershot
2 Very large eyes
3 Round skull with deep stop
4 Ears small, high-set, cropped or natural; if natural, semi-erect
5 Back level and short
6 Tail docked to about one-third, held high
7 Small, round feet

Color: red, belge (mixed reddish brown and black), black and tan, or black
DQ: dudley or butterfly nose, overshot, hanging tongue, white spot or blaze anywhere on coat

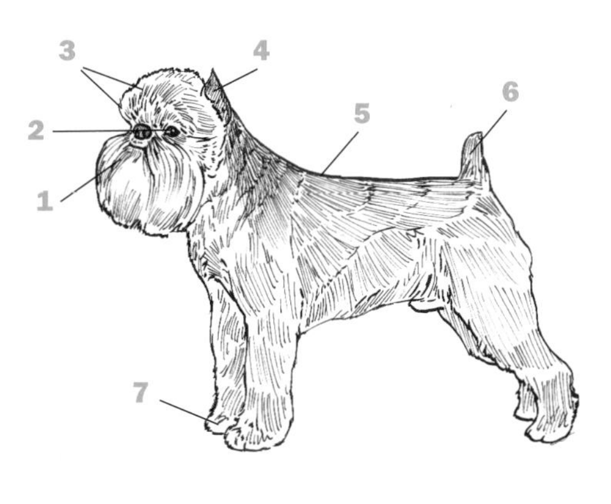

at Belgian dog shows. Around this same time there is some suggestion that additional crosses were made with the Yorkshire Terrier and English Toy Spaniel, the latter further contributing to the Brussels Griffon's head configuration. By the early 1900s, the little street urchin had risen to the heights of popularity in Belgium and found itself in great demand by nobility. Although its numbers were decimated by World War I, the breed recovered and has since gained ardent admirers around the world. In some countries, only the red rough-coated dogs are classified as the Brussels Griffon; black rough-coated dogs are known as the Belgian Griffon; and smooth-coated dogs are known as the Petit Brabancon.

TEMPERAMENT
The spunky Brussels Griffon is full of itself, brimming with self-confidence and gusto. It is bold, playful, stubborn, and mischievous. It is usually good with other dogs and pets. It tends to bark and climb, and some can be escape artists. It make a saucy companion for a family wanting an entertaining, sensitive pet. However, sensitivity and size make it a poor choice for families with young children. It can be difficult to housetrain and may suffer from separation anxiety.

UPKEEP
The Brussels Griffon is an active breed, always on the lookout for action. It needs daily mental and physical stimulation, but its small size makes such stimulation possible with a robust indoor game. It also enjoys a short walk on leash. The rough coat needs combing two or three times weekly, plus shaping by stripping every three months. Grooming for the smooth coat is minimal, consisting only of occasional brushing to remove dead hair.

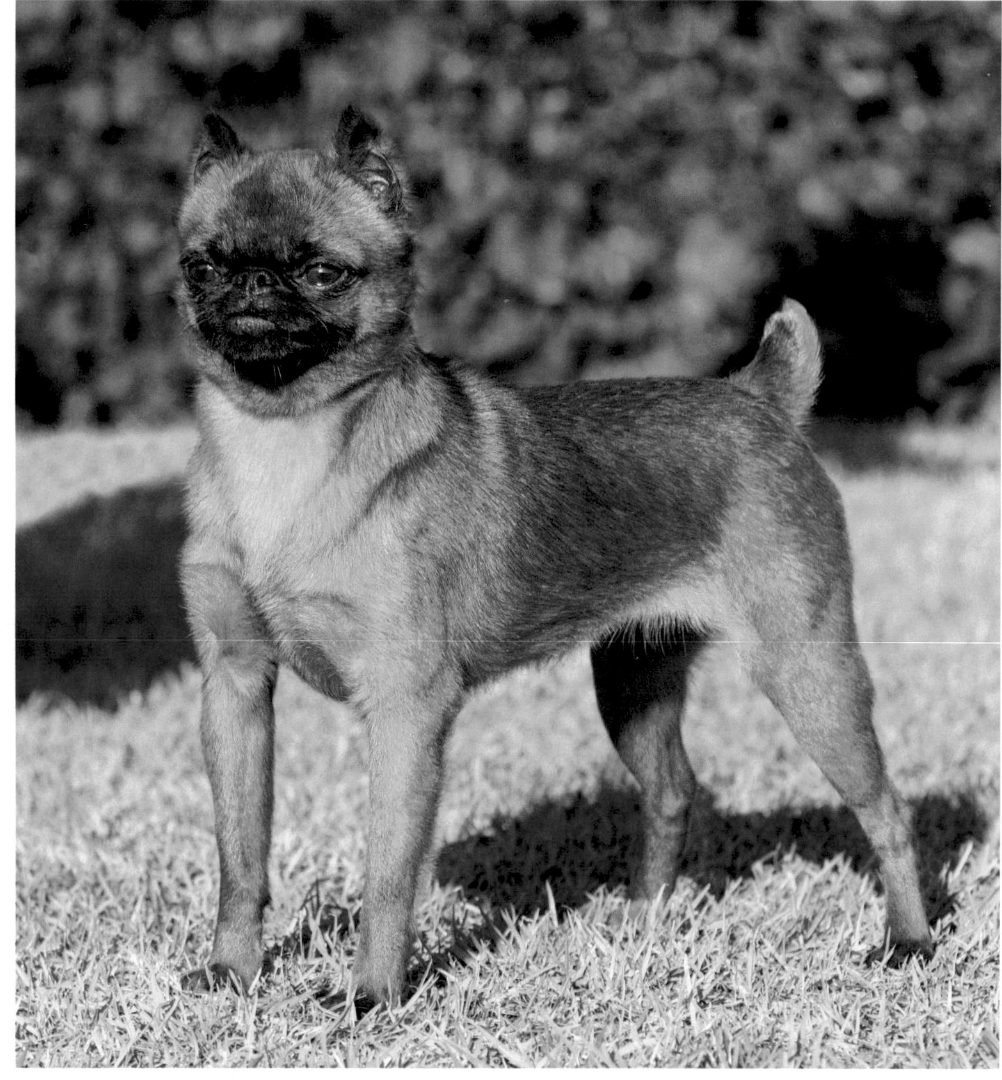

HEALTH
- Major concerns: none
- Minor concerns: none
- Occasionally seen: weak bladder, patellar luxation, distichiasis, cataracts, PRA, CHD, Legg-Perthes
- Suggested tests: eye, (hip), knee
- Life span: 12–15 years
- Note: Caesarean sections are often required.

FORM AND FUNCTION
The Brussels Griffon is square-proportioned, thickset, and compact. It has good bone for its size. Its movement is a purposeful trot, with moderate reach and drive. In temperament it is full of self-importance, and its carriage reflects this attitude. Its almost human expression attracts attention and admirers. Its coat can be rough, with hard wiry hair, which is longer around the head; or smooth, with a short glossy coat.

Cavalier King Charles Spaniel

AT A GLANCE

Energy level:	■■■	Watchdog ability:	■■■	POPULARITY: Very popular
Exercise requirements:	■■■	Protection ability:	■	FAMILY: Spaniel
Playfulness:	■■■■	Grooming requirements:	■■■	AREA OF ORIGIN: England
Affection level:	■■■■■	Cold tolerance:	■■■	DATE OF ORIGIN: 1600s
Friendliness toward dogs:	■■■■■	Heat tolerance:	■■	ORIGINAL FUNCTION: Flushing small birds, lapdog
Friendliness toward other pets:	■■■■■			
Friendliness toward strangers:	■■■■■	WEIGHT: 13–18 lb		TODAY'S FUNCTION: Companion
Ease of training:	■■■■	HEIGHT: 12–13″		OTHER NAME: None

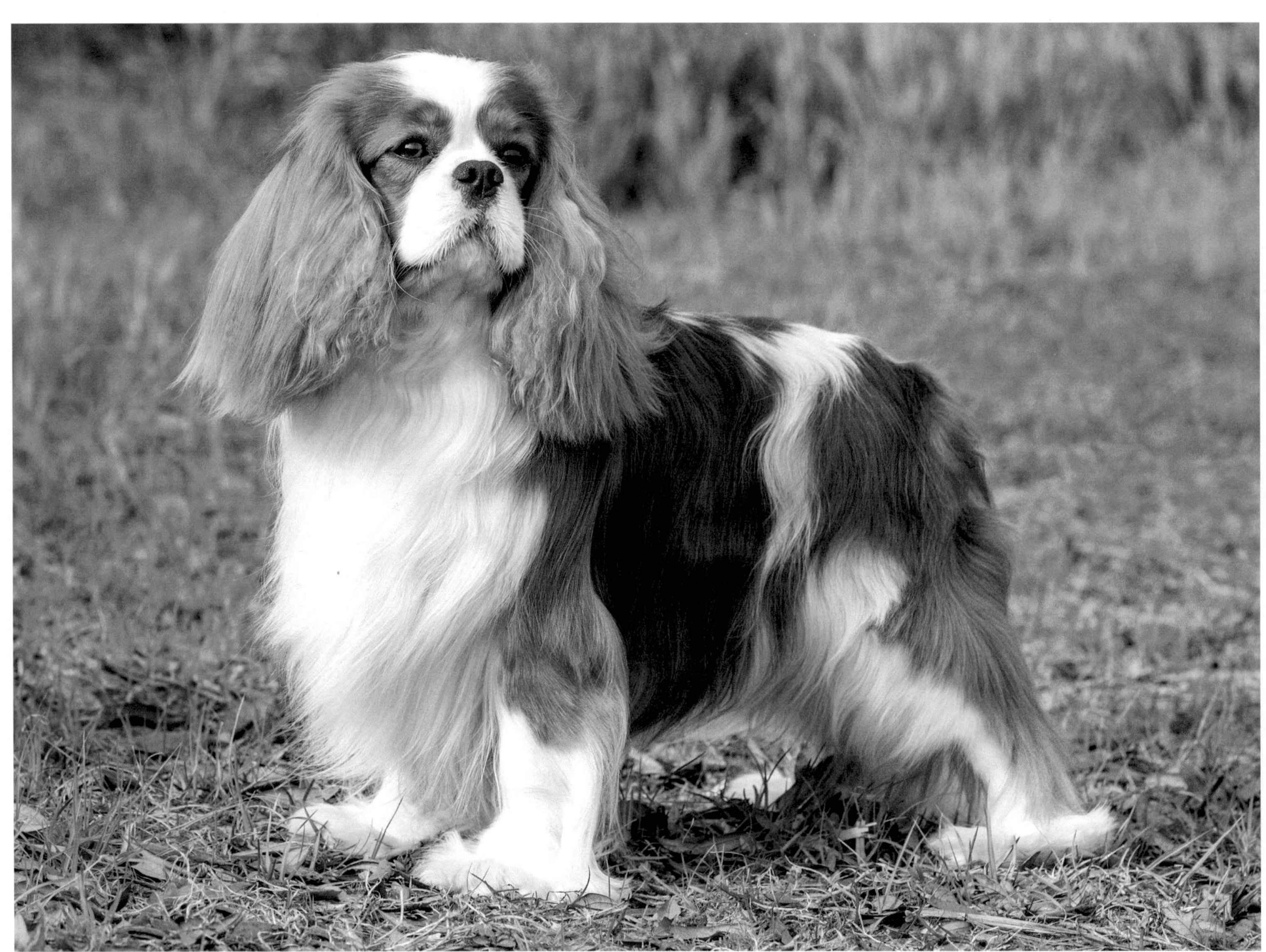

HISTORY

As its name implies, the Cavalier King Charles Spaniel is derived from spaniel roots. The European toy dogs were probably the result of breeding small spaniels to Oriental toy breeds such as the Japanese Chin and perhaps the Tibetan Spaniel. These Tudor lapdogs, known as "comforter spaniels," served as lap and foot warmers, and even surrogate hot water bottles. In addition, they served the vital function of attracting fleas from their owners' bodies! The toy spaniels became especially popular because they appealed to all members of the family. In the 1700s, King Charles II was so enamored with his toy spaniels that he was accused of ignoring matters of state in favor of his dogs. The dogs were so closely associated with him that they became known as King Charles Spaniels. After his death, the

ILLUSTRATED STANDARD

1 Full muzzle
2 Large, round eyes, with cushioning beneath
3 Ears high-set and long
4 Level topline
5 Compact seat with long hair
6 Tail carried happily and in motion when the dog is moving; may be docked with no more than one third removed
7 Long feathering on feet

Color: ruby (solid red), Blenheim (red and white), black and tan, tricolor
DQ: none

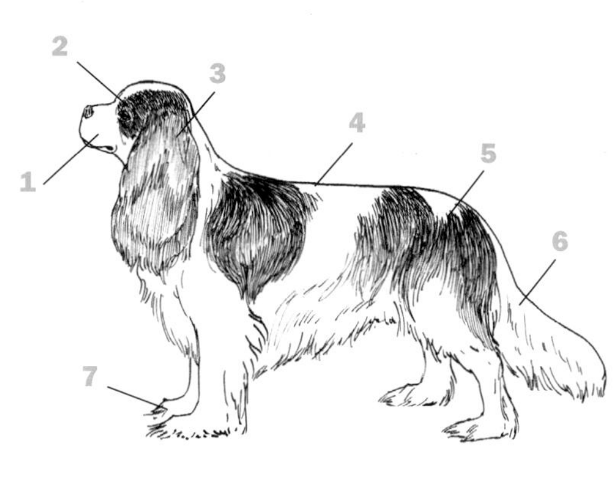

Duke of Marlborough took over as the major advocate of the breed; the red and white "Blenheim" color, which was his favorite, is named after his estate. The King Charles Spaniel continued to grace the homes of the wealthy for generations, but with time a shorter-nosed dog was preferred. By the early 1900s, the few dogs that resembled the early members of the breed were considered to be inferior. A twist of fate occurred when a wealthy American, Roswell Eldridge, came to England and offered outlandish prize money for the best "pointed-nosed" spaniels, most resembling the old type. Breeders bred their old-type dogs together in an effort to gain the prize, and in so doing, many came to appreciate the old type. Ironically, these dogs, named Cavalier King Charles Spaniels in honor of the Cavalier King, eventually outstripped their short-nosed counterparts in popularity, becoming one of the most popular breeds in England. They were slower to catch on in America, and many Cavalier owners fought AKC recognition in an effort to control the problems that so often accompany popularity. In 1996, the AKC recognized the Cavalier. Its popularity continues to grow.

TEMPERAMENT

The Cavalier in many ways fits the bill as an ideal house pet. It is sweet, gentle, playful, willing to please, affectionate, and quiet. It equally enjoys sharing time on the couch or on a walk. It neither digs nor barks excessively. It is amiable toward other dogs, pets, and strangers. Outdoors, its spaniel heritage kicks in, and it loves to explore, sniff, and chase.

UPKEEP

The Cavalier needs a fair amount of exercise every day, either in the form of a moderate walk on leash or a romp in a safe area. Its long coat needs brushing every other day.

HEALTH

- Major concerns: mitral valve insufficiency, CHD, syringomelia
- Minor concerns: patellar luxation, entropion
- Occasionally seen: retinal dysplasia
- Suggested tests: cardiac, hip, knee, eye
- Life span: 9–14 years

FORM AND FUNCTION

The Cav is an elegant, royal, toy spaniel, slightly longer than tall, with moderate bones. It retains the build of a working spaniel, yet in a smaller version. Its gait is free and elegant, with good reach and drive. Its silky coat is of moderate length, with a slight wave permissible. Long feathering on the feet is a breed characteristic. A hallmark of the breed is its gentle, sweet, melting expression.

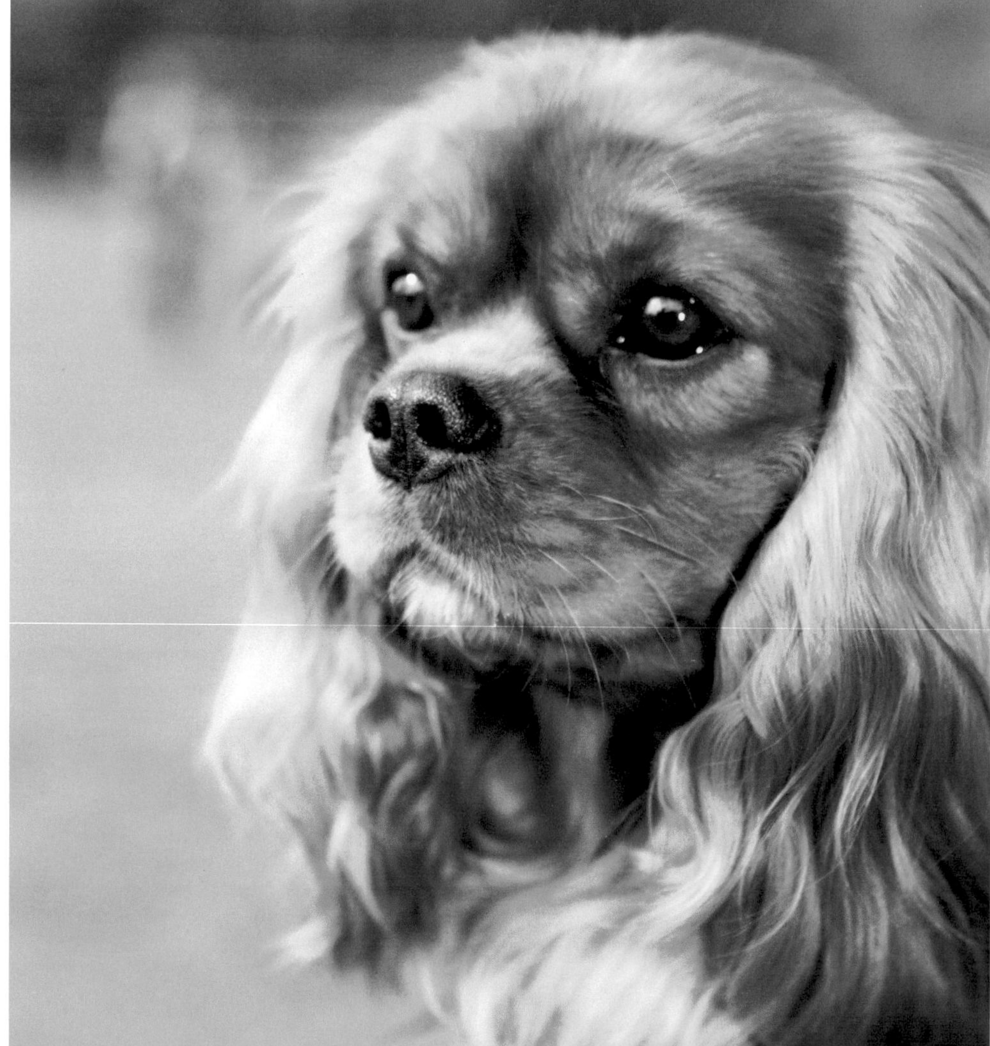

Chihuahua

AT A GLANCE

Energy level:	■■■■■	Watchdog ability:	■■■■■	POPULARITY: Very Popular
Exercise requirements:	■	Protection ability:	■	FAMILY: Primitive
Playfulness:	■■	Grooming requirements:		AREA OF ORIGIN: Mexico
Affection level:	■■	Smooth:	■	DATE OF ORIGIN: 1500s
Friendliness toward dogs:	■	Long:	■■	ORIGINAL FUNCTION: Ceremonial
Friendliness toward other pets:	■■■	Cold tolerance:	■	TODAY'S FUNCTION: Companion
Friendliness toward strangers:	■	Heat tolerance:	■■■■	OTHER NAME: None
Ease of training:	■■			

WEIGHT: not to exceed 6 lb
HEIGHT: 6–9"*

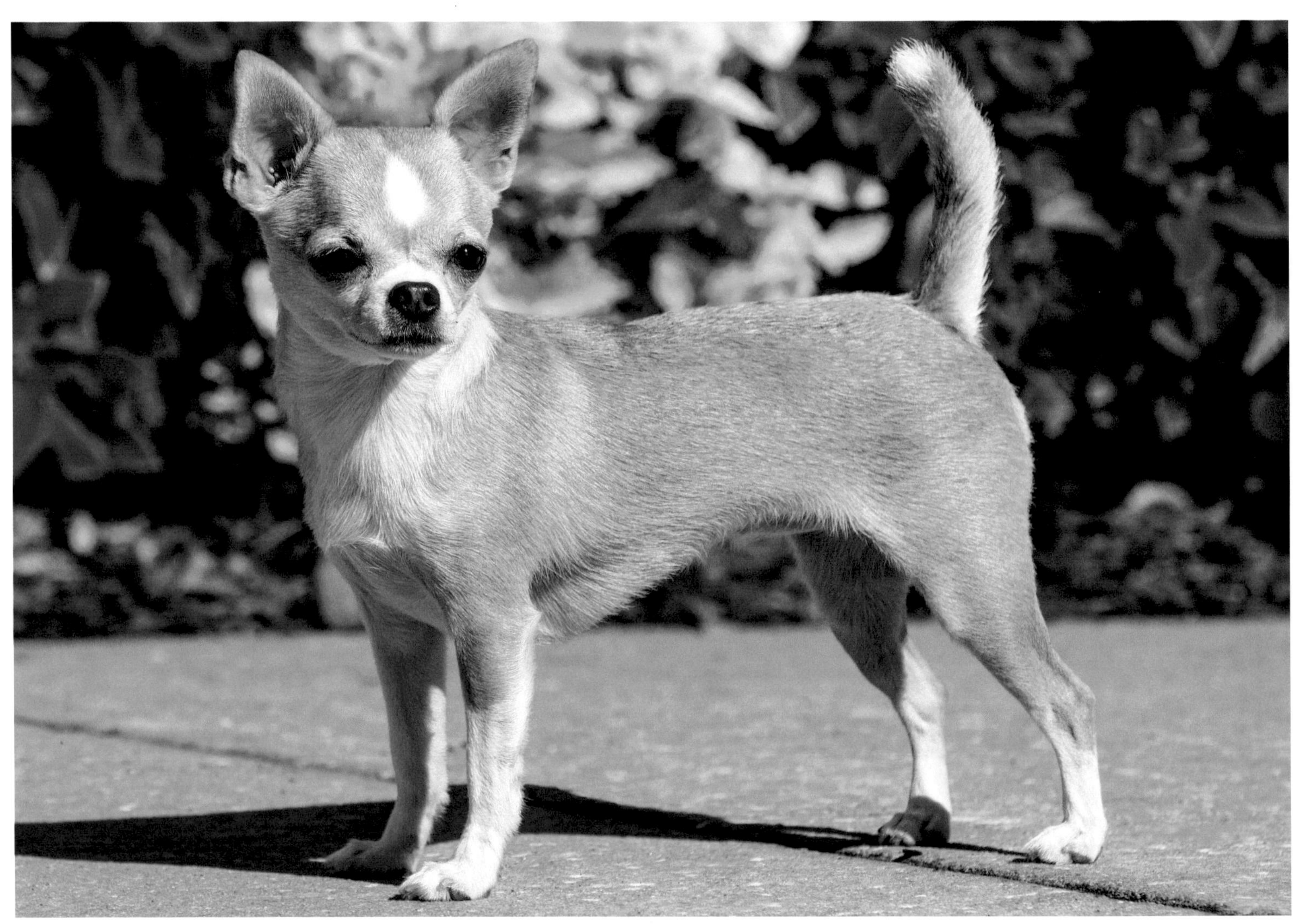

HISTORY

The smallest breed of dog, the Chihuahua has a controversial history. One theory holds that it originated in China and was brought to the New World by Spanish traders, where it was then crossed with small native dogs. The other theory contends that it originated entirely in Central and South America, descending from the native Techichi, a small mute dog that was sometimes sacrificed in Toltec religious rituals. A small red dog was believed to guide the soul to the underworld, and every Aztec family kept such a dog that was sacrificed and buried with any deceased family member. To make matters worse for the Techichi, the Toltecs and their conquerors, the Aztecs, often ate dogs and the Techichi may have sometimes been on the menu. Despite what may have been short lives,

ILLUSTRATED STANDARD

1 Moderately short, slightly pointed muzzle
2 Apple dome skull
3 Large, erect ears
4 Level topline
5 Tail carried either up, out, or over the back
6 Dainty feet

Color: any
DQ: over 6 lb in weight; broken down or cropped ears; cropped tail, bobtail; in long coats, too thin coat that resembles bareness

the Techichis apparently were well cared for during life by the priests or their families. In fact, the most likely origin of the Chihuahua is a combination of these theories: the native Techichi was probably crossed with tiny hairless Chinese dogs, but again the date when this occurred is controversial. The Chinese dogs may have been brought over when a land bridge spanned the Bering Strait, or they may have been brought later by Spanish traders. When Cortes conquered the Aztecs in the sixteenth century, the little dogs were abandoned and left to fend for themselves. About 300 years later, in 1850, three tiny dogs were found in Chihuahua, Mexico. A few were brought to the United States, but they aroused only moderate attention. Only when Xavier Cugat ("the rhumba king") appeared in public with a Chihuahua as his constant companion did the breed capture the public's hearts. It experienced a meteoric rise in popularity and has continued as one of America's most popular breeds.

TEMPERAMENT

The saucy Chihuahua has earned its place as a favored toy dog because of its intense devotion to a single person. It is reserved with strangers but good with other household dogs and pets. Some try to be protective, but they are not very effective. Some may be quite bold; others may be timid. It is often temperamental. Some bark.

UPKEEP

The Chihuahua is a lively dog that nonetheless can get its exercise running from room to room indoors. It enjoys exploring the yard or going for a short walk on leash and especially enjoys accompanying its owner on outings. It hates the cold and seeks out warmth. Coat care for the smooth is minimal. Care of the long coat entails brushing two to three times a week.

HEALTH

- Major concerns: none
- Minor concerns: pulmonic stenosis, hydrocephalus, patellar luxation, KCS, hypoglycemia
- Occasionally seen: none
- Suggested tests: cardiac, knee, eye
- Life span: 14–18 years
- Note: A soft spot (molera) in the skull (due to incomplete fontanel closure) is a common breed trait.

FORM AND FUNCTION

The Chihuahua is graceful, small, and compact, slightly longer than it is tall. It has a saucy expression and alert, terrier-like attitude. It should move out at a swift pace with good reach and drive. Its coat can be smooth, with soft, glossy hair, or long, with soft straight or wavy coats and fringed ears.

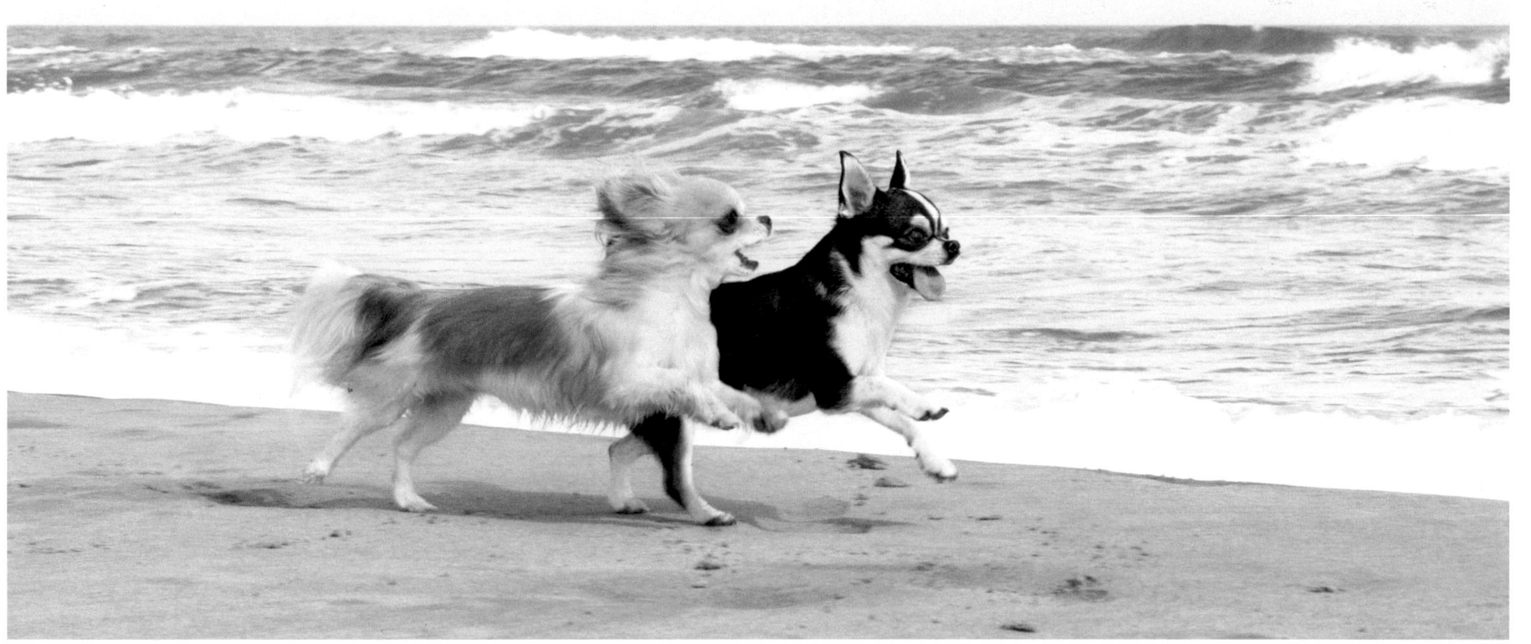

Chinese Crested Dog

AT A GLANCE

Energy level: ■■■
Exercise requirements: ■
Playfulness: ■■■■
Affection level: ■■■■
Friendliness toward dogs: ■■■
Friendliness toward other pets: ■■■■■
Friendliness toward strangers: ■■■■■
Ease of training: ■■■

Watchdog ability: ■■■■
Protection ability: ■
Grooming requirements:
Hairless: ■■■
Powderpuff: ■■■
Cold tolerance: ■
Heat tolerance: ■■■■

WEIGHT: 5–12 lb*
HEIGHT: 11–13″

POPULARITY: Somewhat popular
FAMILY: Primative, hairless
AREA OF ORIGIN: China
DATE OF ORIGIN: 1200s
ORIGINAL FUNCTION: Ratter, lapdog, curio
TODAY'S FUNCTION: Companion
OTHER NAME: None

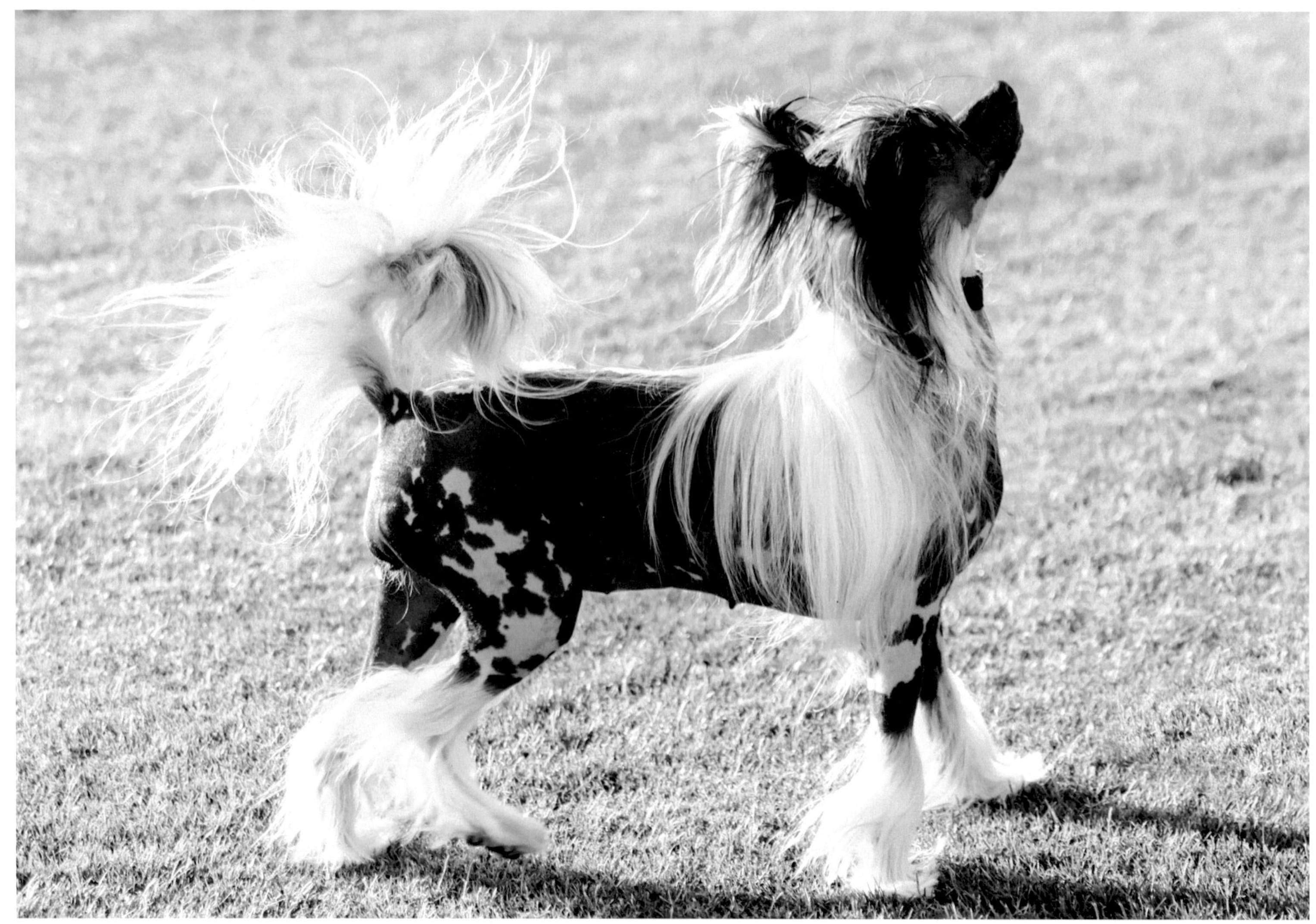

HISTORY

The origins of the Chinese Crested are difficult to trace. Hairless dogs seem to arise by mutation all over the world, but they have been principally perpetuated in Central and South America. The Chinese Crested is the exception, apparently arising in Africa and brought to China as early as the thirteenth century. Chinese seafarers are said to have kept the dogs on ship as non-flea-bearing ratters and curios and to trade them with local merchants wherever they called. Thus, the breed was distributed to Turkey, Egypt, South Africa, and possibly Central and South America. Only in the 1800s were they recorded in Europe, with paintings and later, photographs, including dogs of Chinese Crested type. In the late 1800s, the breed found a proponent in the American Ida Garrett, who popularized several types of hair-

ILLUSTRATED STANDARD

1 Almond-shaped eyes
2 Wedge-shaped head
3 Ears large and erect
4 Level topline with slightly sloping croup
5 Tail carried gaily
6 Moderate tuck-up
7 Breastbone is not prominent
8 Hare feet

Color: any
DQ: none

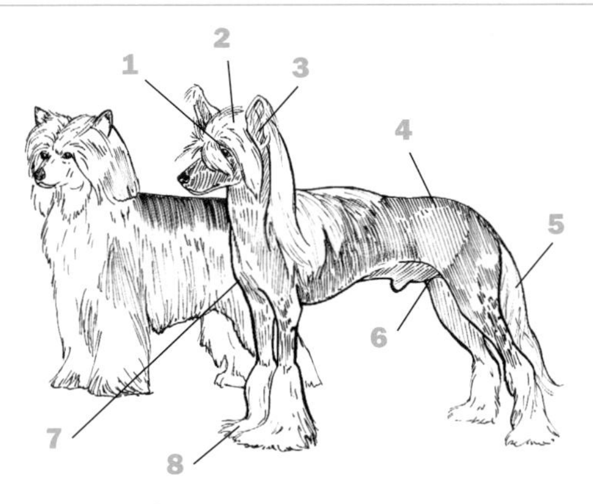

less dogs. With the help of a handful of committed breeders (including the famed Gypsy Rose Lee), the Chinese Crested gradually gained admirers in both America and Europe. In 1991—after a century of effort—the breed was recognized by the AKC. The Chinese Crested quickly became popular with dog showing enthusiasts, but the breed has been slower to attract average pet owners. As the breed gets more exposure, this situation is almost certain to change.

TEMPERAMENT

The Chinese Crested is a combination of playful pixie, gentle lapdog, and sensitive companion. It is devoted to its family and willing to please; it is also good with other dogs, pets, and strangers. Its demeanor should be gay and alert.

UPKEEP

The Crested enjoys a romp outside, but it hates the cold. It is small enough that it can get sufficient exercise with vigorous inside games. Hairless varieties will need a sweater for cold weather outings. This is not a breed for outdoor living. Powderpuff coat care entails brushing every day or two. The muzzle is usually shaved every two weeks in Puffs. The Hairless needs regular skin care such as application of moisturizer, sun block, or bathing to combat blackheads. Most Hairless need some stray hairs that appear on the body to be removed prior to showing.

HEALTH

- Major concerns: PRA, glaucoma, lens luxation
- Minor concerns: deafness, seizures, patellar luxation
- Occasionally seen: Legg-Perthes
- Suggested tests: eye, hearing, knees, cardiac
- Life span: 13–15 years
- Note: The Hairless is susceptible to blackheads, sunburn, wool allergy, and tooth loss. The Hairless has irregular dentition and thinner enamel.

FORM AND FUNCTION

The Chinese Crested is fine boned and slender, among the most elegant and graceful of breeds. It is slightly longer than tall. Its gait is lively and agile. It has an alert, intense expression. In the Hairless variety, soft silky hair is found only on the head (crest), tail (plume), and feet and lower legs. The skin of the hairless areas is smooth and soft. In the Powderpuff the entire dog is covered with soft silky coat of moderate density and length. The hairless condition is caused by one dominant gene. Two such genes cause prenatal death. Thus, every hairless Crested has one gene for hairlessness and one for long hair. Powderpuffs have two genes for long hair.

English Toy Spaniel

AT A GLANCE

Energy level: ■
Exercise requirements: ■
Playfulness: ■ ■ ■
Affection level: ■ ■
Friendliness toward dogs: ■ ■ ■ ■
Friendliness toward other pets: ■ ■ ■ ■
Friendliness toward strangers: ■ ■
Ease of training: ■ ■ ■

Watchdog ability: ■ ■ ■ ■
Protection ability: ■
Grooming requirements: ■ ■ ■
Cold tolerance: ■ ■ ■
Heat tolerance: ■

WEIGHT: 8–14 lb
HEIGHT: 10–11″*

POPULARITY: Rare
FAMILY: Spaniel, Companion
AREA OF ORIGIN: England
DATE OF ORIGIN: 1600s
ORIGINAL FUNCTION: Flushing small birds, lapdog
TODAY'S FUNCTION: Companion
OTHER NAME: King Charles Spaniel

HISTORY

The English Toy Spaniel and the Cavalier King Charles Spaniel share identical early histories. They began as one breed, probably resulting from crosses of small spaniels with Oriental toy breeds. Some evidence supports the theory that Mary, Queen of Scots, brought the first toy spaniels to Scotland with her from France. These "comforter spaniels" became very popular with the wealthy classes, and served as foot and lap warmers as well as delightful companions. They reached their height of early popularity during the seventeenth century reign of King Charles II, who so doted on his dogs that the breed was soon being called King Charles Spaniels—the name by which the breed is still known in England. These early dogs were all black and tan; other colors were developed later, with the first Duke of

ILLUSTRATED STANDARD

1 Slightly undershot
2 Broad, square jaw
3 Large eyes
4 Domed skull with deep stop
5 Large head with a plush, chubby look
6 Low-set, long ears, fringed with heavy feathering
7 Tail docked 2–4″ in length, carried at or slightly above horizontal, with long, silky hair

Color: solid red, black and tan, or either of these colors on a white background
DQ: none

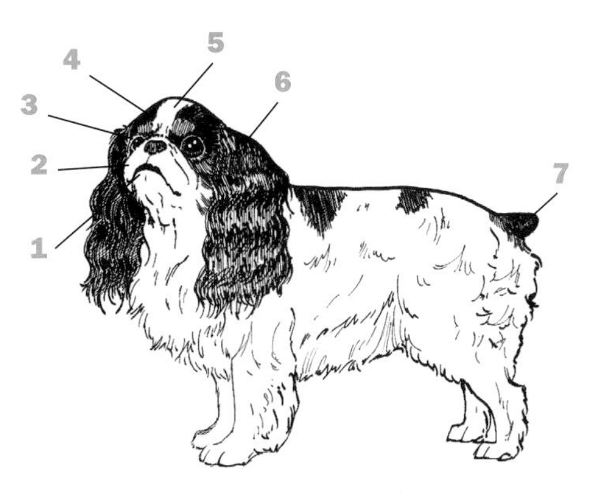

Marlborough credited with developing the red and white "Blenheims," named after his estate. The red and white coloration may have come from crosses with Chinese Cocker Spaniels. The duke's spaniels were said to be good hunting dogs for woodcock. Most proponents of the breed were more interested in having an eye-catching lapdog than a hunting dog, and in the ensuing centuries the King Charles Spaniel was bred down in size and selected for a rounder head and flatter nose. In America, the name was changed to English Toy Spaniel and is shown as two varieties: the red particolored Blenheim and black and tan particolored Prince Charles, and the red solid-colored Ruby and black and tan solid-colored King Charles. Sometimes called "E.T.s" or "Charlies," the breed has continued to find favor with owners desiring an aristocratic but fun-loving lapdog.

TEMPERAMENT

The English Toy Spaniel enjoys rollicking romps. It is a lapdog par excellence, gentle, amiable, calm, and quiet, yet it is playful and attentive. It is devoted to its family and reserved with strangers. It is somewhat stubborn.

UPKEEP

Although it enjoys a nice walk on leash or a fun game in the house or yard, the English Toy Spaniel is not overly active and its exercise needs can be met with minimal effort. It does not do well in heat. Its long coat needs combing twice weekly.

HEALTH

- Major concerns: patellar luxation
- Minor concerns: early tooth loss, entropion
- Occasionally seen: PDA
- Suggested tests: (knee), eye, heart
- Life span: 10–12 years
- Note: A soft spot in the skull (due to incomplete fontanel closure) sometimes occurs in young dogs and is usually not a problem. Fused toes are not considered abnormal. Hydrocephalus occurs but may be overdiagnosed. The breed is sensitive to anesthesia.

FORM AND FUNCTION

Square-proportioned, compact and cobby, the English Toy Spaniel is profusely coated with a silky, flowing coat. The coat can be straight or slightly wavy. It has heavy fringing, including feathering on the feet. The hallmark of the breed, however, is its head and expression. The head should be domed, with lustrous dark eyes and well-cushioned face, creating a soft appealing expression.

Havanese

AT A GLANCE

Energy level:	■■■■	Watchdog ability:	■■■■	POPULARITY: Very Popular
Exercise requirements:	■■■	Protection ability:	■	FAMILY: Barbichon
Playfulness:	■■■■■	Grooming requirements:	■■■	AREA OF ORIGIN: Cuba
Affection level:	■■■■■	Cold tolerance:	■■	DATE OF ORIGIN: Ancient times
Friendliness toward dogs:	■■■■	Heat tolerance:	■■■	ORIGINAL FUNCTION: Lapdog, performer
Friendliness toward other pets:	■■■■			TODAY'S FUNCTION: Companion
Friendliness toward strangers:	■■■■■	WEIGHT: 7–13 lb		OTHER NAME: Bichon Havanais
Ease of training:	■■■■	HEIGHT: 8.5–11.5″		

HISTORY

The Havanese is one of the Barbichon (later shortened to Bichon) family of small dogs originating in the Mediterranean in ancient times. Spanish traders brought some of these dogs with them as gifts for Cuban women, allowing them to establish trading relationships. In Cuba, the little dogs were pampered as the special pets of the wealthy. They became known as Habeneros, and eventually some found their way back to Europe, where they were called the White Cuban. They became quite popular, not only as pets of the elite but also as performing dogs. Their popularity as pets waned, however, and their stronghold remained in the circus, where they performed throughout Europe as trick dogs. Eventually the breed declined in numbers to such an extent that it was almost

ILLUSTRATED STANDARD

1 Large, almond-shaped eyes
2 High-set drop ears of medium length
3 Topline straight but rising slightly from withers to rump
4 Tail set high and arcing over the back
5 Round feet

Color: all colors or combination of colors, including white

DQ: under 8.5″ or over 11.5″; total absence of black or chocolate on eyerims, nose, or lips; coarse, wiry coat; smooth, flat coat

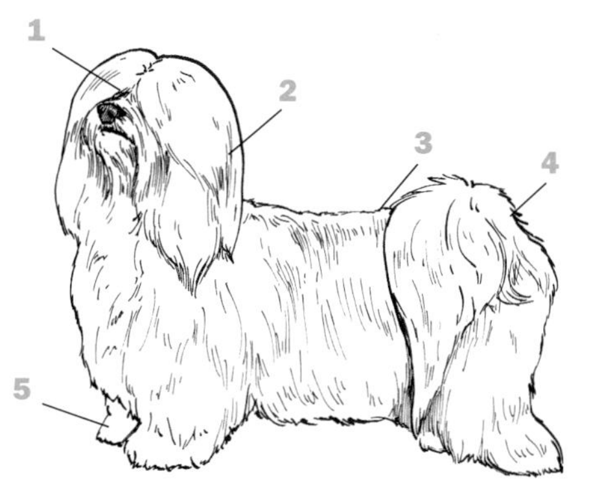

extinct not only in Europe but also in its native Cuba. A few remained in Cuba, however, and three families with their Havanese left Cuba for the United States during the 1950s and 1960s. Most present-day Havanese descend from these dogs. It has gradually aroused attention from dog fanciers and pet owners, and in 1996 the first Havanese entered an AKC show ring, and was accepted for regular recognition as a member of the Toy Group as of the first day of 1999. The Havanese is also known as the Havana Silk Dog.

TEMPERAMENT

This is a busy, curious dog; it is happiest when it is the center of attention. It loves to play and clown and is affectionate to its family, children, strangers, other dogs, and pets—basically everyone! The Havanese is willing to please and learn easily, but it tends to be vocal.

UPKEEP

Although energetic, the Havanese can have its exercise needs met with a short walk or a good play session. Coat care entails brushing two to four times a week. This is a non-shedding dog, which means that loose hairs are caught in the outer hairs, tending to tangle, unless they are combed out.

HEALTH

- Major concerns: none
- Minor concerns: patellar luxation
- Occasionally seen: chondrodysplasia, Legg-Perthes, elbow dysplasia, portacaval shunt, mitral valve insufficiency, deafness
- Suggested tests: knee, eye, hip, (cardiac), hearing
- Life span: 12–14 years

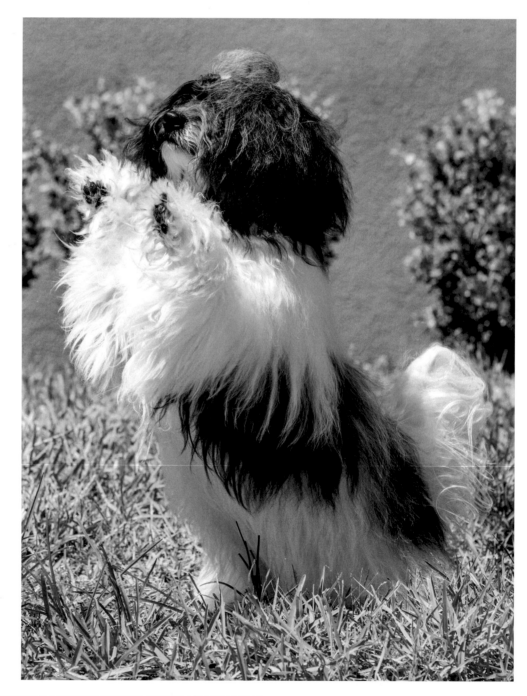

FORM AND FUNCTION

The Havanese is a small, sturdy, short-legged dog. Its unique gait is exceptionally lively and springy, accentuating the dog's happy nature. The coat is double, with both under and outer coat soft. The profuse outer coat is very long, reaching 6 to 8 inches in length, and ranges from straight to curly, with wavy preferred. The curly coat is allowed to cord. The expression is gentle.

Italian Greyhound

AT A GLANCE

Energy level:	■■■■	Watchdog ability:	■■■
Exercise requirements:	■■	Protection ability:	■
Playfulness:	■■■	Grooming requirements:	■
Affection level:	■■■■■	Cold tolerance:	■
Friendliness toward dogs:	■■■■	Heat tolerance:	■■■■
Friendliness toward other pets:	■■■■		
Friendliness toward strangers:	■■	WEIGHT: 7–14 lb*	
Ease of training:	■■■	HEIGHT: 13–15″	

POPULARITY: Somewhat popular
FAMILY: Sighthound
AREA OF ORIGIN: Italy
DATE OF ORIGIN: Ancient times
ORIGINAL FUNCTION: Lapdog
TODAY'S FUNCTION: Lure coursing
OTHER NAME: Piccolo Levrieve Italiani

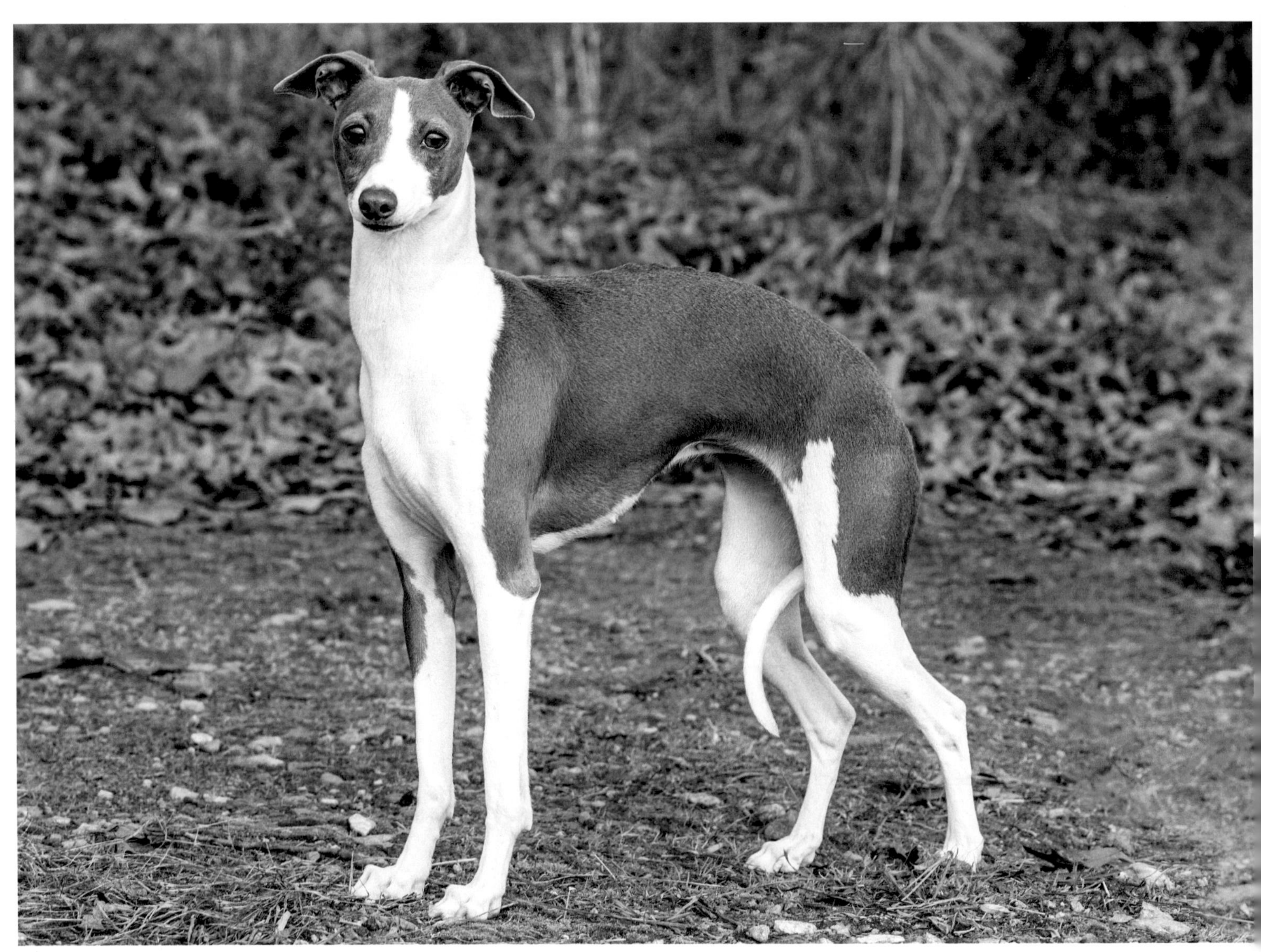

HISTORY

The Italian Greyhound has been around for many centuries, but exactly how and when this miniaturized Greyhound was developed has been lost in time. Evidence of dogs resembling the Italian Greyhound can be found in art dating nearly 2,000 years ago from Turkey, Greece, and other areas around the Mediterranean. By the Middle Ages, miniaturized Greyhounds could be found throughout southern Europe, but they found special favor with Italian courtiers. The breed came to England in the seventeenth century, quickly becoming as popular with nobility there as they had been in their Italian homeland. In 1820, the Italian Greyhound was one of only two toy breeds mentioned in a book about dogs. The Italian Greyhound continued to find favor, reaching its peak during the reign of Queen

ILLUSTRATED STANDARD

1 Long, narrow head
2 Slight stop
3 Small, folded ears
4 Back curved and drooping at hindquarters
5 Deep, narrow chest
6 Hare feet

Color: any color but brindle or black and tan
DQ: brindle markings; tan markings in the areas normally found on black and tan dogs of other breeds

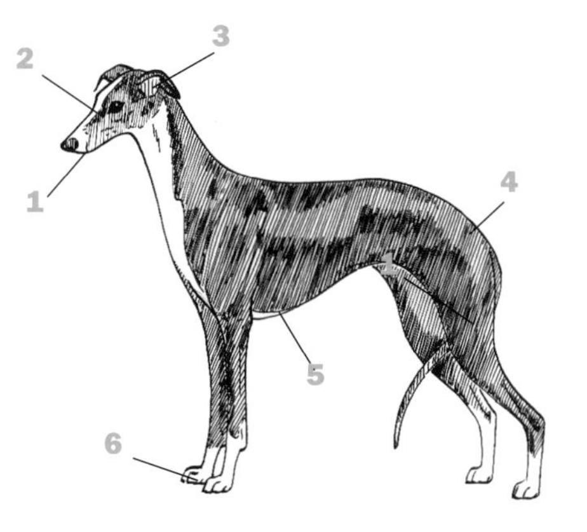

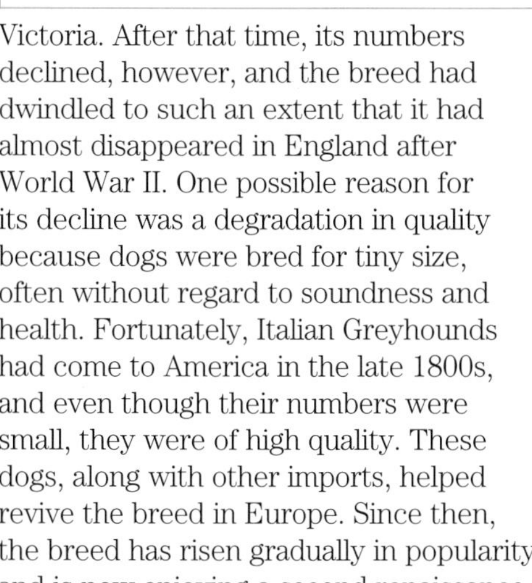

Victoria. After that time, its numbers declined, however, and the breed had dwindled to such an extent that it had almost disappeared in England after World War II. One possible reason for its decline was a degradation in quality because dogs were bred for tiny size, often without regard to soundness and health. Fortunately, Italian Greyhounds had come to America in the late 1800s, and even though their numbers were small, they were of high quality. These dogs, along with other imports, helped revive the breed in Europe. Since then, the breed has risen gradually in popularity and is now enjoying a second renaissance.

TEMPERAMENT

A sighthound in a small package, the Italian Greyhound shares its larger relatives' characteristics. It loves to run and chase. It is extremely gentle and sensitive. Reserved, often timid, with strangers, it is devoted to its family and is good with children, other dogs, and pets. However, it can be easily injured by boisterous children and larger dogs.

UPKEEP

The Italian Greyhound likes a daily romp outdoors, but it hates the cold. Its exercise needs are best met with a good walk on leash or even a rollicking game indoors. It also likes to stretch out and sprint in a fenced area. Care of the fine short hair is minimal, consisting only of occasional brushing to remove dead hair. Regular brushing of the teeth is important in this breed.

HEALTH

- Major concerns: periodontal disease
- Minor concerns: epilepsy, leg fractures, patellar luxation, PRA
- Occasionally seen: color dilution alopecia, cataract, Legg-Perthes, hypothyroidism, portacaval shunt
- Suggested tests: knee, eye, hip, thyroid
- Life span: 12–15 years
- Note: The breed is susceptible to leg and tail fractures. It shares the sighthound sensitivity to barbiturate anesthesia.

FORM AND FUNCTION

Essentially a slender miniature Greyhound, the Italian Greyhound is exceptionally elegant and graceful. It embodies the same qualities that enable the full-sized Greyhound to run at top speed using the double-suspension gallop: a curvaceous outline with a slight arch over the loin and good rear angulation. Its gait is high stepping and free. The coat is short and glossy like satin.

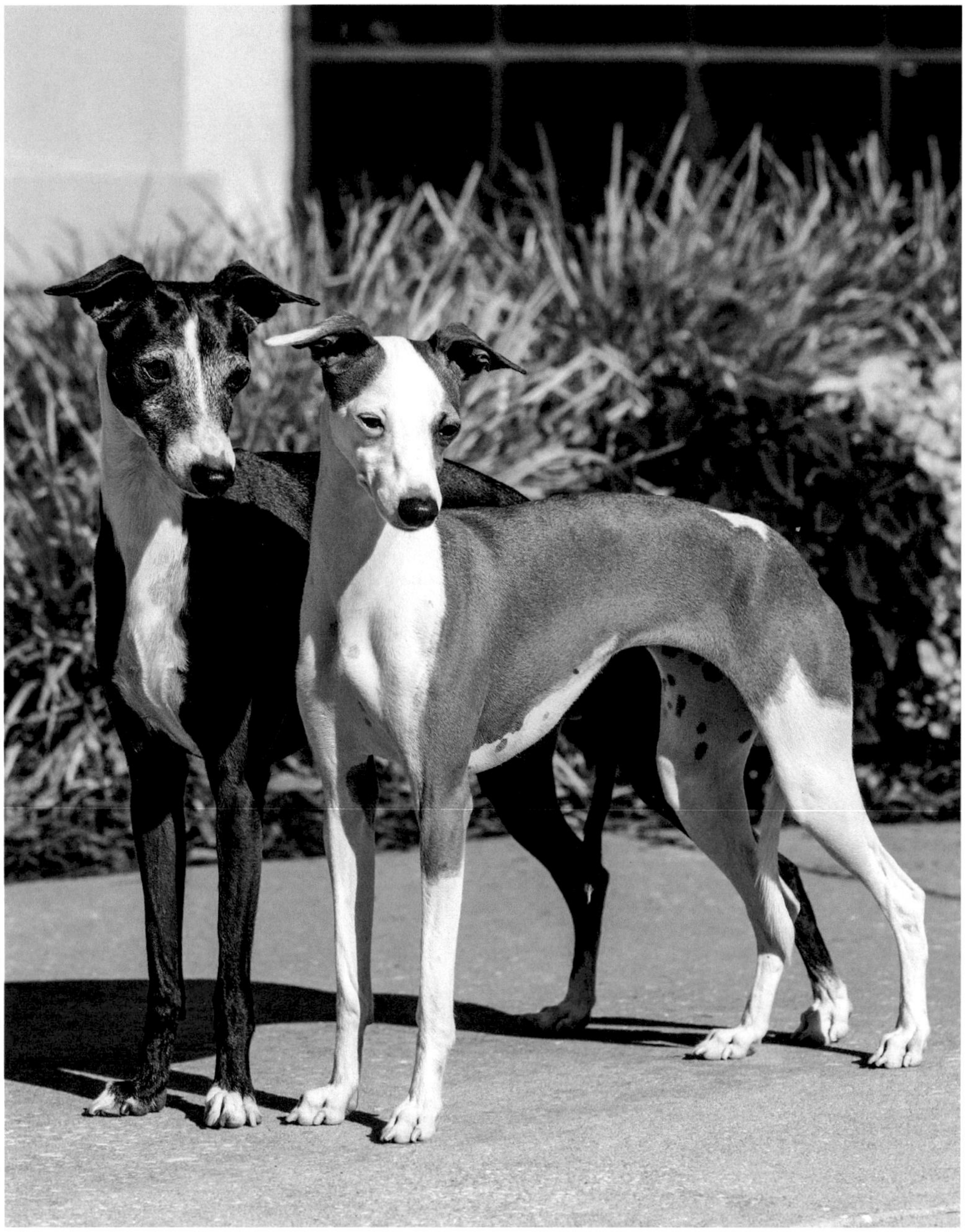

Japanese Chin

AT A GLANCE

Energy level:	■■■	Watchdog ability:	■■■■■
Exercise requirements:	■	Protection ability:	■
Playfulness:	■■■■	Grooming requirements:	■■■
Affection level:	■■■■■	Cold tolerance:	■■
Friendliness toward dogs:	■■■■	Heat tolerance:	■■
Friendliness toward other pets:	■■■■		
Friendliness toward strangers:	■■■■■	WEIGHT: 4–7 lb*	
Ease of training:	■■■	HEIGHT: 8–11″	

POPULARITY: Somewhat uncommon
FAMILY: Oriental
AREA OF ORIGIN: Japan
DATE OF ORIGIN: Ancient times
ORIGINAL FUNCTION: Lapdog
TODAY'S FUNCTION: Companion
OTHER NAME: Japanese Spaniel

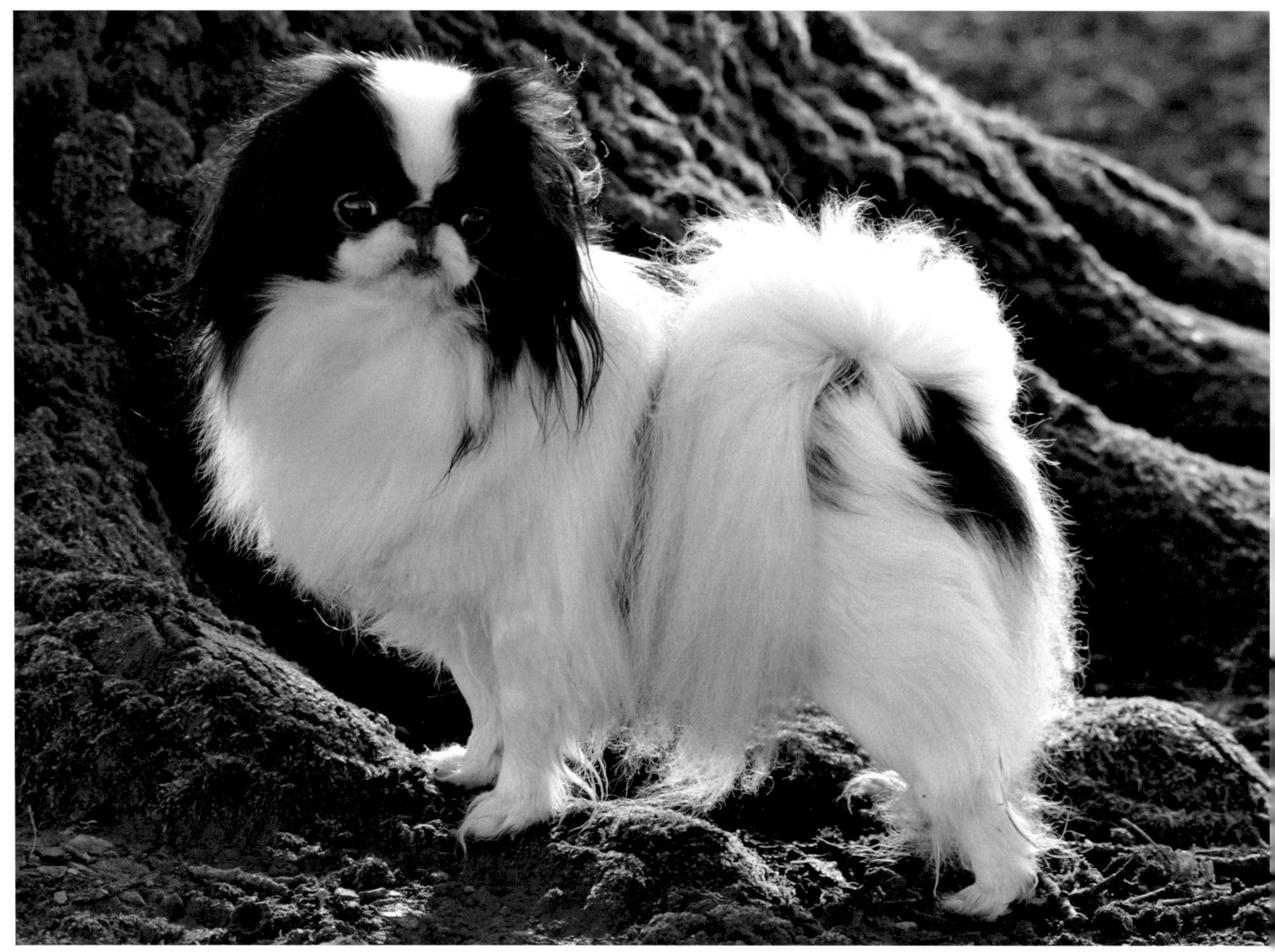

HISTORY

Despite its name, the Japanese Chin is actually of ancient Chinese origin, probably sharing a close relationship with the Pekingese. Like the Pekingese, the Chin was kept by Chinese aristocracy, and sometimes presented as a gift to visiting nobility. Different stories exist about how it arrived in Japan: Zen Buddhist teachers may have brought them some time after A.D. 520, a Korean prince may have taken some to Japan in A.D. 732, or a Chinese emperor may have presented a pair to a Japanese emperor about a thousand years ago. However it got there, it gained great favor with the Japanese Imperial family and was kept as a lapdog and ornament; some particularly small Chins were reportedly kept in hanging "bird" cages. Portuguese sailors first traded with Japan in the sixteenth

ILLUSTRATED STANDARD

1 Slightly undershot
2 Large, broad head with short, broad muzzle
3 Large, round, wide-set eyes
4 Deep stop
5 Upturned nose set on level with middle of the eyes
6 Small, hanging, V-shaped ears
7 Tail carried arched over the back and flowing to either side of the body
8 Well-feathered hare feet

Color: black and white, red and white, or black and tan and white
DQ: none

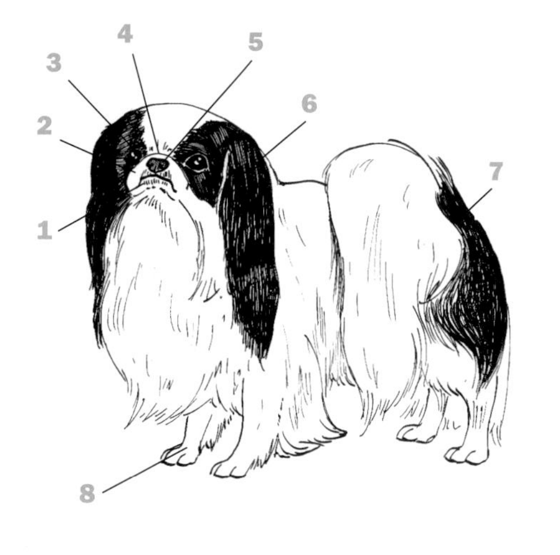

century and may have been the first to bring Chins to Europe. The first official record of Chins coming to Europe was in 1853, however, when Commodore Perry presented a pair from his trip to Japan to Queen Victoria. In the succeeding years, traders brought back many more Chins, selling them in Europe and America. The breed was recognized by the AKC in the late 1800s as the Japanese Spaniel. These early imports were larger than modern Chins, and it is possible that some crossing with English Toy Spaniels may have occurred to reduce size. World War I ended the steady supply of importations, but the breed had already gained a strong foothold. It maintains a modest popularity in America, but still enjoys its greatest popularity in Japan.

TEMPERAMENT

The Japanese Chin is a devoted companion, relishing a warm lap as much as a boisterous game. It is sensitive and willing to please, tending to shadow its owner. It is a friend to all: strangers, dogs, and pets. Its playfulness and gentleness make it a good child's companion for equally gentle children. The breed has been described as almost catlike, some even climb.

UPKEEP

The Japanese Chin is lively but small enough that its exercise needs can be met with a short walk, romp, or game. It does not do well in hot humid weather. Some Chins tend to wheeze. The long coat needs combing twice weekly.

HEALTH

- Minor concerns: patellar luxation, KCS, entropion, cataract, heart murmur
- Occasionally seen: achondroplasia, epilepsy, portacaval shunt
- Suggested tests: knee, eye, cardiac
- Life span: 10–12 years
- Note: The breed is sensitive to anesthesia and does not tolerate heat well. It is also prone to corneal abrasions.

FORM AND FUNCTION

Small, lively, and aristocratic, the Japanese Chin is a square-proportioned small dog. It has a bright inquisitive expression, distinctly Oriental. A small amount of white shows in the inner corners of the eyes, imparting a look of astonishment. Its gait is stylish, lively, and light. The single coat is abundant, straight, and silky, tending to stand out from the body. The overall appearance is one of Oriental aristocracy.

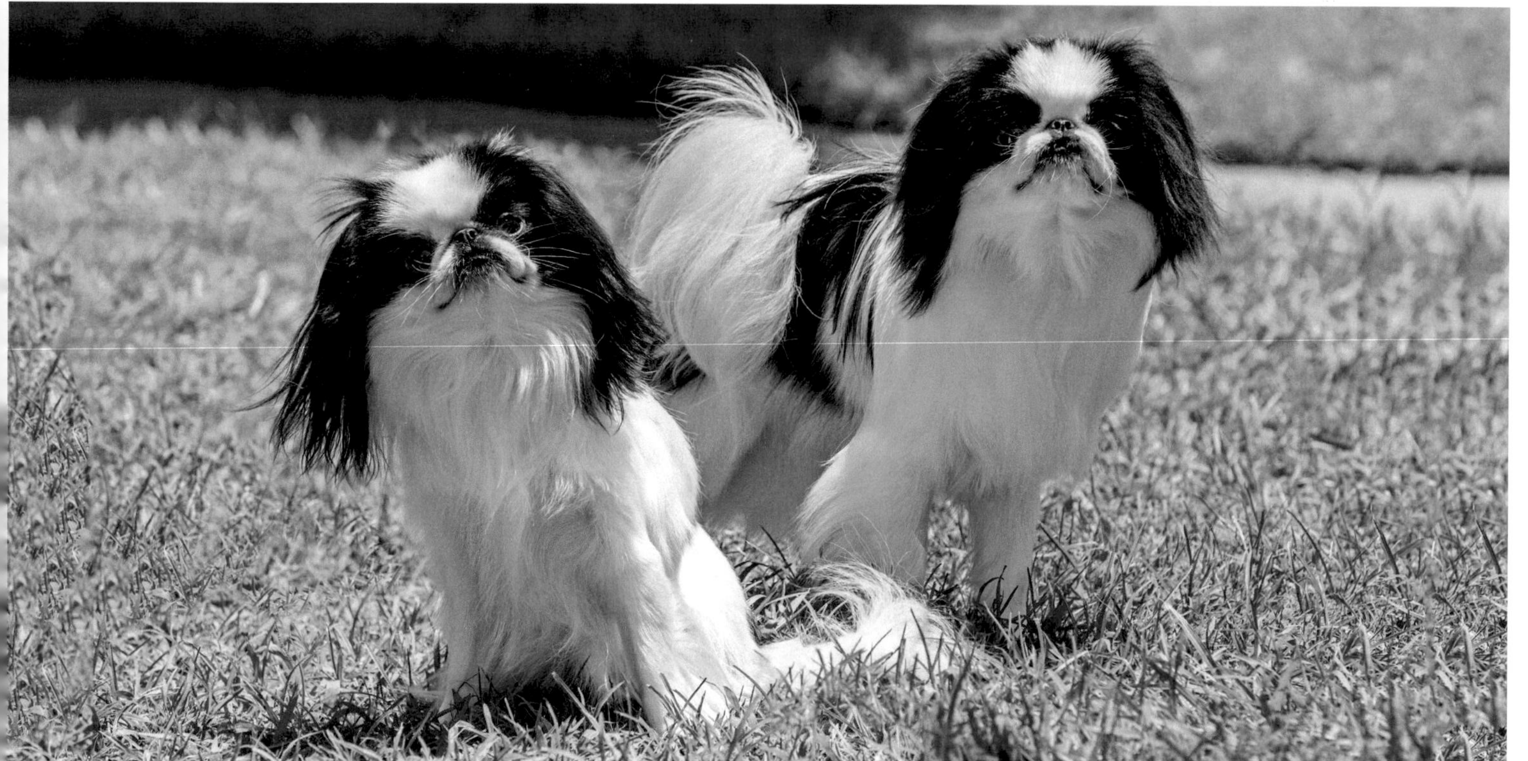

Maltese

AT A GLANCE

Energy level:	■■■■	Watchdog ability:	■■■■■	POPULARITY: Popular
Exercise requirements:	■	Protection ability:	■	FAMILY: Barbichon
Playfulness:	■■■■	Grooming requirements:	■■■	AREA OF ORIGIN: Malta
Affection level:	■■■	Cold tolerance:	■■■	DATE OF ORIGIN: Ancient times
Friendliness toward dogs:	■■■	Heat tolerance:	■■	ORIGINAL FUNCTION: Lapdog
Friendliness toward other pets:	■■■			TODAY'S FUNCTION: Companion
Friendliness toward strangers:	■	WEIGHT: under 7 lb, preferably 4–6 lb		OTHER NAME: Bichon Maltiase
Ease of training:	■■■	HEIGHT: 9–10″		

HISTORY

The Maltese is the most ancient of the European toy breeds, and among the oldest of all breeds. The island of Malta was an early trading port, visited by Phoenician sailors by 1500 B.C. Maltese dogs are specifically mentioned in writings as early as 300 B.C. Greek art includes dogs of Maltese type from the fifth century on; there is evidence that they even erected tombs to favored Maltese. Although the dogs were often exported and subsequently widely distributed throughout Europe and the Orient, the core population on Malta remained relatively isolated from other dogs, resulting in this distinctive pure-breeding dog that bred true for centuries. Though the Maltese's hallmark is its long, silky, dazzling white hair, early Maltese came in colors other than white. By the early fourteenth century, Maltese had been brought to England, where they became the darlings of upper-class

ILLUSTRATED STANDARD

1 Fine muzzle of medium length
2 Round eyes
3 Low-set drop ears covered with long hair
4 Level topline
5 Tail carried over the back, its tip lying to the side
6 Small, round feet

Color: white
DQ: none

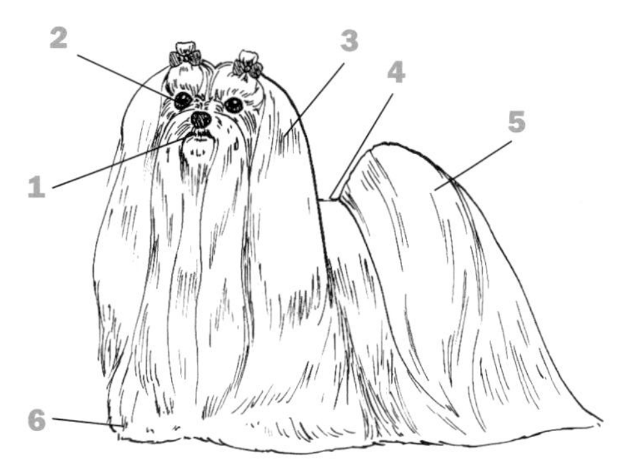

ladies. Writers of the succeeding centuries continually commented upon their diminutive size. Still these little dogs were never commonplace, and an 1830 painting entitled "The Lion Dog from Malta—Last of His Race" suggests that the breed may have been in danger of extinction. Soon after, two Maltese were brought to England from Manila. Although originally intended as a gift for Queen Victoria, they passed into other hands, and their offspring became the first Maltese exhibited in England. At this time, they were called Maltese Terriers, despite the lack of terrier ancestry or characteristics. In America, the first Maltese were shown as Maltese Lion Dogs around 1877. The name lion dog probably arose from the habit of dog fanciers, particularly those in the Orient, of clipping the dogs to look like lions. The AKC recognized the breed as the Maltese in 1888. The Maltese slowly increased in popularity, and now it ranks as one of the more popular toys.

TEMPERAMENT

Long a favorite lapdog, the gentle Maltese fills this role admirably. It also has a wild side, and it loves to run and play. Despite its innocent look, it is bold and feisty and may challenge larger dogs. It is reserved with strangers. Some bark a lot.

UPKEEP

The exercise requirements of the Maltese are easily met with indoor games, a romp in the yard, or a short walk on leash. The coat needs combing every one or two days; show coats may be "wrapped" for protection. The white coat may be difficult to keep clean in some areas. Pets may be clipped for easier care, but then an essential trait of the breed is lost.

HEALTH

- Major concerns: none
- Minor concerns: patellar luxation, open fontanel, hypoglycemia, hydrocephalus, distichiasis, entropion, dental problems, hypothyroidism, portacaval shunt
- Occasionally seen: deafness, shaker syndrome
- Suggested tests: knee, eye, cardiac
- Life span: 12–14 years

FORM AND FUNCTION

Even though the breed is known for its coat, its body structure, facial expression, and overall carriage are essential components of the type. The Maltese is a diminutive dog with a compact, square body, covered all over with long, flat, silky, white hair hanging almost to the ground. The expression is gentle yet alert. It is a vigorous dog, with a jaunty, smooth, flowing gait. The well-built Maltese seems to float over the ground when trotting.

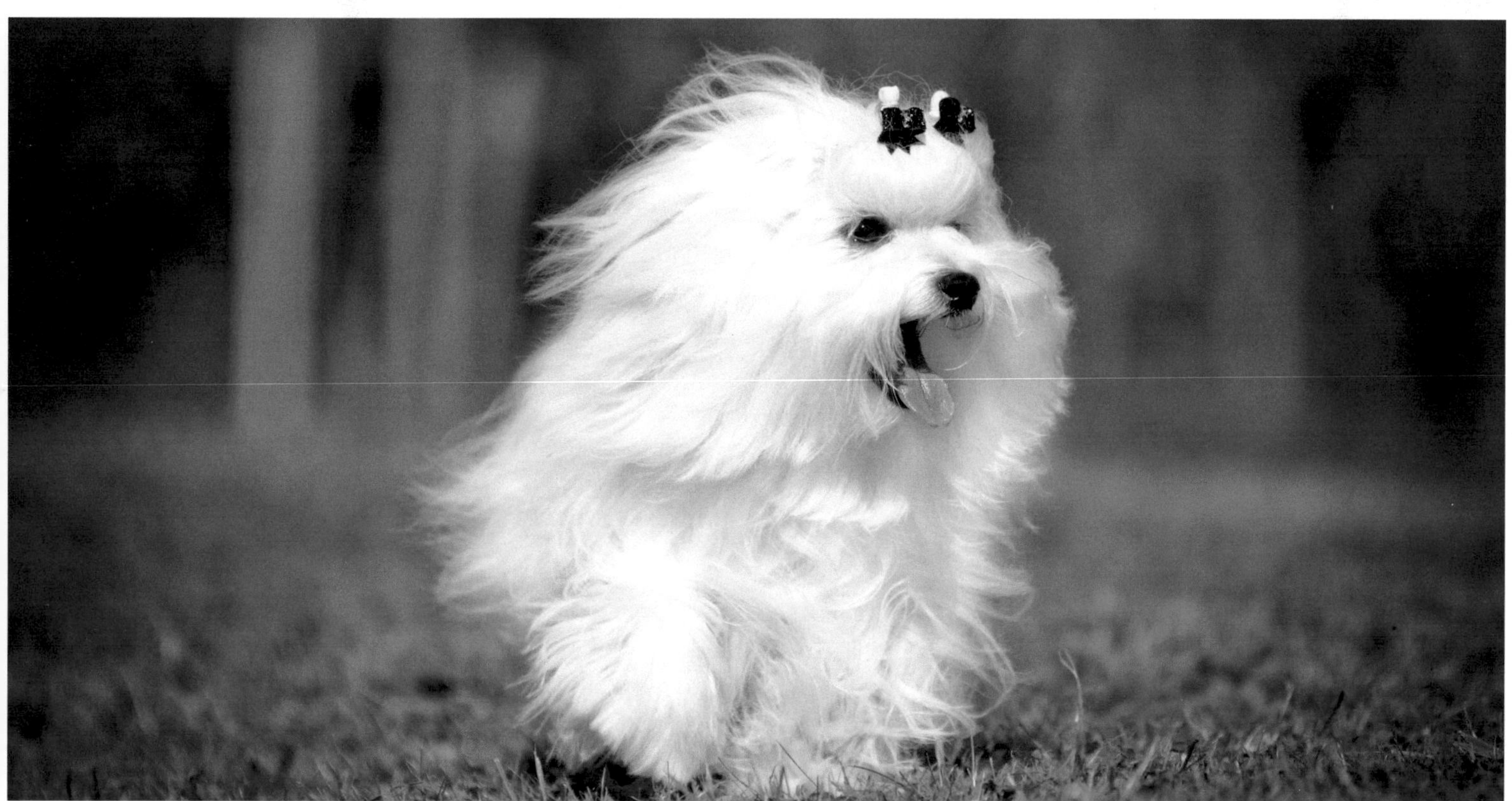

Toy Manchester Terrier

AT A GLANCE

Energy level:	■ ■ ■ ■
Exercise requirements:	■
Playfulness:	■ ■ ■ ■
Affection level:	■ ■ ■ ■
Friendliness toward dogs:	■
Friendliness toward other pets:	■ ■
Friendliness toward strangers:	■
Ease of training:	■

Watchdog ability:	■ ■ ■ ■ ■
Protection ability:	■
Grooming requirements:	■
Cold tolerance:	■
Heat tolerance:	■ ■ ■ ■

WEIGHT: under 12 lb (usually 6–8 lb)
HEIGHT: 10–12″

POPULARITY: Uncommon
FAMILY: Terrier
AREA OF ORIGIN: England
DATE OF ORIGIN: About 1860
ORIGINAL FUNCTION: Hunting small rodents
TODAY'S FUNCTION: Companion
OTHER NAME: English Toy Terrier, Black and Tan Toy Terrier

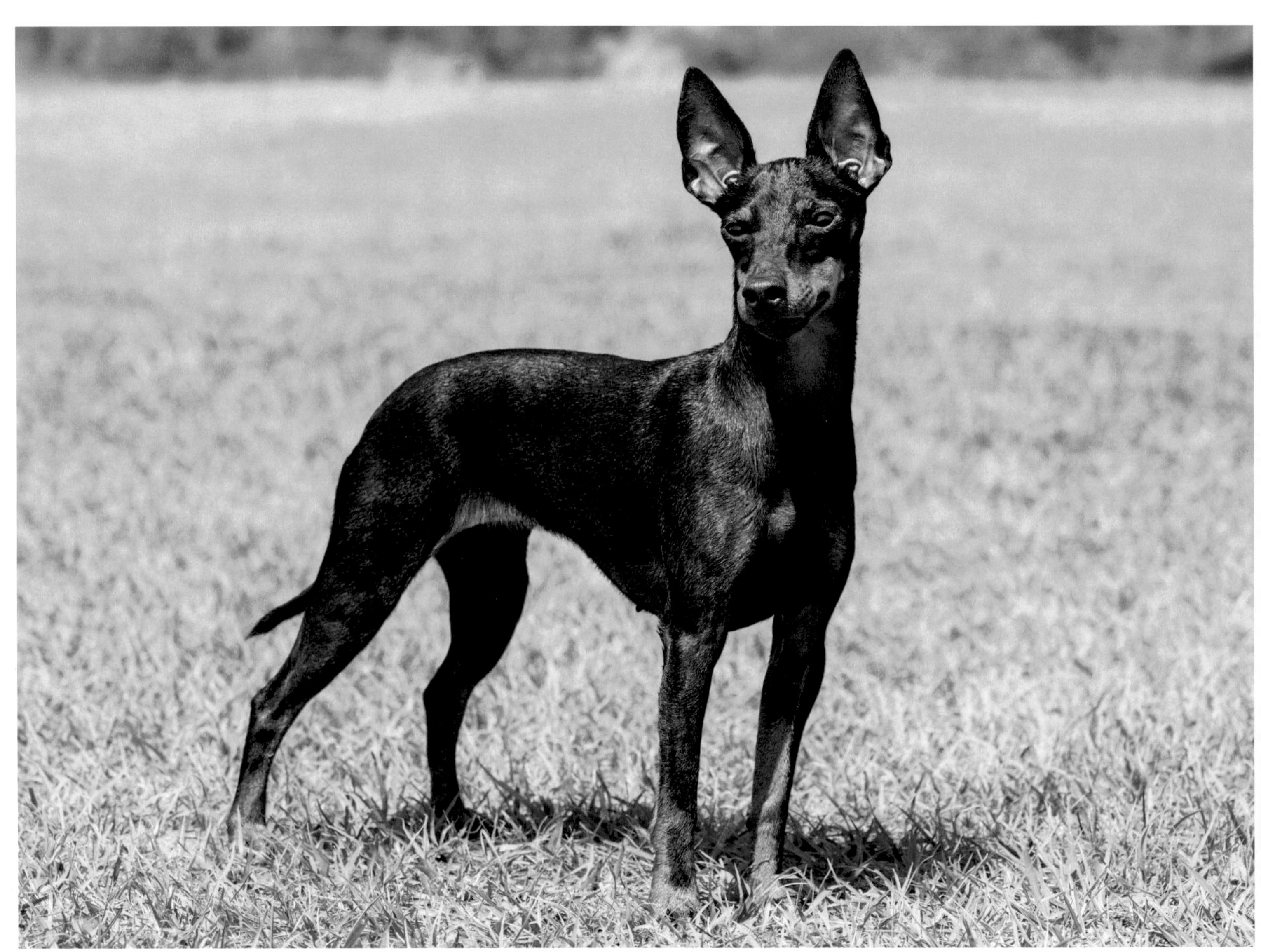

HISTORY

One of the preeminent dogs of England was the Black and Tan Terrier, a breed valued for its rat-killing prowess since the sixteenth century. Rat-killing dogs were valuable not only for ridding homes of vermin but also for the entertainment value of betting upon how many rats a dog could kill in an allotted time. Manchester, England, was populated by workers who looked to their rat-killing contests and dog-racing contests for entertainment. It was only natural that eventually a cross between the Black and Tan Terrier ratter and the Whippet racer would be made, and the result was the dog known since about 1860 as the Manchester Terrier. At times the Manchester Terrier was considered no different from its Black and Tan Terrier forebears, and it was not until 1923 that

ILLUSTRATED STANDARD

1 Small, almond-shaped eyes
2 Head resembles a blunted wedge in profile and from front
3 Naturally erect ears
4 Slight arch over loin
5 Tapered tail carried in a slight upward curve
6 Tucked up abdomen

Color: black and tan, with a black "thumbprint" patch on the front of each foreleg and "pencil marks" on the top of each toe

DQ: cropped or cut ears; patch of white over ½″ at its longest dimension; any color other than black and tan

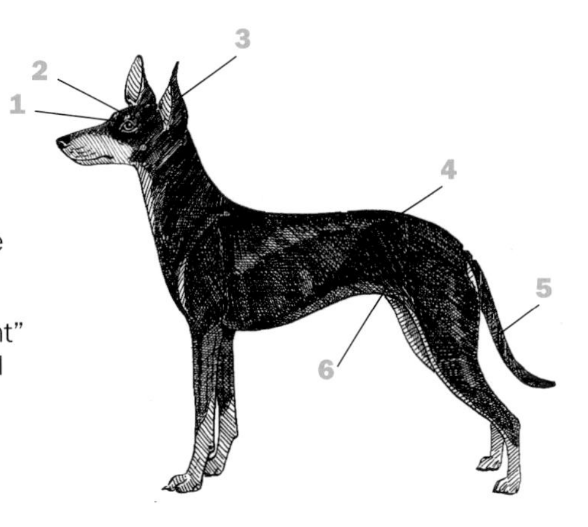

the name was officially changed back to Manchester Terrier. Other breeds have probably been intermingled with the Manchester during its development, most notably the Italian Greyhound. This may account for the breed's wide size range. An early standard of 1881 described the existence of a toy variety even then. The smaller dogs were in high demand, and breeders resorted to inbreeding to achieve even smaller specimens, which eventually led to exceedingly small frail dogs. Upon realizing the state of these dogs, breeders endeavored to breed a miniature, but not tiny, version. The result is the Toy Manchester Terrier. The AKC initially considered the Manchester and Toy Manchester separate but interbreeding breeds. In 1959, they were changed to be two interbreeding varieties of one breed. Besides size, the Toy Manchester differs from its larger counterpart in that cropped ears are not allowed. The Toy Manchester Terrier is also known as the English Toy Terrier.

TEMPERAMENT

Although true to its terrier heritage when it comes to scrappiness and hunting instincts, the Toy Manchester is among the gentlest and most sensitive of breeds. It is playful with its family, yet reserved, sometimes even timid, with strangers. The Toy Manchester Terrier is inquisitive and may chase small pets.

UPKEEP

The Toy Manchester enjoys a romp outdoors, but it hates the cold. Indoors, it appreciates a soft, warm bed. Coat care is minimal, consisting of occasional brushing to remove dead hair.

HEALTH

- Major concerns: none
- Minor concerns: vWD, cardiomyopathy
- Occasionally seen: Legg-Perthes, hypothyroidism, deafness, PRA, patellar luxation
- Suggested tests: eye, hip, DNA for vWD
- Life span: 14–16 years

FORM AND FUNCTION

The Toy Manchester Terrier is a miniature version of the standard Manchester. As such it is sleek, racy, and compact. It is slightly longer than it is tall, with a slightly arched topline. Its gait is free and effortless, not hackney. Its expression is keen and alert, and its coat is smooth and glossy.

Miniature Pinscher

AT A GLANCE

Energy level: ■■■■■
Exercise requirements: ■■
Playfulness: ■■■■■
Affection level: ■■■
Friendliness toward dogs: ■■
Friendliness toward other pets: ■
Friendliness toward strangers: ■
Ease of training: ■

Watchdog ability: ■■■■■
Protection ability: ■
Grooming requirements: ■
Cold tolerance: ■
Heat tolerance: ■■■

WEIGHT: 8–10 lb*
HEIGHT: 10–12.5″, with 11–11.5″ preferred

POPULARITY: Somewhat popular
FAMILY: Pinscher
AREA OF ORIGIN: Germany
DATE OF ORIGIN: 1600s
ORIGINAL FUNCTION: Small vermin hunting
TODAY'S FUNCTION: Companion
OTHER NAME: Reh Pinscher, Zwergpinscher

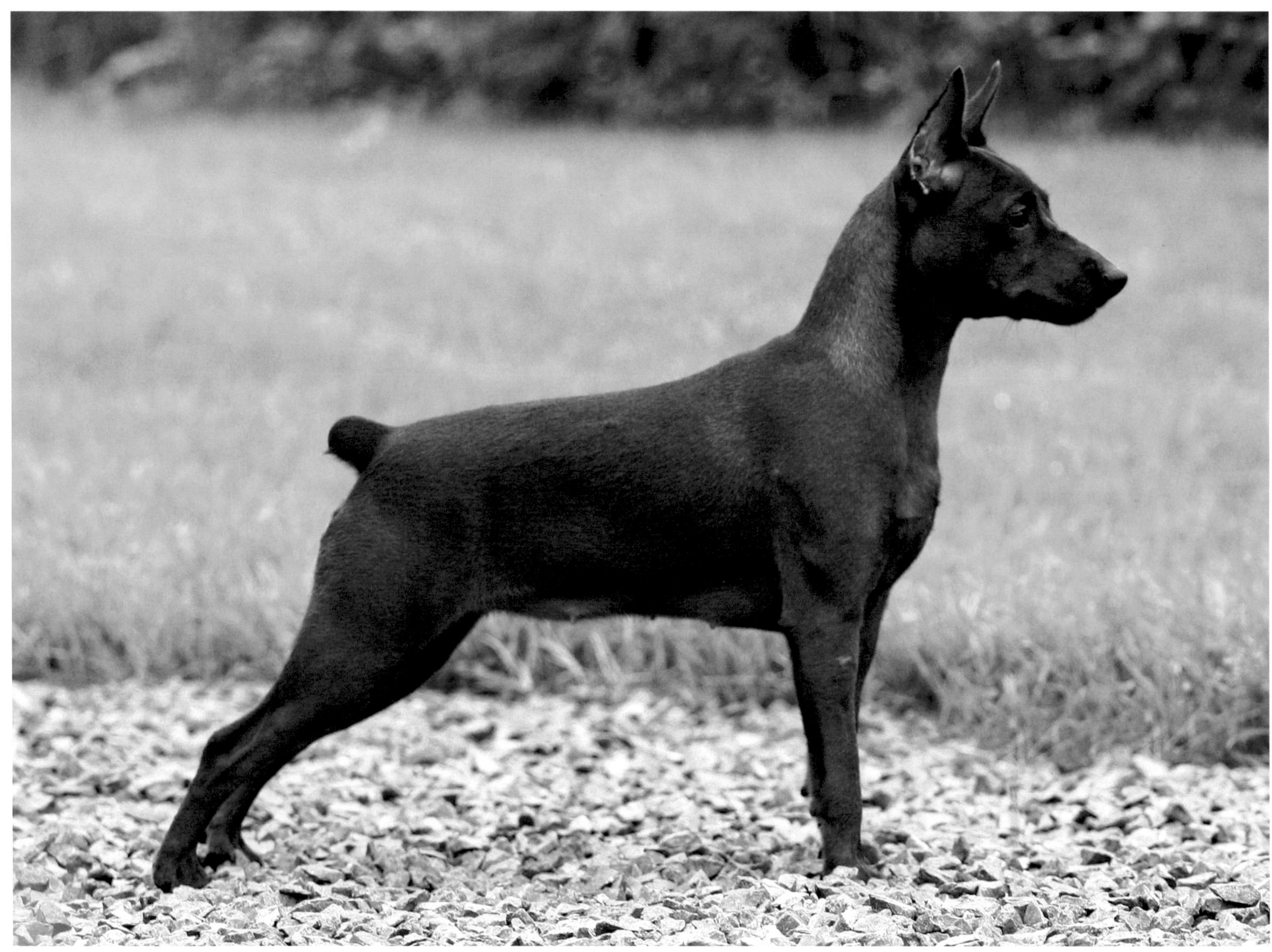

HISTORY

The Miniature Pinscher is not a miniature version of the Doberman Pinscher. In fact, the Min Pin is the older of the two breeds. Clues about the Miniature Pinscher's origin are scarce, but it is noteworthy that a cat-sized red dog resembling a Min Pin is depicted in a seventeenth century painting. By the nineteenth century, several paintings include dogs of distinct Min Pin type. These dogs probably resulted from crossing a small short-haired terrier (German Pinscher) with the Dachshund and Italian Greyhound. Many of the traits from these breeds can be seen in today's Min Pins: the strong body structure, feistiness, and black and tan coloration of the German Pinscher; the fearlessness and red coloration of the Dachshund; and the elegance, playfulness, and lithe movement

ILLUSTRATED STANDARD

1 Narrow tapering head
2 Strong muzzle
3 Erect ears, cropped or natural
4 Tail held erect and docked
5 Small cat feet

Color: clear red, stag red, black and tan
DQ: under 10″ or over 12.5″ in height; any color other than listed; thumbmark (patch of dark hair on the front of the foreleg between the foot and wrist); white anywhere exceeding ½″ in its longest dimension

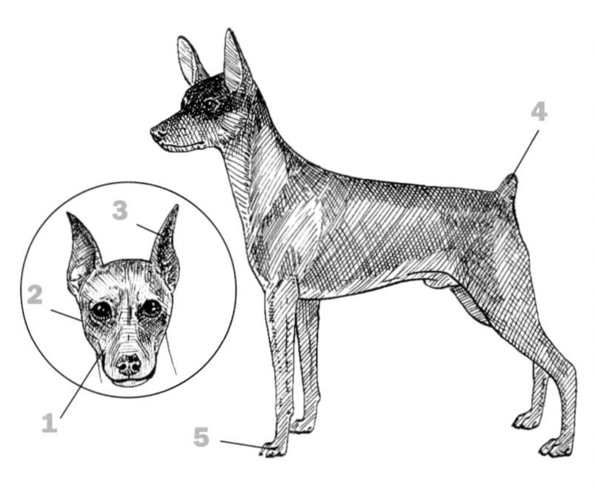

of the Italian Greyhound. Yet the Min Pin is more than the sum of its parts; it is perhaps the world's most energetic breed! These little German spitfires were developed into a distinct breed, the "reh pinscher" in the early 1800s, so named because of their resemblance to the small red German roe (reh) deer. Pinscher simply means terrier. The emphasis in the late 1800s was on breeding the tiniest specimens, resulting in crippled ugly dogs. Fortunately, the trend was reversed, and by 1900, the emphasis had returned to elegance and soundness. The breed quickly became one of the most competitive and popular show dogs in pre-World War I Germany, but after the war, the breed experienced a plunge in numbers. Its future was left to those dogs that had been exported before the war. Its popularity continued to grow in America, and it received AKC recognition in 1929. Dubbed the king of toys, the Min Pin slowly accumulated admirers and is presently one of the more popular toy breeds in the United States.

TEMPERAMENT

Among the most energetic of all breeds, the Min Pin is a perpetual motion machine. It is busy, inquisitive, playful, bold, and brash. It retains terrier-like traits and tends to be stubborn and independent. It can be scrappy with other dogs and may chase small animals. It is reserved with strangers but affectionate to its family.

UPKEEP

The Min Pin needs lots of activity. Because of its small size, its exercise needs can be met indoors or out; regardless, it needs several play sessions every day. It hates the cold. Its coat is virtually carefree, requiring only occasional brushing to remove dead hair.

HEALTH

- Major concerns: none
- Minor concerns: Legg-Perthes, cervical (dry) disk, patellar luxation, hypothyroidism, heart defects, MPS VI
- Occasionally seen: PRA
- Suggested tests: knee, (hip), (eye), (DNA for MPS)
- Life span: 12–14 years

FORM AND FUNCTION

The square-proportioned Min Pin has a compact, sturdy body with moderate tuck up and sort coupling. Its hallmark traits are its spirited animation, complete self-possession, and high-stepping hackney gait. It is upstanding and alert. The coat is smooth, hard, and short. It is among the most athletic of toy breeds.

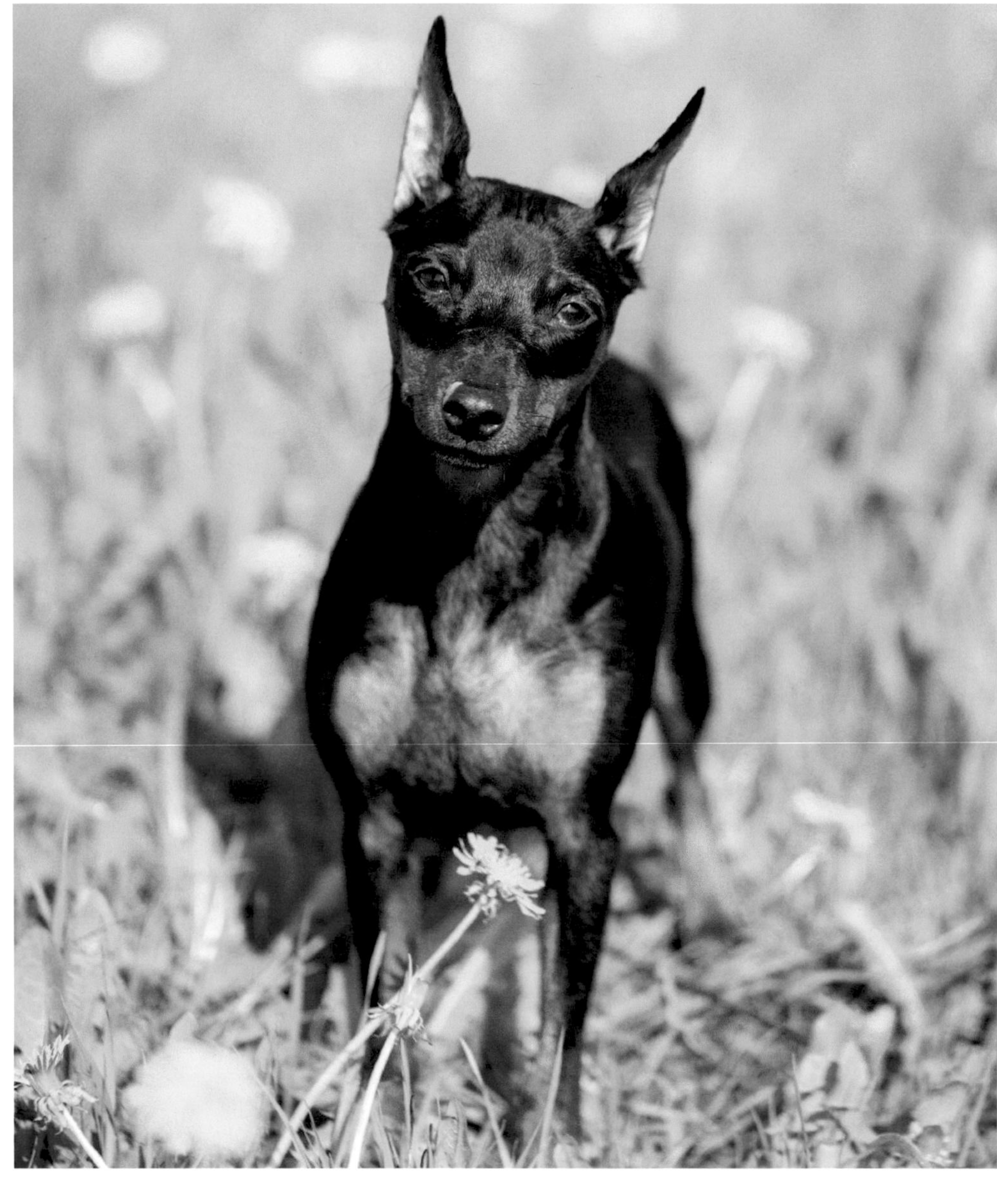

Papillon

AT A GLANCE

Energy level:	■■■■	Watchdog ability:	■■■■■
Exercise requirements:	■	Protection ability:	■
Playfulness:	■■■■■	Grooming requirements:	■■■
Affection level:	■■■■■	Cold tolerance:	■
Friendliness toward dogs:	■■■■	Heat tolerance:	■■■
Friendliness toward other pets:	■■■■		
Friendliness toward strangers:	■■■■	WEIGHT: 4–9 lb*	
Ease of training:	■■■■■	HEIGHT: 8–11″	

POPULARITY: Popular
FAMILY: Spaniel, Companion
AREA OF ORIGIN: France
DATE OF ORIGIN: 1500s
ORIGINAL FUNCTION: Lapdog
TODAY'S FUNCTION: Companion
OTHER NAME: Epagneul Nain (Phalene is also known as Continental Toy Spaniel)

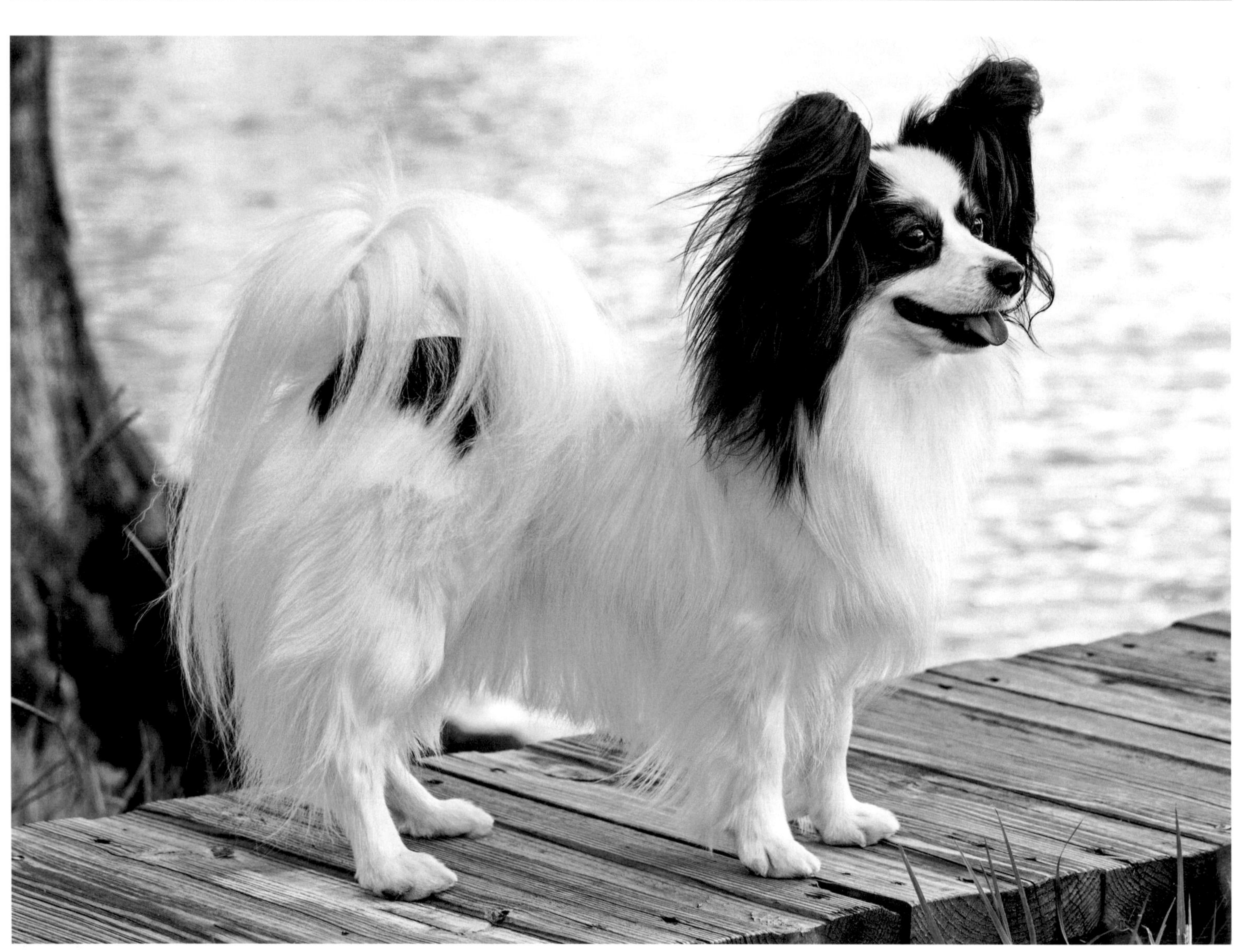

HISTORY

The name Papillon is French for butterfly, which the face and ears of this spritely little dog should resemble. The Papillon has its roots in the dwarf spaniels so popular throughout Europe from at least the sixteenth century. These little dogs were extremely popular with the nobility; as time went on, Spain and Italy became the centers of dwarf spaniel breeding and trading. The court of Louis XIV of France was particularly fond of these little dogs and imported many of them. At one time the Papillon was known as the Squirrel Spaniel because it carried its plumed tail over its back in the same way a squirrel does. These early dogs had drooping ears, but through some unknown event, some dogs sported erect ears. Both drop- and erect-eared Papillons could be found in

ILLUSTRATED STANDARD

1 Round eyes
2 Small, rounded head with fine muzzle
3 Ears erect or dropped
4 Backline straight and level
5 Long tail carried arched over body and covered with a long plume
6 Belly tucked up
7 Forelegs slender and fine-boned
8 Elongated hare feet

Color: white with patches of any color
DQ: over 12″ in height; all white dog or dog with no white

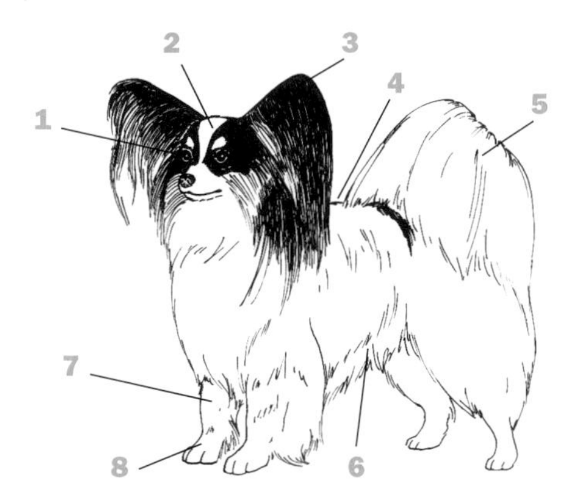

the same litter. Even today both ear types are equally correct, although the erect-eared dog is much more popular. In America, the drop-eared Pap is known as the Phalene, which is French for moth, whereas in Europe it is called the Epagneul Nain or Continental Toy Spaniel. By 1900, the Papillon was well represented at French dog shows and soon afterward was being shown in England and America. These earlier exhibits tended to be larger than those seen today, and were mostly solid colored, usually of some shade of red. Selective breeding has resulted in a smaller dog that is distinguished by its striking colors broken by patches of white. A symmetrically marked face with white blaze adds to the butterfly appearance. The Papillon has become one of the more popular toy dogs, functioning equally well as a loving pet, beautiful show dog, and adept obedience and agility competitor.

TEMPERAMENT

One of the most obedient and responsive of the toy breeds, the vivacious Papillon is also gentle, amiable, and playful. It is friendly toward strangers, other dogs, and pets. It is very good with children although it can be injured by rough play. Some can be timid.

UPKEEP

The lively Papillon thrives on mental stimulation, and it enjoys a daily walk on leash as well as challenging games indoors or out. Its coat needs brushing twice weekly.

HEALTH

- Major concerns: none
- Minor concerns: patellar luxation, seizures, dental problems
- Occasionally seen: vWD, PRA, open fontanel, intervertebral disk disease, allergies
- Suggested tests: knee, eye, (vWD), cardiac
- Life span: 12–15 years

FORM AND FUNCTION

The Papillon is a small, dainty, elegant dog of fine-boned structure, slightly longer than it is tall. Its gait is quick, easy, and graceful. Its abundant coat is long, silky, straight, and flowing. Its hallmark characteristic, besides its friendly temperament and alert expression, is its butterfly ears.

Pekingese

AT A GLANCE

Energy level:	■	Watchdog ability:	■■■■■
Exercise requirements:	■	Protection ability:	■
Playfulness:	■	Grooming requirements:	■■■■■
Affection level:	■■	Cold tolerance:	■■■
Friendliness toward dogs:	■■■	Heat tolerance:	■
Friendliness toward other pets:	■■■■		
Friendliness toward strangers:	■■	WEIGHT: not to exceed 14 lb	
Ease of training:	■	HEIGHT: 6–9″*	

POPULARITY: Somewhat uncommon
FAMILY: Oriental
AREA OF ORIGIN: China
DATE OF ORIGIN: Ancient times
ORIGINAL FUNCTION: Lapdog
TODAY'S FUNCTION: Companion
OTHER NAME: Lion dog, Peking Palasthund

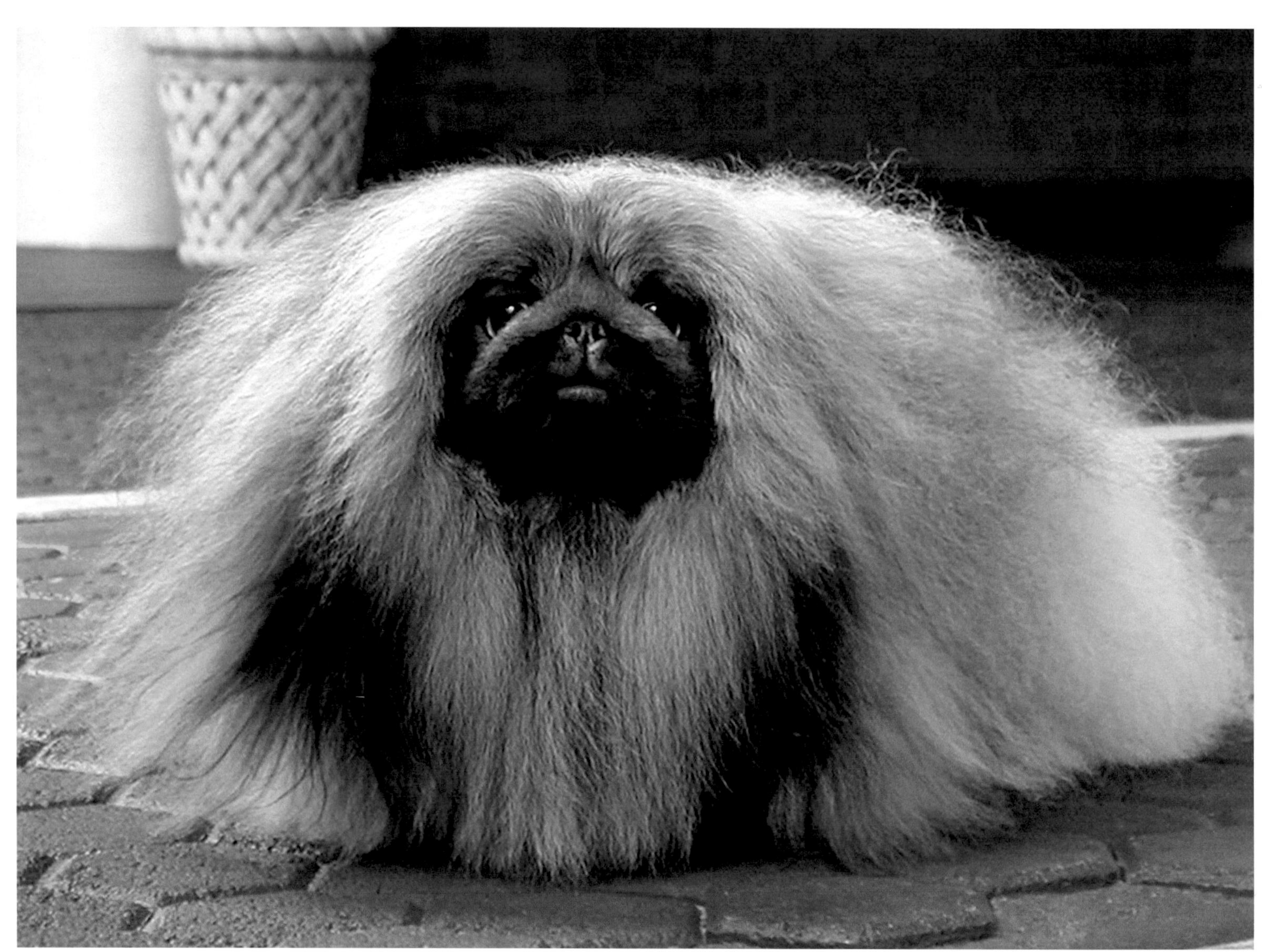

HISTORY

The Pekingese owes its existence to the Lamaist form of Buddhism in China, in which the lion was an exalted symbol of Buddha, sometimes appearing in miniaturized form. The Foo dogs then in existence bore some resemblance to a lion and were carefully bred to accentuate this similarity. In fact, these dogs eventually came to be known as lion dogs. Extensive breeding programs fell under the auspices of palace eunuches, with no expense spared. At the height of their favor (during the T'ang dynasty from A.D. 700 to A.D. 1000) many of these lion dogs were literally treated as royalty, pampered by personal servants. Smaller Pekingese were called sleeve dogs because they could be carried in the large sleeves of their Chinese masters. In 1860, the imperial summer palace

ILLUSTRATED STANDARD

1 Slightly undershot
2 Nose positioned at a height between the eyes
3 Large, round eyes
4 Flat profile
5 Wrinkle extends over the bridge of the nose in an inverted V
6 Massive, broad, flat skull
7 Heart-shaped ears
8 Tail carried over back
9 Front feet large, flat, and turned slightly out

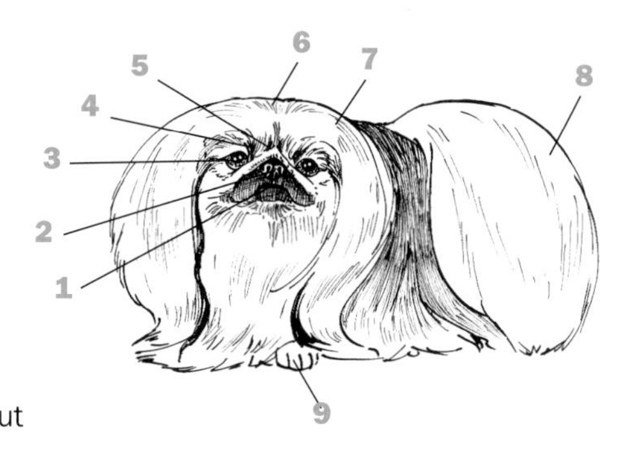

Color: All colors and patterns are allowable
DQ: weight over 14 lb

was looted by the British. Among their loot were five royal lion dogs, which were taken back to England. One was presented to Queen Victoria, and it, along with the other four, caused such interest among dog fanciers that there arose great demand for more of these dogs. Still, their numbers rose slowly, remaining for decades a dog only for the wealthiest of owners. With time, the breed became more readily available. It was extremely popular in the late 1900s but has since fallen greatly in numbers. It remains one of the most competitive show dogs, however.

TEMPERAMENT

The Pekingese is decidedly not a sissy lapdog. It is a courageous character that will not start a fight but will not back down from one. It tends to be aloof around strangers but this is not a breed-wide trait. Many are outgoing. It is loving but it is independent and not overly demonstrative. Its stubbornness is legendary. Although playful around family members, it may not be athletic or playful enough to satisfy many children. It will not tolerate rough handling by children, and can be injured by careless children.

UPKEEP

The Pekingese enjoys a leisurely walk outdoors, but it is equally happy to romp inside. It can easily die of heat prostration. It must be kept in air conditioning in warm weather. It is an ideal apartment dog. The coat will mat unless combed at the very least weekly, preferably more often. The overnose wrinkle should be cleaned daily to avoid infection. The coat around the anus must be inspected daily for soiling. Pekingese tend to snore!

HEALTH

- Major concerns: none
- Minor concerns: elongated soft palate, stenotic nares, KCS, patellar luxation, disticiasis, trichiasis, skin fold dermatitis
- Occasionally seen: urolithiasis
- Suggested tests: knee, (eye)
- Life span: 13–15 years
- Note: The breed is sensitive to anesthesia and does not tolerate heat well. It is also prone to corneal abrasions. Puppies must often be delivered by caesarean.

FORM AND FUNCTION

The Pekingese is a compact dog with a pear-shaped body, heavy forequarters and lighter hindquarters. It is slightly longer than it is tall, with a stocky, heavy build. Its image is lionlike. It should imply courage, boldness, and self-esteem rather than prettiness, daintiness, or delicacy. Its gait is dignified and unhurried, with a slight roll resulting from its wider, heavier forequarters. It has a thick undercoat, and its outer coat is long, coarse, straight, and stands off. It forms a mane around the shoulders. The Pekingese must suggest its Chinese origins in its lionlike appearance, bold and direct character, and distinctive expression.

Pomeranian

AT A GLANCE

Energy level:	■ ■ ■ ■
Exercise requirements:	■
Playfulness:	■ ■ ■ ■
Affection level:	■
Friendliness toward dogs:	■
Friendliness toward other pets:	■ ■ ■
Friendliness toward strangers:	■
Ease of training:	■

Watchdog ability:	■ ■ ■ ■ ■
Protection ability:	■
Grooming requirements:	■ ■ ■
Cold tolerance:	■ ■ ■
Heat tolerance:	■ ■ ■

WEIGHT: 3–7 lb, preferably 4–5 lb
HEIGHT: 8–11″*

POPULARITY: Very popular
FAMILY: Spitz
AREA OF ORIGIN: Germany
DATE OF ORIGIN: 1800s
ORIGINAL FUNCTION: Companion
TODAY'S FUNCTION: Companion
OTHER NAME: None

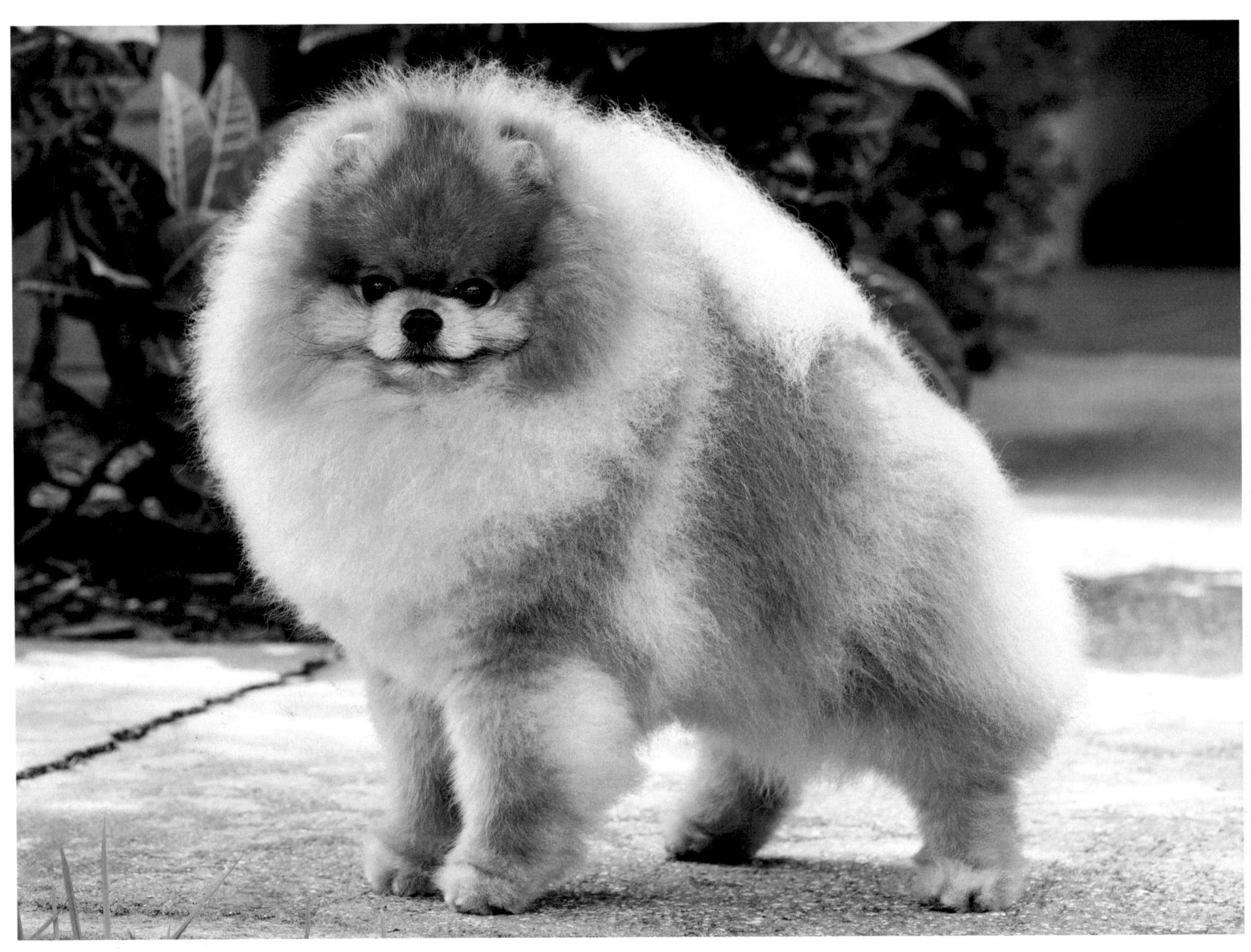

HISTORY

The smallest member of the spitz family, the Pomeranian boasts tough sledding dog ancestors. Exactly when it began to be bred down in size is not known; nor is it known exactly where this miniaturization took place, although Germany, and specifically, Pomerania, is the most likely locale. The breed's likely ancestor was the Deutscher Spitz. Only when the breed was taken to England was it dubbed the Pomeranian, but these early dogs were not the "Poms" known today. They weighed as much as 30 pounds and were often white. In fact, the Japanese Spitz closely resembles these early Pomeranians and very likely descends from them. Although the Pomeranian was recognized by the English Kennel Club in 1870, it was not until Queen Victoria brought a Pomeranian from Italy

ILLUSTRATED STANDARD

1 Short neck
2 Almond-shaped eyes
3 Wedge-shaped head
4 Small, high-set, erect ears
5 Tail arched over back and carried flat
6 Compact feet

Color: all colors and patterns allowed
DQ: none

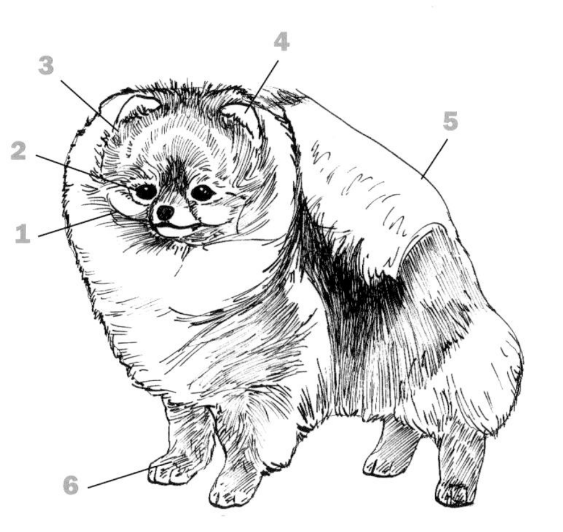

FORM AND FUNCTION

The Pomeranian is a small, square-proportioned, miniature spitz with a cobby, rounded body. It shares the spitz characteristics of small ears, double coat, and curled tail. It has an alert, foxlike expression. Its gait is smooth and free with good reach and drive. The soft thick undercoat combined with the longer harsh outer coat, standing off from the body, combine to give the dog a unique puffy appearance. This look is further accentuated by the thick ruff and a head carriage that is naturally upgazing.

that its popularity grew. The queen's Pomeranians were rather large gray dogs, and even then most fanciers preferred smaller, more colorful specimens. By 1900, Poms had been recognized by the AKC, and dogs were being shown in both England and America in an array of colors. The Pomeranian has continued to be bred down in size; at the same time, an emphasis on coat has led to its unsurpassed "puff-ball" appearance. This miniature sled dog always attracts admirers and is a very popular pet and show dog.

TEMPERAMENT

Bouncy, bold, and busy, the Pomeranian makes the most of every day. It is curious, playful, self-confident (even cocky), and attentive, ever ready for a game or adventure. It is reserved toward strangers. Some can be aggressive toward other dogs. Some bark a lot.

UPKEEP

The Pomeranian is active but diminutive, needing daily exercise but able to meet its needs with indoor games or short walks. Its double coat needs brushing twice weekly, more when shedding.

HEALTH

- Major concerns: patellar luxation
- Minor concerns: open fontanel, hypoglycemia, shoulder luxation, PRA, entropion
- Occasionally seen: tracheal collapse, PDA, Legg-Perthes
- Suggested tests: knee, eye, cardiac, hip
- Life span: 12–16 years

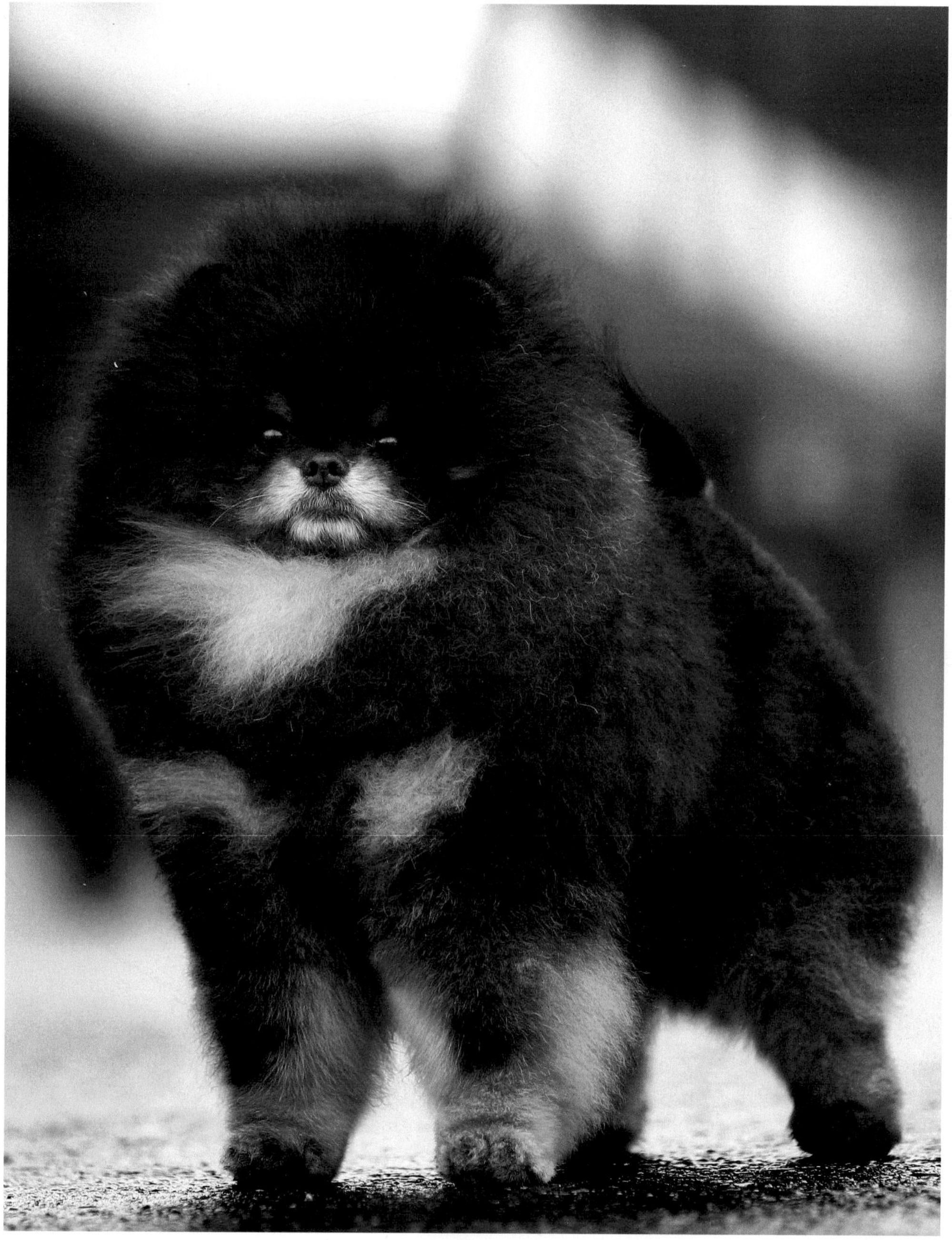

Toy Poodle

AT A GLANCE

Energy level:	■■■■	Watchdog ability:	■■■■■	POPULARITY: Most popular
Exercise requirements:	■■	Protection ability:	■	FAMILY: Water Dog
Playfulness:	■■■■■	Grooming requirements:	■■■■■	AREA OF ORIGIN: Central Europe
Affection level:	■■■■	Cold tolerance:	■■	DATE OF ORIGIN: 1500s
Friendliness toward dogs:	■■■	Heat tolerance:	■■■	ORIGINAL FUNCTION: Lapdog
Friendliness toward other pets:	■■■			TODAY'S FUNCTION: Companion, agility
Friendliness toward strangers:	■■■■	WEIGHT: 4–8 lb*		OTHER NAME: Caniche
Ease of training:	■■■■■	HEIGHT: not to exceed 10″		

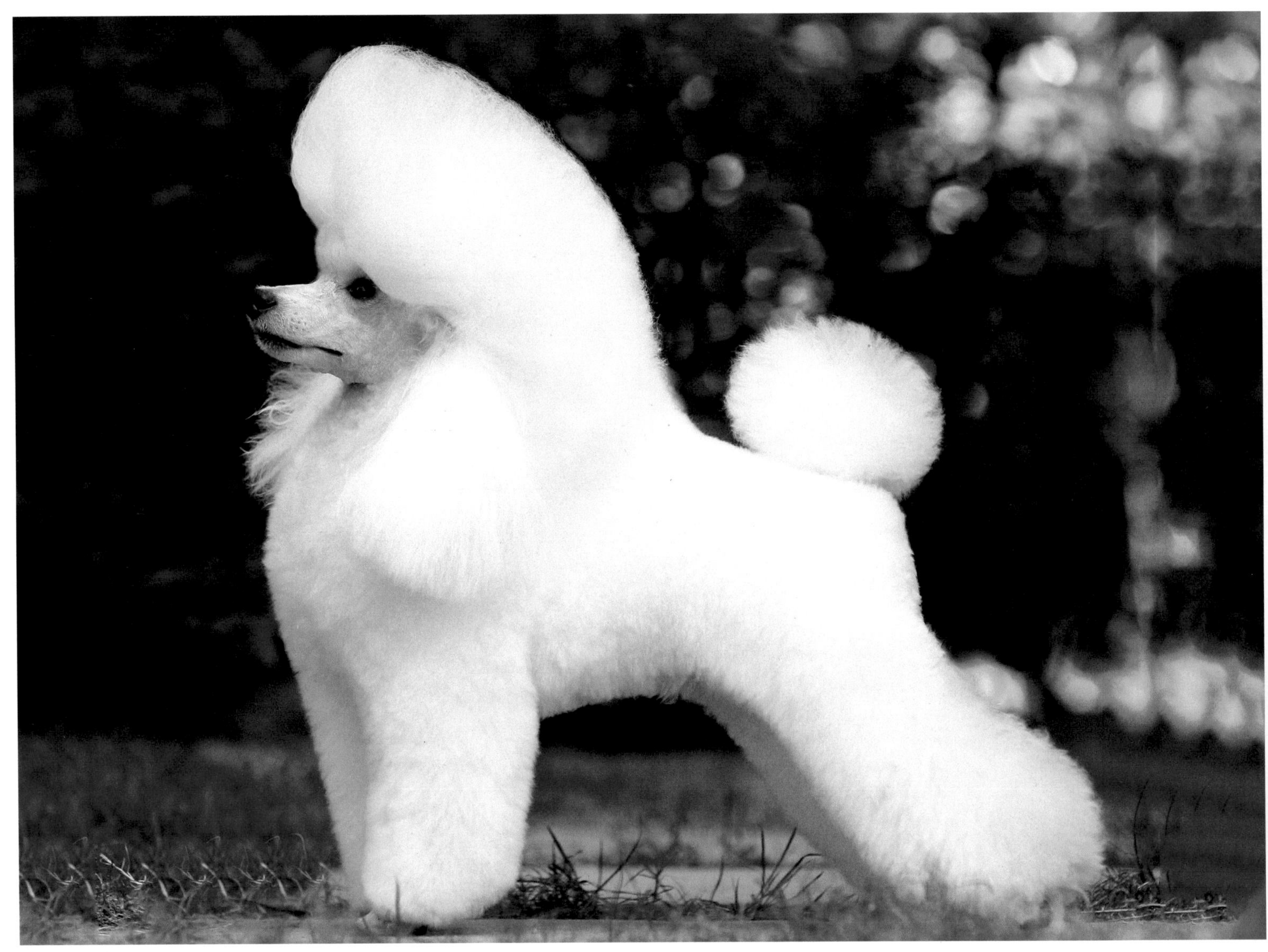

HISTORY

Although the Poodle is most often identified with France, its earliest ancestors were probably curly-coated dogs from central Asia that assisted with herding and followed many routes into various parts of Europe. Interwoven in their ancestry are also several rough-coated water dogs. Perhaps the earliest incarnation of the Poodle was the Barbet, a curly-coated dog distributed in France, Russia, Hungary, and elsewhere. It is the German version, however, that exerted most influence on the modern Poodle. In fact, the word poodle comes from the German word *pfudel*, meaning puddle or "to splash," probably reflecting the dog's water abilities. In France, it was known as *caniche* or *chien canard*, both referring to its duck-hunting abilities. Thus, from herding and water roots the

ILLUSTRATED STANDARD

1 Long, fine, chiseled muzzle
2 Slight but definite stop
3 Oval eyes
4 Tail straight and carried up; docked
5 Level topline
6 Small, oval feet

Color: any solid color
DQ: over 10″ in height; a dog in any but one of the specified clips; a dog not a solid color

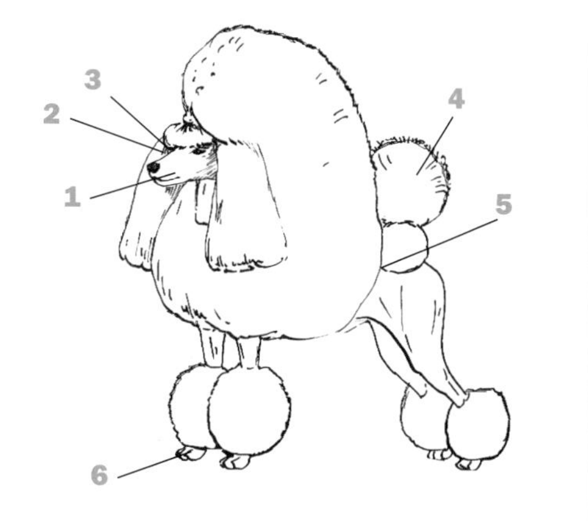

Poodle became a talented water-hunting companion. The Poodle was also drawn into service as a military dog, guide dog, guard dog, wagon puller for performers, and eventually, a circus performer. Its coat was shorn close to facilitate swimming, but left slightly longer on the chest for warmth in cold water. Although some believe the puffs of hair around the leg joints and tail tip were for protection when hunting, other evidence suggests that they arose as decoration during the Poodle's performing days. The Poodle found favor as an elegant companion for fashionable ladies. It became favored by French aristocracy and eventually became the national dog of France. Its characteristic clip was accentuated, and a successful effort was made to perfect the smaller specimens. Poodles entered the show ring in the late 1800s. Some of the early show Poodles were shown in corded coats, in which the hair is allowed to mat in long thin tresses rather than be brushed out. While eye-catching, the upkeep was difficult and the trend died out by the early 1900s, being replaced by the bouffant styles still in vogue. At the same time Poodle popularity in America waned, so that, by the late 1920s, Poodles had almost died out in North America. In the 1930s, the breed staged a comeback that eventually placed it as the most popular dog in America for decades.

TEMPERAMENT

The pert and peppy Toy Poodle is one of the brightest and easiest breeds to train. It is alert, responsive, playful, lively, sensitive, and eager to please. It is devoted to its family. Some can be reserved with strangers; some may bark a lot.

UPKEEP

Poodles need a lot of interaction with people. They also need mental and physical exercise. The Toy Poodle's exercise needs can be met with a short walk or even indoor games. Its coat should be brushed every day or two. Poodle hair, when shed, does not fall out but becomes caught in the surrounding hair, which can cause matting if not removed. Clipping should be done at least four times a year, with the face and feet clipped monthly. Although most Poodles are professionally groomed, owners can learn to groom their own dog.

HEALTH

- Major concerns: PRA, patellar luxation, Legg–Perthes, epilepsy
- Minor concerns: trichiasis, entropion, lacrimal duct atresia, cataract
- Occasionally seen: urolithiasis, intervertebral disk degeneration
- Suggested tests: eye, knee, (hip), DNA for PRA
- Life span: 12–14 years

FORM AND FUNCTION

The Poodle is a square, proportioned dog with proud carriage and elegant appearance. It should move with a light, springy, effortless stride. The Poodle stems from working retriever stock, and its conformation should reflect its athletic background. The coat is curly, harsh, and dense. The traditional clips stem from the function of the coat in protecting and insulating the dog's joints and chest.

Pug

AT A GLANCE

Energy level:	■■■	Watchdog ability:	■■■■■
Exercise requirements:	■■	Protection ability:	■
Playfulness:	■■■■	Grooming requirements:	■■
Affection level:	■■■■	Cold tolerance:	■■■
Friendliness toward dogs:	■■■	Heat tolerance:	■
Friendliness toward other pets:	■■■		
Friendliness toward strangers:	■■	WEIGHT: 14–18 lb	
Ease of training:	■■■	HEIGHT: 10–11″*	

POPULARITY: Popular
FAMILY: Mastiff, Bull
AREA OF ORIGIN: China
DATE OF ORIGIN: Ancient times
ORIGINAL FUNCTION: Lapdog
TODAY'S FUNCTION: Companion
OTHER NAME: Mops, Carlin

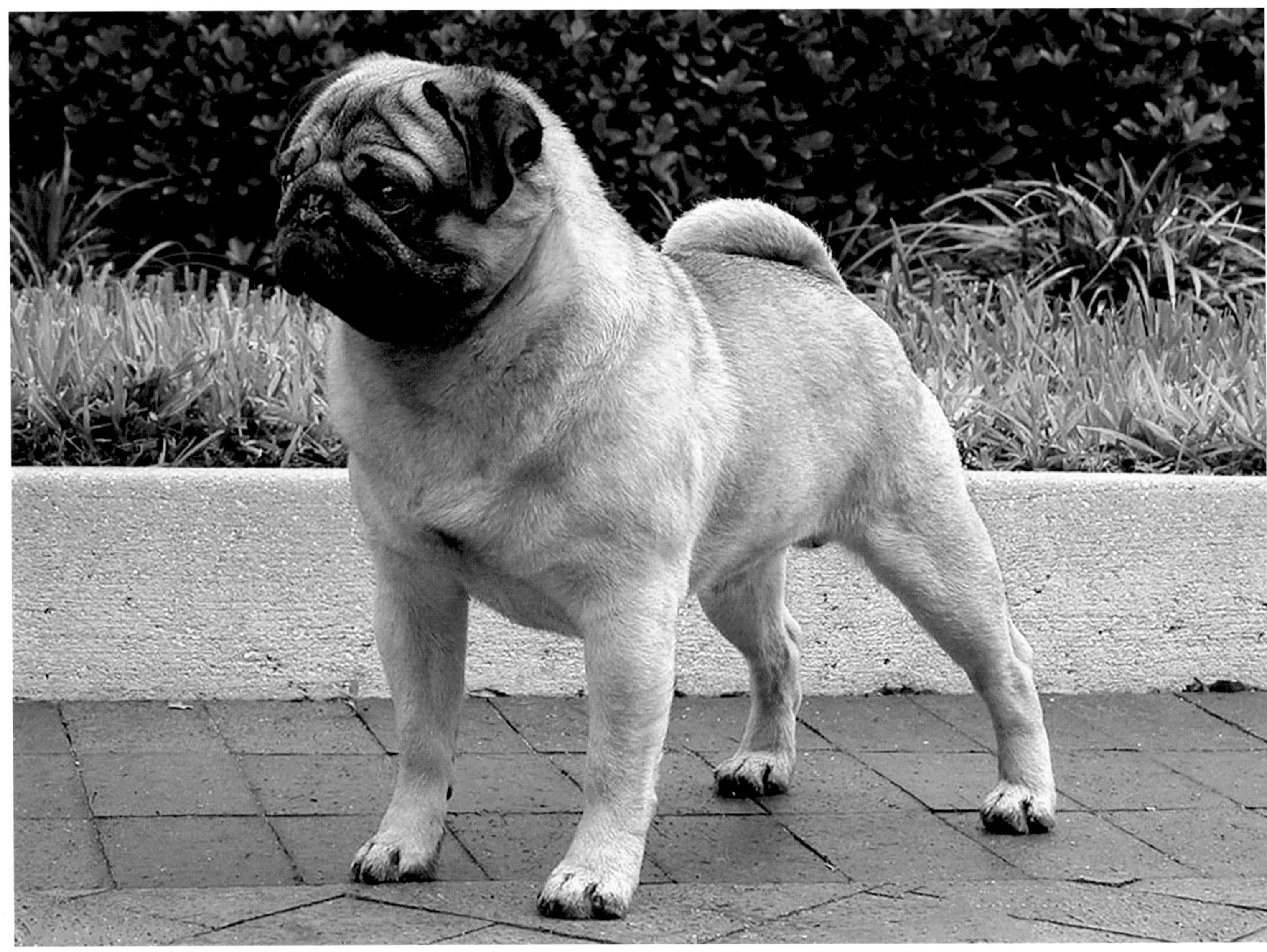

HISTORY

The Pug has been known by many names: Mopshond in Holland (which refers to its grumbling tendencies); Mops in Germany, and Dutch or Chinese Pug in England. The word *Pug* is derived either from the Latin *pugnus* meaning fist, as the head may have resembled a clenched fist, or from the marmoset "Pug" monkeys that were popular pets in the eighteenth century and that the Pug dogs somewhat resemble. Whatever the name, one thing is true: the Pug's official motto "Multum in Parvo" (a lot in a little) fits it exactly. The Pug is somewhat of an exception in the Toy Group because it is perhaps the only one to be descended from mastiff forebears. Although its exact ancestry has been lost in antiquity, the Pug retains many mastiff characteristics. This is an ancient breed, one of several miniaturized

ILLUSTRATED STANDARD

1 Slightly undershot
2 Short, square muzzle
3 Large, prominent eyes
4 Massive, round head
5 Thin, small ears, either rose or button
6 Tail curled as tightly as possible over hip; double curl preferred

Color: silver, apricot-fawn, or black, with black muzzle or mask, ears, cheek moles, and trace down back
DQ: none

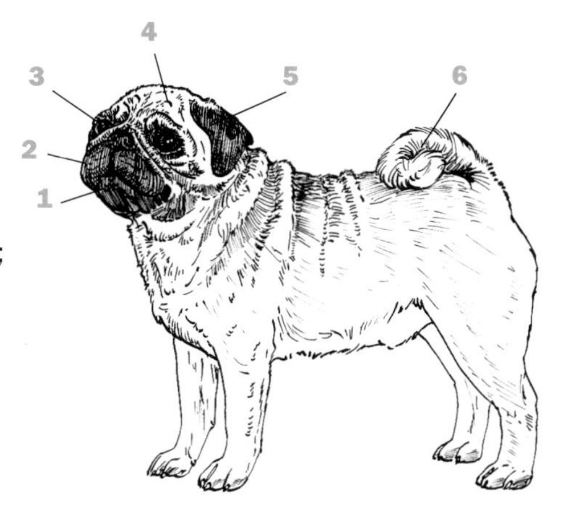

HEALTH

- Major concerns: Pug dog encephalitis, CHD, brachycephalic syndrome
- Minor concerns: elongated palate, stenotic nares, patellar luxation, Legg-Perthes, entropion, KCS, skin infections, hemivertebra
- Occasionally seen: seizures, nerve degeneration, distichiasis, allergies, demodicosis
- Suggested tests: eye, hip, knee, DNA Pug dog encephalitis
- Life span: 12–15 years
- Note: The Pug cannot tolerate heat and is sensitive to anesthesia. It is prone to corneal abrasion and obesity.

in the Orient, where it was a favorite pet of Buddhist monasteries in Tibet many centuries ago. In China, the facial wrinkles were an essential breed feature, most notably the "prince mark," or vertical wrinkle on the forehead, which bore a resemblance to the Chinese character for "prince." Pugs probably came to Holland by way of the Dutch East India Trading Company. Here they became quite popular and were recognized as the official dog of the House of Orange after one saved the life of Prince William by sounding an alarm at the approach of Spanish soldiers in 1572. By 1790, the Pug could be found in France; Napoleon's wife Josephine used her Pug to carry messages to Napoleon when she was imprisoned. Pugs were first brought to England during Victorian times and became incredibly popular with the wealthy, displacing the King Charles Spaniel as the favored royal breed. Pugs of Victorian England usually had cropped ears, further accentuating their wrinkled faces. Several Pugs were brought to England from China in 1886. A year earlier, the breed had been recognized by the AKC. Since that time, it has remained popular as both a pet and show dog.

TEMPERAMENT

A delightful blend of dignity and comedy, the Pug is an amiable, playful, and confident companion. It can be stubborn and headstrong, but it is pleasant and generally willing to please. It loves to cavort and show off.

UPKEEP

The Pug needs daily exercise, either in the form of a lively game or a moderate walk on leash. It does not do well in heat and humidity. It needs minimal coat care but daily cleaning of facial wrinkles. Its smooth coat needs only occasional brushing to remove dead hairs; however, the wrinkles need regular cleaning and drying to prevent skin infections. The Pug wheezes and snores.

FORM AND FUNCTION

Square-proportioned, compact and of a cobby build, the Pug is a large dog in a little space. The gait is strong and jaunty, but with a slight roll of the hindquarters. The distinctive expression is soft and solicitous. The forehead has large, deep wrinkles. The coat is fine, smooth, and short.

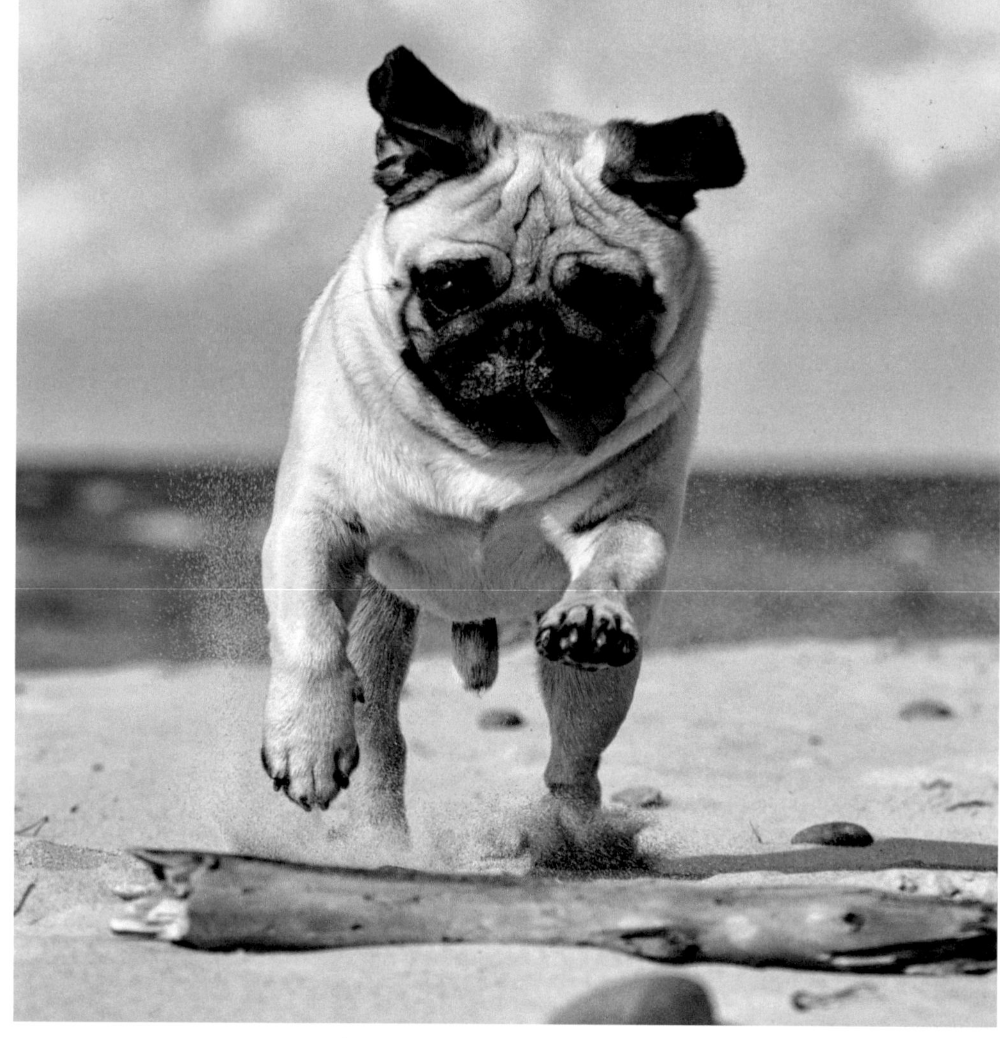

Shih Tzu

AT A GLANCE

Energy level:	■■■	Watchdog ability:	■■■	POPULARITY: Very popular
Exercise requirements:	■	Protection ability:	■	FAMILY: Oriental
Playfulness:	■■■■	Grooming requirements:	■■■■	AREA OF ORIGIN: China and Tibet
Affection level:	■■■■	Cold tolerance:	■■	DATE OF ORIGIN: Ancient times
Friendliness toward dogs:	■■■■	Heat tolerance:	■	ORIGINAL FUNCTION: Lapdog
Friendliness toward other pets:	■■■■			TODAY'S FUNCTION: Companion
Friendliness toward strangers:	■■■■	WEIGHT: 9–16 lb		OTHER NAME: Chrysanthemum Dog
Ease of training:	■■	HEIGHT: 8–11″ (ideally 9–10.5″)		

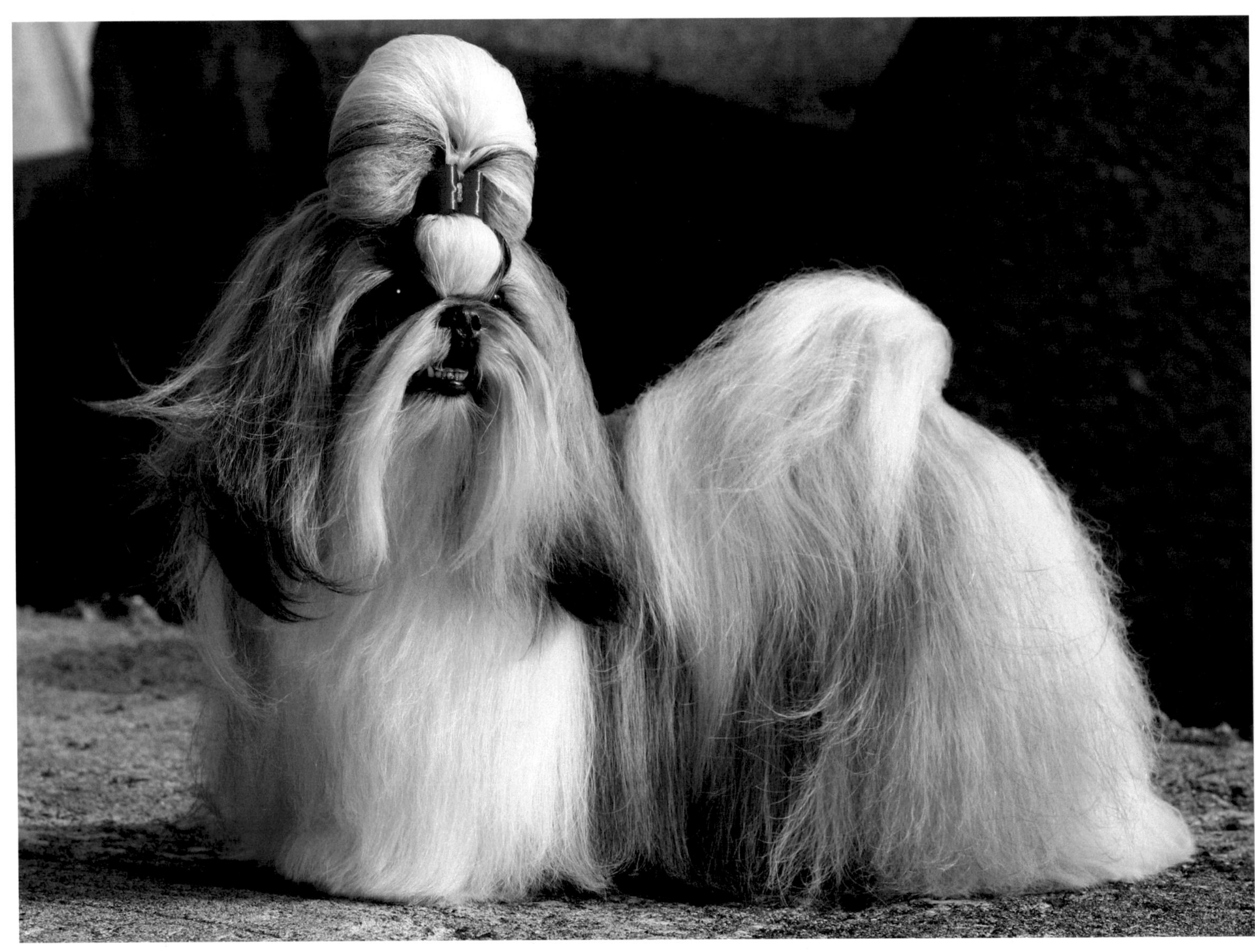

HISTORY

The Shih Tzu (or more properly, Shih Tzu Kou) means Lion Dog, designating the breed as one of the most esteemed animals in China because of its association with Buddhism. Even though the Shih Tzu is most often associated with China, it probably originated in Tibet as early as the seventeenth century, where it enjoyed status as a holy dog. The Shih Tzu as it is known today developed most distinctively in China during the reign of the Dowager Empress Cixi (Tz'u-shi, 1861–1908). The Shih Tzu and Pekingese share similar histories; however, the Shih Tzu can usually be differentiated from the Pekingese in Chinese art by the presence of bumps on the tops of the head, denoting a topknot, or pien-ji. The Shih Tzu was a favored house pet during the Ming dynasty and was highly prized

ILLUSTRATED STANDARD

1 Undershot bite
2 Short, square muzzle
3 Domed skull with definite stop
4 Round, broad head
5 Level topline
6 Tail carried well over back
7 No waist or tuck-up

Color: any
DQ: none

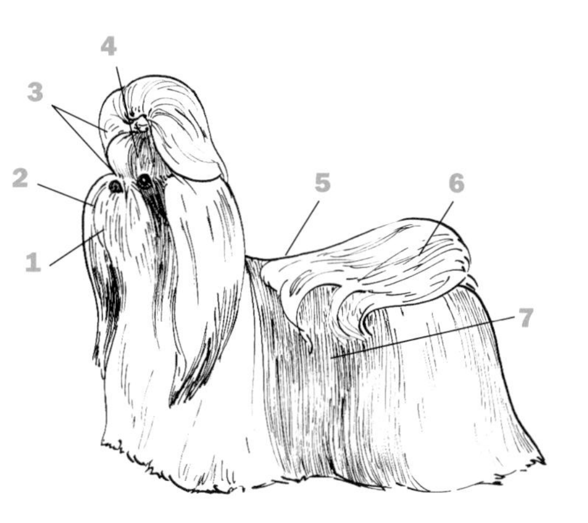

by the royal family. When the British looted the Imperial Palace, most of the dogs were lost, and the breed suffered a great setback. The Shih Tzu was first exhibited in China as the Lhassa Terrier or Tibetan Poodle. In 1935, it was exhibited as the Lhassa Lion Dog; by that time, it was becoming very popular. A similar state of confusion existed in England, where the Lhasa Apso and Shih Tzu were both lumped together as the Apso (meaning shaggy). In 1934, soon after the Apso was first shown, it was divided into two separate breeds, with the smaller, wider-skulled, shorter-nosed dogs from Peking dubbed Shih Tzu, their colloquial Chinese name. In 1952 a single Pekingese cross was authorized to improve certain points, but such crosses have never again been permitted. In the United States, the breed began to become extremely popular in the 1960s, leading to AKC recognition in 1969. Its popularity has continued to grow, and it is one of the most popular toys.

TEMPERAMENT

The spunky but sweet Shih Tzu is both a gentle lapdog and a vivacious companion. It has an upbeat attitude and loves to play and romp. It is affectionate to its family and good with children. It is surprisingly tough and does have a stubborn streak.

UPKEEP

Despite its small size, the Shih Tzu needs daily exercise. Because of its small size, it can meet its requirements with vigorous indoor games or short frolics outside or with short walks on leash. It does not do well in hot humid weather. Its luxurious coat needs brushing or combing every other day; puppies should be taught to accept grooming from a young age. Pets may be clipped.

HEALTH

- Major concerns: CHD
- Minor concerns: renal dysplsia, entropion, trichiasis, PRA, KCS, otitis externa, portacaval shunt, inguinal hernia, patellar luxation
- Occasionally seen: cataract, dental problems
- Suggested tests: eye, hip, DNA for renal dysplasia
- Life span: 11–14 years

FORM AND FUNCTION

Compact, yet slightly longer than it is tall, the Shih Tzu hides a sturdy body beneath its mantle of luxurious hair. It has a smooth, effortless stride with good reach and drive. Even though its function is that of companion, it should nonetheless be structurally sound. Its expression is warm, sweet, and wide-eyed, imparting the impression of trust and friendliness. The long, dense coat is double and fairly straight.

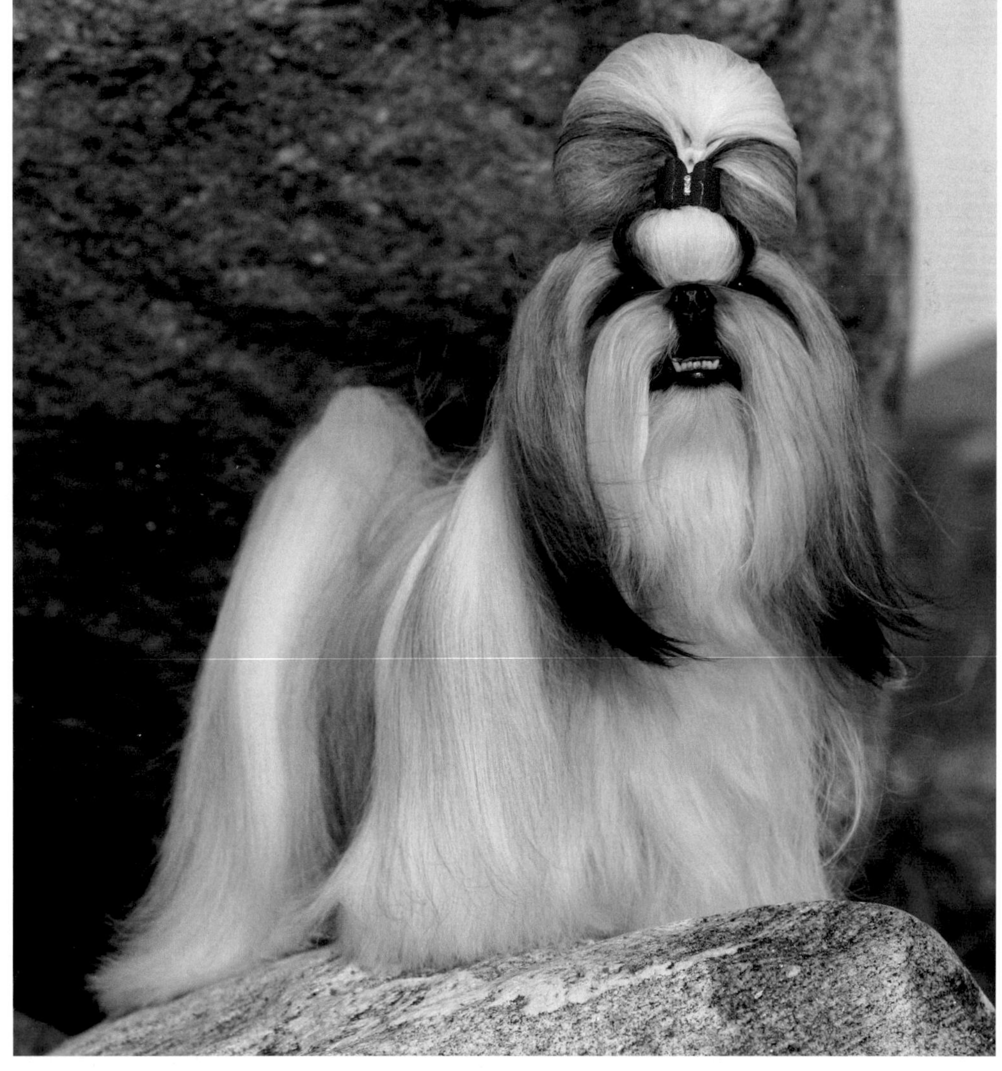

Silky Terrier

AT A GLANCE

Energy level:	■■■■	Watchdog ability:	■■■■■
Exercise requirements:	■■	Protection ability:	■
Playfulness:	■■■■	Grooming requirements:	■■■
Affection level:	■■■	Cold tolerance:	■■■
Friendliness toward dogs:	■■■	Heat tolerance:	■■■
Friendliness toward other pets:	■■■		
Friendliness toward strangers:	■■■	WEIGHT: 8–11 lb*	
Ease of training:	■■■	HEIGHT: 9–10″	

POPULARITY: Somewhat uncommon
FAMILY: Terrier
AREA OF ORIGIN: Australia
DATE OF ORIGIN: Late 1800s
ORIGINAL FUNCTION: Companion, small vermin hunting
TODAY'S FUNCTION: Earthdog trials
OTHER NAME: Sydney Silky, Australian Silky Terrier

HISTORY

In the late 1800s, Yorkshire Terriers were brought to Australia from England. These dogs had striking steel blue and tan coat coloration and were bred with the native blue and tan Australian Terriers in an effort to improve the latter's coat color while retaining its more robust conformation. Both the Yorkshire Terrier and the Australian Terrier were rather recent developments from crosses of a number of other terrier breeds. Some of the descendents from these crosses were shown as Yorkshire Terriers and some as Australian Terriers. A few, however, were exhibited under a new name, Silky Terriers, because it was felt that they were the beginning of a separate breed, intermediate in size and coat length between its parental stock. Interbreeding these Silkies did, in fact, produce a true breeding strain within a

ILLUSTRATED STANDARD

1 Small, almond-shaped eyes
2 Flat skull with shallow stop
3 Small, V-shaped, erect ears
4 Level topline
5 Docked tail carried high
6 Small cat feet

Color: blue and tan
DQ: none

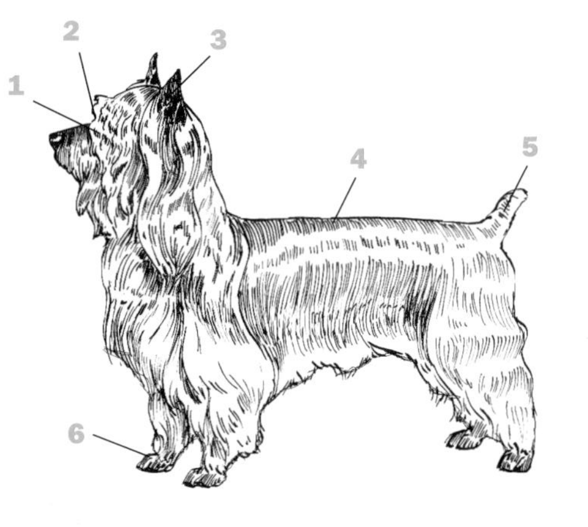

short time. Because the breed was developed in two separate areas of Australia, separate breed standards were drawn up from each area in 1906 and 1910, with weight being the major disagreement. In 1926, a revised standard encompassing all areas was accepted, with accepted weights being somewhat of a compromise. The breed was popularly known as the Sydney Silky Terrier in Australia until it was changed to Australian Silky Terrier in 1955. In America, the name was changed to Silky Terrier in 1955, just prior to its recognition by the AKC. Although not a rare breed, the Silky Terrier has been somewhat slow to attract admirers and is only moderately popular.

TEMPERAMENT

The Silky Terrier is no mellow lapdog. It is bold, feisty, inquisitive, and playful, ever ready for action—a terrier at heart. It can be aggressive toward other dogs or pets. It is clever, but tends to be stubborn, and can be mischievous. It tends to bark a lot.

UPKEEP

This is an active breed requiring slightly more exercise than most toys. It enjoys a moderate walk on leash, but it especially likes the chance to nose around on its own in a safe area. Much of its exercise requirements can be met with vigorous indoor games. Its coat needs brushing or combing every other day.

HEALTH

- Major concerns: none
- Minor concerns: patellar luxation, Legg–Perthes
- Occasionally seen: diabetes, epilepsy, tracheal collapse, allergies, Cushing's
- Suggested tests: knee, eye
- Life span: 11–14 years

FORM AND FUNCTION

The Silky Terrier is a miniature version of a working terrier, and as such retains the essential features of a vermin hunter. It is somewhat longer than tall, and though of refined bone, it should nonetheless have sufficient strength and substance to suggest that it could kill small rodents. The gait is free and light-footed; the expression is piercingly keen. The straight, single coat is silky and glossy, following the body outline rather than falling to the floor.

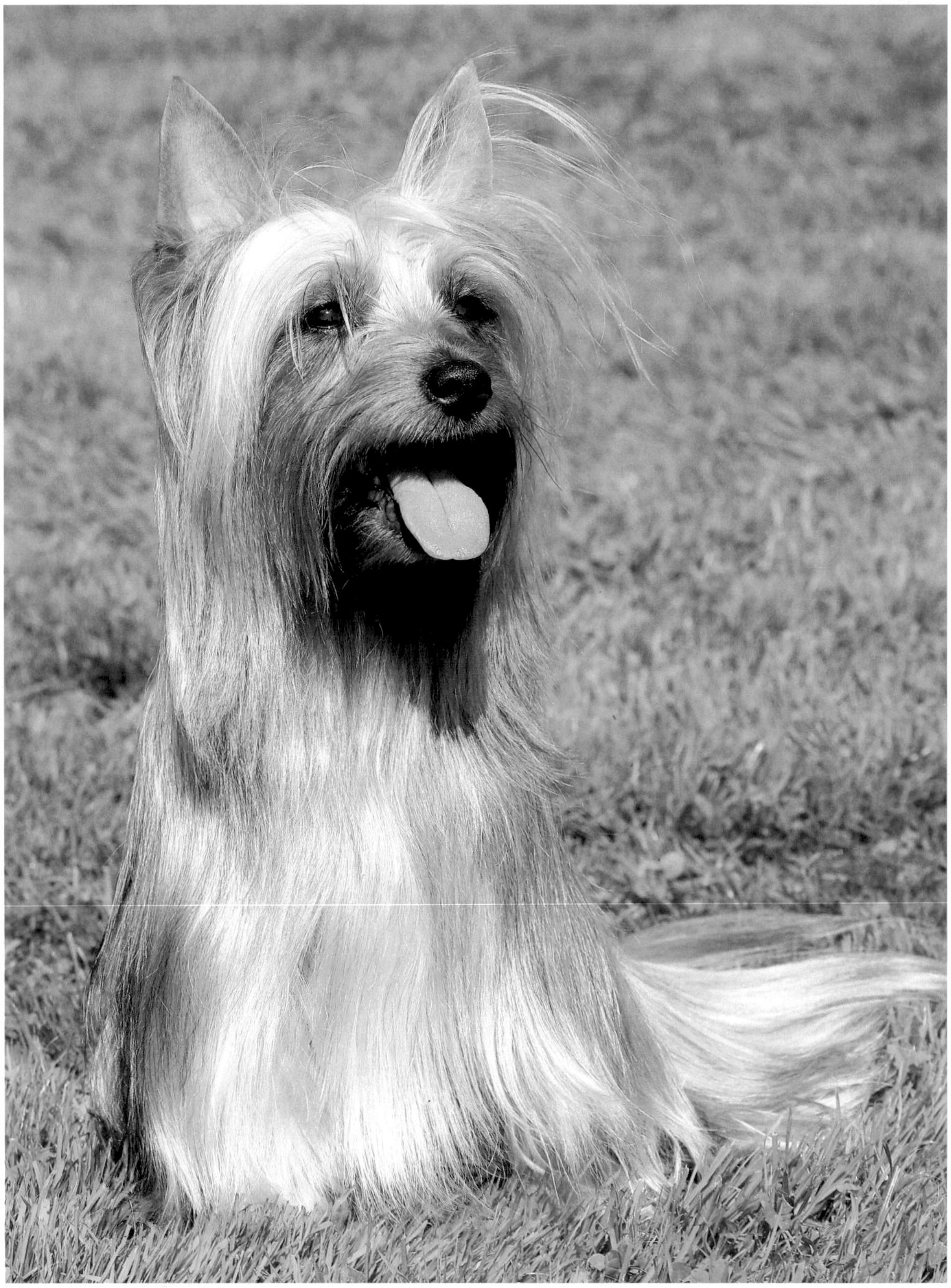

Toy Fox Terrier

AT A GLANCE

Energy level:	■ ■ ■ ■	Watchdog ability:	■ ■ ■ ■ ■
Exercise requirements:	■ ■	Protection ability:	■ ■
Playfulness:	■ ■ ■ ■ ■	Grooming requirements:	■
Affection level:	■ ■ ■ ■ ■	Cold tolerance:	■
Friendliness toward dogs:	■ ■ ■	Heat tolerance:	■ ■ ■
Friendliness toward other pets:	■ ■ ■		
Friendliness toward strangers:	■ ■	WEIGHT: 3.5–7 lb	
Ease of training:	■ ■ ■ ■	HEIGHT: 8.5–11″ (9–11″ preferred)	

POPULARITY: Uncommon
FAMILY: Terrier
AREA OF ORIGIN: United States
DATE OF ORIGIN: Early 1900s
ORIGINAL FUNCTION: Vermin control
TODAY'S FUNCTION: Companion
OTHER NAME: American Toy Terrier, Amertoy

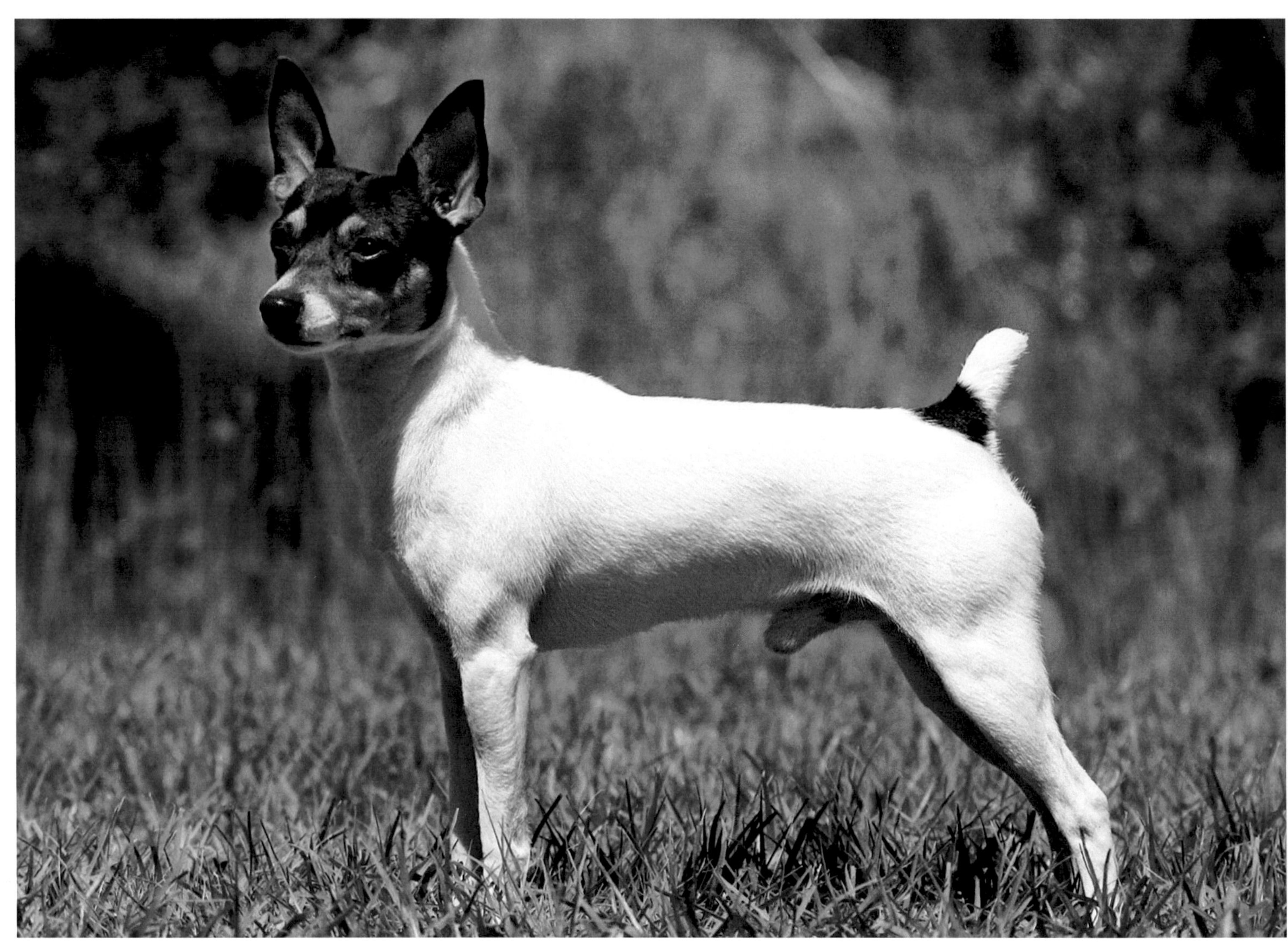

HISTORY

Smooth Fox Terriers have long been a favorite of farmers and pet owners. American farmers found smaller individuals, or what they called runts, were especially scrappy, as well as handy for catching rodents around the farm. Pet owners found them especially entertaining and handier for having around the house. In the early 1900s these smaller fox terriers were crossed with several toy breeds, including the Toy Manchester Terrier, Chihuahua, and possibly Italian Greyhound. The result was a smaller version of the Smooth Fox Terrier with a few important differences. The fiery temperament was still there, but tempered a bit…just a bit. The smaller dogs were still registered with the UKC as Smooth Fox Terriers, but in 1936 the UKC granted them their own name and breed status. The Toy Fox Terrier is easier for many people to live with, without sacrificing the traits that drew them to

ILLUSTRATED STANDARD

1 Round somewhat prominent eyes
2 Erect, pointed, high-set ears
3 Level topline
4 Moderate tuck-up
5 Straight pasterns
6 Small oval feet
7 High-set tail, held erect, docked to third or fourth vertebra

Color: tri-color; white, chocolate and tan; white and tan; or white and black, all with predominately colored head and more than 50 percent white on body
DQ: under 8.5″ or over 11.5″; ears not erect on dog over six months old; dudley nose; undershot, wry mouth or overshot more than 1/8″; blaze extending into eye or ears; any but stated color combinations; more than 50 percent white on head; less than 50 percent white on body; head and body spots of different colors

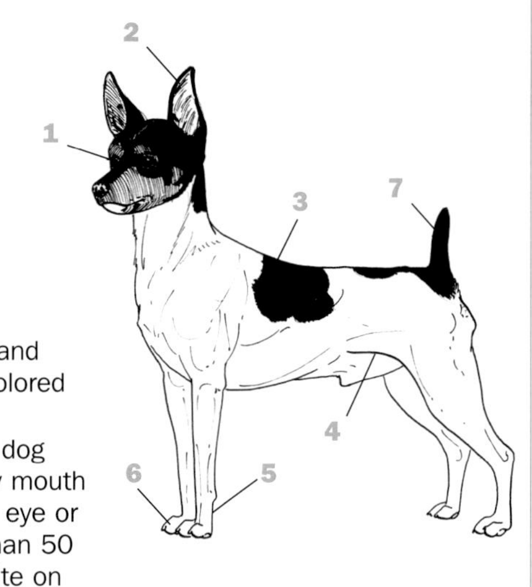

HEALTH

- Major concerns: none
- Minor concerns: patellar luxation, Legg-Perthes, demodicosis, congenital hypothyroidism with goiter
- Occasionally seen: vWD, lens luxation
- Suggested tests: knee, DNA for congenital hypothyroidism, DNA for lens luxation, (vWD)
- Life span: 13–14 years

FORM AND FUNCTION

The Toy Fox Terrier has all the same traits that make the Smooth Fox Terrier such a successful hunter—just in a diminutive package. This is an athletic, agile, and graceful dog with surprising strength and the stamina to frolic all day. The gait is smooth and effortless. The coat is short and smooth, perfect for caressing.

the Fox Terrier family in the first place. They remained one of the most popular non-AKC companion breeds in the country until 2003, when they entered the AKC show ring for the first time.

TEMPERAMENT

TFTs are TNT in a small bundle. Feisty and fun-loving, they are hunting terriers at heart and will spend hours investigating the yard, your cabinets, and places you never knew existed. They love to play with people and toys, and make excellent companions for careful older children; however, they do not tolerate inconsiderate handling. They can entertain for hours and are also content to snuggle on a warm lap during recess. This is a one-family, even one-person, breed that doesn't warm to strangers initially. The TFT's intelligence, energy, and penchant for showing off make it a quick study and impressive trick dog.

UPKEEP

Upkeep consists of making sure the TFT is supplied with toys, playmates, and an appreciative audience. It needs the opportunity to exercise its mind and body, but it can do so in a small area. Without sufficient attention, exercise, and training, it can dig and bark. The Toy Fox Terrier appreciates a warm, soft bed or lap. It does not care to be wet or cold, and should wear a sweater and even protective earmuffs in cold weather. Coat care is wash and wear.

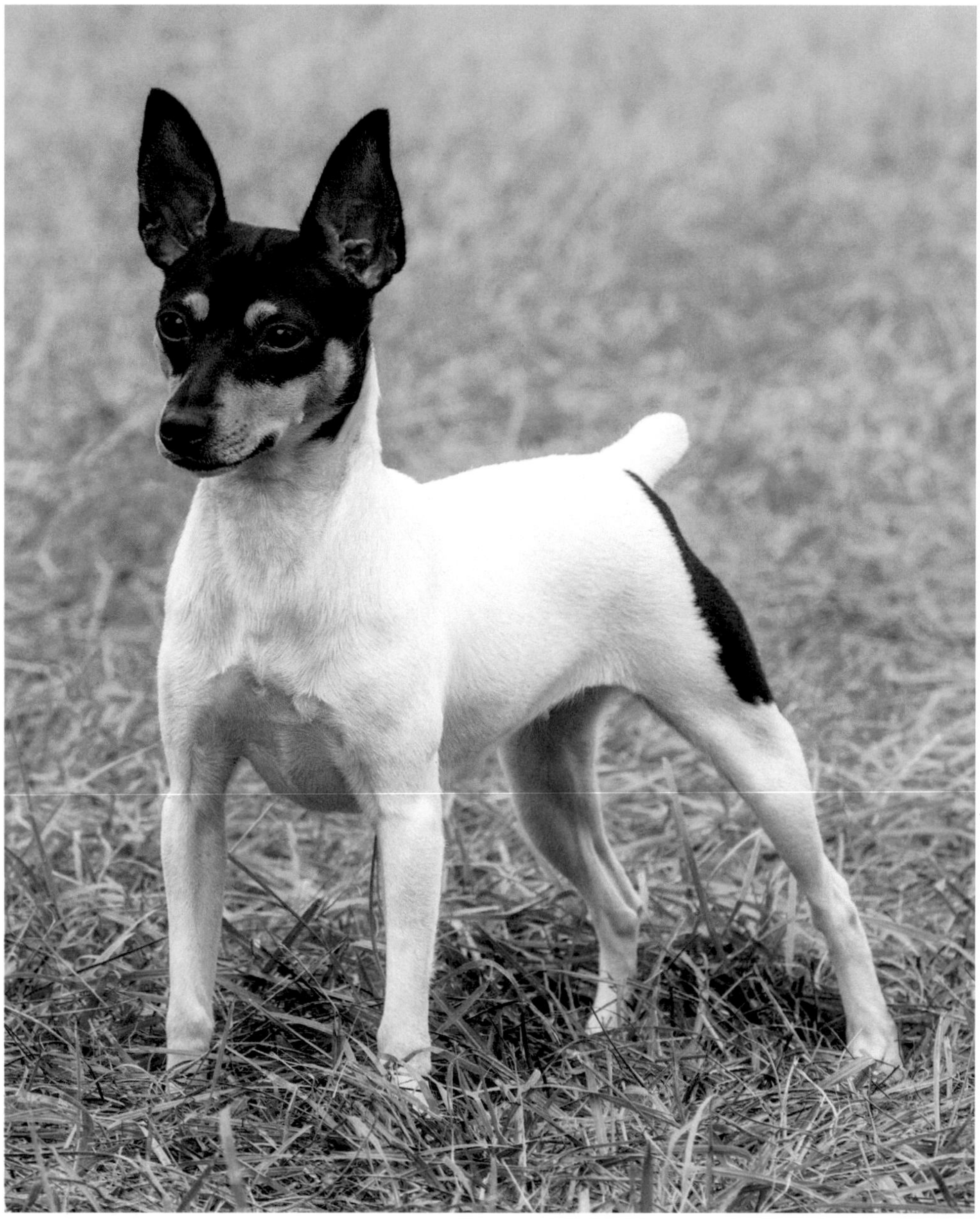

Yorkshire Terrier

AT A GLANCE

Energy level:	■■■■	Watchdog ability:	■■■■■	POPULARITY: Most popular
Exercise requirements:	■	Protection ability:	■	FAMILY: Terrier
Playfulness:	■■■■	Grooming requirements:	■■■■	AREA OF ORIGIN: England
Affection level:	■■■	Cold tolerance:	■	DATE OF ORIGIN: 1800s
Friendliness toward dogs:	■■	Heat tolerance:	■■	ORIGINAL FUNCTION: Small vermin hunting
Friendliness toward other pets:	■■			TODAY'S FUNCTION: Companion
Friendliness toward strangers:	■■■	WEIGHT: not to exceed 7 lb		OTHER NAME: None
Ease of training:	■■	HEIGHT: 8–9″*		

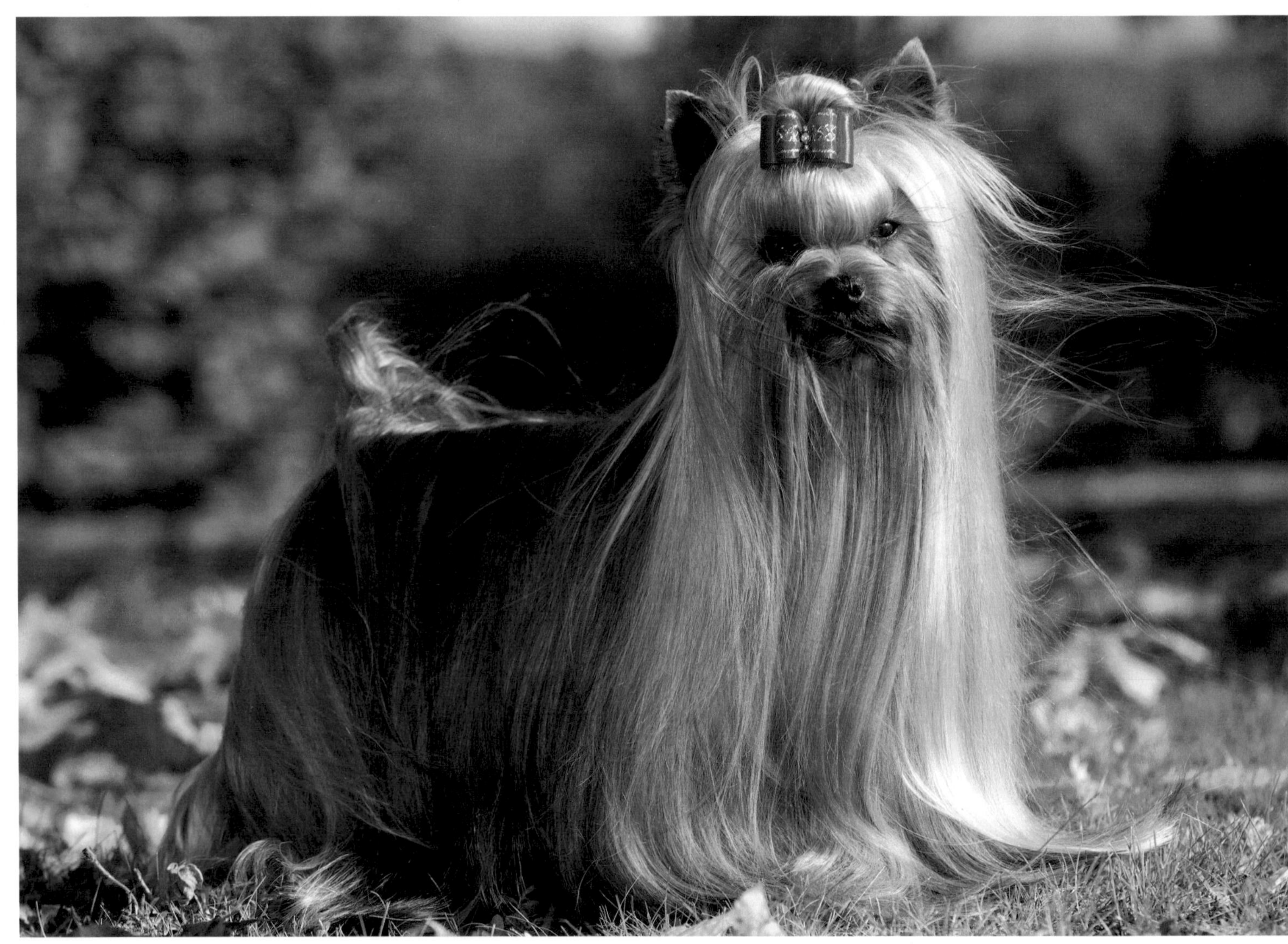

HISTORY

The Yorkshire Terrier doesn't look like a product of the working class, nor does it look like a ratter, but it is both. In fact, the Yorkshire area of England is known for producing fine animals, and it is thought that the Yorkie was no accident but rather the result of purposeful crosses between a variety of terriers, probably including the Waterside Terrier, Clydesdale Terrier, Paisley Terrier, rough-coated English Black and Tan Terrier, and perhaps even the Skye Terrier and Dandie Dinmont Terrier. The Waterside Terrier was one of its major progenitors; these were small blue-gray dogs with fairly long hair, usually weighing around 10 pounds, brought from Scotland by weavers. Because of its modest roots, the Yorkshire Terrier was initially looked down upon by the wealthier dog fanciers. Even the most snobbish could not deny the breed's obvious beauty, however, and in short order, Yorkies were gracing show rings

ILLUSTRATED STANDARD

1 Medium-sized eyes
2 Small, V-shaped ears, carried erect
3 Small head, rather flat on top
4 Level topline
5 Tail docked to a medium length and carried slightly higher than the level of back
6 Round feet

Color: blue and tan; Yorkshire Terriers are born black, gradually attaining their blue and tan coloration as they mature
DQ: none

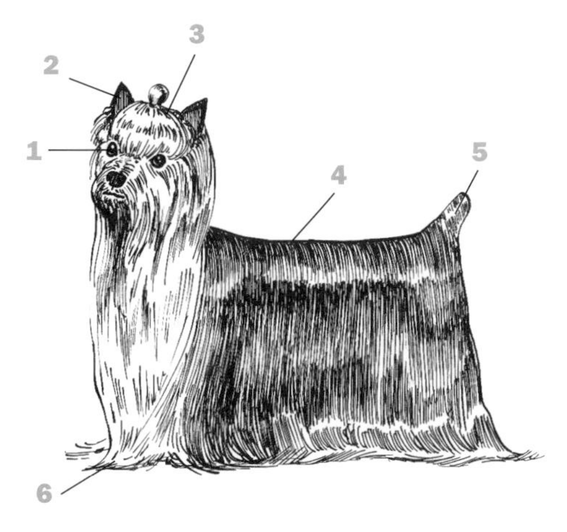

and the laps of wealthy mistresses. By 1880, Yorkies had come to America, but the breed varied so much in size that there was great confusion concerning how big a Yorkshire Terrier should be. Many of these early Yorkies weighed between 12 and 14 pounds. By 1900, fanciers on both sides of the Atlantic had decided that the small size was preferable and made a concerted effort to breed a smaller Yorkie with even longer coat. They were successful, and the modern Yorkshire Terrier is one of the smaller and most luxuriously coated dogs in existence. These traits, along with its terrier heritage, have placed it as a consistent favorite with pet owners and show fanciers alike.

TEMPERAMENT
The Yorkshire Terrier seems oblivious of its small size, ever eager for adventure and trouble. It is busy, inquisitive, bold, stubborn, and can be aggressive to strange dogs and small animals—in other words, it is true to its terrier heritage. Although some tend to bark a lot, it can easily be taught not to do so.

UPKEEP
Yorkies tend to exercise themselves within the home, but they also need to have interaction in the form of games. They appreciate a short walk outdoors on leash and enjoy the chance to explore a safe area. The long coat needs brushing or combing every day or two.

HEALTH
- Major concerns: none
- Minor concerns: patellar luxation
- Occasionally seen: portacaval shunt, PRA, tracheal collapse, Legg-Perthes
- Suggested tests: knee, eye, (hip), (thyroid)
- Life span: 14–16 years

FORM AND FUNCTION
The Yorkie's terrier heritage can be seen in its sharp, intelligent expression, confident carriage, and compact body. It is a diminutive breed, however, now more noted for its long, silky hair, which should be fine, glossy, and perfectly straight. Color is a hallmark of this breed, with the blue a dark steel blue and the tan a clear tan.

This is the most diverse of all groups, sometimes considered a catchall for breeds that defy categorization elsewhere or that no longer have a tenable function. Some prefer to call it the Companion Group because these dogs tend to have in common at least a recent background of being bred solely for companionship purposes. The background of these dogs is so varied, however, that it would be unrealistic to classify them as generally better companions than any other group. Each breed must be evaluated on its own merits in this group.

THE NON-SPORTING GROUP

American Eskimo Dog

AT A GLANCE

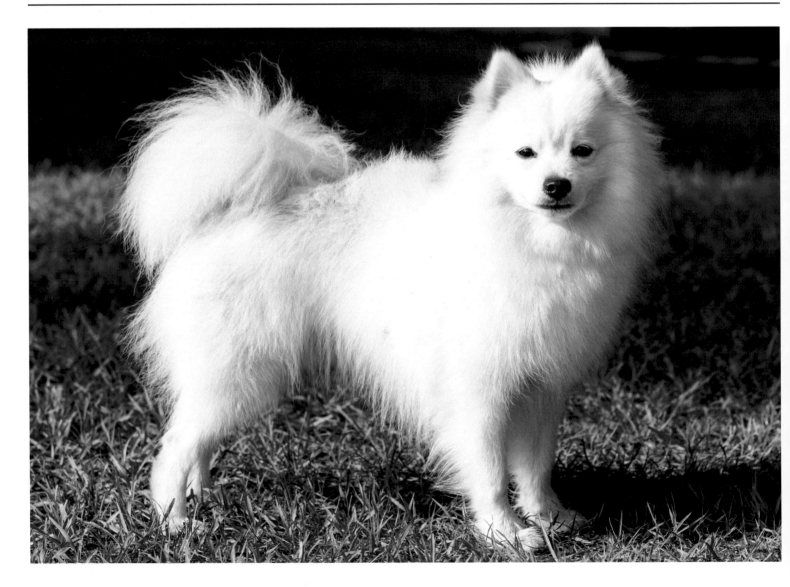

Energy level:	■■■
Exercise requirements:	■■■
Playfulness:	■■■■
Affection level:	■■■
Friendliness toward dogs:	■■
Friendliness toward other pets:	■■
Friendliness toward strangers:	■■
Ease of training:	■■■■

Watchdog ability:	■■■■■
Protection ability:	■
Grooming requirements:	■■■
Cold tolerance:	■■■■
Heat tolerance:	■

WEIGHT: standard: 20–40 lb*; miniature: 11–20 lb*; toy: 6–10 lb*
HEIGHT: standard: 15-19″; miniature: 12–15″; toy: 9–12″

POPULARITY: Uncommon
FAMILY: Spitz
AREA OF ORIGIN: United States
DATE OF ORIGIN: Early 1900s
ORIGINAL FUNCTION: Watchdog, performer, farm worker
TODAY'S FUNCTION: Companion
OTHER NAME: None

HISTORY

As the prototypical spitz, the Eskie (as it is often called) is just as often simply called spitz by pet owners. In fact, the American Eskimo Dog descended from one of the varieties of spitz developed in Germany, with influences from other spitz breeds such as the Keeshond, Pomeranian, and Volpino Italiano. Ironically, it was the success of these other breeds that held the Eskie back. Although the Keeshond originally came in several colors, when it was decided to accept only gray specimens, the white Keeshonden were suddenly excluded. When the Pomeranian standard was drawn up to exclude dogs over 8 pounds, larger dogs were excluded as Pomeranians. Thus, by the early 1900s, there was two groups of medium-sized white dogs that, although pure-breds,

ILLUSTRATED STANDARD

1 Black lips, nose, and eye rims
2 Softly wedge-shaped head
3 Erect, triangular ears
4 Lionlike ruff
5 Compact body
6 Oval feet

Color: white or white with biscuit cream
DQ: any color other than white or biscuit cream; blue eyes; height under 9" or over 19"

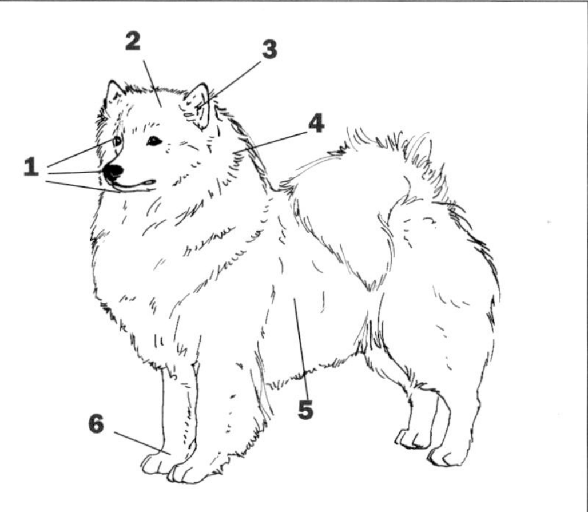

were excluded from their breeds. Their fate is unknown, but it is likely that they became pets of the working people. When European workers came to America, they brought these dogs with them as general farm workers and watchdogs. The UKC began registering them in 1913. In the 1920s the American Spitz (as it had come to be called) became a favorite of circus performers. Spectators often left the circus with a new purchase and family member—an offspring of one of the dazzling performers. Many present-day Eskies can be traced back to their circus ancestors. After World War I, the breed's name was changed to American Eskimos, to remove any Germanic sound from the name. Most Eskies were kept as pets and farm dogs. It wasn't until 1994 that the AKC recognized the breed. The Eskie remains a dog of the people, far more popular as a companion than as a competitor.

TEMPERAMENT

The American Eskimo is bright, eager to please, lively, and fun loving—in short, an enjoyable and generally obedient companion. True to its spitz heritage, it is independent and tenacious and loves to run, especially in cold weather. But it is among the most biddable of spitz breeds, and it is calm and well-mannered inside. Because of their watchdog origins, Eskies can be wary of strangers, and may not be the best choice for homes with small children, other dogs, or pets unless well supervised.

UPKEEP

The Eskie is energetic and needs a good workout every day. The extent of the workout depends on the size of the dog, with the larger Eskies needing a good jog or long walk and the smaller Eskies needing only a vigorous game in the yard or short walk. Eskies like cool weather. The double coat needs brushing and combing twice weekly, more often when shedding.

HEALTH

- Major concerns: none
- Minor concerns: CHD, PRA, patellar luxation
- Occasionally seen: diabetes
- Suggested tests: hip, eye, (knee), DNA for PRA
- Life span: 12–14 years

FORM AND FUNCTION

The Eskie is built along classic Nordic Spitz lines. It is compactly built, slightly longer than tall. The stand-off, double coat resists soaking and provides insulation against the cold. The small thick ears are also cold resistant. Its trot is agile and bold. The expression is keen and alert.

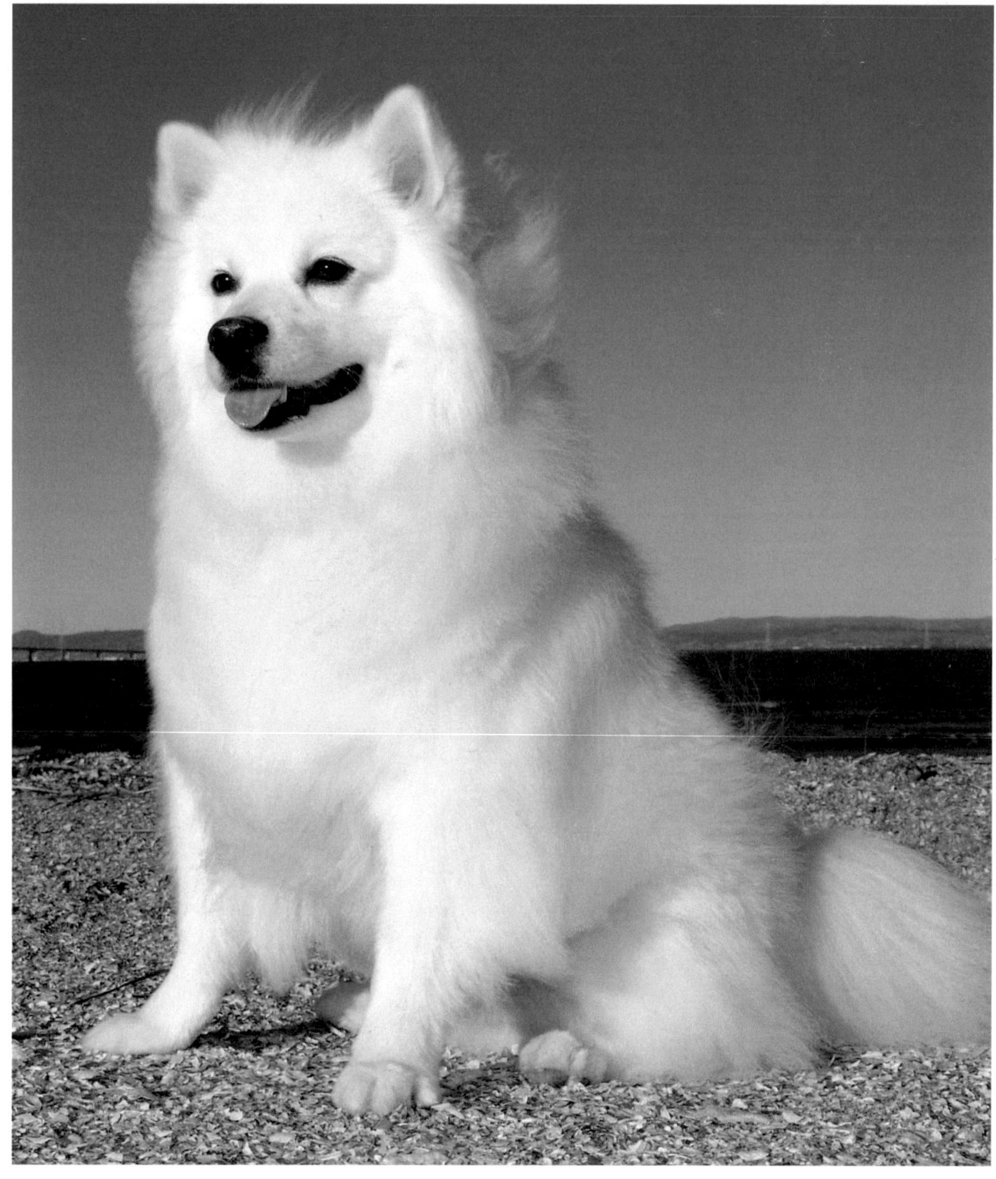

Bichon Frise

AT A GLANCE

Energy level:	■■■■	Watchdog ability:	■■■■	POPULARITY: Popular
Exercise requirements:	■■	Protection ability:	■	FAMILY: Barbichon, Water Dog
Playfulness:	■■■■■	Grooming requirements:	■■■■■	AREA OF ORIGIN: Mediterranean area
Affection level:	■■■■■	Cold tolerance:	■■■	DATE OF ORIGIN: Ancient times
Friendliness toward dogs:	■■■■	Heat tolerance:	■■■	ORIGINAL FUNCTION: Companion, performer
Friendliness toward other pets:	■■■■			TODAY'S FUNCTION: Companion
Friendliness toward strangers:	■■■■■	WEIGHT: male: 11–16 lb*; female: 10–15 lb*		OTHER NAME: Bichon Tenerife, Bichon a Poil Frise
Ease of training:	■■■■	HEIGHT: 9.5–11.5″		

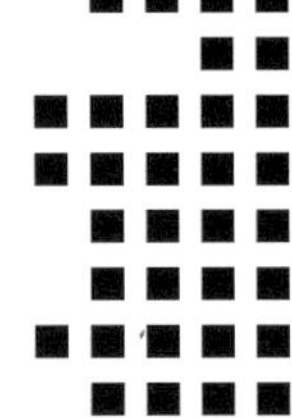

HISTORY

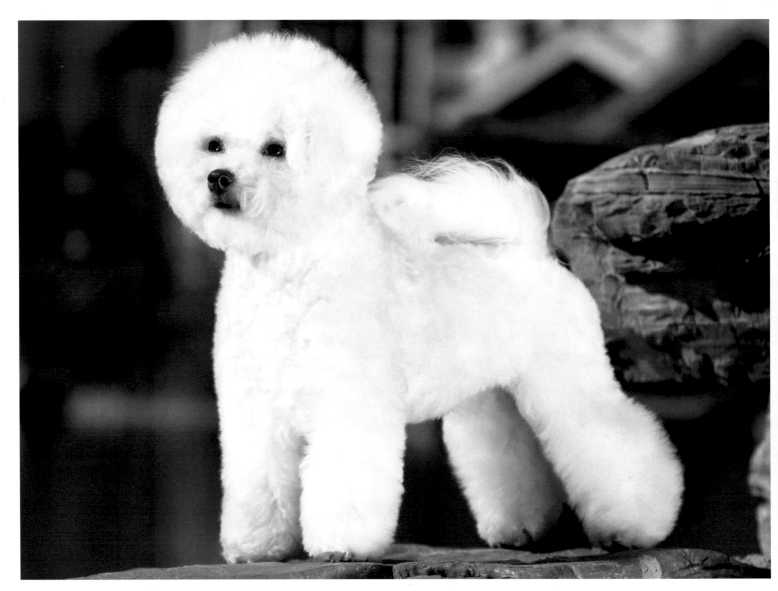

The Bichon Frise has its roots in the Mediterranean, originally produced by crossing the Barbet (a large water dog) with small coated, often white dogs. This cross eventually produced a family of dogs known as barbichons, which was later shortened to bichons. The bichons were divided into four types: the Maltaise, Bolognese, Havanese, and Tenerife. The Tenerife, considered to be one of the sources of the Bichon Frise, developed on the Canary Island of Tenerife, probably having been taken there by Spanish seafarers in ancient times. In the fourteenth century, Italian sailors brought specimens back from the island to the Continent, where they quickly became favored pets of the upper class. Following a series of French invasions of Italy in the 1500s, the little dogs (known there as Bolgnese) were

ILLUSTRATED STANDARD

1 Round, dark eyes
2 Drop ears
3 Level topline except for slight muscular arch over loin
4 Plumed tail curved over back
5 Moderate tuck-up
6 Round feet

Color: white, may have cream shadings
DQ: none

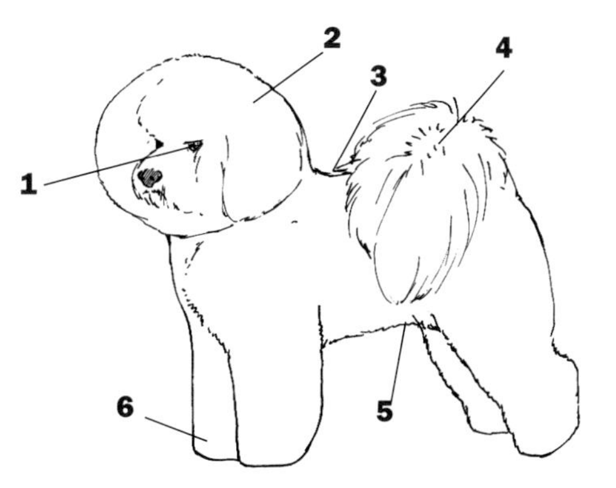

adopted by the French. They were special pets of Francis I and his successor, Henry III. They also enjoyed popularity in Spain, but for some reason, the breed's popularity waned throughout Europe. It experienced a brief resurgence during the reign of Napoleon III in the early nineteenth century, but once again it quickly faded from favor. This began a new chapter in the Bichon's history, as it sank from court favorite to common street dog. The Bichon survived, however, because of its propensity for performing tricks, and it teamed with peddlers and organ grinders to entertain passersby for money. With the advent of World War I, the little dogs were nearly lost. A few dogs were brought back home by soldiers, but no real effort to save the Bichon was made until a few French breeders began an earnest effort to establish the breed. In 1933, the FCI adopted a breed standard and officially named it the Bichon Frise. The breed was threatened again, this time by World War II. It was not until it came to America in the 1950s that its future became secure. Even then, the Bichon Frise did not catch on until its grooming was updated and it received greater publicity in the 1960s. The breed suddenly caught the attention of fanciers and was recognized by the AKC in 1971.

TEMPERAMENT

Perky, bouncy, and playful, the Bichon Frise's happy-go-lucky outlook endears it to all. It is friendly toward strangers and other dogs and pets, and it is very good with children. It is sensitive, responsive, and affectionate, as eager to cuddle as it is to play. It doesn't like to be left alone, and it can bark a lot. It can be hard to housetrain.

UPKEEP

The Bichon is an active dog that needs vigorous indoor games or, better, a romp in the yard or a short walk on leash daily. The white powderpuff coat needs brushing and combing every other day, plus scissoring and trimming every month. It doesn't shed, but the loose hairs become entangled in the coat and can mat. It may be difficult to keep white in some areas.

HEALTH

- Major concerns: patellar luxation, Cushing's, allergies
- Minor concerns: cataract, CHD
- Occasionally seen: liver disease, Legg-Perthes
- Suggested tests: hip, knee, eye, DNA for PRA
- Life span: 12–15 years

FORM AND FUNCTION

The striking powder-puff appearance of the Bichon derives from its double coat, with a soft dense undercoat and coarser, curly outercoat, causing the coat to stand off the body and even spring back when patted. This is a merry, agile breed with an effortless and efficient gait. Its looks, combined with its fitness, make this sturdy little dog a popular family addition. Its soft, inquisitive expression enables it to worm its way into many hearts and laps.

Boston Terrier

AT A GLANCE

Energy level:	■■■	Watchdog ability:	■■■■■	POPULARITY: Very popular
Exercise requirements:	■	Protection ability:	■	FAMILY: Terrier, Mastiff, Bull
Playfulness:	■■■	Grooming requirements:	■	AREA OF ORIGIN: United States
Affection level:	■■■	Cold tolerance:	■	DATE OF ORIGIN: 1800s
Friendliness toward dogs:	■■■	Heat tolerance:	■	ORIGINAL FUNCTION: Ratting, companion
Friendliness toward other pets:	■■■■			TODAY'S FUNCTION: Companion
Friendliness toward strangers:	■■■	WEIGHT: 10–25 lb* (25 lb maximum)		OTHER NAME: None
Ease of training:	■■■	HEIGHT: 15–17″*		

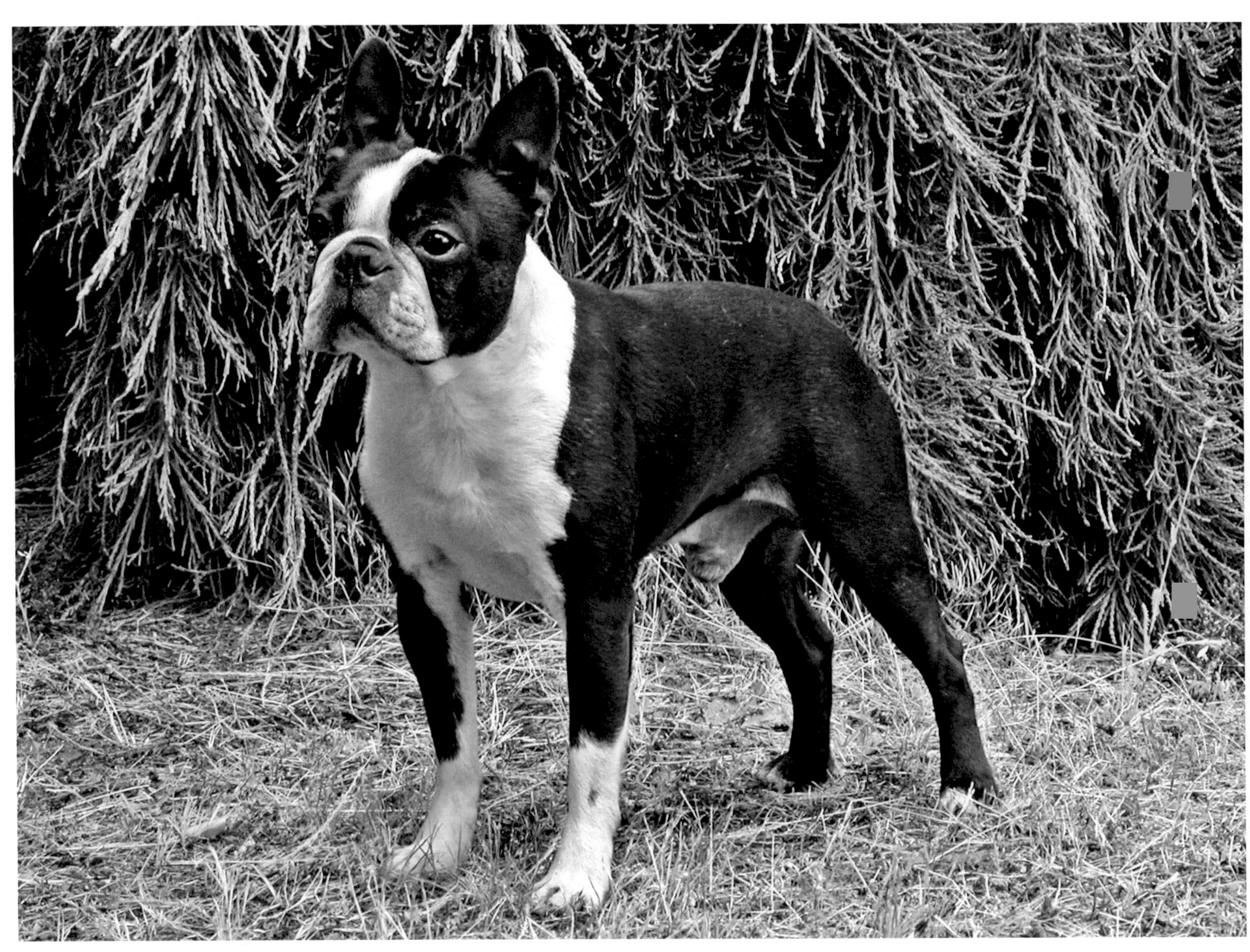

HISTORY

Unlike most breeds, the origin of the Boston Terrier is well documented. Around 1865, the coachmen employed by the wealthy people of Boston began to interbreed some of their employers' fine dogs. One of these crosses, between an English Terrier and a Bulldog, resulted in a dog named Hooper's Judge. Although Judge weighed over 30 pounds, he was bred to a smaller female, and their son was in turn bred to another smaller female. Their progeny, probably interbred with one or more French Bulldogs, provided the foundation for the Boston Terrier. By 1889, the breed had become sufficiently popular in Boston that fanciers formed the American Bull Terrier Club, but this proposed name for the breed was not well received by Bull Terrier fanciers. The breed's nickname, roundheads, was

ILLUSTRATED STANDARD

1 Alert, kind expression
2 Large, round eyes
3 Abrupt brow
4 Square, wrinkle-free skull
5 Small, erect ears, natural or cropped
6 Short, straight or screw tail carried below level of back
7 Small, round feet

Color: brindle, seal, or black with white markings on muzzle, between eyes, and forechest, and possibly white collar and lower legs

DQ: blue eyes; dudley nose; docked tail; liver or gray; lack of required white areas

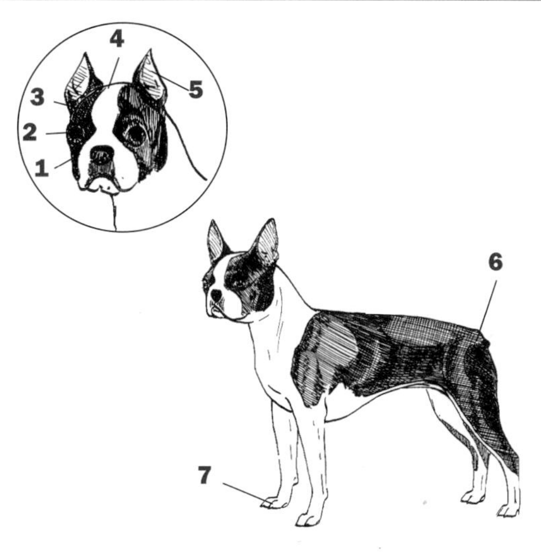

similarly inappropriate. Shortly after, the breed was named the Boston Terrier, after its birthplace. The Boston's rise from nonexistence to AKC recognition was meteoric by modern standards, as the breed was recognized by the AKC in 1893, less than 20 years after the breed was born. Breeders continued to seek greater consistency. In early years, color and markings were not particularly important, but by the early 1900s, the breed's distinctive markings had become an essential breed feature. The handsome little Boston Terrier quickly gained favor throughout America, ranking as one of the most popular breeds in the early to middle 1900s and retaining great popularity today.

TEMPERAMENT

The Boston is devoted and sensitive to its owner's wishes and moods. It is well-mannered indoors but saucy and playful (especially enjoying ball chasing) whenever the chance arises. Somewhat stubborn, it is nonetheless clever and learns readily. It is reserved with strangers, and some may be aggressive toward strange dogs. Some bark a lot.

UPKEEP

This is a lively dog that needs daily exercise and interaction with its people. It loves games, and most of its exercise requirements can be met with a romp in the yard or a short walk on leash. Some Bostons wheeze and snore, and many don't tolerate heat well. The coat requires only minimal care, an occasional brushing to remove dead hairs.

HEALTH

- Major concerns: none
- Minor concerns: patellar luxation, stenotic nares, elongated soft palate, allergies
- Occasionally seen: deafness, seizures, cataract, demodicosis
- Suggested tests: knee, eye, hearing
- Life span: 10–14 years
- Note: This breed does not tolerate the heat and is sensitive to anesthesia. It is prone to corneal abrasions. Caesarean deliveries are commonly needed.

FORM AND FUNCTION

The Boston Terrier is a compactly built, square-proportioned, short-backed, clean-cut dog. It should convey the impression of determination, strength, sturdiness, liveliness, and style, with a graceful carriage. It retains many of the attributes of its Bulldog ancestors, but in a clean-cut package that makes a handy house companion. Its short fine coat, with distinctive markings, adds to its dapper appearance.

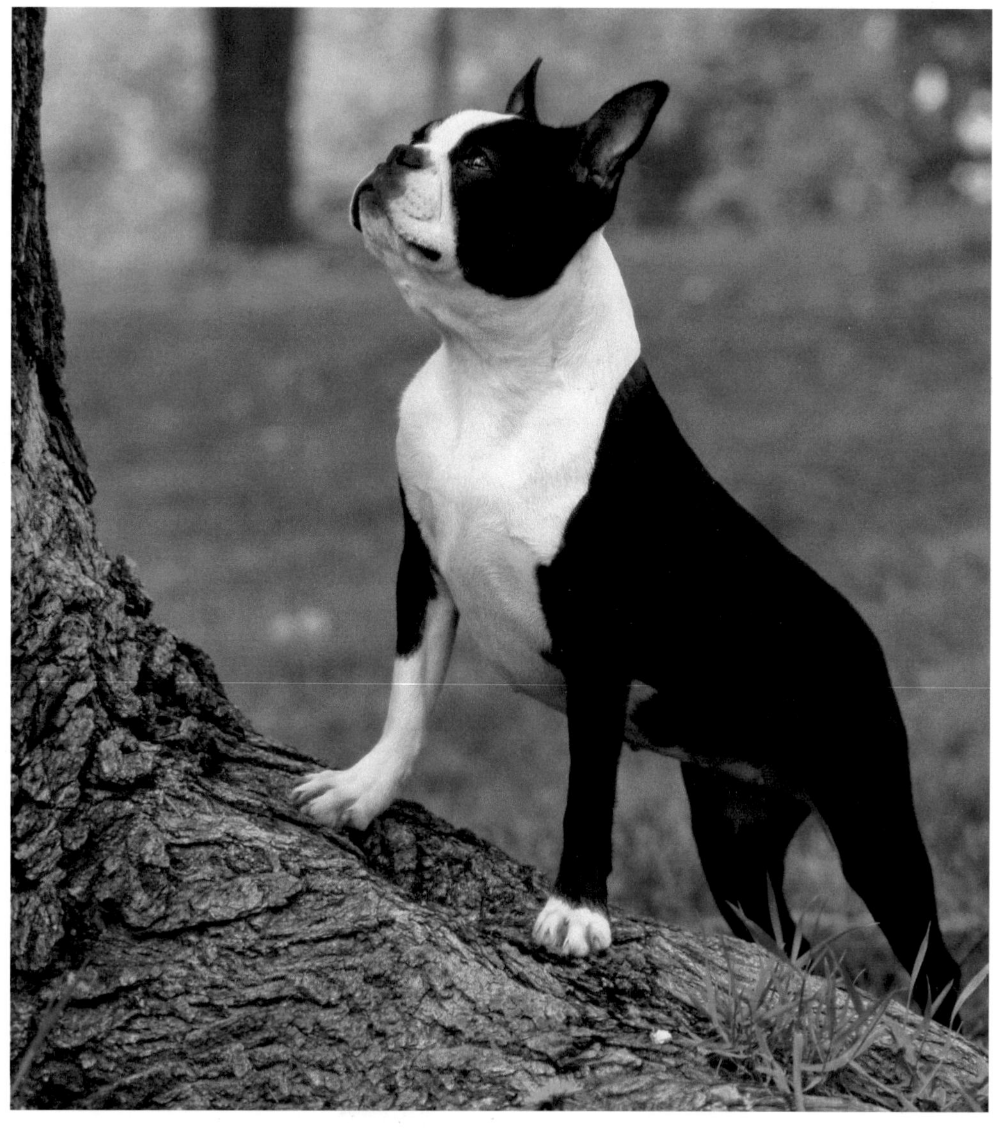

Bulldog

AT A GLANCE

Energy level: ■
Exercise requirements: ■
Playfulness: ■■■■
Affection level: ■■■■■
Friendliness toward dogs: ■
Friendliness toward other pets: ■■■■
Friendliness toward strangers: ■■■■
Ease of training: ■■

Watchdog ability: ■
Protection ability: ■■
Grooming requirements: ■■
Cold tolerance: ■
Heat tolerance: ■

WEIGHT: male: 50 lb; female: 40 lb
HEIGHT: 12–15″*

POPULARITY: Most popular
FAMILY: Mastiff, Bull
AREA OF ORIGIN: England
DATE OF ORIGIN: Early 1200s
ORIGINAL FUNCTION: Bull baiting
TODAY'S FUNCTION: Companion
OTHER NAME: English Bulldog

HISTORY

With the most distinctive mug in dogdom, the Bulldog has an equally distinctive history. The Bulldog's origin lies in the cruel sport of bull baiting, which originated in England around the thirteenth century. The dog's purpose was to attack and madden the bull by grabbing it, usually by the nose, and not releasing its grip. Not only was this considered entertainment, but it also was believed that a bull's meat was tastier if the bull was baited before being butchered. Some Bulldogs were also set against bears for bear baiting, purely for entertainment. Bulldog owners set great store by their dog's ferocity and, especially, fortitude in the face of pain—so much so that horrifying stories exist of owners proving their dog's toughness by demonstrating that it would hang onto the bull despite being tortured or mutilated

ILLUSTRATED STANDARD

1 Head and face covered with wrinkles; dewlap present
2 Undershot
3 Pendent flews completely overhanging massive jaws
4 Short, broad muzzle turned upward, tip of nose set between the eyes
5 Broad head
6 Wheel back
7 Short, straight or screwed tail, carried low
8 Hind legs longer than forelegs
9 Rounded ribs

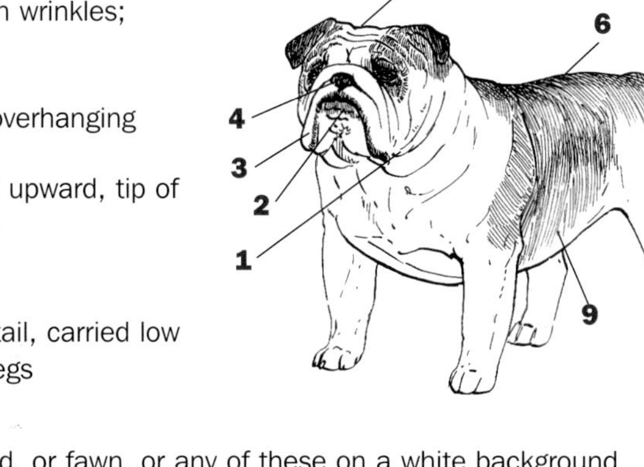

Color: brindle, solid white, red, or fawn, or any of these on a white background
DQ: brown or liver-colored nose

by the owner. In 1835, bull baiting was outlawed, and a new phase began for the Bulldog. Some efforts were made to have the dogs fight one another, but this was clearly not the Bulldog's forte. Now a dog without a cause, the breed's popularity plummeted. By all rights, the breed should have become extinct, except that it had gained so many ardent admirers that they set out to rescue the Bulldog by selecting against ferocity while still maintaining—and often accentuating—its distinctive physical characteristics. So successful were they that the Bulldog became an extremely amiable character, with a personality not at all like its "sourmug" might suggest. Its tough steadfast persona led it to be identified as a national symbol of England. Its amiable clownish personality belies its appearance, and the Bulldog is a popular pet.

TEMPERAMENT

Despite its "sourmug," the Bulldog is jovial, comical, and amiable, among the most docile and mellow of dogs. It is willing to please, although it retains a stubborn streak. It is very good with children. Most are moderately friendly toward strangers. Although some can be aggressive with strange dogs, the breed is quite good with other pets.

UPKEEP

The Bulldog appreciates a daily outing but cannot tolerate hot humid weather, which can be deadly. It should not be expected to jog or walk great distances, or to jump from any heights. Most Bulldogs cannot swim. Most Bulldogs wheeze and snore, and some drool. Coat care is minimal, but facial wrinkles (and any folds around the tail) should be cleaned daily.

HEALTH

- Major concerns: ventricular septal defect, CHD, KCS, stenotic nares, elongated soft palate, shoulder luxation, internalized tail
- Minor concerns: entropion, ectropion, distichiasis, CHD, elbow dysplasia, cherry eye, patellar luxation, demodicosis, tracheal hypoplasia
- Occasionally seen: urethral prolapse, vaginal hyperplasia
- Suggested tests: (hip), (elbow), knee, cardiac, (eye), tracheal hypoplasia
- Life span: 8–12 years
- Note: It cannot tolerate heat. Special precautions must be taken when anesthetizing a Bulldog. Caesarean deliveries are commonly needed. Hip radiographs show most Bulldogs to be dysplastic but few show overt symptoms.

FORM AND FUNCTION

The Bulldog's heavy, thick-set, low-slung body with wide shoulders gives it a low center of gravity, a vital asset when fighting a large animal. The massive head, of which the circumference should equal at least the height of the dog at the shoulder, gives ample room for muscular attachment for the strong, wide jaws. The undershot bite allows a tight grip, at the same time giving breathing room through the nose. The limbs are sturdy, the gait loose-jointed, shuffling, and rolling—this is not a breed that needs to run! The coat is fine and glossy.

Chinese Shar-Pei

AT A GLANCE

Energy level:	■■■
Exercise requirements:	■■■
Playfulness:	■
Affection level:	■
Friendliness toward dogs:	■
Friendliness toward other pets:	■■■
Friendliness toward strangers:	■
Ease of training:	■

Watchdog ability:	■■■■■
Protection ability:	■■■■
Grooming requirements:	■■
Cold tolerance:	■■■
Heat tolerance:	■■

WEIGHT: 45–60 lb
HEIGHT: 18–20″

POPULARITY: Somewhat popular
FAMILY: Mastiff, Oriental
AREA OF ORIGIN: China
DATE OF ORIGIN: Ancient times
ORIGINAL FUNCTION: Dog fighting, herding, hunting, guardian
TODAY'S FUNCTION: Companion
OTHER NAME: Chinese Fighting Dog

HISTORY

The Chinese Shar-Pei may have existed in the southern provinces of China since the Han dynasty (around 200 B.C.). Certainly by the thirteenth century strong evidence in the form of writings describing a wrinkled dog point to the breed's existence. Its origins are unknown, but because only it and the Chow Chow have blue-black tongues, and both come from China, it is likely that they share some common ancestry. The Shar-Pei's history is difficult to trace because most records relating to its past were lost when China became communist. At this time Shar-Peis were the working breed of peasant farmers, fulfilling roles of guard dog, wild boar hunter, and dog fighter. After the nation became communist, most of China's dogs were eliminated, with only a few

ILLUSTRATED STANDARD

1 Abundant dewlap and folds of loose skin around neck
2 Broad full "hippopotamus" muzzle
3 Blue-black tongue and mouth (lavender in dilute colors)
4 Small, sunken, almond-shaped eyes
5 Large head framed with profuse wrinkles
6 Small, high-set, triangular ears lying flat
7 High-set, thick, tapering tail curled over to side of back

Color: any solid color including sable
DQ: pricked ears; solid pink tongue; absence of a complete tail; not a solid color; albino

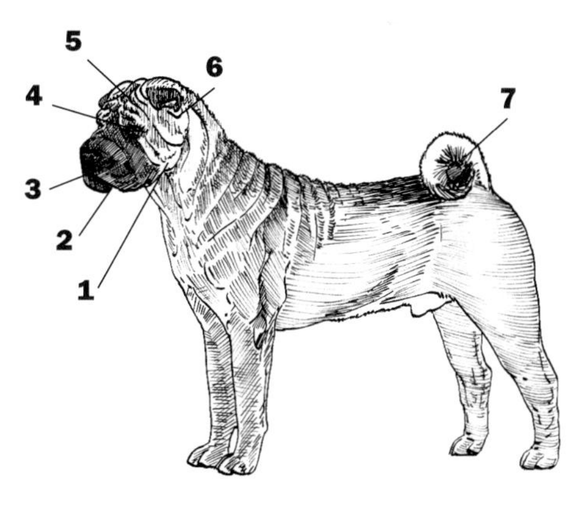

remaining outside of the cities. A few Shar-Peis were bred in British Hong Kong and Taiwan, and the Hong Kong Kennel Club recognized the breed in 1968. Around this same time, a few specimens came to America, but the turning point occurred with a 1973 article alerting American fanciers to the breed's perilously low numbers. Touted as the world's rarest dog, fanciers vied to obtain the few available Shar-Peis. The breed has since been brought from the brink of extinction to the height of popularity, and it is one of the most recognizable breeds in America. Though known for its loose skin and profuse wrinkles, which are superabundant in puppies, the wrinkles of adults may be limited only to the head, neck, and shoulders.

TEMPERAMENT

The Shar-Pei is self-assured, serious, independent, stubborn, and very much self-possessed. Although not particularly demonstrative, it is devoted and very protective of its family. It is reserved, even suspicious, toward strangers. It can be aggressive toward other dogs and may chase livestock and other animals, although it is generally good with other family pets.

UPKEEP

The Shar-Pei needs daily mental and physical stimulation, but its needs can be met with lively games throughout the day or a good long walk. The coat needs only weekly brushing, but wrinkles need regular attention to ensure that no irritations develop within the skin folds.

OTHER CONSIDERATIONS

The name Shar-Pei means sandy coat, referring to the gritty sandpaper texture of the coat. When rubbed backward, the prickly coat can be uncomfortable, and even cause welts on the skin of an occasional sensitive person.

HEALTH

- Major concerns: entropion, CHD
- Minor concerns: patellar luxation, allergies, otitis externa, lip and skin fold pyodermas, hypothyroidism, amyloidosis (renal)
- Occasionally seen: megaesophagus
- Suggested tests: hip, knee, elbow, eye, thyroid
- Life span: 8–10 years
- Note: Some dogs get Shar-Pei fever, a periodic inflammatory response caused, as a result of the mutation, causing skin wrinkling.

FORM AND FUNCTION

The Shar-Pei is compact and square, with a head slightly large for its body. Its signature wrinkles enabled it to twist away when grabbed by a dog when in a fight. Its stiff bristly coat further afforded protection against bites. The coat can be of either brush (not to exceed 1 inch) or horse (very short) types, both it should be extremely harsh, straight, and stand off the body. The small, close ears and small, sunken eyes afford further protection. The gait is free, with good reach and drive. The wide, powerful jaws, scowling expression, and hippopotamus muzzle create a look unique to the breed.

Chow Chow

AT A GLANCE

Energy level:	■
Exercise requirements:	■■
Playfulness:	■
Affection level:	■■
Friendliness toward dogs:	■
Friendliness toward other pets:	■■■
Friendliness toward strangers:	■
Ease of training:	■

Watchdog ability:	■■■■■
Protection ability:	■■■■
Grooming requirements:	
Smooth:	■■
Rough:	■■■■
Cold tolerance:	■■■■■
Heat tolerance:	■

WEIGHT: 45–70 lb*
HEIGHT: 17–20″

POPULARITY: Somewhat popular
FAMILY: Spitz, Oriental
AREA OF ORIGIN: China
DATE OF ORIGIN: Ancient times
ORIGINAL FUNCTION: Guardian, cart puller, food source
TODAY'S FUNCTION: Companion
OTHER NAME: None

HISTORY

The Chow Chow has some spitz characteristics. Because of this, it has been proposed that the Chow Chow either descends from spitz forebears or is itself an ancestor of some of the spitz breeds. Unfortunately, the origin of the breed has been lost in time, but it has been known in China for hundreds, if not thousands, of years. Its original purpose may have been as a hunting dog, sniffing out and even pointing birds for the nobility. The breed declined in quality and numbers after the Imperial hunts were ended, but a few pure descendents were kept in isolated monasteries and wealthy households. Other accounts contend that the breed was a source of fur pelts and food in Manchuria and Mongolia. One of the most distinctive features of the breed is its black tongue, which was also the

ILLUSTRATED STANDARD

1 Blue-black tongue and black mouth
2 Scowling, dignified expression
3 Padded button of skin above the inner corner of each almond-shaped eye
4 Broad, flat skull
5 Small, triangular ears carried erect
6 Tail carried close to back
7 Rear legs are almost straight
8 Round feet

Color: solid red, black, blue, cinnamon, and cream

DQ: drop ear; spotted or nonblack nose (except blue dogs may have gray nose); top or edge of tongue red or pink or spotted red or pink

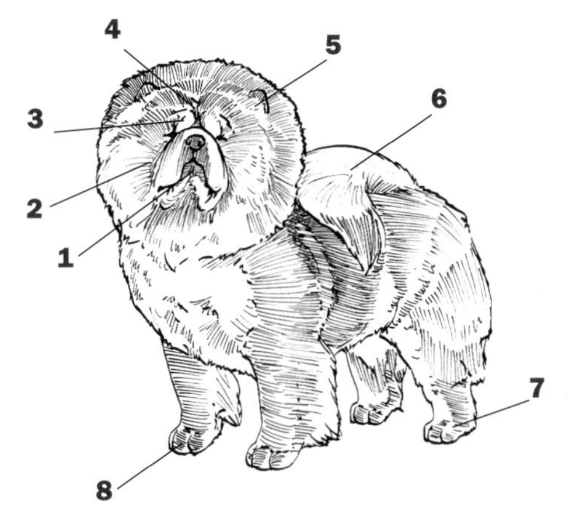

basis for its more common names in China. Only when dogs were brought to England along with other Chinese importations in the late 1700s was the name Chow Chow adopted. The name is probably derived from a term simply meaning Oriental knick knack and assorted curios, and may have come to be applied to the dogs because they were lumped into a ship's log of cargo. These early imports were, in fact, looked upon as curios. Not until the late 1800s was the breed imported to England and then America in earnest. Queen Victoria's interest in these dogs helped draw attention to the breed. AKC recognized the Chow Chow in 1903. The breed's distinctive noble look has always attracted fanciers, but in the 1980s the breed soared in popularity, peaking as the sixth most popular breed in America. Its numbers have since declined dramatically.

TEMPERAMENT

Dignified, even lordly, the Chow Chow conducts itself with reserve. It is not very demonstrative, even with its family, and is somewhat suspicious of strangers. It is independent and stubborn. It can be aggressive toward other dogs but is generally good with other household pets. It is serious and protective, devoted to its family.

UPKEEP

This is an alert breed that needs regular, but not strenuous, outdoor activity. It does not do well in hot humid weather. Its needs are best met with casual morning or evening walks in warm weather or several short play sessions throughout the day. The smooth type needs brushing once weekly; the rough type needs brushing every other day, and daily when shedding.

HEALTH

- Major concerns: CHD, entropion, patellar luxation
- Minor concerns: elbow dysplasia, cataract, distichiasis, PPM, gastric torsion, stenotic nares, glaucoma, elongated palate
- Occasionally seen: renal cortical hypoplasia
- Suggested tests: hip, elbow, eye, knee, thyroid
- Life span: 8–12 years

FORM AND FUNCTION

The Chow is an Arctic-type dog, powerful, squarely built, and sturdy with heavy bone and strong muscular development. It is a breed suited for a number of tasks, rather than specializing in one, and its build reflects its ability to hunt, herd, pull, and protect. It can have either a rough coat, which is straight and offstanding or a smooth coat, which is hard and smooth; both coat types have wooly undercoats, providing ample insulation from the cold. The characteristic straight angulation of the hind legs produces a short, stilted gait unique to the breed. The scowling expression and black tongue are essential components of breed type.

Coton de Tulear

AT A GLANCE

Energy level:	■■■■
Exercise requirements:	■■
Playfulness:	■■■■
Affection level:	■■■■■
Friendliness toward dogs:	■■■■■
Friendliness toward other pets:	■■■■■
Friendliness toward strangers:	■■■■■
Ease of training:	■■■■
Watchdog ability:	■■
Protection ability:	■
Grooming requirements:	■■■■■
Cold tolerance:	■■■
Heat tolerance:	■■■

WEIGHT: male: 9–15 lb; female: 8–13 lb
HEIGHT: male: 10–11″; female: 9–10″

POPULARITY: Uncommon
FAMILY: Barbichon
AREA OF ORIGIN: Madagascar
DATE OF ORIGIN: 1500s
ORIGINAL FUNCTION: Companion
TODAY'S FUNCTION: Companion
OTHER NAME: None

HISTORY

The Coton de Tulear (pronounced co-TAWN day-too-LEE-are) means Cotton of Tulear in French, with cotton referring to its coat and Tulear coming from the sea port at the tip of the island of Madasgascar. These dogs' ancestors, which are also ancestors to the Bichon Frise, Maltese, and Bolgnese, were kept as ratters and companions on sea trading ships. One of these ships sunk off Tulear, and several little white dogs survived and came ashore. Some became feral and mixed with native dogs. In the 17th century, the native Merina people adopted the dogs and presented them to the Merina nobility. When the French laid claim to Madagascar in the late 17th century, French nobility adopted the dogs and decreed no commoners could own them. They became known as the Royal Dog of Madagascar. When Madagascar attained independence in the mid 1900s, tourism increased and visitors took Cotons home with them. The first Coton came to America in 1974. The Fèdèration Cynologique Internationale (FCI) recognized the Coton in 1987, increasing demand

ILLUSTRATED STANDARD

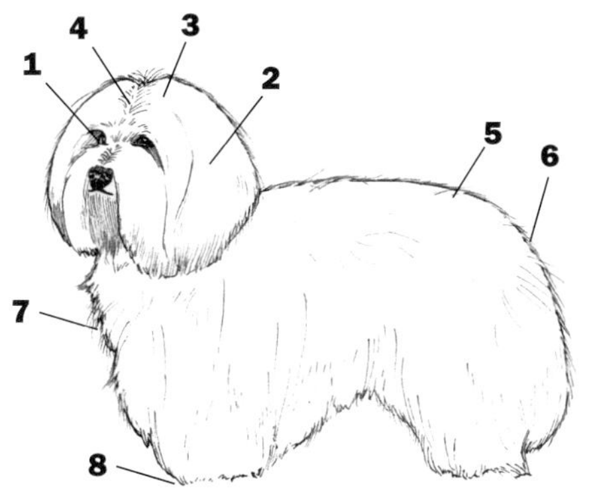

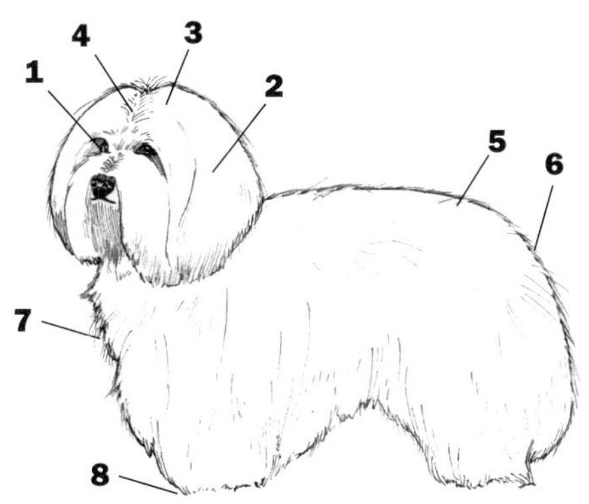
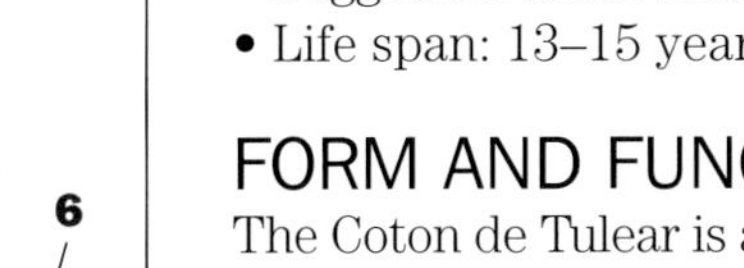

1 Wide-set, rounded, dark eyes with black rims
2 High-set, triangular drop ears, carried close
3 Slightly rounded skull as seen from the front
4 Slight stop
5 Graceful arch beginning over the loin carrying through the croup
6 Low-set tail, curved over so hair rests on back when on the move
7 Pronounced forechest
8 Small, round feet

Color: white; some slight shadings of gray or tan are permitted on ears; light tan shadings are permitted on 5 percent of the body of an adult
DQ: males under 9.5″ or over 12″; females under 8.5″ or over 11″; eye color other than brown or black; total lack of pigment on the eye rim, nose, or lips; black on the body coat; no tail

and depleting native stocks. In 1992, Madagascar began limiting the number of exported Cotons. There is some disagreement about the proper type of the breed between the prominent breed clubs (and even accusations of impure breeding), further fueled by disagreement over pursuing AKC recognition. Against the wishes of many breeders, the AKC admitted the Coton de Tulear into the Non-Sporting group in 2014.

TEMPERAMENT

The Coton is a playful, merry, boisterous companion, eager to entertain and please. It is very affectionate and loves to be loved. It gets along with strangers, children, other dogs, and other pets. It is easily trained. It is calm inside. Although not a big barker, it can still produce an assortment of vocalizations. It's not much of a guard dog and is a hopeless protection dog.

UPKEEP

The Coton is active indoors and can run off most of its energy with lively games inside or in the yard. However, walks are also necessary for mental stimulation. Although shedding is minimal, coat care is the breed's biggest challenge because it tangles and mats easily. Brush with a pin brush daily. Any leaves or twigs in the coat must be removed immediately before they cause a tangle. Weekly bathing is recommended.

HEALTH

- Major concerns: none
- Minor concerns: patellar luxation
- Occasionally seen: CHD
- Suggested tests: knee, hip
- Life span: 13–15 years

FORM AND FUNCTION

The Coton de Tulear is a hardy, sturdy yet small dog. Although bred as a companion, it once survived on its own. Its hallmarks are its bright personality and profuse, white, cottony coat. The approximately 4 inch coat has the texture of soft cotton. It is dense and abundant and stands off the body. It's believed its texture allows air to circulate within it, insulating the dog from heat and cold. The white coloration is another breed hallmark. However, puppies may be born with spots, mostly around the head and ears, which fade with age.

Dalmatian

AT A GLANCE

Energy level:	■■■■	Watchdog ability:	■■■■	POPULARITY: Somewhat popular
Exercise requirements:	■■■	Protection ability:	■■■	FAMILY: Unkown
Playfulness:	■■■	Grooming requirements:	■■	AREA OF ORIGIN: Yugoslavia
Affection level:	■■■■■	Cold tolerance:	■■	DATE OF ORIGIN: Ancient times
Friendliness toward dogs:	■■■	Heat tolerance:	■■■	ORIGINAL FUNCTION: Carriage dog
Friendliness toward other pets:	■■■			TODAY'S FUNCTION: Companion, mascot
Friendliness toward strangers:	■■■	WEIGHT: 40–60 lb*		OTHER NAME: None
Ease of training:	■■■	HEIGHT: 19–23″		

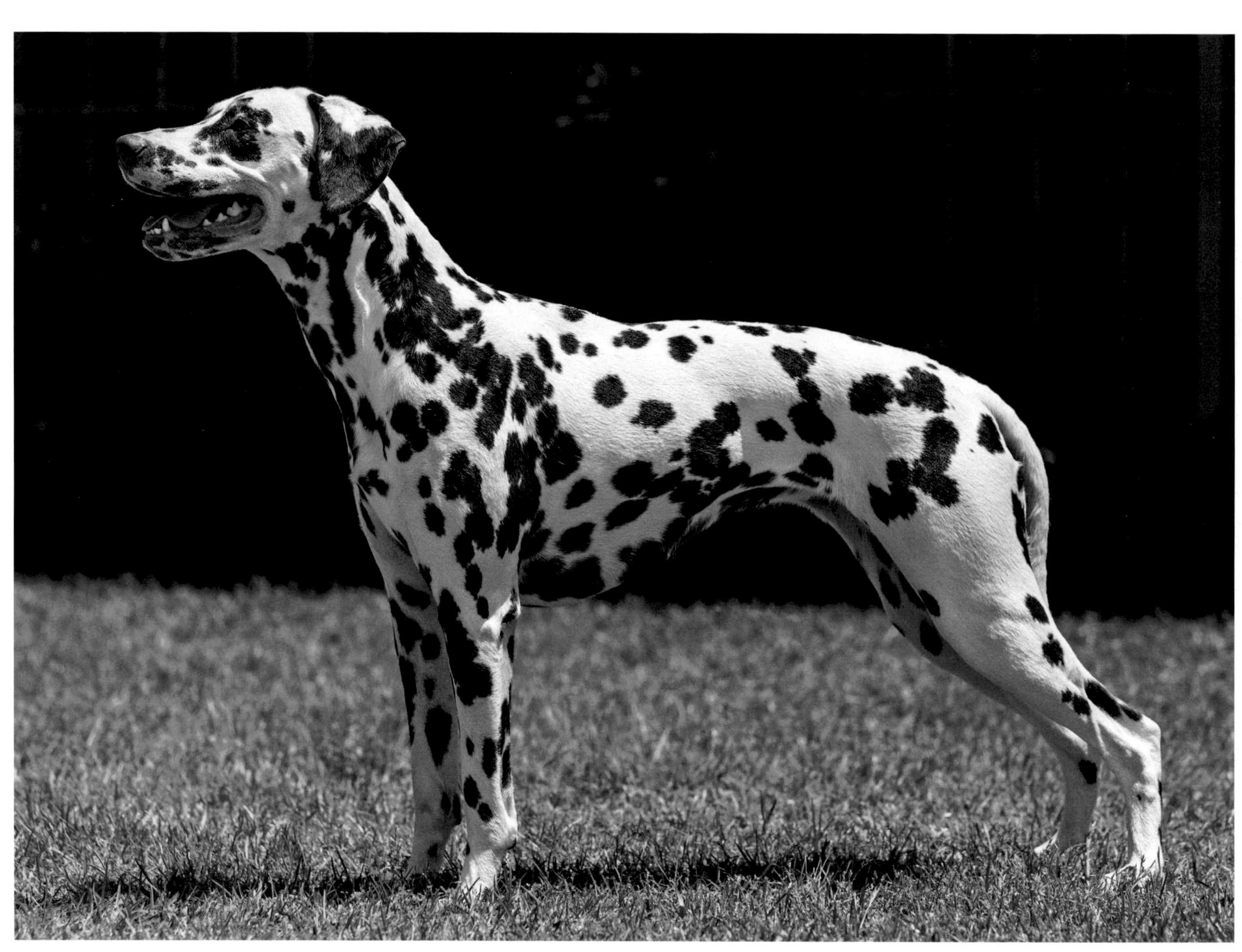

HISTORY

The spotted Dalmatian is the most distinctly patterned breed of any dog, but the origin of its coat pattern is unknown. In fact, although art evidence points to an ancient origin, the time and place of the breed's birth is also unknown. It gets it name from Dalmatia, a region in western Yugoslavia, but it probably did not originate there. Their ancestors may have included a small version of the spotted Great Dane or pointers, though this, too, is conjectural. Even the breed's original function is unclear, but that is more likely because of its use in so many roles rather than any lack of employment. These roles included war dog, sentinel, shepherd, draft dog, ratter, retriever, bird dog, trailer, and even circus dog. It was as a coach dog in Victorian England, however, that the Dalmatian found its

ILLUSTRATED STANDARD

1 Rounded eyes; brown, gold, or blue
2 Flat skull
3 Rounded, high-set, medium-sized ears
4 Tail carried with a slight upward curve
5 Round feet

Color: black or liver spots on white background; spots should be round, well defined, and preferably separated; Dalmatians are born white and develop spots in 2–3 weeks
DQ: height over 24″; overshot or undershot; any markings other than black or liver; patches

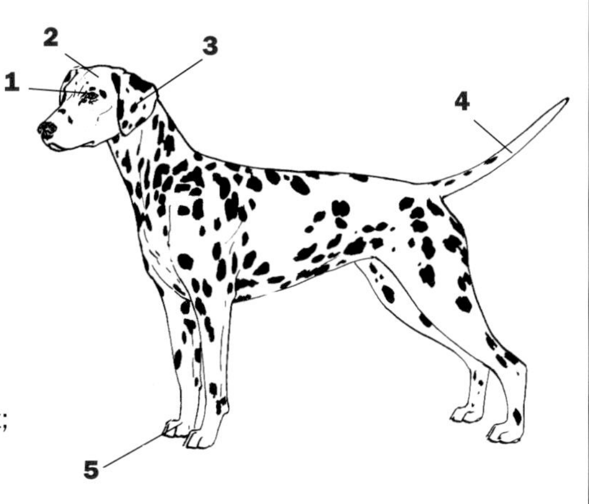

niche. The coach dog served both a practical and esthetic role; it protected the horses from marauding dogs and added a touch of style to the procession. The dogs would trot alongside, in front, or beneath the axle (considered the most elegant position) of the coach; interestingly, some evidence exists that coaching position may have a hereditary component. Some of these early dogs apparently had cropped ears. With the advent of the automobile, the Dalmatian lost its place in high society, and its popularity declined. It continued as a coach dog for horse-drawn fire engines, and this association led to its adoption as the modern "fire-dog." The Dal was AKC recognized in 1888. Its flashy coloration has always ensured that it has been popular as a pet and show dog; however, it has had extreme ups and downs in popularity. Impulse buying followed movies featuring Dalmatian stars, followed by a backlash when so many of these unprepared homes were ill suited for Dalmatian ownership and laid the blame on the breed.

TEMPERAMENT

Bred to run for miles, the Dalmatian retains this tireless enthusiasm. It is a playful, eager companion that must get daily hard exercise in a safe area if it is expected to behave at home. It loves to run and may roam. It may be aggressive toward strange dogs, but it is generally good with other pets and is especially good with horses. It may be too energetic for young children. It tends to be reserved toward strangers. It can be stubborn.

Note: Deaf Dalmatians present special training and behavioral challenges.

UPKEEP

The Dalmatian needs a lot of regular exercise and attention. It needs more than a short walk on leash; it makes a good jogging companion. It can also have its needs met with vigorous games and runs. The coat needs only occasional brushing.

HEALTH

- Major concerns: deafness, urinary stones
- Minor concerns: allergies, seizures, iris sphincter dysplasia, hypothyroidism
- Occasionally seen: CHD
- Suggested tests: hearing, hip
- Life span: 12–14 years
- Note: A unique defect of the Dalmatian is its inability to metabolize uric acid into allantoin, which leads to the tendency to form urinary calculi (stones).

FORM AND FUNCTION

The Dalmatian is a square-proportioned, athletic dog of good substance and sturdy bone. It is built for efficiency at the trot and great endurance, and its movement should be steady and effortless. The expression is alert and intelligent; the coat short and sleek. The distinctive spots are an essential point of type; solid patches (distinguished from masses of spots by the patch's sharply defined, smooth edges) are a disqualification.

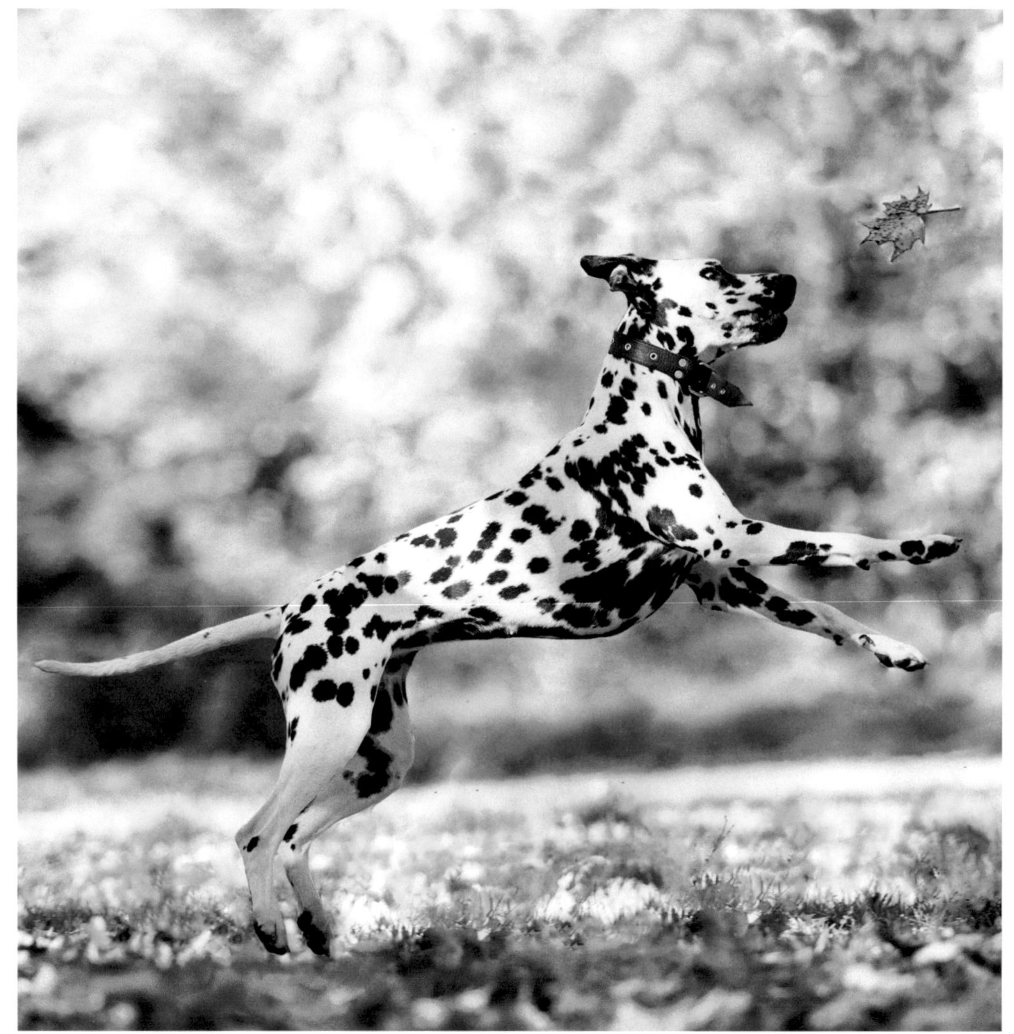

Finnish Spitz

AT A GLANCE

Energy level:	■ ■ ■
Exercise requirements:	■ ■ ■
Playfulness:	■ ■ ■
Affection level:	■ ■ ■
Friendliness toward dogs:	■ ■ ■
Friendliness toward other pets:	■ ■ ■
Friendliness toward strangers:	■
Ease of training:	■ ■ ■

Watchdog ability:	■ ■ ■ ■
Protection ability:	■ ■ ■
Grooming requirements:	■ ■ ■
Cold tolerance:	■ ■ ■ ■
Heat tolerance:	■ ■

WEIGHT: male: 31–36 lb; female: 23–29 lb*
HEIGHT: male: 17.5–20″; female: 15.5–18″

POPULARITY: Very rare
FAMILY: Spitz
AREA OF ORIGIN: Finland
DATE OF ORIGIN: Ancient times
ORIGINAL FUNCTION: Hunting birds and small mammals
TODAY'S FUNCTION: Hunting
OTHER NAME: Suomenpystykorva, Finsk Spets

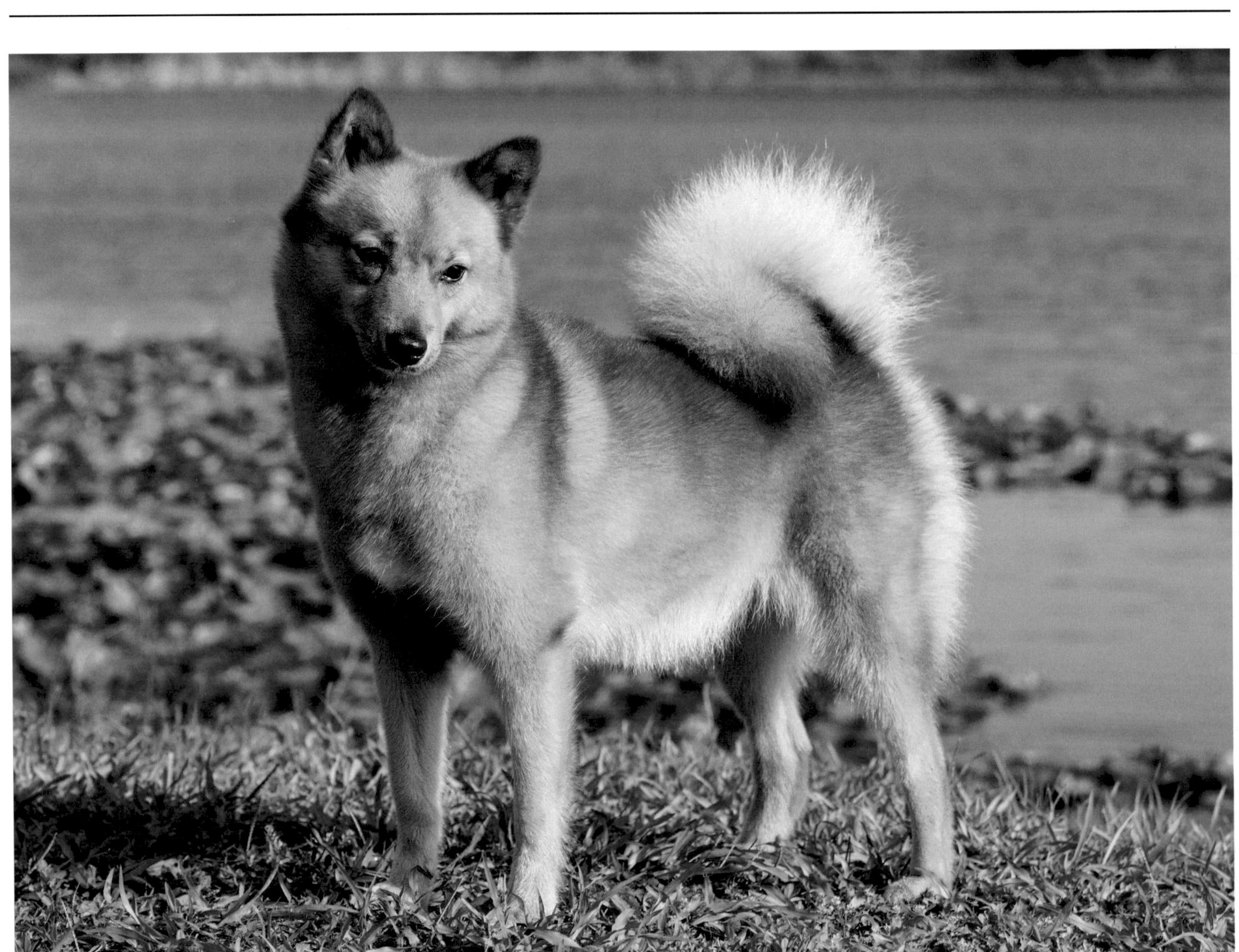

HISTORY

The Finnish Spitz originated from ancestral northern spitz dogs that accompanied early Finno-Ugrian tribes as they journeyed across Eurasia to Finland. These dogs probably originated as camp followers and watchdogs, later developing into hunting dogs. The breed remained pure, not by design but by isolation until the early 1800s. When other groups of people brought their dogs to the region in the 1800s, interbreeding almost obliterated the pure Finnish Spitz. In the late 1800s, two Finnish sportsmen spotted some dogs that had apparently not been interbred, and they were so impressed that they determined to rescue the imperiled breed. Early names for the breed included Suomenpystykorva (Finnish Cock-Eared Dog) and Finnish Barking Bird Dog. When it first came to

ILLUSTRATED STANDARD

1 Foxlike head and expression
2 Pronounced stop
3 Almond-shaped eyes
4 Small, high-set, erect ears
5 Plumed tail curving forward and round to lie against either thigh
6 Round feet

Color: shades of golden-red (puppies are born with a black overlay that disappears by around 8 weeks of age)
DQ: none

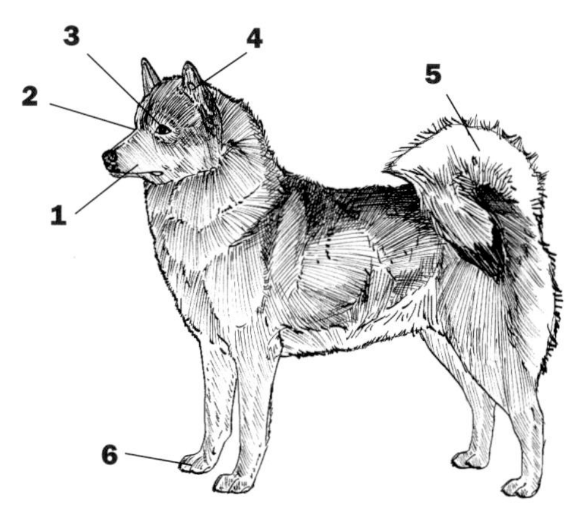

England it was called the Finsk Spets (derived from its Swedish name), but in 1891, the name was officially changed to Finnish Spitz. The breed gained its nickname of Finkie after its arrival in England in the 1920s. It wasn't until the 1960s that Finkies began to be bred in the United States. The breed was officially admitted into the Non-Sporting Group in 1988. Although prized primarily as a pet in America, it is still used for hunting in Finland. There they hunt the capercaille (a turkeylike bird) and black grouse, although they will hunt virtually anything from insects to elk if given the chance. The dogs work by ranging out from the hunter, locating the bird, and barking loudly. If the bird moves, they follow it until it lands and then resume barking. Some claim that the barking mesmerizes the game. Conformation champions in Finland must first prove themselves in the field; their barking talents are so valued that they select a King Barker each year. The Finnish Spitz is the national dog of Finland.

TEMPERAMENT

Like most spitz breeds, the Finkie is independent and somewhat stubborn, although it is more hunting oriented than other spitz breeds. It is alert, inquisitive, and playful, but it is also sensitive, tending to be devoted to one person. It is a breed conscious of its place in the dominance hierarchy, and some males can try to be domineering. It is good with children, and generally good with other pets, but it can be aggressive to strange dogs. It is reserved, even aloof or suspicious, with strangers. In keeping with its barking heritage, the Finkie is proud of its barking ability and likes to show it off—loudly!

UPKEEP

This is an active and lively breed and needs daily exercise, either a long walk on leash or a run in a fenced area. As a hunting breed, care must be taken that they do not go off on a hunt by themselves. Its double coat needs brushing one or two times weekly, more often when shedding. It is not oily so that the Finkie has little doggy odor; in fact, the Finkie is a particularly clean breed.

HEALTH

- Major concerns: none
- Minor concerns: CHD, diabetes
- Occasionally seen: patellar luxation, epilepsy
- Suggested tests: hip
- Life span: 12–14 years

FORM AND FUNCTION

The Finnish Spitz has a foxlike appearance, incorporating the typical traits of a northern breed: small erect ears, dense double coat, and curled tail. It is square-proportioned, and without exaggeration, quick and light on its feet. It has the conformation and temperament to hunt actively and tirelessly under the coldest of conditions. Its double coat, consisting of a short soft undercoat and harsh straight outer coat about 1 to 2 inches long, provides insulation from the snow and cold, allowing it to hunt tirelessly under the coldest of conditions.

French Bulldog

AT A GLANCE

Energy level: ■■■
Exercise requirements: ■
Playfulness: ■■■
Affection level: ■■■
Friendliness toward dogs: ■■■
Friendliness toward other pets: ■■■■
Friendliness toward strangers: ■
Ease of training: ■■

Watchdog ability: ■■■
Protection ability: ■
Grooming requirements: ■
Cold tolerance: ■■■
Heat tolerance: ■

WEIGHT: not to exceed 28 lb
HEIGHT: 11–13″*

POPULARITY: Most popular
FAMILY: Mastiff, Bull
AREA OF ORIGIN: France
DATE OF ORIGIN: 1800s
ORIGINAL FUNCTION: Lapdog
TODAY'S FUNCTION: Companion
OTHER NAME: Bouledogue Francais

HISTORY

In the nineteenth century, the Bulldog was fairly popular in England, especially around Nottingham. Some of these Bulldogs were quite small, weighing less than 25 pounds. When many of the lace workers of the region went to France for work in the mid 1800s, they took their "Toy" Bulldogs with them. The French women, especially, were attracted to these little Bulldogs, especially those with erect ears (a common but disliked feature in England). Dog dealers brought more of the clownish little dogs to France, where they soon became the rage of Paris. The dogs were dubbed Bouledogue Francais. French breeders sought to consistently produce the erect "bat ears," much to the chagrin of English breeders. By the late 1800s, the breed had caught the attention of the

ILLUSTRATED STANDARD

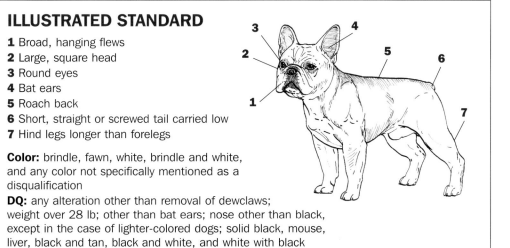

1 Broad, hanging flews
2 Large, square head
3 Round eyes
4 Bat ears
5 Roach back
6 Short, straight or screwed tail carried low
7 Hind legs longer than forelegs

Color: brindle, fawn, white, brindle and white, and any color not specifically mentioned as a disqualification

DQ: any alteration other than removal of dewclaws; weight over 28 lb; other than bat ears; nose other than black, except in the case of lighter-colored dogs; solid black, mouse, liver, black and tan, black and white, and white with black

upper class and had moved into some of the finer homes in France. Around this same time, American visitors to France brought several back to America and began to breed the dogs in earnest. Amid continued controversy over which ear type was correct, an American club was formed and, in 1898, sponsored one of the most elegant dog shows (just for French Bulldogs) ever held. The gracious setting attracted wealthy spectators, and the Frenchie had soon conquered America. Their popularity among high society soared, and by 1913 they were among the most popular show dogs in America. The breed has since been passed by many others in popularity, but it still boasts some of the most elite and ardent fans in dogdom.

TEMPERAMENT

The French Bulldog is a clown in a lapdog. It enjoys playing and entertaining its family, as well as cuddling and snoozing with its favorite person. It is amiable, sweet, companionable, and willing to please.

UPKEEP

The Frenchie has minimal exercise requirements, although it is a fun-loving dog. It enjoys a romp outdoors, but it doesn't do well in hot, humid weather. Most cannot swim. A short walk on lead is sufficient to meet most of its physical needs. The Frenchie snores and may wheeze and drool. It requires minimal coat care, but its facial wrinkles should be regularly cleaned.

HEALTH

- Major concerns: brachycephalic syndrome (stenotic nares, elongated soft palate), intervertebral disk disease, CHD, allergies
- Minor concerns: patellar luxation, hemivertebra
- Occasionally seen: distichiasis
- Suggested tests: hip, knee, eye, cardiac
- Life span: 9–11 years
- Note: This breed does not tolerate heat well and may be sensitive to anesthesia. CHD seldom causes symptoms or problems. Caesarean deliveries are common.

FORM AND FUNCTION

The Frenchie shares many of the traits that made its Bulldog ancestors so successful in the bull baiting arena: low center of gravity, wide body, heavy bone, muscular build, and large, square head. It has soft loose skin forming wrinkles about the head and shoulders. Unlike the Bulldog, it has an alert, curious expression, which is aided by its bar ears. Also, unlike the Bulldog, its movement is unrestrained and free, with reach and drive. It is a hardy, entertaining home companion and a solid lapdog.

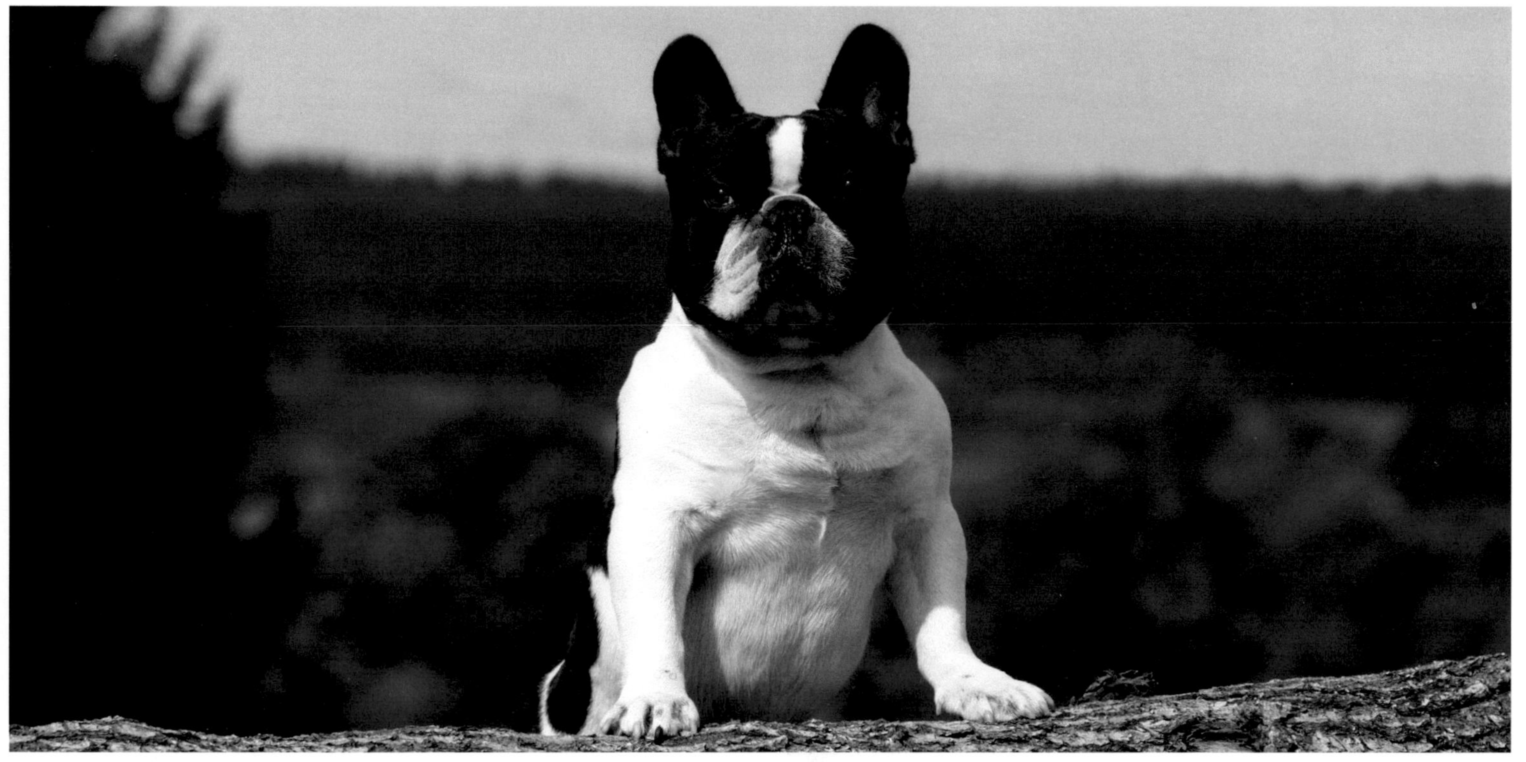

Keeshond

AT A GLANCE

Energy level:	■■■	Watchdog ability:	■■■■■	POPULARITY: Somewhat uncommon
Exercise requirements:	■■■	Protection ability:	■	FAMILY: Spitz
Playfulness:	■■■	Grooming requirements:	■■■	AREA OF ORIGIN: The Netherlands
Affection level:	■■■■■	Cold tolerance:	■■■■	DATE OF ORIGIN: 1700s
Friendliness toward dogs:	■■■	Heat tolerance:	■■	ORIGINAL FUNCTION: Barge watchdog
Friendliness toward other pets:	■■■■			TODAY'S FUNCTION: Companion
Friendliness toward strangers:	■■■■	WEIGHT: male: about 45 lb; female about 35 lb*		OTHER NAME: Wolf Spitz
Ease of training:	■■■	HEIGHT: male: 18″ (17–19″ acceptable) female: 17″ (16–18″ acceptable)		

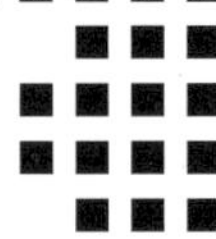

HISTORY

The Keeshond (plural: Keeshonden) is one of the family of spitz dogs, although its exact origin is undocumented. It seems to have been well established in Holland at least since the eighteenth century as a companion and watchdog. The breed later became known as the barge dog because it was often kept as a watchdog on the small vessels navigating the Rhine River. By a stroke of fate, the breed became entangled in the political events of Holland in the years preceding the French Revolution. The leader of the Patriot faction was a man named Kees de Gyselaer, who in turn owned a barge dog named Kees. The dog Kees appeared in so many political cartoons that he and his breed—a dog of the people—became the symbol of the Patriots. Unfortunately for the Keeshond, the Patriots did not prevail, and many Keeshond owners disposed of their dogs lest they be identified with the

ILLUSTRATED STANDARD

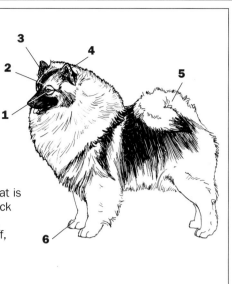

1 Almond-shaped eyes
2 Distinctive "spectacles" add to alert expression
3 Wedge-shaped skull when viewed from above
4 Small, high-set, triangular ears carried erect
5 Tail tightly curled over back, lying flat and close to body
6 Round feet

Color: mixture of gray, black, and cream; undercoat is pale, and tips of the outercoat hairs are black; black muzzle, ears, tail tip, and spectacle lines reaching from the outer eyes corners to the ears; lighter ruff, shoulders, trousers, legs, feet, and tail plume
DQ: none

losing party. To make things worse for the Keeshond, the barges that floated the Rhine became larger, and the small Keeshond became less favored as a barge dog. Nonetheless, the breed did survive, although with a low profile, through the efforts of a few loyal river boatmen and farmers. In 1920, the Baroness van Hardenbroek began an effort to rescue the surviving members. She was so successful at winning friends for the breed that the Keeshond was in England by 1925. AKC recognition soon followed in 1930. So much did the Keeshond recover in its native land that it is now the national dog of Holland.

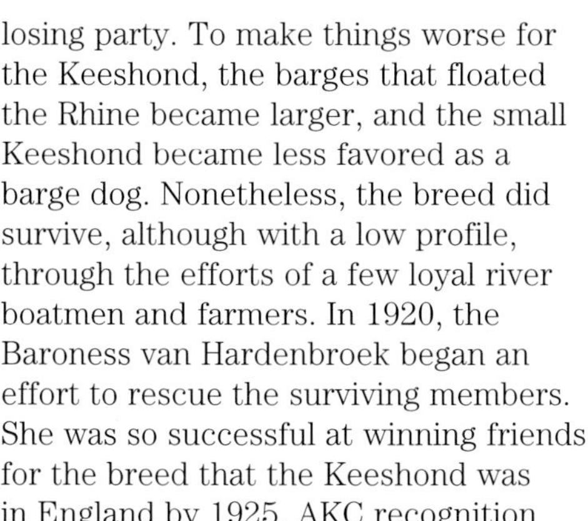

TEMPERAMENT
The Keeshond combines many traits of the best housedogs: fairly energetic and playful, very attentive and loving, and ready for adventure yet content to take it easy. It is sensitive and learns readily. It makes a good companion for a child or adult. It is friendly to all but, nonetheless, an alert watchdog.

UPKEEP
This is a lively breed that can have its exercise needs met with moderate exercise. A good walk on leash, combined with a vigorous game, can satisfy its needs. The double coat needs brushing once or twice weekly, and more when shedding.

HEALTH
- Major concerns: none
- Minor concerns: CHD, epilepsy, skin problems, patellar luxation, elbow dysplasia
- Occasionally seen: renal cortical hypoplasia, tetralogy of Fallot, mitral valve insufficiency
- Suggested tests: hip, knee, elbow, eye
- Life span: 12–14 years

FORM AND FUNCTION
The Keeshond is a square-proportioned, sturdy dog of Northern type. It is an all-purpose dog, a generalist rather than a specialist, and its build reflects this. The gait of the Keeshond is distinctive: clean, bold, and brisk, with only slight to moderate reach and drive. It has a long straight harsh outer coat standing off from its body, a good mane, and a thick downy undercoat—all imparting superb insulation from cold and damp.

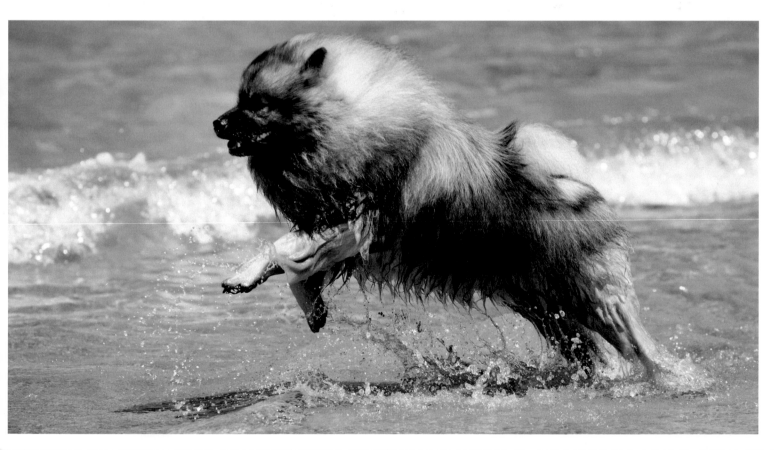

Lhasa Apso

AT A GLANCE

Energy level:	■■■
Exercise requirements:	■■
Playfulness:	■■■
Affection level:	■■■
Friendliness toward dogs:	■■
Friendliness toward other pets:	■■■
Friendliness toward strangers:	■
Ease of training:	■

Watchdog ability:	■■■■■
Protection ability:	■
Grooming requirements:	■■■■
Cold tolerance:	■■■
Heat tolerance:	■■

WEIGHT: 13–15 lb
HEIGHT: 10–11″ (females may be smaller)

POPULARITY: Somewhat popular
FAMILY: Oriental
AREA OF ORIGIN: Tibet
DATE OF ORIGIN: Ancient times
ORIGINAL FUNCTION: Companion, watchdog
TODAY'S FUNCTION: Companion
OTHER NAME: None

HISTORY

The origin of the Lhasa Apso has been long lost; it is an ancient breed bred and revered in the villages and monasteries of Tibet. Its history is intertwined with Buddhist beliefs, including a belief in reincarnation. The souls of lamas were said to enter the sacred dog's bodies upon death, thus imparting an added reverence for these dogs. The dogs also performed the role of monastery watchdog, sounding the alert to visitors, thus giving rise to their native name of Abso Seng Kye (Bark Lion Sentinel Dog). It is likely that the breed's western name of Lhasa Apso is derived from its native name, although some contend that it is a corruption of the Tibetan word rapso, meaning goat (in reference to its goatlike coat). In fact, when the breed first came to England, it was known as the Lhassa Terrier, although it is in no

ILLUSTRATED STANDARD

1 Fairly narrow head covered with heavy furnishings, especially whiskers and beard
2 Level or slightly undershot bite
3 Medium-sized eyes
4 Narrow skull, not quite flat
5 Pendant, heavily feathered ears
6 Tail carried over back in a screw
7 Round feet

Color: any
DQ: none

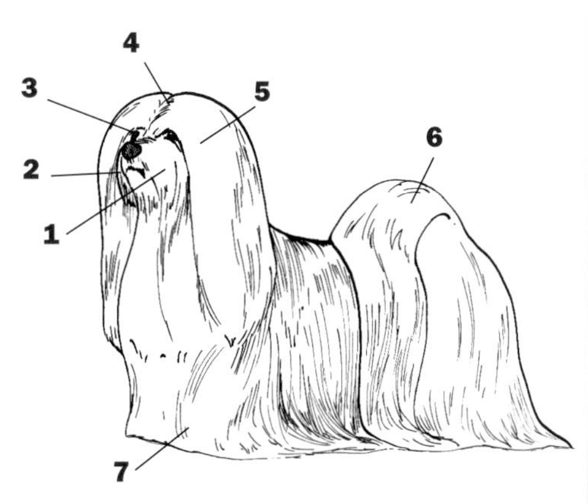

way a terrier. The first Lhasa Apsos were seen in the Western world around 1930, with some of the first dogs arriving as gifts of the thirteenth Dalai Lama. The breed was admitted into the AKC Terrier Group in 1935, but it was reassigned to the Non-Sporting Group in 1959. After a slow start, the Lhasa quickly outpaced its fellow Tibetan breeds to become a popular pet and show dog.

TEMPERAMENT

Despite its lapdog appearance, the Lhasa is a tough character. It is independent, stubborn, and bold. Although it is eager for a romp or game, it will be happy as long as it is given exercise. It will also happily snooze beside its owner. These characteristics make it an excellent small companion in adventure. It is somewhat reserved with strangers. It is not an excessive barker.

UPKEEP

The Lhasa is an active dog, but its relatively small size makes it possible to meet its energy needs either with short walks or vigorous play sessions in the yard, or even home. It makes a fine apartment dog. The long coat needs brushing and combing every other day, always misting the coat first. Bathing every week or two will help prevent mats.

HEALTH

- Major concerns: patellar luxation
- Minor concerns: entropion, distichiasis, PRA, renal cortical hypoplasia
- Occasionally seen: CHD, urinary stones, vWD, sebaceous adenitis
- Suggested tests: knee, eye
- Life span: 12–14 years

FORM AND FUNCTION

The Lhasa Apso is longer than it is tall, with a strong loin. Although the breed has never been used for purposes requiring great athleticism, it should nonetheless have a strong loin and well-developed quarters and thighs. The head is well covered with a good fall over the eyes and good whiskers and beard, imparting a dignified, almost lion-like look. The bite should be either level or slightly undershot. The coat is heavy, straight, long, and hard.

Löwchen

AT A GLANCE

Energy level:	■■■■	Watchdog ability:	■■■■	POPULARITY: Very rare
Exercise requirements:	■	Protection ability:	■	FAMILY: Water Dog, Barbichon
Playfulness:	■■■	Grooming requirements:	■■■■	AREA OF ORIGIN: France, Germany
Affection level:	■■■	Cold tolerance:	■■■	DATE OF ORIGIN: 1500s
Friendliness toward dogs:	■■■■	Heat tolerance:	■■■	ORIGINAL FUNCTION: Companion
Friendliness toward other pets:	■■■■			TODAY'S FUNCTION: Companion
Friendliness toward strangers:	■■■	WEIGHT: 8–18 lb*		OTHER NAME: Little Lion Dog
Ease of training:	■■■	HEIGHT: 12–14″		

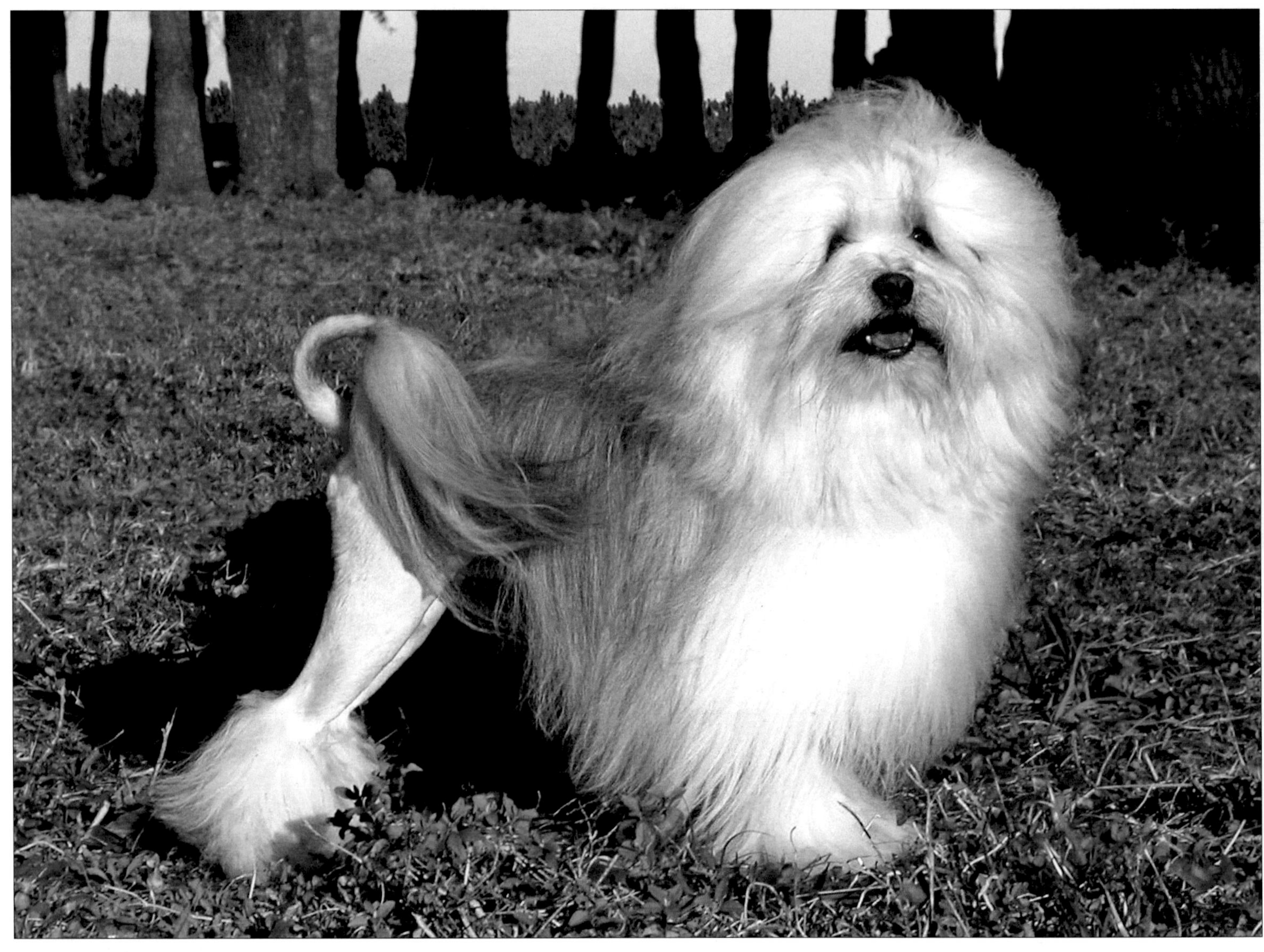

HISTORY

Löwchen (pronounced Lerv-chun) means Little Lion Dog, and in France the breed is known as Le Petit Chien Lion. The Löwchen shares common roots with other members of the Bichon family, which also includes the Bichon Frise and Havanese, among others. Germany, Russia, and France have all laid claim to the breed. The exact time and place of its origin is obscure, but dogs resembling the Löwchen, sporting the distinctive lion trim, can be found in sixteenth-century German art. In the traditional lion trim, the coat is clipped short from the last rib to and including the hindquarters down to the hock joint. The front legs are clipped from elbow to just above the pastern. The feet are clipped, and about half the tail is clipped, leaving a plume at the tip. Any long hair is to be left unshaped. In the

ILLUSTRATED STANDARD

1 Relatively board muzzle
2 Eyes large, round, and forward looking
3 Moderately defined stop
4 Skull broad and relatively flat
5 Pendant ears
6 Topline level
7 Tail set high and carried in a cup-handle fashion when the dog is moving
8 Slight tuck-up

Color: any colors or combinations
DQ: any trim other than specified; shaping or scissoring of the long coat

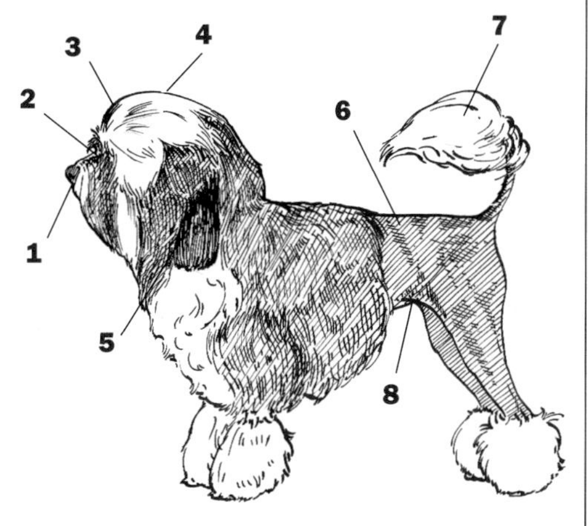

1960s, the breed's numbers had dwindled to perilous numbers; through the efforts of two breeders, several related dogs from Germany were brought to Britain. Because of their small numbers, these dogs were interbred extensively and formed the basis of the breed in Britain as well as America. The Löwchen entered the AKC Miscellaneous class in 1996 and was admitted as a member of the Non-Sporting Group as of the first day of 1999.

TEMPERAMENT

This is a lively, inquisitive, affectionate dog. It is a mixture of playful spirit and calm soul mate, a good companion for a quiet family. It is willing to please and responsive to commands, and it is devoted to its family. Some may bark or dig a lot.

UPKEEP

The Löwchen can receive ample exercise with a short walk or active game every day. It enjoys a mental challenge. Its coat needs brushing or combing about every other day. Clipping to maintain the traditional lion trim must be done every month or two. Many pet owners prefer to keep their dogs in a puppy clip.

HEALTH

- Major concerns: none
- Minor concerns: patellar luxation
- Occasionally seen: cataract, PRA
- Suggested tests: knee, eye, hip
- Life span: 13–15 years

FORM AND FUNCTION

The Löwchen is a compact small dog, very slightly longer than it is tall, with strong, sturdy—but never coarse—bone. Its gait is effortless with good reach and drive, and it proudly carries its head and tail. Its coat is dense and long, moderately soft with a slight to moderate wave. It is traditionally clipped in a lion trim. The Löwchen has a relatively short, broad topskull and muzzle, and its expression is alert, bright, and lively.

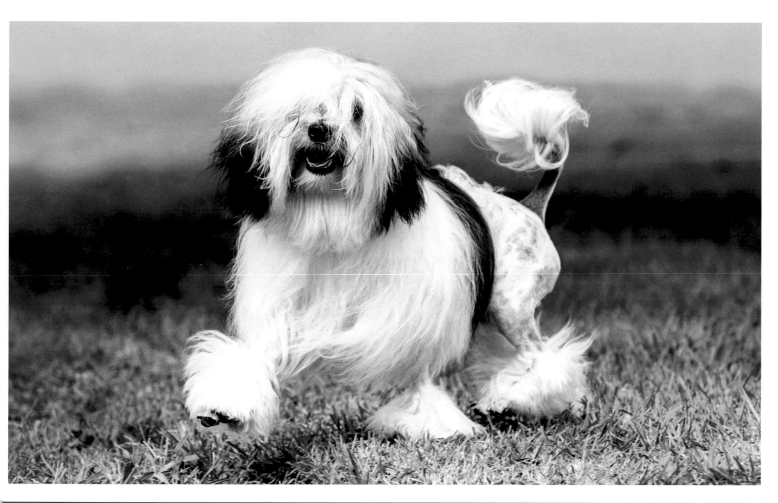

Norwegian Lundehund

AT A GLANCE

Energy level:	■■■■	Watchdog ability:	■■■■■	POPULARITY: Very rare
Exercise requirements:	■■■	Protection ability:	■■■	FAMILY: Spitz
Playfulness:	■■■	Grooming requirements:	■■	AREA OF ORIGIN: Norway
Affection level:	■■■	Cold tolerance:	■■■■	DATE OF ORIGIN: 1500s or earlier
Friendliness toward dogs:	■■■	Heat tolerance:	■■■	ORIGINAL FUNCTION: Puffin hunting
Friendliness toward other pets:	■■■			TODAY'S FUNCTION: Companion
Friendliness toward strangers:	■■	WEIGHT: 13–16 lb*		OTHER NAME: Puffin Dog
Ease of training:	■■	HEIGHT: male: 13–15″; female: 12–14″		

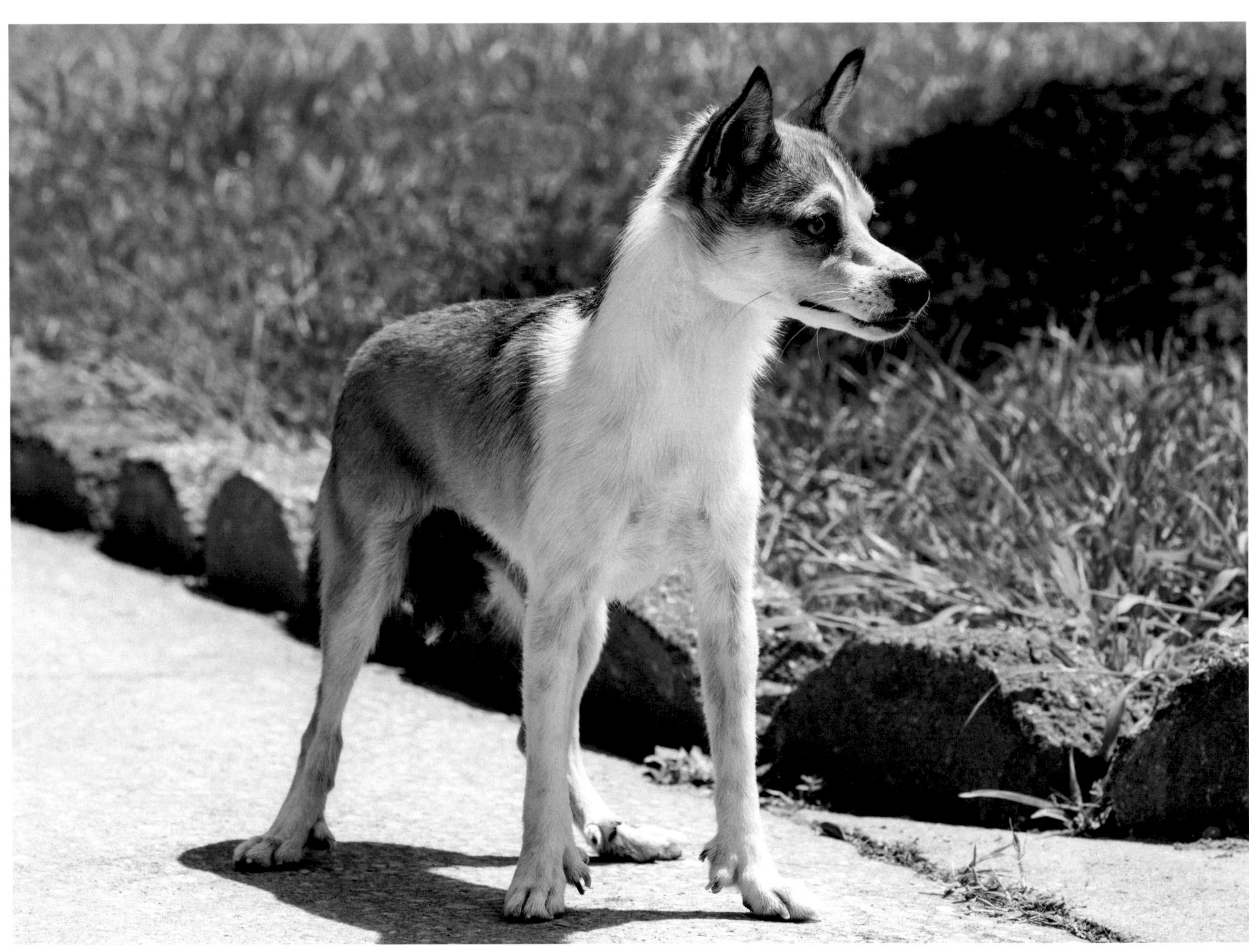

HISTORY

It's the world's most flexible dog and the only dog to have six toes on each foot. These traits have helped the Lundehund perform a dangerous job for hundreds of years. *Lundehund* means Puffin Dog in Norwegian. The Lundehund comes from Norway's Lofoten Islands, where puffin birds ("lundes") nest in narrow caves and tunnels in the islands' cliffs. Only the Lundehund could climb the cliffs and squeeze deep into the twisting tunnels to catch these birds. A good Lundehund could catch 30 puffins a night during their nesting season, supplying the village with tasty meat and valuable down feathers. Lundehunds performed this task at least since the 1500s. By the early 1900s, most puffins were being caught with nets, not dogs. The dogs, neglected and hungry, attacked the sheep and subsequently

ILLUSTRATED STANDARD

1 Wedge-shaped head
2 Almond-shaped eyes, yellow-brown to brown; light are preferred
3 Medium-sized, triangular, erect ears; very mobile; ear leather can be folded up, backward, or at right angles to shut ear openings
4 Level back, short loin, and slightly sloping croup
5 High-set, medium length tail; hanging when at rest; out or over back when in motion
6 Slightly outward-turned, oval feet with at least six fully developed toes, five of which should reach the ground
7 Hind feet are slightly turned out with at least six toes

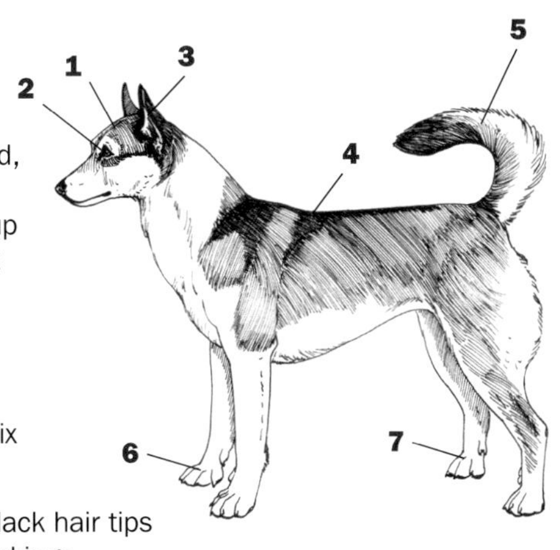

Color: all shades of tan to reddish brown, with black hair tips and white markings; or white with red or dark markings
DQ: none

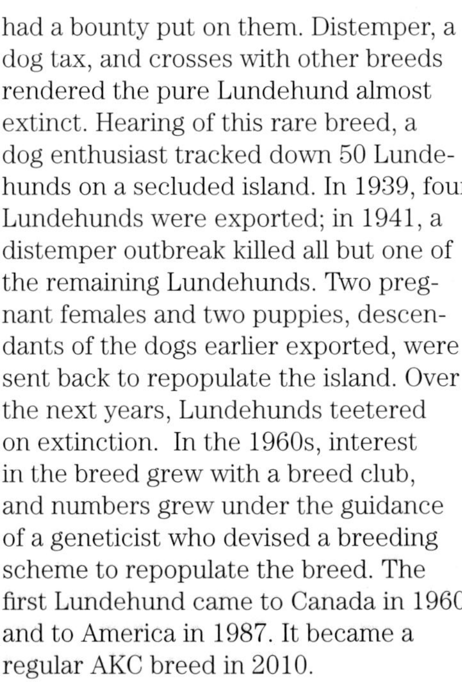

had a bounty put on them. Distemper, a dog tax, and crosses with other breeds rendered the pure Lundehund almost extinct. Hearing of this rare breed, a dog enthusiast tracked down 50 Lundehunds on a secluded island. In 1939, four Lundehunds were exported; in 1941, a distemper outbreak killed all but one of the remaining Lundehunds. Two pregnant females and two puppies, descendants of the dogs earlier exported, were sent back to repopulate the island. Over the next years, Lundehunds teetered on extinction. In the 1960s, interest in the breed grew with a breed club, and numbers grew under the guidance of a geneticist who devised a breeding scheme to repopulate the breed. The first Lundehund came to Canada in 1960 and to America in 1987. It became a regular AKC breed in 2010.

TEMPERAMENT

Lundehunds are more primitive in their behavior than many breeds, very inquisitive and independent. They are free thinkers, which can be challenging when training. They can climb and tunnel, so few things are out of their reach. They have a strong prey drive but can get along with other pets if raised with them. They are very alert and can bark a lot. Most tend to be reserved with strangers but not aggressive. They are excellent watch dogs and will protect by barking, not biting. If not socialized extensively as puppies, they can be sound sensitive or shy.

UPKEEP

Lundehunds are busy dogs, climbing on things and checking out crannies. They need a good walk or vigorous play session every day. They particularly enjoy the chance to explore new places or any activity that engages their active minds. Some can be difficult to housetrain. Coat care consists of a weekly brushing; more often when shedding. A dog with symptomatic Lundehund syndrome can present feeding challenges and needs a special diet.

HEALTH

- Major concerns: Lundehund gastroenteropathy syndrome
- Minor concerns: none
- Occasionally seen: none
- Suggested tests: none
- Life span: 8-12 years

Note: Every Lundehund probably has Lundehund syndrome, a collection of potentially serious gastrointestinal problems, though some show no signs.

FORM AND FUNCTION

The Lundehund uses its strong extra toes to help it grasp the rocky cliffs and to dig under boulders. It must be flexible to squeeze in and out of tight curving passages. It can bend its head backward so the top of the head touches its back, and it can extend its forelegs straight out to either side (this results in a peculiar rotary movement when the dog trots). It can close its ear openings, blocking out debris. It has elongated rear foot pads for better traction. It also has two fewer teeth than other dogs. Otherwise, the general conformation is typically spitz. The Lundehind should be neither coarse nor heavy, but athletic and agile. It is slightly longer than tall. It has a double coat; medium-length, harsh outer coat; and soft undercoat.

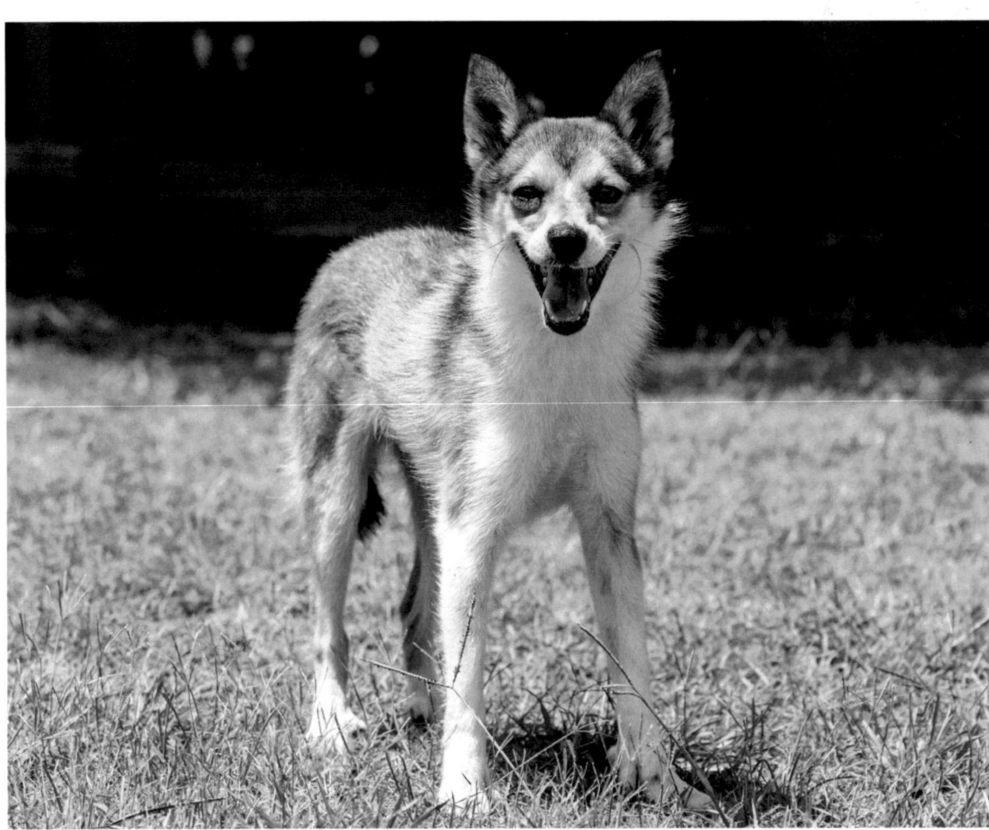

Poodle (Standard and Miniature)

AT A GLANCE: STANDARD

Energy level:	■■■	Watchdog ability:	■■■■■	POPULARITY: Most popular
Exercise requirements:	■■■■	Protection ability:	■■■■	FAMILY: Water Dog
Playfulness:	■■■■	Grooming requirements:	■■■■■	AREA OF ORIGIN: Germany and Central Europe
Affection level:	■■■	Cold tolerance:	■■■	DATE OF ORIGIN: 1500s
Friendliness toward dogs:	■■■	Heat tolerance:	■■■	ORIGINAL FUNCTION: Water retrieving, performer
Friendliness toward other pets:	■■■■			
Friendliness toward strangers:	■■■	WEIGHT: 45–65 lb*		TODAY'S FUNCTION: Obedience, agility
Ease of training:	■■■■■	HEIGHT: over 15″ (usually over 21″)		OTHER NAME: Barbone, Caniche

AT A GLANCE: MINIATURE

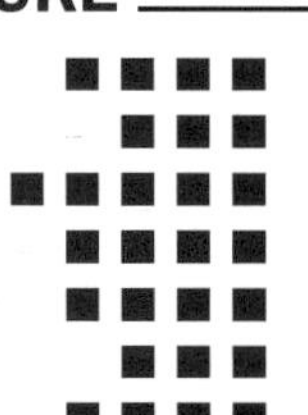

Energy level:	■■■■	Watchdog ability:	■■■■■	POPULARITY: Most popular
Exercise requirements:	■■■	Protection ability:	■	FAMILY: Water Dog
Playfulness:	■■■■■	Grooming requirements:	■■■■■	AREA OF ORIGIN: Germany and Central Europe
Affection level:	■■■■	Cold tolerance:	■■■	DATE OF ORIGIN: 1500s
Friendliness toward dogs:	■■■■	Heat tolerance:	■■■	ORIGINAL FUNCTION: Water retrieving, performer
Friendliness toward other pets:	■■■			
Friendliness toward strangers:	■■■■	WEIGHT: 12–18 lb*		TODAY'S FUNCTION: Obedience, agility
Ease of training:	■■■■■	HEIGHT: 10–15″		OTHER NAME: Barbone, Caniche

ILLUSTRATED STANDARD

1 Long, fine, chiseled muzzle
2 Slight but definite stop
3 Oval eyes
4 Level topline
5 Tail straight and carried up, docked
6 Small, oval feet

Color: any solid color
DQ: Miniature: over 15″ in height, or 10″ or less; Standard: 15″ or less in height; a dog in any but one of the specified clips; a dog not a solid color

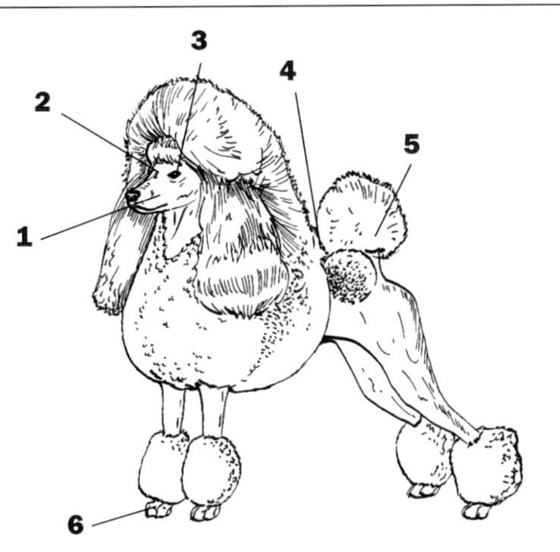

HISTORY
The history of the Standard and Miniature Poodle is described with the Toy Poodle history in the Toy Section.

TEMPERAMENT
Miniature: The Miniature Poodle is lively, amiable, playful, eager to please, responsive, smart, and obedient—small wonder that it has remained one of the most popular varieties of dog for so long. It is sensitive, tending to be devoted to one person, and initially reserved with strangers. It is good with children, other pets, and dogs. Some tend to bark a lot.

Standard: Among the very smartest and most obedient of dogs, the Standard Poodle combines playful exuberance with a zest for life's adventures. It retains its hunting heritage, and loves to run, swim, and retrieve. It gets along well with everyone, although it is somewhat reserved with strangers. It is excellent with children.

UPKEEP
All Poodles need a lot of interaction with people. They also need mental and physical exercise. A brief but challenging obedience or play session, combined with a walk, should be part of every Poodle's day. Standard Poodles will need more exercise and may especially enjoy swimming. They should preferably be brushed every other day or weekly for shorter coats. Poodle hair, when shed, does not fall out but becomes caught in the surrounding hair, which can cause matting if not removed. The pet clips are easier to maintain and can be done every four to six weeks.

HEALTH
Miniature
- Major concerns: PRA, Legg–Perthes, patellar luxation, epilepsy
- Minor concerns: trichiasis, entropion, lacrimal duct atresia, cataract, glaucoma, distichiasis
- Occasionally seen: urinary stones, intervertebral disk degeneration
- Suggested tests: eye, knee, hip, DNA for PRA
- Life span: 13–15 years

Standard
- Major concerns: sebaceous adenitis, gastric torsion, Addison's
- Minor concerns: distichiasis, entropion, cataract, CHD, epilepsy
- Occasionally seen: PDA, vWD
- Suggested tests: (skinpunch for SA), eye, hip
- Life span: 10–13 years

FORM AND FUNCTION
The Poodle is a square-proportioned dog with proud carriage and elegant appearance. It should move with a light, springy, effortless stride. The Poodle stems from working retriever stock, and its conformation should reflect its athletic background. The coat is curly, harsh, and dense, forming a water resistant barrier. If corded, it should hang in tight even cords. The traditional clips stem from functional and decorative tradition; acceptable clips for show purposes are the puppy (for puppies only), English saddle, Continental, and (for some nonregular classes only) sporting. The Poodle should always appear active, intelligent, and elegant. It has a proud bearing and air of distinction.

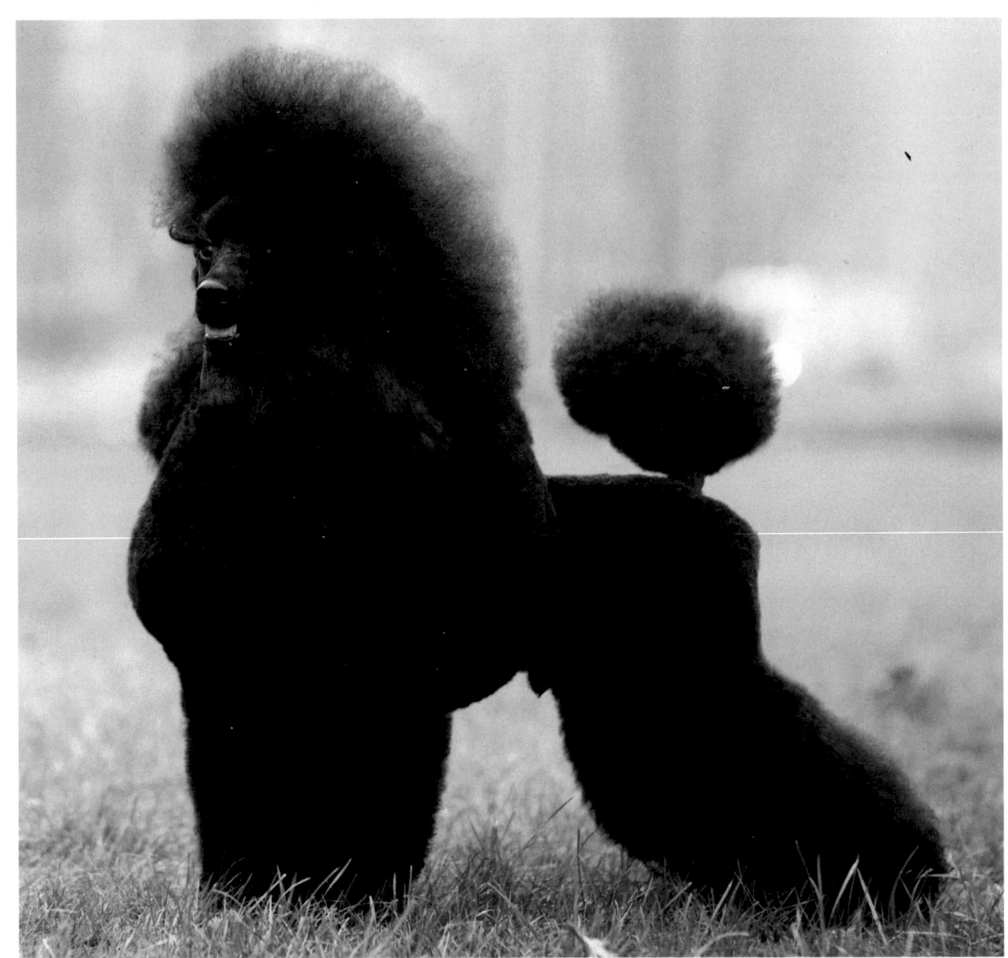

Schipperke

AT A GLANCE

Energy level:	■■■■	Watchdog ability:	■■■■■	POPULARITY: Uncommon
Exercise requirements:	■■■	Protection ability:	■■■■	FAMILY: Spitz
Playfulness:	■■■	Grooming requirements:	■■	AREA OF ORIGIN: Belgium
Affection level:	■■■■	Cold tolerance:	■■■	DATE OF ORIGIN: 1600s
Friendliness toward dogs:	■■■	Heat tolerance:	■■	ORIGINAL FUNCTION: Barge dog, watchdog, ratter
Friendliness toward other pets:	■■■			
Friendliness toward strangers:	■■	WEIGHT: male: 12–16 lb*; female: 10–14 lb*		TODAY'S FUNCTION: Companion
Ease of training:	■■■	HEIGHT: male: 11–13″; female: 10–12″		OTHER NAME: None

HISTORY

The origin of the Schipperke is controversial. One plausible theory is that it originated as a dog of the boatmen who traveled between Brussels and Antwerp. The Flemish word for boat is *schip*, and Schipperke is thus thought to mean little boatman. The breed was less commonly called Schipperke by Belgian townspeople, however, who more often referred to it as spitz. The other plausible theory of origin is that it was a dog of tradesmen guilds and middle-class households, who wanted a small watchdog and ratter. The breed resembles a miniature Belgian Sheepdog, and it is possible that Schipperke derives from the word for shepherd, *scheper*. In fact, a breed of dog intermediate in size was one known in the region. Although small black tailless dogs are mentioned in Belgian writings of the fifteenth and sixteenth centuries, definite evidence of Schipperkes is not found until 1690. A group of Brussels shoemakers

ILLUSTRATED STANDARD

1 Foxlike face
2 Small eyes
3 Small, triangular, high-set, erect ears
4 Appearance of being slightly higher at shoulders than rump
5 Docked tail so that tail is not visible
6 Small, round feet

Color: black
DQ: drop ear; any color other than black

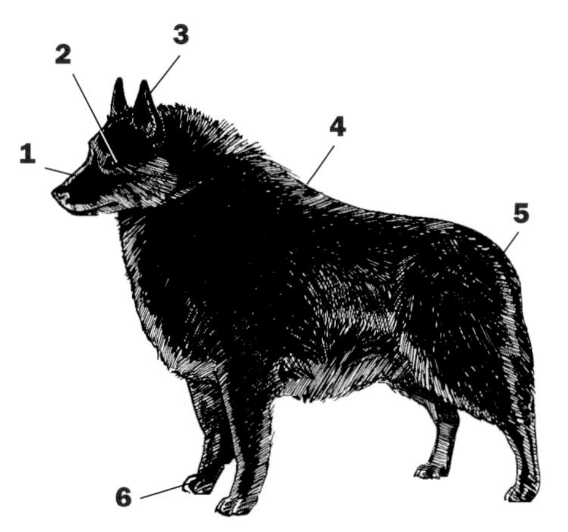

organized regular Schipperke competitions, taking special pride in adorning their companions with ornate brass collars. By the nineteenth century the breed was so popular in central Belgium that it was virtually the only house dog found there, and it was acknowledged as the national dog. In 1885 Queen Marie Henriette acquired a Schipperke she saw at a dog show. After people saw the little dog with her, it sparked great interest in the breed from people of all classes, and the workman's companion thus became companion to the elite. At the same time, the breed's numbers were depleted by exports to England, where they had become extremely fashionable. Most people in Belgium considered the breed common and preferred more exotic breeds. In the late 1880s, a group of Belgian Schipperke fanciers grouped to try to save the breed, setting forth the breed's desirable points. Soon after, the first Schipperke came to America. It aroused little interest at first, but it has since amassed a modest but loyal following.

TEMPERAMENT

The Schipperke is a bold companion, even though it can be an independent and headstrong one. This little dynamo is happiest when busy, poking its nose into every cranny and ever on the lookout for adventure. It is reserved with strangers and an alert watchdog. It can make an amiable and pleasant house dog but needs daily exercise.

UPKEEP

The active nature of this breed makes exercise—both mental and physical—imperative. Its small stature makes getting that exercise fairly easy, however. Either a vigorous game in the yard or a moderate walk on leash will usually suffice to meets its needs. Its double coat needs weekly brushing, more when shedding.

HEALTH

- Major concerns: MPS IIIB
- Minor concerns: Legg-Perthes, epilepsy, hypothyroidism
- Occasionally seen: entropion, distichiasis, PRA, CHD
- Suggested tests: thyroid, DNA for MP IIIB, knee
- Life span: 13–15 years

FORM AND FUNCTION

The Schipperke is a small, cobby dog, square-proportioned, appearing to slope from shoulders to croup. This appearance is helped by its double coat, which forms a stand-out ruff, cape, and culottes. The foxlike face is questioning and mischievous, even impudent. The trot is smooth and graceful. This is an agile, active dog developed as a watchdog and vermin hunter.

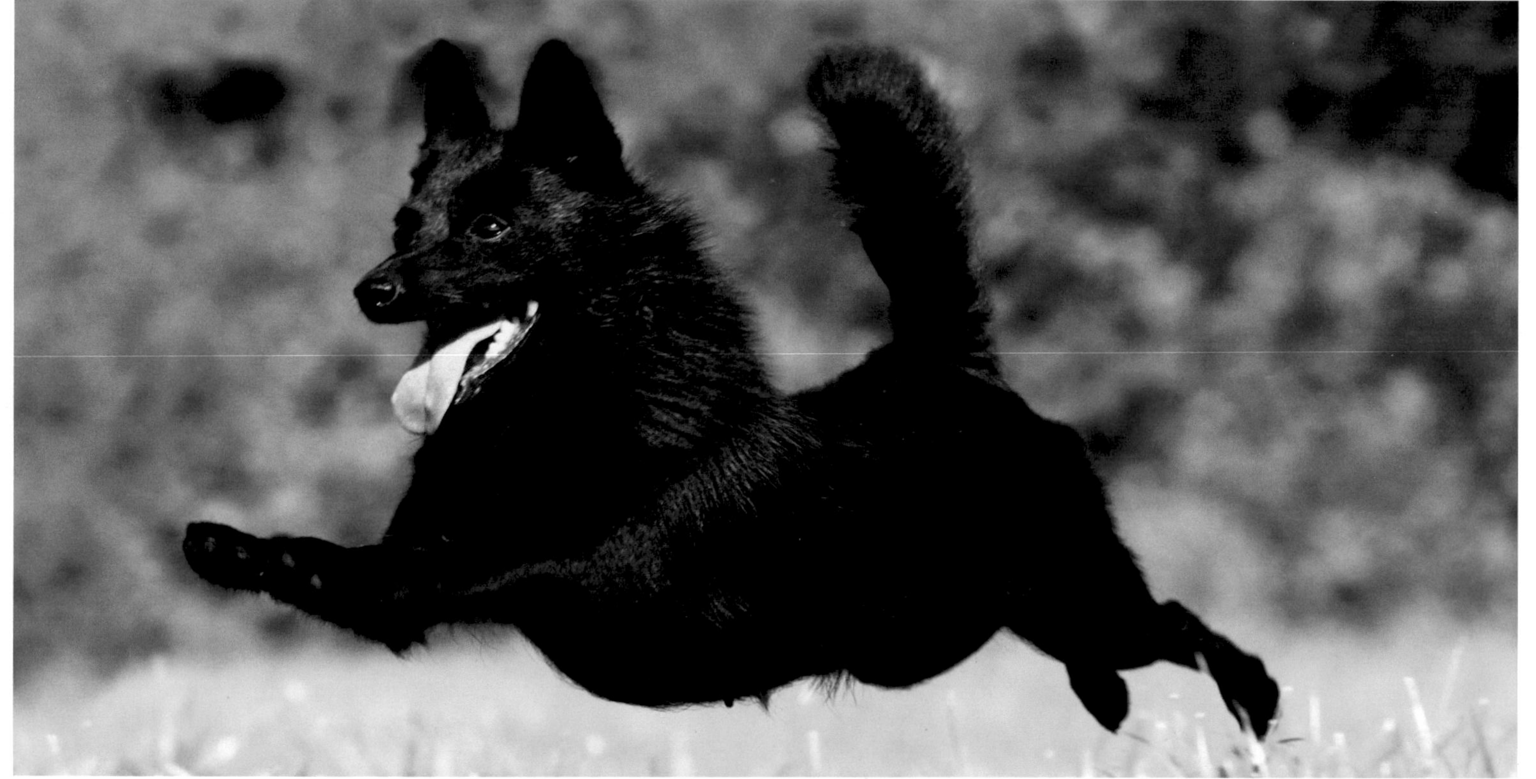

Shiba Inu

AT A GLANCE

Energy level:	■ ■ ■	Watchdog ability:	■ ■ ■ ■ ■	POPULARITY: Somewhat popular
Exercise requirements:	■ ■ ■	Protection ability:	■ ■ ■	FAMILY: Spitz
Playfulness:	■ ■ ■	Grooming requirements:	■ ■ ■	AREA OF ORIGIN: Japan
Affection level:	■ ■ ■	Cold tolerance:	■ ■ ■ ■	DATE OF ORIGIN: Ancient times
Friendliness toward dogs:	■ ■	Heat tolerance:	■ ■	ORIGINAL FUNCTION: Hunting and flushing small game
Friendliness toward other pets:	■ ■			
Friendliness toward strangers:	■ ■ ■	WEIGHT: male: 23 lb; female: 17 lb (averages)		TODAY'S FUNCTION: Companion
Ease of training:	■ ■	HEIGHT: male: 14.5–16.5″; female: 13.5–15.5″		OTHER NAME: Brushwood Dog, Japanese Small-size Dog

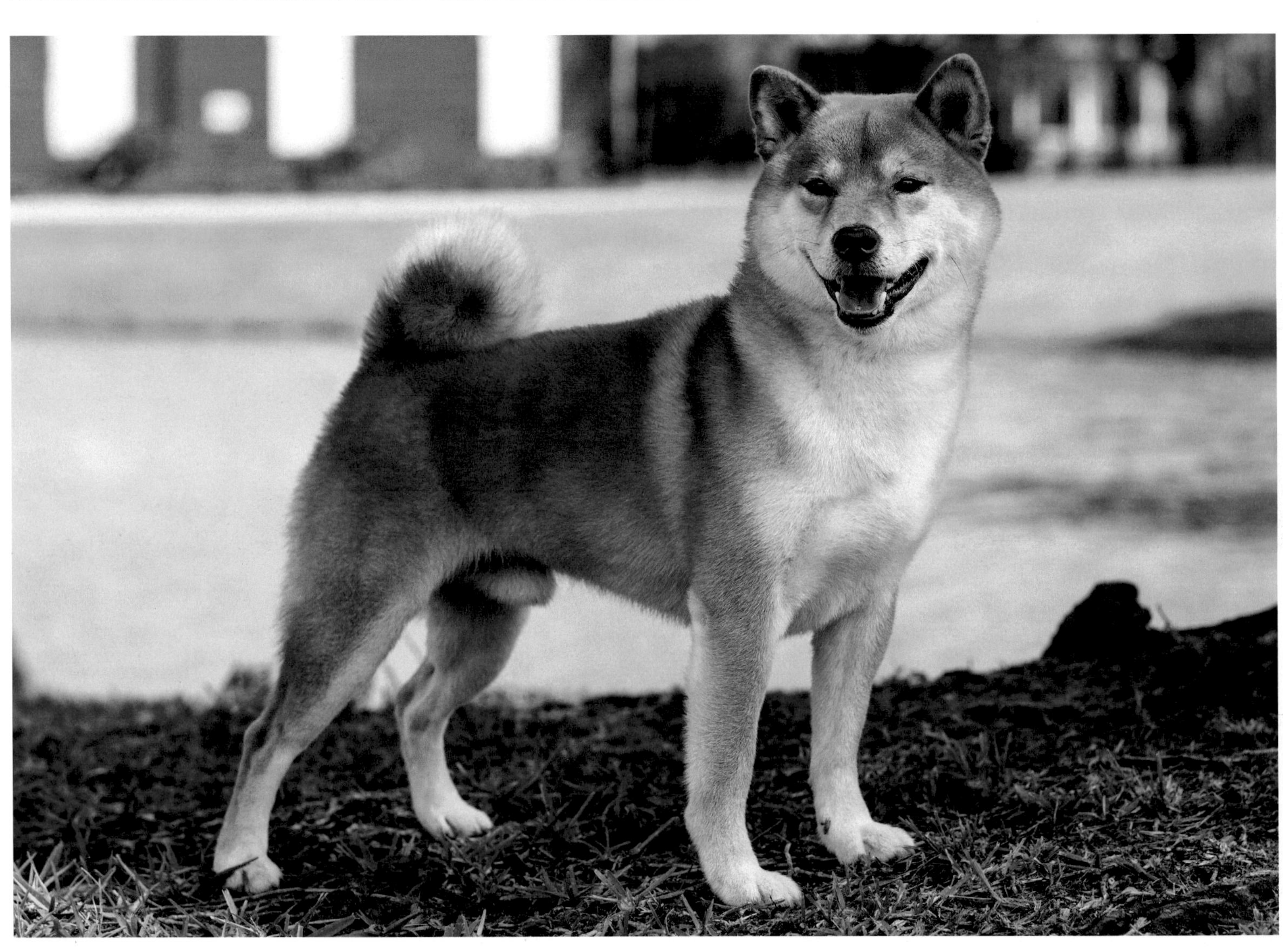

HISTORY

Native Japanese dogs are divided into six breeds. Of these, the smallest and probably most ancient is the Shiba Inu. In fact, one theory about the name shiba is that it simply denotes small; however, it may also mean brushwood in reference to the brilliant red brushwood trees that so closely matched the breed's red coat and through which they hunted. These theories have resulted in the Shiba's being nicknamed the little brushwood dog. The origin of the Shiba is unclear; but it is clearly of spitz heritage and may have been used as early as 300 B.C. as a hunting dog in central Japan. Although they were used mostly to flush birds and small game, they were occasionally used to hunt wild boar. Three main types existed and each was named for its area of origin: the Shinshu Shiba (from the Nagano Prefecture), the Mino Shiba (from the Gifu Prefecture), and the Sanin Shiba (from the northeast mainland). After World War II, the breed was nearly

ILLUSTRATED STANDARD

1 Moderate stop
2 Somewhat triangular eyes
3 Small, triangular ears, tilting forward
4 Topline straight and level
5 Tail curled over back
6 Well-developed forechest
7 Cat feet

Color: red, red sesame (red with black overlay), or black and tan, with cream to white ventral shading
DQ: males over 16.5″ or under 14.5″ in height; overshot or undershot bite

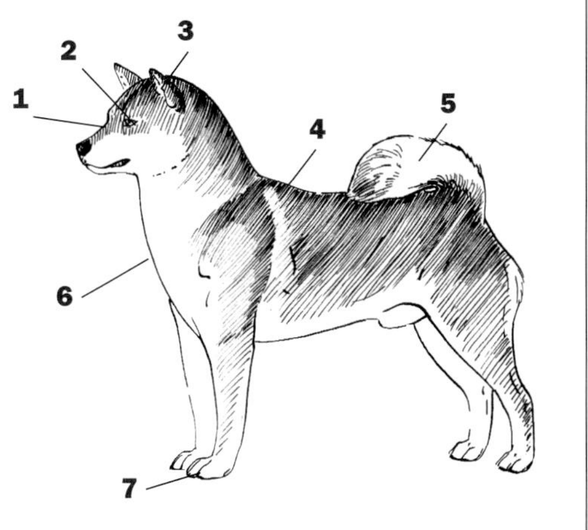

FORM AND FUNCTION

The Shiba Inu is moderately compact, being slightly longer than it is tall. It has typical traits of dogs from northern heritage: small erect ears, thick fur, powerful body, and curled tail. Its expression is bold, spirited, and good natured. The gait is light, quick, and agile, with an effortless, smooth stride. The double coat consists of a strong straight outer coat with a soft undercoat, imparting great insulation. These traits enabled the Shiba to hunt small game through dense cover.

lost, and it was further decimated by distemper in 1952. In an attempt to save the Shiba Inu, the different types were interbred, crossing the heavier-boned dogs from mountainous regions with the lighter-boned dogs from other regions. As a result, the Shiba survived as one breed with some variation in bone substance. The first Shiba came to America in 1954 and was officially recognized by the AKC in 1993. Since then, Shibas have achieved a staunch following, and their popularity continues to grow.

TEMPERAMENT

Bold, independent, and headstrong, the Shiba is brimming with self-confidence. It is lively outdoors, yet calm indoors, as long as it gets daily exercise. It may be aggressive with strange dogs of the same sex and may chase small animals. It is a hardy breed, ready for adventure. Some tend to be headstrong and domineering. It is territorial, alert, and reserved with strangers—ingredients making for an excellent watchdog. It is quite vocal; some bark a lot.

UPKEEP

The Shiba needs a daily workout, either in the form of a vigorous game in the yard, a long walk, or a good run in a fenced area. Its double coat needs brushing one or two times weekly, more when shedding.

HEALTH

- Major concerns: patellar luxation
- Minor concerns: allergies, cataract
- Occasionally seen: CHD, distichiasis, PPM, PRA
- Suggested tests: knee, hip, eye
- Life span: 12–15 years

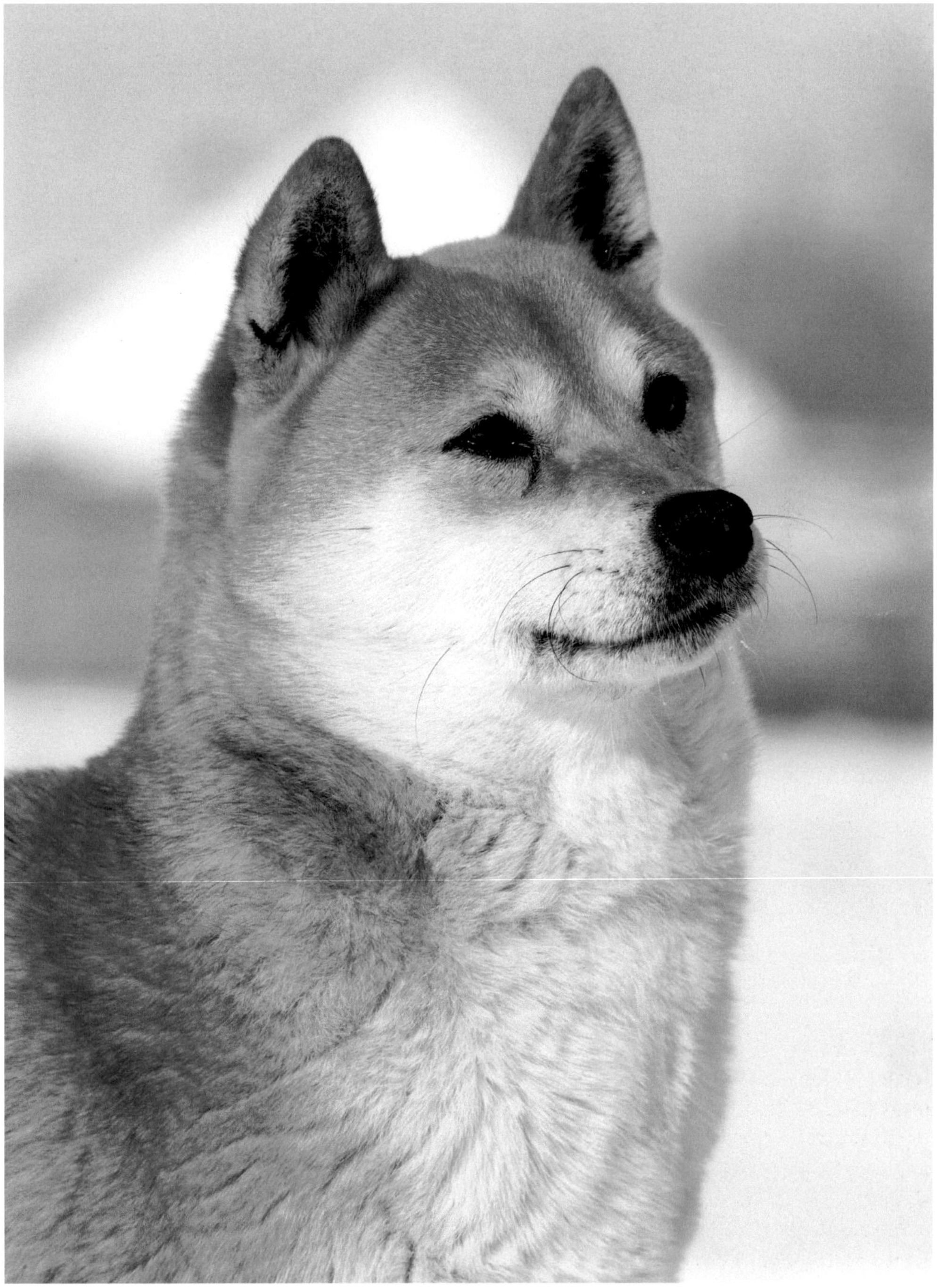

Tibetan Spaniel

AT A GLANCE

Energy level:	■ ■ ■
Exercise requirements:	■ ■
Playfulness:	■ ■ ■
Affection level:	■ ■ ■
Friendliness toward dogs:	■ ■ ■ ■
Friendliness toward other pets:	■ ■ ■ ■
Friendliness toward strangers:	■
Ease of training:	■ ■ ■

Watchdog ability:	■ ■ ■ ■ ■
Protection ability:	■
Grooming requirements:	■ ■ ■
Cold tolerance:	■ ■ ■
Heat tolerance:	■ ■

WEIGHT: 9–15 lb
HEIGHT: about 10″

POPULARITY: Uncommon
FAMILY: Oriental
AREA OF ORIGIN: Tibet
DATE OF ORIGIN: Ancient times
ORIGINAL FUNCTION: Watchdog, companion
TODAY'S FUNCTION: Companion
OTHER NAME: None

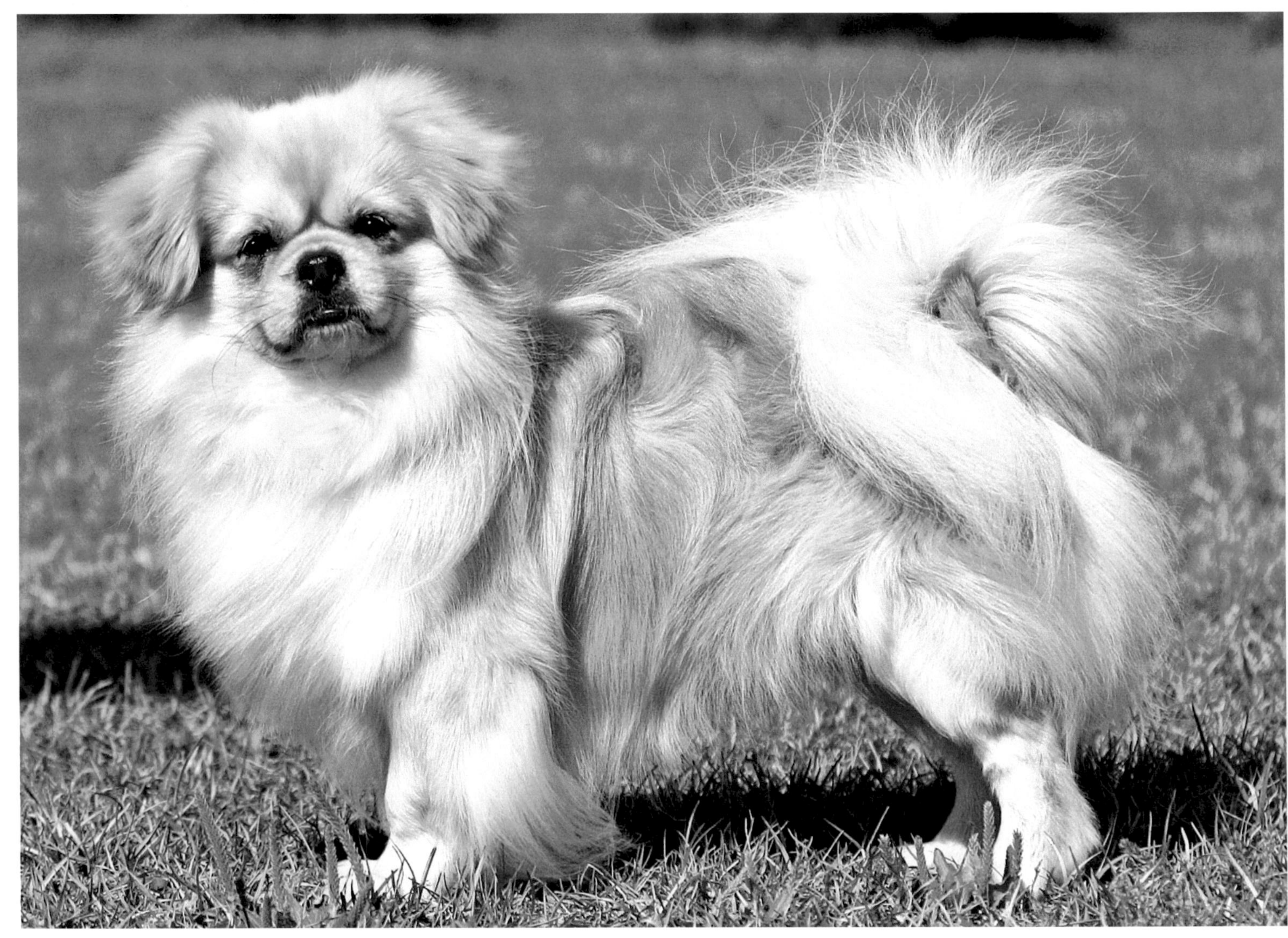

HISTORY

The Tibetan Spaniel's history is interwoven with the Buddhist beliefs of Tibet. The Lamaist form of Buddhism regarded the lion as an important symbol, as it was said to follow Buddha like a dog. The little lionlike dogs that followed their Lama masters were regarded as symbols of the sacred lion and were thus highly valued. The Chinese also cultivated a lion dog, the Pekingese, and dogs from each country were often presented between countries, encouraging some interbreeding between the Tibetan and Chinese dogs. Although breeding occurred in the villages, the best breedings were products of the monasteries, which usually bred only the smallest specimens. The little dogs served more than a decorative purpose; they perched on the monastery walls and sounded the alarm when strangers or wolves approached. They also served as prayer dogs, turning the prayer wheels by means of small treadmills. Although the

ILLUSTRATED STANDARD

1 Slightly undershot
2 Blunt muzzle
3 Small head
4 Slightly domed skull
5 Oval eyes
6 Pendant ears
7 Tail carried in a gay curl over back, richly plumed
8 Hare foot with long feathering

Color: all colors and mixtures; white allowed on feet
DQ: none

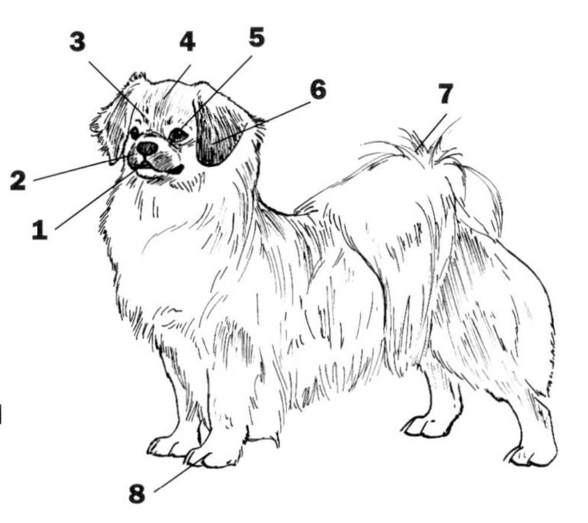

first Tibby came to England in the late 1800s, no concerted breeding program was attempted until the 1920s, when the Griegs (known for promoting the Tibetan Spaniel) obtained several specimens. Only one of their dogs, Skyid, survived World War II, but its descendants can be found in modern pedigrees. The start of most Western Tibbies dates from around 1940, when several dogs came to England by way of an English couple living in Sikkim. It wasn't until the 1960s that the breed came to America, and only in 1984 did it receive AKC recognition. This sacred dog has been slow to garner fanciers, but it is worshiped by those who have adopted it.

TEMPERAMENT

The Tibetan Spaniel is independent, bold, and stubborn, but it is also sensitive and biddable. It has a happy attitude, enjoying games and outings with its family. It also enjoys snoozes next to its special person. It is an exceptionally enjoyable and fastidious housedog. It is amiable with other dogs and animals, but reserved with strangers.

UPKEEP

The Tibbie's exercise needs are minimal, but daily. Its needs can be met by games inside the house or yard, or with a short walk on leash. This breed is suited for apartment life and does not like hot weather. Its coat needs brushing and combing twice weekly.

HEALTH

- Major concerns: none
- Minor concerns: patellar luxation, cataract
- Occasionally seen: PRA, portacaval shunt
- Suggested tests: knee, eye, (DNA for PRA)
- Life span: 12–15 years

FORM AND FUNCTION

The Tibbie is slightly longer than it is tall. Its head is small in proportion to its body; its wide eye set gives it an "apelike" expression. The mouth is undershot. The gait is quick moving, straight, and free. The coat is double, with a flat-lying, silky outer coat of moderate length and a longer mane. The tail is plumed, and long feathering grows from between the toes.

Tibetan Terrier

AT A GLANCE

Energy level:	■ ■ ■	Watchdog ability:	■ ■ ■ ■	POPULARITY: Somewhat uncommon
Exercise requirements:	■ ■ ■	Protection ability:	■	FAMILY: Oriental
Playfulness:	■ ■ ■	Grooming requirements:	■ ■ ■ ■	AREA OF ORIGIN: Tibet
Affection level:	■ ■ ■ ■	Cold tolerance:	■ ■ ■	DATE OF ORIGIN: Ancient times
Friendliness toward dogs:	■ ■ ■	Heat tolerance:	■ ■ ■	ORIGINAL FUNCTION: Herder, good luck, companion
Friendliness toward other pets:	■ ■ ■			
Friendliness toward strangers:	■ ■	WEIGHT: average 20–24 lb, may be 18–30 lb		TODAY'S FUNCTION: Companion
Ease of training:	■ ■ ■	HEIGHT: male: 15–16″; female: slightly smaller		OTHER NAME: Dhokhi Apso

HISTORY

The history of the Tibetan Terrier is as shrouded in mystery as the mountains and valleys from whence it comes. The Tibetan Terrier was bred in Lamaist monasteries nearly 2000 years ago. The dogs were kept not as workers, but as family companions that might occasionally help out with the herding or other farm chores. They were known as "luck bringers" or "holy dogs." Much of the breed's history is speculation or myth; one story claims that a major access route to their valley was obliterated by an earthquake in the fourteenth century. Few visitors hazarded the treacherous journey to the "Lost Valley" after that; the few that did were often given a luck-bringer dog to help them on their return trip. As befitting any bringer of luck, these dogs were never sold, but they were often presented as special gifts of gratitude. So

ILLUSTRATED STANDARD

1 Small amount of beard
2 Marked but not exaggerated stop
3 Profusely coated with a fall of hair covering the eyes and foreface
4 Pendant, heavily feathered ears
5 Tail falls forward over the back
6 Large, flat, round feet

Color: any
DQ: none

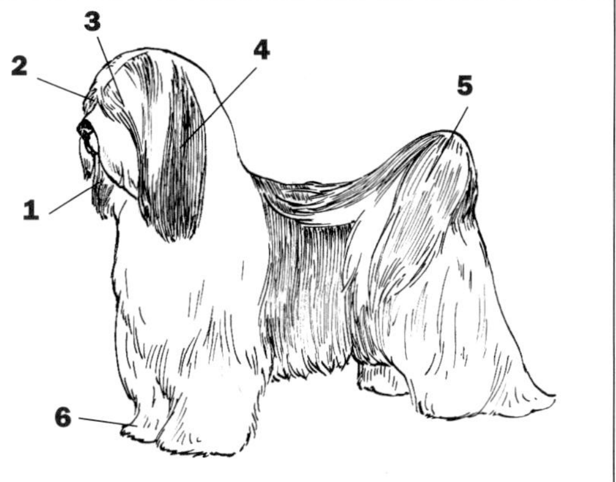

FORM AND FUNCTION

The Tibetan Terrier evolved as an all-purpose dog, able to accompany its owner on any job. It is square-proportioned, compact, and powerfully built. Its double coat, consisting of a profuse fine, long (straight or slightly wavy) outer coat and a soft wooly undercoat, provided protection from the harsh Tibetan climate. Long hair falls forward over the eyes and foreface. The feet are large, flat, and round, producing a snowshoe effect for maximum traction in difficult terrain. The stride is free and effortless.

it was that in 1920 Dr. A. Grieg, an Indian physician, was given one of the special dogs in return for medical treatment. Dr. Grieg became interested in the breed, obtained additional dogs, and began to breed and promote them. The Tibetan Terrier first became recognized in India, and by 1937 it had made its way into English dog shows. From there it came to America in the 1950s and was admitted to AKC registration in 1973. Incidentally, the Tibetan Terrier is in no way a terrier, having only been given that name because it was of terrier size.

TEMPERAMENT

Gentle and amiable, the Tibetan Terrier makes a charming, dependable companion both indoors and out. It is equally up for an adventure in the field, a game in the yard, or a snooze in the house. It is sensitive, very companionable, and willing to please.

UPKEEP

The Tibetan Terrier likes to run and explore, and needs daily exercise in a safe area. Its needs can also be met by a vigorous game in the yard or a moderately long walk on leash. Its long coat needs thorough brushing or combing once or twice a week.

HEALTH

- Major concerns: lens luxation, PRA
- Minor concerns: patellar luxation, cataract, CHD, ceroid lipofuscinosis, hypothyroidism
- Occasionally seen: distichiasis, deafness
- Suggested tests: eye, hip, hearing, DNA for lens luxation, DNA for lipofuscinosis
- Life span: 12–15 years

Xoloitzcuintli

AT A GLANCE

Energy level:	■■■
Exercise requirements:	■■■■
Playfulness:	■■■
Affection level:	■■■■
Friendliness toward dogs:	■■■■
Friendliness toward other pets:	■■■
Friendliness toward strangers:	■■■
Ease of training:	■■■

Watchdog ability:	■■■■■
Protection ability:	■■■■
Grooming requirements:	■■
Cold tolerance:	■
Heat tolerance:	■■■■■

WEIGHT: standard: 20–35 lb*; miniature: 13–22 lb; toy: 9–15 lb
HEIGHT: standard: over 18–23″; miniature: over 14–18″; toy: 10–14″

POPULARITY: Rare
FAMILY: Primitive
AREA OF ORIGIN: Mexico
DATE OF ORIGIN: Ancient
ORIGINAL FUNCTION: Religious
TODAY'S FUNCTION: Companion
OTHER NAME: Mexican Hairless, Tepezcuintli

HISTORY

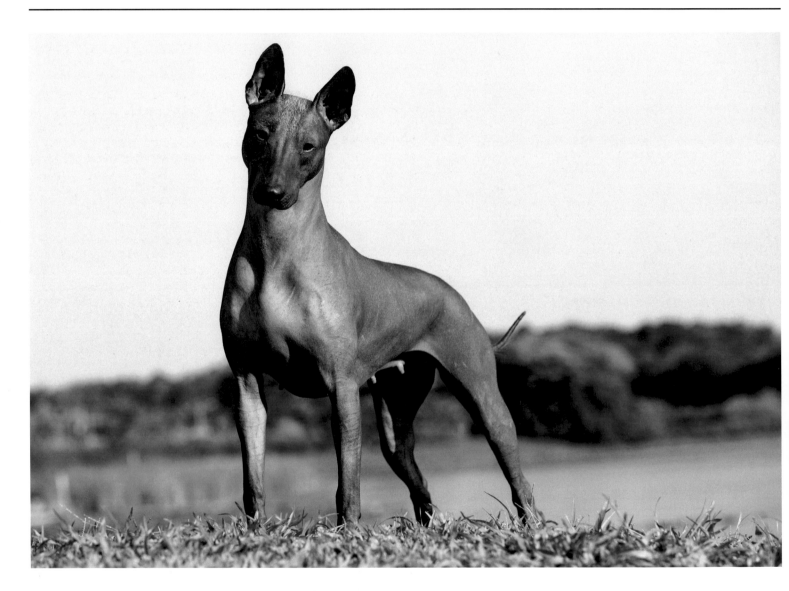

Clay statues of dogs resembling today's Xoloitzcuintli were interred in Mayan, Colima, and Aztec burial sites dating back 3,000 years. The dogs were believed to guide their masters' souls through the underworld. Aztec mythology asserted that Xolotl, the Aztec god of lightning and death, made the Xoloitzcuintli (pronounced show-low-eet-SQUINT-lee) from the "bone of life," imparting physical and spiritual healing power to the dogs. The name combines Xolotl with "itzcuintli," Aztec for "dog." The dogs were found throughout Mexico and parts of Central and South America safeguarding against spirits and intruders and healing people. They were sometimes sacrificed and even eaten on special occasions. The hairless dogs were first described by Columbus in his 1492 journal. After the Spanish Con-

ILLUSTRATED STANDARD

1 Almond-shaped, medium-size eyes.
2 Large, elegant ears, set high, thin texture
3 Stop not pronounced
4 Muzzle longer than skull
5 Hairless dogs may lack premolars or incisors
6 Level topline, slight arch over loin
7 Low-set tail reaching to hock, carried in a low graceful curve
8 Hare feet

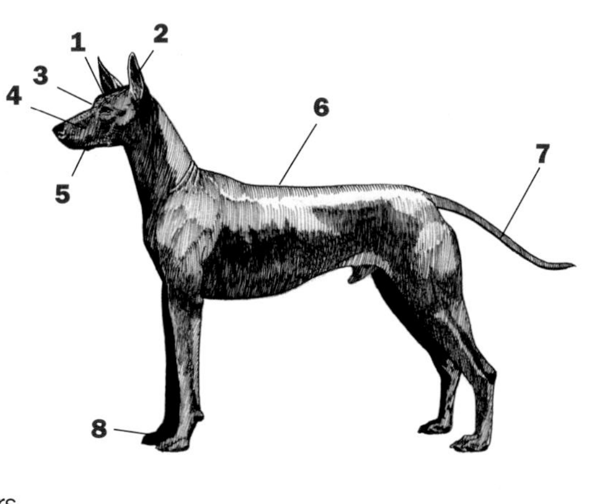

Color: dark uniform color preferred—from black, gray black, slate, to red, liver or bronze; white markings permitted
DQ: under 10″ or over 24″ tall; cropped ears

quest, Xolos (their short name) were almost lost, surviving mostly in remote areas. In 1887, the AKC registered the breed as the Mexican Hairless, but numbers and interest remained low and they were dropped from AKC ranks in 1959—the only breed ever dropped from AKC's roster. Meanwhile, in 1953, several British and Mexican dog authorities, realizing the breed's tenuous existence, searched remote Mexico and returned with ten Xolos. In 1956, the breed was recognized by the kennel association in Mexico and was also named the official dog of Mexico. Interest grew there, and eventually in the United States. In 2007, the AKC recognized the Xoloitzcuintli with three size divisions: Standard, Miniature, and Toy. The gene that causes hairlessness in the Xolo is the same as that in Chinese Cresteds, and the Xolo may descend from ancient Asian hairless dogs. It is a single dominant gene (dogs with two copies die as embryos), so all hairless Xolos have one hairless gene and one coated gene. The same gene causes some dental anomalies. About one third of Xolos are coated.

TEMPERAMENT

As a primitive breed, Xolos are not hop-to-it obedience dogs. They do like to please, but they're also independent thinkers. They tend to be calm but inquisitive, devoted but not fawning, self-assured but not overly trusting of strangers. They get along fairly well with other dogs and pets. They are alert watchdogs, and are not excessive barkers. Some can be escape artists.

UPKEEP

All Xolos need daily exercise. The toy size can get its quota with a walk around the block or an indoor play session, but the larger size will need a long walk or jog. A coated Xolo needs occasional brushing. A hairless Xolo needs no brushing but does need the skin to be wiped or bathed frequently to prevent acne or blackheads, especially when young. If the skin is dark it shouldn't need sunscreen, but it might if the skin is light. Hairless dogs need a sweater in cold weather. The skin of hairless dogs is very thick and hide-like, so it is surprisingly tough.

HEALTH

- Major concerns: none
- Minor concerns: acne
- Occasionally seen: patellar luxation (toys)
- Suggested tests: none
- Life span: 11–14 years

FORM AND FUNCTION

The Xolo combines grace and strength equally and is moderate in all aspects of type and conformation—never extreme or overdone. All three sizes are slightly longer than tall, and they are lean and sturdy with medium, oval-shaped bone. The gait is effortless with good reach and drive. The coated variety has a short, flat coat. The hairless variety has no coat or almost no coat, often with short, coarse hair on the top of the head, the feet, and the last third of the tail. The skin is tough and protective. Hairless dogs feel warmer to the touch than coated ones, but they have the same body temperature. This warmth may have helped people think they could cure ailments, as they functioned much like a hot water bottle. Today they are companions and guardians.

Dogs of this group have the desire and ability to control the movements of other animals, most often sheep and cattle. In some species, this is accomplished by stalking and staring, in others by barking, and in others by nipping. Some herders have gathering tendencies, whereas others have driving tendencies. All have in common the ability to work using both their owner's commands and their own judgment. Herding breeds make intelligent and devoted partners.

THE HERDING GROUP

Australian Cattle Dog

AT A GLANCE

Energy level:	■■■■■	Watchdog ability:	■■■■■
Exercise requirements:	■■■■■	Protection ability:	■■■■
Playfulness:	■■■■	Grooming requirements:	■■
Affection level:	■■■■	Cold tolerance:	■■■
Friendliness toward dogs:	■■■	Heat tolerance:	■■■
Friendliness toward other pets:	■■		
Friendliness toward strangers:	■■	WEIGHT: 35–45 lb	
Ease of training:	■■■■■	HEIGHT: male: 18–20″; female: 17–19″	

POPULARITY: Somewhat popular
FAMILY: Livestock, Herding
AREA OF ORIGIN: Australia
DATE OF ORIGIN: 1800s
ORIGINAL FUNCTION: Cattle herding
TODAY'S FUNCTION: Cattle herding, herding trials
OTHER NAME: Queensland Heeler, Blue Heeler, Hall's Heeler

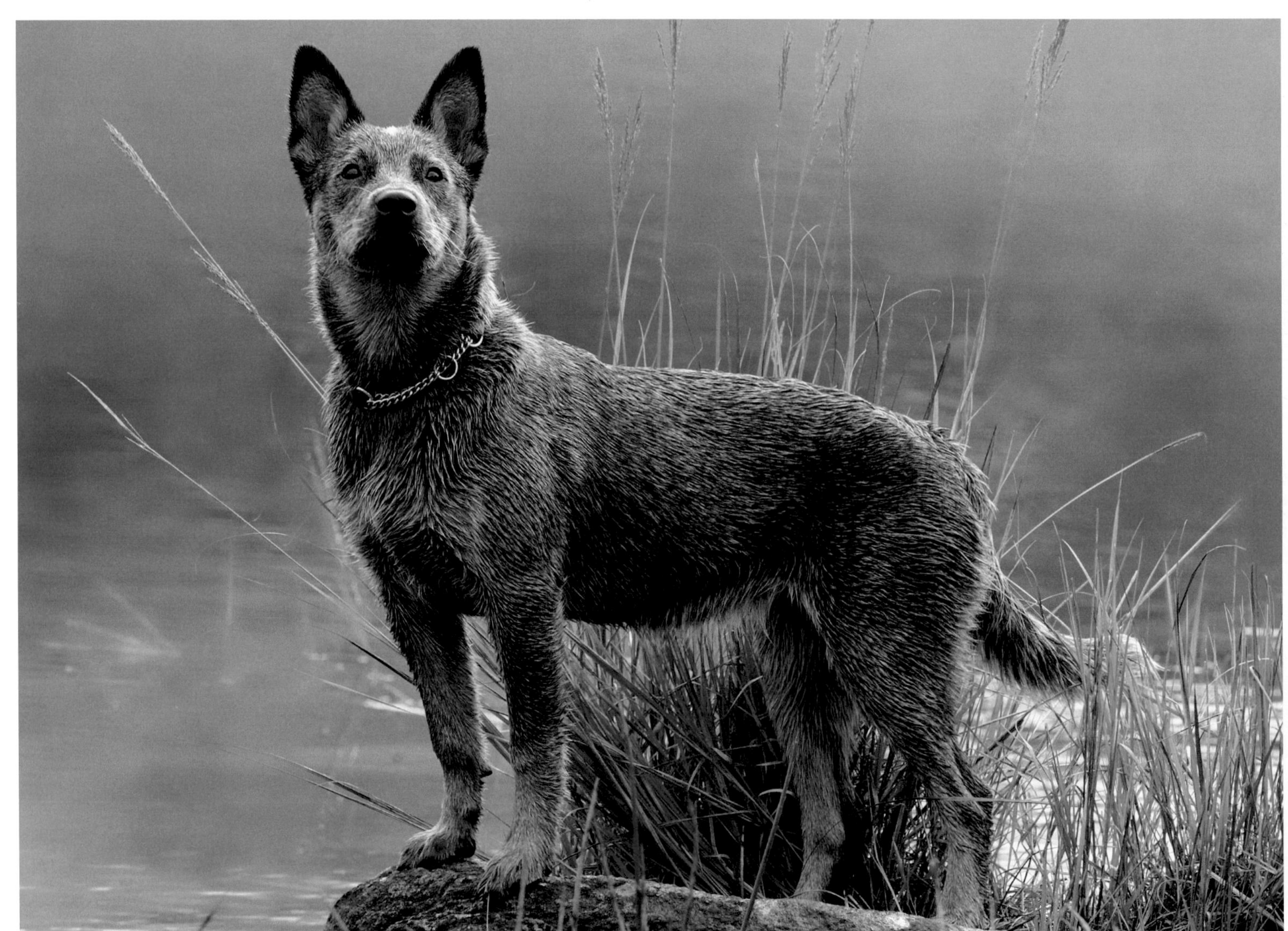

HISTORY

In the early 1800s, vast land areas in Australia became available for grazing cattle. The cattle raised on these lands became so wild and intractable that the traditional European herding breeds that had proved satisfactory on tamer cattle were no longer suited for the job. A dog was needed that could withstand traveling long distances over rough terrain in hot weather and that could control cattle without barking (which only served to make wild cattle wilder). In 1840, a man named Hall bred some smooth blue merle Highland Collies to Dingos, producing a strain known as Hall's Heelers. One particularly influential stud was a dog named Bentley's Dog, who is credited with stamping the white blaze found on the head of Australian Cattle Dogs today. Other breeders crossed their Hall's Heelers with other breeds, including the Bull Terrier, Dalmatian, and, later, Black and Tan Kelpie, a sheepherding breed.

ILLUSTRATED STANDARD

1 Medium-sized, oval eyes
2 Broad skull
3 Rather small pricked ears
4 Level topline
5 Tail set low, hanging in slight curve
6 Round feet

Color: blue or blue-mottled with or without other markings; red speckled; puppies are born white but get their color within a few weeks
DQ: none

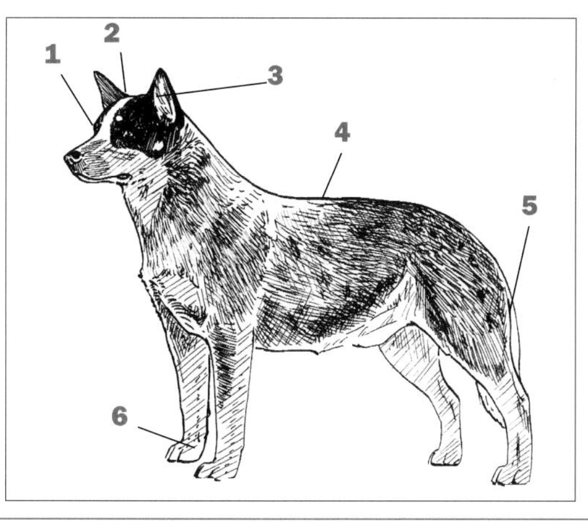

The result was a dog with the herding instincts of the Collie and Kelpie, the endurance, ruggedness, and quiet style of the Dingo, and the horse sense and protectiveness of the Dalmatian, all with a distinctively patterned coat. As the dogs became increasingly vital to the cattle industry of Queensland, they gained the name Queensland Blue Heeler. They later became known as Australian Heeler, and then Australian Cattle Dog. A standard for the breed, emphasizing its Dingo characteristics, was drawn up in 1897. The Australian Cattle Dog was slow to catch on in America, however, perhaps because it bore little resemblance to established herding breeds. When given a chance, it proved its merits and was welcomed as a herder and pet. The AKC recognized the breed in 1980.

TEMPERAMENT

Smart, hardy, independent, stubborn, tenacious, energetic, and untiring—these are all traits essential to a driver of headstrong cattle, and all traits of the Australian Cattle Dog. Given challenging mental and hard physical exercise daily, it is among the most responsive and obedient of dogs. It tends to nip at heels of running children, but is good with older children.

UPKEEP

The Australian Cattle Dog was bred to be active and tireless. A good jog or long workout, coupled with obedience lessons or other intellectual challenges, is essential every day; a bored ACD can be destructive. It is happiest when it has a job to perform, and especially when that job is herding. It is unsuited for apartment life. Its coat needs brushing or combing weekly to remove dead hairs.

HEALTH

- Major concerns: CHD, OCD, deafness, PRA, elbow dysplasia
- Minor concerns: none
- Occasionally seen: cataract, lens luxation, PPM, vWD
- Suggested tests: hip, hearing, eye, elbow, DNA for PRA, DNA for lens luxation
- Life span: 10–13 years

FORM AND FUNCTION

The Australian Cattle Dog is of moderate build, enabling it to combine great endurance with bursts of speed and extreme agility necessary in controlling unruly cattle. It is sturdy and compact, slightly longer than it is tall. Its gait is supple and tireless, and it must be capable of quick and sudden movement. Its weather-resistant coat consists of a short, dense undercoat and moderately short, straight outer coat of medium texture.

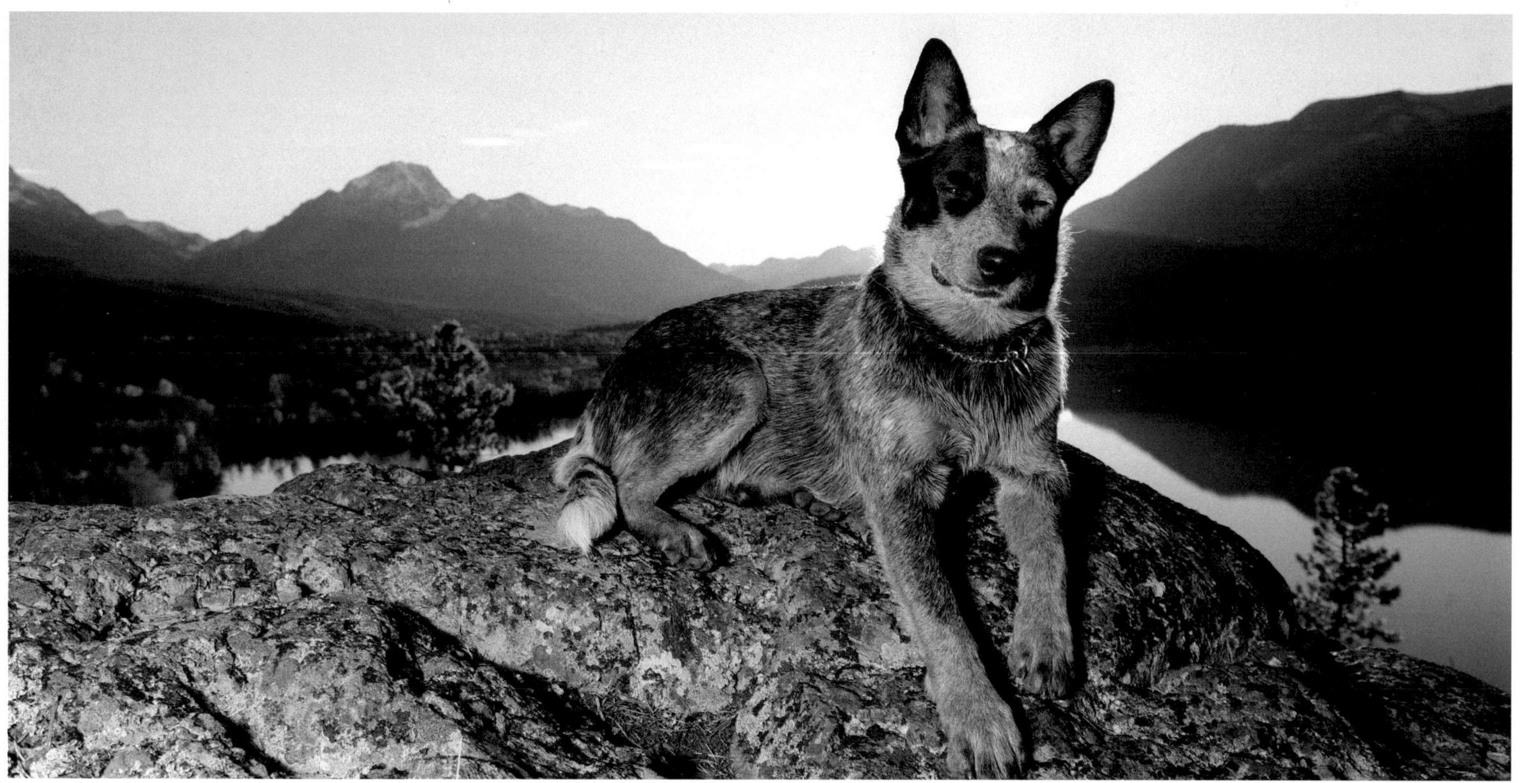

Australian Shepherd

AT A GLANCE

Energy level:	■■■■	Watchdog ability:	■■■■■	POPULARITY: Very popular
Exercise requirements:	■■■■■	Protection ability:	■■■■	FAMILY: Livestock, Herding
Playfulness:	■■■■■	Grooming requirements:	■■■	AREA OF ORIGIN: United States
Affection level:	■■■■	Cold tolerance:	■■■	DATE OF ORIGIN: 1800s
Friendliness toward dogs:	■■■	Heat tolerance:	■■■	ORIGINAL FUNCTION: Sheep herding
Friendliness toward other pets:	■■■			TODAY'S FUNCTION: Sheep herding, herding trials
Friendliness toward strangers:	■■	WEIGHT: male: 50–65 lb, female: 40–55 lb		
Ease of training:	■■■■■	HEIGHT: male: 20–23″; female: 18–21″		OTHER NAME: None

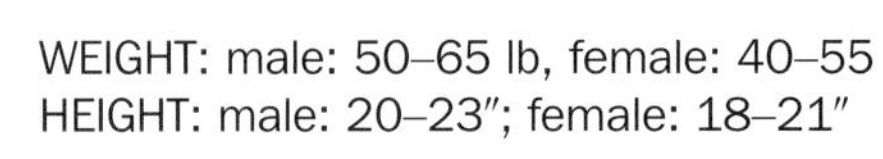

HISTORY

The Australian Shepherd is not really an Australian breed, but it came to America by way of Australia. One popular theory of the breed's origin begins during the 1800s when the Basque people of Europe settled in Australia, bringing with them their sheep and sheepdogs. Shortly thereafter, many of these shepherds relocated to the western United States, with their dogs and sheep. American shepherds naturally dubbed these dogs Australian Shepherds because that was their immediate past residence. The rugged area of Australia and western America placed demands on the herding dogs that they had not faced in Europe, but through various crosses and rigorous selection for working ability, the Basque dog soon adapted and excelled under these harsh conditions. The breed kept a low profile until the 1950s, when they were featured in a popular trick-dog act that performed in rodeos and was featured in

ILLUSTRATED STANDARD

1 Moderate, well-defined stop
2 Eye color is brown, blue, amber, in any combination or with flecks
3 Triangular, high-set ears; at attention they break forward and over or to the side
4 Straight, strong, level back
5 Tail docked close or naturally bobbed
6 Feet oval

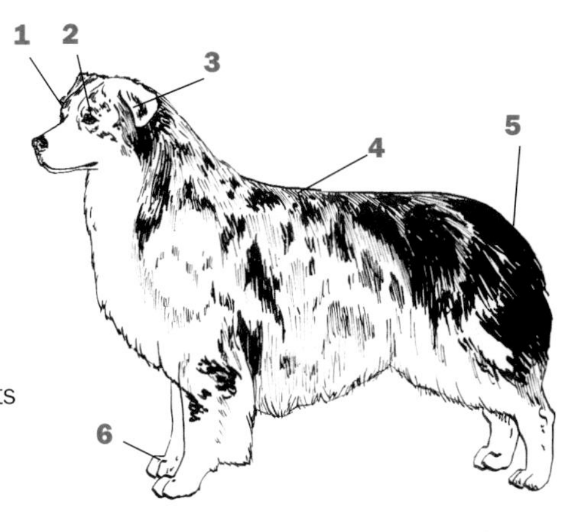

Color: blue merle, black, red merle, or red, all with or without white markings and/or tan points
DQ: undershot; overshot more than 1/8″; white body splashes (white on body between withers and tail or on sides between elbows and back of hindquarters)
Note: The Australian Shepherd Club of America standard contains more disqualifications; they are not included here.

film. Many of these dogs, owned by Jay Sisler, can be found in the pedigrees of today's Aussies. The first Aussie was registered with the International English Shepherd Registry, now known as the National Stock Dog Registry. In 1957 the Australian Shepherd Club of America (ASCA) was formed and subsequently became the largest Aussie registry in America. Because many ASCA members felt that AKC recognition was not desirable for their breed, proponents of AKC recognition formed the United States Australian Shepherd Association. The AKC recognized the Australian Shepherd in 1993. Its popularity according to AKC statistics underestimates the popularity of this breed as a pet because a large proportion of this working breed remains unregistered with the AKC. It is among the most versatile of breeds, excelling at conformation, obedience, herding, and agility competition. The Aussie is also adept at working cattle; in fact, some believe its close working style is more suited to cattle than to sheep.

TEMPERAMENT

The Australian Shepherd has a great deal of stamina and is loving, bold, alert, confident, independent, smart, and responsive. If it doesn't get a chance to exercise and challenge its strongly developed mental and physical activities, it is apt to become frustrated and difficult to live with. With proper exercise and training, it is a loyal, utterly devoted, and obedient companion. It is reserved with strangers, and has a protective nature. It may try to herd children and small animals by nipping.

UPKEEP

This breed needs a good workout every day, preferably combining both physical and mental challenges. Its coat needs brushing or combing one to two times weekly.

HEALTH

- Major concerns: cataract, CEA
- Minor concerns: CHD, nasal solar dermatitis, Pelger-Huet syndrome, iris coloboma, CEA, hypothyroidism
- Occasionally seen: lumbar sacral syndrome, epilepsy, PRA, distichiasis, elbow dysplasia
- Suggested tests: hip, eye, (thyroid), (DNA for CEA), elbow
- Life span: 12–15 years
- Note: This breed is often sensitive to ivermectin. Merle-to-merle breedings result in some offspring that are homozygous merle, which is detrimental to health, commonly resulting in deafness and blindness. Natural bobtail-to-natural bobtail breedings can result in some offspring with serious spinal defects.

FORM AND FUNCTION

This is an athletic dog of medium size and bone; it is lithe, agile, and slightly longer than it is tall. It is muscular and powerful enough to work all day, without sacrificing the speed and agility necessary to cope with bolting livestock. Its gait is free and easy, and it must be able to change direction or speed instantly. Its double coat is weather resistant, with the outer coat of medium texture and length, straight to wavy. The expression is keen, intelligent, and eager.

Bearded Collie

AT A GLANCE

Energy level:	■■■■
Exercise requirements:	■■■■
Playfulness:	■■■■
Affection level:	■■■■
Friendliness toward dogs:	■■■
Friendliness toward other pets:	■■■
Friendliness toward strangers:	■■■
Ease of training:	■■■

Watchdog ability:	■■■■
Protection ability:	■■
Grooming requirements:	■■■■
Cold tolerance:	■■■■
Heat tolerance:	■■■

WEIGHT: 45–55 lb*
HEIGHT: male: 21–22″; female: 20–21″

POPULARITY: Uncommon
FAMILY: Herding
AREA OF ORIGIN: Scotland
DATE OF ORIGIN: 1800s
ORIGINAL FUNCTION: Sheep herding
TODAY'S FUNCTION: Herding trials
OTHER NAME: None

HISTORY

The Bearded Collie probably originated from the central European Magyar Komondor or Lowland Polish Sheepdog. In fact, records show that in 1514 two Lowland Polish Sheepdogs were brought to Scotland by Polish traders. Although dogs strongly resembling Bearded Collies are depicted in art dating from the eighteenth century, hard evidence of the breed cannot be found until the early nineteenth century, when the first breed description was published. These dogs were tireless herders of sheep and drovers of cattle over rough terrain in the cold Scottish mists. Long popular as a herding dog in Scotland, after the Victorian era the breed also gained favor as a show dog. Two strains, the Border strain, which was brown and white with a slightly wavy coat, and the Highland strain, which had a gray and white coat, have since been interbred and merged into one breed. After World War I, the

ILLUSTRATED STANDARD

1 Beard
2 Large, wide-set eyes with soft expression, framed by long eyebrows
3 Broad, flat skull
4 Level topline
5 Low-set tail carried low, with slight upward curve at end

Color: any shade of gray or chocolate; white may appear as a blaze, or on tail tip, feet, and chest; tan points may also occur
DQ: none

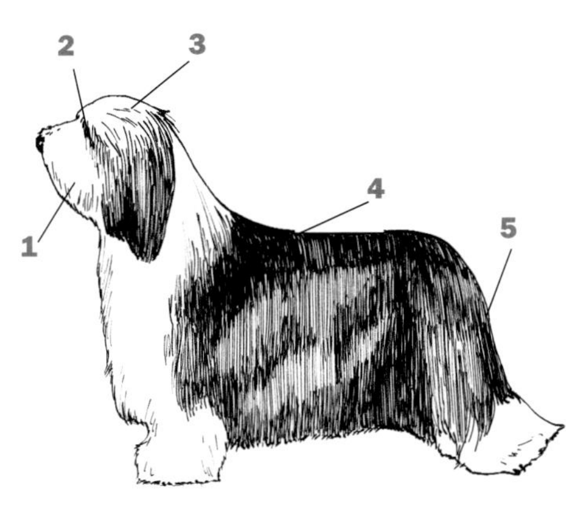

Beardie was once again bred solely for work. Their value as stock dogs made it difficult for outsiders to acquire one from their shepherd owners. Eventually, however, a few breeders interested in showing Beardies were able to bring some dogs to England and then to America. The AKC recognized the breed in 1977. It has since become a prominent show dog and continues as a capable herder, although it is more popular as a competitor in herding trials than as an actual working dog.

TEMPERAMENT

The boisterous Beardie is lively and playful, full of enthusiasm and energy. It is smart and obedient, but it is an independent thinker with a clownish sense of humor. It likes children, but it may be too rambunctious for small children and may try to herd them when playing.

UPKEEP

This active dog needs either a good jog, a very long walk, or a vigorous play session every day. It especially enjoys herding. Its long coat needs brushing or combing every other day.

HEALTH

- Major concerns: none
- Minor concerns: CHD, epilepsy, colonic disease, pemphigus, Addison's
- Occasionally seen: CHD, PRA, PPM, cataract, vWD
- Suggested tests: hip, eye, thyroid
- Life span: 12–14 years

FORM AND FUNCTION

The Beardie is a medium-sized dog with a long, lean, strongly made body, which gives the impression of both strength and agility. Its gait is supple and powerful, with good reach and drive. The ability to make sharp turns, quick starts, and sudden stops is essential in a sheep herding breed, and the Beardie must be able to keep this activity up for a long period of time under all conditions. Its coat is double with a soft, furry undercoat. The outer coat is flat, harsh, and fairly straight; it is sufficient to protect the dog but not so much as to obscure the dog's lines. The Beardie's expression is bright and inquiring.

Beauceron

AT A GLANCE

Energy level:	■■■■	Watchdog ability:	■■■■■	POPULARITY: Rare
Exercise requirements:	■■■■	Protection ability:	■■■■■	FAMILY: Herding
Playfulness:	■■■	Grooming requirements:	■	AREA OF ORIGIN: France
Affection level:	■■■	Cold tolerance:	■■■	DATE OF ORIGIN: 1500s
Friendliness toward dogs:	■	Heat tolerance:	■■■	ORIGINAL FUNCTION: Herding, guardian
Friendliness toward other pets:	■■			TODAY'S FUNCTION: Herding, guardian, police
Friendliness toward strangers:	■	WEIGHT: 65–85 lb*		OTHER NAME: Berger de Beauce, Bas-Rouge
Ease of training:	■■■■■	HEIGHT: male: 25.5–27.5″; female: 24–26.5″		

HISTORY

The Beauceron is an entirely French breed, dating back as far as the late 1500s. It originated in the plains area surrounding Paris known as La Beauce. The largest of the French sheepdogs, it was used as a general-purpose farm dog, driving and protecting sheep and sometimes, cattle, and guarding its family. In 1863 two types of plains flock-herding and guarding dogs were differentiated: the long-coated Berger de Brie (Briard) and the short-coated Berger de Beauce (Beauceron). The Société Centrale Canine registered the first Berger de Beauce in 1893, and the first breed club was formed in 1922. Well known as the preferred herding dog in France, the breed remained virtually unknown outside of France. The French army employed Beaucerons as messenger dogs

ILLUSTRATED STANDARD

1 Large, slightly oval eyes
2 High-set, natural or (more often) cropped
3 Straight, strong topline
4 Tail carried low, with terminal slight J-hook
5 Strong, round feet
6 Double rear dewclaws

Color: black and tan or black, gray, and tan (merle with tan points)
DQ: height outside of limits; nose any color but black; four or more missing teeth; overshot or undershot mouth with loss of contact; yellow or spotted eyes; tail lacking or docked; lack of double dewclaws on either rear leg; absence of markings; white spot on chest exceeding 1″ in diameter; more gray than black (in tricolor)

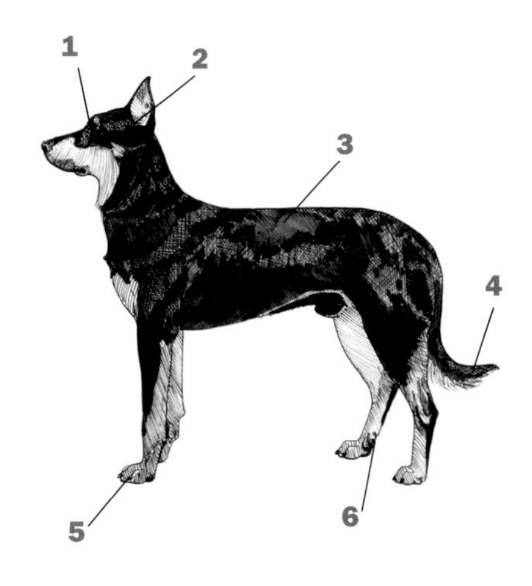

on the front lines during both world wars. The breed's uncanny ability to follow directions, follow trails, and detect mines still makes them a respected military and police dog. They also serve their families as protection dogs. In the 1960s a concerted effort was made to preserve the qualities of native French breeds, and since that time, the Beauceron's popularity in France and elsewhere has grown. In 1980 the Beauceron Club of America formed, and in 2001 the AKC admitted the Beauceron into the Miscellaneous class. They are making their presence felt by excelling in obedience, tracking, agility, Schutzhund, and of course, herding.

TEMPERAMENT

Beaucerons are intelligent and adept at any task involving learning, memory, and reasoning. They are courageous and calm, and make reliable guardians. This is an extremely loyal breed that is eager to please; however, if not properly trained, the Beauceron can run the family. Beaucerons are patient with children, but can be overwhelming to them or try to herd them. They may be wary of strangers and do not take to strange dogs. They can get along with other family pets.

UPKEEP

This is a dog with an active mind and athletic body, and it needs mental and physical exercise every day. Without adequate stimulation, the Beauceron can become bored and destructive. Don't get a Beauceron unless you commit to taking time to train and exercise it regularly. Coat care is minimal, consisting of brushing once a week or so.

HEALTH

- Major concerns: CHD
- Minor concerns: gastric torsion
- Occasionally seen: cardiomyopathy
- Suggested tests: hip, eye, cardiac
- Life span: 10–12 years

FORM AND FUNCTION

The Beaceron is not a dog of extremes, but is a solid, balanced dog as befitting a true multipurpose dog ready to do a long day's work. Its body is powerful yet agile, its jaws strong, its gait fluid, effortless, and ground covering. The head is not held high when moving, but is lowered to the level of the back, as is typical of herding dogs. Its outer coat is straight, dense, and coarse, of medium length; this, combined with a dense undercoat, offers weather-resistant protection. An unusual trait is the presence of double dewclaws on the hindlegs, which seem to be a French tradition for herding and flock dogs. Although they serve no function, they were perhaps at one time associated with the best herders, and are now a breed trademark.

Belgian Malinois

AT A GLANCE

Energy level:	■ ■ ■ ■
Exercise requirements:	■ ■ ■ ■ ■
Playfulness:	■ ■ ■ ■
Affection level:	■
Friendliness toward dogs:	■ ■ ■
Friendliness toward other pets:	■ ■ ■
Friendliness toward strangers:	■
Ease of training:	■ ■ ■ ■ ■

Watchdog ability:	■ ■ ■ ■ ■
Protection ability:	■ ■ ■ ■ ■
Grooming requirements:	■
Cold tolerance:	■ ■ ■
Heat tolerance:	■ ■ ■

WEIGHT: 60–65 lb*
HEIGHT: male: 24–26″; female: 22–24″

POPULARITY: Somewhat popular
FAMILY: Livestock, Herding
AREA OF ORIGIN: Belgium
DATE OF ORIGIN: 1800s
ORIGINAL FUNCTION: Stock herding
TODAY'S FUNCTION: Security, police, military, contraband detection, assistance, herding trials, Shutzhund
OTHER NAME: Malinois, Chien de Berger Belge

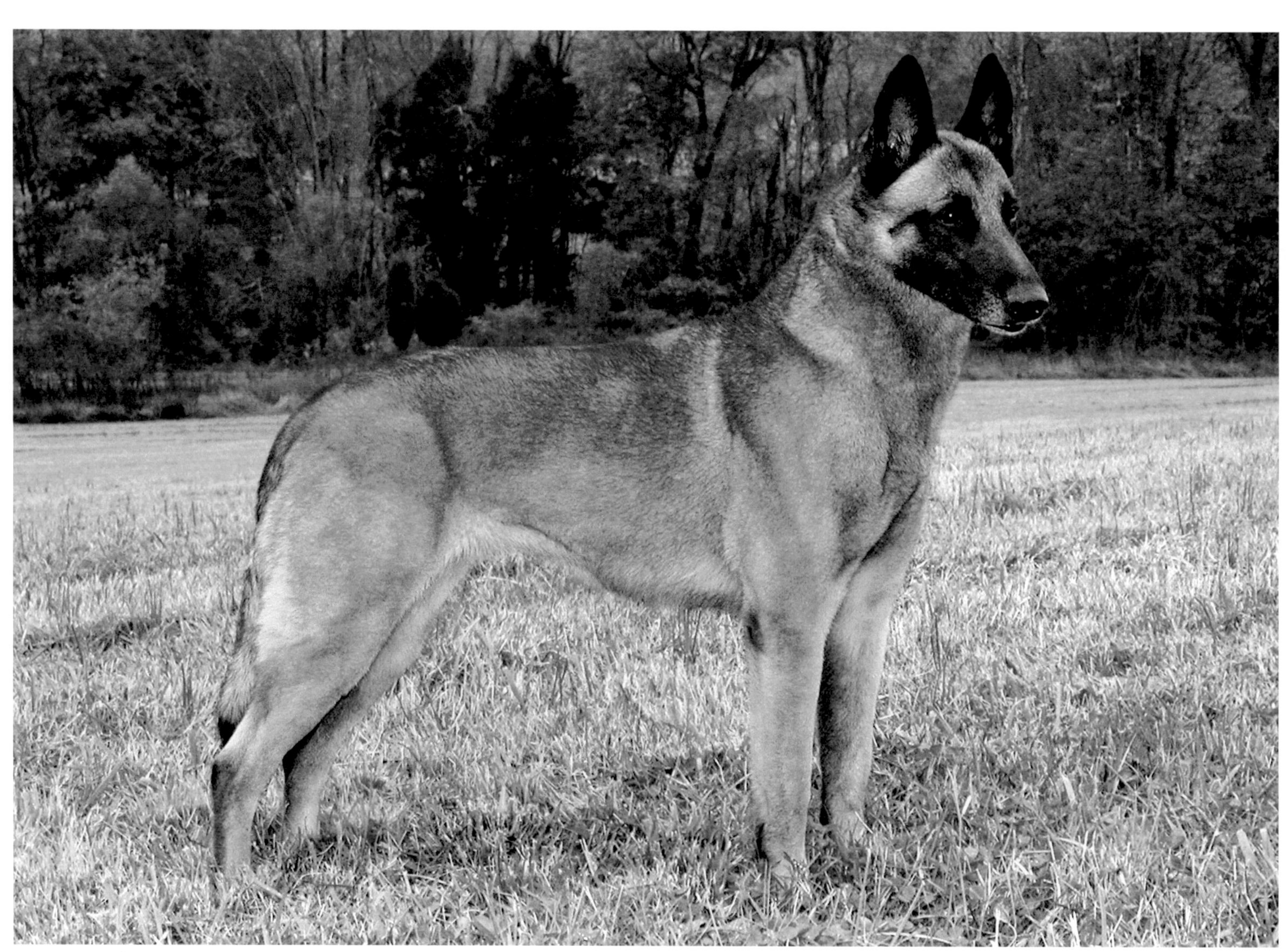

HISTORY

The Belgian sheepherding breeds, collectively known as Chiens de Berger Belge, shared their early history as general-purpose shepherds and guard dogs of Belgium. As working dogs, they were bred for ability rather than esthetics, and no careful records were kept. Thus, when dog shows became popular in the late 1800s, it was not clear if Belgium had any recognizable breeds with which they could tout their national pride. In 1891, Professor Reul was asked to study the native dogs to see if they could be sorted into distinct breeds. He found a group of similar dogs that differed only in coat type and color, all of which were grouped as Belgian Shepherds. The short-haired variety was developed in the area around Malines, and so became known as the Belgian Malinois. It remains the most

ILLUSTRATED STANDARD

1 Almond-shaped eyes
2 Flat skull
3 Ears stiff, erect, and in the shape of an equilateral triangle
4 Level topline
5 Tail raised with slight curve when dog is moving
6 Cat footed

Color: rich fawn to mahogany, with black-tipped hairs; black mask and ears
DQ: males under 23″ or over 27″; females under 21″ or over 25″; ears hanging or semi-pricked; undershot bite in which two or more incisors fail to make contact with incisors of other jaw; cropped or stumped tail

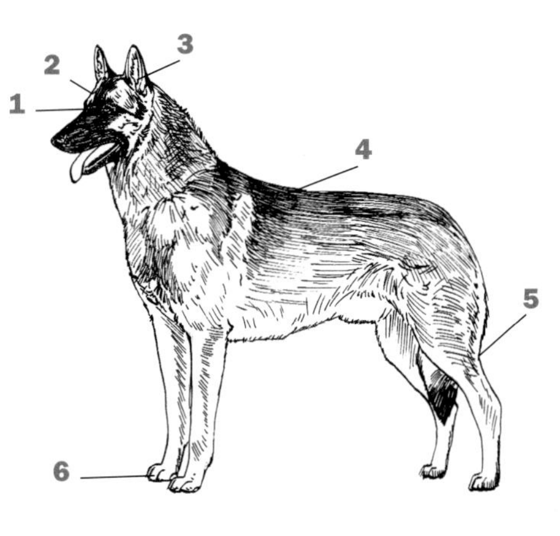

HEALTH

- Major concerns: none
- Minor concerns: CHD, elbow dysplasia
- Occasionally seen: PRA, cataract, pannus, hemangiosarcoma
- Suggested tests: hip, elbow, eye
- Life span: 10–12 years

FORM AND FUNCTION

The Belgian Malinois is a sturdy dog of square proportion with moderately heavy, but oval, bone. It is elegant, with very proud head carriage. The overall impression is of power without bulkiness. The gait is smooth and easy, seemingly effortless rather than hard driving. Such a gait gives the impression of tirelessness. The Malinois has a tendency to run in a wide circle rather than a straight line. Its coat is fairly short, straight, and hard, with a dense undercoat. Its expression is intelligent and questioning.

popular of the Belgian shepherd breeds in its native land, but has had a rockier road in America. Between 1911 and World War II, the Malinois enjoyed a good deal of popularity in America. After the war, registrations plummeted, and it was rare to find a Malinois entered in competition. When the breeds were separated in 1959, Malinois registrations began to grow once again, but they still fell far behind the other Belgian breeds. More recently, the Malinois is becoming popular because of its reputation as one of the preeminent police dogs in the world, surpassing even the German Shepherd in demand. Thus, even though it may not be seen in many homes or show rings, it is making its presence known as a keeper of the peace throughout the world.

TEMPERAMENT

Intense best describes the Belgian Malinois. This is a high-energy breed with a need for regular mental and physical stimulation. It is alert, smart, and serious, an ideal watchdog and guard dog. It is aloof with strangers and can be aggressive toward other dogs and animals. Some can be domineering. When confined, it often runs in sweeping circles in an effort to stay on the move. It is protective of its home and family.

UPKEEP

The Malinois is a high-energy dog that needs a lot of exercise. Its needs cannot be met with a leisurely walk on leash. It instead needs a good jog or a vigorous play session. It especially enjoys herding. Its coat needs weekly brushing, more when shedding.

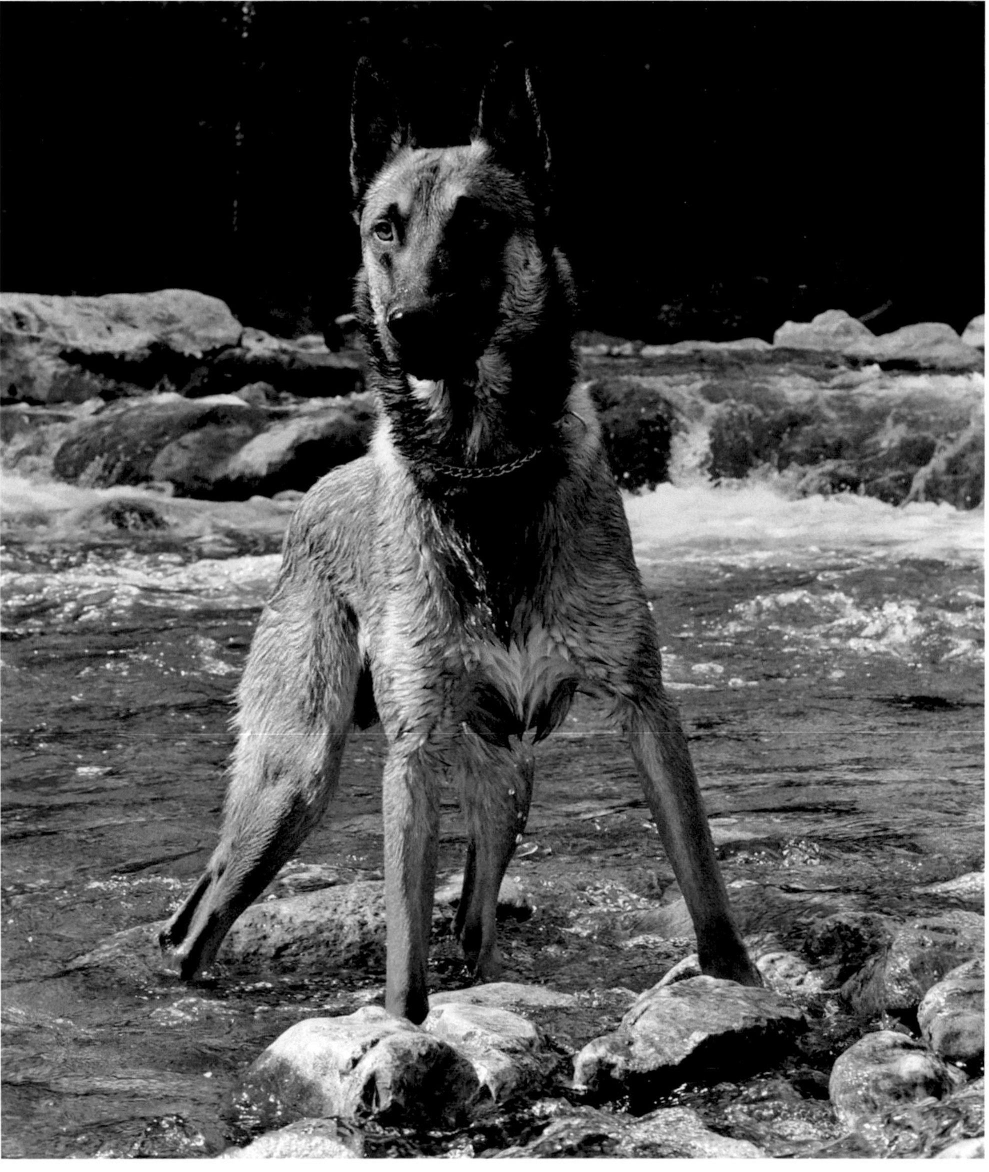

Belgian Sheepdog

AT A GLANCE

Energy level:
Exercise requirements:
Playfulness:
Affection level:

Friendliness toward dogs:
Friendliness toward other pets:
Friendliness toward strangers:
Ease of training:

Watchdog ability:
Protection ability:
Grooming requirements:
Cold tolerance:
Heat tolerance:

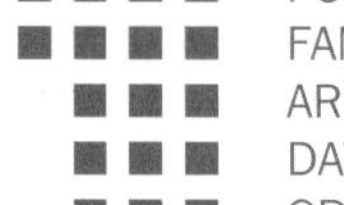

WEIGHT: male: 55–75 lb*, female: 40–60 lb*
HEIGHT: male: 24–26″; female: 22–24″

POPULARITY: Uncommon
FAMILY: Livestock, Herding
AREA OF ORIGIN: Belgium
DATE OF ORIGIN: 1800s
ORIGINAL FUNCTION: Stock herding
TODAY'S FUNCTION: Herding trials, Schutzhund
OTHER NAME: Groenendael, Chien de Berger Belge

HISTORY

The Belgian Sheepdog, Belgian Tervuren, and Belgian Malinois began as three local variations of one breed, which was known as the Belgian Shepherd or Continental Shepherd. The dog that was heir to the name Belgian Sheepdog was originally known as the Groenendael variation of the breed. Like all the Belgian shepherds, it was a working farm dog expected to both herd and guard. It differed from the others because it had a rather long, black coat. In 1910 these dogs were officially dubbed Groenendael after the kennel that had selectively bred the black dogs since 1893 (just after the Belgian Shepherds were recognized as a breed). By this time, the breed had gained some repute as a police dog and was already employed in this capacity in America. In World War I, they continued to shine as sentry dogs, messengers, and even draft dogs. It was here that they captured the attention of the public, and they soon enjoyed a fair

ILLUSTRATED STANDARD

1 Almond-shaped eyes
2 Moderate stop
3 Flat skull
4 Stiff, erect ears in the shape of a triangle
5 Level topline
6 Tail raised with slight curve when dog is moving, held low when at rest
7 Cat footed

Color: black
DQ: males under 22.5″ or over 27.5″; females under 20.5″ or over 25.5″; ears hanging; cropped or stumped tail; any color other than black; viciousness

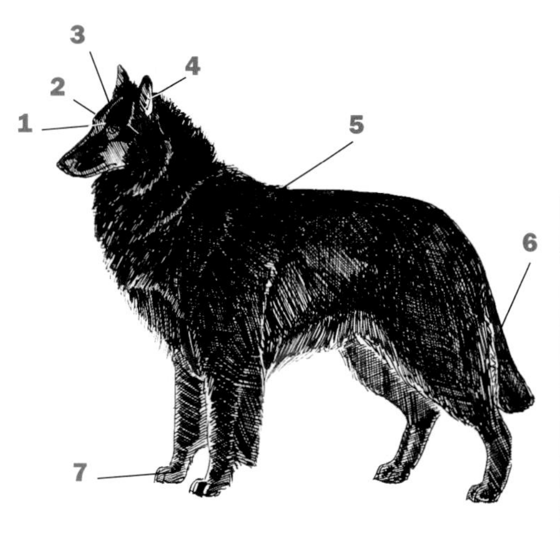

amount of popularity after the war. In 1959, the three Belgian Shepherd breeds were divided into separate breeds, with the Groenendael subsequently known as the Belgian Sheepdog. With its shimmering black coat, it is the most striking of the Belgian breeds, and that fact, along with its versatile abilities, has won it many faithful supporters.

TEMPERAMENT

Ever watchful and on the move, the Belgian Sheepdog glides in large circles. It is playful, alert, watchful, and protective, a tough, independent, and intense dog. It is aloof with strangers and can be aggressive toward other dogs and animals. Some can be domineering. It is intelligent and biddable, but independent. It is protective of its home and family.

UPKEEP

The Belgian Sheepdog needs a good deal of exercise, either a good long jog or a long, strenuous play session. It needs room to move during the day and does best with access to a yard. Its double coat needs brushing and combing twice weekly, more when shedding.

HEALTH

- Major concerns: none
- Minor concerns: seizures, skin disorders, allergies, hypothyroidism
- Occasionally seen: CHD, PRA, pannus, elbow dysplasia, hemangiosarcoma
- Suggested tests: hip, elbow, eye
- Life span: 10–12 years

FORM AND FUNCTION

The Belgian Sheepdog is an elegant, square-proportioned dog that is alert and agile with proud carriage. Its bone is moderately heavy. As a dog expected to herd for long hours, its gait is smooth, tireless, and effortless rather than driving. It has a tendency to move in a circle rather than a straight line. It has an extremely dense undercoat along with an outer coat of abundant guard hairs that are long, well-fitting, and straight. The texture should be medium-harsh, not silky, for protection. The undercoat is extremely dense in cold weather for insulation. The opening of the ear is protected by tufts of hair. Its expression is intelligent and questioning; its black coloration is striking.

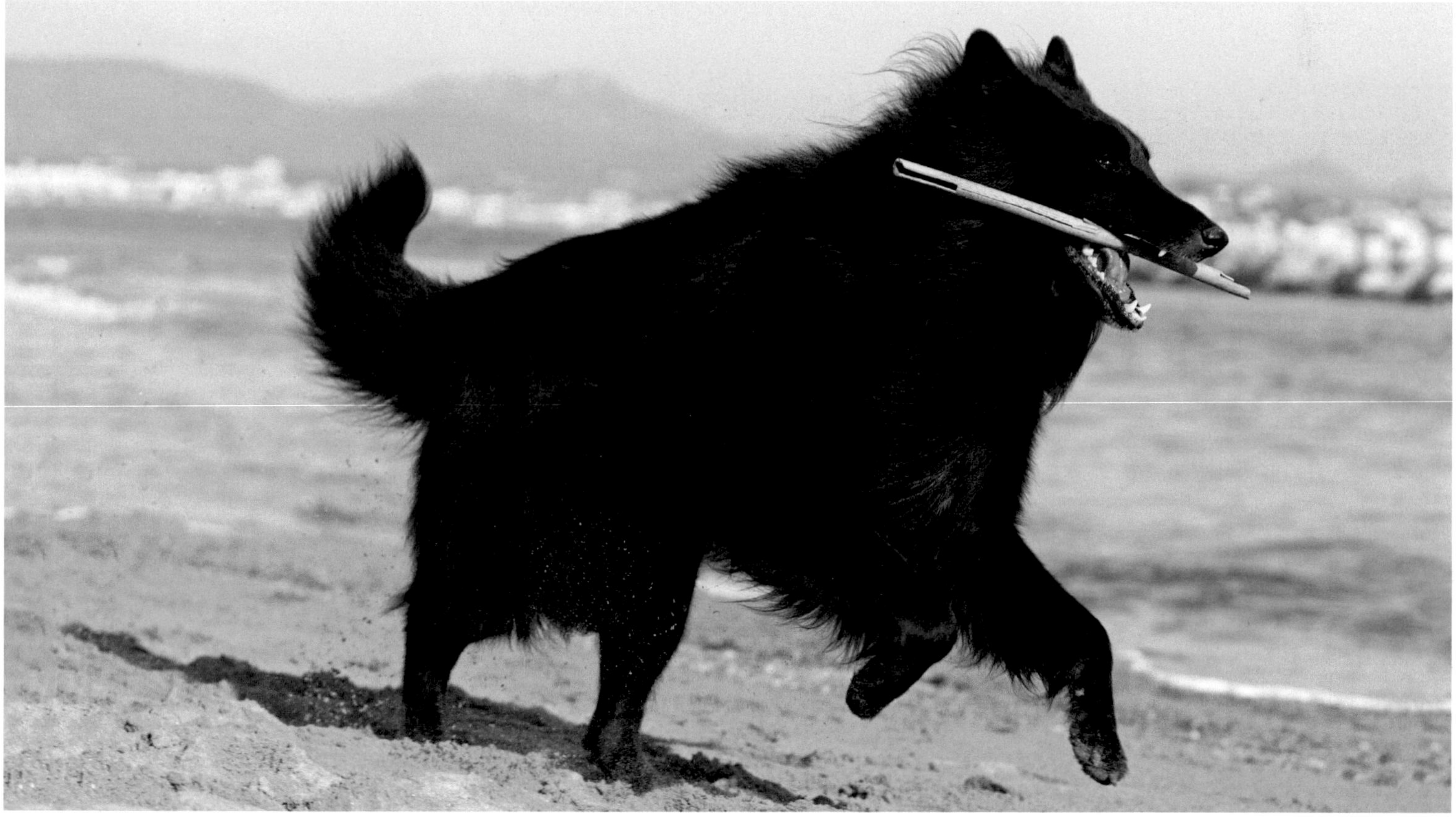

Belgian Tervuren

AT A GLANCE

Energy level:	■■■■	Watchdog ability:	■■■■■
Exercise requirements:	■■■■■	Protection ability:	■■■■■
Playfulness:	■■■■	Grooming requirements:	■■■
Affection level:	■■■■	Cold tolerance:	■■■
Friendliness toward dogs:	■■■	Heat tolerance:	■■■
Friendliness toward other pets:	■■■		
Friendliness toward strangers:	■	WEIGHT: male: 55–65 lb*, female: 40–50 lb*	
Ease of training:	■■■■■	HEIGHT: male: 24–26″; female: 22–24″	

POPULARITY: Uncommon
FAMILY: Livestock, Herding
AREA OF ORIGIN: Belgium
DATE OF ORIGIN: 1800s
ORIGINAL FUNCTION: Stock herding
TODAY'S FUNCTION: Herding trials, Schutzhund
OTHER NAME: Tervuren, Chien de Berger Belge

HISTORY

The Belgian Tervuren is one of four Belgian shepherd breeds, all sharing the same origins but distinguished by different coat types and colors. They are the wire-haired Laekenois, the short-haired Malinois, the long black-haired Groenendael, and the long anything-but-black-haired Tervuren. All these herding–guard breeds were interbred before and after their recognition as one breed (the Belgian, or Continental, Shepherd) in 1891. The Tervuren was named after the village of Tervuren, where one of the breed's earliest proponents lived. The Tervuren lagged behind the other shepherd breeds in popularity, perhaps hindered by its less flashy color and disagreements over exactly what colors were desirable. The first Terv was registered in America in 1918, but the breed's num-

ILLUSTRATED STANDARD

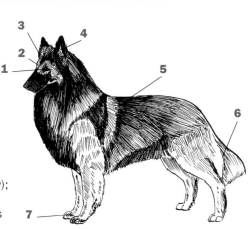

1 Almond-shaped eyes
2 Moderate stop
3 Flat skull
4 Stiff, erect, triangular ears
5 Level topline
6 Tail raised with slight curve when dog is moving, held low when at rest
7 Cat footed

Color: rich fawn to russet mahogany with black overlay (becoming darker with maturity); black mask and ears

DQ: males under 23″ or over 26.5″, females under 21″ or over 24.5″; ears hanging; undershot bite in which two or more incisors fail to make contact with incisors of other jaw; cropped or stumped tail; solid black, solid liver, or any area of white except for a small white patch on the chest, tips of toes, chin, and muzzle

bers remained so low that they died out by the Depression. The Tervuren had to be almost recreated after World War II from long-haired offspring of Malinois parents. In 1959 the Belgian Shepherd was divided into three breeds, and the Tervuren was on its own. The Tervuren has since captured the eye of many fanciers because it is the most elegant of the three breeds. It now enjoys moderate popularity. The Belgian Tervuren is a versatile dog and is used less in guard work, but more in herding, than are its Belgian Shepherd counterparts.

TEMPERAMENT

Alert, watchful, and energetic, the Tervuren is an active and dependable companion that functions best when given daily mental and physical exercise. It enjoys playing and running outside, and can be a well-mannered companion inside as long as it is given sufficient exercise. It is smart and obedient, but independent. It is aloof with strangers and can be protective of its family. It may nip at the heels of children in an attempt to herd them.

UPKEEP

The Terv needs strenuous activity, either a long walk or jog or an invigorating play or work session every day. It especially enjoys herding, which is the ideal exercise. Its double coat needs brushing and combing twice weekly, more often when shedding.

HEALTH

- Major concerns: seizures
- Minor concerns: CHD, elbow dysplasia, allergies, hypothyroidism, PRA
- Occasionally seen: PPM, pannus, cataract, hemangiosarcoma
- Suggested tests: hip, eye, elbow
- Life span: 10–12 years

FORM AND FUNCTION

This breed combines elegance and strength. It is square-proportioned and of medium bone. It is noteworthy for its exceedingly proud carriage. Its movement is lively, graceful, and seemingly tireless, exhibiting an easy, effortless gait rather than a hard-driving action. It has a natural tendency to move in a circle rather than a straight line. It combines a dense undercoat with an outer coat consisting of abundant guard hairs that are long, well-fitting, straight and of medium harshness. Its expression is intelligent and questioning.

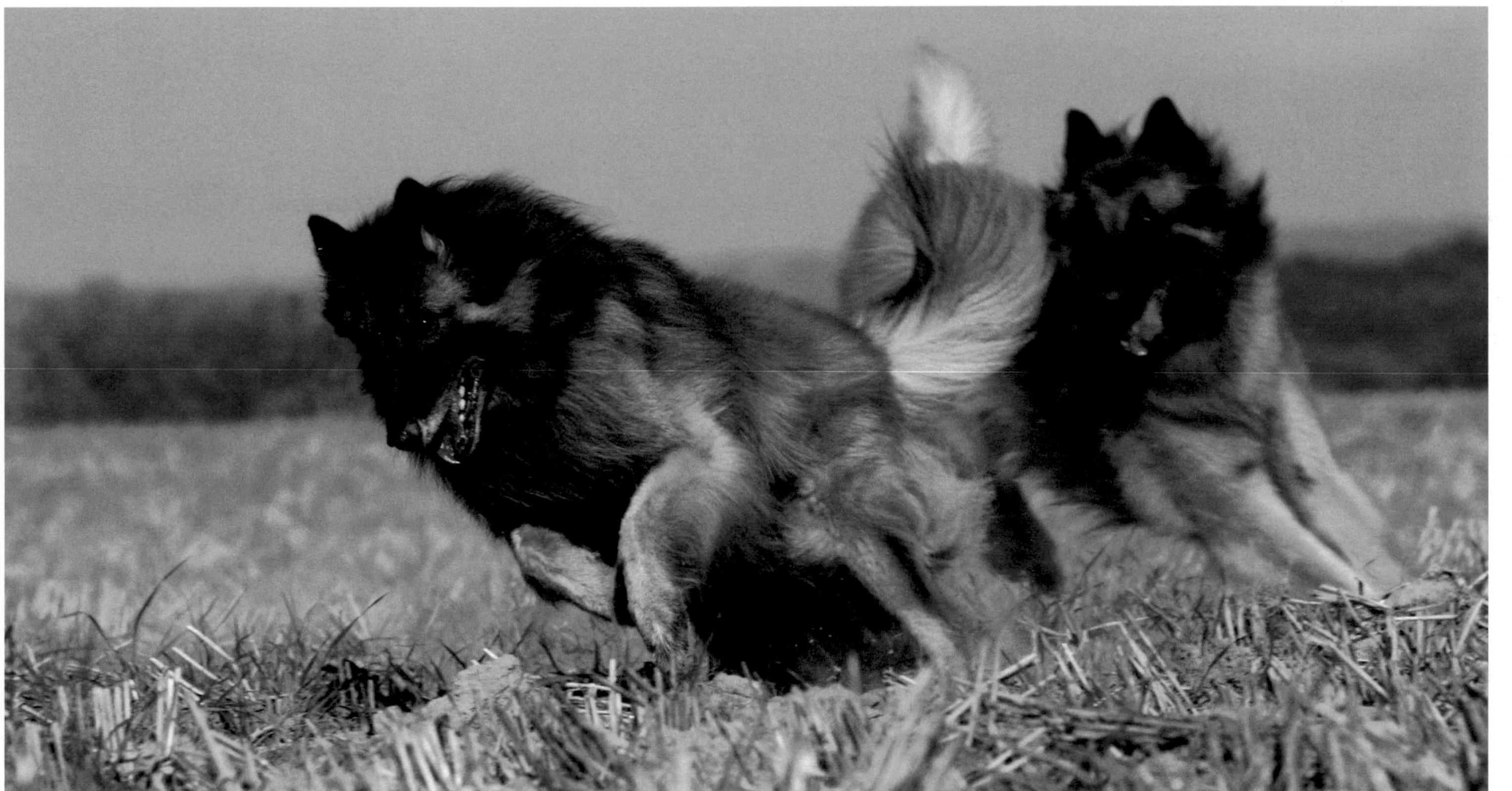

Bergamasco

AT A GLANCE

Energy level:	■■■
Exercise requirements:	■■■
Playfulness:	■■■
Affection level:	■■■■■
Friendliness toward dogs:	■■■
Friendliness toward other pets:	■■■
Friendliness toward strangers:	■■■■
Ease of training:	■■■■

Watchdog ability:	■■■■
Protection ability:	■■■
Grooming requirements:	■■
Cold tolerance:	■■■■■
Heat tolerance:	■■■

WEIGHT: male: 70–84 lb, female: 57–71 lb
HEIGHT: male: 23.5″; female: 22″

POPULARITY: Very rare
FAMILY: Livestock, Herding
AREA OF ORIGIN: Italy
DATE OF ORIGIN: Ancient
ORIGINAL FUNCTION: Sheep and goat drovers and guardians
TODAY'S FUNCTION: Sheep and goat drovers
OTHER NAME: Bergamasco Sheepdog, Cane da Pastore Bergamasco

HISTORY

The Bergamasco's ancestors probably originated in ancient Persia, where they helped nomadic sheepherders tend flocks as they wandered through rugged mountainous terrain. As nomadic populations migrated with their dogs, the Bergamasco's ancestors settled in the Alps, where the dogs bred with local breeds and further evolved to withstand the harsh climate. It's likely that similar sheepdogs, including the Komondor, Puli, Polish Lowland Sheepdog, Briard, and Pyrenean Sheepdog all derived from these same progenitor dogs from Persia. Initially, they were probably flock guardians, but as the flocks needed to be moved they doubled as flock drovers, which encouraged a more biddable yet free-thinking and friendlier temperament. Those that settled in the Italian and southern Swiss

ILLUSTRATED STANDARD

1. Large head with domed backskull
2. Pronounced stop
3. Thin, hanging ears covered with soft, wavy hair
4. Backline slopes slightly downward toward rear
5. Thick tail just reaching the hock, last third curved; carried just above backline when in motion
6. Oval, well-feathered feet
7. The coat forms flocks, or flat layers of felted hair

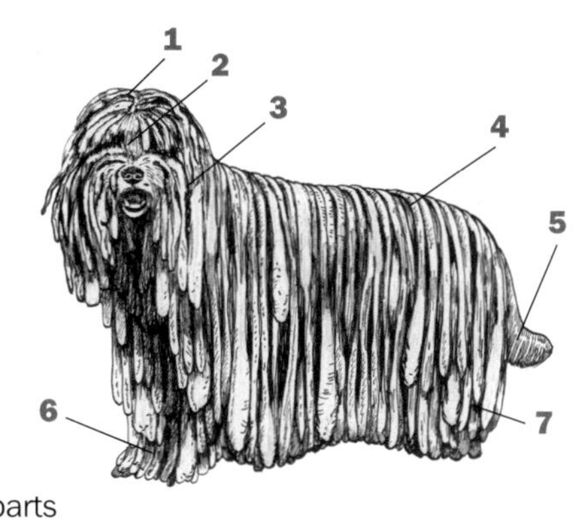

Color: gradations of gray (including merle) with dull black and fawn or isabella shadings on lower parts of flocks from discoloration; white markings acceptable but must cover no more than 1/5th of the body
DQ: full blue eyes; dudley nose; overshot more than 1/8″; undershot; white on more than 1/5th of the body

Alps were called Cana da Pastore Bergamasco after the seasonal shepherds from the city of Bergamo who came to work in the mountain region. They were important components of sheep and goat farming until World War II, after which sheep and goat farming declined. The dogs, too, declined in numbers due to the novelty of new foreign breeds. In the 1960s, Dr. Maria Andreoli undertook a concerted effort to revive the breed. Now the dogs are once again used in the Italian and Swiss Alps as goat and sheep herders. The first Bergamascos came from Italy to the United States in the mid-1990s. They were accepted into the AKC Miscellaneous Class in 2011 and as a member of the Herding Group in 2015.

TEMPERAMENT

The breed evolved as an independent problem solver, eager to fulfill the shepherd's tasks but doing so without step by step guidance. Thus, it is obedient unless it sees a better way to achieve the desired result. Bergamascos learn new tasks quickly but are not clownish performers of unnecessary tricks. They can be good home guardians, but are very friendly once introduced to visitors. They are fun-loving and gentle with family and generally good with other dogs and pets. They are poor protection dogs, as they are not aggressive.

UPKEEP

Bergamascos are much mellower than other herding breeds, requiring a couple of medium to long walks a day rather than jogging or sprinting. They are excellent hiking companions where the pace is slower. They need more companionship than extreme exercise. They enjoy cold weather. A Bergamasco in full coat can swim, but the drying process takes so long it's not recommended. Felting occurs between 9 to 12 months and can happen on its own or by splitting the mats (called flocks). Once the flocks are formed, very little care is needed, requiring little to no brushing and a couple of baths a year. The natural oils of the coat keep them generally dirt and odor free. Washing and drying the coat takes a full day. The coat does not shed.

HEALTH

- Major concerns: none
- Minor concerns: none
- Occasionally seen: some orthopedic problems in sterilized dogs
- Suggested tests: (hip)
- Life span: 12–15 years

FORM AND FUNCTION

The distinctive coat consists of three types of hair called wooly hair (outer wooly fine hair), goat hair (long, straight, and rough), and undercoat (oily dense undercoat that provides waterproofing). All three types of hair combine to form thick, flattened, felt-like mats called flocks to provide an armor of sorts. Because hair is never shed, the flocks grow throughout the dog's life, reaching the ground by about 6 years of age. Beneath the coat, the dog is heavy-boned but trim. The Bergamasco is slightly longer than tall. Its movement is a mix of trot and irregular leaping.

Berger Picard

AT A GLANCE

Energy level:	■■■■	Watchdog ability:	■■■
Exercise requirements:	■■■■	Protection ability:	■■
Playfulness:	■■■	Grooming requirements:	■■
Affection level:	■■■■	Cold tolerance:	■■■
Friendliness toward dogs:	■■■■	Heat tolerance:	■■■
Friendliness toward other pets:	■■■		
Friendliness toward strangers:	■■■	WEIGHT: 50–70 lb	
Ease of training:	■■■■	HEIGHT: male: 23.5–25.5"; female: 21.5–23.5"	

POPULARITY: Very rare
FAMILY: Livestock, Herding
AREA OF ORIGIN: France
DATE OF ORIGIN: Unknown
ORIGINAL FUNCTION: Sheep and cattle herding
TODAY'S FUNCTION: Sheep and cattle herding
OTHER NAME: Picardy Shepherd

HISTORY

Dogs resembling today's Berger Picard are depicted as early as the 14th century, and some breed historians believe it originated during the second Celtic invasion of Gaul around 400 B.C. Harsh-coated sheep and cattle herding dogs were abundant throughout Europe; in the mid-1800s those in France were classified according to coat length as the Berger de Beauce (shorthaired—today's Beauceron); Berger de Brie (longhaired—today's Briard); and later, medium length, the Berger de Picardie (today's Berger Picard). Berger (pronounced bare-ZHAY) means "shepherd" and Picard (pronounced pee-CARR) refers to the region of France. Although they were exhibited at some of the first dog shows, they didn't have the suave show dog look and were never popular in that role. Only in 1925 did the French Shepherd Club recognize them as a separate breed. World Wars I and II decimated the breed, as fighting took place in their

ILLUSTRATED STANDARD

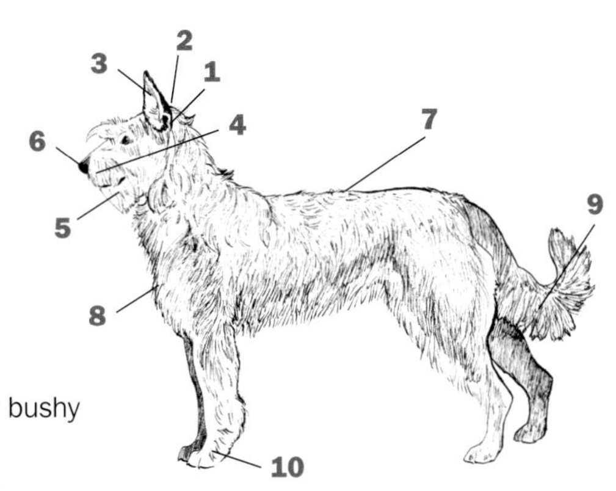

1 Strong, rectangular head narrowing slightly from ears to muzzle; parallel planes separated by a slight stop
2 Medium-sized, oval eyes—medium to dark brown in color
3 Moderately large (4–5″ long) erect ears with slightly rounded tips, not tipped forward
4 Powerful, slightly tapering muzzle with blunt end
5 Moustache and beard not overly long or bushy
6 Large, black nose
7 Level topline with slightly sloping croup
8 Prominent prosternum
9 Tail reaches the hock; slight crook or "J" at the tip, never curled over back
10 Round feet

Color: fawn (with or without dark trim on the ears and gray underlay) or brindle
DQ: Males under 22.5″ or over 26.5″; females under 20.5″ or over 24.5″; undershot or overshot bite with no contact between upper and lower incisors; yellow eyes; non-erect ears; absent, docked, or kinked tail; solid black or white, pied, spotted, or harlequin; entirely white foot or white bib on chest

fields and food for dogs was scarce. It has been claimed that some Picards were used to smuggle matches and tobacco over the Belgian border—the dog's back was shaved, where they placed a goatskin pouch, hair side up, that blended in with the dog's coat. Breeders searched Picardy after World War II for dogs to rebuild the breed, and in the early 1950s found the dogs that would become the foundation of the modern Picard. By the 1970s, occasional Picards were being brought to America. In 2002, Hollywood producers cast the breed in the starring role of the movie, "Because of Winn Dixie," playing the role of a mixed breed. A group of fanciers worked to promote the breed responsibly and it entered the AKC Herding Group in 2015.

TEMPERAMENT
The Picard is lively and alert, even-tempered, confident, and responsive to commands. They can be both stubborn and extremely sensitive, as they were bred to think for themselves but be responsive to skittish sheep. They may be aloof with strangers but are good with other dogs and pets. They make excellent watchdogs, and even good protection dogs, as well as comical companions. They are not excessive barkers.

UPKEEP
As a dog bred to work all day, Picards need a lot of activity, both mental and physical. A daily jog along with challenging games is necessary. Herding is their favorite activity, but they also enjoy obedience and agility training. The coat does not mat and because it has low oil content, it seldom smells or needs bathing. Some plucking of excess hair around the ears may be desirable for show dogs.

HEALTH
- Major concerns: none
- Minor concerns: PRA, difficulty breeding
- Occasionally seen: CHD, OCD, distichiasis, sensitivity to barbiturate anesthesia
- Suggested tests: hip, eye
- Life span: 13 years

FORM AND FUNCTION
The Berger Picard is a medium-sized, sturdily built, athletic dog with a rustic appearance. It is slightly longer than tall. The coat may have a slight wave and is shaggy and rough, about 2-3 inches long. It should never be shaped or scissored. The outer coat is harsh and crisp, providing protection against the elements; the undercoat is soft, short, and dense, providing insulation and warmth. The rough eyebrows, beard and moustache, along with the slight ruff on the sides and front of the neck are called "griffonage" and impart a distinctive look to the face. The gait is effortless and fluid, with the head lowered almost to level for greater efficiency, allowing them to work all day.

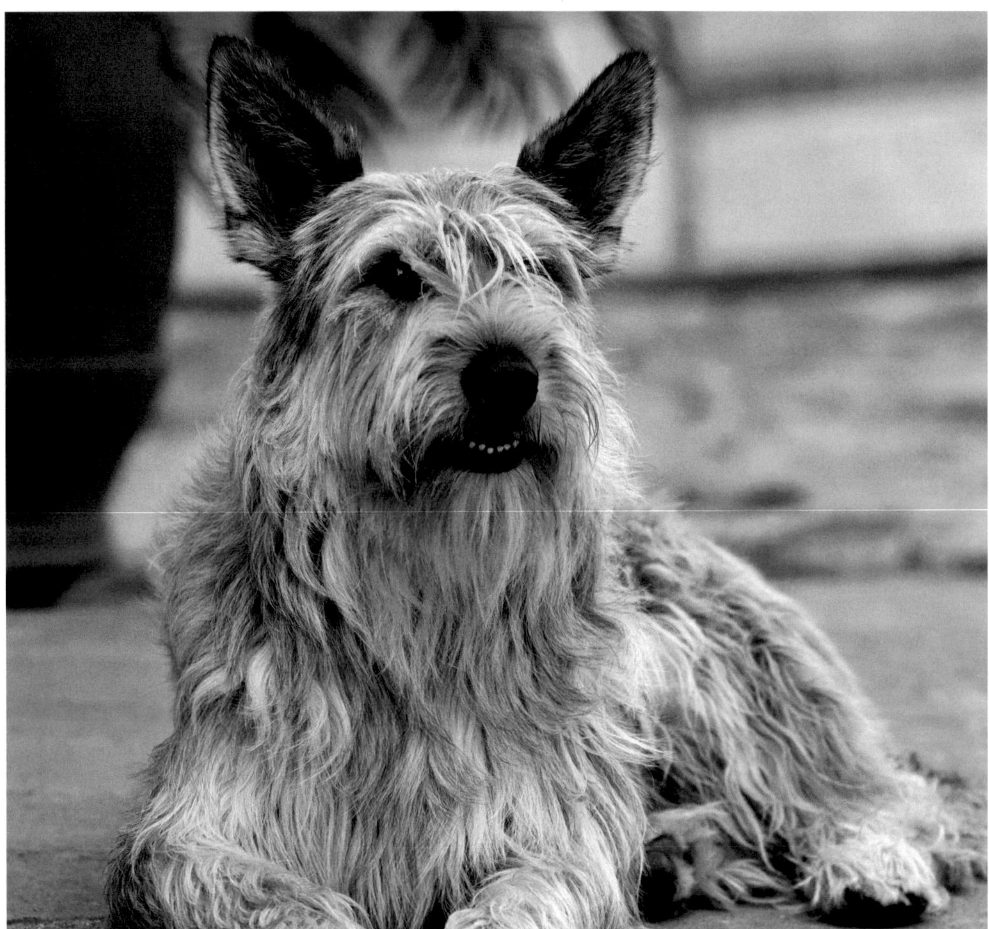

Border Collie

AT A GLANCE

Energy level:	■■■■■
Exercise requirements:	■■■■■
Playfulness:	■■■■
Affection level:	■■■
Friendliness toward dogs:	■■■
Friendliness toward other pets:	■
Friendliness toward strangers:	■■
Ease of training:	■■■■■

Watchdog ability:	■■■■
Protection ability:	■■■
Grooming requirements:	■■■
Cold tolerance:	■■■
Heat tolerance:	■■■

WEIGHT: 30–45 lb*
HEIGHT: male: 20–23″; female: 18–21″

POPULARITY: Popular
FAMILY: Livestock, Herding
AREA OF ORIGIN: Great Britain
DATE OF ORIGIN: 1800s
ORIGINAL FUNCTION: Sheep herder
TODAY'S FUNCTION: Sheep herder, herding trials, obedience
OTHER NAME: None

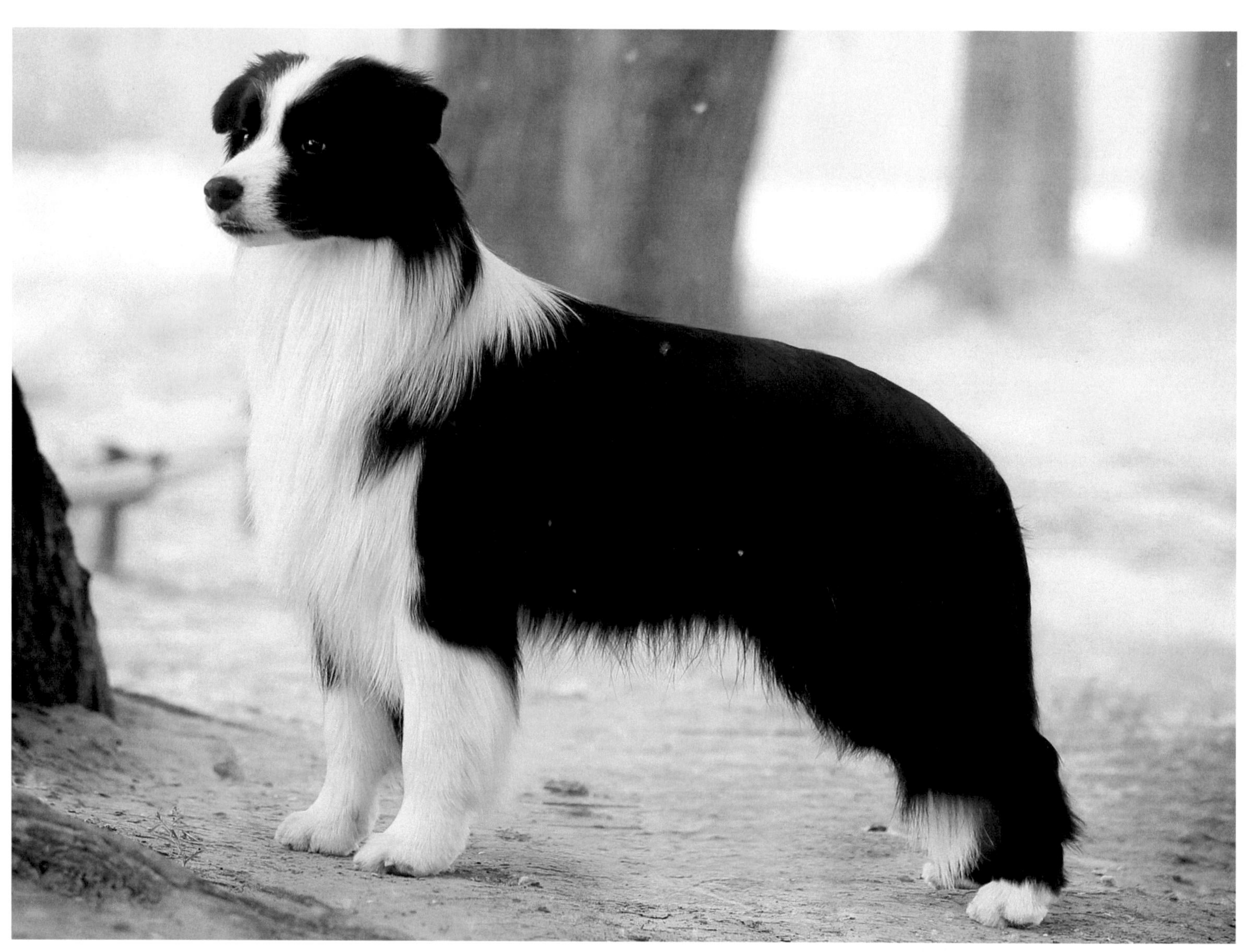

HISTORY

The consummate sheepdog, the Border Collie is the result of over a century of breeding for function above all other criteria. In the 1800s, a variety of sheep herding dogs with differing herding styles existed in Great Britain. Some were "fetching" dogs, dogs having an innate tendency to circle stock and bring them back toward the shepherd. Most of these were noisy dogs, tending to nip and bark as they performed their job. Boasts of the superiority of certain dogs were only natural; in 1873 the first actual sheepdog trial was held in order to settle some of these boasts. This contest would indirectly lead to the first Border Collies, by way of a dog named Hemp, who so distinguished himself in trials that he sired a great number of offspring. He herded not by barking and nipping, but

ILLUSTRATED STANDARD

1 Oval eyes, blue eyes allowed in merles only
2 Ears carried erect or semierect
3 Topline level with slight arch over loins
4 Tail set and carried low
5 Feet oval

Color: solid, bicolor, tricolor, merle, and sable, of various colors; solid white not allowed
DQ: none

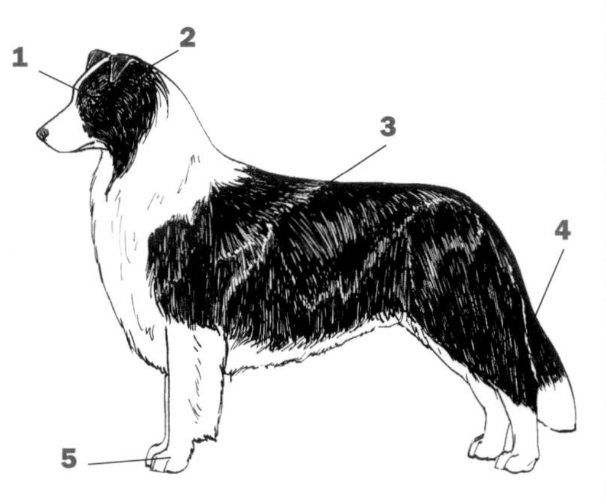

by calmly staring at the sheep ("giving eye") intimidating them into moving. Hemp is considered to be the father of the Border Collie. In 1906, the first standard was drawn up, but unlike the physical standards of most breeds, this was a description of working ability, with no regard to physical appearance. This emphasis has shaped the breed ever since. In fact, the dogs were still referred to simply as sheepdogs; only in 1915 was the name Border Collie first recorded, in reference to the dog's origin around the English and Scottish borders. The Border Collie came to America and instantly dazzled serious shepherds with its quick herding and obedience capabilities. In fact, the latter opened a new door for the breed as one of the top competitive breeds in obedience trials. Having worked hard to gain the reputation of one of the smartest breeds of dogs, a breed unspoiled by cosmetic emphasis, many Border Collie fanciers actively fought AKC recognition as a show dog. In 1995, however, the AKC recognized the breed and herded it into the show ring.

TEMPERAMENT

The Border Collie is a bundle of mental and physical energy awaiting its chance to be unleashed on the world. Among the most intelligent and obedient of breeds, it is nonetheless a disastrous housedog if it is not given a challenging job every day. Given sufficient exercise, it is a dependable and loyal companion. It is intent on whatever it does and tends to stare, which can be unnerving to other animals. It also likes to chase other animals. It is reserved, even protective, toward strangers. Without a job, BCs can be destructive and can develop harmful, compulsive habits.

UPKEEP

Few dogs are as work oriented as the Border Collie. This is a dog that needs a job. It needs a lot of physical and mental activity every day to satisfy its quest for work. This is a dog that cannot live in an apartment and that should preferably have ready access to a yard. Its coat needs brushing or combing twice weekly.

HEALTH

- Major concerns: CHD
- Minor concerns: PRA, lens luxation, CEA, PDA, OCD, deafness, seizures, hypothyroidism
- Occasionally seen: cerebellar abiotrophy, ceroid lipofuscinosis, compulsive behavior
- Suggested tests: hip, eye, (thyroid), (DNA for CEA)
- Life span: 10–14 years

FORM AND FUNCTION

This is a medium dog of strong bone, slightly longer than it is tall, combining grace, agility, substance, and stamina. Its trot is smooth, ground covering, and tireless, moving with stealth and strength. It is able to change speed and direction suddenly. The Border Collie must be able to display incredible agility even after working for long periods. The coat can be either smooth or rough. The smooth coat is short all over the body; the rough coat is medium to long in length and flat to slightly wavy in texture. Its expression is intelligent, alert, eager, and full of interest, a reflection of its temperament.

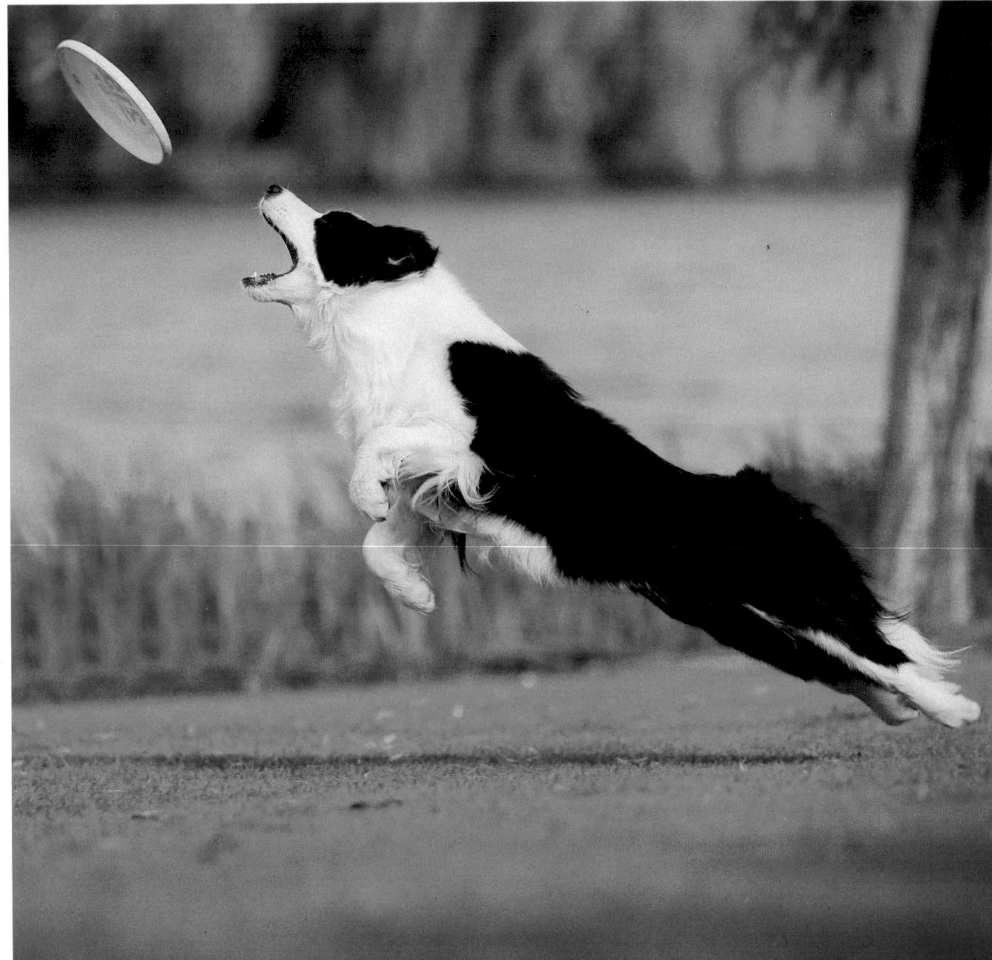

Bouvier des Flandres

AT A GLANCE

Energy level:	■■■
Exercise requirements:	■■■■
Playfulness:	■■
Affection level:	■■■
Friendliness toward dogs:	■■■
Friendliness toward other pets:	■■■
Friendliness toward strangers:	■■■
Ease of training:	■■■
Watchdog ability:	■■■■■
Protection ability:	■■■■■
Grooming requirements:	■■■■
Cold tolerance:	■■■■
Heat tolerance:	■■

WEIGHT: 69–90 lb*
HEIGHT: male: 24.5–27.5″; female: 23.5–26.5″

POPULARITY: Somewhat uncommon
FAMILY: Livestock, Herding
AREA OF ORIGIN: Belgium
DATE OF ORIGIN: 1600s
ORIGINAL FUNCTION: Cattle herding
TODAY'S FUNCTION: Security, herding trials
OTHER NAME: Belgian Cattle Dog

HISTORY

The Bouvier des Flandres served farmers and cattle merchants in controlling cattle in the great farmlands of southwest Flanders and on the French northern plain. In fact, *bouvier* means cowherd or oxherd in French, although the dogs were formerly more often called *Vuilbaard* (dirty beard) or *koe hond* (cow dog). Besides its main duty as a cattle drover, the Bouvier was an all-around farm dog, functioning also as a livestock and farm guard and draft dog. As expected from a dog selected to perform a variety of tasks, these working dogs were of a variety of types, colors, and even sizes. This wide variety also reflected the fact that this was a working dog, and breeding stock was chosen by ability, not pedigree or esthetics. The derivation of the breed is not docu-

ILLUSTRATED STANDARD

1 Thick beard, mustache, and eyebrows
2 Oval eyes
3 Flat skull
4 High-set, rough-coated ears; if cropped, triangular
5 Tail docked to two or three vertebrae, carried upright when in motion
6 Rounded feet

Color: from fawn to black, including salt and pepper, gray, and brindle
DQ: none

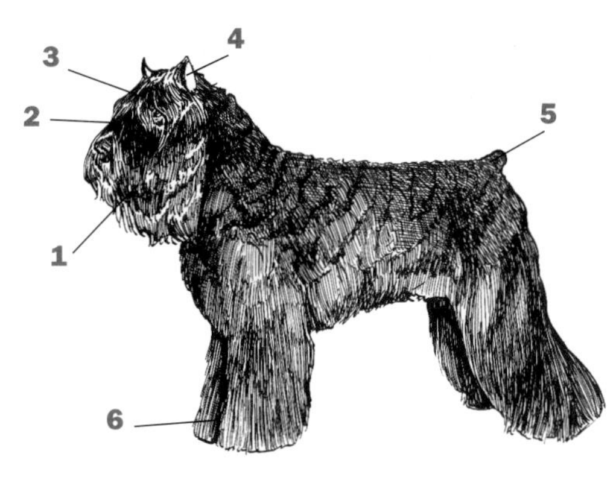

mented but may have included mastiff, sheepdog, and possibly even spaniel breeds. The first breed standard, drawn up in 1912, reflected this diversity of types and signaled a growing interest in the breed from dog fanciers. In the midst of its rising popularity, most of the Bouviers were lost in World War I—although some Bouviers served as ambulance and messenger dogs during the war. One of the few survivors was of such superior quality that the breed was successfully revived through his progeny. This dog, Champion Nic de Sottegem, can be found in virtually every modern Bouvier pedigree. In 1922, a revised standard further defined the desirable Bouvier type, and helped pave the way to a more homogeneous breed. When the first Bouviers entered American show rings in 1931, they aroused much attention among dog fanciers. The breed has never become extremely popular, but it is well known at dog shows and herding trials.

TEMPERAMENT

The Bouvier is loyal, devoted, fearless, and protective. Given daily exercise, it is calm and well-mannered indoors, but ready for an adventure in the great outdoors. It is independent and confident of its own judgment, yet willing to please. It can be domineering. It is reserved, even protective, toward strangers and can be aggressive with strange dogs. It is very good with children, although it may nip at heels in play. It is not an excessive barker or digger.

UPKEEP

The Bouvier des Flandres needs daily exercise and daily interaction, and a lot of both. It loves the chance to herd, but its requirements can also be met with a good jog, a very long walk, or a vigorous play session. Its harsh coat needs combing once or twice weekly, plus scissoring and shaping (clipping for pets and stripping for show dogs) every three months.

HEALTH

- Major concerns: CHD, glaucoma, elbow dysplasia, SAS
- Minor concerns: hypothyroidism
- Occasionally seen: none
- Suggested tests: hip, elbow, cardiac, (eye)
- Life span: 10–12 years

FORM AND FUNCTION

This is a versatile breed able to perform a variety of functions, including cattle herder, draft dog, and guard. As such, it combines great strength with agility and endurance. The Bouvier is a compact, short-coupled dog, of square proportion and rugged appearance. Its gait is free, bold, and proud. Its weatherproof coat is tousled and double, with a fine undercoat and a harsh, dry outer coat. It is trimmed (if necessary) to a length of about 2.5″. The head is accentuated by a beard and moustache, which adds to the dog's bold and alert expression.

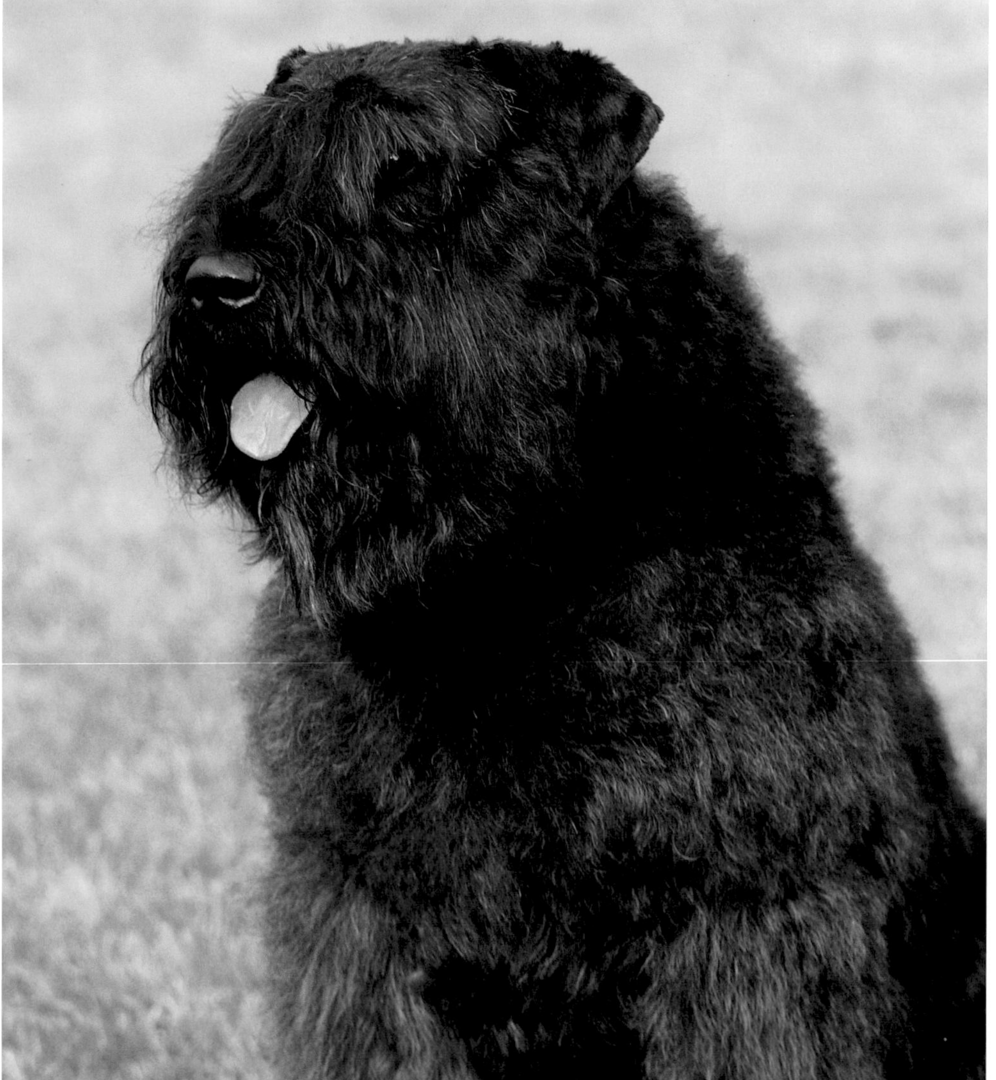

Briard

AT A GLANCE

Energy level:	■■■	Watchdog ability:	■■■■■	POPULARITY: Uncommon
Exercise requirements:	■■■■	Protection ability:	■■■■■	FAMILY: Livestock, Herding
Playfulness:	■■■	Grooming requirements:	■■■■	AREA OF ORIGIN: France
Affection level:	■■■	Cold tolerance:	■■■	DATE OF ORIGIN: 1300s
Friendliness toward dogs:	■	Heat tolerance:	■■	ORIGINAL FUNCTION: Herding and guarding sheep
Friendliness toward other pets:	■■■			
Friendliness toward strangers:	■	WEIGHT: male: 75–100 lb*, female: 50–65 lb*		TODAY'S FUNCTION: Herding trials
Ease of training:	■	HEIGHT: male: 23–27"; female: 22–25.5"		OTHER NAME: Berger de Brie

HISTORY

The Briard is one of four French sheepdog breeds, the others being the Beauceron, Picardy, and Pyrenean. It is the oldest of the four breeds, with dogs resembling Briards depicted in art from as long ago as the eighth century, and more definitive evidence by the fourteenth century. These early dogs were known as Chien Berger de Brie (Shepherd Dog of Brie), giving rise to the belief that the breed originated in the province of Brie; however, it may also be a corruption of Chien d'Aubry, referring to the dog of Aubry de Montdidier that avenged his master's murder (according to fourteenth-century legend). The name Briard was not used until 1809. Originally employed as a herd protector, the Briard was expected to tackle wolves if the need arose. Briards also protected the

ILLUSTRATED STANDARD

1 Wide muzzle with mustache and beard
2 Large, calm eyes
3 High-set ears; natural ear is straight, lying away from the head and covered with hair, cropped ear is long with rounded tip.
4 Tail carried low and ending in curve (called a crochet)
5 Two dewclaws on each hindleg
6 Rear toes turn out slightly

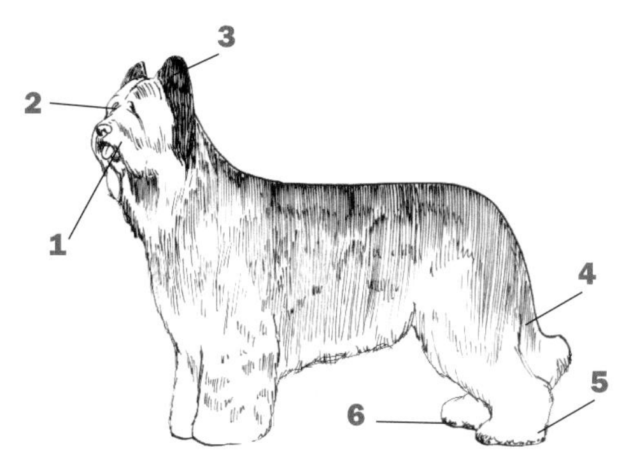

Color: all uniform colors except white (includes black, tawny, and gray shades)
DQ: under minimum size limits; yellow or spotted eyes; nose any color other than black; non-existent or cut tail; spotted or white coat, or white spots exceeding 1″ in diameter

flock and estates against human intruders. After the French Revolution, which resulted in the land being divided into smaller sectors, it was important that the flocks be kept close to home, and the Briard turned its talents to herding, rather than guarding sheep. Only around 1900 did it become a show dog. The first breed standard was written in 1897, but it was replaced by another in 1909. Briards came to America very early, with evidence that both Lafayette and Thomas Jefferson brought some of the first specimens to the New World. These dogs did not have a lasting influence, however. The Briard was the official dog of the French army in World War II. After World War I, American soldiers brought some Briards to America, and this was the beginning of the modern American Briard. Popularity of the breed has been modest in America, but it remains the most popular sheepherder in its native France.

TEMPERAMENT

Devoted and faithful, the Briard is a loving and protective companion. It is independent, intelligent, and self-assured, but it is also willing to please and eager to serve as a partner in adventure. It is reserved with strangers. It can be aggressive with other dogs and may nip at people's heels when playing. It tends to stay at home and may attempt to keep the family's children home as well! Young Briards need a lot of socialization.

UPKEEP

This is a dog that needs a good amount of activity and interaction every day. Its favorite exercise is the chance to herd, but it can also be satisfied with a long walk or jog, or a long play session coupled with a little training. Its long coat needs brushing or combing every other day or mats can form.

HEALTH

- Major concerns: gastric torsion, CHD
- Minor concerns: nightblindness
- Occasionally seen: PRA, heart problems
- Suggested tests: hip, eye, (cardiac), DNA for night blindness
- Life span: 10–12 years

FORM AND FUNCTION

The Briard is square or slightly longer than it is tall and powerful without being course; the overall appearance is one of handsome form. The Briard is a boundary herder, acting as a "moving fence" to keep a flock in an unfenced area. This requires the dog to be an independent thinker. It is a loose-eyed, upright herder. Its movement has been described as "quicksilver," with supple, light strides that give the impression of gliding. Its undercoat is fine and tight, and its outer coat is coarse and dry, lying flat in long, slightly wavy locks. On the shoulders, the coat's length is 6 inches or more. The questioning confident expression is enhanced by the longer eyebrows, as well as the long-appearing head.

Canaan Dog

AT A GLANCE

Energy level:	■■■	Watchdog ability:	■■■■■	POPULARITY: Very rare
Exercise requirements:	■■■■	Protection ability:	■■■	FAMILY: Livestock, Herding, Primitive
Playfulness:	■■■	Grooming requirements:	■	AREA OF ORIGIN: Israel
Affection level:	■■■	Cold tolerance:	■■■	DATE OF ORIGIN: Ancient times
Friendliness toward dogs:	■■■	Heat tolerance:	■■■	ORIGINAL FUNCTION: Sentry, messenger, assistance
Friendliness toward other pets:	■■■■			
Friendliness toward strangers:	■■	WEIGHT: male: 45–55 lb; female: 35–45 lb		TODAY'S FUNCTION: Herding trials
Ease of training:	■■■■	HEIGHT: male: 20–24″; female: 19–23″		OTHER NAME: Kalef K'naani, Kelev Cana'ani

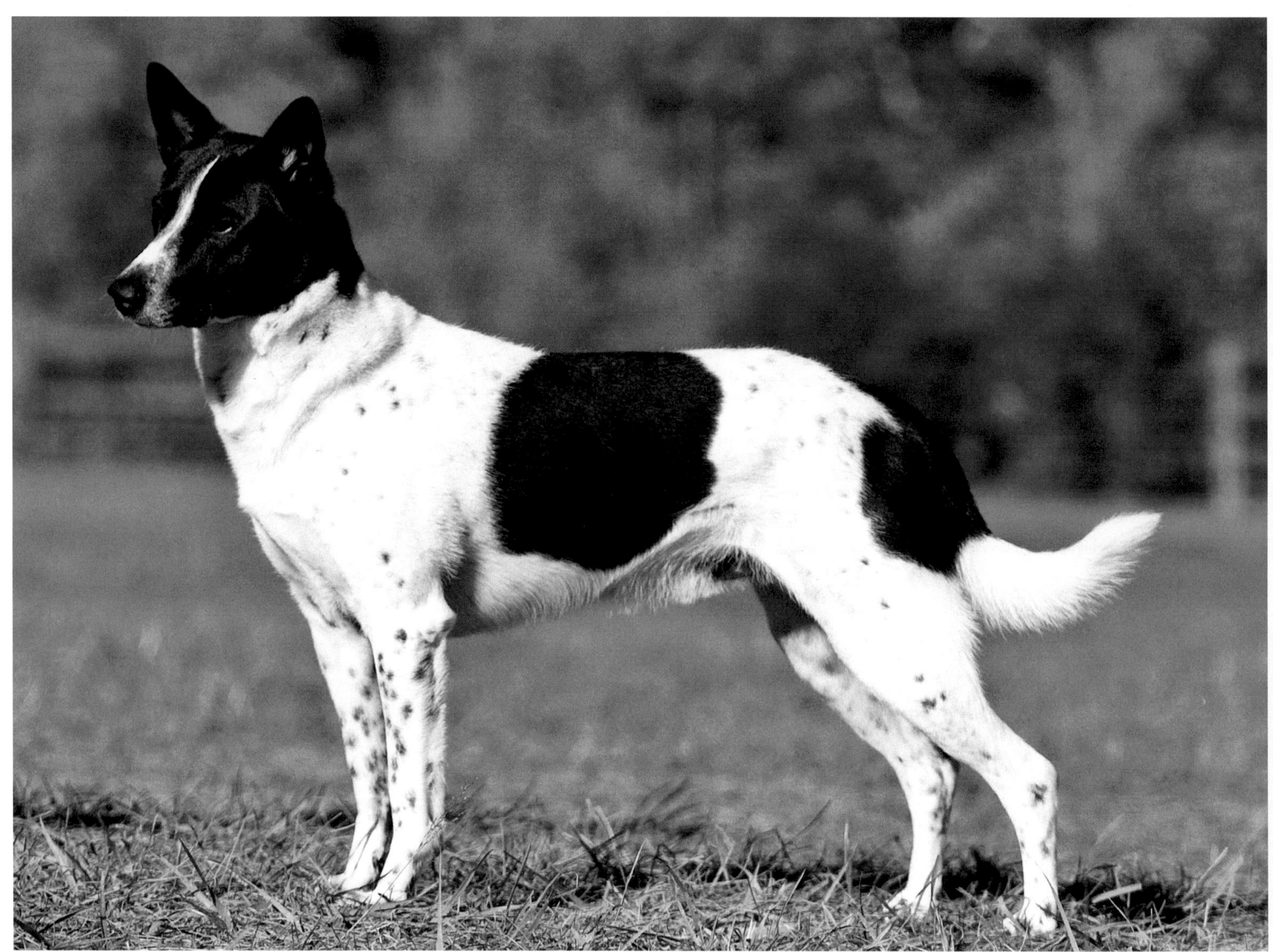

HISTORY

Canaan Dogs have evolved through hundreds, and perhaps thousands, of years of hardship. It is thought that the breed originated in the biblical land of Canaan and were known as Kelev Kanani (Dog of Canaan). When the Israelites were dispersed from their homeland by the Romans 2000 years ago, most of the Israeli dogs were left to fend for themselves in the Sebulon Coastal Plain and Negev Desert. Bedouins captured male puppies from the wild to raise as guard and livestock dogs. When the Israeli Defense Force tried to develop service dogs in the 1930s, the traditional European service breeds weren't able to adapt to the harsh climate. The Canaan Dog owes its existence primarily to the efforts of one woman, Dr. Rudolphina Menzel. Her search for a more suitable military dog

ILLUSTRATED STANDARD

1 Almond-shaped eyes
2 Elongated head, wedge-shaped from above
3 Ears erect and set low, slightly rounded tip
4 Topline level with slight arch over loin
5 Tail set moderately high, may be carried over back when excited
6 Cat feet

Color: may be either predominantly white with mask with or without additional color patches, or solid color with or without white trim; the mask should be symmetrical and must completely cover both eyes and ears

DQ: males under 20″ or over 25″; females under 18″ or over 23″; gray or brindle; all white

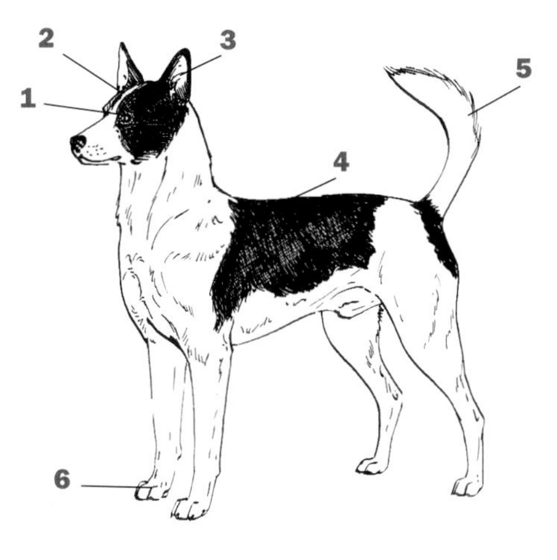

led her to the native feral dogs. Several dogs were captured, and a breeding and training program was begun. The dogs quickly proved their worth, serving as sentry dogs, messengers, mine detectors, Red Cross helpers, and even locators of wounded soldiers during the Second World War. They were trained as guide dogs for the blind in the 1950s but were too small and independent to be widely successful. Perhaps no other breed of dog has ever risen from feral roots to become such a useful and dedicated companion in so short a time. Efforts have continued to recruit feral Canaan Dogs to widen the gene pool, but loss of habitat, mixing with other breeds, and government eradication to prevent rabies has decimated the feral population. The first Canaan Dog came to America in 1965. Not the flashiest of breeds, the Canaan's understated good looks may have made many people overlook it, despite its companionship credentials. Nonetheless, it slowly attracted admirers, and the AKC finally admitted it into the Herding Group in 1997. The breed has remained obscure despite its attractive attributes.

TEMPERAMENT

Not only does the Canaan Dog excel as a herder, but it has also proven itself in a variety of tasks involving dependability and obedience. This is an intelligent, devoted, docile dog that is quite tractable and willing and quick to please. It is aloof toward strangers and protective of its family. The Canaan Dog is generally good with other household pets and dogs, but it may be aggressive toward strange dogs. It is a natural guardian and some tend to bark a lot.

UPKEEP

Few breeds can claim as pure a working heritage as the Canaan Dog. This dog will not be happy just sitting around. It needs lots of exercise and mental and physical challenges. These needs can be met with herding exercise, a long jog, a strenuous game session along with a challenging training session. Its coat needs brushing about once a week to remove dead hairs.

HEALTH

- Major concerns: none
- Minor concerns: CHD
- Occasionally seen: elbow dysplasia
- Suggested tests: hip, elbow, (eye), knee), (thyroid)
- Life span: 12–13 years

FORM AND FUNCTION

The Canaan Dog resembles none of the other herding breeds, arising from a completely different background. Nonetheless, it shares similar traits needed in any dog that must herd for hours. It is a medium-sized, square-proportioned dog of moderate substance that combines strength, agility, and endurance. It is not exaggerated in any way. Its movement is athletic and graceful, with a brisk, ground-covering trot. It is able to change directions instantly. It has a double coat, with a short, soft undercoat that varies in density according to climate, and a straight, flat-lying, harsh outer coat, with a slight ruff. This breed must adapt to great extremes in weather ranging from hot days to cold nights.

Collie

AT A GLANCE

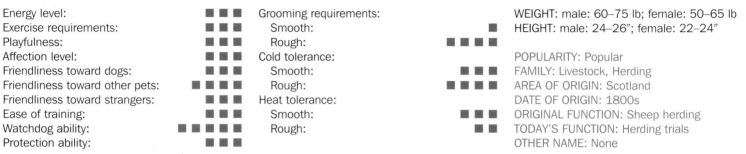

Energy level: ■■■
Exercise requirements: ■■■
Playfulness: ■■■
Affection level: ■■■
Friendliness toward dogs: ■■■
Friendliness toward other pets: ■■■■
Friendliness toward strangers: ■■■
Ease of training: ■■■
Watchdog ability: ■■■■■
Protection ability: ■■■

Grooming requirements:
Smooth: ■
Rough: ■■■■
Cold tolerance:
Smooth: ■■■
Rough: ■■■■
Heat tolerance:
Smooth: ■■■
Rough: ■■

WEIGHT: male: 60–75 lb; female: 50–65 lb
HEIGHT: male: 24–26″; female: 22–24″

POPULARITY: Popular
FAMILY: Livestock, Herding
AREA OF ORIGIN: Scotland
DATE OF ORIGIN: 1800s
ORIGINAL FUNCTION: Sheep herding
TODAY'S FUNCTION: Herding trials
OTHER NAME: None

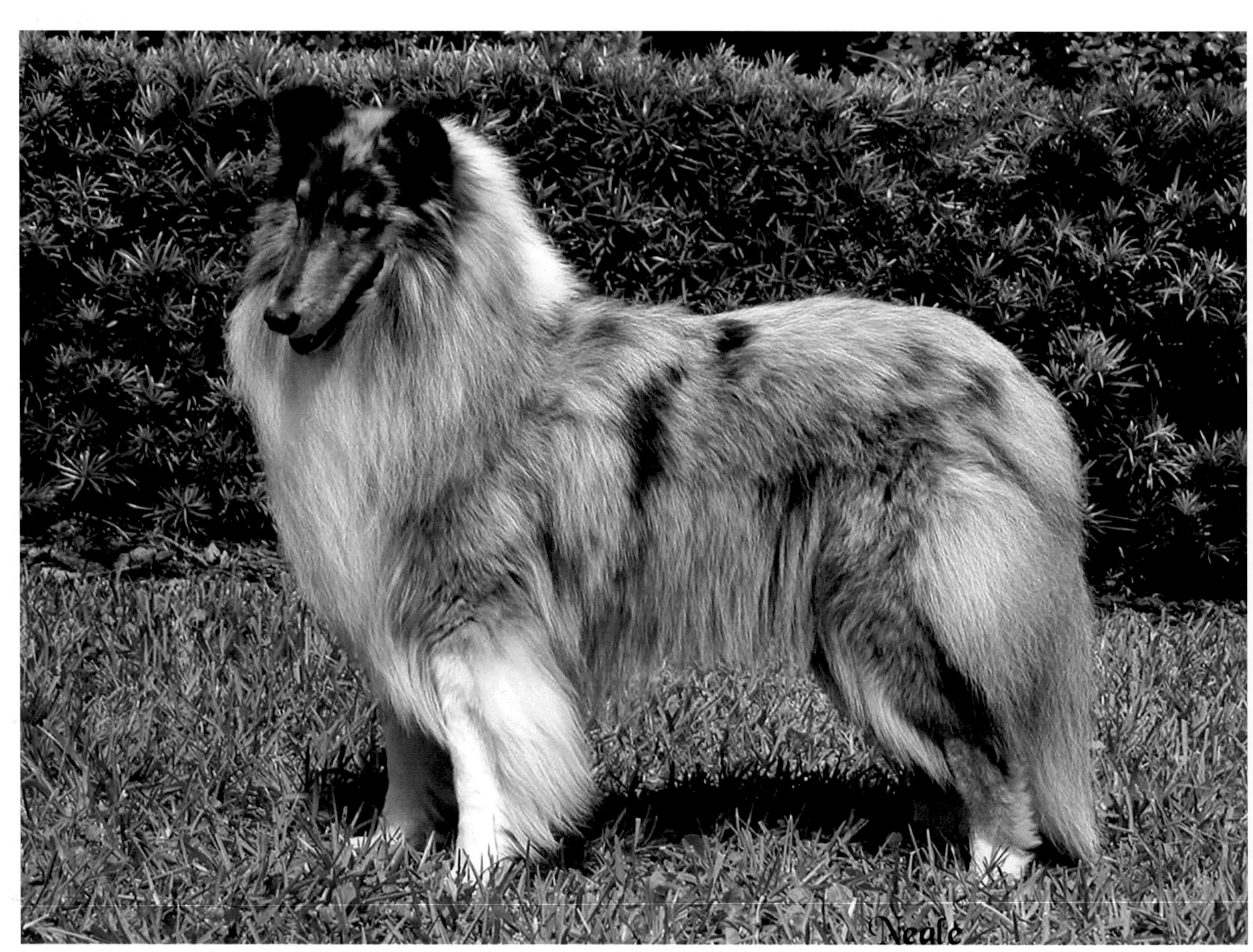

HISTORY

The derivation of the Collie is as obscure as the derivation of its name. One theory of the breed's origins is that it was derived from the same root stock as the Border Collie. One theory of the name's origin is that it was derived from a Gaelic word meaning useful, which certainly described the useful farm or stock dogs valued by the Celts who first settled on the British Isles. Although sheepherding and guarding are some of the most ancient of canine services, evidence of the Collie dates only from about 1800. Both rough- and smooth-coated "Scotch" collies existed by that

ILLUSTRATED STANDARD

1 Head resembles a blunt lean wedge from profile and front views
2 Slight stop
3 Flat skull
4 Small ears, carried semierect when alert with the top quarter tipping forward
5 Medium-sized, almond-shaped eyes
6 Strong, level back
7 Tail carried low
8 Small, oval feet
9 Heavily frilled neck

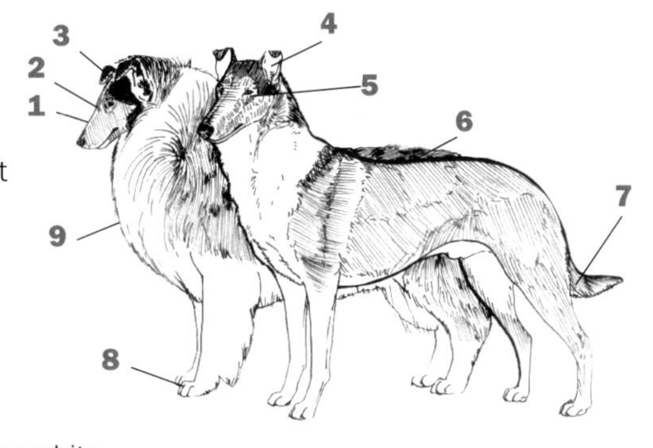

Color: sable and white; tricolor, blue merle; white (predominantly white, preferably with markings)
DQ: none

time. Smooth-coated littermates were chosen as drovers, and rough-coated dogs were to stay out with the flock in all weather. As the breed caught the interest of dog fanciers, both rough- and smooth-coated Collies became taller and more refined. The rough-coated Collie was especially influenced by the progeny of a dog named Old Cockie, born in 1867 and thought to be responsible not only for setting type but also for popularizing the sable color. In 1860 Queen Victoria became enthusiastic about the breed and added her first Collie to her kennel. Under her sponsorship, the Collie's popularity grew with dog fanciers and the upper class. By 1886 a standard was drawn up that still describes the breed as it is today. Meanwhile, as sheepherding became more important in America, settlers brought Collies with them to the New World. America's social elite brought back fine Collies from Europe, and soon the Collie could be found in some of the most prestigious estates in America. Later the Collie found a champion in Albert Payson Terhune, whose stories about Collies heightened their popularity with people from all walks of life. The most famous Collie of all, the movie and television star Lassie, further popularized the breed, helping to make the Rough Collie one of the all-time favorite breeds in America. The Smooth Collie has never shared the same popularity.

TEMPERAMENT

The Collie is gentle and devoted, a mild-mannered friend to all. It is a dog with a working heritage, and it needs daily mental and physical exercise or it can become frustrated. It is sensitive, intelligent, and willing to please, although it is sometimes a bit stubborn. It can nip at heels in play. Some may bark a lot.

UPKEEP

A good walk or jog on leash or a fun play session is needed every day. Herding is an excellent exercise. The coat of both varieties needs weekly brushing to remove dead hair, with the Rough requiring more time.

HEALTH

- Major concerns: none
- Minor concerns: CEA, PRA, gastric torsion, dermatomyositis, demodicosis
- Occasionally seen: seizures, microphthalmia, CHD, cyclic neutropenia
- Suggested tests: eye, (DNA for CEA), DNA for PRA, DNA for drug sensitivity
- Life span: 8–12 years
- Note: Often sensitive to ivermectin. Homozygous merles may have visual or hearing problems.

FORM AND FUNCTION

The Collie is an active, lithe, strong dog that combines strength, speed, and grace. Its gait suggests effortless speed as well as the ability to change speed and direction instantly, as required in herding dogs. The coat can be of two types, both with a soft, abundant undercoat. The outer coat of the Smooth variety is short, hard, and flat; that of the Rough variety is straight, harsh, abundant, and long, particularly on the mane and ruff. The Collie's expression is an important hallmark of the breed, and depends upon the shape and balance of the skull and muzzle, as well as the characteristics of the eyes and ears. It should be bright, alert, and intelligent, traits accentuated by a fairly refined head.

Entlebucher Mountain Dog

AT A GLANCE

Energy level:	■■■■
Exercise requirements:	■■■■
Playfulness:	■■■■
Affection level:	■■■
Friendliness toward dogs:	■■■
Friendliness toward other pets:	■■■
Friendliness toward strangers:	■■
Ease of training:	■■■

Watchdog ability:	■■■■■
Protection ability:	■■■■■
Grooming requirements:	■■■
Cold tolerance:	■■■■■
Heat tolerance:	■■

WEIGHT: 45–65 lb*
HEIGHT: male: 17–21″; female: 16–20″

POPULARITY: Rare
FAMILY: Mastiff
AREA OF ORIGIN: Switzerland
DATE OF ORIGIN: 1800s
ORIGINAL FUNCTION: Herding
TODAY'S FUNCTION: Herding
OTHER NAME: Entlebucher Sennenhund, Entlebucher Cattle Dog

HISTORY

The Entlebucher Mountain Dog (pronounced ENT-lee-boo-ker or ENTEL-boo-ker) is the smallest of the four Swiss Mountain Dogs (the others being the Appenzeller, Bernese Mountain Dog, and Greater Swiss Mountain Dog). These dogs are also collectively known as Sennehund, which translates to the herdsman's dog. All of these dogs descend from molossus type dogs that accompanied the Romans through Helvetia over 2,000 years ago. The two smaller Swiss Mountain breeds (the Entlebucher and Appenzeller) drove dairy cows in from mountain pastures, while the larger ones were livestock guardians and draft dogs. The first description of a dog (the Entlebucherhund) from the valley of Entlebuch was in 1889. At the time, the Entlebucher and Appenzeller were lumped as the

ILLUSTRATED STANDARD

1 Muzzle slightly shorter than skull
2 Slightly small, almond-shaped eyes
3 Ears pendulous, not too big, set high and wide
4 Flat skull
5 Sturdy, level topline
6 Natural or docked tail equally acceptable
7 Slightly rounded feet

Color: black and tan pattern with white extremities (except short tail), blaze, and from chin to chest
DQ: no undercoat; blue or yellow eyes; overshot or undershot; wry mouth

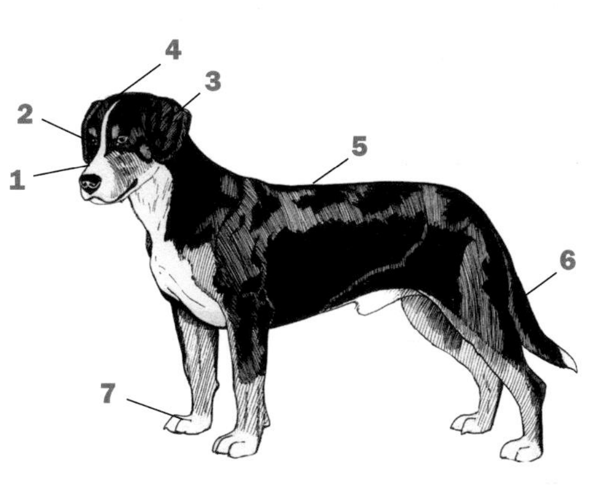

same breed. In 1913, four of the small naturally bobtailed dogs were exhibited, and Professor Albert Heim, the expert on Swiss breeds, advocated their independent recognition. Nonetheless, crosses with German Shepherd Dogs in the early 1900s threatened the breed. World War I further threatened them; after the war not a single one could be found. Efforts of several breeders resulted in a breed standard and club in 1926, and 17 Entlebuchers were located. The Entlebucher became eligible to compete in AKC herding events in 2007 and in the AKC Herding Group in 2009. Entles can be born with naturally short tails, but the trait cannot breed true.

TEMPERAMENT

The Entlebucher is extremely devoted and loyal, tending to stay close to its family. They learn quickly but retain an independent nature, not afraid to make their own choices—especially if they feel they have the upper hand. They are excellent watchdogs and tend to be protective. Their loud bark may be their best protective asset. They tend to be suspicious of strangers. They are generally good with other dogs and pets; however they may try to herd other pets and children! Although males particularly can be aggressive toward other dogs, most are pretty mellow unless provoked.

UPKEEP

Entles are active dogs that like to run and roughhouse. They need a good, long play period or hike daily, plus activities such as agility, obedience, or tracking to challenge their mind. They are fairly quiet indoors as long as they are tired! They are strong for their size. The coat should be brushed once or twice a week, more when shedding. They prefer cool weather.

HEALTH

- Major concerns: CHD
- Minor concerns: PRA, ectopic ureter
- Occasionally seen: cataract
- Suggested tests: DNA for PRA, hip, eye
- Life span: 11–13 years

FORM AND FUNCTION

The Entlebucher is a medium-sized, compact, strongly muscled, elongated drover with ample bone. His herding style is driving, getting behind cattle and pushing them along. This requires an active, nimble, tough, and tireless dog. Too small a dog lacks the necessary power and too large lacks the necessary agility needed for the task. The Entle is longer than tall in a ratio of about 10 to 8. The coat is short but dense, with a harsh close-fitting outer coat for protection and a dense undercoat that supplies warmth without causing overheating. The bright markings may emphasize the dog to the cattle it is herding. The gait is fluid and ground-covering.

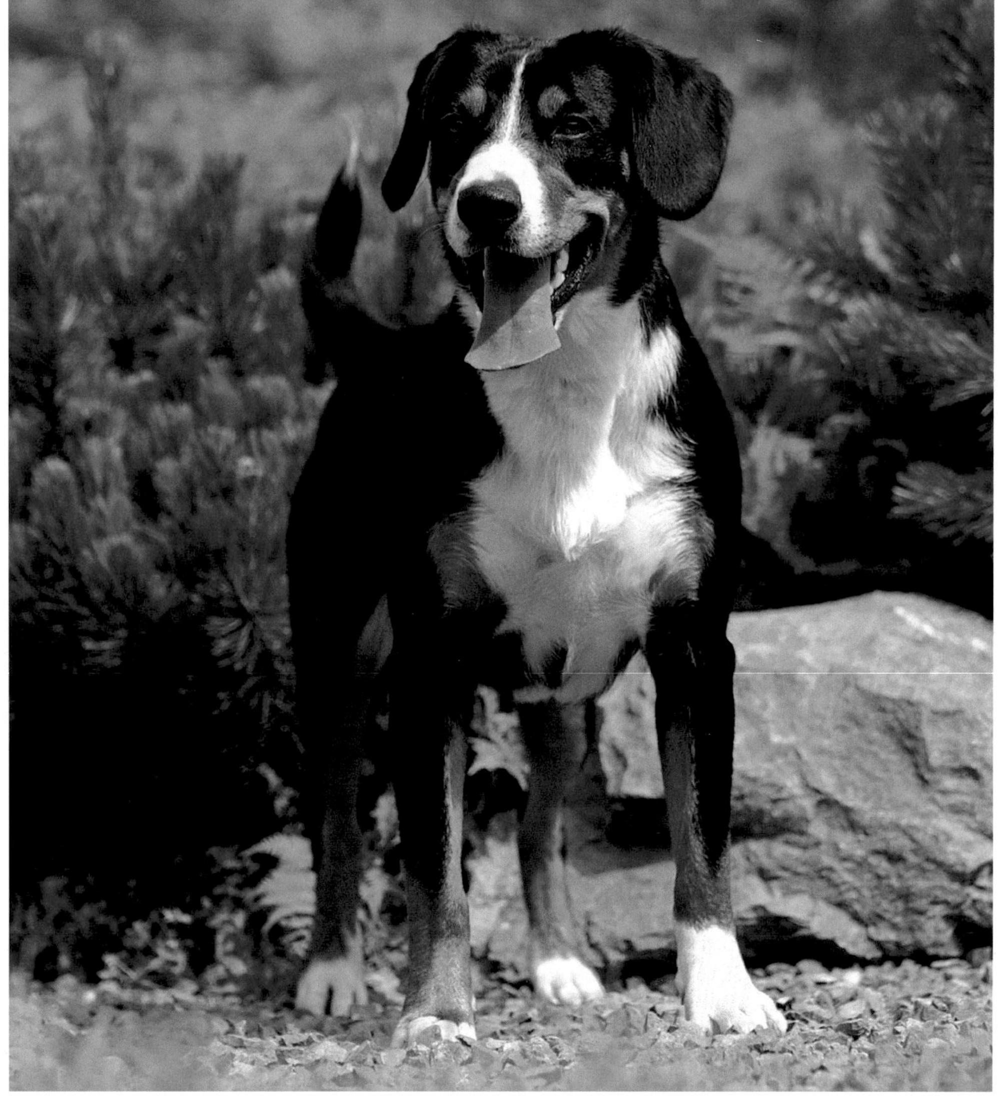

Finnish Lapphund

AT A GLANCE

Energy level:	■■■■	Watchdog ability:	■■■■■	POPULARITY: Very rare
Exercise requirements:	■■■■	Protection ability:	■■	FAMILY: Spitz
Playfulness:	■■■	Grooming requirements:	■■■■	AREA OF ORIGIN: Finland
Affection level:	■■■	Cold tolerance:	■■■■■	DATE OF ORIGIN: Ancient
Friendliness toward dogs:	■■■	Heat tolerance:	■	ORIGINAL FUNCTION: Herding reindeer
Friendliness toward other pets:	■■■			TODAY'S FUNCTION: Herding
Friendliness toward strangers:	■■	WEIGHT: 33–53 lb*		OTHER NAME: Suomenlapinkoira
Ease of training:	■■■■	HEIGHT: male: 18–21″; female: 16–19″		

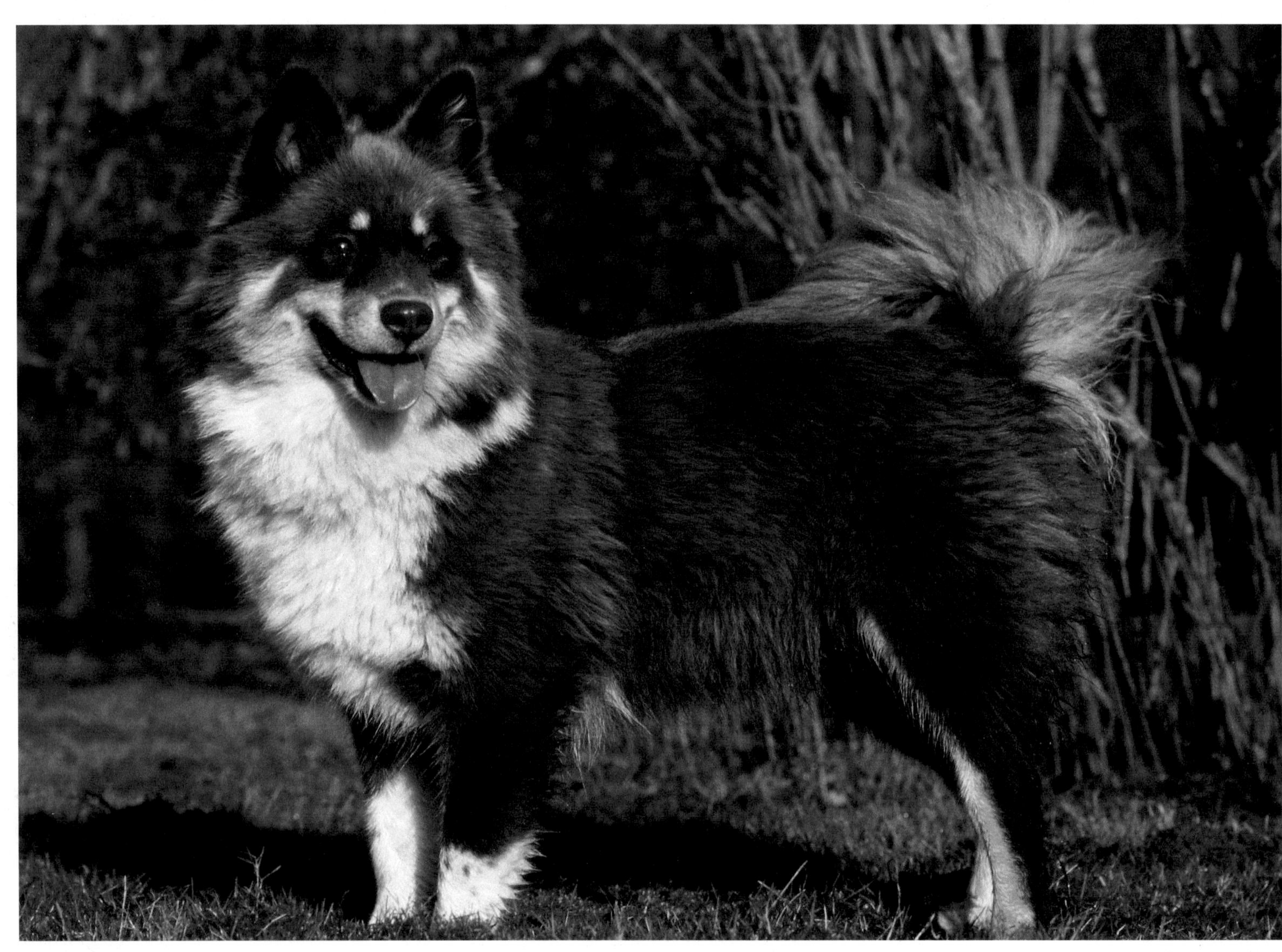

HISTORY

Ancient cave paintings and archeological digs suggest the nomadic Saame in Lapland (northern Finland, Sweden, and parts of Russia) have used spitz-type dogs to herd reindeer for centuries, perhaps for thousands of years. The dogs, which were little known to the outside world, worked as gatherers, not drovers, to keep the herds together. In the 1900s, their use as herders diminished as snowmobiles took their place and the Saame became less nomadic. Invasions during World War II further damaged the remaining population, and a distemper outbreak after the war almost wiped them out completely. Realizing the breed could be lost without intervention, a group of Finnish dog breeders collected dogs, adopted a breed standard, and gained recognition by the Finnish Kennel Club in 1945. Both shorter and longer haired dogs were included together, as both often appeared in the same litters

ILLUSTRATED STANDARD

1 Slightly domed skull, depth is equal to breadth
2 Well defined stop
3 Small to medium triangular ears, set far apart, rounded at tip; erect or tipped
4 Oval eyes
5 Rather high-set tail covered with profuse coat, carried over back or to side when moving
6 Oval feet, covered with thick hair even between pads

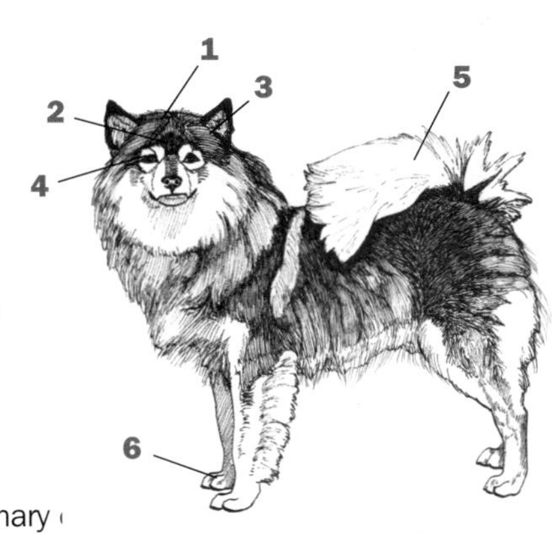

Color: all colors are permitted, but the primary
secondary colors allowed on head, neck, chest, underside of the body, legs, and tail; slightly wedged-shaped head with planes of muzzle and skull nearly parallel
DQ: none

of the breed, then called Lapponian Shepherd Dogs. In 1967, the long-coated variety was recognized separately as the Lapinkoira, or Finnish Lapphund. The short-coated variety was called the Lapinporokoira, or Lapponian Herder. The Finnish Lapphund is now known as the Suomenlapinkoira in Finland, where it is one of the most popular breeds. The breed remained largely unknown in America. In 1987, an effort was made to establish them in America. Breed numbers grew slowly. The UKC recognized the Finnish Lapphund in 1994; and in 2011, the Finnish Lapphund became a member of the AKC Herding Group.

TEMPERAMENT
Lappies are gentle and devoted companions. They learn quickly but can also be independent and strong-willed. They were never bred to be guard dogs and tend to be submissive toward people. The breed has won many obedience awards in their native land. They get along well with other dogs and pets. Befitting their herding heritage, they bark when excited but, generally, not otherwise. They are very alert and aware of their surroundings.

UPKEEP
As a breed developed to be on the move, the Lapphund enjoys an active lifestyle. They enjoy a long hike or vigorous game, preferably every day. They thrive on mental challenges, so training activities such as agility or obedience are helpful. Although an active breed, they are relatively calm indoors even if they miss a day of exercise. Their coat is thick and requires brushing once or twice a week—more during shedding season—to prevent matting. They much prefer cool weather.

HEALTH
- Major concerns: none
- Minor concerns: PRA, cataract
- Occasionally seen: CHD
- Suggested tests: DNA for PRA, eye, hip
- Life span: 12–14 years

FORM AND FUNCTION
The Finnish Lapphund is a medium-sized dog with the look of a northern breed and the temperament of a herding breed. Bred to work outside, north of the Arctic Circle, it is strongly built and thickly coated. The breed has a greater substance than its size would suggest. Its bone is substantial and muscles are well developed. It is very slightly longer than tall, although the abundant coat can mask this. The coat is thick and profuse, with a straight, long outer coat that is very harsh and water-repellant. The undercoat, which is vital for insulation, is soft, very dense, and plentiful. Finnish Lapphunds must be agile and capable of sudden bursts of speed. They have a medium but powerful-appearing stride. Because reindeer are not as fearful of dogs as are many herded stock, working Lappies are constantly vigilant to avoid being trampled.

German Shepherd Dog

AT A GLANCE

Energy level:	■■■
Exercise requirements:	■■■■
Playfulness:	■■
Affection level:	■■■
Friendliness toward dogs:	■
Friendliness toward other pets:	■■■
Friendliness toward strangers:	■■
Ease of training:	■■■■■

Watchdog ability:	■■■■■
Protection ability:	■■■■■
Grooming requirements:	■■
Cold tolerance:	■■■
Heat tolerance:	■■■

WEIGHT: 75–95 lb*
HEIGHT: male: 24–26″; female: 22–24″

POPULARITY: Most popular
FAMILY: Livestock, Herding
AREA OF ORIGIN: Germany
DATE OF ORIGIN: 1800s
ORIGINAL FUNCTION: Sheep herder, guardian, police dog
TODAY'S FUNCTION: Police, contraband detection, assistance, herding trials, Schutzhund
OTHER NAME: Alsatian, Deutscher Schaferhund

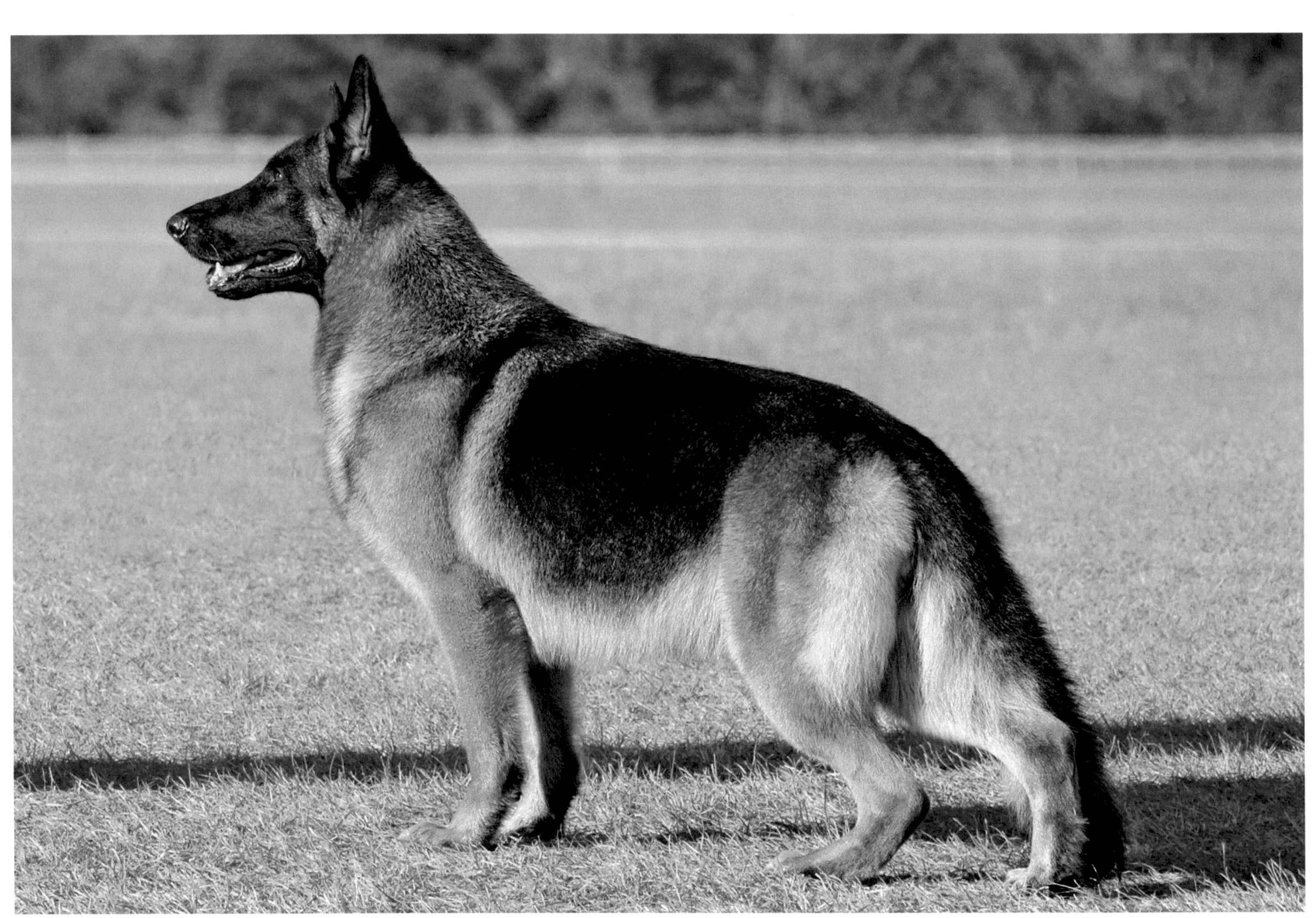

HISTORY

Despite an outward appearance slightly resembling a wolf, the German Shepherd Dog is a fairly recently developed breed and, contrary to naíve beliefs, it is no more closely related to the wolf than any other breed of dog. The breed is the result of a conscious effort to produce the ideal shepherd, capable of herding and guarding its flocks. Perhaps never in the history of any breed has such concerted effort been put into improving a dog, mostly due to the formation in 1899 of the Verein fur Deutsche Scharferhunde SV, an organization devoted to overseeing the breeding of the German Shepherd. Breeders sought to develop not only a herding dog but also one that could excel at jobs requiring courage, athleticism, and intelligence. In short order, the German Shepherd had proved itself a more than capable police dog, and subsequent breeding strove to perfect its abilities as an intelligent and fearless companion and guardian. During

ILLUSTRATED STANDARD

1 Chiseled, strong head
2 Medium-sized, almond-shaped eyes
3 Moderately pointed ears, carried erect
4 Withers higher than and sloping into the level back
5 Tail bushy, hanging in a slight curve
6 Feet short

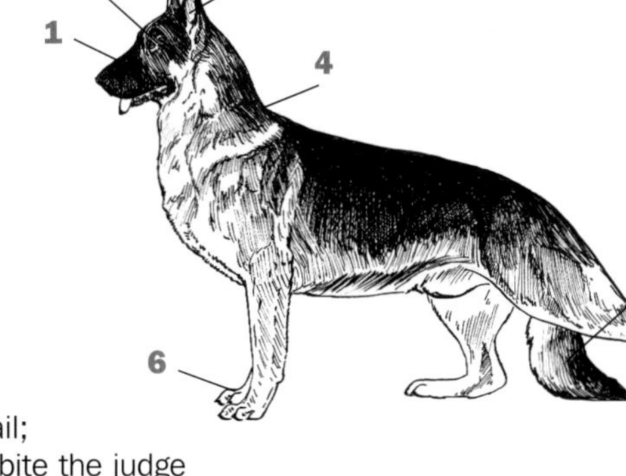

Color: most colors, other than white, are permissible.
DQ: cropped or hanging ears; nose not predominantly black; undershot; docked tail; white coloration; any dog that attempts to bite the judge

World War I, it was the obvious choice for a war sentry. At the same time, the AKC changed the breed's name from German Sheepdog to Shepherd Dog, and Britain changed it to Alsatian Wolfdog, both attempts to dissociate the dog from its unpopular German roots. The Wolfdog was later dropped as it caused many people to fear the dogs. In 1931, the AKC restored the breed's name to German Shepherd Dog. The greatest boon to the Shepherd's popularity came in the form of two dogs, both movie stars: Strongheart and Rin Tin Tin. The German Shepherd held the number one spot in American popularity for many years. Although presently it has dropped from the top spot, the German Shepherd remains as one of the most versatile dogs ever created, serving as a police dog, war dog, guide dog, search-and-rescue dog, narcotics- or explosives-detecting dog, show dog, guard dog, pet—and even shepherd.

TEMPERAMENT

Among the most intelligent of breeds, the German Shepherd Dog is so intent on its mission—whatever that may be—that it is virtually unsurpassed in working versatility. It is utterly devoted and faithful. Aloof and suspicious toward strangers, it is protective of its home and family. It can be domineering. It can be aggressive toward other dogs, but it is usually good with other pets.

UPKEEP

This breed needs daily mental and physical challenges. It enjoys a good exercise session as well as learning session. Its coat needs brushing one or two times weekly.

HEALTH

- Major concerns: CHD, elbow dysplasia
- Minor concerns: panosteitis, vWD, degenerative myelopathy, cauda equina, hot spots, skin allergies, malignant neoplasms, pannus, cataract, gastric torsion, perianal fistulas, cardiomyopathy, hemangiosarcoma
- Occasionally seen: pancreatic insufficiency
- Suggested tests: hip, elbow, (DNA for myelopathy)
- Life span: 10–12 years
- Note: GSDs are especially susceptible to a potentially fatal systemic fungal infection from *Aspergillus*.

FORM AND FUNCTION

The German Shepherd Dog has an outline of smooth curves on a body that is longer than it is tall. It is strong, agile, and substantial. Its gait is exceptionally outreaching and elastic, covering the ground in great strides. It has a double coat, with the outer coat consisting of dense, straight or slightly wavy, harsh, close lying hair of medium length.

Icelandic Sheepdog

AT A GLANCE

Energy level:	■■■■
Exercise requirements:	■■■■
Playfulness:	■■■■
Affection level:	■■■■
Friendliness toward dogs:	■■■■
Friendliness toward other pets:	■■■■■
Friendliness toward strangers:	■■■■■
Ease of training:	■■■■

Watchdog ability:	■■■■■
Protection ability:	■
Grooming requirements:	■■■■
Cold tolerance:	■■■■■
Heat tolerance:	■

WEIGHT: 20–40 lb*
HEIGHT: male: 18″; female: 16.5″

POPULARITY: Rare
FAMILY: Spitz
AREA OF ORIGIN: Iceland
DATE OF ORIGIN: Ancient
ORIGINAL FUNCTION: Herding sheep, cattle, horses
TODAY'S FUNCTION: Herding
OTHER NAME: Iceland Spitz, Iceland Dog, Friaar Dog, Íslenskur Fjárhundur

HISTORY

The Icelandic Sheepdog's ancestors originated in Norway, journeying to Iceland with Norwegian Vikings in 874—which is why they're also known as the "dog of the Vikings." DNA analysis indicates they are closely related to the Karelian Bear Dog of Russia. Once in Iceland, they were used to herd sheep, cattle, and horses. Iceland experienced some severe famines, during which most dogs were killed so people could eat. Only the best dogs were allowed to live. By the Middle Ages, the dogs became known for their profuse coats and were often exported to England to become pets of the aristocracy. A report from 1492 says the Icelanders demanded high prices for their dogs but would give their children away because they couldn't feed them. Icelandic Sheepdogs continued to be popular

ILLUSTRATED STANDARD

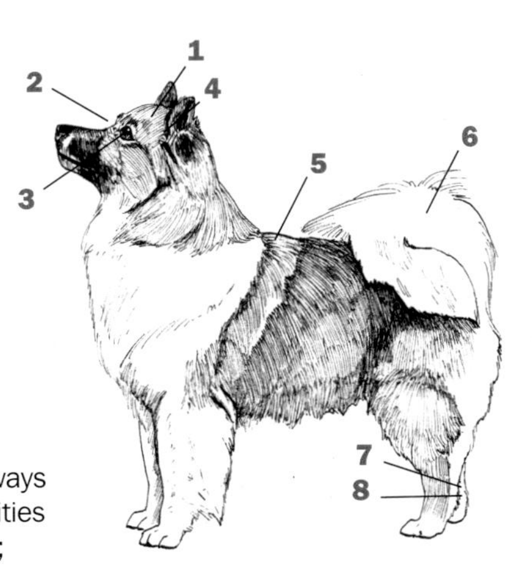

1 Somewhat domed skull, slightly longer than muzzle
2 Clearly defined stop, neither steep nor high
3 Medium-sized, almond-shaped eyes
4 Medium-sized, erect ears
5 Level, muscular, and strong back
6 High-set tail, curled over and touching the back
7 Dewclaws required; may be double
8 Rear dewclaws required; well-developed double dewclaws desirable

Color: a single color (chocolate, gray, black, or shades of tan) should be predominant; white is always present, most often on the face, collar, and extremities (or as a background for patches of the main color); black masks may occur on tan or gray dogs
DQ: none

exports to Europe in the sixteenth and seventeenth centuries and were even mentioned by Shakespeare. Accounts from Iceland up to the twentieth century mention Icelandic Sheepdogs and their various jobs, including herding, finding lost sheep in the snow, rounding up ponies, and gathering puffins. A dog tax imposed in 1869 caused the breed's population to plummet. Additionally, crosses to other breeds almost obliterated the original Icelandic Sheepdog. Iceland banned importation of dogs in 1901, but the first census of Icelandic Sheepdogs located only 20 of the original type. Meanwhile, they were recognized as a breed in Denmark in 1898 and in England in 1905. The breed remained rare, with few typical specimens in Iceland by 1950. Several were brought to America and then England. The Icelandic Kennel Club formed in 1969 to monitor the breed, which was finally seen as part of Iceland's heritage. The AKC recognized the Icelandic Sheepdog in 2010.

TEMPERAMENT

Icelandic Sheepdogs are energetic and alert, ready to play, run, or seek out adventure—preferably at the sides of their people. They are friendly toward all, including strangers, other dogs, and other pets. Although highly responsive, they are also free thinkers—their job often required them to work on their own. If they think they are right they will often ignore commands to the contrary. They tend to bark when alerted or excited.

UPKEEP

These active dogs are happiest when they're on the move and in the cold. They enjoy mental challenges and do well at obedience, agility, and other training activities. They are calm and easygoing inside, even if they miss a day of exercise. Like all double-coated breeds, they shed a lot, especially twice a year. Regular brushing and bathing will cut down on hair. The short coat requires about fifteen minutes a week, and the long coat about an hour a week.

HEALTH

- Major concerns: CHD
- Minor concerns: none
- Occasionally seen: cryptorchidism
- Suggested tests: hip
- Life span: 11–14 years

FORM AND FUNCTION

The Icelandic Sheepdog is a Nordic herding spitz with typical pricked ears; curled, bushy tail; and double, stand-off coat. These features all help insulate it against frigid weather. The breed has two coat types, long and short. Both are double, thick, and waterproof with a fairly coarse outer coat and thick, soft undercoat. It is a medium-sized (or slightly under medium) dog, longer than tall. The dog covers ground efficiently when trotting, displaying both agility and endurance.

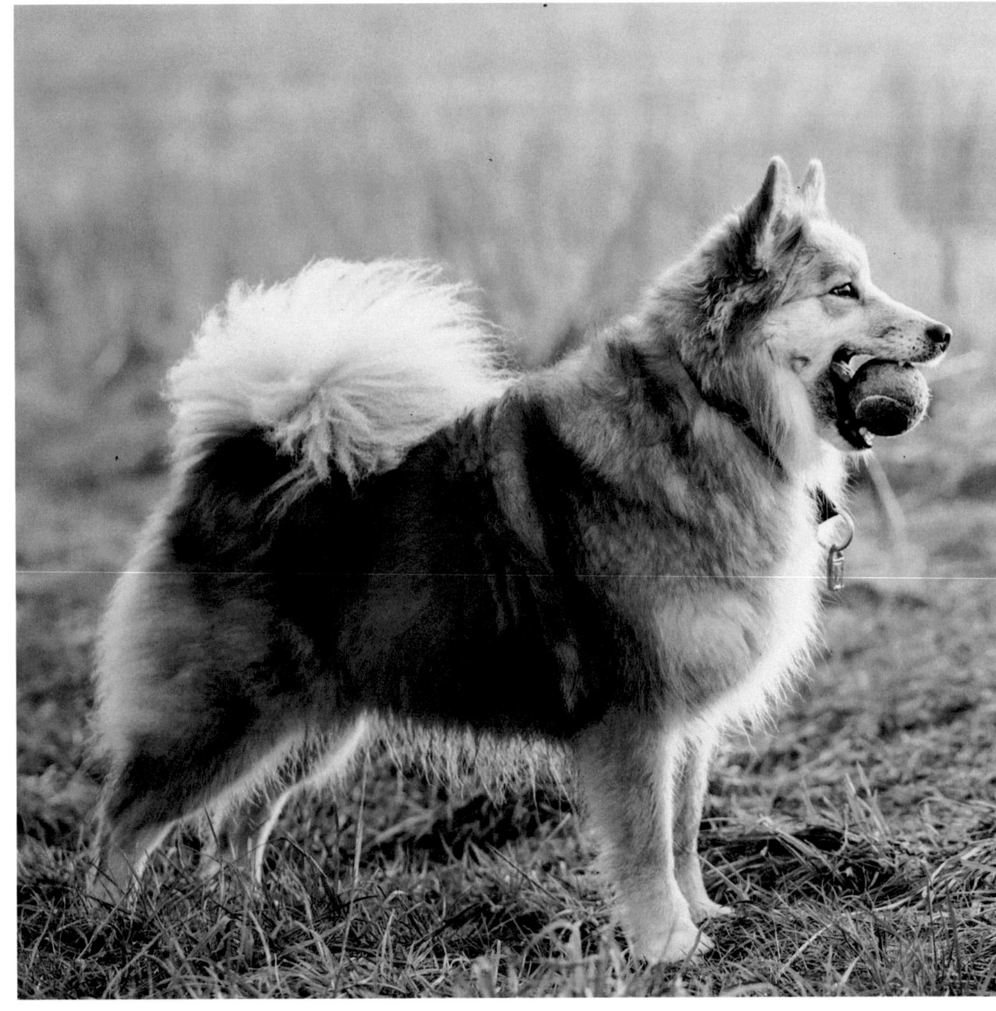

Norwegian Buhund

AT A GLANCE

Energy level:	■■■■■	Watchdog ability:	■■■■■	POPULARITY: Very rare
Exercise requirements:	■■■■■	Protection ability:	■■■	FAMILY: Spitz
Playfulness:	■■■■■	Grooming requirements:	■■■	AREA OF ORIGIN: Norway
Affection level:	■■■■■	Cold tolerance:	■■■■	DATE OF ORIGIN: Ancient
Friendliness toward dogs:	■■■	Heat tolerance:	■■■	ORIGINAL FUNCTION: Herding various livestock
Friendliness toward other pets:	■■■■			TODAY'S FUNCTION: Herding
Friendliness toward strangers:	■■■	WEIGHT: male: 31–40 lb; female: 26–35 lb		OTHER NAME: Norsk Buhund
Ease of training:	■■■■	HEIGHT: male: 17–18.5″; female: 16–17.5″		

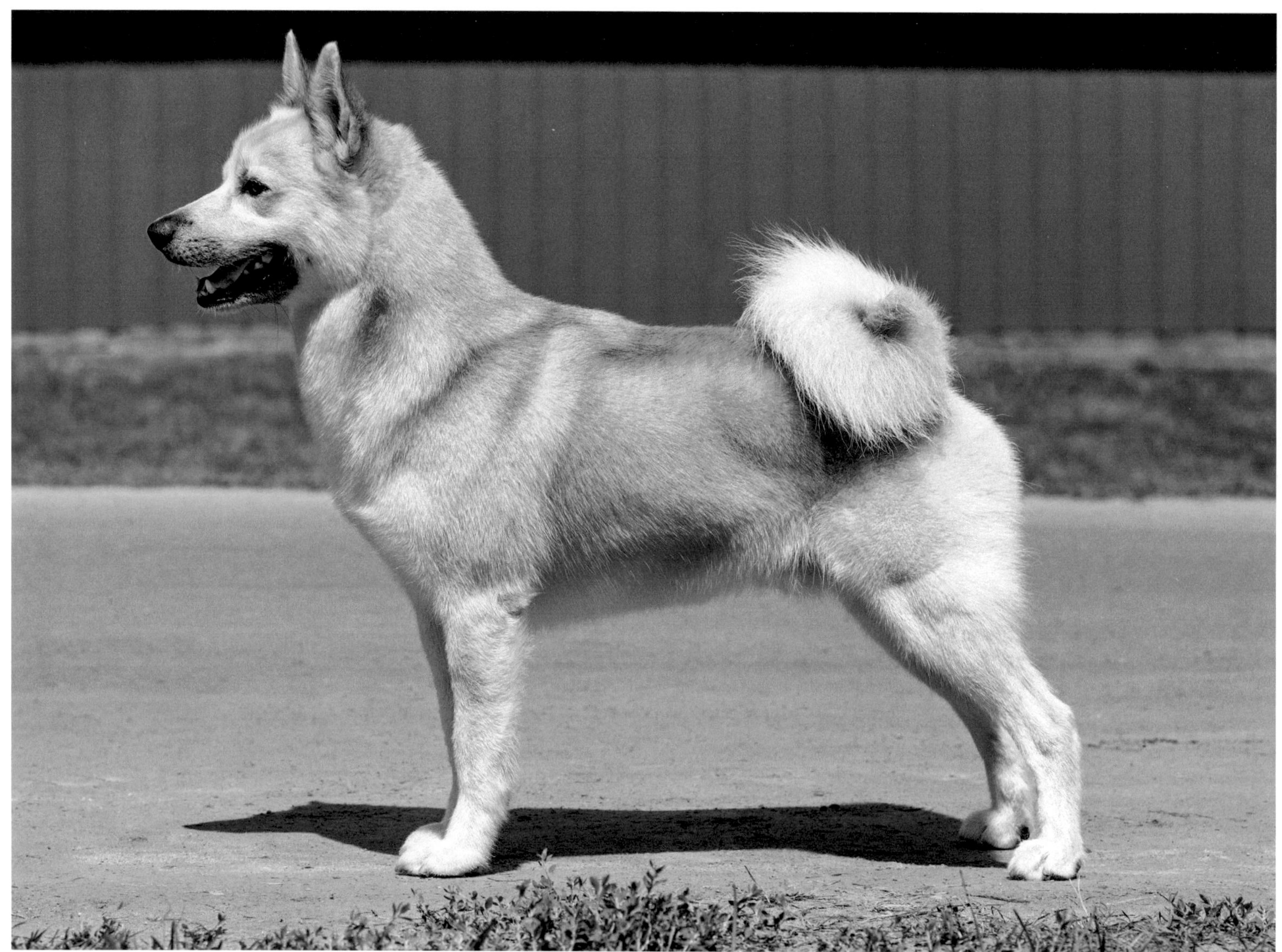

HISTORY

Remains of spitz-type dogs have been found in Norway's oldest archeological sites and in Viking grave sites from 900 A.D. The dogs traveled with the Vikings and were buried with them to continue their various duties in the afterlife. Today's Buhund is the direct descendant of these dogs. The name Buhund roughly translates to farm (or homestead or mountain hut) dog. In many areas, every farm had one to herd and watch over sheep, cattle, pigs, reindeer, and various small livestock. Shepherds spent summers in mountain huts with their dogs to help control and watch the stock. The land was rocky, with steep slopes, and the dogs had to work on their own to gather stock, often finding and flushing them by barking. During shearing, they could walk over the sheeps' backs to get from one

ILLUSTRATED STANDARD

1. Wedge-shaped, almost flat skull; parallel with the bridge of the nose
2. Muzzle about the same length as backskull
3. Stop well defined but not too pronounced
4. Dark, oval-shaped eyes
5. Medium-sized, prick ears with pointed tips
6. Level back
7. Tail set high, tightly curled and carried over the back's centerline
8. Oval feet

Color: wheaten (pale cream to bright orange) or black; white permissible in a narrow collar, narrow blaze, feet, tail tip, and small patch on chest
DQ: more than 0.5″ under height or 1″ over height; overshot or undershot mouth

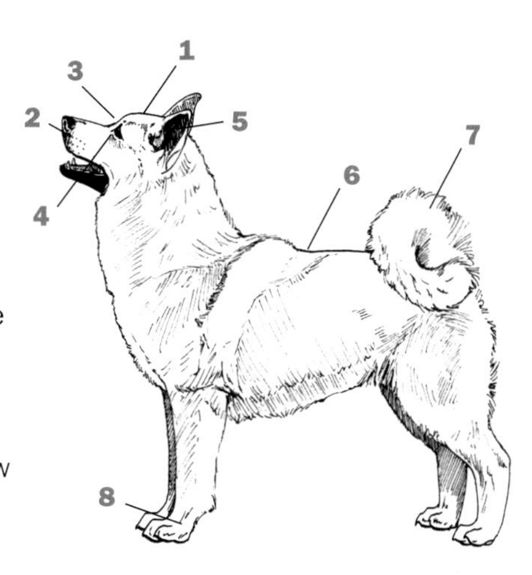

side of a flock to the other. The Buhund remained an essential part of Norwegian farm life for centuries, until the importation of other breeds diminished their population in the early 1900s. The breed was first exhibited in agricultural shows in 1913. In the 1920s, Buhund shows were held with state-run sheep and goat shows, rekindling interest in the breed. The Norsk Buhund Club was founded in 1939. The Buhund came to England after World War II, and later, to America. The Norwegian Buhund Club of America was formed in 1983. The Buhund became a member of the AKC Herding Group in 2009.

TEMPERAMENT

Affectionate, cheerful, and full of energy, the Buhund is a great companion for active families. They are eager to please and are considered one of the easier to train spitz breeds, although they are still somewhat independent thinkers. This breed likes to keep busy and if not given plenty of work or play, they can devise games that may not be acceptable. They are excellent watchdogs but can be overly exuberant barkers.

UPKEEP

Buhunds are active and playful. They need a good workout every day in the form of a long jog or energetic activities such as retrieving, agility, or especially, herding. Given sufficient exercise, they are calm indoors, although prone to bark. The coat is medium to short but double. It sheds freely (especially twice a year) but does not tangle. Brushing a few times a week, plus regular bathing, will keep shed hair down.

HEALTH

- Major concerns: none
- Minor concerns: CHD
- Occasionally seen: cataract
- Suggested tests: hip, eye
- Life span: 12–14 years

FORM AND FUNCTION

The Buhund is a typical northern breed of the spitz type, with erect ears, full and curled tail, and double coat—all of which protect it against the cold. It has a square build, with moderate substance and bone. Its slightly less than medium size makes it large enough to control all types of livestock but small enough to be agile and economical. They are quick and sure-footed; their herding style is that of a loose-eyed upright breed, with a natural tendency to circle and gather. The gait is free and effortless, and temperament alert, self-confident, and lively. The outer coat is thick and hard but rather smooth. The undercoat is soft and dense.

Old English Sheepdog

AT A GLANCE

Energy level:	■■■	Watchdog ability:	■■■
Exercise requirements:	■■■	Protection ability:	■■■
Playfulness:	■■■	Grooming requirements:	■■■■
Affection level:	■■■■■	Cold tolerance:	■■■■
Friendliness toward dogs:	■■■	Heat tolerance:	■■
Friendliness toward other pets:	■■■■■		
Friendliness toward strangers:	■■■■	WEIGHT: male: 70–90 lb; female: 60–80 lb*	
Ease of training:	■■	HEIGHT: male: 22″ and up; female: 21″ and up	

POPULARITY: Somewhat popular
FAMILY: Livestock, Herding
AREA OF ORIGIN: England
DATE OF ORIGIN: 1800s
ORIGINAL FUNCTION: Sheep herding
TODAY'S FUNCTION: Herding trials
OTHER NAME: None

HISTORY

The Old English Sheepdog originated in the west of England, possibly from the Bearded Collie or Russian Owtcharka. The breed was the answer to the need for a strong dog capable of defending the flocks and herds from the wolves that existed at one time in England. By the middle of the nineteenth century, these dogs were used mainly to drive cattle and sheep to market. As working dogs, they were exempt from dog taxes, but their tails had to be docked as proof of their occupation. This custom continues in modern times and has led to their nickname Bobtail. The breed was first exhibited in the late 1800s, and by the early 1900s the breed was a popular show exhibit. The Old English was recognized by the AKC in 1905. Early Old English Sheepdogs could be brown,

ILLUSTRATED STANDARD

1 Eyes brown or blue (or one of each)
2 Well-defined stop
3 Skull capacious and rather broad
4 Medium-sized ears, carried flat to head
5 Lower at withers than at loin
6 Round hindquarters
7 Tail naturally bobtailed or (more often) docked close to body
8 Small, round feet

Color: any shade of gray, grizzle, blue, blue merles with or without white markings
DQ: none

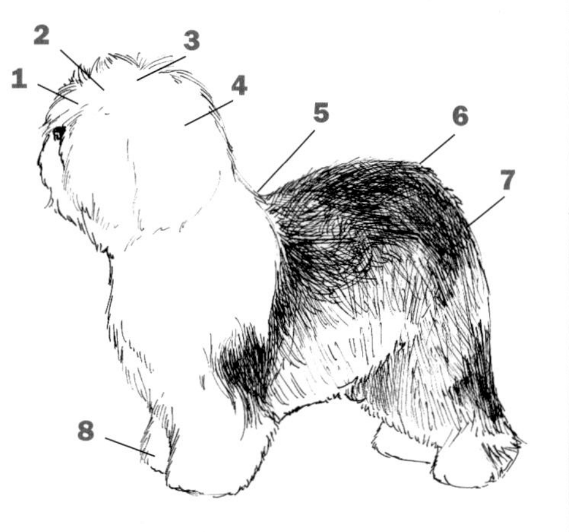

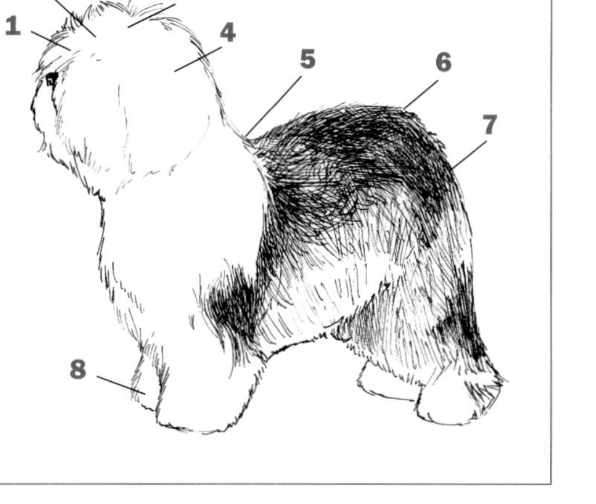

but were later restricted to shades of gray with white. Although the modern Bobtail is very similar to the early specimens, it has a more profuse coat and compact body. Popularity as a pet was slower to grow, until the 1970s when the breed became a favorite media animal. Its popularity exploded with pet owners wanting an exotic but lovable mop. Since that time, its numbers have gradually declined, but the OES still remains a well-known breed. It is now more often seen as a pet or show dog than a working dog.

TEMPERAMENT

The amiable Old English is jolly but gentle. At home, it is a well-mannered house pet that often amuses its family with comical antics. It thrives on human companionship and is very much a homebody. It is extremely devoted to its family and protective of family members, tending children as flock members. It is friendly toward strangers. Some can be headstrong.

UPKEEP

The Old English Sheepdog needs daily exercise, either a moderate to long walk or a vigorous romp. It particularly enjoys herding. Its coat needs brushing or combing every other day, or it may form mats. It may tend to track in debris.

HEALTH

- Major concerns: CHD
- Minor concerns: gastric torsion, otitis externa, retinal detachment, cataract, deafness, PRA, cerebellar ataxia, hypothyroidism
- Occasionally seen: none
- Suggested tests: hip, eye, thyroid, (hearing)
- Life span: 10–12 years

FORM AND FUNCTION

This is a square-proportioned, thick-set dog, combining agility with strength. Its compact body is broader at the rump than shoulders. A distinguishing characteristic is the topline, which is lower at the withers than the loin. Its gait is free and powerful, ground covering, yet gives the appearance of being effortless. It may pace or amble at slower speeds. Its ambling gait is sometimes described as a "bearlike" roll or shuffle. The coat is profuse, but not excessive. It consists of a waterproof undercoat and a hard, shaggy outer coat that is neither straight nor curly. The expression is intelligent. The Bobtail's bark should be loud, with a "pot-casse" ring to it.

Polish Lowland Sheepdog

AT A GLANCE

Energy level:	■■■■	Watchdog ability:	■■■■■	POPULARITY: Very rare
Exercise requirements:	■■■■	Protection ability:	■■■■	FAMILY: Livestock, Herding
Playfulness:	■■■■	Grooming requirements:	■■■■	AREA OF ORIGIN: Poland
Affection level:	■■■■	Cold tolerance:	■■■■	DATE OF ORIGIN: Ancient
Friendliness toward dogs:	■■■	Heat tolerance:	■■	ORIGINAL FUNCTION: Sheep herding
Friendliness toward other pets:	■■■■			TODAY'S FUNCTION: Sheep herding, companion
Friendliness toward strangers:	■■	WEIGHT: 30–35 lb*		
Ease of training:	■■■■	HEIGHT: male: 18–20″; female: 17–19″		OTHER NAME: Polski Owczarek Nizinny, PON

HISTORY

The Polish Lowland Sheepdog is known in much of the world as the Polski Owczarek Nizinny (pronounced pole-ski off-chair-ick na-gin-nee), and even in America it goes by its nickname, the PON. The breed's origins probably reach back to Central Asia from one or more Tibetan breeds, such as the Tibetan Terrier, which were probably introduced to Eastern Europe by Tibetan traders. The long-coated Tibetan dogs were probably interbred with corded-coated Hungarian sheepdogs introduced by the Huns in the fourth century. While large flock-guarding dogs staved off large predators, the smaller PONs worked with shepherds to move and control sheep, and also kept watch against intruders. Unlike larger dogs, they didn't scare the sheep and they could work all day. They

ILLUSTRATED STANDARD

1 Oval eyes
2 Heart-shaped drop ears
3 Level topline
4 Short, low-set tail, no longer than two vertebra; may be docked
5 Heavy bone
6 Oval feet

Color: All colors are acceptable
DQ: none

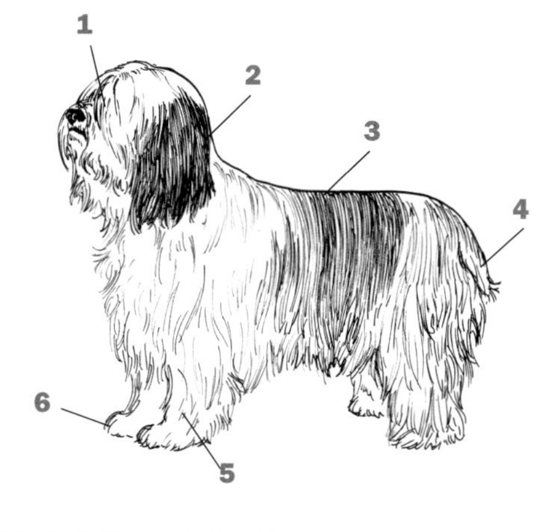

worked on the Polish lowlands for centuries until interest in purebred dogs and livestock swept through Europe in the late 1800s and early 1900s. This, combined with Polish national pride following World War I, created interest in promoting and selectively breeding the PON. Several PONs left the plains to live and work on large estates. In 1924 PONs were shown at a Warsaw poultry and dog show. PONs breeders were in the midst of starting a registry when Germany invaded Poland in 1939. Most dogs had to be abandoned, but legend has it that a Warsaw PON named Psyche was valued for her ability to predict incoming bombs, alerting people to take cover in shelters. Only about 150 PONs remained after the war, but several fanciers sought to reconstitute the breed. The first PONs were registered with the Polish Kennel Club in 1957. A PON named Smok was influential in modeling the breed standard, which was approved in 1959. PONs were exhibited at the World Dog Show in 1965, exposing them to dog fanciers from around the world. In 1987 eight fanciers formed the American Polski Owczarek Nizinny Club. In 2001 the PON was admitted to the AKC under the English translation of its name, Polish Lowland Sheepdog.

TEMPERAMENT

Lively and loyal, the PON has been shaped by centuries of work as a shepherd. This is a territorial breed that is often wary of strangers; however, to those it knows it is very affectionate. A PON's bark is one of its best friends, and the typical PON shows it off often. The PON has an independent and even willful side. It learns quickly, but sees no use in following commands blindly. Despite its shaggy dog look, the PON can be a serious dog. PONs are good with considerate children, most other pets, and most other dogs, although if challenged by a dog, they will hold their own.

UPKEEP

The PON is not a cuddly overgrown lapdog, but a serious worker that needs a job to be satisfied. This dog needs to exercise its body and mind daily. It flourishes when allowed to herd or learn agility. The PON does not accept extended confinement, but does best living inside and working and playing outside. Its coat needs considerable care, preferably brushing every couple of days.

HEALTH

- Major concerns: CHD
- Minor concerns: none
- Occasionally seen: none
- Suggested tests: hip, eye
- Life span: 10–14 years

FORM AND FUNCTION

The PON is a cobby, medium-sized dog, slightly longer than tall, giving it great agility. It is strong and muscular, enabling it to control livestock. It has a fluid gait, with long stride, allowing it to trot effortlessly for hours. It is inclined to amble, which can act as a reconnaissance energy-efficient gait. Toeing in is considered natural. The coat is long, dense, shaggy, and double, providing great protection against the elements. The PON is shown naturally, without scissoring.

Puli

AT A GLANCE

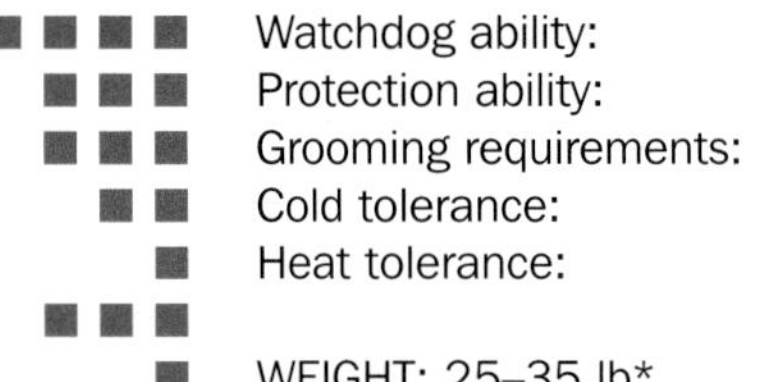

Energy level:	■■■■	Watchdog ability:	■■■■■	POPULARITY: Rare
Exercise requirements:	■■■	Protection ability:	■■■■■	FAMILY: Livestock, Herding
Playfulness:	■■■	Grooming requirements:	■■■■■	AREA OF ORIGIN: Hungary
Affection level:	■■	Cold tolerance:	■■■■	DATE OF ORIGIN: Middle Ages
Friendliness toward dogs:	■	Heat tolerance:	■■	ORIGINAL FUNCTION: Sheep Herding
Friendliness toward other pets:	■■■			TODAY'S FUNCTION: Herding trials
Friendliness toward strangers:	■	WEIGHT: 25–35 lb*		OTHER NAME: Hungarian Puli, Hungarian Water Dog
Ease of training:	■■	HEIGHT: male: ideally 17″; female: ideally 16″		

HISTORY

Around the ninth century the Magyar tribes came from the eastern Urals to occupy the central Danube area, intermingling with Turkish people along the way. They brought with them various sheepdogs, including the forebear of the modern Puli. The Puli's resemblance in body structure to the Tibetan Spaniel has led some to surmise that the latter may have played a role in the Puli's development. Whatever the origin, the small dogs were agile sheepherders, able even to turn a sheep by jumping on its back. The black color was important so that it could be easily spotted by the shepherd among the sheep. Thus, the Magyar's larger dogs were probably used as nighttime guards, and the small black dogs as daytime herders. After the decimation of Hungary by invaders in the sixteenth century, the country

ILLUSTRATED STANDARD

1 Almond-shaped eyes
2 Skull slightly domed
3 Ears V-shaped, hanging, medium-sized
4 Back level
5 Tail carried over back, blending into backline
6 Feet round

Color: solid black, rusty black, gray, and white
DQ: none

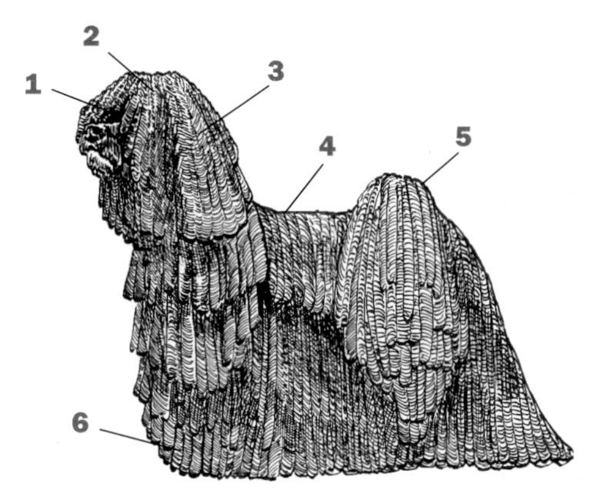

was repopulated by people, sheep, and dogs from western Europe. These dogs interbred with the native Pulik to produce the Pumi, and then the Puli and Pumi were interbred to such an extent that the original Puli breed was nearly lost. In the early 1900s, an effort began to resurrect the Puli; the first standard was written in 1925. Around that time, Pulik in Hungary varied greatly in height from large "police" through medium "working" to small "dwarf" sizes. The medium-sized dogs were most representative of the traditional herding Puli and were established as the desired size. In 1935, the United States Department of Agriculture imported several Pulik in an effort to improve herding dogs in America. This effort was thwarted by war, but the breed's working ability became known in America, and by 1936 the AKC recognized the Puli. The breed's fame spread farther throughout Europe as a result of Hungarians fleeing the war, bringing with them their dogs. The modern Puli remains an adept herder, but it enjoys only modest popularity as a pet or show dog.

TEMPERAMENT

A mop on springs, the Puli is full of bouncing energy. It is busy and curious and needs daily exercise. This smart dog is also headstrong and tough. It can be aggressive toward other dogs. Alert and watchful, it is also protective of its family. It barks a lot.

UPKEEP

This is an energetic breed on the lookout for a job, preferably something to herd. It can be satisfied with a good walk or jog, or a lively game and training session, however. Its coat can hold debris. Its nonshedding coat can be brushed or corded; if brushed, it needs brushing every one to two days. If corded, the cords must be regularly separated because the coat tends to hold dirt; bathing is time consuming and drying takes as much as one day. Pets can be clipped.

HEALTH

- Major concerns: CHD
- Minor concerns: none
- Occasionally seen: PRA, deafness, degenerative myelopathy, patellar luxation
- Suggested tests: hip, eye, (hearing), knee, DNA for myelopathy
- Life span: 10–15 years

FORM AND FUNCTION

The Puli is a compact dog of square proportion and medium bone. Its gait at a trot is quick stepping, but neither far reaching nor mincing. It is of utmost importance that the Puli be able to change directions instantly, and it is quick, agile, and even acrobatic. Its weatherproof coat consists of a soft, wooly, dense undercoat and a wavy or curly outer coat. This coat will form round or flattened cords, but it may also be brushed out.

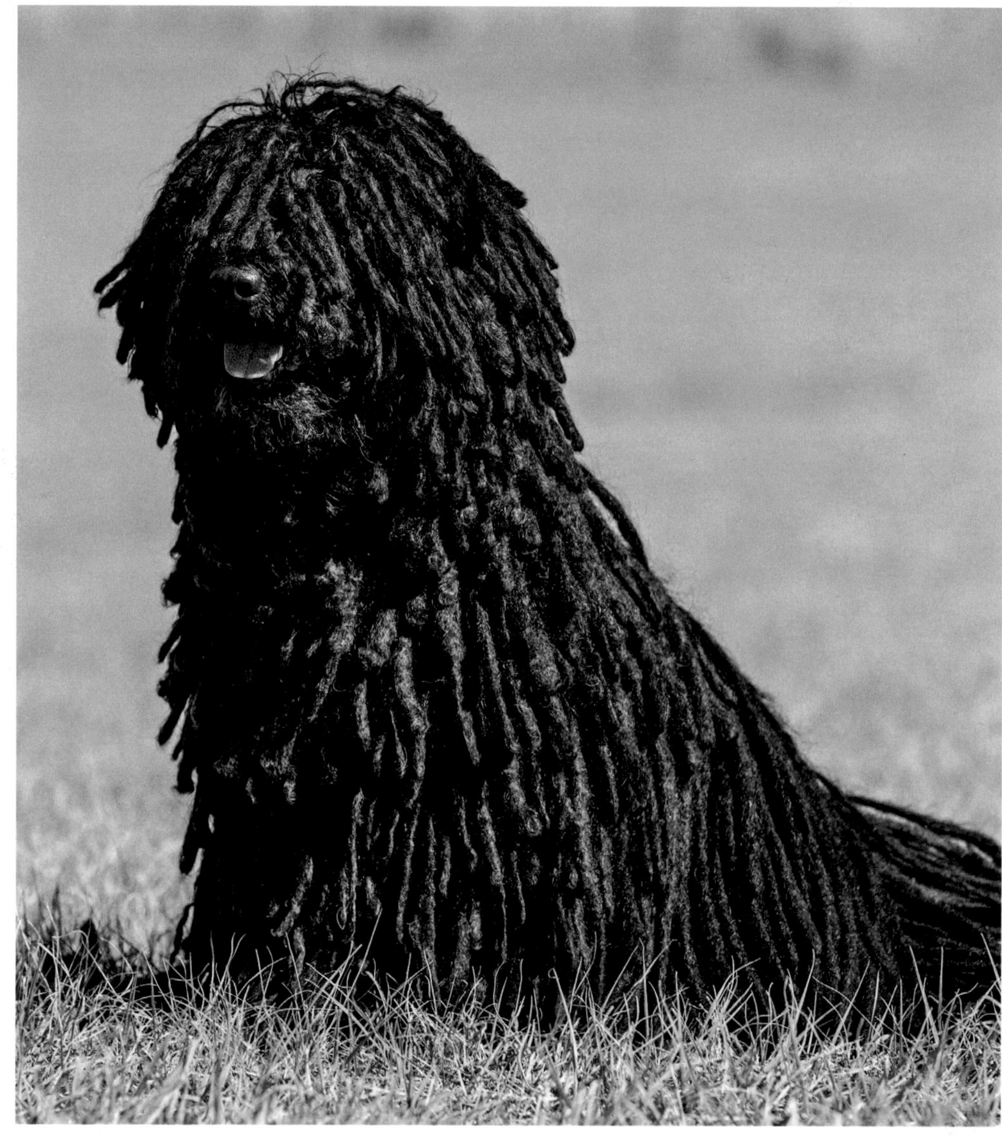

Pyrenean Shepherd

AT A GLANCE

Energy level:	■■■■■
Exercise requirements:	■■■■
Playfulness:	■■■■■
Affection level:	■■■■■
Friendliness toward dogs:	■■
Friendliness toward other pets:	■■
Friendliness toward strangers:	■■
Ease of training:	■■■■

Watchdog ability:	■■■■■
Protection ability:	■■■
Grooming requirements:	■■■■
Cold tolerance:	■■■
Heat tolerance:	■■■

WEIGHT: 15–30 lb*
HEIGHT: Rough-faced: male: 15.5–18.5″; female: 15–18″; Smooth-faced: male: 15.5–21″; female: 15–20.5″

POPULARITY: Very rare
FAMILY: Herding
AREA OF ORIGIN: France
DATE OF ORIGIN: Ancient
ORIGINAL FUNCTION: Herding
TODAY'S FUNCTION: Herding, service dog, agility, obedience
OTHER NAME: None

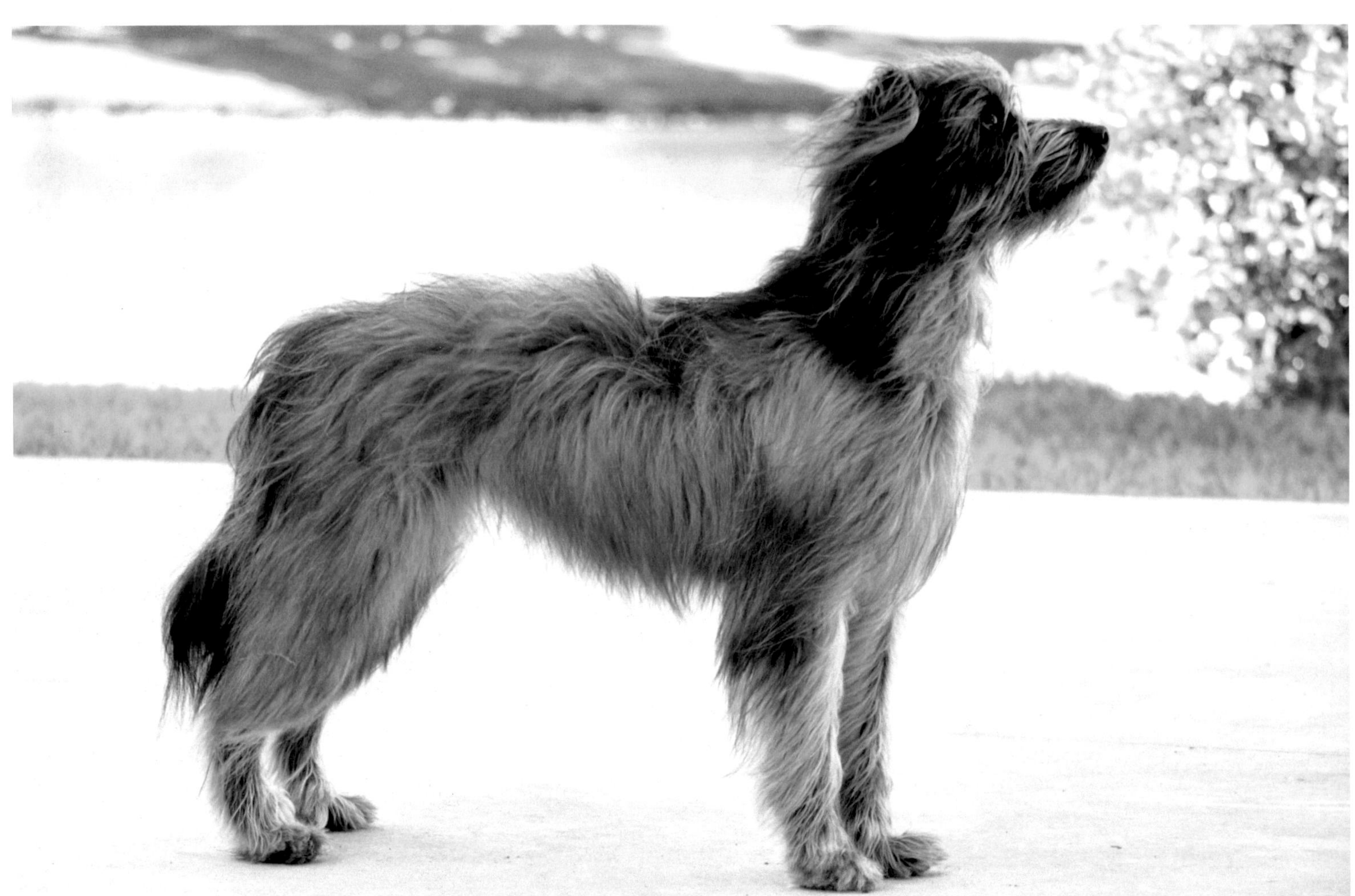

HISTORY

Sheep and goat herding were well established in the Pyrenees Mountains of southern France by 6000 B.C., and bones of small dogs were found in the region long before then. By Medieval times, shepherds and their dogs are mentioned in accounts of Pyrenean life. The quick and agile small dogs controlled the flocks while the larger ones, Great Pyrenees, guarded them. Just two Pyrenean Shepherds can control a flock of 1,000 sheep; they may cover 25 miles a day. In 1858, a Pyrenean Shepherd was with the shepherdess Bernadette Soubirous at Lourdes when the Virgin Mary appeared to her, giving the breed the designation as "the dog who saw God." During World War I, many hundreds of Pyr Sheps (as they are called for short) served as couriers and as search and rescue dogs. The officer in charge of war dogs proclaimed them "the most intelligent, the most cunning, the most able, and the fastest" of the breeds. In 1905, an association was formed to preserve the Pyr Shep and Great Pyrenees. Although some Pyr Sheps came to America in the 1800s with

ILLUSTRATED STANDARD

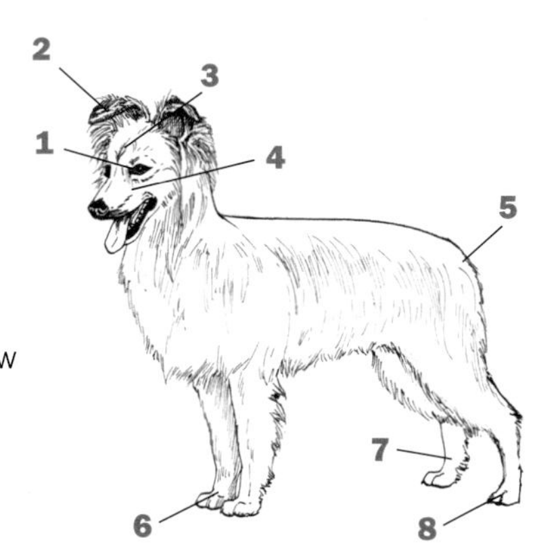

1. Almond-shaped, open eyes
2. Ears either cropped straight across to stand erect; or natural, semi-prick with a third to half falling forward or sideways
3. No marked stop
4. Muzzle slightly shorter than skull; slightly longer and pointier in Smooth-Faced.
5. Tail docked, natural bob, or naturally long; set low and carried horizontally or lower; crook at end
6. Oval feet
7. Single or double dewclaws may be present on rear legs
8. Hind feet toe out slightly

Color: all shades of tan, with or without black hairs; all shades of gray; merle; brindle; black; black with white not exceeding 30 percent of the body
DQ: below minimum height; above maximum height by more than 0.5″; missing pigment on eye rims; blue eyes on any dog other than merle; nose other than black; overshot or undershot; white exceeding 50 percent of the body

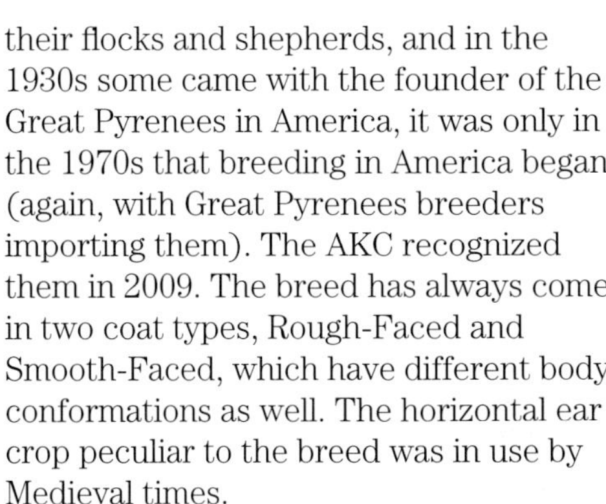

their flocks and shepherds, and in the 1930s some came with the founder of the Great Pyrenees in America, it was only in the 1970s that breeding in America began (again, with Great Pyrenees breeders importing them). The AKC recognized them in 2009. The breed has always come in two coat types, Rough-Faced and Smooth-Faced, which have different body conformations as well. The horizontal ear crop peculiar to the breed was in use by Medieval times.

TEMPERAMENT

The Pyrenean Shepherd is strongly oriented toward working and herding. It is extremely active, attentive, and obedient, and is among the very top breeds for agility, obedience, and herding. It is a versatile herder, both driving and gathering. It is distrustful of strangers, but strongly devoted to and affectionate with its family. Some can be very shy. Some get along well with other dogs and pets, but some can have jealousy issues. They can bark exuberantly, and are good watchdogs.

UPKEEP

This is among the most active, work driven, and responsive of all breeds. The Pyrenean Shepherd must have an outlet for its racing mind and body every day. It should have a vigorous run or long jog several times a week and some sort of mental challenges daily. Without this, it can be frustrated and destructive; with it, it can be the most impressively smart and well-behaved dog around. Both coat types require less care than they would seem. Weekly brushing should suffice.

HEALTH

- Major concerns: none
- Minor concerns: CHD, patellar luxation, epilepsy, PDA, choroidal hypoplasia
- Occasionally seen: none
- Suggested tests: hip, heart, eye, patella
- Life span: 14–16 years

FORM AND FUNCTION

A small, sinewy, light-boned dog, the Pyrenean Shepherd is a superb athlete, incredibly agile and ready for action. It should be in lean condition, with just enough flesh to cover the bones; the ribs should be readily felt. The Rough-Faced dog is clearly longer than tall; the Smooth-Face appears more square. Both Smooth-Faced and Rough-Faced (including both demi-long and long-haired coat types), are born in the same litters. The Rough-Faced dog's coat can be of almost flat demi-long or long hair. Demi-long dogs have culottes on the rump. Longhaired dogs have harsh wooly hair that may cord, especially on the elbows, croup, and thighs. The hair on the muzzle lengthens toward the cheeks, giving a windblown look. The Smooth-Faced dog's muzzle has short hair on the muzzle and legs, with the body hair 2 to 3 inches long on the body, and some feathering on the legs. The Pyr Shep's flowing gait is said to "shave the earth."

Shetland Sheepdog

AT A GLANCE

Energy level:	■ ■ ■	Watchdog ability:	■ ■ ■ ■ ■	POPULARITY: Very popular
Exercise requirements:	■ ■ ■	Protection ability:	■	FAMILY: Livestock, Herding
Playfulness:	■ ■ ■	Grooming requirements:	■ ■ ■ ■	AREA OF ORIGIN: Scotland (Shetland Island)
Affection level:	■ ■ ■	Cold tolerance:	■ ■ ■	DATE OF ORIGIN: 1800s
Friendliness toward dogs:	■ ■ ■ ■	Heat tolerance:	■ ■ ■	ORIGINAL FUNCTION: Sheep herder
Friendliness toward other pets:	■ ■ ■ ■			TODAY'S FUNCTION: Sheep herding, herding trials
Friendliness toward strangers:	■	WEIGHT: about 20 lb*		
Ease of training:	■ ■ ■ ■ ■	HEIGHT: 13–16″		OTHER NAME: None

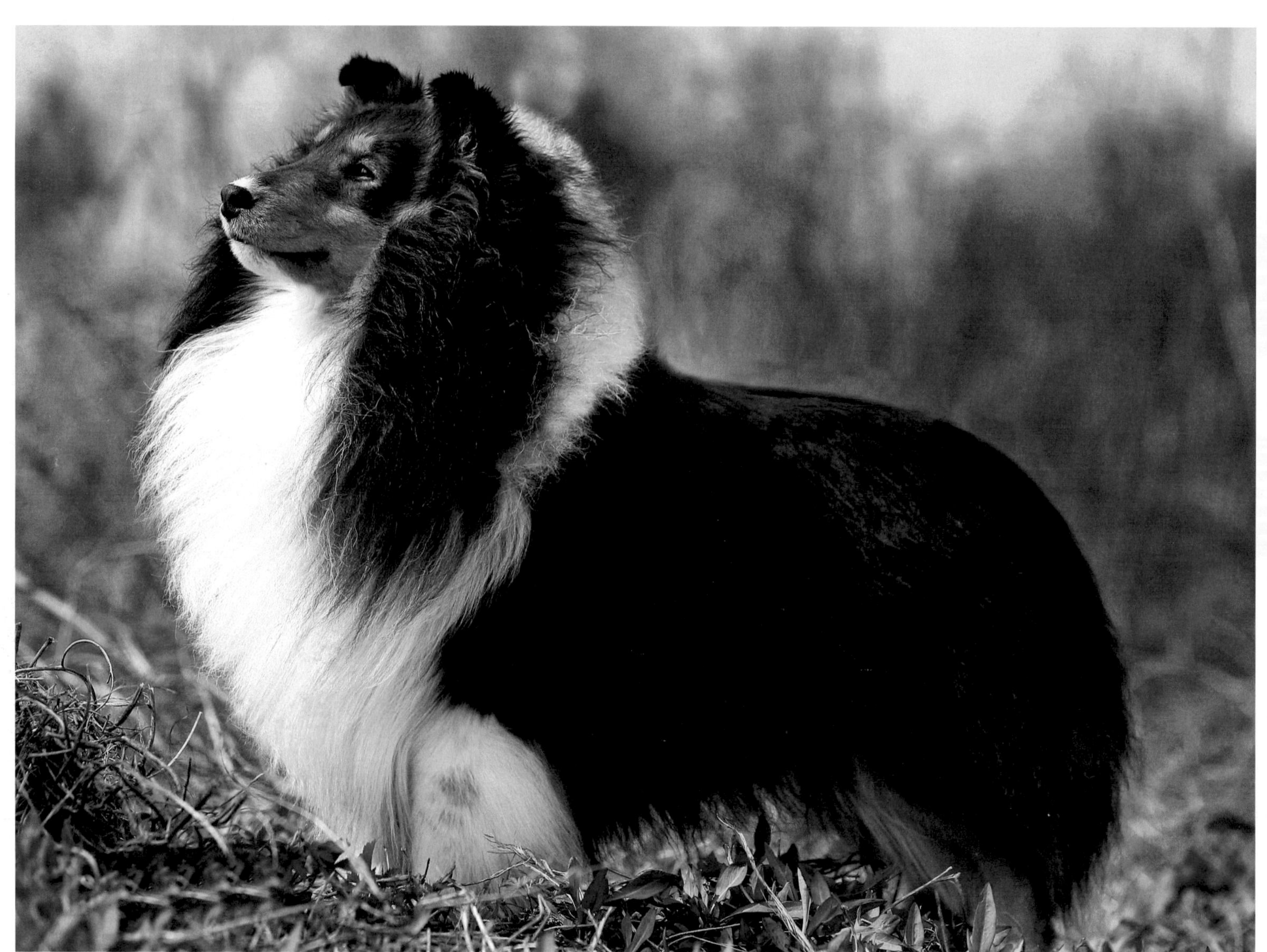

HISTORY

The ancestors of the Shetland Sheepdog were the herding dogs of Scotland that also provided the root stock for the Collie and Border Collie. Some of these dogs were quite small, measuring only about 18 inches in height. The Shetland Sheepdog almost certainly is derived from these early Collie type dogs, which then were further developed on the Shetland Islands. Some Iceland dogs may have also played a role, and perhaps even a black and tan King Charles Spaniel. The paucity of vegetation favored smaller livestock, and the animals needed to herd them were proportionately smaller. In a land with few fences, an adept herder was essential to keep livestock away from cultivated land. As an all-around farm dog, they herded not only sheep but also ponies and chickens. In some

ILLUSTRATED STANDARD

1 Head forms a long, blunt wedge viewed from front or side
2 Almond-shaped eyes
3 Skull flat
4 Small ears, carried erect with top fourth tipping forward
5 Tail carried low
6 Feet oval

Color: black, blue merle, and sable, marked with varying amounts of white and/or tan
DQ: above or below 13–16″; brindle color

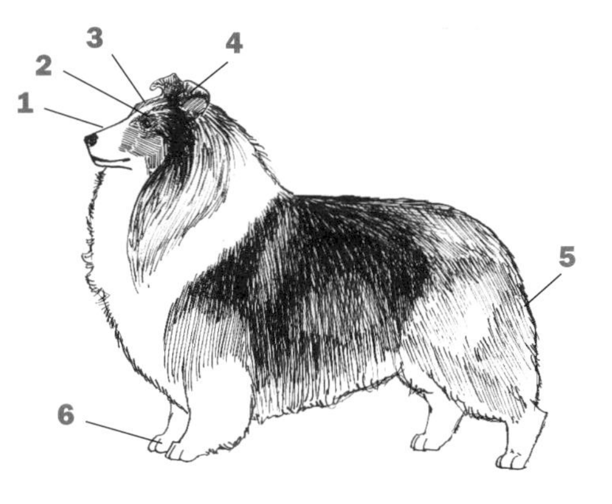

remote areas, it was customary to keep all animals in the family's home building during winter, and the amiable herding dog no doubt worked its way right into the family part of the home. Because of their isolation from the rest of the world, the breed was able to breed true in a comparatively short time. The British naval fleet used to frequent the islands for maneuvers, and often bought puppies to take home to England. Early dogs were referred to as Toonie dogs (Toon being the local Shetland word for farm), but they were initially shown (around 1906) as Shetland Collies. Collie fanciers objected to the name, so it was changed to Shetland Sheepdog. The breed is far more often referred to by its nickname of "Sheltie," however. In the early years in England breeders often discreetly crossed Shelties with rough-coated Collies in an attempt to improve on their Collie characteristics. This practice led to oversized Shelties, however, and has long since stopped. Following the immense popularity of the Collie, the Sheltie became the answer to the family wanting a loyal striking pet of smaller size, and is one of the most popular breeds in the world.

TEMPERAMENT

The Shetland Sheepdog is extremely bright, extremely sensitive, and extremely willing to please. This combination makes for a dog that is very obedient, quick to learn, and utterly devoted to its family. It is not only gentle, playful, amiable, and companionable, but also excellent with children, although it can nip at heels in play. It is reserved and often timid toward strangers. It barks a lot.

UPKEEP

The Sheltie is energetic, but its exercise needs can be met with a good walk, short jog, or active game and training session. Its thick coat needs brushing or combing every other day.

HEALTH

- Major concerns: dermatomyositis
- Minor concerns: CEA, PRA, trichiasis, cataract, CHD, hemophilia, hypothyroidism, Legg-Perthes, patellar luxation, allergies
- Occasionally seen: PDA, deafness, epilepsy
- Suggested tests: eye, hip
- Life span: 12–14 years
- Note: May be sensitive to ivermectin. Merles should not be bred to merles because homozygous merle is lethal or detrimental to health.

FORM AND FUNCTION

The Shetland Sheepdog is a small, agile dog, longer than it is tall. Its gait is smooth, effortless, and ground covering, imparting good agility, speed, and endurance essential in a herding dog. It has a double coat, with a short, dense undercoat and a long, straight, harsh outer coat. The hair of the mane, frill, and tail is abundant. Its expression is gentle, intelligent, and questioning. Although it resembles a Rough Collie in miniature, subtle differences distinguish the breeds.

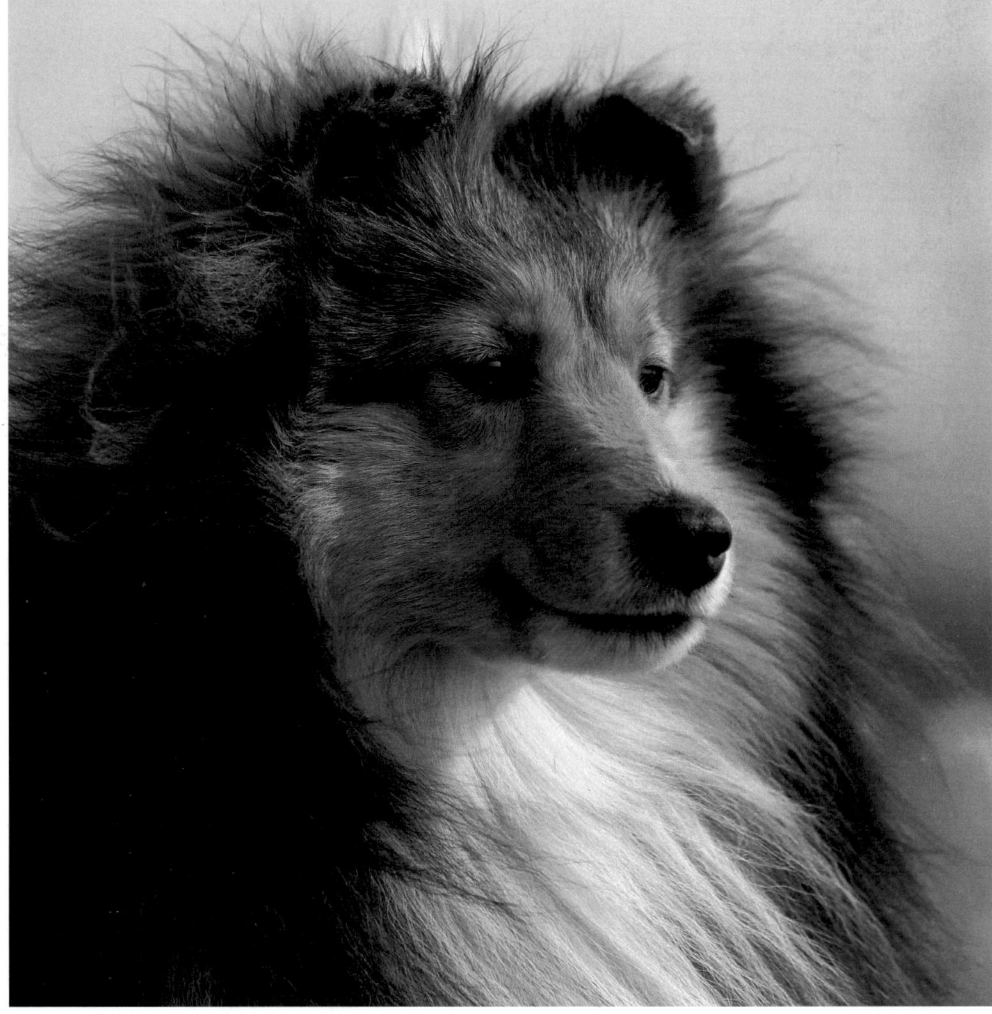

Spanish Water Dog

AT A GLANCE

Energy level:	■ ■ ■ ■	Watchdog ability:	■ ■ ■ ■ ■	POPULARITY: Very rare
Exercise requirements:	■ ■ ■ ■	Protection ability:	■ ■ ■ ■	FAMILY: Water Dog
Playfulness:	■ ■ ■ ■	Grooming requirements:	■ ■	AREA OF ORIGIN: Spain
Affection level:	■ ■ ■ ■	Cold tolerance:	■ ■ ■ ■	DATE OF ORIGIN: At least 1100s
Friendliness toward dogs:	■ ■ ■	Heat tolerance:	■ ■ ■ ■	ORIGINAL FUNCTION: Versatile herder, farm dog, water work
Friendliness toward other pets:	■ ■ ■			
Friendliness toward strangers:	■ ■	WEIGHT: 31–48 lb*		TODAY'S FUNCTION: Herding
Ease of training:	■ ■ ■ ■ ■	HEIGHT: male: 17.5–19.75″; female: 15.75–18″		OTHER NAME: Perro de Agua Espanol, Turco Andaluz

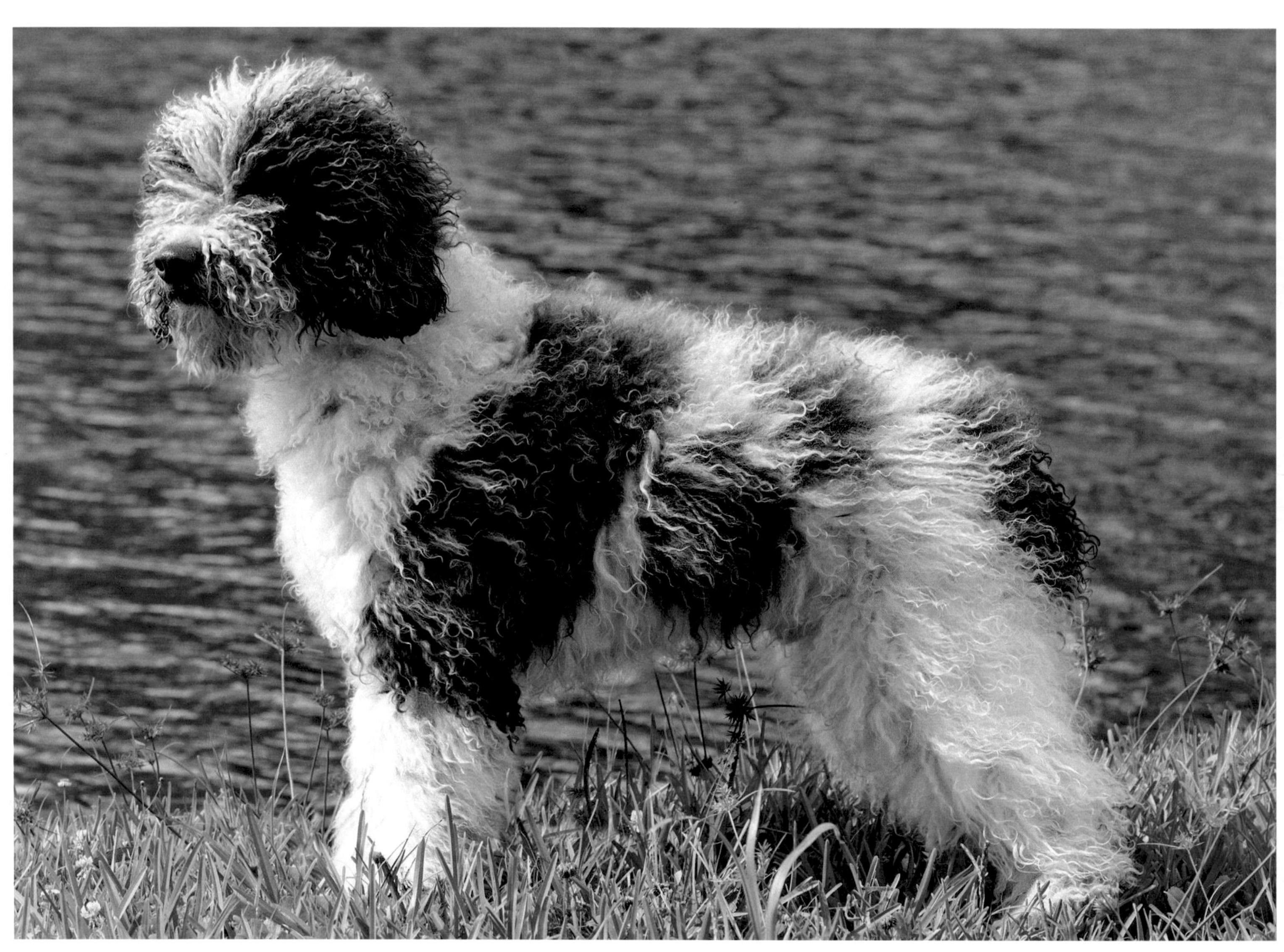

HISTORY

The early history of the Spanish Water Dog is largely speculative, with various theories having their ancestors arising in North Africa, Turkey, Hungary, and even Spain. By 1100 A.D., there are clear references to the dogs in literature. They were used for different tasks in different parts of the Iberian Peninsula. In the northern coastal regions and fishing ports they were all-purpose water dogs, jumping in the water to retrieve fishing tackle, nets, and mooring lines. They may have also been used as hunting dogs. In the central and southern regions they herded and guarded sheep, goats, and cattle, and again, perhaps hunted small game. The Industrial Revolution in Spain gradually drove many dogs out of work, with some jobs being taken over by mechanized means and by destroying coastal fishing areas from

ILLUSTRATED STANDARD

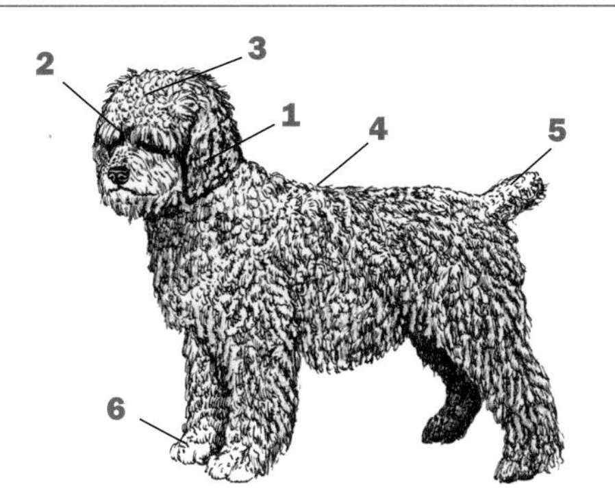

1 Drooping, triangular ears; the tips should not reach past the inside corner of the eye
2 Stop apparent but not abrupt
3 Broad, flat skull
4 Level topline
5 Tail traditionally docked between the second and fourth vertebra; or can be natural bob or any length
6 Round feet

Color: solid black, brown, beige, or white; or one of these colors with white
DQ: parti-colored, where the second color isn't white; tri color, tan point; smooth or wavy coat

pollution. Some dogs remained working as herders, and in 1975 two breeders began an effort to revive the breed. They gathered dogs from all regions, but they mostly gathered Andalucian herding dogs. By 1980 a breed club was established in Spain, and in 1985 the Spanish Kennel Club recognized the breed. In the United States, the UKC recognized them in 2001 and the AKC in 2015. This is an incredibly versatile breed; besides herding they are frequently used as search and rescue dogs, as drug and explosives detection dogs, and they have even been trained as circus dogs.

TEMPERAMENT

This high-energy breed likes activity and challenges. It is intelligent and has an intense desire to please, and is thus highly trainable. It is very affectionate and likes to constantly be with its people. It gets along well with other dogs and pets but is naturally suspicious of strangers. The SWD is protective of its home and family. Like many herding dogs, SWDs can herd children and can be overly sensitive to sudden stimuli. They make excellent watchdogs.

UPKEEP

The SWD needs daily mental and physical challenges that can be met with a long walk, jog, or vigorous games, plus activities like agility, herding, obedience, or water retrieving. Given adequate exercise, it is a calm housedog. The SWD has a non-shedding coat that, over time, tends to form cords. It should never be brushed, and when bathed it should be blotted, not rubbed, dry. The Spanish Water Dog was traditionally sheared once per year, along with the sheep, but now the coat is maintained between one and five inches in length. If cording is desired, there is a natural area of uncorded hair nearest the skin.

HEALTH

- Major concerns: CHD, allergies
- Minor concerns: hypothyroidism
- Occasionally seen: congenital hypothyroidism with goiter (CHG), exocrine pancreatic insufficiency, PRA, cataract, distichiasis
- Suggested tests: DNA for CHG, DNA for PRA, eye, hip, autoimmune thyroiditis test
- Life span: 12 years

FORM AND FUNCTION

The Spanish Water Dog is a sturdy, medium-sized athlete suited for herding, hunting, and assisting fishermen. It is solidly built with moderate bone, neither coarse nor refined. It is slightly longer than tall. The coat is a single coat with distinctly curly hair with wooly texture, adapted to the variable humidity and drought conditions of its homeland. The coat is never brushed but allowed to form curls or cords that cover the entire body, including the head. Its movement is effortless and ground covering, with good reach and drive.

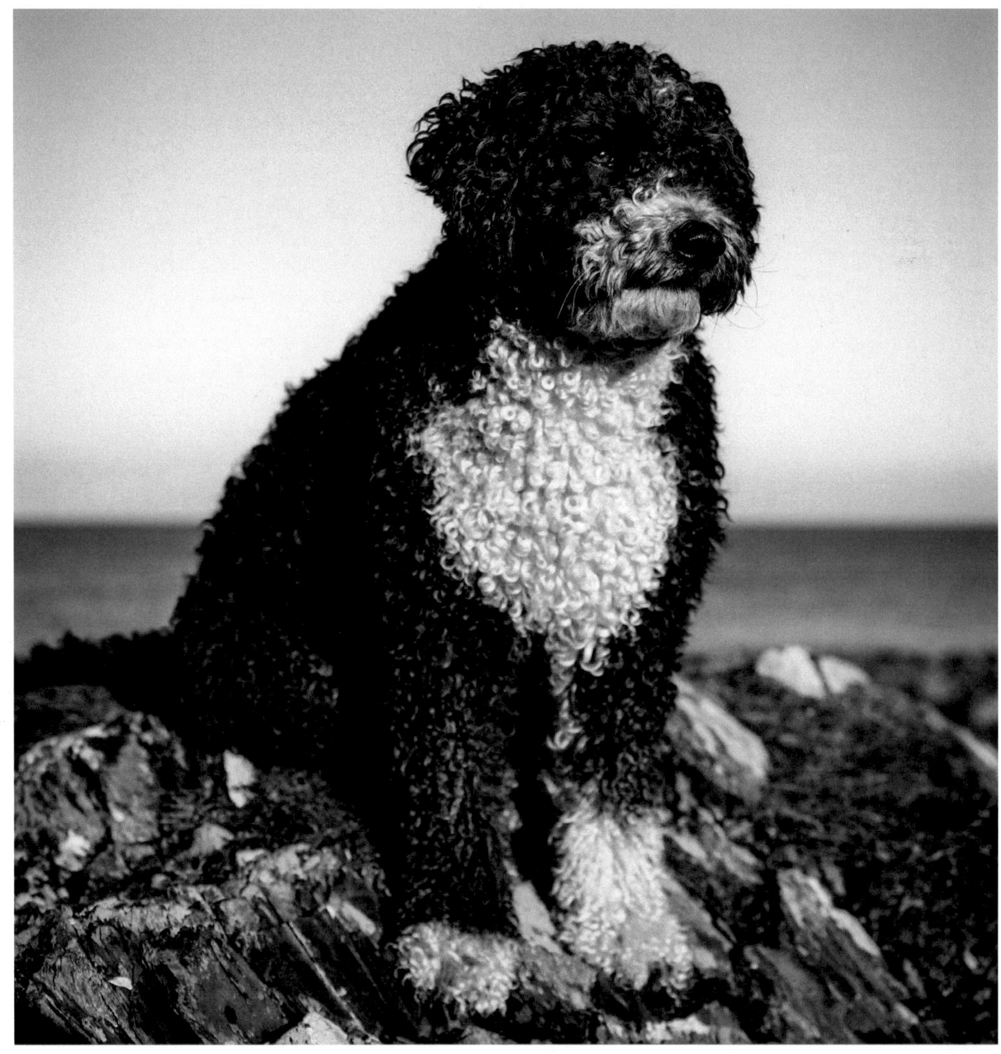

Swedish Vallhund

AT A GLANCE

Energy level:
Exercise requirements:
Playfulness:
Affection level:
Friendliness toward dogs:
Friendliness toward other pets:
Friendliness toward strangers:
Ease of training:

Watchdog ability:
Protection ability:
Grooming requirements:
Cold tolerance:
Heat tolerance:

WEIGHT: 22–35 lb.*
HEIGHT: male: 12.5–13.5″; female: 11.5–12.5″

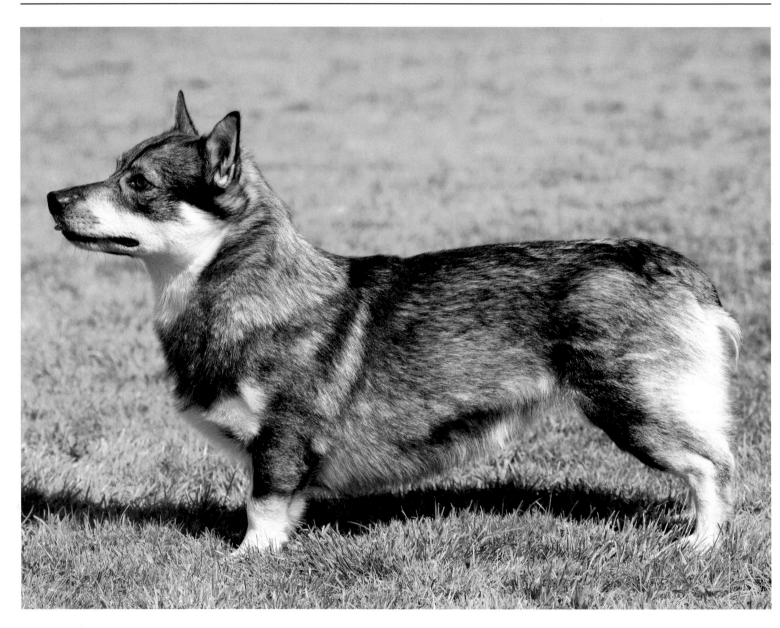

POPULARITY: Very rare
FAMILY: Spitz
AREA OF ORIGIN: Sweden
DATE OF ORIGIN: Viking times
ORIGINAL FUNCTION: Herding, farm dog
TODAY'S FUNCTION: Herding
OTHER NAME: Västgötaspets

HISTORY

The Swedish Vallhund, sometimes referred to as "the little Viking dog," is a dwarf spitz breed that has been used as a farm dog for centuries, possibly since Viking times, when it was known as the Vikingarnas Dog. It herded cattle, controlled vermin, and acted as a watchdog. Interbreeding with Welsh Corgis in the eighth or ninth century has been reported, which accounts for similarities between the breeds. Very little is known of the breed's early history. By 1942, the breed was almost extinct. Two Swedish enthusiasts, Count Bjorn Von Rosen and Karl Gustav Zettersten, began an effort to save the breed, locating one male (named

ILLUSTRATED STANDARD

1 Head rather long and lean, forming a wedge from skull to nose tip
2 Oval eyes
3 Pointed, prick ears set at the outer edge of the skull
4 Stop well defined
5 Level topline
6 Long, stub, or bob tail
7 Short, oval feet, pointing straight forward

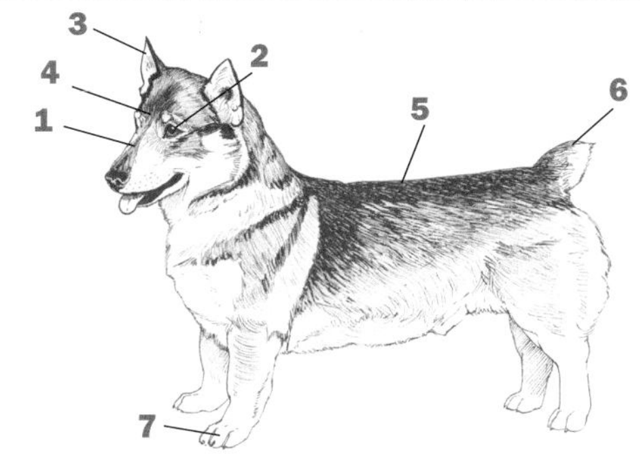

Color: sable in colors of gray through red, lighter harness markings are essential; a well-defined mask with lighter hair around eyes, on the muzzle, and under the throat is desirable

Mopsen) and three females (named Vivi, Lessi, and Topsy), which they used as the foundation for the revived breed. After only one year of exhibition showing, they were recognized by the Swedish Kennel Club as the Svensk Vallhund, which translates to Swedish herder. The name was changed in 1964 to *Västgötaspets*, named after the Swedish province Vastergotland where the revived breeding program originated. The breed came to England in 1974 and was fully recognized as the Swedish Vallhund by the Kennel Club there in 1985. The first Vallhunds came to the United States from England in 1983. They entered the AKC Miscellaneous Class in 2006 and the AKC Herding Group in 2007, but have remained mostly unknown to the general public. Despite being bred from a limited gene pool, the breed is known for its hardiness and health. It exhibits several primitive traits, including a long span of time between estrous seasons.

TEMPERAMENT

The Swedish Vallhund is a confident dog that doesn't let its short stature hold it back. It is energetic and playful when circumstances allow, but calm and mellow when need be. It learns quickly and is eager to please, but has a streak of independence. It enjoys mental challenges and can be too inquisitive for its own good. It is sweet but not fawning. It usually gets along well with other dogs and animals. It's good with considerate children, but can nip heels in play. It can be wary of strangers. It is an excellent watchdog but is not aggressive. It can tend to bark enthusiastically.

UPKEEP

Vallhunds need a medium to high level of activity. A long walk or short jogging venture, along with a mentally challenging game, will usually satisfy their exercise needs. Herding is their favorite activity, but they also enjoy agility. Coat care consists of weekly brushing. They enjoy cold weather but can handle heat as well.

HEALTH

- Major concerns: none
- Minor concerns: CHD
- Occasionally seen: retinopathy, patellar luxation
- Suggested tests: hips, DNA for retinopathy
- Life span: 13–15 years

FORM AND FUNCTION

The Swedish Vallhund is low to the ground (height to length of body is 2:3), enabling it to herd sheep and other farm animals by nipping at their hocks while avoiding their kicks. It is longer legged, shorter bodied, and less stocky compared to Corgis, giving it slightly more speed and agility. Its teeth are large for its skull, helping it when hunting vermin. The medium-length coat is double, with coarse guard hairs and an insulating undercoat to protect against harsh weather. Tails can be any length, from naturally bobbed to full length, even within the same litter, and do not appear to affect function.

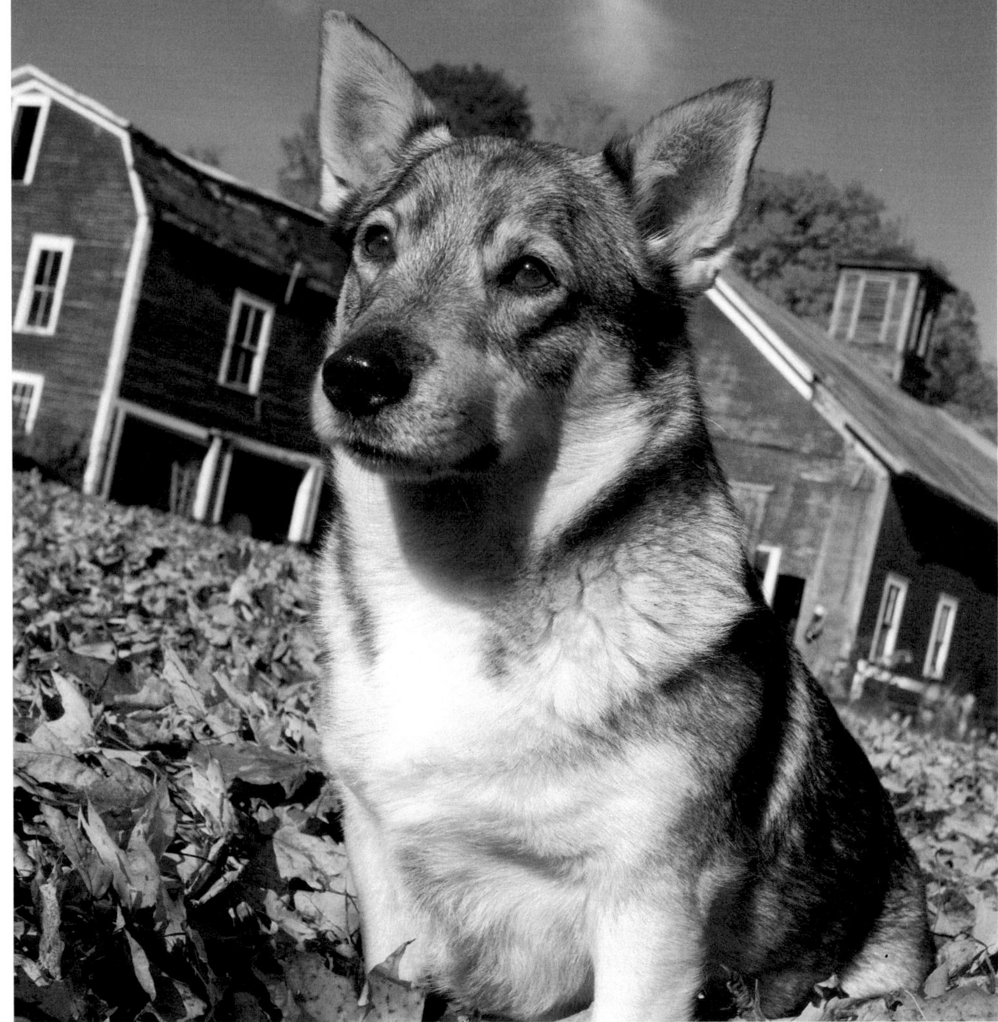

Cardigan Welsh Corgi

AT A GLANCE

Energy level:	■■■
Exercise requirements:	■■■
Playfulness:	■■■
Affection level:	■■■
Friendliness toward dogs:	■■
Friendliness toward other pets:	■■■■
Friendliness toward strangers:	■■■
Ease of training:	■■■■

Watchdog ability:	■■■■■
Protection ability:	■■■■
Grooming requirements:	■
Cold tolerance:	■■■
Heat tolerance:	■■■

WEIGHT: MALE: 30–38 lb; female: 25–34 lb
HEIGHT: 10.5–12.5″

POPULARITY: Somewhat uncommon
FAMILY: Livestock, Herding
AREA OF ORIGIN: Wales
DATE OF ORIGIN: Ancient times
ORIGINAL FUNCTION: Cattle drover
TODAY'S FUNCTION: Cattle drover, herding trials
OTHER NAME: None

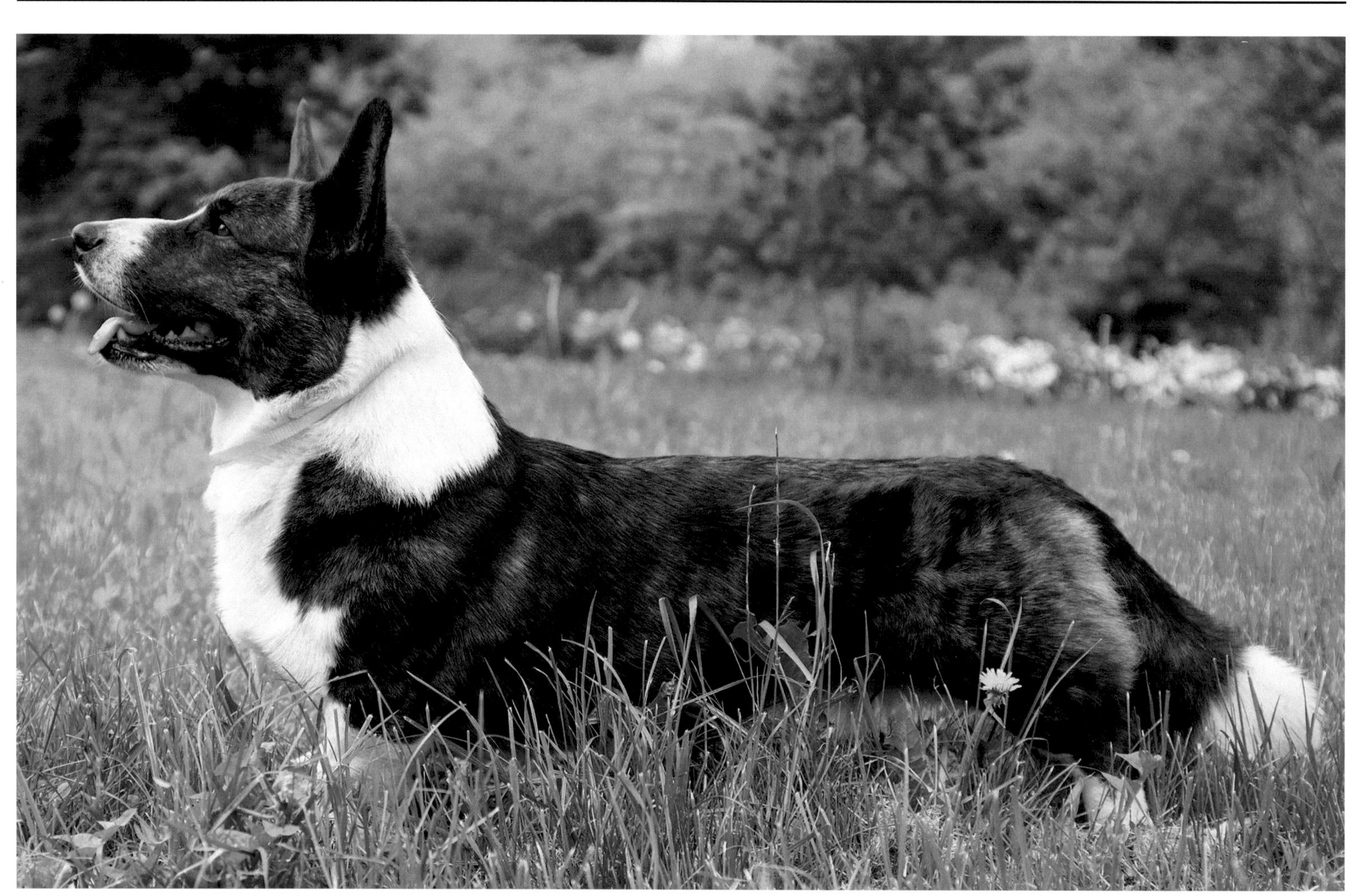

HISTORY

One of the earliest breeds to come to the British Isles, the Cardigan Welsh Corgi was brought from central Europe to Cardiganshire, South Wales centuries ago. Its derivation is unknown, though it may have been influenced by the extinct English turn-spit dog, a short-legged, low-bodied dog used to turn spits in kitchens. Initially used as a family protector and even helper in the hunt, it was only later that the Corgi found its true forte. In a time when the land available to tenant farmers was determined by how much acreage their cattle occupied, it was to the farmer's advantage to have scattered, far-ranging stock. Thus, a dog that would drive, rather than herd, the cattle was an invaluable aid, and the Corgi stepped right into this role, nipping at the cattle's heels and ducking their kicks. In fact the word Corgi probably is derived from Cor (to gather) and Gi (dog). The original Corgis were supposed to measure a Welsh yard (slightly longer than an English yard) from nose to tail-tip, and in parts of Cardiganshire the breed was called the yard-long Dog or Ci-llathed. When the Crown lands were later divided, sold, and fenced, the need for drovers was lost, and the Corgi lost its job. Kept by some as a guard and companion, nonetheless, it became a luxury that few could afford, and it became perilously close to extinction. Crosses with other breeds had been tried, but most were not particularly

ILLUSTRATED STANDARD

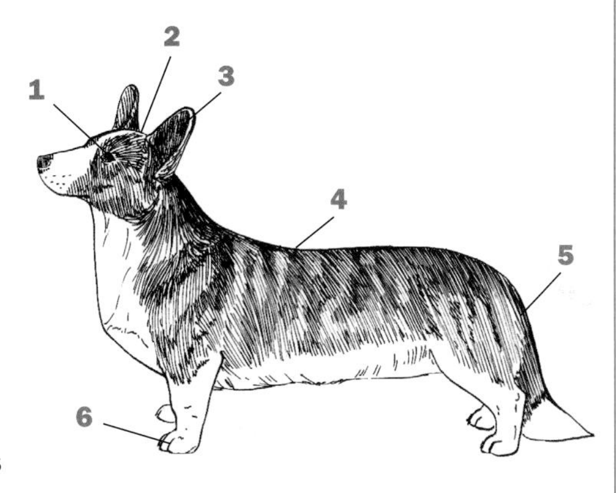

1 Medium to large eyes
2 Moderately flat skull
3 Large ears, slightly rounded at tip
4 Level topline
5 Tail set and carried fairly low, not curled over back
6 Feet large and round, front feet pointing slightly outward

Color: all shades of red, sable, and brindle; also blue merle or black, both with or without tan or brindle points; white flashings common
DQ: blue or partially blue eyes in non-merle dogs; drop ears; non-solid black nose in non-merle dogs; color predominantly white; any color other than specified

FORM AND FUNCTION

The Cardigan is a low-set dog, approximately 1.8 times longer than it is tall, with moderately heavy bone. It is a small but powerful dog capable of the agility, speed, and endurance necessary to drive cattle for extended periods. Its small size allowed it to duck under the cattle's hooves should they kick at the dog. Its gait is free, smooth, effortless, and ground covering. Its double coat consists of a soft thick undercoat and slightly harsh outer coat of medium length. Its expression is alert, gentle, and watchful, yet friendly.

successful. The exception was the cross with the brindle herder, and present-day Cardigans are the products of this slight herder influence. The first Cardigans were shown around 1925. Until 1934, the Cardigan and Pembroke Welsh Corgis were considered one breed, and interbreeding between the two was common. The first Cardigans came to America in 1931, and AKC recognized the breed in 1935. For some unknown reason, the Cardigan has never enjoyed the popularity of the Pembroke Corgi, and remains only modestly popular.

TEMPERAMENT

Fun-loving and high spirited, yet easygoing, the Cardigan is a devoted and amusing companion. This is a hardy breed, capable of a day dodging kicks, so it is agile and tireless. At home it is well mannered, but it is inclined to bark. It tends to be reserved with strangers and can be scrappy with other dogs.

UPKEEP

The Cardigan needs a surprising amount of exercise for its size. Its needs can best be met with a herding session, but a moderate walk or vigorous play session will also suffice. Its coat needs brushing once a week to remove dead hair.

HEALTH

- Major concerns: CHD
- Minor concerns: degenerative myelopathy
- Occasionally seen: PRA, urinary stones
- Suggested tests: hip, eye, (DNA for PRA)
- Life span: 12–14 years

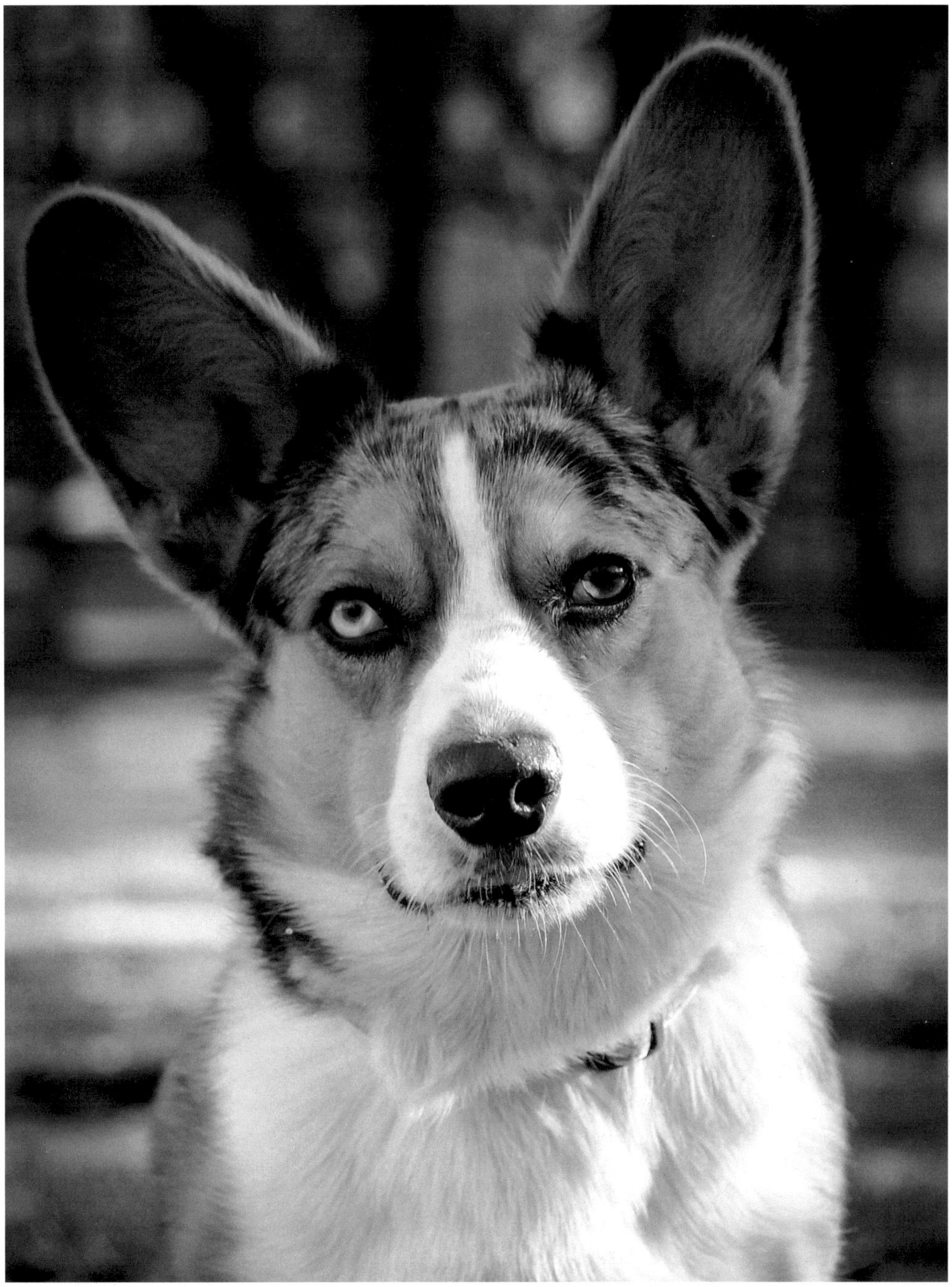

Pembroke Welsh Corgi

AT A GLANCE

Energy level:	■ ■ ■
Exercise requirements:	■ ■ ■
Playfulness:	■ ■ ■
Affection level:	■ ■ ■ ■
Friendliness toward dogs:	■ ■ ■
Friendliness toward other pets:	■ ■ ■ ■
Friendliness toward strangers:	■ ■ ■ ■
Ease of training:	■ ■ ■ ■

Watchdog ability:	■ ■ ■ ■ ■
Protection ability:	■ ■ ■ ■
Grooming requirements:	■
Cold tolerance:	■ ■ ■
Heat tolerance:	■ ■ ■

WEIGHT: male: 27 lb; female: 25 lb (ideally)
HEIGHT: 10–12″

POPULARITY: Very popular
FAMILY: Livestock, Herding
AREA OF ORIGIN: Wales
DATE OF ORIGIN: 1100s
ORIGINAL FUNCTION: Cattle drover
TODAY'S FUNCTION: Cattle drover, herding trials
OTHER NAME: None

HISTORY

The Corgi was an essential helper to the farmers of South Wales. Although these little dogs specialized in herding cattle, nipping at their heels and then ducking under their kicking hooves, they were almost certainly also used in herding sheep and even Welsh ponies. Despite claims for the antiquity of the breed, it is difficult to trace its origins or even authenticate its existence in early times. A Welsh cattle dog is mentioned in a book of the eleventh century, however. Although it certainly shares its past with the Cardigan Welsh Corgi, the Pembroke was developed separately, in Pembrokeshire, Wales. As a hard-working dog, the Corgi was out in the fields when many of the early dog shows were being held. Only in 1926 did a club form and the breed enter the show ring. The first exhibits were straight from the

ILLUSTRATED STANDARD

1 Eyes oval and medium-sized
2 Head foxy in shape and appearance
3 Flat skull
4 Ears erect, tapering to rounded point
5 Tail docked as short as possible
6 Feet oval, turned neither in nor out
7 Forearms turned slightly inward

Color: red, sable, fawn, black and tan, all with or without white flashings
DQ: none

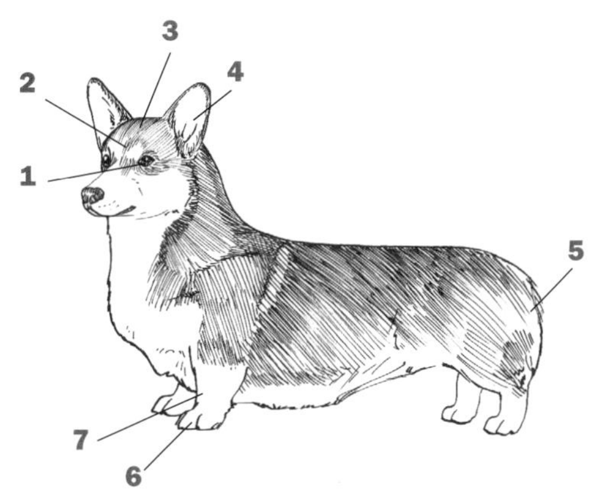

farm and aroused only modest attention. Breeders subsequently strove to improve upon the breed's inherent good looks and were rewarded with increased popularity. The obvious differences between the Pembroke and Cardigan were troublesome to judges—the Pembroke is smaller, with sharper features, a more foxlike expression, and characteristically no tail. In 1934, the Cardigan and Pembroke Corgis were divided into two separate breeds, after which the Pembroke soared in popularity. Its appeal was heightened when it became the favorite of King George VI and, subsequently, Queen Elizabeth II. By the 1960s, the Pembroke had become one of the most popular pet breeds all over the world, but especially in Britain. This popularity has since waned slightly, but far more Pembrokes can be found herding in backyards than in farmyards today.

TEMPERAMENT

Quick and quick-witted, the Pembroke Welsh Corgi has an active mind and body. It needs daily physical and mental exercise to be at its best in the house. It is devoted and willing to please, fun loving, amiable, and companionable. It is very good with children, although it can nip at heels in play. It is usually reserved with strangers. Many bark a lot.

UPKEEP

The Pembroke loves to herd, and a daily herding session would be ideal to meet its exercise requirements. It can do fine without herding, however, as long as it gets a moderate walk on leash or a good play and training session off leash. Coat care consists only of brushing once a week to remove dead hairs.

HEALTH

- Major concerns: intervertebral disc disease, CHD
- Minor concerns: epilepsy, degenerative myelopathy
- Occasionally seen: vWD, PRA, lens luxation, urinary stones
- Suggested tests: hip, eye
- Life span: 11–13 years

FORM AND FUNCTION

The Pembroke Welsh Corgi is moderately long and low, less heavily boned than the Cardigan Welsh Corgi. Its movement is free and smooth, with good reach and drive. This is a breed that needs to be quick and agile, even after herding all day, in order to avoid the cattle's kicking hooves. It combines a weather-resistant undercoat of medium length with a coarser outer coat of slightly longer length. Its expression is intelligent and interested, foxy, but not sly.

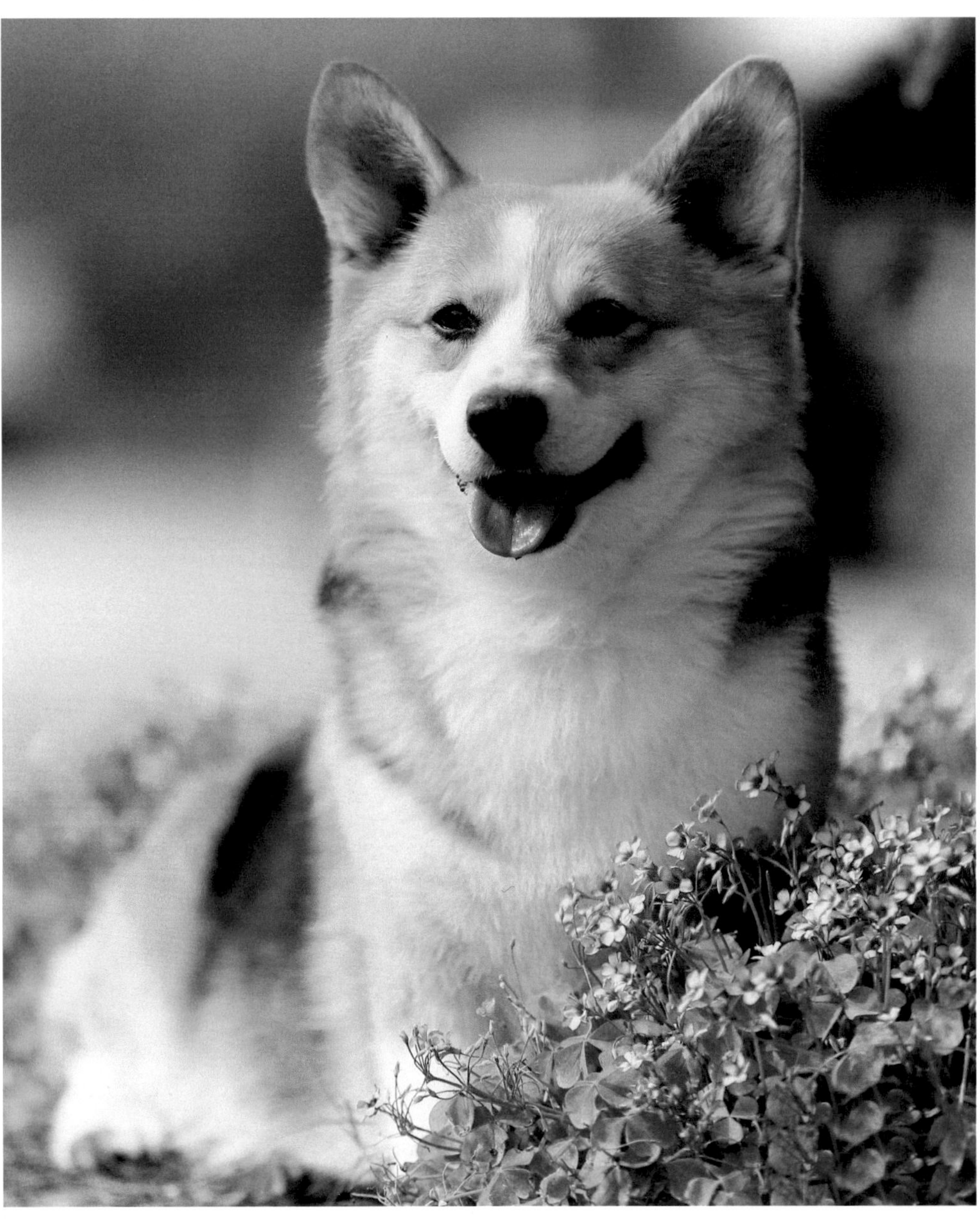

Definitions of Medical Conditions

ABBREVIATIONS USED IN THIS BOOK

ASD: Atrial septal defects
BAER: Brainstem Auditory Evoked Potential
CEA: Collie eye anomaly
CHD: Canine hip dysplasia
CPRA: Central progressive retinal atrophy
CTP: Thrombocytopenia
HOD: Hypertrophic osteodystrophy
JLPP: Juvenile Laryngeal Paralysis and Polyneuropathy
KCS: Keratoconjunctivitis sicca
L2 HGA: L-2 hydroxy-glutaric aciduria
MPS: Mucopolysacharidosis
MVI: Mitral valve insufficiency
OCD: Osteochondritis dissecans
PDA: Patent ductus arteriosus
PDP1: Pyruvate Dehydro Genase Phosphatase 1
PFK: Phosphofructokinase deficiency
PK: Pyruvate kinase deficiency
PPM: Persistent pupillary membrane
PRA: Progressive retinal atrophy
RD/OSD: Retinal dysplasia/Ocuskeletal dysplasia
VKH: Vogt-Koyanagi-Harada-like syndrome
vWD: von Willebrand's disease

DEFINITIONS

Achondroplasia: Type of dwarf-ism with shortened limbs.

Acute moist dermatitis ("hot spots") Area of extremely itchy and inflamed skin.

Addison's (hypoadrenocorticism): Insufficient secretions by the adrenal cortex.

Amyloidosis: Abnormal deposits of amyloid protein in organs, often kidneys, resulting in progressive organ dysfunction.

Ataxia: Incoordination.

Atrial septal defects (ASD): Hole in the wall separating the right and left atria of the heart.

Axonal dystrophy: Problem affecting nerve transmissions.

Basenji enteropathy: Severe progressive intestinal malabsorption resulting in protein loss, intractable diarrhea, and weight loss.

Brachycephalic syndrome: Group of upper airway abnormalities, including stenotic nares and elongated soft palate, affecting breathing in flat-faced dogs.

Canine hip dysplasia (CHD): Abnormal hip assembly wherein the head of the femur does not fit snugly into the pelvic socket.

Cardiomyopathy: Enlargement of the heart resulting from dysfunction of the heart muscle.

Cataract: Opacities of the lens of the eye.

Cauda equina syndrome: Group of neurological signs resulting from compression of the spinal nerves of the lumbosacral vertebral region.

Central progressive retinal atrophy (CPRA): Degeneration of retinal cells beginning with those serving central areas of vision.

Cerebellar abiotrophy: Degeneration of brain neurons, causing progressive incoordination.

Ceroid lipofuscinosis: Metabolic disorder in which a waste product accumulates in brain cells and leading to abnormal neurologic function.

Cherry eye: Tear gland protrudes beyond the "third eyelid," resulting in bright red bulge in the inner corner of the eye.

Chondrodysplasia: Type of dwarfism.

Ciliary dyskinesia: Deformation of cells that normally have cilia, small hair-like appendages that aid in movement of mucous (such as in the lungs and nose).

Colitis: Inflammation of the large bowel causing diarrhea.

Collie eye anomaly (CEA): Congenital abnormalities of varying degrees found in the rear of the eye.

Colonic disease: Large bowel disease.

Compulsive behavior: Behavior that is repeated to excess, to the extent it interferes with normal behavior.

Copper toxicosis: Accumulation of copper in the liver, resulting in chronic hepatitis.

Corneal erosion: Loss of the outer layers of the cornea; can lead to cornea ulcers.

Corneal opacities (corneal dystrophy): Deposits of white or silver spots on the central cornea.

Craniomandibular osteopathy: Abnormal development of the jaw involving excessive bone formation.

Cushing's (hyperadrenocorticism): Excessive secretion of cortisol from the adrenal gland.

Degenerative myelopathy: Progressive loss of coordination and strength beginning in the hind quarters.

Demodicosis: Generalized demodectic mange, a condition caused by the *Demodex* mite to which certain breeds are more susceptible.

Dermatomyositis: Systemic connective disease causing inflammation of both skin and muscles.

Dermoid sinus: Tubular indentation leading from the skin along the midline of the back, sometimes extending into the spinal canal.

Diabetes mellitus: Deficiency in insulin production or utilization.

Digital hyperkeratosis: Thickening of the foot pads leading to cracked, infected, and painful pads.

Distichiasis: Abnormal eyelashes along the lid, irritating the eye.

Ectropion: Outward puckering of the eyelids, leaving a gap between the lid and eye.

Elbow dysplasia (ununited anconeal process): Elbow joint laxity eventually leading to arthritic changes.

Elongated soft palate: Abnormal extension of the soft palate, such that it interferes with breathing.

Entropion: Inward rolling of the eyelids, often irritating the eye.

Epilepsy: Brain disorder resulting in periodic seizures.

Esophageal achalasia: Failure of the walls of the esophagus to relax enough to allow food to pass into the stomach, resulting in regurgitation.

Familial nephropathy: Hereditary impaired kidney function.

Fanconi's syndrome: Reabsorptive defects resulting in kidney failure.

Fragmented coronoid process: Developmental flaw in which a fragment of the ulnar bone of the foreleg never fuses, leaving a chip floating in the elbow, resulting in lameness.

Gastric torsion (gastric dilation-volvulus): Often called "bloat"; twisting of the stomach that traps the stomach contents and gases, and can lead to death if untreated. It is most common in large, deep-chested breeds.

Glaucoma: Increased intraocular pressure.

Globoid cell leukodystrophy: Gradual destruction of white matter in the brain, eventually fatal.

Glycogen storage disease: Deficiency of enzymes required for normal glycogen metabolism, resulting in variable symptoms including weakness.

Hemangiosarcoma: Malignant tumor of the lining of blood vessels, often affecting the heart or spleen, and usually fatal.

Hemivertebra: Partially formed wedge-shaped vertebrae.

Hemophilia A (factor VIII deficiency): Deficiency in clotting factor VIII leading to excessive bleeding.

Hemophilia B (factor IX deficiency): Deficiency in clotting factor IX leading to excessive bleeding.

Histiocytosis: Rapidly progressive malignant cancer infiltrating many parts of body, often including the lungs, liver, spleen, and central nervous system.

Hydrocephalus: Increased accumulation of fluid in the brain. Highest incidence in toy and brachycephalic breeds.

Hypertrophic osteodystrophy: Inflammation of the bone growth plates during periods of rapid growth in large breeds, resulting in lameness.

Hypoglycemia: Abnormally low level of glucose in the blood.

Hypomyelination: Abnormally low amounts of myelin in peripheral nerves, resulting in weakness of limbs.

Hypothyroidism: Decreased production of thyroid hormone, often caused by an auto-immune response. One of the most wide-spread disorders in dogs.

Inguinal hernia: Protrusion of abdominal contents through the inguinal canal.

Intervertebral disk disease: Abnormality of the disks that normally provide cushioning between the vertebra.

Intracutaneous cornifying epithelioma: Benign skin tumor.

Iris coloboma: Pits in the iris (colored portion) of the eye.

Keratoconjunctivitis sicca: Decreased tear production of the eye causing a dry eye and corneal damage.

Lacrimal duct atresia: Abnormally small duct that drains tears from the eye.

Laryngeal paralysis: Paralysis of the larynx, causing noisy or difficult breathing.

Legg–Perthes disease (Legg–Calvé–Perthes): Destruction of the head of the femur bone due to decrease in blood supply.

Lens luxation: Displacement of the lens of the eye.

Lick granuloma: Thickened area of skin, usually of a leg, caused by excessive and often compulsive licking.

Lip fold pyoderma: Infection of the skin around the folds of the lips.

Lumbar-sacral syndrome: Group of neurological signs resulting from compression of the spinal nerves of the lumbosacral vertebral region.

Lupus: Autoimmune condition.

Lymphedema: Swelling due to poor drainage of the lymph system.

Megaesophagus: Paralysis and enlargement of the esophagus, resulting in regurgitation of food.

Meningitis: Inflammation of the membranes surrounding the brain and spinal cord.

Mitral valve insufficiency: Degeneration of the mitral valve of the heart, allowing blood to flow backward into the left atrium and resulting in enlargement of the heart.

Mucopolysacharidosis IIIB: Recessively inherited fatal disease resulting from the lack of an enzyme, giving rise to brain disease.

Muscular dystrophy: Progressive degeneration of skeletal muscles.

Narcolepsy: Episodes of sudden deep sleep.

Narrow palpebral fissure: Abnormally small opening between the eyelids.

Nasal solar dermatitis: Inflammation of the nose surface from exposure to sunlight.

Necrotic myelopathy: Loss of insulating myelin from the spinal cord, resulting in paralysis.

Open fontanel: Incomplete closure of the bones of the skull, resulting in a soft spot on top of the head.

Osteochondritis dissecans: Degeneration of bone underlying the cartilage of joint areas, most often seen in young, fast growing dogs of larger breeds.

Osteosarcoma: Malignant bone cancer. More common in large and giant breeds.

Otitis externa: Infection of the outer ear, including the ear canal. Most common in dogs with long, hanging ears receiving little ventilation.

Pancreatic insufficiency: Inadequate digestive enzyme production by the pancreas, resulting in poor nutrient absorption.

Pancreatitis: Inflammation of the pancreas.

Pannus (chronic superficial keratitis): Corneal inflammation with abnormal growth of vascularized pigment.

Panosteitis: Excessive formation of bone growth in some joints of young dogs resulting in intermittent lameness.

Patellar luxation: Abnormally shallow groove in the knee, so that the knee cap slips in and out of position, causing lameness. Most common in small dogs.

Patent ductus arteriosus: Failure of the embryonic blood vessel connecting the pulmonary artery to the aorta to go away in the postnatal dog, resulting in improper circulation of blood.

Pelger–Huet: Abnormal development of blood neutrophils.

Pemphigus: Auto-immune disease of the skin.

Perianal fistula: Draining tract around the anus.

Persistent pupillary membrane: Abnormality in which strands of iris tissue is stretched across the pupil.

Persistent right aortic arch: Failure of the embryonic right aorta to go away in the postnatal dog, resulting in constriction of the esophagus.

Phosphofructokinase deficiency: Deficiency in a red blood cell enzyme, causing anemia.

Polyneuropathy: Weakness or paralysis of limbs due to problems in peripheral nerves.

Portacaval shunt (portasystemic shunt): Failure of embryonic blood vessels within the liver to go away in the postnatal dog, allowing blood to bypass liver processing, resulting in neurological and other symptoms.

Premature closure of distal radius: One of the two bones of the foreleg stops growing before the other, resulting in malformation of the leg.

Progressive posterior paresis: Paralysis of one or both hind limbs.

Progressive retinal atrophy: A family of diseases all involving gradual deterioration of the retina leading to blindness.

Prolapse of nictitans gland: Hypertrophy of the gland of the third eyelid.

Protein wasting disease: Loss of protein through the kidneys (protein-losing nephropathy: PLN) or intestines (protein-losing enteropathy: PLE) resulting in diarrhea and weight loss.

Pug dog encephalitis: Fatal inflammation of the brain.

Pulmonic stenosis: Congenital narrowing of the opening in the heart between the right ventricle and pulmonary artery, eventually causing heart failure.

Pyruvate kinase deficiency: Deficiency of a particular red blood cell enzyme, causing premature destruction of red blood cells and resulting in anemia.

Rage syndrome: Sudden episode of aggression without apparent warning.

Renal cortical hypoplasia: Failure of both kidneys to function normally.

Renal disease: Unspecified kidney disease.

Renal dysplasia: Abnormal development and function of the kidneys.

Retinal detachment: Detachment of the retina from the back of the eye, leading to partial visual loss.

Retinal dysplasia: Abnormal development of the retina.

Retinal folds: Folds in the retinal layer. Many disappear with maturity.

Schnauzer comedo syndrome (follicular dermatitis): Skin disease characterized by blackhead formation.

Scotty cramp: Periodic generalized cramping of the muscles, usually precipitated by excitement; associated with problem with metabolism of a neurotransmitter (serotonin).

Sebaceous adenitis: Inflammation of the sebaceous glands, resulting in scaly debris, hair loss, and infection.

Shaker syndrome: Episodic diffuse muscular tremors and incoordination.

Shar-pei fever: Recurrent bouts of unexplained fever, often with joint inflammation.

Shoulder luxation: Dislocation of the shoulder.

Skin fold dermatitis: Skin infection caused by moisture and bacteria trapped within deep folds of skin.

Skin fragility (Ehlers-Danlos syndrome, cutaneous asthenia): Tissue disease causing extremely fragile skin.

Spiculosis: Abnormally bristle- or spike-like hairs interspersed among normal hairs.

Stenotic nares: Abnormally small nostrils, sometimes interfering with breathing.

Subvalvular aortic stenosis: Abnormally narrow connection between the left ventricle and the aorta, eventually leading to heart failure.

Syringomyelia: Spinal cord disease characterized by fluid-filled cavaties, causing pain, stiffness, and weakness.

Tail fold dermatitis: Infection of the skin around the tail base due to excessive skin folds or an "inset" tail.

Tetralogy of Fallot: Pulmonic stenosis combined with a defect in the ventricular septum results in de-oxygenated blood being pumped throughout the body.

Thrombocytopenia: Lowered platelet number in the blood, leading to excessive bleeding.

Thrombopathy: Abnormality of blood platelets.

Tracheal collapse: Loss of rigidity of the trachea, leading to weakness of the trachea and breathing problems. Most common in small breeds.

Trichiasis: Eyelashes arising from normal origin are misdirected into the eye, causing irritation.

Tricuspid valve dysplasia: Malformation of one of the valves in the heart.

Urethral prolapse: Protrusion of part of the mucosal lining of the urethra through the external urethral orifice.

Uric acid calculi: Bladder stones resulting from an abnormality in the excretion of uric acid.

Urolithiasis: Formation of urinary stones.

Vaginal hyperplasia: Overly enlarged vaginal tissue, sometimes protruding through the vulva. More common in giant breeds.

Vogt-Koyanagi-Harada-like syndrome (uveodermatologic syndrome): Auto-immune disease leading to progressive destruction of melanin containing tissues, including those in the eye and skin.

von Willebrand's disease (vWD): Defective blood platelet function resulting in excessive bleeding, caused by a deficiency in clotting factor VIII antigen (von Willebrand factor).

Wobbler's syndrome (cervical vertebral instability): Abnormality of the neck vertebrae causing rear leg incoordination or paralysis.

Zinc responsive dermatosis: Thickened, scaly skin condition that responds to zinc supplementation.

Index of Breed Entries

(AKC names in bold)

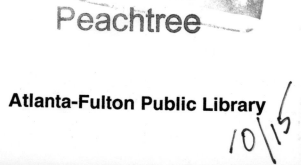